Praise for Robert Fisk's *Pity the Nation*

"Robert Fisk is one of the outstanding reporters of this generation. As a war correspondent he is unrivalled."

—*The Financial Times*

"*Pity the Nation* is a remarkable chronicle of death and disorder in and around Lebanon. . . . Perhaps Fisk's greatest accomplishment is that he has survived all of his years in Beirut with his passion and moral bearings intact."

—*The Los Angeles Times*

"[Fisk's] specialism is Clausewitz's 'continuation of politics by other means.' He does not pad the corridors of power or draw pompous conclusions. He is a reporter of war. He grabs us by the sleeve and says, 'Come quick. Witness what I have witnessed. Make of it what you will.' "

—*The Sunday Times*

"For those who seek to understand why Terry Waite was kidnapped, why an airliner was destroyed over Scotland and why the partisans of religions based on compassion wage merciless war in Beirut, this excellent book provides clear answers. As a record of the experience of modern war, it is outstanding."

—*Scotland on Sunday*

By the same author

The Point of No Return: *the Strike which Broke the British in Ulster*

In Time of War: *Ireland, Ulster and the Price of Neutrality 1939–45*

Pity the Nation

THE ABDUCTION OF LEBANON

Robert Fisk

A TOUCHSTONE BOOK
Published by Simon & Schuster
New York   London   Toronto
Sydney   Tokyo   Singapore

TOUCHSTONE
Simon & Schuster Building
Rockefeller Center
1230 Avenue of the Americas
New York, New York 10020

Originally published in Great Britain by André Deutsch
Limited
First Touchstone Edition 1991
Published by arrangement with Atheneum Publishers, a
division of Macmillan Inc.
TOUCHSTONE and colophon are registered
trademarks of Simon & Schuster Inc.
Manufactured in the United States of America

1   3   5   7   9   10   8   6   4   2

Library of Congress Cataloging in Publication data
Fisk, Robert.
Pity the nation: the abduction of Lebanon/Robert Fisk.
—1st Touchstone ed.
p.   cm.
Includes bibliographical references and index.
1. Lebanon—History—1975–   I. Title.
DS87.F55   1991
956.9204′4—dc20   91-19739
CIP
ISBN: 0-671-74770-3

For Lara

Pity the nation that is full of beliefs and empty of religion.

Pity the nation that wears a cloth it does not weave, eats a bread it does not harvest, and drinks a wine that flows not from its own wine-press.

Pity the nation that acclaims the bully as hero, and that deems the glittering conqueror bountiful.

Pity the nation that despises a passion in its dream, yet submits in its awakening.

Pity the nation that raises not its voice save when it walks in a funeral, boasts not except among its ruins, and will rebel not save when its neck is laid between the sword and the block.

Pity the nation whose statesman is a fox, whose philosopher is a juggler, and whose art is the art of patching and mimicking.

Pity the nation that welcomes its new ruler with trumpetings, and farewells him with hootings, only to welcome another with trumpetings again.

Pity the nation whose sages are dumb with years and whose strong men are yet in the cradle.

Pity the nation divided into fragments, each fragment deeming itself a nation.

Khalil Gibran
The Garden of the Prophet
(London, Heinemann, 1934)

Contents

Preface

In the spring of 1978, on Easter Sunday, on a winding little hill road outside the village of Qana in southern Lebanon, I was interviewing two farmers in a tobacco field when an Israeli tank suddenly drove over the nearest ridge and opened fire on us. As if in a movie – and first experiences of such warfare tend to have a distinctly unreal air about them – we flung ourselves into the undergrowth as a series of great orange flames bubbled around us, the sound of the explosions so loud that the inside of my head hurt for hours afterwards.

Behind us, in a little forest of silver birch trees, Palestinian guerrillas had been setting up a makeshift mortar position, and we had driven blithely past them a few minutes earlier, unaware that we were passing through their front line. The tank coming over the ridge at Qana was Israel's front line and it was shooting at what its crew supposed to be 'terrorists' – which meant at the time that they were firing at any human being that they could see in front of their vehicle. It was a hot mid-morning and on the tape-recording which I was making at the time, you can still hear the cicadas hissing from the bushes seconds before the first shell comes whizzing down the road towards our car.

As we drove frantically away in our hatch-back – clinging to the farmers who had flung themselves onto the tailboard – my microphone was pressed against my chest. Today, listening to the tape of our hysterical shouting and the sound of the detonations, I can still clearly hear the pumping of my own heart – a sort of unsteady drum-beat that increases in tempo by the millisecond – as Bob Dear, the Associated Press photographer in the car, screams at his Armenian colleague Zavem Vartan: 'Zigzag, zigzag.' It is impossible to recreate the sort of panic we felt then or the circumstances in which we experienced our fear. Today, the recording sounds almost comical, my voice rising to a lunatic tenor as I blurt out meaningless descriptions of the shells, of our car turning the corner of the roadway with its tyres shrieking on the hot surface.

It was in fact ten years before I did relive the experience, not with a cassette player but with a page from the thousands of notes, memoranda and reports that I kept in Lebanon from 1976 to the present. Arriving back at the AP Bureau in west Beirut, I had fired off a single computer message to the foreign desk of *The Times*, exhorting them to use my dispatch and beginning the note to my paper with the melodramatic announcement: 'I almost got killed today.'

But why should a newspaper reporter put his life in jeopardy? For the satisfaction of writing a news report, a 'story' as we journalists inaccurately call it, for the preposterous concept of a 'scoop' which few of one's colleagues would anyway wish to share? Certainly not for any search for excitement. Indeed, the report I eventually filed over the AP's wire to *The Times* was ultimately pushed onto an inside page by news from Washington that the United States had arranged a ceasefire which brought the war in southern Lebanon to a temporary halt.

I think I was in Lebanon because I believed, in a somewhat undefined way, that I was witnessing history — that I would see with my own eyes a small part of the epic events that have shaped the Middle East since the Second World War. At best, journalists sit at the edge of history as vulcanologists might clamber to the lip of a smoking crater, trying to see over the rim, craning their necks to peer over the crumbling edge through the smoke and ash at what happens within. Governments make sure it stays that way. I suspect that is what journalism is about — or at least what it should be about: watching and witnessing history and then, despite the dangers and constraints and our human imperfections, recording it as honestly as we can.

Academic historians see their role differently. They go to the primary sources, to the documents of opposing sides in a conflict, to the minutes of Cabinet meetings and committees and military field signals. I can understand the pleasure of that particular search for truth; my last book, a history of Ireland during the Second World War, required years of research in British and Irish archives and included 56 pages of references, two appendices and a four-page bibliography. But no such documentary evidence is forthcoming in the Middle East just now. In Israel, scholars can research the early years of the Jewish state, but there are no contemporary documents available for those who wish to study Israel's catastrophic involvement in Lebanon over the past 14 years. When they left Beirut in 1982, the PLO took some of their files with them on the evacuation boats to Tunisia and Yemen. A few fell into Israeli hands. Most were destroyed in Beirut before the Israelis entered the city. Syrian records on Lebanon should in theory be housed behind the imposing façade of the new state archives building at the end of Kuwatly Street in Damascus, an edifice of titanic proportions in front of which sits a statue of Hafez el-Assad, the president who still wishes to be the vanguard of the Arab world. These files, needless to say, are not available for public inspection.

So this is not an academic book. Nor is it in any formal sense a history of the war in Lebanon, nor of Israel's involvement in that conflict. Readers who are looking for a chronological account of these events should turn to *The Tragedy of Lebanon* by Jonathan Randal of the *Washington Post*, or to what is perhaps the most comprehensive work on the 1982 invasion of Lebanon, *Israel's Lebanon War* by the Israeli

writers Ze'ev Schiff and Ehud Ya'ari.* The most powerful analysis of
the period is contained in Noam Chomsky's *The Fateful Triangle: The
United States, Israel and the Palestinians*, a book of great detail and even
greater anger which concludes that 'as long as the United States remains
committed to an Israeli Sparta as a strategic asset ... the prospects are
for further tragedy: repression, terrorism, war, and possibly even a
conflict that will engage the superpowers ...'†

Mikhail Gorbachev's ascendancy in Moscow suggests that this last
grim prognosis may be exaggerated. But since these books were published, the political crisis in the Levant has grown ever darker. The
Palestinian uprising in the Israeli-occupied West Bank must finally have
convinced those Israelis who wanted to destroy the PLO in Lebanon of
the futility of the 1982 invasion; and the Islamic revolution unleashed
in Lebanon by Israel's catastrophic adventure created a climate so
ferocious that no Westerner could go on living in the country without
fear of assassination or abduction. One of my best friends, a man who
gave me more encouragement than anyone else to write this book —
Terry Anderson, the bureau chief of the AP in Beirut — was taken
hostage not far from my home on 16 March 1985, and endured more
than four years of captivity, chained to the walls of basements and under
constant threat of execution. There were days in 1986 when I was
myself so frightened of being kidnapped that I would drive to work in
west Beirut at up to 90 mph or stay closeted at home for fear that I too
would be taken to join my friend in his torment.

Through all these 13 years, however, I had exercised a journalist's
magpie-like instinct to hoard; not just the dispatches which I sent to *The
Times* — sometimes three reports daily — but every computer message,
memorandum and personal note which I wrote, even those scribbled on
old copy paper and envelopes. The detritus of a journalist's life — the
angry telex demands for confirmation that reports have arrived safely at
The Times, the infuriating requests from London for clarification of
place names in the midst of battle, my own urgent pleas for advance
expenses — were stuffed into unused laundry sacks and duty-free bags
from Beirut airport. I kept mountains of notebooks and newspaper
cuttings, of readers' letters — both kind and insulting — of press
statements and photographs.

* *The Tragedy of Lebanon: Christian Warlords, Israeli Adventurers and American Bunglers* by
Jonathan Randal (London, Chatto and Windus, 1983); *Israel's Lebanon War* by Ze'ev Schiff
and Ehud Ya'ari (London, George Allen and Unwin, 1985).
† *The Fateful Triangle: The United States, Israel and the Palestinians* by Noam Chomsky
(London, Pluto Press, 1983), pp. 468–9. For background, readers might also consult David
Gilmour's *Lebanon: The Fractured Country* (London, Sphere, 1987), Kemal Salibi's *Crossroads
to Civil War: Lebanon 1958–1976* (New York, Caravan, 1976) and Edward Said's *The
Question of Palestine* (New York, Times Books, 1979), a book which in many ways presages
the disaster which was to befall both Lebanese and Palestinians in 1982.

Rummaging through them all, I found small brown and pink slips of paper printed in Arabic ordering the menfolk of Beirut to take their families and flee their homes if they valued the lives of their wives and children – the very leaflets that the Israeli jets dropped from the skies over the Lebanese capital in 1982. There were anonymous broadsheets from the fledgeling Lebanese resistance movement in southern Lebanon warning informers of their imminent execution, even – in one battered shopping bag – a severed set of plastic and steel handcuffs that Israeli troops had used to bind the hands of a blindfolded prisoner in Tyre. I had kept pieces of Israeli and Syrian shells, parts of an Israeli cluster bomb, a massive hunk of shrapnel from a shell fired into the Chouf mountains by the USS *New Jersey*, the Second World War battleship and the most powerful naval vessel afloat, whose guns proved to be as ineffectual in the Lebanon war as the foreign policy of the government which sent it there.

Snapshots and photographs lay among all these files and notes, pictures, some of them more than half a century old, which began to contain a message, as if in some strange way the images were telling their own special story about Lebanon's history. Photographs of Armenians on their 1915 death march. Of the doomed Jews of pre-war Poland, of the Arabs of Palestine, of Muslim and Christian Lebanese families before they lost their homes, kidnappers' snapshots of American hostages, Lebanese suicide bombers, hundreds of missing Palestinians, faces smiling, complacent or in fear. As I wrote my book but without my at first being aware of it, these pictures began to form a ghostly and tragic theme, as if they were themselves a witness to events, providing a permanency which the unfolding drama failed to retain, freezing for all time lives which had been mutilated or destroyed.

Many of the files cover the Iranian revolution, the Soviet invasion of Afghanistan and the Iran – Iraq war, school exercise books in which I had laboriously written out my dispatches in fountain-pen. But most of the papers are from Lebanon, recording its destruction as a nation and as a people over more than a decade. These are the archives upon which I have principally drawn to write this book, which is why it is the work of a reporter rather than of a historian.

Why, a reader may ask, is Lebanon important? Because it remains the most volatile, dangerous nation in the Middle East. Because it is the country in which another Middle East war – which looks ever more likely – will probably be fought. It is, too, the only state in the region in which two powerful armies – Syria's and Israel's – still hold foreign territory. Lebanon contains the largest army of Palestinian guerrillas, most of them only 30 miles from the Israeli border. It is where so many hostages, Western and Arab, remain in torment. In just 15 years, it humiliated the West, brought shame upon Israel, corrupted the Syrians and destroyed itself. Its tragedy is a historic one that cut down the lives of Arabs and Israelis, Americans and French, that has reached – through the Western hostages–the smallest American towns. Its disaster is part of our own history.

A complete list of those who have helped me can be found in the acknowledgements. It would probably never have been written but for Terry Anderson, who frequently appears himself in these pages. While I wrote it, he lay in despair in the underground prisons of west Beirut, weeping with frustration that he could not see his wife or hold the baby daughter whom he had seen only in photographs, taking comfort from the Bible, learning to read French from two old and torn newspapers. Sometimes he was held less than a mile from my own home. He had raged to his colleagues at the use of the word 'terrorist', claiming that it was a pejorative expression that should either be applied to all sides in Lebanon or not at all. It was he who first pointed out to me how often the Israeli prime minister, Menachem Begin, referred during the 1982 Lebanon invasion to the Second World War and to the Holocaust; which is why, while Terry was suffering in his dungeon, I was looking at the crematoria and ash pits of Auschwitz concentration camp.

I also owe a special debt of gratitude to Charles Douglas-Home, who was foreign editor and then editor of *The Times* during the Lebanon War until he died of cancer in October 1985. He stood by me most loyally when I was in danger and always printed my reports without changing them – even though they invariably conflicted with the increasingly right-wing editorials that appeared in *The Times*. After Terry's kidnap, Charlie took a very pragmatic view of my presence in Lebanon, an attitude which I much admired. If I as his correspondent thought *The Times* should maintain its coverage of the country, if I thought this was important to the paper and if I was personally prepared to stay on there, then I should stay. Which is why I went on living in west Beirut and was able to go on chronicling its story for this book. To Charlie's successor as editor, Charles Wilson, I am also grateful; he came to Lebanon one memorable week in the autumn of 1984, trudged around the militia positions of the Chouf mountains, was arrested by the Israelis and handed over to their own proxy Lebanese gunmen and travelled by night across the Beirut front line to help me write my report on the second suicide attack on the American Embassy in Lebanon. Throughout his trip, he would daily tell me that 'You're a bloody fool if you don't get all this down in a book.' Even when the British Foreign Office sent him a hectoring formal note to tell him I should be withdrawn from Lebanon for my own safety, he deferred to my judgement, and so I stayed on; it was a courageous decision for an editor to take, for had I fallen victim to Beirut's kidnappers he would have been personally held to account. I must thank Times Newspapers for allowing me to use passages from my series 'The Land of Palestine' in this book and for permission to quote from the various personal memoranda that passed between myself and my London office.

Neither *The Times* nor its editors nor any of those who are thanked in the acknowledgements are in any way responsible for the views expressed here; in some cases, they may take great exception to what appears in these pages. Having attacked my newspaper reports on various occasions, there is no reason why the Israelis, Palestinians and Syrians should not try to condemn what I have written here. For there is one basic, almost elemental logic that a journalist confronts in Beirut: armies at war – like their governments – are best observed with a mighty degree of scepticism, even cynicism. So far as armies and militias go, there are no good guys in Lebanon.

But this is not intended to be an overtly political book. If it asks any questions, it primarily tries to explore why the things I saw in Lebanon actually happened. In some ways, it is a personal search into the roots of the violence that I have witnessed.

Few Arabs can bring themselves to dwell upon the attempted annihilation of the Jews of Europe, because they do not wish to encourage sympathy for the Israelis. Equally, few Israelis can talk of their postwar history without reference to the Holocaust – yet they are often unwilling to sympathise with Arab suffering. This book begins in a location which both sides, for their different reasons, may find inappropriate: not in Lebanon but in the frosts of Poland.

The events and the people in this book, however, speak for themselves and readers must draw their own conclusions. I suggest no answers and offer no solutions.

West Beirut 1990

Acknowledgements

I am indebted to Lebanese, Palestinians, Syrians, Israelis, Europeans and Americans. Many helped me in my reporting of events in Lebanon before I decided to write this book. They include former Lebanese president, the late Camille Chamoun, Bashir Gemayel, the Phalangist leader and president-elect of Lebanon who was murdered in September 1982, Hussein Moussavi of 'Islamic Amal' in Baalbek and former Lebanese president Suleiman Franjieh.

The following, however, specifically helped me over the past five years in the knowledge that I was researching and writing this book: Terry Anderson, Associated Press bureau chief in Beirut who was kidnapped in 1985, General Franco Angioni, commander of the Italian multinational force contingent in Beirut, Yassir Arafat, the Palestine Liberation Organisation chairman, Neal Ascherson of *The Observer*, Uri Avneri, Israeli journalist in Tel Aviv, Nabih Berri, the leader of the Shia Amal militia and Lebanese minister of justice, Roger Boyes of *The Times* in Warsaw, Lieutenant-General William Callaghan, commander of the United Nations Interim Force in Lebanon (UNIFIL), Dany Chamoun, leader of the Christian 'Tigers' militia, Edward Cody of the *Washington Post*, Szymon Datner, Holocaust survivor in Warsaw, the late Charles Douglas-Home, editor of *The Times*, General Emmanuel Erskine, General Callaghan's predecessor as UNIFIL commander, Scheherezade Faramarzi of the Associated Press, William Foley of *Time* magazine, the late Pierre Gemayel, founder of the Phalange Party, Colonel Timothy Geraghty, commander of 24th Marine Amphibious Unit, Beirut, Timur Goksel of UNIFIL, Juan Carlos Gumucio of *Diario 16* and *The Times*, Philip Habib, President Reagan's special envoy in Lebanon, the late Major Sa'ad Haddad of the 'South Lebanon Army', His Majesty King Husain of Jordan, the late Iskandar Ahmed Iskandar, Syrian information minister, Geoffrey Kemp of the US National Security Council, Brigadier-General Ghazi Kenaan, head of Syrian army intelligence in Lebanon, Khalil Jerardi, leader of the Lebanese Islamic resistance in southern Lebanon who was murdered in 1985, Christina Joelsson of Finland, Walid Jumblatt, the Druze leader, Konstantin Kapitanov of *Literaturnaya Gazeta*, Mahmoud Khadra, director of south Lebanon civil defence service, David Kimche, former director general of the Israeli foreign ministry and former head of the Israeli Mossad intelligence service, Malgorzata Kuczynska of *The Times* in Warsaw, Gerry Labelle of AP, Colonel James Mead, commander of US 32nd Marine Amphibious Unit, Beirut, Donald Mell of AP, Farouk Nassar of AP, Eileen Powell of AP, Jonathan Randal of the *Washington Post*, Bassem Sabbagh, editor of *As Safir*, Peggy Saye, sister of Terry Anderson, former Lebanese prime minister Saeb Salam, Mona es-Said of *As Safir* newspaper, Dr Amal Shama'a of the Barbir Hospital,

Beirut, General Specter of the Israeli air force, Earleen Tatro of the AP, Nicolas Tatro of the AP, Anne Todd, widow of Canadian television reporter Clark Todd, Karsten Tveit of Norwegian television, Terry Waite, the Archbishop of Canterbury's special envoy in Lebanon who was kidnapped in 1987, Khalil Wazzir (Abu Jihad), PLO military commander who was murdered in 1988, Charles Wilson, editor of *The Times*, and Habib Zeidan, headmaster of the Sidon elementary school. I would also like to thank Steve Cox and Esther Whitby, my editors at André Deutsch and Sandra Oakins, who designed and drew the maps for this book.

Many Lebanese, Palestinians and Syrians recounted their memories and gave advice but asked not to be named. To them go all my thanks. Only I am responsible for the conclusions in this book.

Chronology of events

1860 Druze—Christian war kills 12,000 Christians. French troops land
      to protect Maronite community.

1914—18 Ottoman rule in Syria collapses during Great War. Mass star-
      vation in Lebanon.

1920 France given mandate for Syria and Lebanon, creates State of Greater
      Lebanon. British hold mandate in Palestine.

1936 Pierre Gemayel founds Phalange Party after visit to Nazi Germany.

1939—45 British and Free French armies invade Lebanon in 1941 and
      capture Beirut from Vichy forces. France promises full inde-
      pendence

1946 French troops leave Lebanon

1948 Creation of State of Israel. Palestinian exodus into Lebanon and
      Jordan.

1958 Civil war in Lebanon as Muslims rally to pan-Arab calls of Egyptian
      President Nasser. US Marines land in Beirut in accordance with
      Eisenhower doctrine of resistance to 'international communism'
      at request of Lebanese President Camille Chamoun.

1964 Palestine Liberation Organisation founded.

1970 PLO guerrillas driven out of Jordan, set up headquarters in Beirut.
      Increase in PLO raids into Israel from southern Lebanon.

1975 Outbreak of Christian Maronite—Muslim civil war after Phalangists
      attack PLO guerrillas in Beirut.

1976 Civil war fighting intensifies. Christians massacre Palestinian inhabi-
      tants of Karantina and Tel el-Za'atar, Palestinians massacre
      Christian inhabitants of Damour. Syria invited by Lebanese
      President Franjieh to intervene in Lebanese fighting. Syrian troops
      enter Lebanon and occupy all but far south of the country.

1978 Israeli army invades southern Lebanon after Israeli civilians killed in
      PLO guerrilla raid. United Nations force (UNIFIL) sent to
      southern Lebanon. Israel forms proxy Lebanese militia in occu-
      pation zone to the south. Syrian army shells Christians in east
      Beirut.

1980—1 Increase in hostilities between Israel, Israeli-backed militias and
      PLO in southern Lebanon.

1982 Syrian troops besiege Syrian city of Hama after Muslim extremist
      uprising. Up to 10,000 people slaughtered. Israeli army invades
      Lebanon after attempted murder of Israeli ambassador to London.
      On plan conceived by Israeli defence minister Ariel Sharon, Israeli
      troops attack Syrian forces in the Bekaa Valley, surround west
      Beirut and demand evacuation of PLO guerrillas and Syrians from
      Lebanese capital. US—French—Italian forces oversee evacuation

of up to 11,000 PLO men. Palestinian women and children remain. Lebanese president-elect Bashir Gemayel murdered after departure of international troops. Israeli forces invade west Beirut, send Christian Phalangist militias into Palestinian camps of Sabra and Chatila. International outcry and demonstrations in Tel Aviv after Phalangists massacre hundreds of civilians in the camps. Israelis withdraw from west Beirut, US–French–Italian multinational forces return to Lebanese capital. Israeli military headquarters in Tyre destroyed in massive explosion.

1983　US Beirut Embassy destroyed by 'Islamic Jihad' suicide bomber. Lebanese and Israeli governments agree on withdrawal of Israeli troops from Lebanon on condition Syrian army also leaves. Syrians refuse to withdraw. Outbreak of fighting between Muslim forces and Lebanese government troops of President Amin Gemayel. Israeli army stages unilateral withdrawal from Chouf mountains east of Beirut to new front lines north of Sidon. French and US military headquarters razed by 'Islamic Jihad' suicide bombers, slaughtering more than 300 servicemen after US warships shell Muslim areas of Lebanon in support of Gemayel's government. Lebanese hold first 'reconciliation' conference in Switzerland. Suicide bomber destroys Israeli military headquarters in Tyre.

1984　Multinational force evacuates Beirut after collapse of Lebanese government army. President Assad of Syria welcomes Gemayel to Damascus. Second Lebanese 'reconciliation' conference in Switzerland fails. Abductions of Westerners in Beirut, including CIA station chief William Buckley, who dies after torture. Fierce Lebanese resistance – mainly by Shia Muslims – against Israeli occupation army in southern Lebanon.

1985　Israeli army withdraws from Sidon. Israel starts 'iron fist' policy of military repression against guerrilla villages in southern Lebanon. Car bomb kills more than 80 civilians in Shia area of Beirut (CIA involvement later reported in Washington). Further abductions of Westerners in Lebanon, including journalist Terry Anderson of Associated Press. Israelis withdraw from Tyre. Shia Amal militia attacks Palestinian Beirut camps. Suicide bombers again attack Israelis and their allies in southern Lebanon.

1986　Shia Amal militia resumes attack on camps. More Westerners abducted. Hundreds of Palestinians die in camp sieges.

1987　Archbishop of Canterbury's envoy Terry Waite disappears in west Beirut while seeking release of US hostages. Shia and Druze militia war in Beirut prompts return of thousands of Syrian troops to Lebanese capital. Palestinian camps siege resumes.

1988　Failure of Lebanese parliament to elect new president. Rival prime ministers take office in west and east Beirut.

1989　General Michel Aoun, Christian Lebanese 'prime minister', declares war on Syrian army in Lebanon. East Beirut besieged by Syrians and their Lebanese militia allies. Aoun abandons his war.

Principal Characters

Yassir Arafat, chairman of the Palestine Liberation Organisation
Hafez el-Assad, Syrian president
Menachem Begin, Israeli prime minister
Nabih Berri, leader of Amal militia and Lebanese minister of justice
Camille Chamoun, former Lebanese president, leader of Lebanese National
   Liberal Party
Dany Chamoun, son of former president, leader of 'Tigers' militia
Brigadier-General Rafael Eitan, Israeli army chief of staff
Suleiman Franjieh, Lebanese president, ally of Syria
Tony Franjieh, son of former president Franjieh
Amin Gemayel, Lebanese president after Bashir Gemayel's murder
Bashir Gemayel, leader of Phalange militia, Lebanese president-elect
Pierre Gemayel, founder of Lebanese Phalange party and militia
Philip Habib, President Reagan's special envoy to Lebanon
Major Saad Haddad, leader of pro-Israeli 'South Lebanon Army' militia
Elie Hobeika, commander of Phalangist militiamen who massacred
   Palestinians at Sabra and Chatila
Khalil Jerardi, south Lebanese resistance leader
Kamal Jumblatt, Druze leader of Progressive Socialist Party
Walid Jumblatt, Druze leader of PSP after his father Kamal's murder
Rashid Karami, Lebanese prime minister
David Kimche, director general of the Israeli foreign ministry, formerly
   head of the Israeli Mossad intelligence service
Hussein Moussavi, leader of Islamic Amal militia in Baalbek
Imam Mousa Sadr, leader of south Lebanese 'Movement of the Deprived'
   (later Amal) until his disappearance in Libya
Elias Sarkis, president of Lebanon
Yitzhak Shamir, Israeli foreign minister, later prime minister
Ariel Sharon, Israeli defence minister and architect of the 1982 invasion of
   Lebanon

The Journalists

Terry Anderson, Associated Press bureau chief, Beirut
Charles Assi, AP office manager, Beirut
Ivan Barnes, foreign news editor of *The Times*
Edward Cody, AP correspondent, Beirut, later *Washington Post* correspondent
Charles Douglas-Home, editor of *The Times*
Scheherezade Faramarzi, AP correspondent, Beirut
William Foley, AP photographer Beirut, later *Time* magazine photographer
François Ghattas, AP chief technician, Beirut

Samir Ghattas, AP correspondent, Beirut
Juan Carlos Gumucio, AP correspondent, Beirut, later CBS bureau chief, Beirut, and reporter for London *Times* and *Diario 16*
Stephen Hindy, AP correspondent Cairo, assigned to Beirut
Loren Jenkins, *Washington Post* correspondent, Beirut
Konstantin Kapitanov, Beirut correspondent of *Literaturnaya Gazeta*
Gerry Labelle, AP news editor, Beirut
Donald Mell, AP photographer, Beirut
Farouk Nassar, AP correspondent, Beirut
Eileen Powell (wife of Labelle), AP correspondent, Beirut
Jonathan Randal, *Washington Post* correspondent, Beirut
Zoheir Saade, AP photo-editor, Beirut
Earleen Tatro, AP correspondent, Beirut, later assigned to AP, Tel Aviv
Nicolas Tatro, AP bureau chief, Beirut, later AP bureau chief Tel Aviv
Clark Todd, Canadian Television correspondent, assigned to Beirut
Karsten Tveit, Norwegian television correspondent, Beirut
Christopher Walker, Jerusalem correspondent of *The Times*
Charles Wilson, editor of *The Times* after Douglas-Home's death

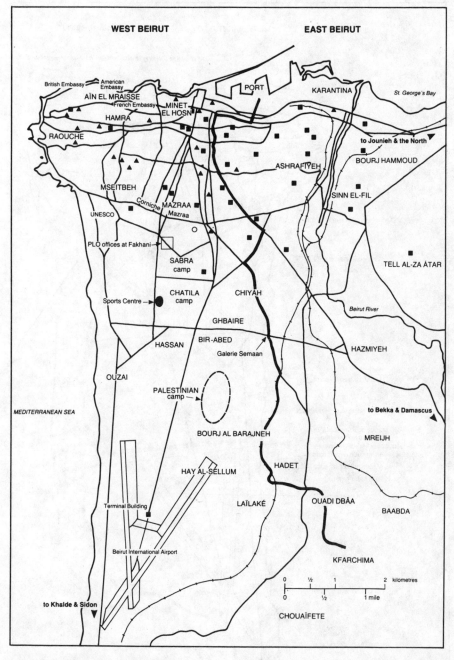

The Divided City of Beirut

WEST BEIRUT   EAST BEIRUT

British Embassy
American Embassy
AÏN EL MRAISSE
French Embassy
MINET EL HOSN
HAMRA
RAOUCHE
MSEITBEH
UNESCO
Corniche
MAZRAA
Mazraa
PLO offices at Fakhani
SABRA camp
Sports Centre
CHATILA camp
CHIYAH
GHBAIRE
HASSAN
BIR-ABED
Galerie Semaan
OUZAI
PALESTINIAN camp
BOURJ AL BARAJNEH
HAY AL-SELLUM
Terminal Building
Beirut International Airport
to Khalde & Sidon
CHOUAÏFETE

PORT
KARANTINA
St. George's Bay
ASHRAFIYEH
BOURJ HAMMOUD
to Jounieh & the North
SINN EL-FIL
TELL AL-ZA ÁTAR
Beirut River
HAZMIYEH
to Bekka & Damascus
MREIJH
HADET
LAÏLAKÉ
OUADI DBÂA
BAABDA
KFARCHIMA

MEDITERRANEAN SEA

0   ½   1   2 kilometres
0   ½   1 mile

━━ front line dividing Christian East and Muslim West Beirut
┿┿ disused railway
▲ mosque   ■ church   ○ hospital

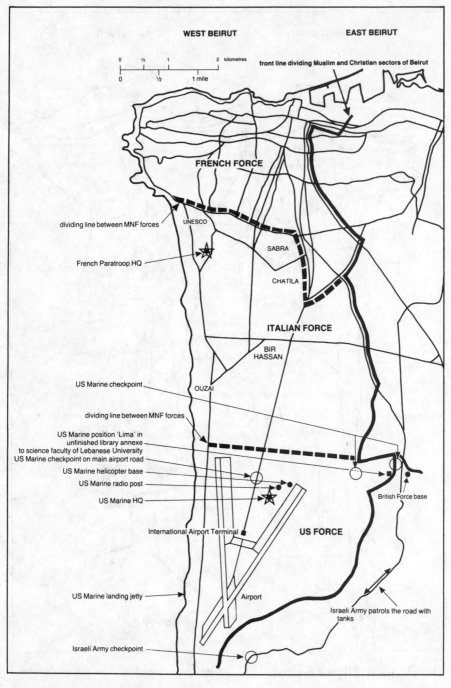

WEST BEIRUT   EAST BEIRUT

front line dividing Muslim and Christian sectors of Beirut

0   ½   1   2 kilometres
0   ½   1 mile

FRENCH FORCE

dividing line between MNF forces   UNESCO

French Paratroop HQ   SABRA

CHATILA

ITALIAN FORCE

BIR HASSAN

US Marine checkpoint   OUZAI

dividing line between MNF forces

US Marine position 'Lima' in
unfinished library annexe
to science faculty of Lebanese University
US Marine checkpoint on main airport road
US Marine helicopter base
US Marine radio post
US Marine HQ

British Force base

International Airport Terminal   US FORCE

US Marine landing jetty   Airport

Israeli Army patrols the road with
tanks

Israeli Army checkpoint

The Multinational Force
in Beirut

front line dividing Christian East and Muslim West Beirut
Multinational Force (MNF)

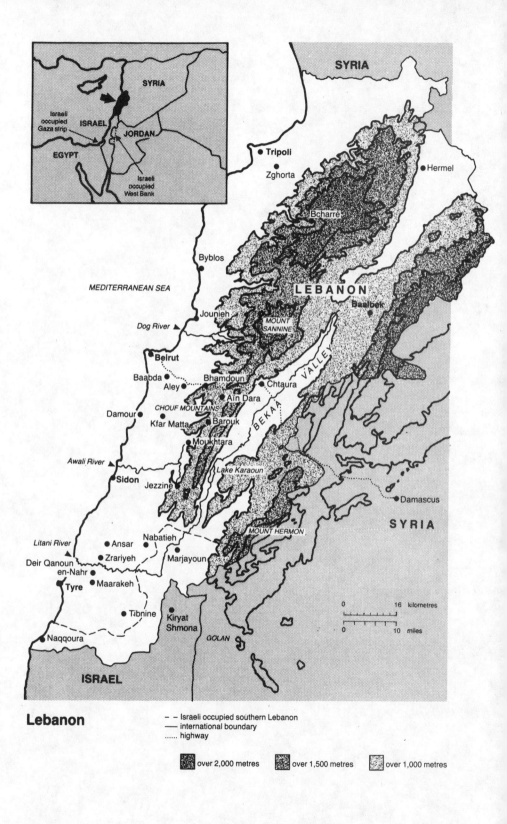

SYRIA

● Tripoli

Zghorta ●

● Hermel

Bcharré ●

Byblos ●

MEDITERRANEAN SEA

L E B A N O N

● Baalbek

Jounieh ●

Dog River ▷

Beirut ●

*MOUNT
SANNINE*

Baabda ●

Bhamdoun ●

● Chtaura

B
E
K
A
A

V
A
L
L
E
Y

Aley ●

● Ain Dara

CHOUF MOUNTAINS

Damour ●

● Barouk

Kfar Matta ●

● Moukhtara

Awali River ▷

Lake Karaoun

Sidon ●

Jezzine ●

● Damascus

S Y R I A

MOUNT HERMON

Litani River

● Ansar   Nabatieh ●

Deir Qanoun ▷ ● Zrariyeh   Marjayoun ●
en-Nahr ●

Tyre ● ● Maarakeh

● Tibnine   Kiryat
Shmona ●

● Naqqoura

GOLAN

	0		16	kilometres

	0		10	miles

ISRAEL

Lebanon

– – Israeli occupied southern Lebanon
—— international boundary
······ highway

▨ over 2,000 metres   ▩ over 1,500 metres   ▦ over 1,000 metres

Inset map:

SYRIA

Israeli
occupied
Gaza strip

ISRAEL

JORDAN

EGYPT

Israeli
occupied
West Bank

1 Sepia Pictures on a Wall

I think that tree roots cannot grow in ash.

Stetkiewicz Wojciech, guide at
Auschwitz concentration camp.

Warsaw, 16 December 1986

It was snowing in Litewska Street; not big, heavy flakes but small, hard,
blinding droplets, almost sleet, that blessed the dull suburban road with
a kind of grey fog. We parked our car on the pavement beside a tiny,
bare tree, its branches glistening with rime. The few people in the street
were hunched in their furs. Winter had attacked Poland more savagely
than usual.

When we climbed to the second floor of number 10 Litewska Street,
it was so dark that we had difficulty in reading the name on the door of
apartment 15. When we pressed the bell, we heard first the paws of a
large dog on the other side and a muffled bark, followed by the sound of
human feet shuffling on the floor. They seemed to take a long time
reaching the door. It opened to reveal an old man, breathing heavily, his
arms at his side, bent slightly but with the eyes of a teenager. Szymon
Datner's expression of permanent youth is an illusion, for it is the result
of suffering.

We introduced ourselves. I am the journalist who has come from
Lebanon, I tell him. He does not smile. He remembered our telephone
call. The dog, a large grey beast with heavy, kind eyes, jogged its paws
on the ground in excitement as Szymon Datner led us into a small room
with a tall bookcase along one wall, so crammed with volumes that
pamphlets and books were squeezed into the shelves at odd angles, in
danger of exploding outwards onto the floor. When he sat down, Szymon
Datner looked smaller and older in his brown zip-up jacket. He placed
us at right angles to him at the wooden table and rested his clasped
hands on the surface with careful formality. 'What can I do for you?' He
was like an archivist, a man of research grown used to the naivety of
undergraduates.

I explained that I was writing a book about Lebanon, about the events that I had witnessed and reported in Lebanon for more than a decade, about why these events happened as they did. I said that I suspected some of the answers lay in the Holocaust; which was why I had come to Poland. Szymon Datner nodded slowly. He was a survivor of the Holocaust, one of the few thousand Polish Jews to have escaped extermination but to have stayed on in the country of their birth. He was a tiny, fragile link, too, to the Israel which I was writing about. He was of the generation of Menachem Begin and Yitzhak Shamir. Begin was born in Brest-Litovsk, which was in Poland and is now in the Soviet Union. Shamir came from the village of Rushova in eastern Poland and went to school at the Hebrew Gymnasium in Bialystok. His gymnastics and music teacher in Bialystok was Szymon Datner.

'I can remember a not tall boy, a very vivid one, smart.' Datner spoke very slowly. 'Everything at the gymnasium was taught in Hebrew except Polish and Polish history. I even taught gymnastics and music in Hebrew. That is the language in which he learned.' Datner still felt the pride of being a schoolmaster. 'Our pupils were brought up in a spirit of love and esteem for Poland – and also of love for Israel. Some of my pupils emigrated to what was then Palestine. Every year, we teachers passed hundreds of pupils through our ranks.' Szymon Datner slowly rose from his chair and shuffled to the corridor, into a small, narrow room with on one side a bed covered by a chequered blanket.

On the facing wall were affixed some faded sepia photographs. In one of them, a class of the late Twenties, the young Jewish boys were sitting stiffly to attention. A boy in the back row was grinning. Another had turned his head at the moment the photograph was being taken. 'Perhaps Shamir is there,' Datner remarked. We looked in vain for the familiar, chubby face. Datner did not know how many of these children left for Palestine, how many stayed behind. Beneath the pictures was a series of smaller photographs; each showed a group of schoolteachers sitting on rows of chairs, the first picture labelled 1926, the last 1938, so that by casting our eyes along the row we could see the teachers growing older, the bright, sometimes humorous faces of the Bialystok Gymnasium staff moving inexorably towards the Holocaust. There was a rather portly man in the front row who may have been the headmaster, and a woman with high, aristocratic features and jet-black hair in the second. In ten years, the portly man grows larger, the woman becomes more beautiful. One tries to detect some change in their expression, some hint of concern in their dark eyes as the cameraman takes what was to be their last group photograph in 1938. There is none.

Did any of these teachers survive the Holocaust, I ask? Szymon Datner places his stubby finger on the left-hand side of the last picture and moves it steadily to the right, past the pudgy teacher. 'I think,' he says – his finger is sliding past the beautiful woman – 'none of them.'

There is a pause. 'Except this one.' He is pointing to the sharp, staring features of Szymon Datner.

There is one more photograph behind the old man's bed, a pale brown picture that must have been enlarged from an earlier, torn print because there is an uneven white line across the bottom. The picture shows a young woman, remarkably pretty, smiling, with dark hair, and two little girls. The woman is Szymon Datner's wife Sosannah. The girls are his daughters Miriam and Shalomit.

He wanted to talk about them. 'When the Nazis came, I was an inmate with my family in the Bialystok ghetto. I joined the underground and went into the woods and became a member of a Jewish partisan group which amalgamated later with Russian and Polish partisans. Half of our people fell in battle. The other half survived.' Szymon Datner waited for several seconds, perhaps because he knew the question I wanted to ask. What happened to Sosannah and Miriam and Shalomit? He still paused because he did not know the complete answer. 'I am not sure,' he eventually replied. 'But it seems to me that they died in the annihilation of the Bialystok Jewish ghetto in 1943. They were hidden in the underground bunker in the home where we lived but they were betrayed to the Nazis by somebody and were executed on the spot, so far as I know. I don't know the place where their remains are. But every night, before I go to bed, I say the Kaddish, the Jewish prayer for the dead, for them.'

Szymon Datner returned to his study. He wanted to know about Lebanon and I asked him what he felt about what had happened there, about those events in Lebanon that had involved Israel, about the invasion of Lebanon in 1982. Datner's parents emigrated to Palestine before the Holocaust although his mother died during the war. 'I went to see my father in Palestine in 1947,' he said. 'I was very glad to see the place where some 100,000 Jews from all over the world had gone before the war. It was a safe haven for them. And I am sure that if it was not for the policy of the British mandate power which forbade the Jews to emigrate to Palestine then, maybe some hundreds of thousands if not millions of the Jews from the countries of Europe occupied by the Nazis could have been saved. Israel is in my opinion the first and last line of defence of the Jewish people all over the world. I am of this opinion today.'

The old man's conviction forced his voice to rise. There was a question I had to ask him and I told him that he might feel he did not want to talk about it. But how could Israel, the nation which of all others understood the horror of mass murder, have allowed the Palestinians of Sabra and Chatila camps in Beirut to have been murdered? The number of Palestinians killed – up to two thousand – bore no relation to the six million Jews who were slaughtered in the Holocaust. But in the camp of

Chatila on the day the massacre ended, my colleagues and I — with bodies lying in heaps around us — had asked that question many times.

Szymon Datner looked in front of him. He understood why I had asked this question. He spoke slowly, choosing each word with great care, his English flawless. 'As far as I know, the Jewish soldiers did not take a direct part in this slaughter. It was a slaughter of innocent people — this is always an abhorrence to Jews. I am not in a position to judge whose fault it was that these terrible crimes took place but I am sure no Jewish hand was involved in this massacre.' He stopped speaking for perhaps ten seconds. There was a point to be made. 'But also I know of another massacre, an abhorrent massacre of Jewish children in a place called Ma'alot which was committed by one or two members of the Palestine Liberation Organisation. As far as I know, more than twenty children fell as victims. Of course, such crimes cannot be justified but only deplored and stigmatised.'

Because of who Szymon Datner was, because of his own personal tragedy, because he was a witness to the unthinkable, it seemed impossible to tell him what we had experienced in our little world; that his excuse for Sabra and Chatila — for that is what it was — was almost identical to the historical parallels employed by tens of thousands of Israelis at the time. The Israeli soldiers who knew what had happened, who had done nothing to prevent the slaughter that was going on a few hundred yards from them, also told us about Ma'alot as we questioned them in west Beirut on 18 September 1982. With just such conviction did they deplore the massacre. We had questioned them incredulously, realising what was the truth; that they had known yet done nothing. But could one question the self-assurance of this gentle old man whose wife and daughters, whose sister, brother, uncles and aunts — at least 30 relatives in all, he thought — had been murdered by the Nazis?

Outside the window of Szymon Datner's study, the snow had grown heavier, the flakes larger, the glass steaming on the inside as the temperature fell in Litewska Street. 'It seems to me,' he said, 'that the safest guarantee for the security of the Jews in Israel would be understanding and friendship between the Israelis and their Arab neighbours. But for marriage that is a result of love and esteem, there must be a precondition; it must be a mutual love, not just a pious desire of the Jews and the Arabs.'

Szymon Datner sat back in his chair. He would say no more about the Palestinians, about those people who also regard the land of Palestine — in which his parents sought safety — as their home. Yet the sense of belonging which Jews and Arab Palestinians felt toward Palestine had curiously passed Szymon Datner by. How many Jews remain in Poland, in this country of the Holocaust, to live among the ghosts of their own departed people? 'Between four and seven thousand,' he suggested bleakly. 'We don't know, for there is one sad fact that must be mentioned – that because they were so frightened by their experiences, many Jews who survived the Holocaust – a great part of them – have until now hidden their provenance. They are hiding behind their Polishness.'

And Szymon Datner? He remarried after the war and his wife, although Jewish, was a prominent member of the Polish Communist Party. Instead of emigrating to the new Israel, he stayed behind to write about the Holocaust, to publish books and booklets and newspaper articles about the annihilation of the Poles and Jews. He had grown weary and his unnaturally young eyes looked tired. He is 84 years old. 'All this is at the root of why I remain to work here,' he said. 'And now I am an old man and I remain only to wait for the bitter end of everybody in this life; to pass away.'

Oswiecim-Brezesc (Auschwitz-Birkenau)

The road to Auschwitz from Cracow was almost covered in snow. It runs through a succession of poor villages and we had to slow often to allow the farmers to pass, great men on wooden carts pulled by thick-necked, snorting horses. There were still wooden cottages beside the fields, long barn-like structures whose roofs sagged in the centre as if they had too long borne oppression. Just once, for a few minutes, a pale pink sun emerged meanly through the grey snow clouds.

About seven miles north of Oswiecim, the traffic was backed up at a railway crossing. We climbed out of our car and stamped our boots in the snow as we waited for the train. It was a long time in coming but we could hear it far away because of its wailing. Polish state railways use diesel locomotives for their main-line passenger services, but out of the forest to our left came a great steam locomotive, a black-painted goliath of pipes and pistons with two big wind-deflectors at the front, shovelling white smoke across the snowfields, pulling behind it a long line of freight cars.

They clicked past us slowly, cattle wagons and flatbed trucks and a big guards van, moving softly off into the cold fog. The drivers watched them with disinterest, climbing into their cars with relief. By the time we reached the town of Oswiecim, the mist had begun to close in. Like many of the towns and cities of eastern Europe – and of Ireland – Oswiecim has two names, a legacy of conquest and colonisation, of shared or defeated cultures, Polish, Russian or German. But this is a place which needs a pseudonym, for who would want to admit that they had made their home at Auschwitz? It is as if the Polish name was essential for any narrative plausibility. How could one otherwise say that the local railway station (trains to Warsaw every three hours) is bright and clean, refurbished with new bricks? Indeed, Auschwitz station has a new digital clock so that rush-hour commuters to Cracow should not miss their connection. There are sidings just down the line that run directly into the 45-year-old factories, the same still-functioning factories built by the Germans for their slave labour, still served by the same track and permanent way. Even Stetkiewicz Wojciech, the official Polish guide to the concentration camp, admits that he lives in a house built for the SS camp staff.

Is this, in the end, part of the banality of evil, the very expression of Hannah Arendt now almost a cliché amid the attempts to understand wickedness? Is it perhaps excusable that the railway branch line just one mile out of Auschwitz station, the most terrible permanent way in the world, somehow exerts a more subtle, more acute fascination than all the evidence of butchery and madness within the camp? For the very same track which carried the millions to the gas chambers is still there, curving gently past the back of some farm cottages, across the laneway through a field to the neat brick and slate gateway of Birkenau. In a hundred photographs, on the covers of innumerable works of Holocaust literature, that geometrical porch had become somehow familiar, a geographical reassurance in a strange land that one comes across as one might suddenly recognise the Great Wall or the Forbidden City even if one had never before been to China. We had seen it in the pictures. There's the Great Wall. Ah yes, this must be Birkenau! And I climbed from the car and walked to the railway line. There were the rails, the iron ties still clenched around them, securing them to the old wooden sleepers. You could run a train into the Auschwitz-Birkenau camp today without any danger of derailment, right up to the selection ramp. It was so cold that my camera lens frosted but I took two pictures of the Birkenau gateway, one from ground level where the snow lay smooth on top of the tracks. Inside, the points were still set for the left-hand siding as if someone had diligently prepared for just one more transport to arrive. I think I supposed that, later, from the photographs some truth might emerge that would help to encompass the enormity of what happened here.

Four days earlier, I had been in Beirut, driving past the Sabra and Chatila Palestinian camps to the airport because I suspected that in Poland, at Auschwitz, lay clues to what I had seen in Lebanon. Yet from the hot, untidy killings of the Middle East to this frozen, methodical place was a journey that should have been taken in a spaceship across light years. No massacre in Lebanon could remotely compare with this in size, in scientific evil. The scale of the Holocaust here − of gypsies and Polish non-Jews as well as Jews − was so unimaginable that the tens of thousands of deaths in Lebanon seemed somehow an irrelevance.

This, of course, is not what history should teach us. Nor is it true. But if that is how I, a stranger, a non-Jew born a year after Hitler's death could think – even briefly – then how is one even to question the survivors or their children? Or, more importantly, how is one to approach the behaviour of the state which was forged – as many of its citizens will tell you – in the very fires of Auschwitz? Every Jewish victim of the Holocaust, as it says at the Yad Vashem memorial outside Jerusalem, was made an honorary citizen of Israel. If this premise is accepted, then to visit Auschwitz is not only a pilgrimage to the largest mass grave in the world but an acknowledgement of its intimate connection to the Middle East and, ultimately, to the tragedy – of inconsequential significance if the equation is to be resolved only with numbers – of another people, indeed of numerous peoples whose own suffering I and my colleagues in Lebanon had witnessed.

Yet here, even the literature of the Holocaust can prove almost as shocking as the actual experience of violence in the Middle East. The night before we travelled to Auschwitz, I had lain in bed in the Hotel Polski in Cracow, listening to the snow shawling its way across the window and reading one of Tadeusz Borowski's short stories of the Birkenau camp, the one called *This Way for the Gas, Ladies and Gentlemen.** After surviving both Auschwitz and Dachau, Borowski gassed himself in 1951. And the book reads as though it has been written by a man who is already partly dead. The prose is stretched to the very limit of meaning, the sense more important than the grammar. The direct speech is ugly. There are whole sentences without verbs. Borowski wrote that 'the living are always right, the dead are always wrong', but in the preface his editor disagrees. What Borowski wrote about Auschwitz, he says, proves that it is the dead who are right.

Borowski identifies himself with a camp Kapo, one of the prisoners who waits for the railway transports to arrive with Jews from Hungary, Holland, France, Germany itself.

... slowly, terribly slowly, a train rolls in, the engine whistles back with a deafening shriek. Again weary, pale faces at the windows, flat as though cut out of paper, with huge, feverishly burning eyes. Already trucks are pulling up, already the composed gentleman with the notebook is at his post, and the SS men emerge from the commissary carrying briefcases for the gold and money. We unseal the train doors. It is impossible to control oneself any longer. Brutally we tear suitcases from their hands, impatiently pull off their coats. Go on, go on, vanish! Men, women, children, some of them know.

The victims are Hungarian Jews who arrived at Auschwitz in 1944 to be murdered – all 400,000 of them in just two months, consumed by

* *This Way for the Gas, Ladies and Gentlemen* by Tadeusz Borowski, introduction by Jan Cott (London, Penguin, 1986), pp. 42–6.

the gas chambers at the rate of 24,000 a day even though the crematoria
could not cope.

They are dragging to the truck an old man wearing tails and a band
around his arm. His head knocks against the gravel and pavement; he
moans and wails in an uninterrupted monotone: 'Ich will mit dem Herrn
Kommandanten sprechen — I wish to speak with the Commandant ...'
Several other men are carrying a small girl with only one leg. Tears are
running down her face and she whispers faintly: 'Sir, it hurts, it hurts ...'
They throw her on the truck on top of the corpses. She will burn alive
along with them.

Should one therefore regard Auschwitz as a place to understand evil
or as a shrine to the dead and all their sufferings? Or merely as a
measure of distance between the experience of those who survived
Auschwitz and those who can never comprehend what that meant? In
Warsaw, we had met an Associated Press correspondent who had travelled
to Auschwitz with a Jewish delegation for a memorial service. 'Two of
them were on the ramp where the selections were made for the gas
chambers,' he had told us. 'There was this man and woman and they
stood there arguing about where Mengele, the camp doctor who did the
medical experiments, had stood. The guy said Mengele stood on one
side and this woman was swearing it was on the other side of the ramp
and she was crying. There were all these TV cameras recording this
poor woman having a nervous breakdown right there, arguing about
where Mengele stood. Can you imagine it?'

His question unwittingly struck at the problem which faces all new-
comers to this place. It is not that what occurred here passes comprehension — which it does — but that it is distanced even from imagination;
which is perhaps why the writing of Primo Levi conveys more reality to
us than the artifacts of Auschwitz, the actual terrifying evidence that
yes, it all happened just as we have always been told. So the surviving
gas chamber in the original Auschwitz camp, the crematorium with the
name of its Erfurt manufacturers still displayed on the oven, the room-
fuls of human hair, the medical experiment block, the piles of spectacles,
the Birkenau railhead, the execution wall, the mass gallows, all serve to
authenticate the accounts of Borowski or Levi rather than as evidence in
their own right — because evidence can only be applied to imaginable
things.

Only the empty tins of Zyklon B crystals, their lids ripped off as if
they were cans of beans emptied by an impatient cook, were somehow
different. The jagged edges of the metal lids demonstrated the impatience
of the German who had poured the contents into the gas chambers.
Let's get this business over quickly, he must have been saying. These
rusty little horrors were part of a routine, and thus imagination could
just encompass them. But other things in the Auschwitz showcases led

nowhere. In one room in the old camp buildings, there are piles of suitcases, most of them bearing the names of their owners. These were a few of the same suitcases that Borowski's camp Kapo and his colleagues so brutally tore from the hands of the Jews in the Birkenau railway sidings. There was nothing unreal about this luggage. The names had been crayoned onto the bags in a hurry, by people who had been given little time to leave their homes and ghettos. One cracked brown suitcase bore a name in childish handwriting, the letters of unequal height. 'Carl Israel Hafner,' it said. 'Vienna 1, Biberstrasse 14.' I wrote down the name and address. Was he, as his handwriting indicated, a small boy perhaps of school age? Could he by some miracle have lived through Auschwitz, perhaps even returning to his old home? What happened to his father and mother or his brothers and sisters? Did any of his family survive the Holocaust?

On my way back to Beirut, I routed my flight through Vienna and took a taxi into the city. It was almost as cold as Poland and Biberstrasse was deep in snow. It was a narrow, respectable street with double-glazed windows to keep out the cold, a thoroughfare that might have seen better days. For number 14 was no longer an apartment. 'Bundesministerium für Land und Forstwirtschaft,' it said over the main door of the building through which, more than 45 years earlier, Carl Hafner must have walked for the last time clutching his ungainly suitcase. The apartment block was now part of the Austrian Ministry of Agriculture. Its interior had been torn out and replaced by offices. Just down the road, the girl in the local post office could not understand my enquiry. There was no way, she said, that her bureau could trace a resident so long absent from the neighbourhood. Even the local Rabbi — for Biberstrasse is still in what is left of the Jewish area of Vienna — had no record of the name. Carl Israel Hafner had simply disappeared. His family, his identity, his very existence had vanished; it was as if the Hafners had never lived; which is what Hitler intended. Only that ancient suitcase with its childish writing shows where Carl Hafner disappeared to.

Wojciech, our Auschwitz guide, understood something of this, perhaps because he had met so many survivors, perhaps because — living with his wife and young son in the old SS house — the evidence of Auschwitz had itself become commonplace. Yet he had other knowledge that provided its own chilling evidence of the realities of Auschwitz. 'Some weeks ago, we had a West German delegation here,' he said. 'They wanted to lay wreaths on the execution wall where the Nazis shot thousands of people, whole families together, the mother and father holding the hands of their children who stood between them as they were killed. Well, we always have to clear the wreaths away after a while, when they die. On this occasion, my colleagues went to clear the stuff away. And when they took one dead wreath from the wall, they found hidden on the back of it a very small plastic swastika. Why would anyone do that?'

If further evidence of the darkness of the mind were needed, one has only to notice the camp guards. Yes, there are camp guards at Birkenau camp *now*, dressed in black, officially appointed by the Polish government to protect Auschwitz. Wojciech explained in an almost matter-of-fact way. 'You see, we believe that nothing should be taken from here but people come here with metal detectors to look for things.' He did not want to continue, for there was clearly something very shaming in what he knew. We pressed him. What could anyone be looking for with metal detectors? 'At night,' he said. 'They have come here at night and they go up to where the ash pits are, where the Nazis put the ash of all the dead. And they look for things. They've been told that some of the men and women, just before they went into the gas chamber, realised what was happening, that they had jewels and things and that they buried them rather than let them fall into the hands of the Nazis. So the people with the metal detectors were coming here at night. To look for jewels. That is why we have the guards.'

Visitors to Auschwitz camp are not normally taken to the ash pits. It was a long drive down an unpaved road thick with ice, a track marked by a row of watchtowers with neat slate roofs and the posts for the barbed wire of an uncompleted Birkenau compound; the Germans were still enlarging Auschwitz when the Red Army arrived to liberate it. Through a rusting gate, we walked into a little forest between rows of tall fir trees. The snow was encrusted onto their bark, for there had been a blizzard in the night, but from time to time in the silence cakes of snow would slide off the upper branches and start a small ghostly landslide deep inside the foliage.

To our right were some stumps of masonry almost obscured by the snow, the remains of one of the four Birkenau gas chambers, destroyed by the camp guards in the last days. And further over, beside the forest wall, was a deep ditch, a trench that cut at a 90-degree angle beside a wall of fir trees where another of those clean, well-built watchtowers nestled amid the branches. This was one of the burning ditches which the Germans used when the crematoria could no longer cope with the 24,000 corpses a day. The bodies were burned in pyramids, on trestles above the trenches; the remains were thrown with all the other ashes, into the small natural lakes beside the clearing.

Wojciech stood there in the snow saying nothing, a museum curator beside the buried ashes of nearly four million people. Most of them were Jews. From above the trees, from far away on the other side of Auschwitz, came the long wail of a steam locomotive. Perhaps it was the same train we had seen in the morning, now taking its empty freight cars back to

Cracow or Warsaw. Its whistle turned into a high shriek that varied in pitch and then became smothered by the fog. The forest was silent. Wojciech said that he had never seen or heard birds here. Nor were there any trees at the shore of the little lakes. 'I think that tree roots cannot grow in ash,' Wojciech said.

But they were really not even lakes, just small frozen ponds with a fringe of undergrowth covered in hoar-frost. If this had been anywhere else, we would have noted the fragile beauty of the place. In any other land, someone would have built a wooden pier into the pond for fishermen or tethered a small boat to the shore. But in another country, if its contents were known, there would at least have been a sign. The last mortal remains of even 30 humans would warrant a stone; the resting place of 300 would need an artist of world renown to design the memorial. And memorials there are indeed at Birkenau between the two railhead gas chambers. But here at this ash pit, there was nothing. If the grave of 300 might be commemorated, how can one represent in words the ashes of 3,000 or 30,000 or − let us be realistic about this little pond − of 300,000?

Somewhere down there in the cold depths beneath the ice were the powdered white bones of cities of people, of generations, of a whole continent. At one edge of the pond, the frosted weeds had been scuffed and from the shore a set of small animal tracks led over the ice, probably a fox taking a short cut across the clearing. But near the centre the surface crust had suddenly been punctured by the animal's paw. The fox had obviously run to the bushes in panic, for his tracks had slithered and scraped their way back across the ice.

I took several monochrome photographs of this little lake with its frosted surface and backdrop of sagging white trees. When I returned to Beirut, I had the pictures developed. But there must have been something wrong with the chemicals used to print the photographs; perhaps they had been diluted before being sold. For after four or five weeks, the pictures of Auschwitz, of the Birkenau railhead, the gas chambers and the ash pits became grainy and less distinct and developed a dark sepia tint like old wartime photographs, the same colour as the snapshots of the doomed Jews on old Szymon Datner's bedroom wall.

2　The Keys of Palestine

> It is a tragedy of both our people. How can I explain in my
> poor English? I think the Arabs have the same rights as the
> Jews and I think it is a tragedy of history that a people who
> are refugees make new refugees. I have nothing against the
> Arabs ... They are the same as us. I don't know that we
> Jews did this tragedy – but it happened.
>
> Shlomo Green, Jewish refugee from the Nazis,
> on learning that his home in Israel was taken from
> a Palestinian family in 1948.

When David Roberts toured the Holy Land, he was an explorer as well
as an artist, a romantic who filtered the hot and crude realities of the
Middle East through a special screen. As he journeyed on horseback
through Palestine and then up the coast of southern Lebanon in the
1830s, he was an adventurer, staying overnight with the governor of
Tyre, crossing the snows of the Chouf mountain chain to the gentleness
of the Bekaa Valley where he sketched the great temples of the Roman
city of Heliopolis.

In the world that he created, there were no wars, no political disputes, no
dangers. His lithographs of Palestinian villages and of Lebanon, of Tyre
and the peninsula of Ras Naqourra, of the temples of Baalbek, are
bathed only in the peace of antiquity, a nineteenth-century dream machine
that would become more seductive as the decades saw the collapse of the
Turkish and then of the British Empire.

For today, Roberts' delicate sketches and water-colours of Ottoman
Palestine can be found in the hallways, bedrooms and living rooms of
tens of thousands of Palestinians in Lebanon. In the dust of the great
Ein Helweh Palestinian camp just east of Sidon, cheap copies of Roberts'
prints – of Nablus, of Hebron, of Jericho and Jerusalem – are hung on
the cement walls of refugee shacks, behind uncleaned glass, sometimes
held in place by Scotch tape and glue. His pictures of Lebanon's
forgotten tranquillity hang in Lebanese homes too. Volumes of Roberts'
prints of Lebanon and Palestine can be bought in stores all over Beirut.
They can be purchased in almost every tourist hotel in Israel. They are a
balm in which anyone can believe.

In Roberts' drawing of Jaffa, the old city seems to bend outwards
with domes and minarets and dusty tracks, watched from a distance by

a pastoral couple with a donkey. At Acre, the ramparts of Richard Coeur de Lion's massive fortress stretch down to a tideless Mediterranean while tiny Arab figures promenade in the dusk past the *serail*. From time to time, the dun-coloured hills are washed with a light green, faint proof for the Palestinians perhaps that the desert bloomed before the Israelis created their state. In his epic landscape of Jerusalem executed in April of 1830, Roberts draws the Holy City in silhouette, its church towers and minarets, the Dome of the Rock, mere grey outlines against a soft evening sky. Six Arabs – their headdress and robes suggest they are Bedouin – rest beside an ancient well of translucent blue water. A broken Roman column lies beside the pool, its mammoth pedestal a reminder of the immensity of history. Roberts' prints have become almost a cliché, corrupted by overuse, representative of both a cause and a dream. If it was like that once, why cannot it be so again, a land of peace and tranquillity?

On the wall of my Beirut home, I have one of Roberts' lithographs of Tyre in southern Lebanon. There in the distance is the great peninsula upon which Alexander built his city, there are the familiar standing Arab figures, the broken Roman masonry in the foreground. One afternoon in 1978, I returned from Tyre after spending 12 hours in the city under Israeli shellfire. The Tyre from which I had travelled was a place of unpaved roads and overflowing sewage, of Palestinian camps and *fedayeen* guerrillas, of guns and sunken ships and the sharp clap of explosions. Could I relate this in any way to the picture on my living-room wall? Was this part of the Lebanon I knew? Was it a scene which in later years I would look at with nostalgia, even longing? For the Roman ruins of Tyre, a few of the old Ottoman harbour warehouses, the little Christian streets near the port, are still there. And the Mediterranean, the great pale green sea that sloshes away at the coastline of Phoenicia, this too still shaped our movements and our lives, provided the essential and unchanging link between that distant, unphotographed world of Roberts and the country in which I now lived.

Reading Roberts' biography, one learns that the world he visited *was* violent: crossing the snows of the Chouf mountains, he was told that there were gunmen on the road to Baalbek – just as there are today. But this picture hung there on my wall with the depth and serenity of a new world. And if I could enjoy the dream, how much easier for those who were born in Israel or Lebanon or Palestine – or for those who wished to live in the land that was Palestine – to believe in it.

Certainly, the Palestinian Arabs can reflect that when Roberts drew Jerusalem, the Jewish population of the land can have numbered scarcely 10 per cent of the total. There had always been a continued physical Jewish presence there over the centuries; it was for the Jews too an ancient homeland. But eight years before Roberts sat on that hilltop above the city, there were only 24,000 Jews living in Palestine.* Browse through the second-hand bookshops of Beirut or Jerusalem, however, and the ghosts begin to appear. In 1835, for example, just five years after Roberts had sketched the recumbent city of Jerusalem, we find the French writer Alphonse de Lamartine returning from a visit there to recommend to his readers in *Voyage to the Orient* that since Palestine did not really constitute a country, it presented remarkable opportunities for imperial or colonial projects.

Within 60 years, the nineteenth-century fascination with the Middle East begins to lose its romantic edge, even for the most mundane travellers. In a broken-backed 1892 edition of John Murray's *Handbook for Travellers in Syria and Palestine* which I bought in an antiquarian bookshop in west Beirut, a volume with a faded title in gold on its pale red cover, I discovered an item entitled 'Muslim Arabs'. These people are, we are told, 'proud, fanatical and illiterate ... generally noble in bearing, polite in address, and profuse in hospitality; but they are regardless of truth, dishonest in their dealings and secretly immoral in their conduct.' The Jews, on the other hand, were in the guidebook's opinion 'the most interesting people in the land ... The Jews of Palestine are foreigners. They have come from every country on earth ... of late years there has been a remarkable influx of Jews into Palestine, but the Turkish government are striving to hinder their settlement by every means in their power.'

These were the authentic reactions of an imperial Britain to a land which covered its transit routes to the Indian empire. Britain encouraged the growth of Zionism in Palestine in the early years of the First World War because she wanted American Jews to ally their country in the war against Turkey. Since the Tsar was already an ally against Germany, it was politically inconvenient to demand an end to anti-semitism in Russia. The idea of settling Jews in Palestine, the British Foreign Office cabled two of its ambassadors in 1916, 'might be made far more attractive to the majority of Jews if it held out to them the prospect that when in course of time the Jewish colonists in Palestine grew strong enough to cope with the Arab population they may be allowed to take the management of the internal affairs of Palestine ... into their own hands ... Our sole object is to find an arrangement which would be so attractive to the majority of Jews as to enable us to strike a bargain for Jewish support.'†

This is cold-blooded business indeed, just as was the Balfour Declaration of 1917 that gave Britain's support to a Jewish homeland providing

* Said, *Question of Palestine*, p. 9.
† Among the most carefully researched works on this period, containing many other examples of Foreign Office pragmatism, is *Britain and Zion: The Fateful Entanglement* by Frank Hardie and Irwin Herrman (Belfast, Blackstaff Press, 1981).

that 'nothing shall be done which may prejudice the civil and religious rights of existing non-Jewish communities in Palestine'. The equally earnest Anglo-French Declaration of 1918 promising the Arabs of former Ottoman colonies their independence if they supported the Allies against the Turks fell into much the same category, although it was not a promise that was intended to be kept. As Balfour himself said the following year, 'in Palestine we do not propose even to go through the form of consulting the wishes of the present inhabitants of the country.' So far as Balfour was concerned, Zionism was 'of far profounder import than the desire and prejudices of the 700,000 Arabs who now inhabit that ancient land [of Palestine]'.* The slaughter on the Somme and at Passchendaele had helped to bring about these conflicting pledges, just as a far more terrible massacre would in the second great European war virtually guarantee the creation of the Jewish state in Palestine. Against these historical profanities, the descendants of those colourfully dressed figures in Roberts' lithographs stood no hope.

The British themselves began their descent of the bloody staircase the moment Balfour blotted his signature in 1917. As Winston Churchill was to write on a different occasion, 'at first the steps were wide and shallow, covered with a carpet, but in the end the very stones crumbled under their feet.' One of the men who had to walk down this precarious companion-way was Malcolm MacDonald, the British dominions secretary in 1938, still vainly attempting to reconcile the desperate promises of the First World War before the outbreak of the Second, trying to preserve order in the British mandate of Palestine by restricting Jewish immigration.

Forty years later, I sat in the drawing-room of his home at Sevenoaks in Kent, watching him shake his head vigorously from side to side as he contemplated the ruins of his own efforts to resolve the Palestine problem. The ghosts were more substantial now. Churchill, a strong Zionist supporter, had fiercely condemned MacDonald in the Commons in 1938 and continued his verbal assault afterwards in the Division Lobby of the House of Commons. 'Churchill accused me of being pro-Arab,' MacDonald said. 'He said that Arabs were savages and that they ate nothing but camel dung.' But the British could avoid turning such disputes into personal grievances with a generosity not available to those who would ultimately be their victims. 'I could see that it was no good trying to persuade him [Churchill] to change his mind,' MacDonald said. 'So I suddenly told him that I wished I had a son. He asked me why and I said I was reading a book called *My Early Life* by Winston Churchill and that I would want any son of mine to live that life. At this point, tears appeared in Churchill's eyes and he put his arms around

* Quoted in Said, *Question of Palestine*, p. 16.

me, saying "Malcolm, Malcolm."' MacDonald sat there in his deep
armchair, savouring this story, an old man contemplating lost opportunities. He was to die four years later. He fussed for a while over a
large teapot, pouring both of us outsize cups of tea. He put down the
pot, stared at the floor for a few seconds and then looked up glowering,
pointed his finger at me in a way that was frightening because it was so
sudden. 'But you are living now in Beirut,' he said, 'because I failed.'

How could he have succeeded? More ghosts, more photographs intervene. The Yad Vashem memorial on the hills west of Jerusalem is
supposed to commemorate the Holocaust. That word 'supposed' may
anger Jewish readers, but Yad Vashem is not so much a memorial as a
political statement. Its documents, its photographs, dictate its theme:
that the Holocaust produced the state of Israel and that anyone who
opposed the creation of that state is on the level of the Nazis. Thus in
the same building as the photographs of SS officers selecting the Jews on
the ramps of Birkenau are news pictures of British paratroopers ordering
the concentration camp survivors away from postwar Palestine. The
British, it says in effect, were like the Nazis; they too were war criminals.
When I first visited Yad Vashem in 1978, I found it a place of un-
answerable accusation. When I went there in 1987, after my journey to
Auschwitz, it seemed somehow facile, an instrument of propaganda that
used the horror of what happened in Auschwitz and Treblinka and all
the other camps to justify not just the existence of Israel but all that
Israel has done since.

It is also a place of accusation against the Arabs of Palestine. For
there are pictures at Yad Vashem of the Grand Mufti of Jerusalem being
greeted in Nazi Germany by Heinrich Himmler. The photographs are
perfectly clear. Here we can see Sheikh Haj Amin al-Husseini shaking
hands with the leader of the SS, there he proudly inspects a volunteer
Muslim contingent of the *Wehrmacht*. On the wall are his words – an
accurate translation – exhorting the German government to prevent the
Jews of Europe going to Palestine. The inference is clear: the Muslim
religious leader of the Palestinian Arabs is also a war criminal. So
why should not his political successors be war criminals? If the Arab
Palestinians who saw in the Nazis some hope of preventing Jewish
immigration into Palestine were on the same level as the SS, were not
those Palestinians who oppose Israel today equally guilty?

The civil war in Palestine that followed the end of hostilities in
Europe inevitably embraced the tired holders of the imperial mandate.
From the desert of political opposition at Westminster, the old Zionist
Churchill contemplated the murder of British troops by Jewish gunmen
and pronounced Palestine a 'hell-disaster'. It was far worse for the Arabs
whose homes lay in that part of Palestine in which the United Nations
had decided to locate the new state of Israel. Those whom Balfour had

described as 'the existing non-Jewish communities of Palestine' were about to undergo their first catastrophe.

The Arab armies that invaded the new Israel were driven out, together with between 500,000 and 700,000 Arab Palestinians whose homes had been in that part of Palestine that was now Israel or in those areas of Arab Palestine that the Israelis captured. For decades after their War of Independence, the Israelis claimed that most of the Arab Palestinians had left of their own free will after·being urged by Arab radio stations to leave their homes and take sanctuary in neighbouring states until the Arab armies had conquered the upstart new Israeli nation. Israeli scholars now agree that these radio appeals were never broadcast and that the allegations were fraudulent. The Palestinian Arabs left their homes because they were frightened, often because they had heard stories — accounts which were perfectly true — of the massacre of Arab civilians by Jewish gangs.

The result was inevitable. While the Jews of Israel exulted in their renaissance, the Arabs of Palestine left in despair. From the camps of Europe, those who had avoided the execution pits and the gas chambers had at last reached the Promised Land about which their cantors had sung at Auschwitz. Here, for example, is how the American journalist I. F. Stone describes the last hours of his voyage to Haifa, aboard a Turkish refugee ship called the *Akbel*, a listing hulk carrying hundreds of concentration camp survivors on their journey to Palestine. The vessel approached the coastline at dawn, somewhere to the north of Mount Carmel.

Shortly before dawn I slept for a while on top of the wheelhouse. I woke to see the dim outlines of a mountain towards the southeast.

As the light increased and the sun rose, a cry ran over the ship.

'It's Eretz Israel.'

We saw Mount Carmel ahead of us and the town of Haifa sleeping in the morning sun below us ... The refugees cheered and began to sing *Hatikvah*, the Jewish national anthem ... People jumped for joy, kissed and hugged each other on the deck.*

And here is the militant Palestinian writer Ghassan Kanafani recalling an Arab family's departure from that same country just a few months later:

At Al-Nakura, our truck parked, along with numerous other ones. The men began to hand in their weapons to their officers, stationed there for that specific purpose. When our turn came, I could see the rifles and guns lying on the table and the long queue of lorries, leaving the land of oranges far behind and spreading out over the winding roads of Lebanon.

---

* *Underground to Palestine, and Reflections Thirty Years Later* by I. F. Stone (New York, Pantheon Books, 1978), pp. 205–6.

Then I began to weep, howling with tears. As for your mother, she eyed
the oranges silently ...*

The feelings of joy and despair in these two passages are almost
equally balanced, and the Jewish cry of delight on seeing the shore-line
of Palestine in the first and the image of Arab guns and hopelessness on
leaving Palestine in the second are even more relevant now than they
were then. The idea that Israel is the final and true refuge of all Jews —
'the first and last line of defence of the Jewish people', as Szymon
Datner called it — is as credible to Israelis today as it was in 1948. And
amid the hovels of Sabra and Chatila in Beirut, in Ein Helweh, in the
Nahr el-Bared camp in Tripoli, in Bourj el-Shemali in Tyre or in
Rashidiyeh further south, the guns and the bitterness and tears that
Kanafani witnessed have congealed into hatred.

Henceforth, the many thousands of Arabs who fled — like the few
thousand who stayed and like the inhabitants of Jerusalem and the West
Bank that would shortly be annexed by Jordan — would call themselves
Palestinians. The Jews of Palestine were now Israelis. And from the
'land of oranges', the new exiles arrived in the West Bank and in
Lebanon and in the Kingdom of Transjordan with an identity — as
'Palestinians' — that applied to a country that no longer existed, that
indeed never did exist as an independent nation. This irony was only
accentuated by the refugees' initial belief that their exile was to be brief,
a few days perhaps, at most a month, after which — in the manner of
other civilians who had abandoned their homes in the midst of battle —
they would return to their houses and fields to resume the life which had
been interrupted by war.

It was for this reason that many of them carefully locked their front
doors when they left their homes. Those who had time also diligently
collected their most important legal documents — the deeds of ownership
to property, the maps of their orange groves and fields, their tax returns
and their identity papers going back to Ottoman times — and packed
them into bags and tins along with family heirlooms and jewellery and
their front door keys. With luck, their homes would not be burgled and
any disputes that might subsequently arise over their property would be
swiftly resolved on production of those impressive-looking deeds, some
of them so old that they bore the colophon of the Sublime Porte.

By one of the more subtle cruelties of Middle East history, the papers
and the keys were to prove the most symbolic and most worthless of
possessions to the Palestinians. They acquired a significance that grew
ever more painful as weeks and then months away from home turned

* *The Land of the Sad Oranges*, quoted in *Dispossessed: The Ordeal of the Palestinians 1917–
1980* by David Gilmour (London, Sidgwick and Jackson, 1981). Gilmour's book is among the
most readable accounts of the Palestinian tragedy in Lebanon.

into years. Younger Palestinians − Palestinians who were born in Lebanon, for example − can remember how their parents angrily threw the keys away in the early 1950s, how the documents that were guarded with such care in the initial days of exile were mislaid or destroyed as their true meaning became clear; because they proved ownership of a world that had disappeared. For the keys − often made of thick grey iron, sometimes with decorated handles − were in a sense a promise of return, a promise that history inevitably broke. The new owners of those homes forbade any return and then changed the locks.

Yet among the half million Palestinians now living in Lebanon, many stubbornly went on cherishing these keys and their titles of ownership in Palestine. When a Palestinian political identity began to emerge after the 1967 Arab−Israeli war − when the West Bank and Gaza Strip were occupied by the Israeli army − the promise contained in these mundane implements and pieces of paper was somehow renewed. Reminders of humiliation once again became priceless possessions, as emotionally valuable as they had once been legally essential. In Lebanon, where the Palestinian war against Israel was focused once the PLO's guerrilla movement was evicted from Jordan in 1970, they were squirrelled away beneath floors or carpets, sometimes stored in rusting biscuit tins, broken suitcases and ancient trunks, often the very containers in which the refugees carried their most valuable belongings from Palestine in 1948.

Each document is signed by a British mandate official and gives in detail the figures of sale and settlement in the name of the Palestinian who inherited or bought the land. Some of the papers are now torn and others have been heavily creased because they have been re-read and re-folded so many times over the past 41 years. But each of them, surmounted by the royal coat of arms and the monogram of King George VI, carries the authority of the British Crown. Laid across a map of Israel, these documents form a patchwork of disputed ownership, a matrix of lands from northern Galilee to Ashqelon for which there are now in existence two perfectly legal deeds: one, in Jerusalem or Tel Aviv or Beersheba, proving irrefutably that the land is now owned by an Israeli, the other − in Beirut or Amman − showing that the rightful owner is a Palestinian Arab. Placed next to each other, the documents are both a territorial and a political contradiction; one is proof of the existence of Israel, the other carries with it the dream of Palestine.

The first time I ever saw one of the keys was in the Chatila camp in Beirut in 1977. I had been interviewing a family − four young brothers, two sisters, their parents, the children's paternal grandmother − about their lives in a city that was now dominated by the Syrian army. Were they watched by the Syrian intelligence service? Probably. Had any of the family been arrested? Perhaps. Did Yassir Arafat truly represent them? Of course. And then — because the deepest questions curiously acquire the least importance in such interviews — did they ever really think they would return to 'Palestine'? At this, the grandmother stood up and shuffled into a little hut-like concrete alcove, her bedroom, and emerged carrying something in a handkerchief. 'It is from our home in Haifa,' she said, unwrapping the cloth. And there was her key, its gun-metal grey shaft rusted brown but the handle still gleaming. How many families kept these keys? They did not know. Only the grandmother was old enough to have lived in Palestine. Her son and his family regarded the instrument as the key to 'their' home, just as they regarded Haifa as 'their' town although they had never been there.

Over the following three years, I was to see the keys again and, more often, the deeds of ownership to lost land. In many cases, they were kept in a container with ageing brown British Palestinian passports, the last used page of which registered their owner's final departure into exile. Before the fighting started in 1948, some Palestinians had even arranged to take a holiday in case of hostilities and had called at the Lebanese consulate in Palestine to pick up a visa for Beirut. An agreeable sort of departure, a legal exit to which no legal re-entry was ever to be forthcoming. But if it was so easy for me to see this evidence and to talk to those who had substantial proof of their ownership of homes in mandate Palestine, surely it would be no more difficult to go to Israel, find those same homes and — the idea had a special excitement about it — to knock on those same front doors. Who would open them?

What I did not realise then — but what I would discover the moment I embarked on my journey to those front doors — was that I had touched upon the essence of the Arab—Israeli war; that while the existence of the Palestinians and their demand for a nation lay at the heart of the Middle East crisis, it was the contradiction inherent in the claims to ownership of the *land* of Palestine — the 'homeland' of the Jews in Balfour's declaration — which generated the anger and fear of both Palestinians and Israelis. The evidence of history, not to mention the physical evidence of those land deeds, suggested a subject of legitimate journalistic inquiry: who legally as well as morally had the right to ownership of the property? To the Palestinians, the question appeared naive, almost insulting. In their eyes, they were not refugees but legal inhabitants of Palestine who were illegally exiled. Their homes had belonged to them, had been taken away from them and were now in the hands of others. Merely to ask the question was to imply that the justice of their cause was in doubt. To the Israelis, however, and to their supporters in the Jewish diaspora, the same question struck at the very morality of Zionism. To knock on those front doors, it transpired, was to cast doubt upon the very legitimacy of the state of Israel.

It mattered not that after weeks of interviews with 35 Palestinian families in Lebanon, I chose to write about the experiences only of those who had no immediate connection with the Palestinian guerrilla movement. It proved of no consequence that I then chose only those four families who still possessed their original Palestine passports, complete land deeds and mandate tax returns. The fact that three of these families had been moderately wealthy in Palestine and had managed to acquire the same social status in their exile — that they behaved and looked like millions of middle-class couples in Europe, or indeed in Israel — only compounded my error. I set off from Beirut for Jerusalem in the late autumn of 1980; and the moment I entered Rafi Horowitz's office in Jerusalem, I realised that I had set myself no easy assignment. Horowitz was an Israeli government spokesman, a middle-aged man with an angry, almost bitter way of explaining what happened to the Arabs of the old Palestine mandate. Every few minutes, he would break off to apologise for his own cynicism. 'You've got to realise that the state of Palestine never existed,' he said. 'The Arabs went to war with us in 1948 to destroy our Jewish state. Please excuse us for winning.'

Outside, in the rainy winter evening, the rush-hour traffic still clogged Jaffa Road. It had taken almost half an hour to reach his office along streets jammed with tourist coaches, the Americans inside staring through the windows at the neon Tel Aviv highway sign that glowed through the drizzle. The advertisement hoardings, the posters on the buses, the names above the shops — all were in Hebrew. A pretty Israeli girl had been selling magazines in the little paper-shop on the corner. 'That'll be two dollars,' she said. 'Have a nice day.' She sounded like a clerk at a Manhattan bookstore. Could this really once have been Palestine?

It is a question that immediately caused irritation in the office of Israel's official spokesman. Ask just who legally owns the land in Israel — who owns the deeds to the houses and orchards and blocks of property parcelled out under the British mandate — and the irritation turns to open annoyance. Horowitz left the room for a moment and returned with a slim red volume entitled *Land Ownership in Palestine 1880–1948*. It was written by Moshe Aumann of the Israel Academic Committee on the Middle East and its 24 pages are sprinkled with quotations stretching back a hundred years — from Mark Twain and Lamartine to Lord Milner and the 1937 Palestine Royal Commission — all of which assert that Palestine was a land of brigandage, destitution and desert before the mass immigration of Jews in the late 1930s.

Aumann, for example, quoted Mark Twain's account of his visit to the Holy Land in 1867 in which the American writer spoke of 'desolate country whose soil is rich enough but is given over wholly to weeds — a silent mournful expanse ... We never saw a human being on the whole route.' Twain is quoted as recording that 'one may ride ten miles, hereabouts, and not see ten human beings' and that 'the hills are barren ...

the valleys are unsightly deserts ... it is a hopeless, dreary, heartbroken land ... Palestine is desolate and unlovely.' The quotations were accurate but one sensed within Aumann's text an underlying idea: not just that Palestine was empty of people — which it assuredly was not — but that perhaps those people who did live there somehow did not deserve to do so; that they were too slovenly to use modern irrigation methods or to plant trees or to build brick houses. That Palestinian Arabs did cultivate the land in the nineteenth century — as a glance at Roberts' lithographs clearly proves — went unnoticed by Aumann, who concluded his thesis by stating that the contention that 95 per cent of the land of the state of Israel had belonged to Arabs 'has absolutely no foundation in fact.'*

To Horowitz, the Palestinians were now refugees, pure and simple. 'When the entity of the mandate ended,' he said, 'two other states — Jewish and Arab — were to have come into existence but the Arab state did not. It was annexed by Jordan. Of course, Arabs owned land here legally in what is now Israel. There are Arabs who owned land and can prove it without any doubt. But these people are now citizens of Arab states that are at war with Israel and they cannot claim possession of this land. As a result of losing the war in 1948 — excuse us for winning — the Arabs became partly a community of refugees. That is part of the Middle East problem.'

There was a pause in Horowitz's peroration. Then he leant forward across his desk. 'You know,' he said, 'you people have a habit sometimes of coming here to Israel with some specific details and thinking that from them you can deduce some universal truth. Forgive me for being a little cynical of that.' There was in reality no need for his self-proclaimed cynicism. Up in Lebanon, where so many of the 1948 Palestinian refugees are concentrated, there is sometimes precious little detail to be had about the land they once owned.

Even memories have been sealed up. One elderly Palestinian in Beirut wanted to draw a map of his olive grove for me and spent ten minutes sketching and re-sketching the roads south of Jaffa. But after a while, the roads on his map began to criss-cross each other in a crazy fashion and it became clear that he had forgotten the geography of his land. 'I am very sorry,' he said, 'but you must understand it has been a very long time ...' There is indeed an opaque quality to the memories that Palestinians like to tell of Palestine. Many now recall how happily Jews and Arabs lived together before 1948, although it is a fact that in some parts of Palestine near civil war existed between the two communities long before that date. Elegiac recollections are buttressed by the Roberts

---

* Land Ownership in Palestine 1880–1948 by Moshe Aumann (Israel Academic Committee on the Middle East, undated), pp. 5–8.

lithographs, pictures which have become part of a deep and dreamlike sleep through which the Palestinians have passed since 1948.

They bear little enough relation to the land that now lies west of Jerusalem. In many places, the Arab villages have disappeared, their names erased from the map. Even the township of Deir Yassin – notorious in Palestinian history as the village in which Jewish gangs massacred 250 Arabs, half of them women and children, in April of 1948 – has vanished. It is now called Givat Shaul and is a mere suburb of Jerusalem, its main street a line of petrol stations, garages and high-rise apartment blocks, more like the Edgware Road or Brooklyn than the scene of a mass murder. Only occasionally can you glimpse the old Palestine. Near the Latroun monastery, for example, and along the back road to Ashqelon, you can briefly catch sight of Arab women picking fruit in the dark orchards, their traditional Palestinian dresses of gold and red embroidery glimmering amid the heavy foliage, descendants of the 170,000 Arabs who stayed behind in 1948. Down in the old Arab quarter of Jaffa, the cosy streets of Roberts' lithographs are all but gone. The Arab houses are little more than shacks separated by acres of devastation where developers have torn down vacated Palestinian homes. While I was searching for some Arab property in the area, I had come across three young Palestinians standing beside a shabby food stall on the waterfront. The three – all were Israeli citizens – were arguing fiercely among themselves about a loan of ten Israeli shekels. One was talking in Arabic. But the other two Palestinians were shouting at each other in Hebrew. After the Palestinian militancy of Lebanon, it was like staring at the wrong side of a mirror: Palestine through the looking glass.

Is this the land to which the Palestinians of the diaspora wish to return? It was not difficult to find the answer in Lebanon. For every Palestinian who expressed doubts about the worth of returning, there were hundreds who would go back to what is now Israel if they had the opportunity to do so, people like David Damiani, a Christian whose family had been in Palestine since the time of the Crusades. Sitting on a thin metal chair above one of west Beirut's noisiest streets, eyes staring intently through heavy framed spectacles, he described his family tree with careful pride. Boutros Damiani was born in Jerusalem in 1687 and his four sons were consuls there for Britain, France, Holland and Tuscany. The last consul in the Damiani family was Ferdinand, who represented Mexico in 1932. David Damiani has an old photograph of him, a slightly pompous-looking man in a top hat surrounded by some Jerusalem worthies and an Englishman or two.

'When Napoleon besieged Jaffa,' Damiani said, 'my ancestor Anton Damiani interceded on behalf of the Muslim population and protected them from French anger – we have an official certificate from the *sharia* court to this effect.' In the early nineteenth century, Lamartine stayed with the Damiani family in Jaffa and mentioned them in *Voyage to the Orient*, the same book in which he advertised the colonial possibilities of Palestine. David Damiani's father Jean owned olive groves, extensive properties in Jaffa, Tel Aviv and Jerusalem and a soap factory which he operated inside the old Turkish *serail* on the hill above Jaffa not far from St Peter's church. The Damianis had bought the decrepit domed buildings from the Jaffa municipality and for several decades after the First World War the name of Damiani was proudly displayed in English and Arabic over the vaulted gateway where Turkish pashas once administered the law.

David Damiani's memories of the time were those of a schoolboy in a safe land. He lived with his five brothers, sister and parents in an old building near the Cliff Hotel in Jaffa and he still remembered the day in 1935 on which Jean Damiani bought the first family car, a magnificent light green Buick saloon costing 350 Palestinian pounds, equivalent then to the same amount in sterling. Damiani senior maintained a chauffeur to take him round the family olive groves. 'Before 1936, the harbour at Jaffa was flourishing,' Damiani recalled. 'There were always 25 or 30 ships moored off the port waiting to load. It was a prosperous place. Arabs and Jews were happy to live in Palestine. Everything was in abundance – fruit, vegetables and foodstuffs of all kinds. People would have lived happily if it wasn't for the troubles instigated by the government and the Jewish Agency.'

It was only when he came to 1936 that Damiani's face grew suddenly cold and his hands, until now resting quietly on his knees, began to move in agitation. 'I remember the general strike starting in 1936. It started on April 19th, a Sunday; and the next day I didn't want to go to school. I was fourteen years old. A bus used to take us to school in the Ajami area of Jaffa but there was no school that day and I was pleased. It was an Arab strike but we were in a safe area. It was middle-class.' Damiani paused here for several seconds. 'When the Arab revolt came in 1938, the Arab leaders used to impose taxes on well-off people. So like many others, my father went to Beirut to get away. In his absence, the factory was run by honest workers. I was still at school but at home I used to look after the accounts for the soap factory. My father did give money to the Arabs to keep his head.'

With the outbreak of the Second World War, life in Palestine returned to normal – 'in a day', according to Damiani – as old enemies temporarily cooperated. When the Allies liberated Lebanon in 1941, David Damiani went to the American University in Beirut to study business administration. It was a gentle enough life and it took only six and a half hours to travel home by taxi from Beirut to Jaffa. The first hint that things were not really changing for the better came in 1945 when, according to Damiani, two Palestinian Jews paid a visit to his father.

'They were both prominent Jews in the town. One was called Jad Machness and the other's name I can only remember as Romano. They proposed to my father that he make a list of all our properties in Palestine so that they could buy them. They said he would then have to take his family to Switzerland. My father would not accept the idea. He told them that we were a very ancient family in Palestine and were much respected. He said that our grandfathers fought for the Holy Land and that we must stick to the Holy Land. Then Romano took me to one side – my father was sitting at his desk – and told me that I had a great future in front of me and that people would be prepared to sell property to the Damianis. He brought out a list of thirteen Arab properties that he wanted me to buy and the resell to the Jews. One of the properties comprised five thousand dunums of land owned by the Latin Patriarchate of Jerusalem near Nablus. He told me that if I bought this land at five pounds a dunum, he and his friends would buy it from me at twenty-five a dunum. He told me he also wanted me to buy land from an Arab magistrate called Aziz Daoudi who had an orange grove near Tel Aviv. "You will make two million pounds," he told me. "Then you can go and live in Switzerland with your family." I told my father and mother about this and my father said: "Is there anything that you lack? Do you lack clothes, food or a home? Why should we do such a dirty business and stain our name, we who for centuries had an excellent reputation?" I turned Romano down.'

When the United Nations resolved upon the partition of Palestine in 1947, the Damianis were in Jerusalem, buying property near Terra Sancta in the Jewish part of the city. 'We thought that if we didn't like the Arab sector of Jerusalem after partition,' Damiani said, 'we would also have property in the Jewish sector. We thought that Jerusalem sooner or later would be an international city. We wanted to put our money in various places so that if one was not safe, the other would be. We did not think of going to live abroad or of buying property outside Palestine. We did not think things would be as bad.'

A year earlier, David Damiani had married Blanche, an 18-year-old Nazareth girl, and set up a home of his own in the Arektenje district of Jaffa. He bought a two-storey house at the end of a narrow street just off the Tel Aviv road and furnished it with new tables, chairs and beds. There was a handsome portico outside and four mock Grecian columns at the back of the front hall that gave the house a museum-like effect. There was no street number but in Beirut years later, David Damiani could remember that his postal address had been Post Office Box No. 582. It was to be the only home he ever owned in Palestine.

'You have to realise,' he said, 'that we didn't think in terms of a Jewish state and an Arab state. We thought the worst that would happen would be a national partition with Jews and Arabs still living in their own homes. But from the beginning of December 1947 until April 1948 there was continuous fighting around Jaffa. In early 1948, people started sending their families outside Jaffa to Nablus, Gaza and Lydda. Some Arabs went to Amman, Egypt, Lebanon or Syria. In Jaffa, life was rendered very difficult. Water pumping by the municipality stopped. The electric wires were cut. The British cooperated with the Jews against the Arabs. Dogs and donkeys were killed and left in the streets to create a health hazard. The city was in chaos and we were afraid that armed men would attack us. I once went to the Ajami police station to ask for protection but the British constable wouldn't open the door to me.'

Palestinians find it almost impossible to recall their final departure from Palestine without considerable emotion, for it was not only a tragedy for individual families but has become a critical moment in modern Palestinian history. The Damiani family made their decision to leave in the third week of April after snipers in Tel Aviv began shooting into the centre of Jaffa, sending at least one bullet into David Damiani's home. They left for Beirut by sea on 25 April.

'My father originally refused to leave Jaffa,' Damiani said. 'But the rest of our family insisted because we did not want him to be endangered. We were peaceful people. We did not care very much for politics. We are still not interested in politics. We locked the front door of our home just before lunchtime. We carried only suitcases and clothes and we had a case with our jewellery and the registry deeds to our lands inside. We never thought we would not be able to go back. If we had thought that, we would never have left. We thought we were going for a month or so, until the fighting died down. We took our front door keys with us but we threw them away some years ago. They are worthless now . . .'

In Jaffa harbour, the Damianis boarded the Italian passenger cruise ship *Argentina*, a comfortable vessel which would take the family on the 16-hour journey to Beirut port. Damiani still has the tickets for the journey. 'When we pulled out of Jaffa, I stood on the stern and looked out over the old city,' he said. 'I could see our soap factory in the *serail* on top of the hill and St Peter's church next to it. Then I did ask myself if we would see this place again; and when Jaffa started to disappear to our starboard, I remember I said to myself: "If this ship could turn round now, I would return to Jaffa." We were foolish. It was too late.'

David Damiani said nothing for several seconds after finishing his narrative but he opened up a battered suitcase and produced from it his old pale brown British Palestine passport and opened the document on page six. There, in the top left-hand corner, is an exit visa. 'Jaffa Port,' it says. '25-4-48'. It still retained the same dark blue colour that it had when it was stamped into the passport by a British policeman 32 years earlier; last exit from Palestine.

David Damiani's life since 1948 was a mixture of family bereavement, hardship and moderate business success. The family spent the summer of 1948 in the Lebanese hill resort of Aley, living on 7,000 pounds they had taken with them from Palestine. By the standards of other refugees, they were well off. 'We heard the radio and saw photographs of the damage in the papers,' Damiani said. 'We wondered who would take care of our orange groves. After about a month, we realised that a catastrophe had taken place. My father was very sad all the time; he was an old man without home, property or money. He died in 1952, a broken man.' Damiani and his wife went to Jordan in 1950 while his brothers looked for work in Beirut. In Amman, he worked for UNRWA — the newly established United Nations Relief and Works Agency for Palestine refugees — and started a small soap factory, but the project was not successful. He became a civil servant in Jordan and then part-owner in a Beirut hotel. In 1949, he had become a Jordanian citizen and in 1954 secured some family money that had been locked in Jaffa bank accounts, making him 'not a rich man, but living'.

Yet he still kept all the family deeds and files. On a clean parchment headed by the British crest were the deeds to his home in Jaffa, bought from his father for 3,493 Palestinian pounds and dated 27 October 1947. He was even able to produce the fragile Turkish deeds to the *serail* in Jaffa and British documents proving family ownership of orange groves in Yazour on the main Jaffa–Jerusalem road (32 dunums), near Holon (76 dunums) and at Beit Dajan (240 dunums) and to property in Jerusalem, part of which was rented to a British assistant district commissioner.

'I once had an opportunity to visit Jaffa again,' Damiani said. 'My wife went but I refused to go there. I would see my house occupied by other people. I am not allowed to dispose of my property or live in it. If you were not allowed to go back and live in your country, how would you feel? And if you could go back, would you stay in Beirut just because you had a nice home there?'

There is something insulting about the way in which a stranger can visit a place which is forbidden to people with infinitely more interest in such a journey. If Damiani could go to Jaffa, most of his fellow exiles are prevented forever from walking in the streets outside their old houses — or knocking on those front doors. The nearest a Palestinian in Lebanon can go to his former family home in what is now Israel is likely to be the orange orchards south of Tyre or the east bank of the Jordan river. A key or a lifeless deed or a cheap Roberts reproduction, perhaps a family snapshot or a tourist postcard of the 1930s, is the nearest that many Palestinian exiles can move in spirit towards the place they regard as their homeland. Blessed be the foreign correspondent who can fly

from Beirut to Athens, therefore, and in the same day pick up an El Al
flight from Athens to Tel Aviv and land at Ben Gurion airport and travel —
faster even than the old direct taxi route from prewar Beirut — to
Jerusalem. Doubly fortunate is the journalist who can within 24 hours
leave Beirut and look upon what is left of the world Damiani lost on that
April day when the *Argentina* sailed out of Jaffa harbour for Beirut,
carrying his family from Palestine for the last time. It was not difficult
to find the ghosts of that world. The Israelis had turned the Damiani
soap factory into a municipal museum but you could still see the
family's name in fading Arabic letters on the archway at one end of the
building. The wind and rain on the little hill above Jaffa had ripped
away at the paint but it was just possible to make out the words 'David
Damiani' to the left of the broken wooden gate.

The rest of the wall was stained with damp and flaking brown paint;
the winters had cut deeply into the fabric of the old *serail*. The museum
had taken over the northern end of the building but the main hall of
what had been Damiani's factory, with its vaulted roof and tunnels, was
in semi-derelict condition, leased on occasion to a firm of Iranian-born
Jews who dealt in Persian art. The outer windows had been smashed
and the cut stone had been severely fissured. Dust lay thickly over the
cracked flagstone floor and only when I ascended a dangerous staircase
did I find a solitary reminder of the business that helped to make the
Damianis one of the richest Arab families in Jaffa. Against a wall was a
corroded iron trolley that was once used for carrying oil in the factory.
It was perhaps as well that David Damiani had not come back.

The first-floor museum for the Ancient History of Tel Aviv—Jaffa just
round the corner was well cared for, although it recorded not the Arab
history of Jaffa but the Biblical history of the land; there was an
exhibition to illustrate the Israelite Royal Period (930 BC) with references
to King David. A large Biblical map of Solomon's life lay beneath a
quotation from the Book of Chronicles chapter 2 verse 16: 'And we will
cut wood out of Lebanon, as much as thou shalt need: and we will bring
it to thee in flotes by sea to Joppa; and thou shalt carry it up to
Jerusalem.' The museum staff knew the name of Damiani, although it
was not recalled with much enthusiasm. 'Do I know the history of this
building?' asked the Israeli Jew in the museum curator's office. He was
a cheerful, tubby-faced man, born in Australia and still using the broad,
flat accents of the Antipodes. 'This place used to be the Turkish administrative headquarters in Jaffa. It was one of the most important places
in the city. Then much later it was bought by a very rich Arab Christian
family called Damiani and they turned this building' — the man paused
in humorous reflection for a moment — 'into a soap factory. In 1948,
this became a Jewish town and we took over the building.' The whole
structure was now owned by the municipality of Jaffa and the museum

hoped to extend its galleries into the rest of the building when money was made available.

When I told the museum official that I had met David Damiani, his eyes opened wider with interest. 'Does he know this is a museum now?' he asked, and then walked over to a glass-fronted bookcase. He withdrew from it a rare bound second volume of *Palestine Illustrated* by François Schotten, published in Paris in 1929. The Israeli flicked through the pages of photographs, sepia prints of Arab peasants and donkey-drawn carts clattering through the streets of a forgotten Palestine, until his thumb came to rest on a picture of workers inside a cavernous hall. And there, sure enough, was the interior of old Jean Damiani's soap factory with a row of moustachioed Palestinians piling up bar after bar of soap around the walls. Each man in the picture was staring blankly at the photographer, a bar of soap in each hand as if caught in the act of some doubtful ritual. 'When you get back to Beirut,' the Israeli said, 'you must ask Damiani if he's got that picture.'

Beneath the hill on which the *serail* huddles, the great iron gates of Jaffa port still stand next to a row of small stone shops, their Arab architecture belied by the Hebrew names above the windows. David Damiani set off from here with his family in April 1948, and it was not difficult to see how clearly the old factory and the church above the city must have stood out on the horizon as the *Argentina* slipped past the tide bar and steamed for Beirut.

Finding Damiani's old home, however, was not quite so easy. The Israelis had turned the old Arab buildings south of the *serail* into a shopping and restaurant precinct, a tastefully laid out tourist attraction in which the best architectural features have been preserved. But no one there had ever heard of the Arektenje area of Jaffa where the newly married Damiani had bought his home. Nor did the Israelis in the market by the Jaffa clock-tower have any idea where it was. It was only when I entered the Arab quarter, a network of dusty roads and wastelands of rubble interspersed with a few small houses just south of the city, that a Palestinian remembered the name. He directed me to a main road on the edge of Jaffa and to a small lane that ran off it to the north. I followed his directions and down a narrow street came to a cul-de-sac dominated by a large white house with a portico over the front door.

Jews and Arabs lived together in the street, speaking each other's language with some fluency, and it was an Israeli Jew who first pointed to the white house. An Arab woman, a Palestinian, was peering from the upper balcony. 'Was this Damiani's house?' he shouted up to her in Arabic and she replied, in Hebrew, that it was. A small Palestinian boy led me up some steps to the side of the building and the woman ushered me inside. It was a light, airy room with some rural paintings on the wall and two small clean bedrooms leading off on each side. Very shyly, the woman introduced herself as Georgette Aboud. She and her husband Louis, a garage owner, had bought the upper floor from a Jewish family and were bringing up their four children there. The little boy, Zohair, was sent to make coffee.

Mrs Aboud led me to the balcony from where it was evident that many of the surrounding buildings — like those elsewhere in the Arab quarter — had been devastated, their roofs smashed in and their windows punched out of their frames. 'The landlords do that,' she said, and pointed to three small cottages that had been vacated and destroyed within the past 24 hours. 'Two Arab families and a Jewish family lived there and the moment they moved out, the landlords broke the houses. They want to build on the land.' Mrs Aboud — she and her husband were both Israeli citizens — seemed resigned to this gradual destruction of the little mixed society around their home. But her family owned only the upper floor of Damiani's old house. 'There is an old man living downstairs,' she said. 'We do not usually see him but he is a kind man. He is a Jew.'

It was growing dark and a sharp wind was coming in off the Mediterranean, blowing up the dust around the house. But downstairs I rang the bell next to the black steel gates and after a while I heard someone coming to the front door. The gate opened to reveal an old man, slightly stooped and staring quizzically at us. He had a thin cardigan over his shoulders to protect him from the breeze. We told him why we had come. 'If you know the man who owned this house, you had better come inside,' he said. And so we followed the old man up the stone steps beneath the portico and into the long hall.

At the far end it was possible to see four mock Grecian columns, painted white and glowing in the light of a single bulb. 'I live here with my two daughters,' the man said and sat down carefully in an armchair beside the columns. There was a little table between us, piled with books upon which lay an old photograph of a man in British army uniform standing next to a beautiful young Jewish girl. 'That was my wife,' the old man said. 'I was in the British army during the war. I have been here eight and a half years now. I bought this floor of the house from an Arab family. I never knew Mr Damiani.'

The man spoke in short sentences, as if trying to strain out of his monologue all but the most essential facts. There was a long silence and then he said with just a trace of a smile: 'I am a sculptor, I am an old man and I am a Jew.' He wanted to talk. His name, he said, was Shlomo Green and he had been a refugee from Romania. He had left his village of Clug on the Romanian–Hungarian border in 1939 and boarded a ship for Palestine just before the outbreak of the Second World War. 'The British navy caught our ship but we were lucky,' he said. 'It was the last ship from which the passengers were permitted to stay legally in

Palestine. I spent a year and a half in a kibbutz then joined the English army for five years. I went from Alamein to Tobruk then to Syria. All my family were sent to Auschwitz. Only my mother survived. They made her a slave labourer. She told me my father died in the camp in 1944. I lost about a hundred relatives in Auschwitz.'

Shlomo Green stopped speaking for a moment. It was a natural coda in his story. He joined the Israeli army in 1948, fought at Latroun and in Galilee and joined up again in 1956 and 1967. His wife had died just over a year earlier; one of his daughters was a teacher in Tel Aviv, the other a painter, and Shlomo Green was himself a sculptor of some distinction. He had had 11 exhibitions in Jerusalem and some of his creations lined the walls of his little home, of David Damiani's home. Shlomo Green was only 62 but he looked much older.

He walked quickly around the room to show off his sculptures and then said: 'Tell me about Mr Damiani. I know nothing about him.' So he sat down again and listened to the story of the Damianis, of their life in Jaffa and of how they fled in 1948, how David Damiani stood on the stern of the ship off Jaffa port and wished he could have turned round then and gone back to his home. If human death is a measure of suffering, then David Damiani would surely have agreed that he had suffered less than Shlomo Green.

But the old Jew sat for a long time in silence as the wind and rain in the darkness outside lashed at the windows of Damiani's old home. Then he looked up quite suddenly with tears in his eyes. 'I am very moved by what you have told me,' he said. 'What can I say? I would like to meet these people. If you can say for me ...' Here he paused, but he wanted to go on. 'It is a tragedy of both our people. How can I explain in my poor English? I think the Arabs have the same rights as the Jews and I think it is a tragedy of history that a people who are refugees make new refugees. I have nothing against the Arabs. I am living here with Arab people in peace and I have some friends among them. They are nice people. They are the same as us. I don't know that we Jews did this tragedy — but it happened. I want only one thing: peace for the new generation and progress. How can I say more than this? I feel at home here.'

In Beirut, I told Damiani of what Shlomo Green had said, of the warm old house with the mock Grecian pillars still standing in the front hall. I repeated the details of how so many of Green's family had been murdered at Auschwitz. Damiani showed no bitterness. 'I wish him happiness,' he said. 'Can you tell him that? Can you tell him please that I wish him happiness?'

It would, however, be an historical untruth to suggest that all Palestinians felt as generously as Damiani towards those who now own the lands that belonged to them. Kanaan Abu Khadra was a case in point, a journalist in mandate Palestine – by all accounts a good one in a crusading and courageous if rather partisan sort of way – who founded and edited a newspaper called *Al Shaab*. In 1946, in the top front page article in the very first edition of his newspaper, whose title in Arabic means 'The People', he urged Arabs to struggle harder to maintain their land in Arab ownership in Palestine. The page carried a map covered in dark smudges. 'These shaded land areas have become the property of the Jews,' the caption said. 'This will become the national homeland of the Jews.' It was a prophetic piece of journalism.

Leafing through bound volumes of those old editions in Beirut, Abu Khadra could still experience the odd moment of journalistic triumph as old newspapermen tend to do, long after their papers have died. 'We had a great paper,' he said. 'By 1948, we had a circulation of 12,000 – the highest in Palestine. I bought a second-hand English flatbed press and issued shares. We were less than self-supporting but we were an independent, neutral paper. We were independent of the Husseinis and the Nashishibis, the big Arab families. It was a national paper. The Jews hated it but we were not against the Jews.'

Abu Khadra's heavily boned face and strong rectangular glasses gave him a slightly fearsome appearance. He was also the kind of editor who would ask you to check the spelling of a place name or the age of a politician (he was born in 1920). He was as exacting in his own business affairs. The old blue suitcase which he carried out of Palestine in 1948 was still stuffed with his files and documents, all neatly labelled and dated – land deeds, deeds of sale, taxes, rents and maps of allotments – together with correspondence with the United Nations about the owner-ship of his family's land. There was a lot of it. Indeed, the Abu Khadras were one of the largest families in Palestine, their orchards and property scattered between Jaffa, Jerusalem and Gaza. There were two Abu Khadra Streets in Jaffa and there still is an Abu Khadra Mosque in Gaza. The family jointly owned 12,000 dunums of agricultural land and about 20 properties in Jaffa. One of Abu Khadra's first memories – and one that he went back to again and again – was of walking with his brothers Rabah and Anwar through his father's olive grove in Jaffa to visit the house of his uncles. The family grew oranges, corn, barley and sugar cane.

'I used to go there every day when I was a boy. My uncles Fawzi and Tawfiq lived in two houses joined together, one of which had been built by my grandfather Ismail. It had three big windows with iron doors and white walls and you used to go| into the house up a flight of steps because there were shops underneath. My cousin Ibrahim lived in a two-storey house a few hundred metres away, just beyond the Tel Aviv – Jaffa port railway line. He had Jewish tenants in the house.' In 1937, Abu Khadra went to study science in Beirut and attended the

American University – as David Damiani was to do four years later – but he did not like the course and returned to Jaffa, eventually settling for a degree in journalism at the American University in Cairo.

He started *Al Shaab* in 1946, with four full-time staff in Jaffa. He was at his desk at the paper when the UN passed its resolution to partition Palestine. He kept working when the war started between the Arabs and the Jews but his last edition came suddenly on 9 March 1948. 'We wanted to print a banner headline above the capture of a Jewish settlement by Lebanese soldiers,' he recalled. 'The British mandate censor, a Jewish man called Arieh Siev – a nice fellow although we never saw eye-to-eye – refused to let us print. On the next day, the district commissioner suspended our paper. My father and mother had died some years before and I lived with my brother Rabah, my sister Rabiha, my wife Sulafa and my baby son. It was originally my father's home; there was a big hall inside the entrance which was also used as a dining-room. Most of the house was white. My father had been a great admirer of Kemal Ataturk – he fought in the Turkish army against the British in Gaza – and Ataturk's picture hung in the living-room.

'About April 15th, my home was mortared. It was in the middle of Jaffa. Two shells hit the roof and one exploded in the corridor during the night. By five in the morning, it was impossible to stay there. We had a car, an English Rover, so we drove to the southern part of the city. We locked the house up but we thought we were going back. People say that the Arabs were told to leave their homes by Arab countries. But in Jaffa it was panic. The city was being destroyed. Some people left babies behind. We were being murdered.' The shelling, according to Abu Khadra, came from Tel Aviv. The family stayed with relatives for ten days, then drove to Ramleh where Abu Khadra's second brother Anwar lived. Abu Khadra remembered stopping at a gas station and finding three bullet holes in his car from snipers. Then he went on to Gaza. By this time, the Egyptian army had entered southern Palestine but Abu Khadra was to watch them, only a few days later, retreating along the beach towards Sinai. The family Rover also became bogged down on the beach road and his brother Anwar suffered a heart attack after spending a night on the open beach. He died of a second attack a few months later.

For days, the Abu Khadras lived in a house in Gaza under nightly air attack. 'We could not move further,' he said. 'We could not move back home and we had reached the end of Palestine.' Abu Khadra became a refugee camp official for the UN in Gaza, leaving in 1951 to become an UNRWA officer in Lebanon. He was later to become owner of a Beirut company that dubbed educational films and translated technical books into Arabic. Yet he took with him to Beirut his old suitcase of deeds and taxes, proof that the Abu Khadras owned their land in Palestine. The documents amounted to a small archive; they even included his Palestine mandate press cards, entitling him 'to pass freely anywhere in Palestine, including areas in which a curfew has been imposed'. There were 1948 tax receipts from the Municipal Corporation of Jaffa and rental agreements for the lease of land to the Royal Air Force. There were deeds for the family home in Jaffa, in the name of his father and dated 1 August 1930, and a map of the Abu Khadras' mortgaged orange orchards at Barqa around the Wadi al Gharbi on the road from Jaffa to Ashqelon.

'The groves were just above the sea,' he said. 'They were magnificent oranges, the best in Palestine. These were the original Jaffa oranges; they were grown in Palestine long before the Israelis came. From my orchard, I could see the steam trains running down the coast to Gaza. I used to hear the locomotive's whistle.' Abu Khadra showed little physical emotion when he talked about the past, but his words were carefully chosen and sometimes very angry. 'It is miserable for us to look back on these things. The West says the Palestinians are better off now and this could be true in some cases. But it is not the point. Palestine is our home. My sister-in-law was allowed to visit Palestine a few years ago. She brought me some oranges from my orchard but I couldn't eat them. I threw them away. I don't realise even now that we will not go back. My kids want to go for a visit and my daughter wants a picture of our home ... I was asked if I wanted to go. But I could not stand the humiliation of crossing the Allenby Bridge – at my age, being stripped and searched by a Zionist, Jew, a Pole, a Russian or a Romanian who is living in my country, in my home, asking me questions and searching me. And it is my country. I think about my land every day. I remember every stone in my house and every tree in my orchards. I am not willing to sign any paper that would release that land to anybody.'

Abu Khadra's faith in legal niceties was only a gesture. He knows what has happened to his land. The trains still run along the coastline south of Jaffa where the family's old orange groves stand. It is no longer a steam locomotive but a fast diesel pulling a trail of red, white and blue carriages, an express that rumbles down to Ashqelon between the orchards and the sea. I could see it from where Abu Khadra used to stand at the edge of his fields in Barqa, although few people knew where Barqa was. 'Was' is the correct word; for Barqa, like hundreds of Palestinian Arab villages, disappeared after 1948.

The Israeli Jews in the little kibbutz a mile or so away had never heard of it, but an old Arab woman in a long dark dress picking fruit pointed up a hill when she heard the name and shrugged her shoulders. The orchards, now part of a large farming combine, stretched across a little hill. The Wadi El Gharbi – mentioned in Abu Khadra's land maps – elicited a faint response in the woman. It is buried today, like the village beneath the trees, their branches heavy with fruit.

The Abu Khadra inheritance in Jaffa was almost equally hard to find. The house which Kanaan Abu Khadra fled in April 1948 had lain in semi-derelict condition for years, its windows partly boarded up. The olive grove through which he used to walk as a boy was submerged beneath a main road and a cluster of lean-to engineering sheds even before 1948. But I found the home which his cousin Ibrahim owned next to the Tel Aviv – Jaffa port railway line. The railway track had been torn up years earlier – a cutting lined with ivy-covered telegraph poles marked it now – but the house, in need of a few coats of paint, was just next to the old railway bridge. One of Ibrahim's former Jewish tenants still lived on the second floor.

David, a small, thin, smiling man with long, sensitive features, welcomed me to his little home. He and his wife were Turkish-born Jews who came to Palestine before the Second World War. They had never left their home, even when the Arab–Jewish front line ran behind the house in 1948. He well remembered Ibrahim Abu Khadra. 'He was a nice enough man,' David said. 'But we saw little of him in 1948. This house was part of the Jewish front line and although Mr Abu Khadra never knew it, we had guns and ammunition stored downstairs. Menachem Begin used to come here during the 1948 battles to this house, and he came up to see us three or four times during the fighting to have coffee and biscuits with us. He was a good man, an agreeable man.'

The war had left its mark, too, on the home of the two uncles whom Abu Khadra so often recalled visiting. Abu Khadra Street had now become Gerulot Street, but the white-stone house was still there, with its three fine, tall windows of delicate iron tracery. The embossed iron doors were rusting and one of them had fallen off its hinges. On the south wall, there were some faint shrapnel marks; several deep bullet holes could be seen beside a window. The ground floor consisted of a key-cutter's stall and some small shops, just as it did when Abu Khadra knew it. Up the flight of steps was a very old door, covered in flaking green paint.

I knocked on it but it was so dilapidated that I could see right through the door frame and into a large room where a man was sitting in a kitchen chair, dressed in trousers and vest. He was suspicious but courteous. 'Yes, this was Abu Khadra's house,' he said. 'It is not his house now.' He was joined at the door by his wife and daughter. He wanted no publicity and he did not want to talk about himself. 'I own this house now,' he said. So I left, and as I walked back to my car, the man watched me from the little steel balcony upon which Kanaan Abu Khadra had played as a boy. His hands were thrust deep in his pockets, his shoulders slightly hunched in the breeze, a man looking after his home.

At least in Jaffa there had been doors to knock upon. The same cannot be said for many thousands of Palestinian houses in what is now Israel. Fatima Zamzam, for example, knew just what had happened to her home and lands. But from her two-room concrete refugee shack, she could now just see Palestine. She still called it that; and indeed, beyond the line of evergreen trees beside the main road south of the Lebanese city of Tyre, I could see above the coastline a faint, thin grey line of hills inside Galilee on the other side of the Israeli frontier. Mrs Zamzam had left her home on the other side of those hills more than three decades earlier and she had never been back.

She lived in the Palestinian camp at Rashidiyeh, a wretched four square miles of breeze-block huts and cabins relieved only by the occasional tree, a straggling plant hanging from a poorly made brick wall and an open sewer that snaked uneasily down the centre of the mud roads. Mrs Zamzam had a tiny garden; a few feet of clay with a stunted flowering cherry tree that shaded the sandbagged air-raid shelter. For Rashidiyeh was coming under shellfire or Israeli air attack almost every day.

She was at first sight a cheerful figure, a plump woman of 65 who wore a brightly patterned dress and whose curly hair showed around the front of her white scarf. She had a heavily lined face, a prominent, almost hawk-like nose, but she had kindly eyes and every so often she would display a vein of sharp humour that suggested her family had to keep their shoes clean when they approached her little parlour. When she told me how she came to be a refugee, she paused reflectively before each statement, conscious that as a foreigner I might not know the history of Palestine before 1948.

'I come from a village called Um Al-Farajh,' she said. 'It was in northern Galilee. My family had three houses in the village. We used to make olive oil to sell to the other villages around. We grew wheat and made flour. My husband was Mustafa Zamzam and we had three orchards — two with olives and one with citrus. We even grew grapes on the side of our houses. We had all kinds of fruit — we had everything. In 1944, we had a new house built just outside the village for my husband and myself. Mustafa got Arab engineers up from Tel Aviv to build it and it cost about 700 Palestinian pounds. Some English tourists even came to take pictures of our home. It was a stone house — white stone — with four rooms upstairs and four rooms downstairs. It was built in an orchard opposite a place where we used to have our old house. It was known in the village as the Island Area. We had seven children — five boys and two girls.'

Mrs Zamzam spoke slowly, a village woman speaking to a stranger, and without warning she stood up and went to her other room, returning a minute or so later with a rusting tin. I could still read the name of the English toffee manufacturer on the lid which she prised off with a knife.

From inside, she took a piece of pale mauve, floppy parchment. It was the 1915 Turkish deed to her family land, heavily stained by damp, the corners torn but the wording and the ornate flowered crest still clearly visible. A Turkish stamp was still affixed to the bottom left-hand corner. 'This shows that my family owned the land,' she said with a simplicity that might have left even a lawyer silent. Then she took a cleaner but still crumpled paper from the tin. *Government of Palestine Certificate of Registration*, it said at the top. 'Land Registry Office of Gelo, Sub-District: Acre. Village: Um Al-Farajh. No. of Land 18151. No. of Doc 52. Block: Al-Habara Kanel. 19 dunums ...' The date is 22 October 1947. The document was in the name of Mustafa Ibn Assaad Shihada Zamzam, Mrs Zamzam's husband, and when she saw that I recognised this type of British mandate deed Mrs Zamzam's face lit up as if a great discovery had been made. Mr Zamzam was dead but his widow regarded the land — not without reason under Islamic law — as rightfully hers.

She said that it never occurred to her or her husband that her village would be harmed or its people endangered. 'We used to visit Jewish people,' she said. 'There was never any problem. We took our sick people to a Jewish doctor. There was a Doctor Kayewe and a Doctor Natani and there was also a lady doctor called Miriam. They were good to us. Sometimes we took our goods to sell in Jewish villages. But one day in 1948, Jewish gangs stopped a truck from our village. They ambushed the truck and killed the driver. Jewish women then shot all the men on board the truck. This happened on the road between Um Al-Farajh and Acre, near the Al-Insherah orchard opposite Nahariya. So no one went to Acre any more.'

According to Mrs Zamzam, Jews then began to shell her village. 'We were surrounded. Other Arabs told us we were surrounded and should move to another village. We tried to use the date palm trees to close the roads — we had only eight English .303 rifles in Um Al-Farajh. The Jewish gangs were just outside. I met a brother-in-law who told me to leave but I stayed another night in our new house just outside the village. The men stayed behind but we left next day. I held my son Hassan who was 40 days old and the small children carried the other babies. We took the keys to the house with us — we lost them here in Rashidiyeh.'

Mrs Zamzam listed the villages through which she travelled — Al Naher, Al Kabil, Al Nahalie, Tashiha and Al Dear — and then she fell into a kind of swoon, wailing as if she was mourning a husband or son and holding her hands to her face. The young Palestinian men who had gathered in the room to hear her story sat quietly, knowing that she would finish her grief and that this was a ritual even if it was a deeply felt one. Mrs Zamzam looked up to the wall of the room where there hung a framed portrait of a young man and woman. The girl was dark-haired with an attractive but serious face; the man was painfully innocent, his handlebar mustache and sleeked-down hair with its sharp parting at odds with his handsome features. It was a photograph of Mrs Zamzam and her husband taken in 1939, six years after their wedding.

Outside Um Al-Farajh as she fled, she had met her brother-in-law Mohamed, who had a car, and he returned briefly to her home to get blankets and clothes for the children. 'We thought we would only be away from our village for a few days,' she said. 'But the Jews entered the village. My husband was in the fields and he saw them blow up our new house. They discovered the olive oil we had left behind and they took all our olive oil machines. The Jews destroyed all the village. Even the cemetery was destroyed — my father had been buried there.'

In May of 1948, the Zamzams crossed the Palestine border into Lebanon at Naqqoura — where the Palestinian writer Kalafani was to describe the misery of the refugees — and rented a house in Tyre for 12 Palestinian pounds a month. 'We moved to Baas camp from there,' she said. 'We had only tents for shelter and we tried to make concrete blocks. Then we came to Rashidiyeh. I thought I would go home when I left but it has been a long time. I have been twenty-nine years in camps now.'

Just as Mrs Zamzam was finishing, there was a shriek from a home-made air-raid siren in the street and a general movement towards the door of the little hut. High up in the deep blue midday sky were the contrails of three Israeli jets. They soared above us up towards Tyre and then turned southwards over the Mediterranean, back towards Galilee. Mrs Zamzam watched all this with equanimity. A year and a half earlier, she had lost her previous camp home when a shell fired from the Israeli-armed Lebanese Christian enclave to the south hit the roof. She had lived almost half her life amid violence.

Throughout our conversation, a loaded Kalashnikov automatic rifle had lain propped against a wall of her living room, left there by a youth who had gone off to drink tea. When I asked Mrs Zamzam what her sons did for a living, a young man interrupted to say that they all worked 'for the revolution'.

When I asked Mrs Zamzam whether she would really go back to Palestine if the frontier was opened, she did not hesitate. 'We are waiting to go back. I hope I am still alive to go back to Palestine again. I would like to die there.' Mrs Zamzam agreed to let me photograph her and she sat a little unsteadily beside the wall of her home just in front of the cherry tree. She stared into the camera as if she was talking to it. But when I suggested that she smile, another young man interrupted to answer for her. 'She cannot smile,' he said bleakly, 'because she has lost her land.'

Mrs Zamzam's land should have been only 25 minutes' drive across the international frontier. It was actually only 15 miles away. But true to the political contours of Lebanon and what is now Israel, I had to fly to Greece, then to Tel Aviv and then take a four-hour car journey to see it, a round-trip of almost a thousand miles. On the way to Mrs Zamzam's land, I looked across the same Lebanese border from the Israeli side and could actually make out in the far distance Mrs Zamzam's camp at Rashidiyeh inside Lebanon. It was a journey that would not have made Mrs Zamzam happy had she been able to make it herself.

For her land now lay underneath a plantation of banana trees a few hundred yards down the road from a bricked-up mosque. Her two-storey white-stone house long ago disappeared. It had vanished as surely as the name of her village had been erased from the map of Israel. The Palestinian Arab hamlet of Um Al-Farajh simply no longer existed.

Just how it came to be extinguished was something of a mystery, and even the Israelis who live in Ben Ami — the farming settlement that has been built on the site — had scarcely heard the name. A young man wearing a yarmulka skullcap and sitting astride a roaring tractor wiped his brow with his arm when I asked for the location of Um Al-Farajh. 'I have never heard of this village,' he said. 'Why do you want to know?'

The mere question had been enough to provoke suspicion. Ben Ami lies just five miles south of the Lebanese border, well within range of the Katyusha rockets which were then being fired by Palestinian guerrillas around Tyre and Rashidiyeh; there were concrete air-raid shelters with iron doors between the bungalows. Barbed wire zigzagged in front of the small houses and large Alsatians snarled at strangers from behind steel fences. The people of Ben Ami were not frightened but they were prepared for an enemy; and visitors interested in the Arab–Jewish war of 1948 were well advised to present convincing explanations for their questions before they stirred memories too deeply.

'So you are writing about those things,' another Israeli said as he stood in a narrow, shaded lane. 'There was an Arab village here but there is nothing left now, you know. All that business is over long ago.' His friend, a tall, bearded man in a black vest with a pair of garden shears in his hand, stared at me without smiling. 'Whose side are you on?' he asked. 'Are you on our side or their side?' He did not bother to explain what he meant by 'their' side. In the event, it was a local veterinary surgeon, a woman with a brisk, hospitable but no-nonsense attitude towards journalists, who invited me into her home and confirmed that this had indeed been Um Al-Farajh. She gave me sandwiches and coffee while I told her of Mrs Zamzam's flight from the village in 1948. She listened carefully to the details of the Palestinian woman's story, of how Jewish gangs had murdered a truckload of Arab villagers shortly before Um Al-Farajh was surrounded and of how the Jews then destroyed Mrs Zamzam's home, the village and even the little Muslim cemetery beside it.

'This certainly was an Arab village,' the Israeli woman said. She spoke charitably of what happened so long ago but her attitude was to grow colder as the evening wore on. She suggested that I speak to a man who had lived nearby in 1948, and after some hours he arrived at the house, a middle-aged Israeli with a lined face and very bloodshot eyes. He spoke only Hebrew and the woman translated for me. I never knew his name; if I wanted to quote him by name, I would have to get permission. Neither of them disclosed from whom this permission would have to be obtained. The newcomer listened in his turn to the description Mrs Zamzam had given me of the events that led her to run away from Um Al-Farajh, occasionally nodding agreement or interrupting to correct her account.

Yes, he said, it was true that the houses had grapes on the outside walls. He himself had seen them when he used to bring olives to the village so that oil could be made from them. Yes, Jewish doctors did indeed care for the Arab villagers then, although Mrs Zamzam had mispronounced the names. It was Dr Kiwi not 'Dr Kayewe' as Mrs Zamzam remembered, and Dr Nathan not 'Dr Natani', but there was indeed a woman doctor called Miriam just as Mrs Zamzam had said. Her family name was Beer; all were now dead. But the man was clearly unhappy about Mrs Zamzam's memory. Did she really have a two-storey house? he wanted to know. All the houses in the village had been small single-storey homes, perhaps only four square metres in area. He was to become even more disenchanted about Mrs Zamzam's record of events.

The first ambush was staged not by Jews but by Arabs, he said. A bus travelling from Haifa to Nahariya in the early spring of 1948 was stopped by Arabs who took the five Jewish passengers from the vehicle and cut their throats. Then it was rumoured that Haj Amin al-Husseini, the Grand Mufti, was travelling from his postwar sanctuary in Lebanon to Acre and there was an ambush at Insherah on the bus believed to be carrying him. When shots were fired at two cars accompanying the bus, one of the vehicles, which had been loaded with ammunition for the Arabs, blew up. This, the man thought, was the ambush to which Mrs Zamzam had referred.

'Um Al-Farajh was not shelled,' the man said, 'although the Jewish forces threw hand grenades near the village of Kubri some kilometres from here. Mrs Zamzam has accurately remembered the way she travelled away from Um Al-Farajh but the Jews never destroyed her village. They never blew up the houses. The mosque is still standing here and one of the stone-built houses of the village is still here. You can see it. And the cemetery was *not* destroyed. It is still here. Some houses fell down later. Mrs Zamzam is correct when she says that the villagers put tree trunks on the road but she seems to have forgotten why this was done. They were afraid of reprisal because the Arabs had just ambushed a relief convoy at Kubri. It had been sent to an isolated kibbutz with food but the Arabs stopped it and killed forty-seven Jews. That is why Mrs Zamzam left Um Al-Farajh. All she forgot to tell you about was the killing of forty-seven Jews.'

It is quite true that the Jewish armoured convoy was ambushed over at Kubri. What is more, the old iron trucks with their armour plating are still lying rusting beside the old Kubri road just where they came to a halt in 1948, the wheels stripped of their tyres but their iron bullet shields still intact. The rifles with which the Jews defended themselves have been welded onto the sides of the vehicles as a memorial. A plaque erected by the Israeli Ministry of Defence pays tribute to Ben-Ami Pachter, the Israeli commando leader who died in the ambush; which is one reason why the name Um Al-Farajh ceased to exist and the name of Ben Ami took its place.

It was also perfectly true, as the Israeli said, that the village mosque was still standing. Its windows and doors had been sealed up with breeze-blocks but the Koranic inscription beneath the roof remained and someone had painted it in the past ten years. The only surviving house of Um Al-Farajh was now used as a storage shed.

It was not so easy to find the cemetery where Mrs Zamzam's father was buried. The same bearded man whom we had already met said that it lay next to the mosque, behind some barbed wire which had been put there to protect it. It was impossible to see it now, he said. But I walked round the barbed wire and crawled inside the little ground that lay beyond. The Muslim cemetery of Um Al-Farajh was a field of rubble and undergrowth, distinguished over most of its area by nothing more than small mounds of earth and scattered, broken stones. Two cement graves had been smashed open, apparently several decades earlier. Just as Mrs Zamzam had said – and contrary to what the Israelis had told me – the cemetery seemed to have been systematically destroyed.

Beside a new gymnasium not far away, an Arab Israeli was sweeping a path. Where was Um Al-Farajh, I asked him, and he led me to a large square of fir trees and pointed to the earth. 'There is Um Al-Farajh,' he said and raised his hands quickly together in the way you might imitate an explosion. There he left me.

So I walked beneath the trees and found just under my feet pieces of old concrete and what might once have been bits of wall. There was what looked like a door lintel. It was cheaply designed, the kind that villagers would have used in their homes. All this time, I was watched by three Israeli farmers standing next to a tractor.

It seemed as if the circular ironies of history in Ben Ami were too strong. The dead Jewish convoy commander had given his name to the land where Mrs Zamzam's village once stood, an Israeli hamlet that was now periodically threatened with rocket-fire from Palestinian guerrillas, perhaps the same men who as children walked with Mrs Zamzam from Um Al-Farajh after the ambush on the Jewish convoy.

My visit might have ended there if my car had not run short of petrol on the road south of Nahariya. The gas station attendant was an Israeli Arab, a young man with light brown hair who assumed I was a tourist and wanted to know what I was doing in the cold far north of Israel in winter. I mentioned Ben Ami and Um Al-Farajh and referred momentarily to Mrs Zamzam, when suddenly the boy's face lit up. 'She is my aunt,' he said.

And so it was that Osman Abdelal took me from the gas station and up to a small Arab village called Mazraa, clustered round the ruins of an old Roman aqueduct. He lived in a small house there with his brothers and sisters, all Israeli citizens who spoke Hebrew and lived and worked in Israel. It was Osman's father Mohamed who had returned in his car for the clothes for Mrs Zamzam's children just before Um Al-Farajh was finally abandoned by the Palestinian Arabs in 1948. The family did not want to talk about politics but they asked about Mrs Zamzam's health. They never went near Ben Ami, they said, and smiled at me. What happened to Mrs Zamzam's house? I asked. 'It is gone,' one of Osman's older sisters replied. 'My mother went to look for it later but it had gone.'

Then what happened to Um Al-Farajh? Osman looked at his brother and sisters. 'They blew it up,' he said. 'My family did not see it but they heard the noise of the explosions. They were already coming here to Mazraa.'

And so Mrs Zamzam's family, perhaps irrevocably split by nationalities, was living only 15 miles apart, divided by the Israeli—Lebanese frontier. If Osman Abdelal and his sisters had climbed the furthest hill to the north, they might have just been able to see Mrs Zamzam's refugee camp at Rashidiyeh. But they had never climbed the hill.

There are, of course, specific Israeli laws to stop Damiani and Abu Khadra and Mrs Zamzam from crossing back in the other direction. There is Israeli 'absentee' legislation and there are land expropriation laws passed on from the British mandate. Palestinians with relatives still inside Israel could pay two-week visits — many, like Damiani's wife, have gone wistfully to look from a distance at the homes they once bought and lived in — and the same Israeli spokesman who referred to the Palestinian Arabs as 'a community of refugees' said that he had himself assisted 40,000 Palestinians to rejoin their families and become Israeli citizens. Yet most exiled Palestinians instinctively reject the idea of taking Israeli citizenship in order to return. The spokesman, Rafi Horowitz, was wrong when he said that Palestinians could not claim their lands because they were citizens of a country at war with Israel. Whatever his or her status, a Palestinian can claim compensation from the Israeli Special Committee for the Return of Absentee Property. But only about 170 Arabs had claimed such compensation in five years; making a claim in the Israeli courts means recognising the state of Israel.

It was a point made to me with some vehemence by Mahmoud Labadi, who was then official spokesman for the Palestine Liberation Organisation in Lebanon, a bespectacled figure every bit as urbane and cynical as his Israeli counterpart. 'Do you really wonder,' he asked me at an embassy function in west Beirut, 'why we won't claim compensation? We don't want compensation – we want our *land*.' He sipped his champagne (Veuve Clicquot 1976) and raised his finger in the air. 'It's invidious for any Palestinian to take a cash payment from the Israelis. It undermines our demand for the return of our homes.'

And he was right, as the Israelis themselves were well aware. They still hoped in 1980 that the Palestinian issue – the demands of Palestinians who lost their homes in what is now Israel – could be dealt with as part of a general Arab–Israeli peace settlement, that the whole two and a half million Palestinian diaspora could be given a lump-sum, once-and-for-all payment of compensation. They do not want the Palestinians back and a glance at the statistics quickly shows why. Well over two million of that diaspora regard themselves as victims of the 1948 war; the half million or so who fled Palestine in 1948 have had children – in many cases grandchildren – who regard themselves as Palestinians. Many Arabs who lost their homes in what became the state of Israel and settled on the West Bank in 1948 became refugees for a second time during the Six Day War in 1967. All these people now regard themselves as having a moral claim to land inside Israel – which is one reason, of course, why the PLO was for so long loath to consider a Palestinian nation outside the boundaries of the Jewish state.

Exactly how much land the Arabs owned in the part of Palestine that became Israel is still disputed. Moshe Aumann concluded from original British figures that in 1948 Jews owned 8.6 per cent of the land and Arabs 20.2 per cent; of which, he claimed, 16.9 per cent was abandoned by Arabs when they thought the neighbouring Arab armies were going to destroy Israel.

But there was one man to talk to in Israel who knew more than anyone else about the land of Palestine. Jacob Manor proved to be the very opposite of David Damiani or Fatima Zamzam. He was academically specific and efficient, a thin ascetic man with a degree in jurisprudence from the Hebrew University and offices in Tel Aviv and Jerusalem.

Manor held the title of Custodian of Absentee Property — the word 'Absentee' giving the curious impression that the absent person could not be bothered to return. He could describe the land registration bureaucracy of the Ottoman Empire, define the intricacies of land expropriation and run off a photocopy of the Israeli Absentee Property Law (1950) in the twinkling of an eye. And everything he did, as he told me several times in his Tel Aviv office, was strictly according to the law.

In his possession were copies of almost every British mandate land registration document, file after file of papers recording in detail the Arab and Jewish owners of property in pre-1948 Palestine. Ask Jacob Manor about the land that belonged to Mrs Zamzam's husband in the village of Um Al-Farajh and he could immediately explain how it came into the hands of the development authority and was then leased to the village of Ben Ami. Each transaction — of which the original owners remained in ignorance — had involved the transfer of money from one Israeli government department to another. If the government expropriates land, then it must pay compensation to the office of the custodian. The custodian can then in theory pay compensation to the original owner — although the land, of course, has gone.

The law is so rigorous and so thorough that it would be difficult to misunderstand the import of the statutory legislation which governs the property of the Palestinian Arabs who fled their homes in 1948 and who — by the same law — cannot return. Manor knew much of this legislation by heart. An absentee, according to the 1950 Israeli law, includes anyone who, between 20 November 1947 and the ending of the State of Emergency, was 'a legal owner of any property situated in the area of Israel ... and who, at any time during the said period, was a national or citizen of the Lebanon, Egypt, Syria, Saudi Arabia, Trans-Jordan, Iraq or the Yemen or was in one of these countries or in any part of Palestine outside the area of Israel ...' An absentee also included anyone who was 'a Palestinian citizen and left his ordinary place of residence in Palestine for a place outside Palestine before 1 September 1948, or for a place in Palestine held at the time by forces which sought to prevent the establishment of the State of Israel or which fought against it after its establishment.'

The definition is broad. For the 'State of Emergency' has not yet ended. And if a Palestinian Arab fled his or her home during the 1948 fighting for an area controlled by Arab forces — even though the individual did not in any way participate in the war — Israeli law effectively deprived the owners of their homes and lands. Jacob Manor made no bones about it. 'Let us suppose,' he said, 'that there is someone called Mohamed and that he was born and lived in Acre. And let us suppose that in 1948, following the fighting, he left his ordinary place of residence for a place of insurrection, then he is an absentee — even if he did not join the Arab forces that were fighting against Israel.'

There is a further clause in the 1950 law that permitted Manor to confirm that a man or woman was not an absentee if that person left his place of residence 'for fear that the enemies of Israel might cause him harm or otherwise than by reason or for fear of military operations'. Manor said he had given this dispensation on 40 occasions. But the law did not take specific account of Arabs who left their homes for fear that *Israeli* forces might cause them harm — the reason most Arabs give for their sudden departure. So much, therefore, for the Damianis, the Abu Khadras and the Zamzams.

Of those who left — well over half a million people — scarcely any had disinherited themselves by claiming compensation under the Israeli Absentees Property Compensation Law of 1973. Only 170 Arabs had made successful applications in five years. The Israelis, of course, do not dispute the legality of the old British mandate deeds. 'There is no dispute about the legality of the mandate papers,' Jacob Manor said. 'There is no dispute about the land unless a claim is made ... compensation for those who claim it for their land and receive it from the authorities is calculated according to the value of the property in 1973 plus the difference in the index of inflation together with four per cent interest.'

Manor sat back in his office chair as he rolled off these statistics. 'I am a very liberal man,' he said. 'I always take a positive view towards any claim.' He himself was an Iraqi Jew and estimated that 150,000 Iraqi Jews were expelled from their country. 'They left all their property. They came here penniless and made a claim to the Minister of Justice. We have a list of all the claimants for the future when there is peace with Iraq.' Manor holds the figures, too, for those Jews who lost all their property in Egypt, Yemen and Morocco after the creation of the state of Israel. The Israelis have in fact scrupulously recorded every dunum and block of lost Jewish property in the Arab world so that it can be placed on the scales of compensation payments when there is any balancing of refugee debts at that final Middle East peace conference.

The Custodian of Absentee Property did not choose to discuss politics. But when I asked him how much of the land of the state of Israel might potentially have two claimants — an Arab and a Jew holding respectively a British mandate and an Israeli deed to the same property — he said he believed that 'about 70 per cent' might fall into this category. If this figure was accurate — and it should be remembered that over half of Israel in 1948 consisted of the Negev desert — then it suggested that Arabs owned a far greater proportion of that part of Palestine which became Israel than has previously been imagined. Jacob Manor seemed unaffected by this fact. 'Do you really believe that the Palestinians want to come back?' he asked. 'Most of them have died. And their children are in good positions now.'

If this extraordinary statement involved a blindness to reality, it provided no warning of the storm of anger and abuse which my series of articles in *The Times* was to generate among Israelis and their supporters in Britain. At some length and in careful detail I had told the story of David Damiani, Kanaan Abu Khadra, Fatima Zamzam and of another Palestinian woman, Rifka Boulos, who had lost land in Jerusalem. To visit their former homes and lands had been like touching history. For I had also told of the lives of those who now lived on or near those lands. Save for one mention of a PLO official in Beirut — the spokesman slugging champagne at the diplomatic reception — Yassir Arafat's organisation did not receive a single reference in the thousands of words I wrote. *The Times* also carried a long interview with Jacob Manor. But the reaction to the articles — a series that dealt with Palestinians as individual human beings rather than as some kind of refugee *caste* manipulated by fanatics and 'terrorists' — was deeply instructive.

On the day that the last of the articles appeared, the Zionist Federation staged a demonstration outside the London offices of *The Times*, some of their supporters holding placards which announced that the paper was 'a new Arab secret weapon' and that the PLO would be the next owner of *The Times*. Shlomo Argov, then Israeli ambassador in London, denounced the series as 'a bold apologia for what is none other than basic PLO doctrine'. In the letters columns of *The Times*, Jewish readers variously suggested that I was 'making a serious attempt to undermine the legal basis of Israel's existence' and that the paper had become 'a platform for the enemies of Israel'. The general drift of critical correspondence suggested that the mere publishing of the series was anti-semitic. Argov himself had written an earlier letter of such hostility that it had to be returned by the paper because its contents were regarded by lawyers at *The Times* as potentially defamatory. When this was first pointed out to the ambassador, he said that he could not be sued for libel since he possessed diplomatic immunity. The Zionist Federation condemned Damiani, Abu Khadra, Mrs Zamzam and Mrs Boulos as 'victims of their own aggression' who had 'remained refugees because they are being used as an instrument of the destruction of the State of Israel.'

Just how such lack of pity could be justified was not vouchsafed. Eric Graus, the Federation's honorary secretary, was involved in a heated argument in the street outside *The Times* building with Louis Heren, who was deputy editor of the paper and a former Middle East correspondent. Heren was actually in Palestine in 1948 and was one of the first correspondents to enter Deir Yassin after the massacre of its Arab residents by Menachem Begin's Irgun gunmen. He found himself bitterly telling Graus of the horrors which he had witnessed during a war in which the Israelis still claim they never committed atrocities. No comment was made by either demonstrators or critical readers – or by the ambassador – about the kindness of Shlomo Green, the old Israeli who showed such compassion towards the Palestinian in whose former home he was now living.*

Generosity, however, was not an emotion that could be found in many Palestinian hearts in Lebanon, and the hatred that burned in 1948 was eagerly taken up by a new generation. I witnessed this phenomenon in tragically symbolic form several months after *The Times* had published my series. In early 1981, the Israelis had staged an air raid against the Rashidiyeh Palestinian camp – where Mrs Zamzam had her home – and I drove down to southern Lebanon from Beirut to report on the attack. The Palestinians had been firing Katyusha rockets into Galilee, the missiles landing not far from the Israeli village of Ben Ami where Mrs Zamzam's Arab village of Um Al-Farajh had once stood. There had been little damage to Galilee or Rashidiyeh in the exchange of fire but, not far from the entrance to the Palestinian camp, I was briefly introduced to a man who was described as the 'leader of joint PLO forces' in Rashidiyeh.

Several seconds passed before I recognised the features of the PLO officer who was defending the Palestinian camp and shelling the area around Ben Ami. It was Hassan Zamzam, Fatima Zamzam's son, the same Hassan who as a 40-day-old baby had been carried by his mother out of Um Al-Farajh in 1948 on the family's road to exile. So now the children of the dispossessed were attacking the children of those who had brought such misery to their Palestinian parents. The war had truly gone full circle.

---

* The complete series of ten articles entitled 'The Land of Palestine' can be found in editions of *The Times* between 15 and 24 December 1980. Editorial comment, readers' letters and a report of the demonstration by the Zionist Federation appeared in the paper between 23 December 1980 and 20 January 1981.

3 The Pied Piper of Damascus

We went to the Olympic Games of 1936 in Berlin. And I
saw then this discipline and order. And I said to myself:
'Why can't we do the same thing in Lebanon?'

Pierre Gemayel *July 1982*

The boy amid the ruins could have been no more than 12 years old and
he looked at us with genuine disinterest, sitting on a broken office
swivel chair in the middle of rue Trablos, scruffy brown hair on top of a
tired, old face. He was wearing khaki dungarees about three sizes too
big for him and a boy's shirt with pictures of Mickey Mouse printed
across the front. In his right hand he held the barrel of a Kalashnikov
rifle, its wooden butt resting on the roadway. In his left he balanced a
glass of scalding hot tea. He was a Lebanese Muslim and he had been
given the gun by the Palestinians who were sitting on the side of the
broken street, sipping their own glasses of tea. They had made him into
a gunman. No, he was a gunboy, something very special to Lebanon,
youth given false maturity. The buildings around us were scorched by
fire, their roofs long fallen in, the façades scored by shoals of bullets,
shattered by artillery fire.

It was hot and the cicadas whispered away in the shadows. Somewhere, perhaps a mile away down the Beirut front line, shells were
bursting in a long, low rumble that ever so slightly changed the air
pressure in rue Trablos. The explosions were dull and heavy; the sort of
noise that an expensive carpet would make if thrown onto a road from a
balcony. Where had we seen this boy before?

There is a boy of about the same age in *Kanal*, Andrzej Wajda's epic
film of the Warsaw uprising. He is seen, just briefly, behind a barricade
in a burning street, his rifle beside him but intent on removing a stone
from his boot while a German Tiger tank moves steadily down the street
towards him. The more menacing the progress of the tank, the more
absorbed the boy becomes in his physical discomfort. The camera
eventually tracks away leaving the boy still shaking his boot, part of the
furniture of the front line.

As we clambered across the rubble towards him, our 12-year-old boy
in 1976 knew that the nearest tank was only 300 yards away. But he also

knew it had been destroyed; like Lebanon and the 40,000 who had died there over the previous 17 months. The canyons of ruins, the heaps of pancaked houses, formed a front line as static as the valleys and mountains to the east of the city. The gunmen and the survivors who came here, the photographers and correspondents and film crews simply walked onto the theatrical stage. The props — ruins, guns, sound effects — were always there.

When we approached the 12 year-old's little aluminium throne with its torn plastic seat and its bent wheels, he looked at us with that special insouciance of the Lebanese militiaman. The gunmen of Lebanon had grown used to the *sahafa*, the press. Sometimes they would take journalists to the front line; sometimes they would risk their lives to help reporters. Or they would rob them or threaten to execute them. One day, in years to come, they would kidnap them, too. Our 12-year-old had plenty of time to make up his mind.

'If you want to see the war, you should go that way,' he said, gesturing wearily in the direction of a gutted restaurant. He put down his glass of tea, lifted the rifle to his shoulder and trudged off into the debris. We followed him, across the street and into the building. It was Al Ajami, once one of Beirut's most prestigious restaurants. We walked into it through the wall, through a shell-hole that had been enlarged by the gunmen for easy access. In the darkness, we padded across the dank, wet velvet floor and out through the kitchen wall into a street whose hollow buildings leaned outwards. Four or five storeys high, they tottered against each other, held up only by the shells of neighbouring structures, their innards shrivelled up by fire, a real Dresden of a street.

What did the boy want to do when he grew up? I asked. 'I want to be a guerrilla commander,' he said in French. An educated gunboy, his intellectual ambitions were limited. He gave us a grin of yellow teeth. He was enjoying himself. And if the war ended? He shrugged. We followed him across the street and down crumbling cement stairs into a fetid basement that stank of excrement, a place two feet deep in sodden papers, envelopes, parcels and stained government forms. Sometime back in 1975 — the date franked on the envelopes — the front line moved across the postal sorting office and the employees must have simply run away during their shift. From the ceiling on the far wall, a shaft of bright, dusty light focused on a rusting office desk. We climbed onto it, put our arms into the shaft of sunlight, grasped the upper edges of the hole and, one by one, hauled ourselves up through a manhole into another street.

The war was definitely in this direction. The air outside snapped with rifle fire. Here the buildings were disfigured almost beyond recognition; some had fallen into the street while others leaned outwards, a hopeless thoroughfare of broken concrete, stones, weeds and pillaged furniture across which had been built a low barricade made of chairs, doors and broken tables. The boy ran across it and we followed him, bent double, as bullets hissed around the disembodied doors, the upturned chairs. On the other side, we jumped over some steps and entered a cavernous, empty doorway, a place of slime and undergrowth. Months of raw sewage had passed down the scarred pavement outside and a thin layer of grass – a bright, sickly, unreal green – had crept over the doorstep and into the building. Beside a dangling traffic light outside, an earth revetment was sprouting bushes.

Six years later I would be back in this same street. Then I would find that the grass had carpeted the rubble and the bushes had begun to climb the torn traffic lights. In 1987, I would be here in rue Trablos again to find that the grass had formed a miniature jungle, that the bushes had become trees that sometimes grew taller than the ruins, small groves and forests of dark, luxuriant foliage moving gently in the hot breeze. Their roots lay deep in the shell-holes and in the earthen barricades which had been erected with such sectarian conviction more than a decade before. It was as if the ecology of the place had chosen to imitate politics. For the whole of central Beirut was being gradually reclaimed by nature, as overgrown as the political system which had so regularly betrayed Lebanon.

How little we had understood in 1976. Then it seemed that the Lebanese civil war was one of those historical tragedies in which opposing communities fought themselves to a standstill only to be reconciled by a central government and foreign economic assistance. The streets would be swept clear, the buildings replaced and rebuilt or repaired. I still possess a tape-recording of a news report I made for Irish radio in which – to a background of Palestinian rifle fire – I hear my own voice informing listeners in the furthest villages of County Mayo that they are listening to 'the last shots of the Lebanese civil war'. Heaps of faded, yellowing newspaper cuttings – their arguments as flawed as the foundations of the front-line ruins – are there to prove our lack of comprehension. Pious indeed were our predictions of recovery. There is *The Times* front page of 16 November 1976, on which I announce that 'the Lebanese civil war – or at least that stage of the conflict that cost ... almost 40,000 lives – came to an end this morning when a Syrian army, 6,000 strong and accompanied by hundreds of tanks and heavy armoured vehicles, occupied the entire city of Beirut.'

Here is a special *Times* supplement, no less, devoted to the future recovery of Lebanon in which I write of the ships returning to Beirut port, of the re-opening of central banking facilities, the renovations at the temples of Baalbek, the arrival of the first postwar tourists – Swedes, of course – who were bussed off to the ruins of the Palestinian camp of Tel al-Za'atar and then to the Bekaa. In 1982, when the Israeli army surrounded Beirut and the Palestinian guerrillas agreed to leave, I was down in those same front lines, invited by a Palestinian gunman to push the last sandbags from his position now that the final ceasefire had been called. The end of the war. Then the Israelis entered west Beirut, their Lebanese militia colleagues massacred the Palestinians in Sabra and Chatila and European armies established themselves in Beirut. The end of the war. The Israelis retreated out of almost all of Lebanon. The end of the war. The Syrian army returned in February of 1987 to repress the anarchy of the Lebanese militias. The end of the war.

Amid the clippings, I find a snapshot of myself sitting on top of a Syrian T-54 battle tank on the Beirut front line at Galerie Semaan; another photograph taken by Zoheir Saade of the Associated Press shows Ed Cody of the AP and myself standing with Syrian troops in the mountains before the 1976 advance on Beirut. Were there no clues to what was really happening? Even our 12-year-old boy is there in the clippings in his Mickey Mouse shirt with his cup of tea and his Kalashnikov rifle, scampering across page one on 25 September 1976, behind that barricade of old doors, travelling with us to page four, column three, into that grassy interior.

It had once been the offices of a film company and inside we found a dozen Iraqi soldiers in battledress, claiming to be Palestinians, members of the Arab Liberation Front. They had been defending the building for 31 days and there was blood on the floor. It trailed across the dust, occasionally halting in dark brown cakes, from room to room, not through the doors sealed up with breeze-blocks but through holes in the walls, holes through which we crawled, troglodytes all. We climbed a narrow and broken staircase towards the top of this building, the boy now at the rear, an Iraqi army captain leading the way. Each landing was almost an inch deep in cartridge cases across which the thin track of dried blood still passed. It led to the highest floor where we found an Iraqi soldier firing an automatic rifle through a narrow aperture in a pile of sandbags, reloading and firing his weapon until he became exhausted. The sound moved through us as the gunman's shoulder and body jerked with the recoil of the rifle, the small boy's face alert, fixated.

The Iraqi leaned to the left and I peered through the crack in the sandbags at the Fattal building, a yellow-painted office block whose window frames had been chewed down to an inch or two by thousands of bullets; the Christian Phalangist front line. It was no different to the building in which we were hiding. Those inside it behaved in precisely the same way. They fired back — so many bullets that they cracked against the outside walls of the film company office in a sheet of sound lasting several seconds. They fired mortars from the roof, the ping-pong noise of the projectile followed by a distant rumble. 'It was bad last night,' the officer said. 'The Phalangists tried to attack us but we beat them back. We had no casualties.' It was, of course, a lie.

Was this all it meant then, the Beirut front line, a mile-wide avenue of sepulchral ruins that stretched from the port all the way out to Galerie Semaan, even to the foothills of the Chouf mountains? How easily we were misled. How simply we believed that this wasteland was the immediate effect of social antagonism, community tension, civil war. How little we realised that the front line was a focus, that it was important to the Lebanese, the only way to define the undefinable, the only method by which those who had suffered – which meant every Lebanese – could uniquely understand the nature of the calamity that had come upon them. In 1976, their government had sent trucks to clear the streets, and the airlines and banks had started to reconstruct their offices. Then the war destroyed it all again. In 1982, the French army had collected the unspent ammunition lying in the rubble and defused unexploded shells. In 1983, the Lebanese–Saudi entrepreneur Rafiq Hariri had paid millions of dollars for the restoration of the city centre. Then the fighting had resumed and the streets were re-seeded with mines. In truth, the Beirut front line could not be repaired, restructured, rebuilt or re-roofed because it had become *necessary* to the Lebanese. It was a reference point without which the tragedy could not be expressed. It represented the cruellest of all front lines, one that lay deep within the minds of all who lived in Lebanon and all who came there.

For we had all been fooled, even the Lebanese themselves. We believed in the idea of national catastrophe, of national renewal, of political renaissance. We thought that an identity existed beyond the civil conflict. We were taken in by the lies which the Lebanese told about themselves; we had to believe we had not seen the blood on the stairs. Just as we were supposed to accept their stories about how this was the only country in which you could ski in the mountains in the morning and swim in the Mediterranean in the afternoon. Like so much else in Lebanon, it was physically possible but we never met anyone who had actually achieved this.

In reality, the story of Lebanon was one of both implosion and explosion, of internal conflict and external pressure, but its tragedy – its history – was one of constantly invading armies, negotiating, cajoling, intimidating, storming their way into Beirut. Lebanon was easy to invade. The country was smaller than Wales, only one fortieth the size of California; the ridge-line of mountain peaks provided Lebanon's epic dimensions, plateaus of snow that seemed to reach up to the moon on winter nights.

Just north of Beirut, at the Nahr al-Kelb, the Dog River, where a doubtful trickle of brown water creeps through a narrow ravine next to a disused railway bridge, inscriptions, steles, cuneiform reliefs and plaques commemorating 25 centuries of armies are carved onto the walls of the gorge. Nebuchadnezzar the Second, Marcus Caracalla's Third Gallic Legion, Greeks, Assyrians, Egyptians and Arabs, the French expeditionary force of 1860, the French mandate troops of General Gouraud, the British army of 1941; all were somehow drawn to mark their passing above the bed of this little stream. The very last inscription is that of President Beshara al-Khoury of Lebanon, who in 1946 recorded the evacuation from Lebanon of what he supposed to be the last foreign troops. Every militiaman in Lebanon should perhaps be taken up to the Dog River to see these memorials to pride and power. The greatest Pharaonic inscription was defaced in antiquity; the disgraced Roman Third Legion had its name hacked away. The remaining monuments have been cracked open by undergrowth or assaulted by time and neglect.

The more recent armies to arrive in Lebanon all suffered similar indignity. The Palestine Liberation Organisation, the Syrians, the Saudis, the North Yemenis, the Sudanese, the Israelis, the Americans, the French, the Italians, even the tiny British contingent, all left Beirut hopeless, humiliated or ashamed. They were welcomed, always welcomed by the happy, friendly, shrewd, suspicious Lebanese. In November 1976, I watched Syrian tanks drive through the suburb of Hazmiyeh, a crewman on the first tank playing a flute. From their balconies, the Christian Lebanese threw rose water and rice at the Syrians, a phenomenon which we journalists archly described as 'a traditional Arab greeting'. Just over five and a half years later, I stood on the same spot and watched the Israelis drive down the same road to be greeted in precisely the same way by the same Christians on the same balconies. 'See how they welcome us,' a cheerful Israeli colonel proclaimed to me then. 'We have come to liberate their country; they have been waiting for us.'

The Israelis came like the Syrians, with expressions of innocence and with promises that they had arrived only to restore the sovereignty of Lebanon. Like all the other armies, they promised to stay not one hour – not one minute – longer than necessary. And then they stayed for months, indeed years, until driven out in pain and indignity. One thing all the armies had in common was a careful explanation of their presence, a specific mandate set out in such complex detail that officials of the Lebanese Foreign Ministry were sometimes still trying to decipher its true meaning when the army in question was retreating out of Lebanon. It was as if in some government department in Washington, Damascus, Paris, Jerusalem, Rome or London, there were people who understood the true meaning of this military involvement and were trying to square the adventure with history. The armies that came to Lebanon marched down a long, dull tunnel that inevitably ended in brown smoke and pieces of flesh.

It has been the fate of the Lebanese militias to inhabit the very ramparts of their own history. Israel's proxy 'South Lebanon Army' militia invested the magnificent crusader Castle of the Sea at Sidon in 1982. The Lebanese national army moved into the Castle of St Louis in Sidon in 1985. For most of the 1975—76 civil war, the massive stone keep of the twelfth-century Castle of St Gilles that still towers over Tripoli was occupied by a Sunni Muslim militia that made its head-quarters in the crusader banqueting hall. Along the great escarpments that form the spine of modern-day Lebanon, above the rivers that vein their way across the country, the crusader castles that once formed the outposts of Christendom are still part of a front line, albeit with the roles of their defenders historically reversed.

At Tibnin, the ruins are the highest point in the last village in southern Lebanon still held by a Muslim militia. From the old tower, you can today look across at the concrete and mud emplacements of the occupying Israeli army two miles to the south. During the civil war, Palestinian guerrillas moved into the far more impressive fortress of Beaufort on the heights above the Litani River, from where they could gaze deep into Israel — or into Palestine as they would insist — and shell the Lebanese Christian villages in between. In 1977, I had crouched in the corridors of Beaufort as Christian militia shells crashed around the castle walls. In the gloom and dust inside, there were fluted columns and small, implacable stone faces with crowns that glared down from the upper walls. Armoured men with swords had clanked down the stairwells here; now the steps were used by gunmen in grubby camouflage fatigues whose rifles lay propped against the walls of the round towers.

After the military disasters of 1192, the Christian soldiers and crusader knights had taken refuge at Beaufort under Renaud, Prince of Sayette, and shut themselves up inside the fortress as the armies of Saladin arrived to lay siege to them. Renaud was eventually tricked into leaving the castle for negotiations with his enemy; Saladin's ring was sent as a token of good faith. But the moment Renaud reached the Saracen lines, he was put into irons; the Christian defenders then watched in horror as he was dragged before the castle and tortured in front of them.

The Muslim Palestinian defenders of Beaufort were ignorant of all this, sitting around the walls in silence when I told them of this historical deceit, dangerous children who must have found something familiar in the old tale of fear, treachery and pain. But when I mentioned that there was a legendary tunnel that ran from the battlements of Beaufort down through the sheer rock to the bottom of the Litani gorge, they leapt to their feet and bounded up one of the staircases. I followed them onto a narrow, crumbling ledge above the ravine where the wind hurled us against the wall. The snows of Mount Hermon streaming northwards, the blue vales of Galilee, the brown waters of the Litani encircled us in that little cyclone, We could be seen, for above the sound of the gale we heard the clatter of bullets tossed by the wind against the ramparts. To the east of the wall, we reached a kind of well, an ancient cistern partly constructed from masonry but also cut into the rock. Here the Palestinians clustered excitedly around the mouth with their backs to the snows of Hermon. From the darkness of the interior of this well came the smell of burned refuse and decaying meat and the stench of urine. Could this be the secret passageway to the Litani, groined by the forces of Christendom to escape from their ancient predicament?

Five years later, the Israelis levelled much of Beaufort with F-16 fighter-bombers and then sent their own troops and Christian militiamen into the rubble. From the castle, armed Jews and Christians now faced Muslim militias to the west where before Muslim gunmen in the keep had faced Christians and Jews to the east and south. In the twelfth century, the Christians in Beaufort had confronted Muslims in both directions. Somehow what is left of Beaufort conspires to embody these political and religious transitions; when the mists lie in the valleys of southern Lebanon, the remaining walls can be glimpsed above the clouds, but because of the peculiar geography of the place — because the ravines and wadis fold in uneven formation and in odd directions — Beaufort always appears to be in a different location, its broken ramparts a nightmare denture which eludes every contour and coordinate. In winter, when the storms bluster in from the Mediterranean and the valleys glow green, the cloud comes down and Beaufort simply disappears.

The Christian Maronites of Lebanon had unwisely associated themselves with the crusaders — this tragic addiction for unhappy alliances was to be developed in later centuries — and the results are still visible in Lebanon today. For with the defeat of European Christendom, the Maronites too retreated, up into the mountains of northern Lebanon where their towns and villages still stand, wedged between great ravines, clinging to the icy plateaus of the Mount Lebanon range. Under assault by Muslim Arabs, they found that these pinnacles provided their only protection and they clung on there, up amid the remains of the ancient cedar forests. They were a pragmatic, brave, distrustful people who learned that responsibility for their continued existence lay exclusively in their own hands, that their ultimate fate depended solely upon their own determination and resources. It was a characteristic that they were to share with all the minorities of Lebanon; and later with the Israelis.

Yet through the centuries the Maronites were able to spread south in Lebanon, through Beirut, into the lands of the Druze and Shia Muslims, the Chouf and the lower Bekaa, settling on the low stony ridge-lines south-east of Tyre. These villages today form the Christian frontier strip still occupied by the Israeli army. Maronite power was consolidated in the aftermath of the civil war against the Druze in 1860, a conflict whose massacres − in which 12,000 Christians died − prompted the French army to intervene in Lebanon on behalf of the Maronites. French warships anchored in Beirut bay and French troops set up their first encampment at Khalde, where Beirut international airport now stands − and where the US Marines were to establish their own doomed military headquarters 122 years later.

This European − or, to be more exact, Euro-Christian − involvement in Lebanon was to be a recurring theme, facilitated by the fact that every community in the land that was to become Lebanon was a minority. In Syria, which then included present-day Lebanon, the people were tribes without a country, in many cases the inheritors of great religious schisms, often dissidents who had themselves been drawn to the mountains of Lebanon by the physical protection which the terrain afforded them.

The Maronites, who took their name from a fifth-century Syrian hermit, had emerged from the great division in the Byzantine Church over the single divine will of Christ. So had the Melchites, whose two communities − Greek Orthodox and Greek Catholics − form a small but economically powerful minority in modern Lebanon. The Druze had originally come from Egypt. Regarded as heretics by orthodox Muslims, they believed in reincarnation and the transmigration of the soul. Yet their real faith − like that of the Christians − was towards their own clan, their villages, their leaders. In the Chouf now, the Druze holy colours hang over the militia checkpoints. Small stone oratories − the Druze have no mosques − stand amid the fields. But it is the Jumblatt family which is the focus of Druze loyalty. Walid Jumblatt represents their political demands and their claim to a seat in the national government.

Similarly, the Shias have disputed the leadership of Islam with the Sunnis since the eighth-century murder of Ali, the son-in-law of the Prophet. The Shias believe that Ali's descendants − the Imams − are the lawful successors of Mohamed. Yet again, the present-day philosophy of the Shias in Lebanon is based as much upon their own political history as it is directed by their religious belief. Under the Sunni Muslim Ottoman Empire in Syria, they were treated with contempt, abandoned to the poverty of the hill villages in southern Lebanon where they had originally come from Mount Lebanon. They were neglected and turned into outcasts with much the same arrogance as that shown by the English Protestants towards the Irish Catholics during the same period.

The Sunnis, adherents of the *sunnah* (practice) of Mohamed − the sayings (*hadith*) ascribed to the Prophet and other Islamic traditions − garnered their commercial power from their close association with

the Mamelukes and then with the Ottoman Turks, an alliance based
on their shared Sunni faith. They were the merchants, traders and
businessmen of the north-east Mediterranean coast who had most to lose
if the Shias could establish themselves in the economic life of the
Levant. Thus Sunni power came to be founded upon Shia poverty, the
first more or less conditional upon the second.

European interference in the Levant had been evident since the 1840s
when representatives of the European powers proposed to the Turks
that Lebanon should be partitioned between Christians and Druze. The
Emir Bashir the Third, who ruled Mount Lebanon for the Sublime
Porte in Istanbul, had been unable to contain the bitter disputes which
had broken out between the two communities. In 1842, the European
proposal – which was to contain the seeds of so much grief in the next
century – was accepted by the Turks; Mount Lebanon was divided into
two sectors, a Christian canton in the north and a Druze canton in the
south, with the main Beirut–Damascus highway marking the boundary
between them. Today on Mount Lebanon, just east of a little Christian
village called Kahhale, the same highway marks the front line between
Christian Phalangist militiamen and gunmen of the Druze Progressive
Socialist Party.

The nineteenth-century European powers only exacerbated the differences between the communities. The French and the Austrians
favoured the Christian Maronites while the British supported the Druze.
The Russians offered protection to the Greek Orthodox. Only after the
civil war broke out between Christians and Druze did the French put
troops ashore, but European 'interest' in Lebanon had already been
clearly established. Thus by 1892, Murray's guidebook to Syria and
Palestine was able to record that 'the Lebanon district is ruled by a
Christian governor, appointed by the Porte, and his authority is guaranteed by the Christian powers of Europe.' In what the book called 'the
Lebanon district' – for Lebanon would not be a separate independent
state for another half century – the writer identified the various religious
communities which inhabited the land: Sunni and Shia Muslims, the
Druze, the Maronite Christians, Greek Catholic and Greek Orthodox
Christians. The book did not mention the small but thriving Jewish
community in Beirut.

In many ways, the Lebanon of 1892 is still identifiable to us, for the
various religious communities – the minority tribes – still live in the
same villages and cities as they did then. The Chouf is the preserve of
the Druze; Sidon and Tripoli of the Sunnis; the south of the Shias; the
mountain chain north of Beirut is the heartland of the Christians. By
1983, with French, Italian and British troops patrolling the streets of
west Beirut, American Marines protecting the city's southern perimeter,
the European community supporting the sovereignty of Lebanon, the

country still seemed to be — as Murray's guide pointed out in 1892 — guaranteed by the Christian powers. The history of the last century in Lebanon thus provided dynamite for the detonation of the past 15 years.

It is surprising that the explosion did not occur earlier, for the sense of betrayal and hatred towards the foreigner was manifest in Lebanon long before. During the First World War, Turkish bureaucracy and a locust plague produced a famine in Lebanon of such proportions that an American woman resident in Beirut was moved to describe for readers of *The Times* how she:

> passed women and children lying by the roadside with closed eyes and ghastly, pale faces. It was a common thing to find people searching the garbage heaps for orange peel, old bones or other refuse, and eating them greedily when found. Everywhere women could be seen seeking eatable weeds among the grass along the roads ...*

The Allies then blockaded the Levant in order to starve the Turkish troops in Palestine and Syria of supplies. Instead, the Turks commandeered the food they needed and the civilian population starved to death. At least 300,000 people died in Syria and Mount Lebanon in this man-made famine brought about by a war of outside powers.† Another American resident in Lebanon was to describe in 1917 how:

> during a two-day journey through the Lebanon with the chairman of the American Red Cross in Bairut [sic] ... the scenes were indescribable, whole families writhing in agony on the bare floor of their miserable huts ... Every piece of their household effects had been sold to buy bread, and in many cases the tiles of the roofs had shared the same fate ... It is conservatively estimated that not less than 120,000 persons have died of actual starvation during the last two years in the Lebanon alone.‡

Among the earliest souvenirs to be hawked to the victorious Allied troops who marched into Beirut on 8 October 1917 was a horrific picture postcard, old copies of which can still be found in the antiquarian bookshop that sells the David Roberts lithographs on Makhoul Street. It depicts the children of a Beirut orphanage in 1915, their matchstick limbs and skull-like faces appended to huge, distended bellies.

The figure of 120,000 Lebanese dead is at least 20,000 higher than the estimated total of fatalities for all the Lebanese wars between 1975 and 1989, including the 1982 Israeli invasion. George Antonius suggested that the true statistic of starvation deaths in all Syria — including present-day Lebanon — may have been as high as 350,000. Taking into account Syria's losses in military service and imprisonment under ill-

---

* *The Times*, 15 September 1916, quoted in *The Arab Awakening: The Story of the Arab National Movement* by the Arab historian George Antonius (New York, Capricorn Books, 1965), p. 204.

† ibid., p. 241.

‡ ibid.

treatment, the country may have lost half a million of its people during the First World War out of a population of well under four million.*

From his self-imposed exile in America, the Lebanese Maronite poet Khalil Gibran — whose verse and drawings have an uncanny similarity to the work of William Blake — was moved to write an angry, ferocious poem quite out of keeping with the gentle, philosophical message for which he is generally remembered:

My people died of hunger, and he who
Did not perish from starvation was
Butchered with the sword;
... They perished from hunger
In a land rich with milk and honey.
They died because the monsters of
Hell arose and destroyed all that
Their fields grew ...
They died because the vipers and
Sons of vipers spat out poison into
The space where the Holy Cedars and
The roses and the jasmine breathe
Their fragrance.†

It was a time of great migration. Many thousands of Lebanese had, like Gibran, travelled to America to escape hardship in the years immediately preceding the First World War. Many of the non-European names among the third class passengers who drowned aboard the *Titanic* were Lebanese.

But the most tragic movement of population was one of emigration *into* Lebanon by the victims of the first European Holocaust, the Armenians. The Turks had used none of the sophisticated machinery that the Nazis were to employ against another minority community less than 30 years later. The one million Armenians slaughtered by the Turks in 1915 were shot or knifed to death, the women often raped before being murdered. There are no ash pits, no identified mass graves. Tens of thousands of Armenians died of thirst and starvation after being forced into the north Syrian desert on the long march south.

True, the Armenians of Beirut have collected some macabre, terrible old photographs that might — had they been studied with more care by the shell-shocked peoples who had just emerged from the First World War — have served as a warning, the shape of things to come. One brown, scratched negative reproduced by the Armenian *Tashnag* militia in Beirut shows a long column of men being led out of an Armenian village by Turkish troops. Each carries a suitcase. Double-take. Is this

* ibid.
† 'Dead Are My People', from *The Treasured Writings of Khalil Gibran* (USA, Castle Books, 1981).

Lake Van or Lvov, western Armenia or eastern Poland? Are the soldiers Ottoman or *Wehrmacht*? Another old print shows a litter of bodies, young men in white shirts, their stomachs already swelling in the heat, lying spread-eagled beside an orchard. In some of the photographs, the Turks who had helped to carry out their government's orders to liquidate the Armenians are standing beside the corpses, grinning into the camera. The only Armenian remains to be saved were found in the desert around Deir Ez-Zohr. A photograph survives of some Armenian priests kneeling in the sand beside a pile of bones.

Today, there is a small octagonal chapel in the Beirut coastal suburb of Antelyas dedicated to the 1915 massacres. The visitor enters the gateway of the Armenian patriarchate and first sees the chapel to the left of the cathedral, a small building of yellow stone which appears to contain some religious relics behind sheets of unwashed glass. Only when you walk out of the sunshine into the shaded interior can you see what lies behind the glass. Neatly arranged in patterns, fixed to the wall with pins, are human skulls, femurs, sockets and pieces of bone from feet and arms. Some of the skulls have been smashed, all are brown with age. These are the human remains that appear in the picture of the priests, from bodies that had already been torn apart by dogs before they were found in the sand. There are perhaps 36 skulls in all and there were at least a million Armenian dead. So each skull represents about 27,777 corpses.

To this day, the Turkish government refuses to acknowledge the slaughter, even though the killings continued after 1915. Perhaps 75,000 more Armenians were butchered during Turkey's 1918 invasion of the Caucasus. As many as a quarter of a million more may have died between 1919 and 1922.*

There are few survivors of the first Holocaust because the Turks tried to kill them all and because age has now claimed most of the rest. When the sick and exhausted Armenians reached Beirut after the Ottoman collapse, they were allowed to build shacks on the swamps of Bourj Hammoud in the east of the city and then to erect houses which look to this day curiously Balkan, their wooden balconies hanging over the narrow streets of Camp Marash. A few of the Holocaust Armenians are in Beirut old people's homes, too senile to record what happened 74 years ago. But old Khoren Pilibossian still lives just off Municipality Square in Bourj Hammoud, up a narrow concrete staircase and through an unpainted wooden door.

He is 90 now, so deaf that we had to shout at him to be heard, so old

---

* For some of the most detailed statistics, see *Armenia: The Survival of a Nation* by Christopher J. Walker (New York, St Martin's Press, 1980), especially p. 230.

that he speaks only Turkish, the language of his oppressors. Many Armenians who lived in Turkish Armenia never spoke their own language. Pilibossian stares at visitors through powerful round spectacles and walks with the help of a cane as he tells his story.

'The Turks took my aunt and uncle from our house in the village of Gessaria,' he said. 'We found their bodies on the street corner. They had been bayoneted.' Here he raised his cane and made a sharp, stabbing motion. In the corner of his cluttered bedroom was a photograph of a woman dressed in black, her sad, unsmiling face staring miserably from the picture. 'It is my sister Florence. The Kurds who worked for the Turks killed her husband and children. They raped her and took her away and forced her to marry one of them. When he died ten years later, she came to Beirut and found us.'

Salvation in Beirut. The Armenians were lucky, for they were the only people this century to flee *to* rather than *from* Lebanon for comfort and protection. Yet their fate is a lesson for others, none more so than for the Palestinians. Like them, Armenian families in Lebanon remain grouped by their original cities and villages. An Armenian whose family came from Erzerum or Kars is neighbour to other Armenians whose parents or grandparents came from the same towns, just as Palestinians from Haifa – or from Mrs Zamzam's village of Um Al-Farajh – now live in refugee camps next to those whose homes were in the same places, sometimes in the very same streets, in what was Palestine. The Armenians – as the Palestinians have often told them – waited too long to fight for their nation.

Camp Marash, where perhaps 150,000 Armenians now live, spawned its own gunmen in the 1980s, the 'Armenian Secret Army for the Liberation of Armenia', whose assassination campaign against Turkish diplomats has provided a violent epitaph for the calcified remains in the Antelyas ossuary. It is the Armenians who live in what is left of the Armenian Republic – in the Soviet Republic of the same name – who perhaps have the only fragile opportunity of one day restoring their nation; just as the Arab inhabitants of the West Bank and Gaza Strip are now the only Palestinians to be able to fight with any effect for their statehood. Political and military impotence is one of the prices that Lebanon exacts of all who enter her frontiers.

This, of course, was not how it seemed to the European powers which held authority over the Middle East after the 1914–18 war. European culture, European political and military power – and specifically French cultural and political influence – began to dominate Lebanon. France's League of Nations mandate extended across Syria and Lebanon, just as the British mandate encompassed Palestine, Transjordan and Iraq – with all the consequences this held for the future. The French now shamefully manipulated the religious minorities within their area to increase their control. They used Druze fighters as a colonial militia just as they used members of the minority Muslim Alawite community in Syria to put down Sunni Muslim nationalist revolt.

The irony behind this — that President Assad is himself an Alawite — has not, of course, been lost on the majority Sunni population who live in Syria today. Until February of 1982, the Beit Azem museum in the Syrian city of Hama contained dozens of torn and faded grey photographs of young Sunni militiamen who had fought the French, who had in some cases been hanged for their acts of defiance. The Azems were the Rockefellers of Hama, a wealthy family of Maecenas-like aristocrats who governed and influenced the city for well over two centuries. Assad Pasha al-Azem was governor of Hama in 1700 and a descendant became prime minister of Syria.

Many of the young men in those faded grey pictures were Azems. The photographs were arranged behind glass in a small anteroom above the door of which was printed the legend: 'The Martyrs of Hama'. There were snapshots of youths with big moustaches and huge muskets over their shoulders, country boys sensing that nationalism rather than colonialism was a path of honour. Some of them were dressed in Ottoman regalia or Arab dress or even French cavalry uniform, serious-looking young men who — in the later pictures — were carrying Lee-Enfield service rifles. These were the Azems who had once served in the French army or even the French air force but who later turned against their French masters — and their minority supporters in Syria — and died fighting them.

Some were sacrificed in later wars. On one wall was a portrait of a man who looked like a young Gary Cooper, hair waved and slicked back, jaw jutting in heroic pose. He was Farid Adib Azem who was shot fighting the Israelis in 1948. In February of 1982, the Sunni fundamentalists of Hama rose up against the Alawite regime. They were cut down and much of the ancient city was destroyed. Perhaps 10,000 — even 20,000 — people died. The photographs of the 'martyrs of Hama' were, of course, burned with them.

The French fully understood that Syrian nationalist sentiment would be opposed to their rule. This, in effect, meant that the Sunnis were their principal antagonists and they thus proceeded to capitalise on the good will of the Christians, their oldest friends, by creating a new state which stripped Tyre, Sidon, Tripoli, the Bekaa Valley and Beirut itself from Syria and added them to the Ottoman sanjak (administrative district) of Mount Lebanon, the very backbone of Maronite Christianity. Syria was cut off from its finest ports and Damascus — the centre of the Muslim Arab nationalist movement opposed to French rule — was weakened at the expense of Beirut and the new Christian-dominated regime. The 'State of the Greater Lebanon' proclaimed by the French

General Gouraud on 31 August 1920 was thus a totally artificial, French-created entity. Its frontiers, over 20 years later, would become the borders of the independent Lebanese state. It was in defence of the presumed 'sovereignty' of this peculiar nation — a product of the Quai d'Orsay rather than the creation of any Arab national aspiration — that countless thousands were to die more than half a century later.

Not surprisingly, the Sunnis led the opposition to this strange, inter-tribal state. The Druze of Lebanon were to join forces with their fellow Druze in Syria in the rebellion against the French in 1925. The Greek Orthodox wanted to be re-united with Syria. So did most of the Sunni inhabitants of Sidon, Tripoli and Beirut. Only the Maronites felt able to drink from the cup of French tutelage and even they quickly found that the chalice contained a special, colonial poison, the effects of which would be passed on to future generations; for by adding such large areas of Muslim Syria to the new 'Lebanon', the French ensured that the Christians' precarious status as the largest religious community would — once the Muslim birthrate increased — be lost. All the more, therefore, would the Christian Maronites need French protection.

Much has been made of the beneficence of French rule in Lebanon; the economy was revitalised, Beirut harbour enlarged, and a network of major roads built to link the country's principal cities. A new judicial system was introduced. The educational system, public health and living standards were improved. But the inhabitants of Lebanon saw these changes in a somewhat different light. When the French introduced a new 'Syro-Lebanese' currency, for example, they pegged the new currency to the collapsing French franc, thus inflicting the weakness of their own monetary system on the Lebanese. The currency management was entrusted to a French bank whose shareholders were said to have prospered at the expense of Arab fiscal autonomy.*

In the schools, French became a compulsory language at the very moment when Arab nationalists were enjoying the linguistic triumph of Arabic over the Turkish of the now broken Ottoman Empire, a victory which had important political implications for the concept of Arab unity.† The teaching of French was seen as a deliberate slight by the Lebanese. The new Lebanese flag was a French-style tricolour. In the law courts, the French language was given equal precedence with Arabic. Many government documents, passports, residence cards, even the road-signs, appeared in both French and Arabic — as they still do in General Gouraud's strangely conceived republic to this day.

The French were well aware of the enmities which they had aroused.

---

* Antonius, *Arab Awakening*, p. 373.
† The rhetoric of this cause — *ittihad* in Arabic — has since obscured the reality that only under the Ottomans did the Arabs actually enjoy any kind of pan-Arab status.

The 1925 Druze rebellion in Lebanon and Syria was put down with great brutality and with the help of gangs of Armenian gunmen who had been armed by the French in order to attack the rebels. And there were other precedents for the future. In the Syrian town of Suwaida, a French force of 3,000 troops was routed by Druze militiamen who then advanced on Damascus. At one point, the insurgents even approached the new Francophile capital of Beirut. The French air force was used to bomb rebel-held areas of Damascus and Druze villages, a bombardment that fell indiscriminately upon the civilians of Syria and Lebanon.

Thus developed in Lebanon a pattern of events which was to recreate itself in increasingly savage form over the coming years. The Maronites were prepared to cooperate with the outside power because they correctly believed that the French wanted a future independent Lebanon which would look to France for protection. The Muslim nationalist parties continued to demand the abolition of the 1920 frontiers, to agitate against French rule and against the pre-independence governments, while the Maronites looked to French *civilisation* for their inspiration. They adopted French Christian names, often spoke French as a first language, were educated at French schools and frequently sent their children to French universities.

In November of 1936, a Franco-Lebanese treaty theoretically recognised the 'independence' of Lebanon but France was permitted to keep an army in the country and thus maintained considerable political control. There were serious disturbances in Beirut and Tripoli which were put down by the new Lebanese administration with the help of French troops. The Christians not unnaturally responded to Muslim protests with alarm. That it represented a threat was clear enough. But how to deal with it and encourage loyalty, impose *discipline* upon the people of the future notional Christian state?

On 16 December 1936, the French-language Lebanese newspaper *L'Orient* did a most unusual thing; it abandoned its normal, sober typographical layout and printed instead across the top of its front page a seven-column photograph of hundreds of young men in well-creased shirts and trousers standing in lines across a field in the rural Beirut suburb of Ein al-Rumaneh. The men in the picture were staring straight in front of them, dedicated to a new cause, the very first *escadrille*, as the caption informed readers, of Lebanon's new blue-shirted Phalange party.

Visitors to the present-day west Beirut offices of *L'Orient-Le Jour*, as the paper is now called, will not find this front page among the back issues. In July of 1982, during the Israeli siege of west Beirut, I had myself prowled through the archives to try and discover the political roots of the Lebanese Phalange, Israel's latest ally in its war against the Palestinians. From outside the newspaper's offices could be heard the murmur of distant artillery as the Israelis and Phalangists fired into the city. From time to time, a shell-burst would shake the windows of the stuffy, hot little room where the paper's forgotten editorial history lay between great covers of bound leather. The entire issue of 16 December 1936 had simply been removed from the file. So had several issues from the previous August when Lebanon's football team under the captaincy of Pierre Gemayel, a Maronite Christian, had travelled to National Socialist Germany to attend the Olympic Games in Berlin. Several of *L'Orient's* editions of that autumn had also disappeared and in later issues, articles about the new Phalange party — the headlines still intact but the accompanying text missing — had been crudely cut from the pages.

I only came across the 1936 front page because it was hanging framed on the right-hand wall of old Pierre Gemayel's office when I went to talk to him in the summer of 1982 in east Beirut. Here, in a high-ceilinged room only 400 yards from the front line — on the Israeli side of the line — the grand old man of the Maronite cause, now aged 77, still held court. He was dressed in the manner of the Thirties with a broad-lapelled jacket, wide cuffs and dark tie firmly attached with a gold clip to a gleaming white shirt. His face was thin and emaciated, drawn together as if it spent each night in some kind of linen press. His hair was combed straight back like a French politician of the Third Republic. He preferred French to Arabic, a language he had anyway never fully mastered.

He had not expected me to ask about his 1936 visit to Nazi Germany. His Phalange was now, after all, a bosom ally of Israel. So he waited for perhaps eight seconds before replying. 'I was the captain of the Lebanese football team and the president of the Lebanese Football Federation,' he said. 'We went to the Olympic Games of 1936 in Berlin. And I saw then this discipline and order. And I said to myself: "Why can't we do the same thing in Lebanon?" So when we came back to Lebanon, we created this youth movement.' Gemayel did not mention Adolf Hitler. Nor did he suggest that the government of the Third Reich used the 1936 Olympiad as a propaganda vehicle for the German Nazi Party. German Jews were forbidden from participating and when Jesse Owens — a black American — won the 100 metres, Hitler walked out of the stadium.

Gemayel saw it all rather differently. 'When I was in Berlin then, Nazism did not have the reputation which it has now,' he said. 'Nazism? In every system in the world, you can find something good. But Nazism was not Nazism at all. The word came afterwards. In their system, I saw discipline. And we in the Middle East, we needed discipline more than anything else.'

Gemayel's youth movement blossomed; indeed, its military descendants were standing guard outside Gemayel's office as we spoke, pistols at their hips, a triangular-shaped cedar tree insignia stitched to their olive-green battledress. After Hitler's demise, the Phalangist movement died out across Europe. Only in Lebanon did it survive, outliving even Franco's political offspring. And in 1982 Gemayel still saw it as he had in the late 1930s, as a movement of renewal that prepared Lebanon's young Christians for independence and civic responsibility.

'We had four hundred years of Ottoman rule in Lebanon,' he said. 'And we asked for our independence. But we had to be mature enough to undertake this independence. And I think we succeeded in our Phalangist youth movement because we created young men who were prepared for politics.' Gemayel's foot tapped up and down as he warmed to his subject, his large oak desk shaking slightly with the vibration. 'We succeeded because we were elected to the Lebanese parliament and we were able to take over from the Turks and French in their ministries.'

But the transition from French rule to Lebanese self-determination had not been an easy one. The French several times reneged on their pledges of future autonomy for the Lebanese. In 1941, after a brief and inauspicious period of Vichy French rule, Lebanon was again occupied by Allied armies; it was the second time in 24 years that British troops had crossed the southern frontier from Palestine. The Australian army won their first Victoria Cross of the Second World War in a tank battle against Vichy forces near the south Lebanese town of Marjayoun — which would in 1978 become the headquarters of Israel's local Christian militia — while in the coastal village of Damour, the future Israeli minister of defence, Moshe Dayan, lost his eye to a Vichy French sniper while fighting as a British soldier.

A Free French administration was installed in Beirut and General de Gaulle quickly made it clear that he intended to keep his forces in Lebanon however much independence the country thought it had been given. Churchill was bitterly opposed to the continuation of the French mandate, but when the Maronite President Beshara al-Khoury and the Sunni Prime Minister Riad Solh also insisted that the French must leave, they were summarily arrested by the French and imprisoned in a castle in the village of Rashaya in the Arkoub region of south-eastern Lebanon. The French wanted to stay. Even the Maronites — including Pierre Gemayel and his Phalange — now demanded their withdrawal.

It was not until 1946 that the French departed from Lebanon and Syria, spitefully shelling Damascus and killing 500 Syrians as they did so. Armies would leave Lebanon this way in the future, firing into its hinterland to persuade themselves that they could abuse their tormentors to the end. But the French also left behind them a nation which was still dominated, both constitutionally and fatally, by the Christian Maronites. In 1943, the Maronites had agreed to an unwritten National Covenant which awarded them the presidency of Lebanon, command of the

Lebanese army and other assets in return for their abandonment of French protection. The Maronites now had to acknowledge that Lebanon possessed what would be described, exactly 40 years later, as an 'Arab identity'.

For another generation, this Covenant was to be held up as a model of political excellence within the Middle East, especially by the Western powers which gave it such approval but which did not have to suffer its consequences. It was supposed to be a paragon of democracy in an Arab world more familiar with dictatorship than freedom. But there were two fundamental flaws in the Covenant. The first was that the Maronite community — which at best constituted only 30 per cent of the Lebanese — was almost certainly outnumbered by the Sunnis or the Shias. There had been no census since 1932 — nor was there ever to be a census again. The myth of a Maronite majority thus had to be accepted by the Muslims for Lebanon's 'democracy' to work. For their part, the Muslims had already given up their claim to reunion with Syria as their price for participation in government under the Covenant.

But whenever the behaviour of either Christians or Muslims was to be challenged in the future, the Covenant itself would inevitably be called into question. And this would reveal that the Covenant's structure was by nature essentially Western, a product of European parliamentary equality grafted on to a newly independent nation whose very existence had been contested by more than half its population for more than two decades. It was, as the Lebanese Maronite publisher George Naccache was to say, compromise elevated to the level of state doctrine; the folly was to have 'treated an historical accident as an element of stability'.* It was, in essence, a system of power-sharing in which offices were distributed according to the notional strength of the communities. Thus the president was a Maronite, the prime minister a Sunni, the speaker of parliament a Shia; even in parliament, there had to be six Christians for every five Muslims.

Power-sharing had a good name in the West. The British instituted a remarkably similar system in post-colonial Cyprus, where a Greek Christian president was appointed alongside a Turkish Muslim vice-president. In the early 1970s, Northern Ireland's politicians were urged to study Lebanon's Covenant by the British government which, in 1974, actually created another power-sharing administration in Belfast. There, the chief executive was to be a Protestant and the deputy chief executive a Catholic with 'Cabinet' seats apportioned according to the two-to-one Protestant majority in the province. The Cyprus model failed when an attempted coup by Greek Cypriots provoked a Turkish invasion. In the

* George Naccache, *Deux négations ne font pas une nation* (1949), quoted in Gilmour, *Fractured Country*, p. 53.

same year, the Belfast model collapsed under the strain of working-class Protestant opposition. Lebanon's own power-sharing institutions lasted longest and only finally fragmented when Muslim—Maronite friction — and foreign interference — became so intense that parliament could no longer elect a president.

It was in any case something of a miracle — and a tribute to the tenacity of the Lebanese — that their Covenant worked for as long as it did. This was partly because of the fantasies in which most of the parties in Lebanon found it convenient to indulge. In 1975, for instance, journalists arriving in Beirut would invariably be told by the Lebanese of the halcyon days which had just ended, of the peaceful Phoenician land in which Christians and Muslims had shown the world that historically religious antagonists could live in peace.

Or, more to the point, how they could live in peace and make money. For as long as Lebanon's economy grew, the dream years were credible even to the Lebanese themselves. The Sunnis and the Maronites were both beneficiaries of the extraordinary wealth that flowed into Beirut. As a financial centre with an open economy, as a trade intersection between Europe and the Middle East with a lucrative port in its capital, as a comparatively 'free' nation amid the dictatorships of the Arab world, Lebanon was to be blessed with the indulgence of both East and West, its modern-day *caravanserais* arriving hourly at the new international airport at Khalde.

The first visions to distort this mirage had appeared on the southern border of Lebanon or from the sea off Beirut in 1946 when the Covenant was barely three years old. But when David Damiani, Fatima Zamzam and her children, Ghassan Kanafani and his family and around 140,000 other Palestinian refugees fled into Lebanon, the Beirut government took comfort — as did the Palestinians themselves — from the hope that they might soon return to their homes. These disturbing images — convoys of refugees, unsanitary tent encampments — were initially refracted because Lebanon had itself vainly assisted the ridiculous 'Arab Liberation Army' in its war against the new Israeli state; for the Lebanese, their own military failure was of greater moment than the fate of those whom they were supposed to be saving. Most of the Palestinians were distributed around Lebanon to settle in UN camps on the fringes of Tyre, Beirut and Tripoli or the old Wavell barracks outside Baalbek. The filthy colonial military compounds so recently evacuated by the British and French provided convenient quarters for those who were now destined to spend most of their lives in exile, even though neither they nor their unwilling Lebanese hosts yet knew that they would have to do so.

From the start, the Palestinians were treated with little love by the Lebanese. Since most of the refugees were Sunnis, the Maronites correctly divined that they were potential allies of Lebanon's Muslims. Some Palestinians with relatives in Lebanon were later to change their nationality and become Lebanese, but most of the refugees were classed as non-citizens and given a pale brown passport – the same colour as the old British Palestine passport – with a cedar tree printed on the front. They could not enter the civil service or acquire the privileges of Lebanese citizenship. It was almost impossible to obtain work permits. Poorly paid employment on Lebanese construction sites–as David Gilmour points out in his *Dispossessed* – was the fate of many of the farmers and labourers of Palestine.

But if this large population of unwilling immigrants did not immediately worry the Lebanese, the emergence of Gamal Abdul Nasser's Arab nationalism could not be ignored. Much later, in 1975, the Lebanese chose not to refer to this period. It occurred during Lebanon's glorious recent history and so only in old magazines or in scratched newsreel films can one sense the phantoms that were even then being made manifest in the streets of Beirut.

On leave in Ireland during a ceasefire in the 1976 fighting, I came across a pile of back issues of the *National Geographic Magazine* in a Dublin bookshop. In the April 1958 edition, I found an article entitled 'Young–Old Lebanon Lives by Trade', by Thomas J. Abercrombie. The sub-head said it all: 'The Land of Cedars, Phoenician Sea Cities, and Crusader Castles Thrives Again as Middleman [*sic*] of the Middle East.' Here was the old dream.

Coloured photographs in the magazine show yachts and surfers in the pale blue waters beside the exclusive Saint-Georges Hotel in Beirut, a folk dance festival on the playing fields of the American University (founded by American Protestant missionaries, 1866), the ancient cedars at Bsharre ('the glory of Lebanon', Isaiah 35:2), the Phoenician port of Byblos ('root of our word "Bible"') and an aerial view of the Bekaa Valley ('an enormous oriental rug unrolled beneath the Anti-Lebanon Range'). There is even a coloured snapshot of President Camille Chamoun in huntsman's dress taking a picnic lunch in the Bekaa with his wife. ('Fluent in English, French, Turkish and Arabic, the President has represented his country in the United Nations. He is an ardent huntsman.')

In his travels around Lebanon, Abercrombie visits Beirut, Jounieh, Byblos, the Cedars and Baalbek and even Beaufort Castle. Mrs Chamoun guides him around the Emir Bashir's palace at Beit Eddine; he is clearly taken in by the mythical Lebanon of happy agrarian masses toiling away under the guidance of a benevolent leader. In the Bekaa, he records, 'birds sang among the reeds and were echoed by a distant chorus from farm workers marching out to potato fields with long hoes over their shoulders. Then coming towards us appeared His Excellency, President

Camille Chamoun ... His graying hair and tanned complexion accentuated the distinguished bearing of his tall, erect frame. A single game bird hung from his belt.'

But then, suddenly, at the very end of his report, Abercrombie writes something quite extraordinary, as if a bright and penetrating light has suddenly fallen upon the land of dreams. He hears that an anti-government demonstration is to take place in the Beirut suburb of Basta — a Shia district which 30 years later will be controlled by pro-Iranian militiamen — and he takes a taxi to investigate:

'You must not go there; you will be killed!' warned my cab driver ... 'No photographs!' shouted one gendarme ... around the corner rushed an angry mob of demonstrators pursued by a squad of gendarmes ... Suddenly the mob turned and began throwing rocks ... Spectators standing on the balconies joined in, filling the air with stones. One of the gendarmes stumbled dizzily and dropped his rifle. The rest of the squad fell to one knee, and I heard the smart click of rifle bolts ... I flattened to the street just as the first shots were fired ... I saw one demonstrator crumple as the rest fled ... Ambulances were screaming back and forth, and then in the distance I could hear the rumble of tanks ...

Shortly afterwards, Abercrombie's journalistic inquisitiveness deserts him. He concludes that the event demonstrates only the 'growing pains of a young republic' which 'after 5000 years of conquerors ... looks forward to a prosperous and peaceful future.' In fact, Abercrombie was watching the start of the first Lebanese civil war, itself the preliminary act in the catastrophe that would tear Lebanon to pieces.

The 1958 war is remembered now not so much for the vicious sectarian battles that occurred in Beirut but for the arrival of the US Marines, who stormed ashore only to find the beaches occupied not by militiamen but by bikini-clad ladies and street urchins who were merely waiting to sell Coca-Cola to the country's latest rescuers. The story is true but it has also become part of the myth. For the reality behind the 1958 conflict was the reawakening of the old dispute between pro-Arab nationalism and pro-Western *Maronitisme*, the same antagonism which had emerged in 1920 when the French created Lebanon.

Now, however, it was Nasser's United Arab Republic — the union of Egypt and Syria into one nation — and the nationalist opposition to the Hashemite regimes in Jordan and Iraq that excited the Muslims of Lebanon, especially the Sunnis. Their interest in Nasser's message of Arab unity was natural, although to President Chamoun it appeared to be a dangerous obsession. Chamoun himself was less of a Francophile than an Anglophile and his contempt for Nasser bore a strange similarity to the equally irrational hatred expressed for the Egyptian leader by Anthony Eden at the time of Suez. Indeed, Chamoun had hoped that Eden's Suez adventure would be successful in deposing Nasser. Eden had regarded Nasser as a fascist in the Mussolini mould. Chamoun saw him — or claimed to see him — as a communist.

Chamoun was leader of his own National Liberal Party, which at that time included a number of conservative Shia and Sunni political leaders. But he treated the democracy about which he boasted to foreign journalists with near contempt when it stood in the way of his domestic ambitions. In the 1957 parliamentary elections, Chamoun's supporters claimed that the opposition were in reality Nasser's candidates; political constituencies were gerrymandered to ensure that Saeb Salam, the most prominent Sunni leader in Beirut, and Kamal Jumblatt, the Druze leader in the Chouf, were defeated. The violent street demonstration witnessed by Abercrombie in Beirut had been in protest at these electoral violations.

Chamoun then attempted to capitalise upon his victory by contemplating a change in the constitution that would allow him a second term as president. The National Covenant had already been weakened by Chamoun's decision to accept the Eisenhower Doctrine, under which the United States promised to use its forces to help any nation which requested assistance against aggressors controlled by 'international communism'. When the Muslim—Druze revolt against Chamoun began with fierce street fighting in Beirut, the Christians noted that the Muslims were using the same pan-Arab rhetoric as Nasser. The rebels were supposedly in league with Egypt; and since Nasser was — in Chamoun's eyes — a communist, then the Eisenhower Doctrine could be invoked. Chamoun called in the US Marines to preserve the sovereignty of Lebanon. The whole structure of the Covenant creaked under the strain as Salam in Beirut and Rashid Karami, the Sunni leader in Tripoli, accused the Chamounists of allying Lebanon with the West. Only the succession to the presidency of the Lebanese army commander Fouad Chehab, and his refusal to commit the army to the struggle, preserved the balance of power in Lebanon.

During the fighting in Beirut large numbers of armed militiamen had appeared on the streets. Christians and Muslims had been the victims of sectarian assassinations. The Lebanese air force had used its Hawker Hunters to attack Muslim positions in the sector of the capital around Fakhani. In Tripoli, Karami's insurgents kept government forces out of the city for several weeks. Yet outside Lebanon, it was as if the battles had never occurred. The economy continued to grow, the banking services increased; by 1962, 38 airlines were flying into Beirut at the rate of 99 flights a day. It was calculated that 65,000 of the country's registered 76,000 road vehicles were used by or for tourists. 'Beirut ... is acquitting herself brilliantly in her new role of tourist "Gateway to the East",' Hachette's Guide to Lebanon boldly announced in 1965.

How did the world remain so blind for so long? In late 1976, Radio

Telefis Eireann, the Irish state television service, decided to produce a documentary on Lebanon and asked me if I could locate any films that depicted the country in the days of peace. The nearest film archive was at the Cyprus Broadcasting Corporation's studios, outside Nicosia. The projectionist there dutifully pulled out can after can of old stock, sometimes so poorly preserved that the nitrate was destroying the footage. The longest documentary, a British film, had been made in 1969. And up on the screen came the familiar images: young women water-skiing past the Saint-Georges, farmers in the Bekaa, the great cedar trees of Bsharre. But then again, a penetrating light: a group of young men with carbines over their shoulders marching through the foothills of Mount Lebanon. The Phalangists look innocent enough with their little moustaches and their campfires amid the fir trees, the stuff of youth movements. Another sequence of frames, this time in the lower, warmer hills of southern Lebanon, where a uniformed officer is teaching some young Muslim men how to load and fire rifles. The voice-over says that the officer is from the Egyptian army.

There is a quick flash of 'unhappier times', of a Hawker Hunter attacking a Beirut apartment block in 1958. The plane jerks across the screen in its bombing run, the camera panning wildly to the building as a cloud of grey and white smoke blossoms from its interior. In 1982, I would stand just where that cameraman stood in 1958 and watch an Israeli jet on the same bombing run, attacking the same block of buildings in west Beirut. The film closed gently, at night, the lights winking along the Beirut skyline.

Footage of a different kind. It is 1972 and I am travelling in a minibus through the Bekaa Valley, *The Times* correspondent in Ireland on holiday in Lebanon, unwittingly choosing to spend my vacation in the country in which I shall much later spend more than 13 years of my life. It is hot and the windows of the bus are open, the smell of orange trees moving through the vehicle, flashes of purple and crimson bougainvillaea brushing against the windows as we approach Baalbek. The Lebanese tourist guide, a small man with a thin moustache, is a Christian. His commentary is all about the past, the very distant past, of Phoenicians and Romans, Assyrians and crusaders — as if the modern history of Lebanon were the story of tourism. The columns of the Temple of Jupiter bake in the sun, white at midday, rose-red in the evening. Beside the Temple of Bacchus, its great stone doorway familiar from the David Roberts lithographs, the floodlighting is being prepared for the Baalbek festival. The Comédie Française is to perform this year.

On the way back to Beirut, we stop in Chtaura for tea and our little Christian guide flourishes a tourist map on the back of which is a photograph of a silver-haired, bespectacled man in a dinner jacket and white bow-tie. He has a sash across his shirt as if he is an ambassador at a diplomatic function. 'An appeal from His Excellency Monsieur Suleiman Franjieh,' says the caption. 'We hope that our meeting with tourists and holidaymakers in our country may be an opportunity to demonstrate the honesty of the Lebanese people, their hospitality, freedom, security and stability which have become an example to others.' But on the highway into Beirut we pass a shanty town on the left-hand side of the road, a place of destitution, of tiny concrete huts, their corrugated iron roofs held down by stones. When I ask our guide who lives there, he glances disapprovingly at the slums. 'Palestinians,' he says. 'They are not part of our people.' It was the Chatila camp.

At Raouche, we watch the water-skiers sliding beneath the tunnel formed by the Pigeon Rocks. The fish restaurants are full. The papers say there has been shooting in the centre of Tripoli far to the north. 'Bandits', the paper reports, have 'taken over' the souk. A jeep passes with members of the Squad 16 paramilitary gendarmerie on board. They are holding automatic rifles and wearing steel helmets. No one – not even the hotel receptionist – can explain why they are there.

On the way back from the classical ruins of Byblos in an old red and green school bus, co-opted by the bus company for the tourist trade, we drive down the coastal highway into Beirut from the north, towards Martyrs' Square, so soon to become the front line. On the road, the Christian driver has pointed out those inscriptions on the walls of the Dog River. There are Muslims and Christians on the bus. Then as we pass the slaughterhouse at Karantina, I ask the Christian driver the reason for the appalling smell. He does not refer to the factory or the tannery beside it but points cruelly instead towards some squalid huts behind a tin wall. 'It's probably the Palestinians,' he says. The war is only three years away.

To 1982 again, to the high-ceilinged room in east Beirut where Pierre Gemayel sits behind his large oak desk. He does not wish to talk further about his visit to Berlin in 1936. But he does not wait to be asked about the Palestinians. He calls them a 'fifth column' and he means it. 'They were a subversive presence here,' he says. 'There was a war, not between us and the Lebanese, but between us and the Palestinians, who tried to conquer Lebanon and take Lebanon and occupy it. They wanted to dissolve Lebanon in the Arab world.' And one is conscious as Pierre Gemayel speaks – unfairly perhaps but the parallel is there – of another, infinitely more vulnerable minority which another government blamed, back in the 1930s, for its own social ills.

There can be no denying the effect of the Palestinian presence upon Lebanon. By 1975, the Palestinian population – swollen by refugees from Israel's conquest of the West Bank in 1967 and from the Jordanian civil war – was around 350,000. But now it was also an armed presence, established by the PLO guerrillas and their leaders who had been forced out of Amman by King Husain. Beirut had become not just the cultural capital of the Palestinian movement but the headquarters for Yassir Arafat's Palestine Liberation Organisation. It was therefore also an 'enemy' capital for the Israelis.

Lebanon had already suffered for the Palestinians' presence. From 1968, the PLO sent raiding parties into Israel from southern Lebanon and the Israelis responded by launching their own revenge raids, often against Lebanese villages. The motive was simple and comparatively cost-free: if the Lebanese villagers allowed armed Palestinians to take shelter among their homes, then they would be made to pay for it in blood. The only way to avoid Israeli attack was to eject the Palestinians from their villages. This, of course, the Lebanese could not do. The Palestinians were armed and the Lebanese were not; and the Lebanese national army was too weak – both militarily and politically – to remove the Palestinians. The PLO, of course, saw its often murderous operations as a sacred duty; they were fighting the occupying power that had taken away the land of the Palestinians.

To legitimise their activities in Lebanon, the PLO could point to the 1969 Cairo agreement, a dubious document drawn up in Egypt between Arafat and the Lebanese army commander which permitted any Palestinian in Lebanon 'to participate in the Palestinian revolution' and to assist in guerrilla operations by safeguarding 'the road to the Arkoub region', the great volcanic escarpment in south-east Lebanon that was now largely controlled by Arafat's Fatah gunmen. The Lebanese, meanwhile, would 'continue to exercise all their prerogatives and responsibilities in all areas of Lebanon ...' This assurance was, of course, meaningless.

The PLO struck at Israeli soldiers and civilians alike, and by 1970 the Israelis were retaliating deep into Lebanon, usually against civilian targets and always with results quite out of proportion to the original Palestinian attack. Thus, for example, when Palestinian rocket fire and a mine explosion had killed two civilians and two soldiers, the Israelis shelled the town of Hasbaya, killing 48 people and wounding another 45. It was another pattern that would be expanded, developed and perfected with ferocity over the coming 15 years.

The Lebanese were powerless to control this conflict between Israel – a foreign nation with which Lebanon was still technically at war – and an increasingly strong Palestinian army of guerrillas who now controlled their own camps in Beirut and elsewhere in Lebanon. Palestinian gunmen stood guard at the entrances of the camps of Sabra, Chatila, Karantina, Tel al-Za'atar and Bourj al-Barajneh in the capital. The Israelis alleged that the Palestinians had created a state within a state, a claim with which few Lebanese would have disagreed.

Whenever the Palestinians attacked Israeli targets abroad, the Israelis invariably assaulted Lebanon. After guerrillas attacked an El Al jet at Athens airport, Israeli troops landed beside Beirut airport and destroyed 13 aircraft belonging to Middle East Airlines (MEA), the country's national carrier, and other Lebanese companies. There were Israeli attacks inside Beirut itself. Three leading PLO figures and the wife of one of them were murdered in their homes in rue Verdun by an Israeli assassination squad on 10 April 1973. In 1974, the Israelis began staging what they called 'pre-emptive' raids, attacks made against Palestinian targets without provocation.

All this had its inevitable effect on relations between Muslims and Christians in Lebanon. The Maronites complained that areas of the country had fallen under Palestinian control, especially the Arkoub, which was now known as Fatahland. The Muslims, however, felt an instinctive sympathy for the Palestinians. Was their cause not also a pan-Arab cause, one for which all Arabs should be fighting? The structure of the Lebanese National Covenant groaned again under the weight of these new pressures. Damascus urged the Lebanese to allow the PLO to continue operations from southern Lebanon while ordering the Syrian security services to ensure that no such activity could be undertaken by Palestinians from Syrian territory. The best-armed – and most opportunistic – of the Palestinian guerrilla movements in Syria was Saiqa ('the lightning bolt'), whose officers were themselves Syrian and whose energies were to be employed almost exclusively against their brother Palestinians.

The Palestinians were thus caught in a moral circle, although they rarely cared to debate the morality of what they were doing to the Lebanese: if they failed to fight the Israelis, then they sacrificed their right of return to Palestine; yet if they did attack the Israelis, they created a new class of refugees among the Lebanese, mostly from the poor Shia community in southern Lebanon. The Maronites would later insist that the Palestinians had helped to destroy Lebanon's democratic freedom. But as Arafat and his colleagues knew full well, the Lebanese state was not beholden to anything so exotic as parliamentary democracy.

For Lebanon was run by the *zaim* (or, more accurately, *zuama*), the 'leaders', the powerful feudal chieftains whom the Lebanese would describe as 'honoured families' but whom the average Westerner would quickly identify as mafiosi. Every community, every tribe, had produced its leaders whose pronouncements, conspicuous wealth, bodyguards, cruelty, education and private armies proved more efficacious than any electoral appeal. Their principal characteristics were a declared love of Lebanon, a publicly expressed desire to respect the National Covenant and a ruthless determination to ensure that their power was passed on to their sons.

The gentle old men who took up the presidency of Lebanon had about them a streak of cold savagery that stunned even the Palestinians. Suleiman Franjieh, the elegantly dressed 'excellency' who expatiated so eloquently on the back of the tourist map about Lebanon's hospitality, security and stability, is widely believed to have participated in the machine-gun massacre of members of the rival Douaihy family near the town of Zghorta in 1957. Although he denied it, at the time he fled to Damascus where the Syrians — never slow to take advantage of those in need — offered him protection and later supported him in his successful candidacy for the presidency of Lebanon in 1970. When his election was disputed by the speaker of the parliament, Franjieh's gunmen brought their firearms into the chamber.

Franjieh's rule had been particularly corrupt; his son Tony was exalted to the Cabinet through a process of nepotism scarcely rivalled elsewhere in the Middle East. But Tony Franjieh's rise was to be short-lived. When Suleiman Franjieh refused to accept the growing Phalangist relationship with Israel in 1977, Pierre Gemayel's son Bashir — destined himself to be elected president of Lebanon — sent his gunmen to the north Lebanese town of Ehden to cut down the young man in whom Franjieh had vested all his hopes. The Phalangists stormed into Tony Franjieh's home, murdered 32 of his supporters and bodyguards and then set about the ritual execution of Suleiman Franjieh's beloved son. According to the old man, the Phalangists first forced Tony and his young wife to watch the shooting of their baby. Then the gunmen made Tony Franjieh witness the murder of his wife. And then the Phalange killed him too.

When Bashir Gemayel's own baby daughter was killed in a car bomb attempt on his life in east Beirut, Suleiman Franjieh, who was now secluded in his home town of Zghorta under the protection of his Marada (Giants) militia, could scarcely suppress his satisfaction. When I asked him for his reaction, he sat hunched behind a table in his little palace, his head hanging down, his half-moon spectacles on the end of his nose. 'I hope,' he said to me, 'that Bashir Gemayel now feels what I felt.'

Camille Chamoun's power was ultimately founded upon his *Nimr* (Tigers) militia, commanded by his son Dany, who was himself to be a declared candidate for the presidency of Lebanon in the aborted 1988 elections. If the Muslim *zaim* were less cruel, they were no less devoted to the system of patronage and family loyalty. Rashid Karami in Tripoli had inherited his father's political power. Kamal Jumblatt's assassination in 1977 led directly to the succession of his son Walid as leader of the Druze and as commander of the 'Leftist Alliance', the agglomeration of Lebanese Muslim and Palestinian guerrillas which generally represented the nationalists. Kamal Jumblatt lived — and Walid still lives — in a magnificent palace of dressed stone at Mukhtara, its courtyards alive with fountains and artificial waterfalls and green-uniformed gunmen.

When his militiamen had stormed onto the Jiyeh coast road and killed the remaining Phalangist defenders there in 1985, I found Walid leaning back in an old wooden chair in one of his palace reception rooms, swigging from a bottle of frozen Czech lager and lamenting the moral improprieties of war. 'There have been people killed, yes,' he said. 'And there has been looting – ah, this damned war!' Walid promised that all displaced Christian civilians would be allowed to return to their homes with appropriate compensation. There was, of course, no such recompense, and I later watched those Christian homes – hundreds of them, even the local Maronite church at Jiyeh – being dynamited to the ground and bulldozed into the earth. As usual with the Druze, there were no prisoners.

These, then, were the scions of Lebanese democracy, men – never women, of course – who amassed personal power as assiduously as they propagated the myth of a stable, pluralistic Lebanon. Walid Jumblatt at least made no secret of his own disillusion, but the dream had to be maintained. Pierre Gemayel in his high-ceilinged office personified this fantasy, lecturing visitors on the achievements of an ordered world which really existed only inside his own office with its Phalangist and Lebanese flags and its old newspaper photograph on the wall. Outside in the street, there were ruins and shell-holes and warnings to drive fast round the port because the snipers were busy again.

'Between 1943 and 1970, Lebanon had its happiest period,' he said. 'We were free and independent. Some countries are rich because they have oil or copper or iron. But the wealth of Lebanon is in private initiative, a wealth that needs social and civic security. The free economic system cannot work with communism or socialism. We had a very special system in Lebanon, a parliamentary democratic system.' Yes, he said, there were equal rights for Lebanon's 17 religious communities, freedom of expression for every man and woman be they Muslim or Christian; it was a land where every man was a friend to the other without distinction. For Pierre Gemayel, myth had become religion. Only the Palestinians were to blame for its destruction. The Shias, the growing community of poor who had suffered more than any other Lebanese, were curiously never mentioned.

The events of the 1975–6 civil war have become a fixation for the Lebanese. Even today, the bookshops of Hamra Street and Sassine Square contain shelves of expensive photographic records of the fighting, coffee table books with colour plates in which readers can study at their leisure and in detail the last moments of a young Muslim militiaman before the firing squad, the anguished eyes of a Palestinian mother pleading for her family before a hooded gunman, a Christian family lying massacred inside their home. It is a kind of catharsis for both the Lebanese and the Palestinians who have long understood the way in which these dreadful events should be interpreted. Victories were the result of courage, of patriotism or revolutionary conviction. Defeats were always caused by the plot: The Plot, the *mo'amera*, the *complot*, undefinable and ubiquitous, a conspiracy of treachery in which a foreign hand – Syrian, Palestinian, Israeli, American, French, Libyan, Iranian – was always involved. Edward Cody of the AP and I once came to the conclusion that in every interview we conducted in Lebanon, a special chair should be set aside for The Plot – since The Plot invariably played a leading role in all discussions we ever had with politicians, diplomats or gunmen.

The 1975–6 fighting may have been the beginning of the final struggle over the Covenant between Arabism and the West, although in physical terms, it involved a series of horrors rather than battles; Black Saturday on the Ring motorway, the Palestinian massacre of Christians in Damour, the Christian massacres of Palestinians at Karantina and Tel al-Za'atar.

Typically, it was an economic dispute between Muslims and Christians in Sidon – involving Muslim fishermen who feared that a new fishing consortium run by Chamoun and other Maronites would destroy their livelihood – that ignited the fire. Maarouf Saad, the leftist mayor of Sidon, was fatally wounded in a fishermen's demonstration and in further fighting the Lebanese national army – largely commanded, of course, by Christians – came into conflict with Muslim gunmen and the more radical of the PLO's Palestinian guerrilla groups.

Those who have always believed that the war was between Maronites and the rest – the forces of the Gemayels and the Chamouns against Lebanese Muslims and Palestinians – can point to the Phalangist massacre, on 13 April 1975, of 27 Palestinians who were travelling by bus through the Beirut suburb of Ein al-Rumaneh. The Maronites were later to claim that there had been provocation for the killings but the attack appeared to have been carefully planned. If it was intended to provoke the Palestinians and the Muslims into armed conflict, it certainly succeeded. Kamal Jumblatt and other nationalist leaders said that they would no longer support a Cabinet that included Phalangists – just as Chamoun, back in 1957, had refused to countenance nationalists in the administration. The more extreme Palestinian groups and, more discreetly, Arafat's Fatah guerrillas – and subsequently the Muslim militias – were drawn into battle with the Phalange. There were moments of truce – the first of hundreds of Lebanese ceasefires – during which the Lebanese persuaded themselves that the war was over. But it was the entente that was at an end. Rashid Solh, the prime minister, spoke darkly of the arrival in Lebanon of several hundred Israeli *agents pro-*

vocateurs whose mission was to destroy the republic. The Plot had arrived in Beirut.

The Sunni Mourabitoun ('Ambushers') militia, which was Nasserist by persuasion and venal by instinct, allied itself with the Popular Front for the Liberation of Palestine – General Command (PFLP–GC). Like George Habash's PFLP, from which it had broken away in a brutal revolutionary schism, it was opposed to Arafat's gun-and-olive-branch approach towards Israel and therefore outside Arafat's control. The two groups drove the Phalangists out of the Kantari district of central Beirut and evicted the Maronite militias from their bunkers in the luxury hotels near the port.

In December 1975, on what was ever afterwards to be known as Black Saturday, four Christians were found shot dead in a car outside the electricity company headquarters in east Beirut. Bashir Gemayel was in Damascus when the news was reported to him. Phalangist officers of the time insist that he told them to kill 40 Muslims in reprisal. Christian roadblocks were therefore set up at the eastern end of the Ring motorway and the first 40 Muslim men to arrive at the Christian checkpoint, some of them travelling with their wives and children in their family cars to homes in east Beirut, were taken beneath the overpass and had their throats cut. When this news became known in west Beirut, Muslim militias followed the Christian example. For hours, civilians of both faiths dutifully queued at these terrible checkpoints at each end of the Ring on the innocent assumption that the gunmen there merely wished to look at their identity papers. Only when they saw the hooded men with blood-covered knives approaching their cars did they realise what lay in store for them. At least 300 Muslims were butchered in this way; an equal number of Christians probably met the same fate.

In January 1976, the Phalange overran Karantina and killed or deported the inhabitants. Arafat had tried to keep his Fatah guerrillas out of the fighting, but when the Phalange and Chamounists laid siege to the Palestinian camps of Karantina and Tel al-Za'atar, the PLO had committed itself to the war on the side of the Muslims and leftists. The PLO could no longer remain out of the war. Arafat allowed his men to join a leftist Lebanese assault on Damour, a pretty Christian coastal village of silk factories and olive groves that lay across the Sidon–Beirut highway. Chamoun's own home was here, a graceful, red-roofed villa whose tennis courts and lawns ran down to the Mediterranean. Chamoun directed the defence of the village before being evacuated by helicopter. The remainder of the Christian population were either evacuated by sea or murdered by the advancing Palestinians.

For the Palestinians, the Lebanon conflict was now a 'war of liberation' in its own right, intimately bound up with the aspiration for a return to Palestine, a conflict in which the Maronite militias became a proxy enemy. 'The road to Palestine', we in Beirut were told by the PLO, lay through Jounieh, that pleasant Maronite port halfway between Beirut and Byblos. It was Salah Khalaf no less, one of the PLO's leading strategists, who announced in May 1976 — when the Palestinians were climbing the eastern flanks of Sannine to attack the Christians in their historic mountain defences — that the road to Palestine should pass through 'Uyun Al-Siman, Aintura and even Jounieh itself to prevent any further threat to the Palestinian presence in Lebanon'.*

This sort of statement required a special kind of arrogance. It showed what many journalists in Beirut had long realised: that the Palestinians regarded *their* cause, *their* country — Palestine — as infinitely more holy, more sacred than the nation in which they had been given refuge. Jounieh, after all, lay to the north of Beirut, not towards Israel in the south. The Palestinians were fighting their way forward — as they were to do many times in the future — *in the wrong direction*.

One hot morning in west Beirut, the Palestinians' Mourabitoun allies even invited journalists down to the American University campus to witness the launching of a newly acquired ground-to-ground missile towards Jounieh. What was this new rocket? the press wanted to know. Would it be used against Israel? The guerrillas duly launched the missile north across the bay of Beirut at Jounieh, the first stage of the projectile falling into the Mediterranean as the warhead sped off towards the sleepy Christian harbour and its unsuspecting inhabitants. The Mourabitoun then held a press conference to explain the significance of this new weapon while the correspondents — few of whom could speak Arabic — waited in patience to know the weight of the warhead, its height and range. A militia spokesman rambled on in Arabic about the need for resistance, the nobility of the struggle against isolationism and the potentialities of the revolution. Unaware that they were being treated to a rhetoric bath, foreign reporters demanded a translation, whereupon Mohamed Salam, a Lebanese AP staffer, turned to them with grim cynicism. 'The man,' he explained to his press colleagues, 'is saying "no comment".'

With good reason, the memory of the 1975–6 war became painful for many Palestinians. West Beirut, which the PLO controlled, was a lawless, anarchic city in which corruption and protection rackets thrived amid gangland feuding and murder. There were genuine attempts to curb these activities but the PLO could do no more than send its 'security units' into the streets to prevent looting. One hot afternoon in June of 1976, I flew into Beirut to find the PLO in open combat *within* west Beirut against Saiqa, who had attacked Arafat's forces on orders

* Qouted in *The Lebanese Civil War* by Marius Deeb (New York, Praeger, 1980), p. 111.

from Damascus. The first body I saw was that of a man lying in a gutter in Raouche, his arms wrapped around his face, one leg hooked above the pavement. He was a Fatah gunman. The Lebanese — Muslim Lebanese — remained locked in their homes while their streets became a battleground for foreigners. This disgraceful phenomenon — of Palestinian fighting Palestinian — was to be repeated with ever greater savagery in the years to come. The Lebanese, it seemed, were brother Arabs when they were allies but foreigners themselves, ignored and disregarded, when internecine feuds had to be resolved within the Palestinian resistance movement.

All but the Palestinians appeared to realise that Syrian military involvement was now inevitable. Yassir Arafat and Kemal Jumblatt had been summoned the previous winter to Damascus, where they told Assad that they were winning the war and wished to move all the way into the Christian heartland. Assad told them he would prevent this at all costs. And when Jumblatt insisted that he would order his men to advance into east Beirut, Assad had angrily walked out of the meeting. The Syrian foreign minister, Abdul Halim Khaddam, visited Lebanon on three occasions to call for ceasefires or appeal for political reforms that might re-establish trust between the two sides. But when in the early summer the Palestinians appeared on the slopes of Mount Sannine and the Christians found themselves in danger of total defeat, a Syrian military intervention in Lebanon became certain. Sure enough, after persuading President Suleiman Franjieh to request their help — a formal prerequisite which the Syrians characteristically demanded for their army's advance — armoured units of President Assad's forces moved into the Bekaa Valley. They were joined, like most of the other foreign armies that came to Lebanon, by a retinue of Lebanese acolytes, of leftist militiamen and Lebanese Baath party functionaries, all of them desperate to explain how delighted they were that the peace-loving Syrians had arrived to save their country.

Armies are much alike. Their soldiers are bored, the tedium relieved only by seconds of frantic danger and usually futile endeavour. In films, they advance in droves of armour across open fields, their soldiers running behind their tanks for cover. Sometimes it is like this in Lebanon. More often, we would come across them when we least expected it; which is how we found the Syrians one hot June morning in 1976. We simply drove over Mount Lebanon on the Damascus highway, turned a corner west of Chtaura where silver birches ran beside the road and there, quite casually, stood a Syrian soldier in combat fatigues, rifle over his shoulder, cigarette in his mouth, a swaggerstick covered in snakeskin in his right hand. He was leaning against a tree.

In the centre of the road was a six-foot colour portrait of President Assad, an artist's impression of the Syrian leader in air force uniform that made him look like an elderly Battle of Britain pilot, eyes narrowed against the sun, gaze fixed on the heavens. The poster had been pinned onto a large wooden board to the top of which had been affixed a very small Lebanese flag. Only when we looked very carefully did we see, behind the poster and almost obscured by the wall of an old quarry, the barrel of a tank.

The soldier idly flapped his hand towards our car. 'Hello to you gentlemen,' he said, surveying the cameras on the back seat with faint disapproval. 'No pictures.' No indeed. 'It is forbidden.' Of course. Behind the gun barrel, we could now see the tank crew sitting on the turret of the T-62, one of them with a cloth tied round his forehead. 'If you take any photographs, we will riddle your car with bullets.' Perhaps this soldier had heard this in the films. In Arabic, the word for bullets — *rassass* — is almost onomatopoeic, and the soldier hissed the word at us. No, we absolutely would not take pictures.

The idle flap of the hand again, and round the next corner was another tank, then a third, hull down in the long grass like old dogs sunning themselves on a lazy day. A second checkpoint where another soldier pushed a handful of printed sheets through the driver's window. Syria had been invited to come to help Sister Lebanon, they announced, and President Franjieh himself had asked them to come. We were next to that restaurant in Chtaura, where the little Christian tourist guide had four years earlier produced the tourist map with President Franjieh's photograph on the back. So this was what Franjieh meant by hospitality.

The Syrians were everywhere, marching beside the highway where it stretched across the Bekaa towards Masnaa, buying sandwiches and wine in the village shops. 'It is always good to have visitors,' one storekeeper told us. 'And it is always nice when they go home again.' But the Syrians were not going home. We found the local Syrian commander basking on the geranium-smothered patio of the Park Hotel, in happier times the retreat of honeymooners. His soldiers, he said, would prolong by an extra day their ultimatum to the Palestinians to leave the mountain ridges between here and Beirut. He too was happy for us to continue our journey — no photographs, of course — and there was every reason why he should have been. For there was not one gunman to be seen in the Bekaa.

A few hours earlier, Ismail Fahmi, the Egyptian foreign minister, had emphasised his country's deteriorating relations with Damascus by claiming that Syria's invasion might produce 'massacre and genocide' in Lebanon. Yet in the Bekaa, this was not true. The Christian town of Zahle, which had been under siege by leftist militias, was now open to visitors and traffic, the Syrians cooperating openly with the local Phalangist defenders. With Syrian approval, the captain of the town's 'defence committee' had set up office in the telephone exchange. For the Syrians had come to protect the Christians.

Just like the French 116 years earlier, the Syrians had entered Lebanon to save the Maronites from defeat. The Maronites needed saving; they were a minority and President Assad understood minorities. The Christians were beholden to the Syrians for this service — for the moment at least — and thus the Syrians could expect compliance from them. So was it any surprise that the Syrians we met that hot day in the Bekaa wanted only to maintain Lebanon's Maronite-dominated institutions, to restore the sovereignty of the Lebanese government, to stay not one hour, *not one minute* longer than necessary?

They also wanted the Palestinians crushed. Assad did not want the civil war to continue, for if Lebanon suffered any more wounds some of its blood might seep into Syria, through those narrow grey wadis in the anti-Lebanon mountain range and down into the plateau beyond, perhaps even infecting Damascus, whose carefully balanced but Alawite-controlled metabolism had so far remained untouched by the epidemic on the other side of the border. Nor did Assad want a new Palestinian state in Lebanon. That was not where Palestine was supposed to be. Palestine was meant to be to the south, beyond Golan, on the West Bank, in Gaza, in Israel itself. The Syrians had no desire to have a revolutionary Palestinian state along their western frontier. Indeed, the Palestinians were soon to wonder whether the Syrians wanted a Palestinian state at all.

Certainly, there was little to recommend Palestinian rule to the inhabitants of Lebanon. By midsummer of 1976, robbery and kidnapping in west Beirut had become an inseparable part of the war. 'Savage wolves' was how Franjieh would describe the Palestinians a few weeks later. On 16 June, the American ambassador to Lebanon, Francis Melloy, was abducted near the Museum crossing on the front line together with Robert Waring, his economic counsellor, and their Lebanese driver. That same evening, their corpses — minus their shoes and socks — were found lying on the beach at Ramlet al-Baida by the Beirut station manager of British Airways. President Ford demanded that the assassins be 'brought to justice', a curious concept in Lebanon just then and one that was predictably ignored. When Arafat satisfied himself of the identity of the three Palestinians responsible, they were sent down to Tyre 'in disgrace'. At least one of them surfaced, rifle in hand, as an officer in the Palestinian forces to fight against the first Israeli invasion a year later.

Ford demanded an evacuation of American citizens. There were to be a lot of evacuations in the coming years, by land, sea and air, each accompanied by promises from departing residents that their absence would only be temporary. In some cases, they meant what they said; by

1986, some foreigners had been evacuated from Lebanon four times in 12 years. The British left first in a convoy of 20 cars fluttering with Union flags, led by the absent ambassador's Austin Princess and a station wagon containing the bodies of Melloy and Waring. The Americans had dignified their departure with a ceremony of shallow and macabre sentiment. Television crews were invited to stand in front of the US Embassy and film a senior member of the staff, in black tie and dark suit, as he slowly wound up the folding door of an inconspicuous, metal-framed garage. Inside were two young men in the full dress uniform of the United States Marines, standing like figures in a wax museum under the television lamps with two flag-draped coffins between them. 'On my left, ladies and gentlemen, is the casket containing the body of Ambassador Melloy ...' It was the soft-shoe *théâtre noir* for prime time television, broken only by the agitated voice of an American security guard wearing a blue T-shirt yelling: 'Come on. Let's not waste time. Let's go.'

The PLO escorted the British through west Beirut and they were replaced at Khalde by Major Hassan Kassar of the Libyan army, a reconnaissance officer for a Libyan-sponsored Arab League peace force that disintegrated some days later. Major Kassar carried a silver cane made from a golf club and dutifully escorted his charges through every militia checkpoint between Beirut and the Syrian front line. When he handed them over to the Syrians, the major received a special word of thanks from representatives of the country which would, ten years later, help the Americans to bomb Libya.

The American operation on the following day was in a class all its own. US Marines sailed a 115-foot landing craft into a converted bathing club on the west Beirut Corniche guarded by armed PLO guerrillas. The vessel was decorated with the American bicentennial logo and American diplomats publicly thanked Palestinian officers who — a few years later — would be vilified by the same nation as 'international terrorists'. Avoiding the stigma of using the word 'Palestinians', Ford would later express his thanks to what he called 'Arab soldiers' who had 'helped' with the evacuation. But Lebanon's foreign community did not view the operation with the same enthusiasm or sense of drama as Ford, who ostentatiously spent the night in the Oval Office in Washington waiting for news of the evacuation. When the landing craft pulled away it was only just over half full, because scarcely a tenth of the American and British citizens in the country wanted to take advantage of the offer. Some of the Americans who stayed behind questioned the motive behind the whole affair; having publicly urged their own citizens to leave, the British Embassy then let it be known that it privately viewed the evacuation as part of Ford's election campaign.

The Palestinians ordered a general strike in protest at Syria's involvement in Lebanon. In Sidon, a sudden Syrian armoured thrust into the city had ended in disaster when Palestinians and Muslim members of the fragmented Lebanese national army – glorying in the name of the 'Lebanese Arab Army' – trapped the Syrian tanks in Riad Solh Street and destroyed every one, burning their crews alive inside. But in the mountains above Beirut, the Syrians advanced. Every day, we would drive up to the mountains and each day the Syrian tanks would be a little closer. The Palestinian guerrillas would squat behind their outposts of earth and rocks up in the cold air among the fir trees, cradling their rocket-propelled grenades and announcing to us that the Syrians would not be permitted to move one more metre – *not one more inch* – along the highway to Beirut. And each time we visited the mountains, we would find the Syrians not an inch nor even a metre but at least a mile nearer to Beirut.

At Bhamdoun, a hill resort with a little railway station, an ornate French signal box and a clutch of mosques and apartment blocks built by the Saudis who had once gone there for their summer holidays, Syrian shellfire had smashed into the shops and flats, punching a hole into the wall of the Carlton Hotel. The Palestinians claimed to be mining the road when we arrived; Palestinian military preparedness was as thorough as usual. Several guerrillas, wreathed in cartridge bandoliers, were reading comics near an empty café where an old man was picking crumbs of bread off a table. There were some Mourabitoun warriors down the road, asleep beside their mine explosives. A Fatah officer with long, dirty hair led us down a slit trench cut into the soft, red earth. And there, across a field filled with long grass and butterflies, were the Syrian tanks. 'We do not want to fight the Syrians any more,' he said. 'The Syrians and ourselves should be fighting the Zionists together. Assad was fooled by secret promises from America.' It was our old friend, The Plot.

Yet the Palestinians could not see the illusory quality of such conspiracies. How else were they to account for the martyrdom of Tel al-Za'atar, the huge Palestinian camp under siege in east Beirut? Its Maronite attackers were able to concentrate all their energies upon their last assault against the Palestinians now that the Syrians had arrived to save Christian Lebanon. Etienne Saqr, who used the name Abu Arz, the 'Father of the Cedars' – one of the more psychopathic of the minor Christian militia leaders – commanded a group which specialised in cruelty, whose men tied Palestinian prisoners to the backs of taxis and then dragged them 12 miles up the motorway to Jounieh. Their carcasses would then be flung into a dried-up riverbed. 'If you feel compassion for the Palestinian women and children,' Abu Arz proclaimed, 'remember

they are communists and will bear new communists.'* Arafat had ordered
the inhabitants of Tel al-Za'atar not to surrender, knowing full well that
they would be defeated. The survivors themselves later said that Arafat
only wanted more martyrs to capture the attention of the world. Bashir
Gemayel's Phalange and Dany Chamoun's Tigers provided thousands of
them, mostly civilians, when they eventually broke into the camp in
August.

The Syrians ensured the continuation of Maronite rule by arranging
for the installation of Elias Sarkis, a banker of political probity whose
rule was to be marked by the further collapse of the country he promised to
save. The Syrians produced 2,000 soldiers and 40 T-62 tanks to guard
his installation ceremony in the Park Hotel in Chtaura. No stranger
honeymooners could have gathered there than the gangs of parliament
members – 67 of them – who were ferried down to the Bekaa in Syrian
helicopters and armoured limousines, guarded by squads of bodyguards
armed with anti-tank rockets. A flight of Lebanese Hawker Hunters
from the Rayak air base, now in Syrian hands, flew over the hotel as
Sarkis expressed his 'unshakeable faith in the ability of our people to
rebuild a new Lebanon based on fraternity, unity and hatred of any
form of partition.'

The Syrians drove effortlessly through the Palestinian positions on
Bhamdoun while the Phalangists attacked the Palestinians further down
the mountains. The Syrians used their tanks against the leftists without
compunction, but by October they were armed with a weapon far more
powerful than their armour: a mandate from the Arab League to enter
Beirut as an 'Arab Deterrent Force'. The Syrians could now move into
the city. Contingents of Saudi, North Yemeni, Sudanese and Emirates
soldiers were to operate with the Syrian army to provide a semblance of
pan-Arab unity, but it was Syrian armour and Syrian troops who would
occupy the Lebanese capital. There was to be no opposition, the Syrians
said. Once in Beirut, all heavy weapons would be collected from the
militias. This was another of the instructions that would be repeatedly
announced, ignored and forgotten over the next decade.

Emboldened by their own good fortune, the Maronites even argued
that they did not need their Syrian saviours in the streets of Christian
east Beirut. It was a premature demand. Down the mountainside above
the city at dawn on 10 November – almost 17 months to the day since
the civil war had begun – there filed column after column of Syrian
tanks, artillery and troop transporters, at least 20 miles of them, clogging
the valleys with clouds of blue exhaust fumes. More than half the 30,000
Syrians to have entered Lebanon were now approaching the city that lay
below them in the early morning heat, its dim perspective merging into

* Qouted in Randal, *Tragedy of Lebanon*, p. 91.

the Mediterranean. Never had a postwar Arab army occupied the capital of a brother — or sister — nation, let alone done so with such formal constitutional approval.

And they were led — incredulity forced us to ask each other later if we had seen it — these legions of men in full battledress were led by a lone soldier in a forage cap sitting atop a T-62 tank, playing a flute. At 35 mph, he travelled down the highway, all the while swaying from side to side on the iron turret, cheeks puffed out, face frozen with concentration as he played his unheard tune, his notes smothered by the thrashing of the tank tracks. The Pied Piper of Damascus led the way into Beirut.

In the Christian village of Kahhale, white flags were hanging from the windows. The local Phalangist headquarters were deserted but a Syrian officer, who had earlier been distributing leaflets describing the Syrian army as 'an envoy of brotherly love and peace', brusquely jumped down from his tank and uprooted a Phalangist sign designating Kahhale a military zone. He contemptuously hurled the notice-board into a ravine. At Hazmiyeh, the Christians threw rose water and rice at the tank crews. Only when the soldiers moved opposite the Palestinian front line at Galerie Semaan — and the familiar crackle of Beirut rifle fire began to make the troops nervous — did the Syrian column come to a halt as if scarcely able to take in its objectives. A disciplined, regular army was about to drive the gunmen from streets which had for so long been ruled by rival guerrillas exacting their own terrible day-to-day justice.

And it was a genuinely historic moment when the first tanks moved past the blocks of apartments in the Beirut suburbs, many of the buildings scorched and smashed by months of fighting. Just half a mile away, we could see the rampart of sand, 20 feet high, behind which the Palestinians lay waiting, unwilling participants in a ceasefire which Arafat himself had already declared sacrosanct. Only a few of the Christian residents appeared to notice that the Syrians had come prepared for more than just a few days' stay. Many of the soldiers had brought their own suitcases and there were truckloads of supplies: not just food and bedding but barrack equipment, construction materials, even parts of prefabricated buildings.

A more transient atmosphere existed on the other side of the front line, just beyond the heaps of dark earth at Galerie Semaan. If the Syrians moved to a coordinated plan, their potential Palestinian opponents still lived on their emotions. On their side of the line, singing was coming from inside the shell-smashed, desecrated church of Saint Michel. The Palestinian gunmen crouching behind the sand embankment across Boulevard Ariss went on watching the Syrian tanks, ignoring the sound. But when we walked inside the church, we found five small Palestinian boys standing in a line just where the altar would have been.

Each was dressed in a miniature guerrilla uniform and each carried a gun. The eldest, who had unwashed brown hair and could have been no more than ten or eleven years old, was holding an automatic rifle in his arms. The boy on his right was grasping a rocket-launcher. The youngest, perhaps only eight, was bowed down under the weight of an M-16 rifle. He had grenades strapped to his chest with military webbing. Under the eyes of a serious, tall Palestinian with a pistol in his holster, they were singing, over and over again: 'Fatah, we are your children and, when we are older, we will be your soldiers.' Stamping their hopelessly outsize boots, they trudged in single file out of the gutted, white-stone church and slogged off over a ditch away from the barricade.

The guerrillas there still ignored them. Instead, they went on watching the Syrian tanks manoeuvring down the road half a mile away, in what had the previous day been the Christian front line. Shells exploded a long way away across Beirut, down by the port. The thump of each explosion sounded like a door being slammed far beneath our feet. One of the Palestinian guerrillas turned irritably to a companion and asked: 'Why don't we shoot at them?' Had he not heard the Arab League spokesman that morning, promising that the Syrian 'peace-keepers' would 'strike with an iron fist' at any resistance?

But then a remarkable event occurred. From behind us, from the Muslim district of Shiyah, came about 20 people, husbands and wives and a few girls in summer dresses and a man with two little boys walking beside him. They were the nearest residents to the front line and most of them had not dared to walk down the boulevard for more than a year. Cars began to draw up amid the rubble and whole families, 60 or 70 people in all, climbed out of them to view the silent barricade. Businessmen and elderly women picked their way over the broken concrete and steel to stare in disbelief at the crippled buildings with their bulging walls and blackened balconies.

The final great act − for everyone thought it was the final act − took place on 16 November. It fell to a platoon of 14 Syrian infantrymen to end the war because, down by the harbour, the 19 months of street fighting were, almost inconceivably, still going on. For to the very last absurd minute, the combatants went on shooting at each other, as if they could not resist one last battle, as if the front line and the war had become inseparable from their own lives.

We discovered the Syrians sheltering under the walls of Avenue Charles Helou as they came under intermittent shellfire, apparently from Palestinian positions a mile away. Their path of advance − from Christian to Muslim sectors − seemed to have been ordained by history. The Syrians had after all come to save the Christians. The soldiers carried rocket-launchers as well as rifles or machine-guns and behind them, spaced along the dual carriageway high above the port, were lines of tanks.

The platoon commander, a short man with a moustache, a cane and a two-way radio, was arguing with a gang of Christian Phalangist gunmen who had not yet vacated their barricades and who were still guarding the streets, wearing revolvers and carrying carbines with telescopic sights. The officer, obviously unnerved by the continued shooting, was trying to persuade the Phalangists to leave the area while at the same time asking them for directions. Every few minutes a shell would swish over the rooftops to explode with a roar in the docks; and more Syrian troops — nearer to the explosions and silhouetted against the sea — could be seen running beside the harbour wall. The Syrian intention was to move right across the front line and, with this in mind, the officer with the radio began to lead the way up the avenue towards Martyrs' Square.

We could see the entrance to the great square at the end of the street. Before the war, it had been a fruit market and bus station; one side of its nineteenth-century Levantine façade had served as the entrance to the soukh. Its centre was once lined with palm trees and its perimeter with cafés. It took us 20 minutes of scrambling through squalid, ruined alleyways before we reached the place, clambering over burnt-out buses and cars to find some Christian gunmen sitting on a pile of earth, smoking cigarettes. But the square was now unrecognisable, every building had been torn down or pummelled by hundreds of shells and rockets. Buses — some of them upside-down and turned into barricades — were strewn across the square while a mountain of upended transport containers formed the last Christian front line. 'Please,' the Syrian officer kept saying to the Phalangists. 'Please leave us now. You can go now.'

The Syrians watched impassively as one of the Christian gunmen produced a camera, the kind of small pocket camera that might be given to a child as a Christmas present. Then the Christians stood up in front of their barricade and put their arms round each other's shoulders. They faced the camera in their dungarees and jeans and cowboy-style holsters and knee-high boots. Two of them put on paper hats which bore the sign of the swastika. A third held out a crucifix. And there, in front of their destroyed city, they had their photograph taken, like a picture for a school magazine. The front line was thus immortalised, firmly affixed to their own existence, a part of them, something to be recalled with nostalgia, something to be understood and wondered at. Then they walked solemnly away.

We waited another half hour behind a pile of sand for the shooting to die down. Round the corner to our right was what we journalists liked to refer to as 'No-Man's-Land', into which no man had ventured for more than a year. At 10.30 precisely, the Syrian officer stood up, studied a large map of Beirut and walked into an open street to the right. The soldiers followed him and so did we. But what we saw was not a street in any real sense of the term. It was an avenue of crumbling, collapsed masonry in which eight- and nine-storey buildings had slid into the spaces between ruins. Ceilings and floors dangled from what had once been a department store.

We walked through this rubble, the Syrian patrol around us, picking our way over concrete and broken typewriters and tailors' dummies and, occasionally, small, grey, live grenades. There was complete silence as we padded through two more streets with walls so bitten away that they looked like lace. Then we came to a smashed yellow stone façade and a doorway that led down into a cellar. Sounds came from inside and from the darkness appeared a man holding a Kalashnikov rifle and wearing a Palestinian scarf. His face was covered in dirt and he grinned at us in a rather frightened way. We had reached the Palestinian front line.

The Syrian soldier nearest to the door held out his arms in friendship. The man embraced the Syrian, starting at the same time to cry. He sobbed on the soldier's shoulder. More Palestinian guerrillas emerged from the darkness — two Palestinian girls with rocket-launchers were among them — and the soldiers began to shout greetings. We walked up a narrow street from their dugout past a doorway whose lintel was matted with grass, the entrance to the old film company offices to which the 12-year-old gunboy had taken us less than two months before.

There on the other side stood the small square where the Lebanese parliament had once met. The parliament building had burned, its roof had collapsed and a large heap of concrete lay around its doors. Just in front of it lay what remained of the ancient forum of Roman *Beyrutus*, three bullet-slashed columns in the middle of the road.

The Mourabitoun gunmen and Palestinians fired their machine-guns in the air to welcome the Syrians, the thousands of bullets ricocheting off the ruins. Had the Lebanese gunmen not been so enthusiastic in their celebrations, they might have noticed a small but symbolic incident which cast a shadow over the Syrians' arrival. As the guns were still being fired, a Syrian tank came lunging up the shattered street where we had just been walking and entered the tiny square. It drove to one side, then turned 90 degrees, its tracks skidding on the rubble. And as the last shots were being fired, the Syrian tank came to rest outside the very door of the building which housed Lebanon's 'democratic' parliament.

It was too soon for anyone to understand the true meaning of what had happened. That afternoon, Ed Cody and I drove up to Galerie Semaan. The Syrians had already broken through the rampart of sand but as we approached, a Palestinian holding a rifle walked up to our car. He was tired, unsmiling, puzzled in an irritated way. 'Where are you going?' *Sahafeen*, we said. 'Where are your papers?' Cody looked at the gunman with a cold, unhappy expression. 'We don't need papers any more,' he replied, rewarding the Palestinian with his familiar, mirthless smile. 'The revolution's over.'

4   The Garden of Earthly Delights

To Beirut ...
From the soul of her people she makes wine,
From their sweat, she makes bread and jasmine.
So how did it come to taste of smoke and fire?

The Lebanese singer, Fayrouz.

A close neighbour of mine in Beirut died in 1986. She wasn't killed. She just died of cancer after spending 26 years in her little ground-floor home on the Beirut seafront. For much of her time, she used to look after stray dogs and cats, guarding them in her apartment, feeding them in the narrow, shady street outside her wrought-iron front door. During one day of what the news agencies used to call 'sporadic bombardment' − an artillery battle that sent the occasional shell swishing over our homes and into the Mediterranean − I found her in the old dirt parking lot opposite the house. She was trying to feed a frightened kitten.

Her death was greeted with Lebanese formality. Death notices appeared on handkerchief-sized posters which were glued to the door of our apartment block, to the walls outside, to the nearest telegraph poles. Neighbours and relatives and distant friends were invited to her house where her son served coffee, remembered his mother and talked politics. All this time, her body lay up in the American University hospital awaiting burial. For this was a difficult business. The kind old lady who looked after cats was a Christian, and she had lived in west Beirut which was Muslim. The front line that divided the city was too dangerous for her family to take her remains to the Christian sector for a funeral.

There was documentation to complete − pages and pages of it signed by the local *mohafez* (governor) − before the Sheikh who presided over the hot, untidy cemetery behind the back wall of the Kuwaiti Embassy could be prevailed upon to allocate my neighbour a few square yards of earth for her eternal rest. There was a little bureaucratic delay here, too, a few formalities to clear up about my neighbour's earthly beliefs. She had been a Christian and this was a Muslim cemetery. And though dead, she had still to be counted a Christian. So prior to burial, he accepted her, in an informal way, into the Muslim faith. Conversion after death. Only Beirut could produce so awesome a phenomenon.

In one sense, posthumous conversion affects all Beirut. Not of religion so much as political strength. The dead endure this stoically enough. No militia or political leader is so powerful – his name never so influential – as when he is dead, enshrined on wall posters and gateposts amid naively painted clusters of tulips and roses, the final artistic accolade of every armed martyr in Lebanon. Bashir Gemayel, Kamal Jumblatt, Imam Mousa Sadr, even Rashid Karami; murdered they may have been, but who could deny their potency now? Their brothers and sons and sisters have had to compete with immortality. In east Beirut, they still display posters of Bashir beaming down from the afterworld in a sheen of celestial light upon a three-dimensional Lebanon, an image which unintentionally represents the nation in the shape of a cheaply constructed coffin. All who live there are dead.

Death is important because it has provided a mandate for the living; what Muslim would now contest the arguments of Khalil Jerardi, the murdered leader of the south Lebanese Islamic Resistance? What Shia would wish – or dare – to dispute Jerardi's thesis that the forces of Islam will one day march to liberate Jerusalem? More than two years after he was torn apart by a bomb on his helicopter, Rashid Karami still speaks to the Sunnis of Lebanon; on the cassettes sold by the street vendors of Hamra Street, Karami still lectures his people on Lebanon's Arab identity, the importance of national unity and the struggle against Zionism. No matter that his classical Arabic is delivered in a preacher's monotone, that the tape costs a dollar, that he was regarded by his enemies as a creature of Syria. His words are now wisdom.

Bashir can be heard regularly on the Voice of Lebanon, broadcasting on behalf of the Phalange from transmitters up the coast above Byblos. It is seven years since he was crushed to death in the bombing of his party headquarters in Beirut, but on the air he still shouts to his supporters. You can hear them cheering him on the recordings. A Lebanon free from all foreign interference, a strong Lebanon, a respected Lebanon. Who would now doubt that this young man would have made a fine president? What Christian would want to recall that it was Bashir's Phalange that entered the camps of Sabra and Chatila in the week of his death to kill up to two thousand of their inhabitants?

In Lebanon, one shot, one bomb, has served to immortalise a cause, to make words unimpeachable, arguments irreproachable. To question the dead is sacrilege of a special kind. Look at the legions of martyrs on the walls of Beirut, all those who followed this wisdom of the dead. Study the confident, smiling eyes of Bilal Fahas, lionised by the Amal militia as *arouss al-jnoub*, the 'bridegroom of the south', his last moments captured by Amal's official war artist, driving his Mercedes car bomb into an Israeli armoured personnel carrier. After a while, a routine started; the martyrs would have their own show on television.

Hours after she immolated herself in an attack against the South Lebanon Army, Sana Mheidli was there on our screens, appearing in her very own posthumous video-cassette. Recorded shortly before she set off on her mission, she is almost radiant, grinning into the camera, expressing her belief in the necessity of sacrifice. She is wearing make-up. She is a very pretty woman and she is speaking to us from the afterlife, still dressed in her combat jacket and red beret. It is as if the dead of Lebanon had constructed some unique passageway between life and death. Did the Maronites not say that Bashir was really pulled from the ruins alive, that he was witnessed being carried to an ambulance? Ambulance 90, they said it was, although we found that no ambulance in Beirut bore that number. Bashir would return one day in Lebanon's hour of need, a Phalangist King Arthur.

And Imam Mousa Sadr, he too is alive, the Shias tell you in southern Lebanon. He disappeared in Libya in 1978, almost certainly murdered by Moammar Ghaddafi, who allegedly suspected him of misappropriating 'revolutionary' funds. But Mousa Sadr, who claimed descendancy from the Seventh Imam, will return, a Twelfth Imam. Meantime, in those street posters, his benevolent face gazes approvingly down upon the photographs of his own Shia martyrs. Between the quick and the dead, he has achieved a special place: all the more alive in the hearts of his people because he is dead.

Beirut is the opposite. Its hopelessness relies upon its resilience. There are those who praise the courage of its people, their valour amid despair, but it is this very capacity for survival, for eternal renewal, that is Beirut's tragedy. If the city were allowed to die — if its airport closed forever, if its imports and exports were frozen, its currency destroyed, if its people gave up — then its war would end. So long has it continued that now it is difficult to think of a Beirut that is not at war. Live there for a few months and you begin to see it as the Lebanese do. You come to regard the city as a normal metropolis; visit Europe, fly into Geneva or Paris, and you feel as if you have entered a glass bubble, an artificial world totally divorced from the 'real' existence of power-cuts and burning garbage heaps and gunmen and constant political instability.

The Lebanese themselves have difficulty in explaining this inversion, in comprehending their own affection for Beirut. Having believed for so long in Lebanon — in the democratic, bucolic, non-existent Lebanon — many of them are unable to fathom why they now live in such misery, in a nation which has provided a grave for more than 100,000 people in 14 years. Perhaps this accounts for the success of Fayrouz. For if in 1940, Londoners sought solace when they heard Vera Lynn singing of nightingales in Berkeley Square, so now the Lebanese who live thousands of miles from their country will pay thousands of dollars in black market concert tickets to hear Fayrouz, the best, the most loved of Lebanese singers, as she chants 'To Beirut':

To Beirut — peace to Beirut with all my heart
And kisses — to the sea and clouds,
To the rock of a city that looks like an old sailor's face.
From the soul of her people she makes wine,
From their sweat, she makes bread and jasmine.
So how did it come to taste of smoke and fire?

Like the country, the city also lived a lie. David Roberts drew Beirut beneath the mountain of Sannine, its avenues of trees gleaming at dusk, its *serail* standing out like a castle above the bay. T. E. Lawrence walked through Beirut as a young man and thought it a delicate town with its red tile roofs and narrow streets. A fine volume of photographs culled from early postcard collections shows what a noble place it used to be. Chocolate and cream tram cars run past Turkish sentry boxes and the façades of porticoed villas. The old streets downtown are smothered in blossom. A snapshot of Ein al-Mreisse — where the apartment building in which I live now stands — shows a cluster of fields running down to the sea, a few magnificent old Levantine houses with windows of lead tracery and narrow stone columns supporting the balconies.

Yet here again, there are phantoms. On a rainy afternoon on leave in London in 1984, I pause with a Lebanese friend at a shop that sells antiquarian newspapers. I am looking for contemporary reports on the Irish famine and Daniel O'Connell and I browse through *The Standard*, published at Blackfriars, an edition of 29 July 1840. And there, on page three, I come across another portent. It is a short report in a single column:

Beyruth.

Anarchy is now the order of the day, our properties and personal safety are endangered, no satisfaction can be obtained, and crimes are committed with impunity. Several Europeans have already quitted their houses and suspended their affairs, in order to find protection in more peaceable countries.

What produced these historical throwbacks? It was as if there were something in the *nature* of Lebanon that made these phenomena occur. Purged of its early Victorian grammar, had I not written an identical report to that of 1840 only a few *days* before I entered this shop?

Then again, in a volume of old prints, a drawing of a nineteenth-century Anglo-French naval bombardment of Beirut, its caption describing how the noise of the artillery could be heard as far away as Sidon. In Beirut, I buy some very old, torn postcards. One shows a tiny warship with a narrow, straight smokestack under a heavy, cloudy sky, riding at anchor below Mount Sannine. 'Aunullah Gunboat 5 minutes before Italian bombardment, Feb. 24. 1912,' says the caption.

Of course, Beirut must have been a friendly old city even if its colleges had about them something rather earnest, over-diligent and severe. In the pictures of the time, the Protestant missionaries who founded the American University in 1866 look a sober lot. President Bliss sits in his private library under a brass chandelier, a grave man whose eyes droop at the same angle as his moustache. There are Persian rugs on the floor, heaps of books lying on the tables. More than a century later, one of his successors would be shot just outside this room. Bliss would recognise little of the Beirut in which the man was to die. The university campus is one of the few surviving features of the city which then even boasted a crusader castle of its own down by the port. It was pulled down early this century so that its stones could be used in new construction. The red roofs have gone. So have almost all the lead tracery windows, the columns and decorated balconies. Between 1950 and 1970, the speculators trashed Beirut in order to build new high-rise apartments, block after block, without sanitation and often without sufficient water supplies, a hot, treeless city; plenty of sweat but no jasmine.

It was in this modern, broken city that the Lebanese of 1976 tried to re-create their dream. The conspicuous façade of wealth and luxury symbolised by the hotels in Phoenicia Street, the Saint-Georges, the banks and commercial offices, had all gone. Instead there swelled warrens of poverty and deprivation, the slums of Hay al-Sellum and Bourj al-Barajneh, Chiyah and Ghobeiri and Haret Hreik, Sabra and Chatila, in which the Palestinian refugees, their sons and daughters, the homeless Lebanese of the civil war, the Shia refugees from the flattened villages in southern Lebanon, all came to share squalor in an urban mass entirely beyond government control.

But the Christian leadership of Lebanon and the Syrian government which was dedicated to its continuation were intent on eradicating not the causes of the recent war, but its memory. The Lebanese henceforth referred to those terrible 17 months as *al-hawadess*, the 'events', as if they were the result of some natural calamity rather than a man-made catastrophe. They wanted to talk about the comradeship that the 'events' engendered rather than the society it destroyed. And since no one discussed the war, no one was trying to discover the lessons which might be learned from the tragedy. Syrian troops occupied the offices of *An-Nahar* and *As-Safir*, the two leading Beirut newspapers, so that their correspondents should clearly understand their new responsibilities. In all the papers appeared pictures of buildings under repair; but there was no debate about political reconstruction, about the efficacy or value of the Lebanese Covenant. Even the Egyptian food riots of 1977 which almost dethroned President Sadat were considered so sensitive that the

Lebanese papers virtually ignored them. Foreign news magazines and newspapers were rigorously censored. The *International Herald Tribune* would appear on the streets with 'windows' cut in its pages almost every day. The English-language *Middle East* magazine would arrive on the newsstands with whole pages missing.

Under Syrian auspices, Phalangist operatives within the Lebanese civil service had also set up a censorship office in east Beirut to which not only the local press but foreign correspondents were ordered to report with their dispatches. Zahi Boustani, one of the most prominent of the Lebanese government censors, would always greet journalists with a warm smile and a strong handshake. He was a tall, handsome man with a Marshal Foch moustache and a sharp command of the English language. He dressed in smart grey suits and his only concession to youthful fashion was a large blue kipper tie with a picture of a woman in eighteenth-century dress on the front.

He was scrupulously, painstakingly polite. All his staff were polite. There were 20 censors of whom only two were Muslims. No local or foreign newspaper was permitted to refer to them; the penalty for doing so could — in theory at least — be five years in one of Beirut's non-existent prisons. Boustani worked in a rectangular room at the top of the staircase, a room whose windows had been covered by hardboard. I had written an innocuous enough dispatch, a brief account of the attempts by President Sarkis to gather in militia arms, but Boustani seemed troubled by it.

'Let me explain', he said. 'I realise that your readers in Britain may wish to have the political affiliations of people here explained to them. But we feel that by now they will be aware of the political labels in Lebanon. For this reason, we no longer refer to people as "left-wing" or "right-wing". We refer to them by their political parties — the National Liberal Party or the Phalange.' But how could one distinguish between Christian and Muslim? 'The war,' Boustani replied, 'was fought between the Lebanese and the Palestinians.'

At this point, he picked up a stubby, felt-tipped red pen and began to delete large passages of my report. I later transmitted it — in its entirety — to *The Times*, with the censored passages reinserted in italics; which is exactly how my paper printed the story the following day. Boustani's work was part of the re-creation of a lie, as meretricious as all the fantasies created about Lebanon:

Brigadier Muhammad al-Kholi, *the head of Syrian military intelligence*, is expected to hold talks with President Sarkis of the Lebanon in the next two days to make final arrangements for the collection of arms *from the armies which fought each other in the nineteen month Lebanese civil war* ... Ever since the war ended in November *with the occupation of Beirut by mainly Syrian troops of the Arab League peacekeeping force*, there have been repeated but vain attempts by the authorities to persuade the various *right and left-wing militia* forces to hand over their heavy artillery ... *

Boustani justified the deletions by claiming that Brigadier al-Kholi was only a colonel, that he was not head of Syrian military intelligence — as everyone knew him to be — that one could not refer to Syrian troops in the context of the Arab League because there were Sudanese and Saudi soldiers in the force; and that the reference to 'right' and 'left' gave the impression of 'disunity'. Boustani was apologetic. 'I am sorry', he said as he excised a long sentence which referred to the attempts by Palestinians in Beirut to keep their arms. 'You just cannot say that.'

Every reference to Phalangist barricades in east Beirut was censored. So was the rising death toll — which then stood at 40 — from a recent bomb explosion. 'We have heard enough about the bomb', Boustani said. He would allow no reference to the funerals of the dead. 'Look,' he said, 'we are not a sectarian society. I am a Christian and over there' — here he pointed to a smallish man who had entered the room — 'is a Muslim.' Then why, I asked, if Beirut was not divided, did my Muslim taxi driver refuse to cross the old front line to the Christian east of the city? Boustani laughed. 'That is his problem.' I asked how the Western press could continue to work under such heavy censorship. 'That is your problem,' Boustani replied. And he was no longer smiling.

Nor did he have any reason to. When Sarkis heard that *The Times* had published my report on Boustani's work, he demanded a copy of the paper which he, like everyone else in Beirut, had been prevented from seeing. And once he had read it, Sarkis immediately suspended censorship of outgoing foreign press reports. It was one of the few independent acts he was to take during his presidency.

Yet the Lebanese had not been alone in forcing facts into a new mould. At Damour, the Christian village 12 miles south of Beirut which had been captured by the Palestinians in January of 1976, the PLO had now installed the survivors of the Tel al-Za'atar massacre in the ruined homes of the former inhabitants. It took some time to arrange a visit to Damour. It was easy to drive there on one's own but no Fatah officer would talk to a journalist unless he was given proof that the reporter really was a journalist and not a spy. Mustapha was our proof. Mustapha was a plump, middle-aged Palestinian functionary with a brown moustache and an irritating habit of using outdated English expressions to show his familiarity with the language. Anything to be stated with emphasis would naturally acquire the accretion 'by golly'. When it rained, it always 'poured cats and dogs'.

And it rained when we drove to Damour, sheets of it that flowed across the windscreen of our car and turned the streets of Damour into

---

* *The Times* 11 January 1977.

fast-running rivers. Mustapha and I and the dull-faced gunman who accompanied him for the last part of the journey had to shout to make ourselves heard against the pounding of rain on the roof of the car. Damour was a place of overwhelming poverty, of dark, sad faces and grief. There was scarcely a soul in the broken village who had not been touched by death. There were few men and the women seemed prematurely old, bent over cooking pots and surrounded by ten, twelve, perhaps fifteen children. Inside each cold, damp hovel with its sputtering oil lamp was one of those framed portraits, sometimes of a middle-aged man wearing a suit and tie — an enlargement of a wedding picture — more often of a youth glaring at the camera with embarrassment and hostility. They were martyrs all, most of them killed in the last minutes of the Tel al-Za'atar siege when the Maronite militias broke through the perimeter and massacred the majority of those who remained.

'This village is a witness to what the *Kata'ib* [Phalangists] did,' Mustapha said as we splashed past a gutted petrol station. 'Everyone here is from Tel al-Za'atar. Everyone lost a member of their family. The *Kata'ib* murdered their relatives. Those people were animals.' But what about Damour? Had not there been a massacre here too? Some of the houses in the little seaside village had been beautiful buildings with large yellow stone facades and with grape-vines strung across their roofs. 'The *Kata'ib* blew them up before they left in the war,' Mustapha said.

He was lying. The buildings had been systematically destroyed by the Palestinians who stormed into this place on 20 January 1976. That was before Tel al-Za'atar but two days after the first news of the Phalangist slaughter of Palestinians at Karantina. The guerrillas' revenge had been merciless. Although many of the people had escaped by sea, at least 350 Christians stayed behind. Twenty were Phalangist militiamen, the rest civilians. It was said — not by Mustapha, of course — that Arafat later wanted to execute the local PLO commander for what he then permitted.

The Christian militiamen were executed. The civilians were lined up against the walls of their homes and sprayed with machine-gun fire. Their houses were then dynamited. The 149 bodies that lay in the streets for days afterwards showed grisly evidence of what the Palestinians had done. Many of the young women had been raped. Babies had been shot at close range in the back of the head. Two hundred other civilians were never seen again. Among those who died was a family called Hobeika and a girl to whom one of the Hobeika boys — a youth called Elie — was said to have been engaged. We would be hearing that name again.

But the plunder did not end there. The cruel young men who follow every civil war army made their way into Damour, some of them as high on hashish as the Phalangists had been at Karantina. Many of them were Lebanese Muslims, part of Jumblatt's 'Leftist Alliance'. Some were Palestinians. And at some point – no one knows exactly which day – they vented their wrath on the old Christian cemetery, digging up the coffins and tearing open the gates of vaults, hurling Damour's past generations across the graveyard. They lay there for days, the long dead, skeletons and withered cadavers still dressed in the nineteenth-century Sunday best in which they had been buried before mandate Palestine even existed.

Of all this, Mustapha said nothing. Instead, he walked up the narrow lane that led to Damour's church. There came the sound of children's voices. The church had been burnt and on one outside wall a huge mural depicted Fatah guerrillas holding AK-47 rifles marching across some low, stony hills. At one end was a large portrait of Arafat; it had been painted with painful accuracy, even down to the PLO chairman's three-day growth of beard. Opposite this mural was a concrete school yard; for the ruined church and the damaged priests' quarters that adjoined it had become a school for the children of Tel al-Za'atar. There were more than 300 of them, sitting in classrooms that had been converted from the priests' bedrooms.

There were Arabic classes in one, Palestinian history in another. On each wall was a map of mandate Palestine with a red and gold star marking the location of Jerusalem. In an art class a boy of 11 was crayoning a panorama of the battle of Tel al-Za'atar, a picture that showed a truly professional eye for the mechanical details of every rifle and anti-aircraft gun. The figures in the drawing – the guerrillas who were holding or manning these weapons – were mere appendages. There was a mosque with a half moon on the dome and a church with a cross over the tower. Who had told him to include those two essential institutions of Middle Eastern history? But what caught our attention were the flights of Israeli jets bombing the camp. They were obviously Israeli because the Star of David had been coloured onto the fuselage and wings of the aircraft. The bombs could be seen falling from the planes. The boy handed the picture to me. I thanked him but did not tell him that I knew – as even he probably knew – that not one aircraft, neither Israeli nor Lebanese, had ever bombed Tel al-Za'atar during the siege.

He had been invited to believe something other than the truth and, like the Lebanese, he had obliged by acquiring a new memory of the reality which he had endured. He was to be one of the fedayeen, the Palestinian guerrillas, for this was a primary training school for just such a future. That was why the mural was on the wall and why the school yard was used for military displays. A Fatah commander, a tall man in a dark green uniform who looked at the children in an exaggeratedly avuncular way and smiled too much, had arrived to watch an exercise in military preparedness.

So one by one, the children — girls as well as boys — appeared in the yard, each dressed in little khaki uniforms. They formed up on three sides of the square, at the fourth side of which was a low wooden bar suspended a foot from the ground by two vertical metal supports. Each child then ran forward, performed a somersault and crawled under the rod of wood to the accompaniment of high-pitched, militant cries of 'Palestine'. If they did not touch the wood, they were cheered by their classmates. If they knocked it off its supports, they were left in miserable silence.

We wondered whether this was how they were supposed to assault Israel, each little guerrilla clambering beneath the electrified fence along the Lebanese border, always preceded, of course, by an obligatory somersault, before helping to identify themselves to the waiting Israeli army by screaming 'Palestine' at the top of their voices. But we were wrong. These children were being trained — although neither we nor they nor their teachers nor that constantly smiling man in the green uniform knew it then — for a far more dramatic event, one in which the Israelis would come to them, rather than the other way round. The Israelis would come all the way to Damour and even walk into this little school yard.

Mustapha was pleased. We had taken photographs of the children, the unhappy subject of Damour's own history had apparently been dropped, and it was no longer raining cats and dogs. Our car bumped down the narrow road through the village. Why did the Palestinians kill the Christians here? I asked. Mustapha was silent for a while. 'Robert,' he said at last, 'you should not believe the propaganda you are told about us. We are the ones who have suffered. Do you not realise what those little children represented?'

The rain had grown heavier and the windscreen wipers could scarcely compete with the downpour once we reached the main highway. I was driving and Mustapha was sitting in the back with the gunman. 'You know,' he continued, 'it may surprise you to know that not all the Christians left Damour. No, there is a Christian lady there now, an old lady who stayed after the Palestinians came and she still lives there, in her own home.' What did she do? 'She keeps birds,' Mustapha said. 'Lots and lots of birds, some in cages. Some are tame and come to her home for food. We all love her.' There was another silence and then I heard the gunman in the back of the car trying to suppress his laughter. What was funny, I asked? The man laughed more loudly, guiltily but uncontrollably. 'The woman,' he said. 'The woman with the birds. She went mad.' I turned round. Both Mustapha and the gunman in the back seat were giggling.

A few days later, Damour was graced with a visit from Arafat himself. He had come to see the relatives of his martyrs. On this occasion, the press were not invited. And with good reason. For the refugees of Tel al-Za'atar had clearly not all adopted the revolutionary approach to reality embraced by the 11-year-old boy artist. They remembered that Arafat had called on their menfolk in Tel al-Za'atar to go on fighting when they were hopelessly surrounded. They recalled how Arafat had appealed to them to turn Tel al-Za'atar into 'a Stalingrad'. And some of them had realised that their families had died because Arafat needed martyrs. So when the PLO chairman arrived, kitted out as usual in his familiar *kuffiah* headscarf and pistol at his hip, several women – according to Palestinian witnesses – stood by their hovels and shouted 'traitor' at him. Some reports said that rotten vegetables were thrown at Arafat. Mustapha had not been on hand to witness this perverse tribute to the courage of Tel al-Za'atar.

But at least the ruins of Damour provided a semblance of normal life for its new inhabitants. The same could not be said of the Beirut camps. Winter is always unkind to the camp-dwellers, but in November 1976 the winter storms attacked Beirut with particular cruelty. At the Sabra camp, for instance, where 30,000 people lived in the damp misery behind chipped and shell-scarred walls, hundreds of hovels were inundated. From the outside, the only sign of habitation was the bent mass of corrugated black tin roofs weighted with stones against the wind, which fanned out across the camp like broken umbrellas. The waterlogged streets, however, were peopled with dozens of small children, wearing filthy clothes and chasing each other through the water which gushed past the front of their stone shacks with their rusting roofs. Children's faces appeared in unlit windows to stare at visitors. Some would hold up babies dressed in huge pyjamas.

When they built the original huts in 1948, the United Nations authorities must have forgotten that Sabra lay in a depression and would turn into a swamp in heavy rain. Some of the streets were six inches deep and the torrent covered the open sewer. The elderly, some of them bare-footed, stumbled wearily through the mire. The streets and the houses emitted a faint but perceptible smell of sewage. The Palestinians were unlikely to forget their suffering in the civil war. About 2,000 women and children were estimated to have died in the shelling of Sabra in 1975 and 1976. Of the 30,000 inhabitants, at least 10 per cent were Lebanese.

Nearly every home was the same: a two-room prefabricated shack with a stove, but no electricity or running water and only an oil lamp and candles for light. Small carpets, the colours faded years ago, glistened with moisture in the doorways. The nightly shelling by the Phalangists had left patches of smashed huts and scorched wood, although there was other, less tangible damage.

Mrs Hasnashi was a beautiful woman of 25 who had married at 13 and had seven children. They stood around her, dripping with rainwater, as she talked in an unemotional voice − even smiling − about the miscarriage she had earlier in the year during a night of shelling. 'There were many rats at the time,' she said. 'The children were frightened of them and at night they would wake up and scream.' It was 15 minutes before Mrs Hasnashi mentioned that her youngest son, a baby of seven months, became paralysed during the bombardment and died.

During her conversation, some Palestinian men arrived. They watched me carefully but without comment. But they nodded with ostentatious agreement when Mrs Hasnashi said that she believed she would yet live in 'a free Palestine'. For the Palestinians, even leaving Sabra presented difficulties. The PLO claimed that few if any refugees wanted to leave the camp; it did not want it said that its people would run away. So anyone wishing to leave Sabra − even if shelling made the camp un-safe − had to seek permission from a 'People's Committee' of Palestinian resistance movements; and if permission was refused, he or she had to stay. Persistent questioning disclosed that anyone who left Sabra without permission and then wished to return was automatically deprived of a portion of food and free blanket allowance, a strangely harsh punishment if so few people really wished to leave Sabra.

The PLO men − for the new arrivals were, of course, camp officials − went on at length about the 'democratic centralism' of the People's Committees. But they did not talk so freely about other camp affairs. Every 50 yards or so through the clogged and muddy streets, guerrillas stood beside sandbagged positions or on the few houses which had concrete roofs. All carried weapons and their uniforms were easily identifiable because Sabra had been ruthlessly if untidily quartered out between the various rival Palestinian factions. Fatah men wore combat jackets, khaki trousers and red berets. George Habash's Popular Front for the Liberation of Palestine were dressed in grubby brown anoraks. Saiqa wore camouflage uniforms, bandoliers of ammunition draped over their shoulders and Palestinian *kuffiahs*. Saiqa were Palestinians but they represented the Syrians in Sabra, another intrinsic truth that no one was supposed to acknowledge.

But there could be no more unprincipled struggle just then than the dishonest, unnecessary little war going on in southern Lebanon. No sooner had the civil war around Beirut been suffocated by the Syrian army than fighting broke out again between the Palestinians and the Israelis. The Syrians had initially offered to secure all Lebanese territory down to the Israeli frontier, a notion which did not appeal to the Israelis. They invented what they called a 'red line' beyond which the Syrians were not expected to move. If they did so, according to spokesmen in Tel Aviv and Jerusalem, Israel would 'not sit idly by'.

It was the first of many such lines that were to be scribbled across

Lebanese maps over the next decade and it would not be the last time that Israel's threatening expression would be employed. Over the next few years, the Israeli government repeatedly announced that it would 'not sit idly by' if the Syrians crossed the 'red line', if the Christians were attacked, if the Palestinians did not leave Beirut, if Lebanese guerrillas continued to assault Israeli occupation troops. But the red lines were ultimately futile. Having discouraged the Syrians from crushing the Palestinians in southern Lebanon, the Israelis now had to deal with the guerrillas themselves.

Initially, the Syrians extended their own area of control and occupation as far south as the Zahrani refinery on the coast road between Sidon and Tyre. They also put a platoon of soldiers under canvas in a little grove of trees east of Nabatieh. Here they were exactly six miles from the nearest point on the Israeli frontier. An armoured personnel carrier was parked by the trees while behind it was an old T-54 tank so smothered in tarpaulins that only its muzzle was visible. As a forward position, it left a lot to be desired. Each time we passed their position – which was only three miles from the back of Beaufort Castle – a Syrian sergeant or corporal would anxiously ask us if we knew something that they did not. Why else were we in Nabatieh, they would demand to know, if we were not expecting an Israeli attack?

Theirs was a dingy existence. The eight rain-soaked soldiers, their wellington boots covered in mud and their rifle ammunition clips swaddled in adhesive tape to keep out the damp, would stand day after day at their windy checkpoint. Their only distraction was an occasional supply trip into Nabatieh, itself an uninspiring town with a single restaurant, a row of old garages and dirty car repair shops and a few poor farms.

When the weather was clear, we would sit by the roadside not far from the Syrians and watch the early morning Israeli reconnaissance flight soaring up in a long thick contrail from Galilee, turning gently high above us, the sun distantly glinting on the plane's tiny wings. We used to think that the ropes of vapour which the jets left across the skies of southern Lebanon were intended to represent the red line. There was no other way in which anyone could draw a coherent political projection upon Lebanon. The plane would trail away to the west, out over the Mediterranean, and the Syrians would go back to their little stoves and cups of hot tea.

The Syrians had always said that their presence in Nabatieh was justified by the need to prevent the movement of heavy arms after the civil war and to stop the fighting which was continuing between the Palestinians and the Phalangists in the border strip north of Israel. The Palestinians and the 'Lebanese Arab Army', the dissident Muslim wing of the old national army which had somehow maintained its wartime identity, would say nothing. We suspected that the Syrians' real concern was the failure of all the civil war militias to hand in their heavy weapons as they were required to do under the terms of their ceasefire agreements with the Beirut government. A series of deep tracks leading across the fields towards Beaufort Castle suggested that trucks had taken some of these weapons up to the old keep from whose battlements even the Syrians were kept at a distance. If some of the heavy artillery used by the Palestinians in the war was inside, the Syrians intended to make sure it stayed there.

For their part, the Israelis would angrily declare that the Syrian presence at Nabatieh constituted a serious military threat. This was news to the eight dejected soldiers on that road of drifting rain outside Nabatieh. Their lonely tank was not likely to force many breaches in Israel's security. But it was part of a routine that was clearly understood by all involved. The Israelis would inform the American ambassador in Tel Aviv of those areas of Lebanon in which they did not wish to see the Syrians. The ambassador would tell the State Department in Washington who would wire the US ambassador in Damascus who would visit the Syrian Foreign Ministry to explain Israel's warning. The Foreign Ministry would then tell the Defence Ministry and the message would be sent across to the army command in Lebanon.

One day in February 1977, the Israelis decided they did not want the Syrians in Nabatieh any more. So the messages sped off across the Mediterranean and the Atlantic and back again to Damascus and eventually down to the pleasant little forest east of the town where the sergeant and corporal and the six other non-coms had spent those rainy months watching the skies. We found them next morning quietly folding their blankets and lifting their camp beds into the back of three badly maintained army trucks. Tel Aviv had spoken.

The reasons were obvious. The Israelis had decided to deal a little more ruthlessly with those villages in southern Lebanon and with the Palestinian guerrillas who had set up their bases in and around them and who, from time to time, fired Katyusha rockets towards the Israeli settlements beyond the border. The Israelis did not want to take on the Syrians. The feeling was mutual so the Syrians left. The two nations could understand this kind of logic. For in order to keep the Palestinians in check, Israel was now adopting precisely the same formula that Syria had employed further north: they had found willing clients who would do the job for them. Just as Saiqa ensured Syria's control over Fatah and the other PLO factions in Beirut, the Israelis discovered willing proxies among the Christians of the far south of Lebanon.

We had first seen evidence of this in the last weeks of 1976. On a rainy morning in late November, I had driven down to the Israeli frontier with Ed Cody of the AP, a tireless reporter and a fluent Arabist who believed firmly and correctly that only by trekking across hundreds of miles of broken roads could one find out what was really going on in Lebanon. In the village of Bent Jbail, we found Palestinian guerrillas occupying the local government offices. We travelled on to the border itself, a frontier marked by two swathes of barbed wire with an earthen track in between that was soft enough to carry the footprints of any intruders who had crossed into Israel. An Israeli soldier in a jeep even drew up on the far side, recognised us as Westerners and asked cheerfully in an American accent: 'Do you guys wanna come over?'

But further on along this road, nearer to Metulla, the socialising came to an end. As we drove beside the border fence, we saw an Israeli truck on the road — on the Lebanese side of the frontier — with a number of bearded gunmen standing by the tailboard. An Israeli officer was standing with them and several Israeli soldiers on the truck were handing down boxes of ammunition and rifles to the gunmen. When the officer saw us, he gave orders to one of the bearded figures who approached our car and screamed abuse at me through the window. 'Get out of here. You have no business here. You will be arrested.' I put the car into reverse and the man stood watching us, pointing his rifle at the windscreen. He and the other bearded men were Phalangists, men who would now form the nucleus of yet another Lebanese militia. It would be called the 'Army of Free Lebanon' and, later, the 'South Lebanon Army', uniformed, trained, paid, armed and commanded by Israel.

But back in those early years there was something deceptive about southern Lebanon. It had to do with the physical beauty of the place, the constant smell of oranges and undergrowth after the rainstorms had moved down from the Golan, the dark fields of tobacco, the way in which we would turn a corner in a winding mud track and be ambushed by a field of crimson and white flowers. In the Arkoub — Fatahland — the valley floor was carpeted in hibiscus and poppies, the walls of the wadis rising high above us with great circles of contrasting colour described in the volcanic stone like giant Swiss rolls made entirely of solid rock. Further down the Arkoub we would find ourselves among poplar trees. Behind them frothed the Hasbani River, its waters frozen from the snows of Mount Hermon; through the trees there stood a Roman bridge, its stones undamaged, its path still marked by the wagon wheels of antiquity.

Most of the inhabitants of southern Lebanon — the majority of them Shias with Christians and Druze living among them — were generous people. A foreigner would always be treated with respect, invited into their homes for lunch or dinner or for endless cups of black spicy coffee so thick that it stuck to the back of your throat for hours afterwards. Husbands would introduce their wives (we would shake hands if the women were Christian, politely touch our chest with our right hand if they were Muslim), and families would bring us into inner rooms to meet numberless brothers and sisters, children, cousins, aunts and mothers. They would sit around us, smiling with big gold teeth, honouring a spirit of hospitality that was part of their lives. After those innumerable coffees, they would talk, gently and carefully but with great honesty, about their predicament. They would tell us whether the Palestinians had been to the village, and if the pro-Israeli militias had threatened them. And they would complain about the corruption of Lebanese politicians, about inflation and the weather.

In times of danger, these people would risk their lives for us, pulling us into their homes to avoid shellfire. Years later, in 1982, when the Israeli army was fighting its way up the floor of the lower Bekaa Valley, firing their artillery indiscriminately onto the villages and roads in front of them, I was driving furiously northwards to escape the path of their advance, past terrified Syrian troops whose vehicles were burning in the fields around them. At the village of Deir al-Ahmar just north of Kfar Meshki, I stopped to ask a couple if the road north had been under air attack. The ground was vibrating with explosions and oily smoke was climbing from the burning trucks to the south. The husband was studying the skies for aircraft but both he and his young wife seized me by the arm, literally propelling me into their home. 'Stay with us,' he said. 'You will be all right. Don't be afraid. We will protect you. Stay in our home.'

They were Greek Orthodox Christians. And in their small concrete house with the windows rattling to the explosions, they produced coffee and sweets and urged me to spend the night in their home. They talked about the war, about their own lives – they had been born in Zahle – about their relatives in Beirut and their fears for them. The man offered to travel with me as far as Chtaura if I was still frightened.

These were honourable, kind people – Muslim and Christian families alike – and it would dawn on some of us as the years went by that if they could endanger themselves to protect us, then we owed them something in return, that perhaps we might sometimes have to take risks with our own lives in order to report their tragedy. They little deserved the fate that awaited them in the coming years, nor the hardness of spirit that they would be forced to develop and subsequently employ against their oppressors, even against us.

The war in southern Lebanon had always been a lie. Take the example of Kfar Kila, a little Shia village exactly a mile from the Israeli frontier. In November 1976 the Phalangists in Beirut produced a press statement, couched in the florid tones that were always adopted on such occasions, to the effect that Christian militiamen in southern Lebanon had captured the village from Palestinians after fierce hand-to-hand fighting. The ramshackle publicity organisation of Kamal Jumblatt's 'Leftist Alliance' denied Kfar Kila's capture but admitted that 'bitter street fighting' had taken place.

A drive down to Kfar Kila, however, showed the village in remarkably good shape. When I arrived there, the small market was crowded with peasants. Village women were scrubbing their household sheets in the stream that bubbled down from the mountain above them and a very old man was kneeling on a worn and threadbare prayer mat beside a tiny whitewashed mosque whose loudspeakers were broadcasting a Koranic recitation on a scratched record. The reason for this pastoral normality became apparent when I asked to see the military commanders in the village. They were sitting on sofas in an attractive villa overlooking a valley to the south, sipping coffee – the same thick, black coffee – out of delicate, hand-painted cups. All were leftists.

For the village never fell to the Phalangists and not one right-wing fighter had ever entered its narrow streets. The artillery 'bombardment' that the Christians launched from two elderly pieces of field artillery did not injure one villager or damage one house. Kfar Kila was as good a place as any to realise the depth of political dishonesty and of family loyalties which so belied the simple, inaccurate statements put out by the parties in Beirut. The village was jointly defended by communists and pro-Iraqi Baathists and other youths, all born within a few square miles. One of the commanders was the apolitical son of the village's oldest family – his parents' palatial and verandaed house could be seen across the valley – and the township's total armour amounted to just under 200 hand-guns. There had not been a Palestinian guerrilla in the place for six months.

Nor was the war around Kfar Kila a simple sectarian matter. The Phalangists occupied Kleia, the nearest Christian community four miles to the north, but, providing they were not combatants, the men and women of the two villages were free to visit each other. The Muslim women of Kfar Kila frequently travelled to Kleia because the Christian village had better shops. The son of the oldest Kfar Kila family, a student in his twenties with a small beard and wearing a gun in a dark leather holster, lacked both the swagger and preoccupations of his opposite numbers in Beirut. One of his cousins was fighting for the Baathists, who he said were receiving 9,000 dollars a month from the Iraqi government, while another cousin was under arms with the right-wing remnants of the old national Lebanese army, stationed in a barracks in Kleia. Kleia was an army village by tradition. The Christian commander of the Lebanese army, General Hanna Saeed, was born there. Although the Phalangist militia in Kleia did not agree with them, the Lebanese soldiers stationed there had said they were prepared to accept a ceasefire with the leftists on condition that the Palestinians did not return.

Arafat's Cairo agreement was unlikely to make much headway in Kfar Kila. Many of the villagers, like their counterparts in the Christian community in Kleia, paid regular visits to the Israeli medical clinic over the frontier and the Muslims had a well-developed hostility towards the Palestinian revolution, as one of the communist militiamen made clear. 'When the fedayeen were here, they did what they wanted and tried to rule us,' he said. 'If they saw something they liked, they stole it. They drew up lists of people they thought did not support the Palestinian cause. If they disliked someone in the village, they arrested him and interrogated him. If a man or woman in Kfar Kila wanted to have nothing to do with politics, the Palestinians accused them of being Israeli agents.'

There were ceasefires throughout 1977, on one occasion arranged after a meeting between Arafat and Sarkis. But the Palestinians saw no reason to take account of the few Lebanese who had chosen to remain in the villages which they turned into front line positions. This was only too obvious at Rachaya Foukhar, a beautiful little Christian hamlet in the foothills of Mount Hermon, a place of small stone houses, a church, a series of stables and several fields full of ancient clay jars, broken apart and lying abandoned in the grass. When I arrived there on 21 September 1977, Israeli shells had been falling around the village all morning. The civilians were in no position to appreciate the more subtle political advantages that the Palestinians might gain from their battles. They were old for the most part, silver-haired women and men with thin-framed spectacles, sleeping each night in their disused church with its brass candelabra and broken candlesticks with sandbags against the chancel window for protection. The young men had long ago left to join the militias in Beirut.

While we were walking around the village, several shells exploded in a cow byre and another hit a small cottage. Many of the people here had relatives killed in the Israeli shelling over the preceding weeks. One old woman stood in the central square and waylaid us to announce in a shrieking voice that she had lost her entire family in the space of a year. In the church, we found the villagers near the altar. They pushed someone towards us, a bespectacled man of education who spoke old-fashioned French and told us he had been asked to speak for the others. They wanted the Palestinians to leave, he said. There were Palestinians in a street beside the church.

'I went to see their officer,' the old man said. 'I asked him please to go, that if he stayed, the Israelis would kill us. He was not interested and told me to go away.' I looked for the guerrillas. They were there, beside the church, just as the old man had said, sitting in a laneway in the shade on the northern side of the building, protected from the shrapnel. They were from Habash's PFLP, but they were not the fighters of Palestinian legend, *kuffiahs* round their heads, rifles in their hands. They were scruffy teenagers, gnawing pieces of stale bread, watching the villagers in a lazy, disinterested sort of way. Their weapons lay among the bushes beside the church. Why did they not leave? I asked their commander. 'Who are you?' He must have been in his early twenties, with hair down to his shoulders. He at least had a chequered black and white *kuffiah* around his neck. *Sahafi*. 'We have nothing to say.' What about the old man? The officer was tired and dirty, in no mood to suffer a journalist. 'Get out of here,' he said.

The war could be paradoxical. In Hasbaya, where in 1860 the Christians took shelter from the Druze during that much earlier civil war, most of the inhabitants were Greek Orthodox Christians who shared their town with a few Maronites and Druze. For 20 months, Palestinian guerrillas had occupied an office in Hasbaya; as a result, the town had come under regular shellfire from Marjayoun, which had become the headquarters for Israel's Lebanese Christian militia. As in Hasbaya, most of the inhabitants of Marjayoun were Greek Orthodox, who lived there with Maronites. So Lebanese Christians had been shelling Lebanese Christians on behalf of the Israelis.

Travelling across these fragile hills and valleys in the months that followed the end of the 1975–6 civil war took on a repetitive quality. We would drive down the long, crowded, pitted old coast road from Beirut and turn inland from Tyre, always finding ourselves on ridge-lines above dry wadis, taking our bearings from the streaks of snow on Hermon or the magenta blue glow of the Mediterranean between the hills, watching fascinated as the dark walls of Beaufort loomed above us when we least expected them.

Just before 1 pm, the first shells of the day. We are in Nabatieh, in July of 1977, months after the departure of the eight Syrian soldiers. The Palestinians are here now. The shells seem to be outside the town, three slightly muffled explosions which a stranger might mistake for a distant thunderstorm had the few shopkeepers still working not hurriedly rattled down their metal shutters in the main street. In the Andalos Café, a corner store with three dining tables and a fading colour photo-graph of Brigitte Bardot on the wall, the young proprietor serves our beer quickly. He stands at the door, squinting towards the sun like a man who thinks that he might actually catch sight of an incoming shell. The roast chicken turns on the spit behind him, growing darker, crisper and eventually black and charred as the proprietor's attention is focused on the hot sky. The town has been shelled by the Lebanese Christians in Marjayoun every day and night for weeks.

Two children wearing cheap plastic sandals run into the café holding pieces of hot metal, tossing them from hand to hand. They grin and hold them up for inspection. There is Hebrew writing on several of the hunks of steel. '*Rhamse liraat*,' says the smaller of the two boys with determination. Five Lebanese pounds, about two dollars. No. There is another rumble of shells. '*Arba*.' Four pounds. When he reaches two, we purchase his shrapnel and throw it into a trash can in the corner of the café. Watched by the proprietor and by Miss Bardot, the elder boy leaps forward, pulls the metal from the garbage and runs away. Palestinians drive down the street in the dust. We can hear a mortar somewhere to the south, firing back at the Christians and the Israelis.

The bombardment lasts half an hour. Afterwards, we watch the smoke rising from the fields outside the town. There used to be 10,000 people here. Now there are perhaps three or four hundred. 'The Israelis shell us, not Lebanese,' says the Andalos proprietor. For him, the Hebrew markings on the pieces of shell are conclusive. He is not interested in the suggestion that the Phalangists are using Israeli ammunition. If that is true, then the shells still come from Israel, he says.

How can one dispute this, especially when we drive through the wadi south of Nabatieh to the hot, dusty hilltop village of Derdghaya where the Palestinian guerrillas – this time leftists from the Democratic Front for the Liberation of Palestine – have their forward headquarters. Typically, they have taken over a Greek Orthodox church. In the converted nave are piled several tons of ammunition, shells and mortars captured from the Christian militiamen when the village of Taibe fell to the PLO three months earlier. Three tons of bullets and shells – still packed in Israeli ammunition crates marked in Hebrew – stand against one wall, and the local Palestinian guard, a man who disconcertingly chain-smokes as he handles a 155mm shell, keeps a collection of Israeli rifles behind a door in the vestry. The Palestinians also have several dozen crates of ammunition which they acquired, they say, from 'other sources'. Bullets from these crates are marked with Chinese characters.

It was, we used to think then, a silly little war. In June 1977, only 20 people were killed from this shelling in all southern Lebanon. In Taibe, which was less than half a mile from the nearest Christian positions, a visitor might safely enjoy a picnic and a bottle of wine beside the road were it not for the giant ants and the occasional six-inch lizards that scuttle through the grass verges.

Lieutenant Fihme, the local Palestinian commander, says he has lost only 21 men dead and injured in three months of fighting here. His enemy is so close that we can occasionally see the Christians on the next ridge-line, walking between the rocks. Yet he seems to find the war a satisfying, necessary affair and always interrupts his description of the shelling with a few phrases to stress the importance of the 'revolutionary' struggle in southern Lebanon.

★   ★   ★

Indeed, back in those hot, lazy months, one could not escape the impression that the war – if that is what it could be called – only continued because it was to the common benefit of all the parties involved. The Palestinians needed some field of action to express their military strength now that the fighting in Beirut was at an end. The Israelis must have realised that a crisis in southern Lebanon provided a permanent excuse for future military intervention. The Lebanese, too, needed the war; it reinforced their appeals for international aid, particularly for military assistance from the United States. For the Syrians, the shooting provided proof of all they had said about Israeli expansionism. Were there not Israeli troops in southern Lebanon? Indeed there were; and unlike the Syrians, they did not have a mandate from anyone but themselves.

Taibe had been captured by the Palestinians on 5 April and, save for an old man, his wife and two little girls, it was a ghost town. The houses were pockmarked with bullets, the gardens overgrown, the streets cracked, the mosque deserted and given over to stray cats. In the early evening, long before sundown, gunfire began to echo and re-echo around the mountains outside Taibe. Lieutenant Fihme admits rather reluctantly that he is not sure who is shooting at whom. It would be difficult to find a more palpable symbol of so disreputable a war.

It was nonetheless real. Most of the villagers had left Ibl al-Saqi when it became part of the Palestinian–Christian front line. It too had a Greek Orthodox church with a shell-hole through the very centre of the tower. It must have been a cosy little village. The houses all had red roofs and some still boasted those magnificent Ottoman balconies. From the cow pens behind the church, you could see all the way into the vale of Galilee. In September 1977 the bullets spat down the streets, cracked into the wall of the church or simply hissed on into the air beyond. The Palestinians were friendly. Tea first, and we would go see the Israeli tanks afterwards. It was ten in the morning, less than an hour since Sarkis' government had accused Israel of moving armour across the border into Lebanon. In a garage, we had taken tea with the Fatah men. They lay around on their torn sleeping bags watching us, too tired to do more than offer more scalding tea from the stove.

No wonder we would always associate the PLO with tea. Cup after cup of tea, the glass almost too hot to touch. Did we want a cigarette? Marlboro? Tea and Marlboros became the story of the Palestinian revolution. The tea was always sweet, the sugar poured into the pot before the glasses were filled. The cigarettes were always offered with a slight flourish, the packet banged against the palm of the hand to ensure that the tobacco was well packed. It was as if the guerrillas did nothing but fire machine-guns at ridge-lines, drink tea, chain-smoke and sleep. Which was more or less the case. At Ibl al-Saqi, we had caught them between sleep and the tea and Marlboros. Later they would fire their machine-guns.

'Come with us.' We crept round the back of the church and ran along an exposed roadway, a disturbing place of chipped tarmac and splinters of wood, the broken lines of a telegraph pole dancing on the road surface beside us. A pit of dried mud with sandbags heaped on top. 'Lie flat on the top and you will see the Israeli tanks.' They were there, silhouetted against the horizon. Holding binoculars, it was possible to steady one's arm on the sandbag embrasure and observe the machine-guns on the turrets of the tanks. Heavy artillery rumbled along the valleys beside us. Through the glasses, I saw a man standing on the rear of a tank, gazing northwards with his arms on his hips.

The Fatah officer here called himself Abu Meyad. He was a thin man with a poorly groomed moustache and no sense of security. 'Look over that wall,' he said casually as we returned towards the church. With the glasses, we could see a man sitting on top of a small concrete structure with a belt-fed machine-gun in front of him. He was wearing a beret and was outlined against the sun in a harmless sort of way. 'Israeli,' Abu Meyad muttered with contempt. It was impossible to see if the man was Israeli or a Lebanese Christian. Perhaps we had been watching him for ten seconds when the wrecked street suddenly filled with gunfire. The soldier above the little concrete bunker had become very dangerous.

Abu Meyad threw himself onto the road. I jumped towards the bushes and fell on top of a very large thistle. For almost a minute, the bullets swept back and forth above our heads, whizzing and slapping into the walls of the buildings behind us, biting into the stonework and showering us with fragments of plaster and concrete. The telegraph pole began to splinter beside me, pieces of wood spinning upwards, the bullets crackling into the metal cones on the top of the pole. The wires on the road began to jig up and down.

Then it stopped. Abu Meyad crawled across towards me and tut-tutted at the thistles sticking out of my shirt and the little red blobs at the base of them. 'You have been wounded,' he smirked. 'We will give you some tea.' Back in the garage. Four more cups of tea. Shells, a lot of them, coming over the roof of the church with a great rushing noise. One blew up inside an empty bungalow and demolished the entire building before our eyes with an explosion that temporarily deafened us. Every 50 seconds, a group of Palestinians − some of them boys of only 13 or 14 − would return the fire with a 75 mm recoilless rifle concealed in a sandpit.

Almost an hour before, we had sat on a quiet hillside behind Ibl al-Saqi while three Palestinians in a Land-Rover erected a 14-foot aerial for their radio in an attempt to listen to the Israeli army's net. We persuaded them to move to the medium wave. Then we had listened, a world away, to the BBC broadcasting from London. A woman newsreader with a careful, very English voice, had informed us that the Israeli prime minister, Mr Begin, was ready to discuss a ceasefire with the Palestinians. One of the Palestinians grimaced when we translated the words. 'So they admit they are in Lebanon,' he said.

Two days later. Inside Beaufort Castle. The ceasefire did not last. No one had intended that it should; which was why Lieutenant Ayman had positioned a green-painted anti-aircraft gun inside a stone archway at the northern end of the keep. Its barrel had been deflected to the horizontal in order to shoot across the gorge of the Litani at the narrow road which ran from the Israeli border into the Christian town of Marjayoun. Every hour or so, a Palestinian boy no more than 13 years old snapped open the breech to check the ammunition then fired off a few rounds. The bullets went hissing across the sky from the 1,000-foot escarpment.

Just to the boy's right, at the end of a corridor, the Palestinians also had a mortar. It too was dutifully employed every hour when it dispatched a rocket with a hollow sound that delighted Lieutenant Ayman. His *kuffiah* was delicately embroidered, almost effeminate, and he ran up to us with childlike excitement every time he gave the order to fire. 'Come on, come, see quickly,' he would say, smiling broadly, and sure enough far beneath us a tree near the river would twitch with the distant explosion. But Ayman admitted that he did not know exactly who was firing the shells that occasionally swept over the castle. Yes, he could show us journalists a whole covey of Israeli tanks on Lebanese territory but by the time he had settled himself on a boulder above the chasm, all he could do was stare crestfallen across the miles of valleys and hills – without a tank in sight – and claim that the Israelis only showed their armour at night.

More lies. All that week, the local authorities in Sidon were claiming that 45,000 refugees had flooded into the town from the battle areas. Thousands of people had abandoned their homes near the Israeli border months before, but in the previous seven days we had seen only three cars driving north; two were hauling cattle trailers. The Israelis reported that the Christian militias had captured three villages, including Ibl al-Saqi. Untrue: it was the arrival of those American-made Israeli tanks that had made southern Lebanon so dangerous. They were real. For once, something was true. Even Egypt felt able to condemn Israeli 'aggression' in southern Lebanon.

The Christian radio station in Beirut was later to announce that Phalangists had overrun several villages, tearing down Palestinian flags, a strange claim since the Palestinians never put up flags on houses in southern Lebanon. The Christians, the radio continued, had captured the village of Khiam just outside Ibl al-Saqi 'after a mop-up operation which left eighteen aliens dead'. Aliens were Palestinians. On 26

September, the Israelis withdrew their tanks. The Christian buffer zone had been slightly broadened by the fighting. Now it stretched almost all the way along the Israeli frontier from the sea to the snows of Hermon.

Always, it was like this. Threats and shooting followed by withdrawal. Each crisis was the greatest crisis since the last greatest crisis, each more desperate in the telling, more devastating in effect. On the day we had sat with Lieutenant Ayman and his colleagues as they eased their boredom by firing their mortar at the end of the Beaufort corridor, Reuters news agency in Beirut had described how shells fell so thickly upon the castle that clouds of black smoke had enveloped the keep. 'Nothing was known of the fate of its defenders,' the agency said. How Ayman and his teenage gunmen would have enjoyed that. They would no doubt have gone along with the story. If they were told about it, they probably did.

Misinterpretation might be a kind way of describing the failure to understand what was really happening then. Somehow, down there in southern Lebanon, we became cut off from the great fissures which were opening across the Middle East. One broiling day in 1977, Ed Cody and I had driven into a scruffy Shia Muslim village north of Bent Jbail to find the usual tea-drinking Palestinians sitting in a field beside the main road, their officer lecturing them about the need to move their mortar positions every 24 hours.

But our attention was caught by a gunman who seemed different from the others. He rested his rifle on his lap while he was sitting on the ground as if he feared that he might suddenly have to use it. He wore a coal-black scarf – not a *kuffiah* – around his neck. And he appeared to speak no Arabic. His English, however, was almost perfect. Could we possibly translate what his officer was saying to him? Cody asked why he spoke no Arabic. 'Because I am not an Arab. I am from Iran.' He grinned brightly at us. 'I am from the opposition in Iran. I have come to learn here how to fight. We understand a common cause with our Palestinian brothers. With their help, we can learn to destroy the Shah.' Cody and I smiled grimly at each other, unimpressed by this precocious young man with his determination to overthrow the most powerful potentate in the Middle East. As we drove away, Cody started laughing. 'What an asshole!' he roared. And I remember agreeing with him. And, of course, we were wrong.

Even the placidity of Tyre – or, as it was momentarily called by its tinpot rulers that autumn, the 'People's Republic of Tyre' – had its deceptions. The lighthouse keeper had been without work for more than a year. True, the Lebanese government was still paying his salary. During the summer, he had been stitching dresses for his one-room shop round the corner where a faded sign proclaimed in white letters: 'Haute Couture de Paris'. But there were no supplies of acetylene gas coming down from Beirut for his lighthouse, and besides, there were few ships. He was an approachable man who happily showed us the squat little red-painted lighthouse outside his front door. When we had climbed to the top, he made a point of telling us that it was possible to see the columns of the ancient Roman city just beneath the sea. He neglected to mention the broken ships that lay all around Tyre harbour.

One of them was resting on the bottom, only its mastheads showing above the waterline. A large freighter was lying on the rocks at 45 degrees with the autumn seas sweeping across her funnel and sloping decks. Strangely, the lighthouse keeper could not quite recall how the ships came to sink. It was, he said, 'difficult to know the facts about recent events'. It paid to have a poor memory during the brief history of the People's Republic of Tyre.

Lebanon's three other major cities — Beirut, Sidon and Tripoli — had been under Syrian military occupation for almost a year but Israel's 'red line' had effectively locked Tyre into its civil war past. Thus the grubby old Phoenician port with its broken economy, its sunken ships and its refugee-swollen population of 55,000 people still remained under the control of the same Lebanese leftist and Palestinian militias that once ruled much of Lebanon. A visit to Tyre was like travelling in a time machine back to the worst days of civil war Beirut.

Not that there was any lack of visible authority in Tyre. At road junctions in the town stood brown-uniformed young men with high-powered rifles, a gendarmerie known, in the semi-official parlance of the local left-wing governors, as 'the Popular Security'. Several of them directed us to the ruins of the classical city where, beside the Roman forum, two armed men in green fatigue trousers guarded the entrance to a beautiful villa. It had once been the home of a curator of antiquities but its garden of crimson flowers and purple-blossomed trees was now enjoyed by the political committee of the People's Republic of Tyre.

The committee — which was discreetly debating whether to drop the 'People's Republic' from the title — was a confusing amalgam of Iraqi-supported Baathists, communists and Nasserites. Its first secretary, Mohamed Faran, was a communist, although he preferred to greet us in the offices of Jumblatt's Progressive Socialist Party 300 yards away, two rooms whose walls were decorated with portraits of the late Kamal Jumblatt. He had been murdered eight months earlier, but already his stature had grown in death. Faran was a mathematics teacher and he listed the good works of his 16 committee members with academic precision: 18,000 dollars a month donated to local hospitals, provision of social services, water and health facilities, almost 1,800 dollars spent on the police each month and ambitious plans for two new public gardens. In the next few weeks, he said, he expected the Lebanese national army to move into southern Lebanon but the committee would insist on remaining in power: just how this would be accomplished – and with whose money – Faran would not disclose, although, when pressed twice on the subject, he said without much embarrassment that 'most of our money comes from Iraq.'

Relations with the local Palestinian leaders were friendly, he insisted, in spite of rumours to the contrary. 'Everyone has their problems, of course,' he said with a smile. 'But our police and their police always sort things out.' One of Faran's recent problems concerned a member of his own committee, a certain Hussein Hamiye, who had fallen into an argument with a Palestinian officer a few weeks before. Hamiye's photograph now graced the walls of Tyre framed in black because at the end of the argument, the Palestinian – currently recovering from wounds in a Sidon hospital – shot him dead. Perhaps naturally, Faran did not mention the affair.

Nor was he particularly forthcoming about those sunken ships, although the Palestinian commander in Tyre, an intelligent and helpful young officer called Kayed, agreed that there had been a few unfortunate incidents in the town. There had been a savage gun battle, for instance, between members of Fatah and Saiqa. And there had been other, more important battles. A more humble leftist activist, though one well known to Faran, remembered how the two leaders of the Popular Front for the Liberation of Palestine – General Command had quarrelled over the ownership of guns and ammunition brought to Tyre from Libya on the Famagusta-registered freighter *Spyros*. As a result, Ahmed Jibril, the more Syrian-orientated of the two leaders, sent frogmen to blow the hull off the *Spyros* as she stood in Tyre roads.

It was the *Spyros* – her name and port of registry still clearly visible above the waves – that now lay broken on the rocks off the harbour with her decks awash. A Tyre harbour worker recalled how the Libyans later spent 7,000 dollars a day paying the locals to unload the wrecked vessel which had reportedly been insured for five million dollars.

Next to the Tyre wharf lay the hulk of a smaller freighter named the *Riri* which Faran's colleague said was mined by the Israelis because they believed she carried guns. The ship, whose masts could just be seen from the lighthouse, had been owned by the father of a friend of Faran; she was allegedly carrying smuggled whisky when she went down. While a vessel which regularly carried guns to Tyre had left the port only two days earlier after apparently arriving with an innocent cargo of cement. Coincidentally, the ship was now under charter to Faran's brother.

A visit to one of Tyre's leading citizens, however – a middle-class, educated man who pleaded with us not to mention his name – suggested that the people of Tyre were not reaping many benefits from their strange society. 'The Palestinians and the leftists both extort money from any businessman here or anyone who is wealthy,' he said. 'At the south end of the town, the people with good houses pay thousands of Lebanese pounds a week in protection money. We want the Lebanese army here to end all this. We cannot say more. If we talk, we are dead.'

It was the same story of publicly expressed good intentions and private corruption all across Lebanon. Most people told us privately that they wanted the Lebanese army to enter their towns. Rarely did it do so and never in Tyre. Security was in any case collapsing even in Beirut. Gun battles broke out between Syrian troops and Palestinian guerrillas in the camps. Fighting between rival militia groups was broken up by the Syrian army with ever-increasing difficulty; it was a task made all the harder by the growing propensity of the Syrians to favour those political groups that supported their presence in the city. Those who did not agree with Syria's role sometimes paid the price.

Kamal Jumblatt was just one of these, although his assassination in March 1977 was a harbinger of things to come. While he was revered by some European leftists as a socialist philosopher, Jumblatt had proved to be one of the more intransigent of the civil war participants, repeatedly demanding a military victory against the Phalangists and haughtily condemning Syria's attempts to bring the conflict to an end. He called frequently for a blood revenge against the Maronites, recalling the 1860 civil war between the Christians and the Druze. On one particularly terrible day of fighting in Beirut, in which scores of civilians had been killed by indiscriminate shellfire from both sides, Jumblatt angrily announced that from then on there would be '*real* war'. Most people felt they already knew what real war was like. Possessed of a facile habit of accusing all his opponents of fascism, Jumblatt refused to travel to Damascus to see President Assad once the war was over and was probably doomed from that moment.

Driving home to Moukhtara with his bodyguards up the high mountain road near Baaqlin, his car was overtaken by a limousine containing at least two gunmen. Jumblatt was sitting in the back of his vehicle, reading *An Nahar*. When the first shots hit his head, most of his brains fell onto the newspaper. The subsequent bloodletting was just as brutal. Christians in villages around that area of the Chouf were murdered in their homes by the Druze, usually by having their throats cut. It mattered not that the act was most probably carried out by Syrian agents. The Syrians had come to Lebanon to rescue the Christians and might have used Christians to perpetrate the crime. Syria denied any involvement in Jumblatt's killing but the point had been made. Cooperation with Syria was something to be refused only after a great deal of thought.

If this development further strengthened Syrian control, it by no means cut into the traditional power of the *zaim*. Camille Chamoun continued for the moment to blame Lebanon's problems upon the Palestinians rather than the Syrians, while Pierre Gemayel's ruthless young son Bashir went out of his way to praise President Assad. Invited to Damascus himself, he willingly went to pay court to Assad, returning with the news that the Syrian president had 'told us some things and views he had about other Arab leaders.' That, he said, 'convinced me he can be trusted.'

Chamoun's approach was more open. He was still a distinguished-looking man with white hair and a gravelly voice, although the huntsman of Abercrombie's 1958 acquaintance had given way to a stooped, elderly figure who would enter the room with his head bowed. A certain *gravitas* had to attend the man who was still Lebanese deputy prime minister, foreign minister and interior minister. At a press conference in early 1977, he arrived without his now familiar, large, heavy-framed spectacles and appeared almost lost, sitting down in an oval chair with baroque coverings. He spoke in a low voice and apparently did not notice when one of his bodyguards, a thin man with a bushy black moustache, walked quietly to the side of a Lebanese cameraman and picked his pocket. He was looking for the man's identity card – which would state his religion – but found that he had instead stolen his driving licence. His victim realised what was happening. 'If you want to know my religion,' the cameraman said, 'why don't you ask? I'm a Muslim.'

Incidents like this one told one more about Chamounism than anything its namesake actually said. On this occasion, Chamoun agreed that confessionalism had played a role in the civil war but insisted that there never had been sectarian discrimination in Lebanon. 'There has never been social inequality,' he said. 'Some areas of Lebanon were not favoured ... but not because they were Muslim. It was because the people in those areas did not want to work. There are people here who are lazy, who don't work.' The Christians had paid 70 per cent of the nation's income tax before the war, yet 50 per cent of benefits payments were made to Muslims. Yes, he said, the Christians had a majority of 52 per cent; if we wished, we could check the figures in last year's news-papers. Later, he would admit that the papers had got their statistics from him. The Palestinians had started the war. They should be made to leave. France and the United States might have to come to the aid of the Christians because 'communist nations' were aiding the Palestinians. The old man had still not learned the lesson of his 1958 blunder. At least his son Dory realised the West could not be counted on for help. 'A senile old man' is how Dory described the Western world when I interviewed him in August of that year.

But then Camille Chamoun reverted to type. He put on those dark glasses and walked across the room to a youth who was standing at the back. The young man was wearing a sports jacket and had prematurely receding hair. Chamoun put a hand on his shoulder and turned proudly towards us. 'Look at this young man,' he said. 'He is one of our brave young "Tigers". It was boys like this – university students, trainee doctors – who fought for us, and thousands of them died.' Thus spoke the deputy prime minister of Lebanon. Within two years, Bashir Gemayel's Phalangists had destroyed Chamoun's militia power base and the 'Tigers' – as Camille Chamoun's other son Dany was to describe them to me afterwards – became 'just little pussy cats'.

Despite all their assurances to the contrary, the Christian *zaim* were still considering partition as the ultimate solution to their declining power. The most obvious symbol of this political drift was the Pierre Gemayel International Airport. Airline guides did not list this particular facility nor define its location high in the mountains of northern Lebanon. Blasted and cut through the rock and forests below the snowline ten miles south of Tripoli, it was Bashir Gemayel's inspiration; nor did it possess the kind of muddy runway and tin shack terminal that its political purposes might have suggested. The Phalangists did share one characteristic with Hitler's Nazi Party which even the Gemayels could scarcely deny: a fascination for things on a grand scale, preferably involving thousands of tons of pre-stressed concrete.

Pierre Gemayel International Airport was thus built to international standards, its huge cement and tarmac runway cleaving the forest for well over a mile, its modern though unfurnished terminal buildings constructed with a spacious control tower and even room for a duty-free shop. Into this Bond-like enterprise, the Christians poured an initial four million dollars. It had to be capable of taking Boeing airliners and it was to be completed within eight months of the end of the civil war. When I travelled up to the village of Hamet to investigate this extravagant project, 17 multicoloured steamrollers and caterpillar construction vehicles were manoeuvring over the surface of the runway.

Every few days, a Syrian patrol would pass by Hamet to observe the progress of the new airport – purely a social call, of course, on their Christian allies. The Maronite construction site manager claimed the whole thing was merely an 'insurance policy' but the Syrians realised full well what this meant. Assad regarded any move towards the partition of Lebanon as a division that would set dangerous precedents in the Arab world, not least in Syria itself.

Syria's greatest security had hitherto been the inability of the Christian barons to decide on the kind of Lebanon they now wanted to live in. Both the elder Gemayel and Camille Chamoun made the usual fashionable noises about the need for unity through recognition of cultural and religious differences, but their two parties could not agree on their ideas. Chamoun wanted a new constitution for Lebanon which would give Christians and Muslims almost complete independence in separate areas with a largely powerless central government to maintain the façade of Lebanese unity. The Chamounists even produced a coloured map of their new Christian statelet with a frontier that snaked uneasily out of east Beirut, wandered in a gerrymandering way through Mount Lebanon and ran down to the sea south of Tripoli. Pierre Gemayel preferred to talk about confederation and 'regionalisation' with a more powerful executive — though one which would still happily represent the Maronites' long-lost numerical superiority.

In principle, the Muslims refused to countenance any notion of dividing the country, basing their rejection on purely nationalist grounds. But there was always a suspicion that in the event of partition, the Christians might somehow take with them the heart of the nation's economy. Equally, the Muslims distrusted the Maronites' contention that partition would only be a last resort for the Christians of Lebanon. If that were so, they asked, then why had the Chamounists gone to the length of writing a new constitution? Why had they been installing new communications and telex lines into the wartime Christian capital of Jounieh? Why were the Phalangists operating their own radio station? And why were the Christians building their airport at Hamet?

In the event, the Syrians decided to foreclose on the whole affair. A few days after the Christians had obligingly put the finishing touches to the runway, several Syrian tanks appeared out of the forest and trundled onto the apron. And there they stayed, until ex-President Franjieh broke with his Maronite partners and was awarded control of his own area of the northern mountains — including Pierre Gemayel International Airport — by the Syrians.

Only Bashir Gemayel could have been blind enough not to have foreseen the outcome. Had he not observed the twin 18-inch posters in the streets of Beirut, on *every street*, sometimes on every house wall? One showed the tired, slightly flabby face of President Sarkis; the other depicted the sterner, less compromising features of President Assad. The question which the Lebanese immediately asked when they saw these portraits was: which is the president of Lebanon? Bashir thought that in the long term both might prove to be irrelevant.

Bashir Gemayel's failure was to some extent excusable. Lebanese leaders were so obsessed with their own predicament after the 1975—6 war that they tended to ignore — or merely to minimise — the developments that occurred elsewhere in the Arab world. Assad, for example, was trying to discover what role President Carter might envisage for Syria in an international Middle East peace conference. He was not going to have the Lebanese interfering with matters of such great moment. The Arab world itself was in a state of almost constant confusion at this time. One morning, the Arabs would awake to hear that the

Americans had agreed with the Soviet Union on a joint approach to an early reconvening of the Geneva peace conference and had talked of the 'legitimate rights' of the Palestinians. Next morning, Arab hopes would be dashed when they heard that Moshe Dayan, the Israeli foreign minister, had rejected any such idea. A Beirut newspaper cartoonist drew a picture of Carter zigzagging on skates towards Geneva while a mystified Arab looked on.

Syria's involvement in Lebanon, however, could not be seen in exclusively political terms. Up in the Bekaa Valley that September of 1977, the first postwar crop of Lebanese hashish was ripening in the fields around Baalbek. Its production, like so much else in Lebanon, was officially illegal. But the 30 wealthy Lebanese families who controlled the crops were both politically and militarily powerful. In case the Lebanese army was rash enough to contemplate spraying the fields with poison from the air, several of the farmers defended their hashish plantations with anti-aircraft guns. One farmer I went down to interview kept a battle-tank beside his house in case of more serious forays. And there were other tanks guarding the fields, Syrian T-54s manned by troops who belonged to the Syrian Special Forces.

The hashish fields spread for miles over the Bekaa, a sea of gentle, dark green bushes that ran sometimes to the very horizon. Cartloads of the stuff would groan down towards Zahle or up towards the presses below Boudai where dealers would willingly divulge details of their most recent profitable trip to Rotterdam. The families of some of the *zaim* were involved in the hashish trade; members of the Lebanese parliament were known to have acquired their wealth from the plant. By 1978, the Lebanese would be exporting an estimated 10,000 tons of hashish. After I made an innocent visit to the Bekaa to report on the harvest, two members of a leading Baalbek hashish family turned up in Beirut to see if I was interested in purchasing their product. My denial of any interest in trading in drugs was to no avail. If I had visited the hashish fields, I was clearly a buyer.

'How much are you interested in taking?'

'I'm not. I am a journalist. I was only interested in writing for my newspaper.'

'Yes, yes. But how much do you want to buy?'

'Really, I'm only a reporter. I do not — I really do not — want to buy your hashish.'

'The price is a deal. A hundred and forty dollars a kilo. Where do you want us to send it?'

'Please . . .'

'We can send it through East Berlin.'

'Look, I DO NOT WANT TO BUY YOUR HASHISH.'

'OK, then opium.'

'Please stop ...'

'We'll put as much as you need out through Damascus International Airport – to the country of your choice.'

And that, of course, was the clue. Syria had come to Lebanon and Syria was now being corrupted by Lebanon, as surely as another great army would soon be corrupted. Lebanon's revenge was to welcome all her invaders and then kiss them to death. The longer they stayed, the longer they needed to stay; and each day, every hour, their presence would be imperceptibly debased and perverted and poisoned.

Those great hot, balmy fields across the Bekaa concealed from all who went there the dangerous, moist centre of this garden of earthly delights. It was like being bitten by a beautiful dragonfly whose wings were of such splendour that the victim did not even feel the nip in the flesh. Later, the skin would itch and the stranger would scratch at the irritation, trying to remember where he had acquired so strange a mark. Much later, the flesh would swell up and give pain and, very often, it would prove fatal.

'Defence Minister Ezer Weizman told a press conference early today that after last Sunday's guerrilla attack near Tel Aviv in which more than 30 Israelis were killed it had been decided to "clean up once and for all terrorist concentrations in southern Lebanon".' Page two of the flimsy green sheet from the Agence France Presse report was still stuffed into my pocket as we drove south from Beirut. We could smell the blossom on the trees, the scent of oranges off the dawn orchards. There were shapes in the semi-darkness, hundreds of them on foot, trudging northwards in the half-light to the east. Above the trees, we could see the smoke from great fires. There was a constant sound, a kind of 'woomph-woomph' noise that shook our car even as we moved on the road. The Israeli air strikes had already begun.

How often we went to war with these pieces of paper pushed into our notebooks or lying on the back shelf of the car, agency tape torn from the machine in the Beirut office the moment we had scrounged enough petrol to take us to Tyre. On Sunday, 11 March 1978, Fatah gunmen from Lebanon had evaded Israeli patrols on the coast near Haifa, killed several tourists on a beach and then hijacked a busload of civilians whom they drove towards Tel Aviv. When the Israeli army stopped the vehicle not far from the city, many of the passengers and all nine Palestinians were killed. In all, 37 Israelis died. The PLO would say later that some of the Israelis were shot down by their own soldiers as they stormed the bus. This may have been the case but it hardly provided an excuse for an attack which was so evidently intended to kill civilians and which would, even more inevitably, bring massive reprisals against the Lebanese.

'I hope,' Weizman said in that agency tape, 'that Syria will understand that it is an operation limited to southern Lebanon, that the Lebanese government will understand that it is a preventative operation, and that the rest of the civilised world will realise that it is aimed essentially at preventing fresh attacks against Israel's civilian population like the ones we have suffered.' The Israelis were later to claim that 108 Israelis had been killed in PLO attacks since 1973. Their invasion was now about to kill an estimated 2,000 people, almost all of them civilians. Some of those about to die were walking up the highway now, just outside our car.

By six, when the sun was streaming down through the pine trees on the road north of the Litani, we had stopped to watch the refugees. I sat beside the trees, recording the path of these frightened people onto a cassette, talking blandly into the microphone, the mike-wire wound round my wrist to stop the rustling sound which would be recorded on the track if it hung free. We had had to force our own way southwards against the crowds, hooting them out of our way because they filled the entire road. There were hundreds of them now on just this one section of roadway, men shepherding their families on foot, women and children crammed into battered cars, all moving at a steady 4 mph up the highway towards Beirut. Still, we heard that sound. 'Whoomph-whoomph' and the movement of the ground beneath us. From high above on that beautiful dawn came the thin whisper of jets.

The people did not look up. Several glanced at us. There was a girl in a long skirt who stared at me tiredly and held out her right hand with a slight movement of her wrist, palm upwards, which in Lebanon is not an appeal for alms but a gesture of despair, a way of saying 'What can we do?' Behind her came a bearded old man leading three camels. He must have come from the most rural areas far to the south, for camels were a rare sight in Lebanon. But there they were, great dismissive beasts walking along with their steady lope, piles of cushions, sheets and crockery tied around their humps.

There were gunmen among the refugees, mostly young communists who lived in the villages to the south and who did not regard this as their war. We did not even see the Palestinian gunmen when they arrived. We were walking back to the car, which was parked on the right-hand side of the road. Zavem Vartan, AP's Armenian photographer, had been driving. Robert Dear, from AP's London bureau, sat in the front with him. Michael Duffy, an AP correspondent from the Rome bureau, occupied the back with me. We had opened the doors of the car when the jeep suddenly drew up next to us, the armed men on the back screaming at us and pointing their Kalashnikovs in our direction.

The tide of refugees did not stop. Few even turned to watch. A woman was sobbing in the front of a car. A cart pulled by a scraggy horse was filled with sleeping children. Vartan was taking a photograph of some farmers as they hauled a plough behind them. One of the gunmen, in a pullover and brown trousers, started shouting: 'No pictures. No pictures.' Another Palestinian in a camouflage jacket with an unkempt black moustache ran to the car, yelling at us, pulling back the bolt on his rifle. CLACK-CLICK. It was a sound we all of us understood. It was in lieu of a warning. Anywhere else, a man might cry 'Stop' or 'Don't move' or, if he went to the movies a lot, he might shout 'Freeze' or 'Hold it right there.' In Lebanon, a man might mutter an obscenity. But then all you would hear was CLACK-CLICK.

I was already inside the car but the man ran to me and pointed the muzzle of the gun through the open window. '*Kuss ukhtak*,' he screamed. 'Your sister's cunt.' If you hate someone in Lebanon, you speak obscenely of their family. The man was so angry that he was shaking, the barrel of the rifle banging against the top of the glass. Through the windscreen, I could see another armed man pulling Vartan back across the road, the Armenian opening his camera and extracting the film, a long thin trail of exposed celluloid that hung guiltily from his hand.

The gunman with the moustache tore open my door. 'Give me the film.' He was shouting so loudly that he was spitting when he roared his instructions. There was no film, I said. I was a reporter, *morasl*, a correspondent. 'The film,' he screamed again. Another Palestinian ran over to us, an older man with a kinder face. 'OK, OK Mister. Get in the car. It's OK.' I climbed back into the car. The newcomer went to rescue Vartan. Dear was sitting in the front of the vehicle, looking at me with relief. Then the door opened again. It was the gunman with the moustache.

'I told you to give me the fucking film.' I stepped out of the car again. Look, there was no film. Look, this is just a tape-recorder, a cassette. 'Cassette,' he hissed. It was as if I had sworn at him. 'Cassette. Your sister's cunt. Give me the fucking cassette.' He seized the microphone from my hand and pulled. I let him have the mike but the mike-wire was still wound round my wrist and it pulled taut as he stepped back. '*Give* it to me, you bastard!' Yes but let me release the wire. He pulled savagely on the mike and the line twisted tighter round my wrist. 'You bastard! You bastard!' he kept shouting. Then he stopped, walked back three paces, held the rifle at waist level and pointed the barrel at my chest. CLACK-CLICK.

Your life does not pass in front of you when this happens. Later I would learn in Lebanon that I had to think very carefully and quickly when things like this occurred. At the time, I stood there like a dog. Please, I said. Please. I felt — it was a very acute sensation and quite overpowering — I felt that the idea of dying did not seem so important, that perhaps this whole business of being killed had been exaggerated. Like the girl who had made that hopeless gesture with the palm of her hand, I stood there in the road and accepted fate. I had run out of ideas. So I said please again.

Then the older man returned. 'It is all right, go, Mister, go.' The man with the moustache lunged towards me and smashed his fist onto the recorder. The lid flipped open and the plastic cassette spun out onto the road. He seized it as if it contained the key to his own salvation, squirrelling it away in his inside pocket like a child. The older man was pushing me into the car. Duffy was shaking beside me. Vartan threw the vehicle forward. Dear sucked on a cigarette.

It had been a salutary experience, for it gave us some idea of the mood of the Palestinians in the combat area that we were approaching. They were angry and frightened and they had already been shelled and attacked from the air. The mood was infectious. We too would become irritable, angry with each other as the dangers increased. Only Bob Dear, the photographer from London, remained immune. He adopted an exclusive approach to the possibility of sudden death, announcing that 'Things are a bit moody around here' when shells fell around us. He was a veteran of other wars in other places.

At the Litani River, Dear insisted on halting the car while he took three or four photographs of the iron bridge as the shells burst around it. The Israelis were planning to occupy Lebanon up to the Litani River. They had helpfully named their invasion 'Operation Litani', thus informing the Palestinians of their strategic objectives before they reached them. The result was predictable. The PLO pulled the majority of its forces back across the river — with the exception of those in the Tyre salient — before the Israelis arrived. The casualties were thus almost all civilians.

None could have been more frightened than the remaining citizens of Tyre. The lighthouse keeper had fled along with the middle-class Shia Muslims in the better part of town. The officials of the People's Republic of Tyre had also taken the road to Beirut. Only a few hundred people remained in the centre of the city, living in the cellars of their houses out on the old peninsula. The rest of the city was occupied by Palestinian guerrillas. They were everywhere.

We reached the deserted waterfront just before ten in the morning. The Israelis were south and east of the city — to the north-east as well, leaving open only the coast road to the Litani. This was the Tyre salient or Tyre 'pocket' as it was later to be called. The Israelis did not want to become involved in street fighting in the city. They assumed the Palestinians would flee along with the Lebanese refugees. They were wrong.

There were gunmen on the seafront, most of them from the Democratic

Front for the Liberation of Palestine, friendly communists and left-wing Palestinians who – unlike other PLO men – saw the war as a political inevitability rather than a disaster. Out in the Mediterranean we could see two small Israeli gunboats. The wash from their bows was clearly visible, their prows cutting back and forth in the water. Every time they fired a shell towards us, there would be a loud empty report followed by a rushing noise. We would see the projectile explode on the beach in a great spray of sand and water. High above us was the perpetual, now familiar sound of jets. Every minute or so, there would be a change in the tone of their high-pitched engines and piles of white and black smoke would pour upwards from the hills to the east. Shells were landing on the outskirts of the city.

There was a DFLP man near us, an older man, perhaps 50 or more, regarding this with almost academic interest. He would draw our attention to the gunboats firing or the shells rushing overhead as if he were a schoolteacher initiating his pupils, teaching them the first facts of war. Learn the difference between incoming and outgoing shellfire. You do not need to duck when the gunman down the street fires his mortar to the south. You cannot see him but the hollowness of the sound tells you that the projectile is being fired *out* of Tyre. When you see the smudge of black smoke beside the gunboat, you should stand behind the wall until you hear the shell exploding. The man pointed upwards at the sky and – climbing like three slow worms – were three lines of tracer smoke. 'SAM missiles,' the Palestinian said. The smoke blossomed into white puffs high in the sky.

The Israelis sent at least 25,000 soldiers into Lebanon to attack this ragtag army of a few hundred Palestinian gunmen. It seemed an extraordinarily large army to commit to Lebanon if the eradication of a few PLO bases was all that was at stake. Menachem Begin, the Israeli prime minister, spoke about Israel's determination 'to root out the evil weed of the PLO'. This sort of metaphor became a constant refrain in Israel. Weeds had to be destroyed, torn out by their roots. The Palestinians – civilians as well as guerrillas – were part of 'a cancer', one of the invading soldiers would later tell us. Once he had retired, one of Israel's senior army officers would compare the Palestinians to 'cockroaches'. Above all else, they were terrorists. Terrorists, terrorists, terrorists. The word was ubiquitous, obsessive, cancerous in its own special way. Terrorists were animals. Animals had to be put down. The PLO was a terrorist organisation. Terrorists, terrorists, terrorists. Israel radio used the word in every broadcast, almost every sentence.

Each morning when we left Beirut, we would tune to Israeli radio, broadcasting from Jerusalem. Every time the newsreader announced that the Israelis were attacking 'terrorist supply lines' beside the sea, we would understand its true meaning. The supply line was always the coast road down which those thousands of refugees were still trying to escape the war. The news reports from Israel would always mean that the road was under heavy shellfire. We drove fast and in great fear, always. 'Israeli forces this morning mounted an assault against terrorist forces on the coast road south of Sidon.' What did this mean? We drove south again.

There were more people on the road, in lorries, farm carts, taxis and old buses, all wearing the desolate expression of people who had abandoned all they owned and had no plans for the future. We had just reached a dusty coastal village called Adloun when we found Palestinian gunmen standing all over the road, shouting and gesticulating frantically at drivers who did not slow down.

We knew that some kind of massacre had occurred when we saw the doctor in a bloodstained white coat standing in front of an old ambulance with his arms outstretched in front of a small crowd. Behind him were two smashed, fire-blackened cars, riddled with bullets and cut open by rocket fire. From the first of these, Palestinians were tugging something heavy and soft out of the doors.

The corpses were congealed together inside the car. One Palestinian youth with a rifle over his shoulder, pulled on an arm that protruded from the door, setting his boots into a crack in the concrete to heave the body out. There was a faint tearing sound and the arm came out detached from the body. He stood there, clutching the disembodied hand in disbelief.

The women and children in the two cars were identifiable by the bright flowered orange traditional dress they wore, but their faces were unrecognisable. One had been beheaded. Another, a young girl, lay curled in the arms of an older woman on the back seat. Another Palestinian youth leaned inside the car and put his arms round her waist and pulled her gently, shyly, towards the door. She folded into his arms but as he pulled her clear of the door, her face slopped off onto the road and the young man dropped her and started to vomit.

Around the two cars, a throng of women stood crying and wailing – a sign of respect for the dead as well as grief in the Arab world – next to a stretcher in which a small child had been laid in two separate pieces. How was one to describe all this? If we were writing fiction or compiling a medical report, perhaps we could dwell on the details of so terrible a scene. An American correspondent who had arrived with us began to cry. 'Oh Jesus Christ! Oh Christ!' he kept saying. He leaned against the ambulance in a state of great distress. 'I suppose all this,' he said, 'is because of what Hitler did to the Jews.'

Lorryloads of refugees were trying to drive past; they slowed down to a crawl and the adults among them could be seen forcing their children to look at the bodies. The children gazed blankly as if they did not understand the meaning of the thing. There had been six people in the second car; like those in the first, they were all dead.

Whatever had cremated these women and children had come suddenly and unexpectedly and the truth quickly emerged. An Israeli raiding party had come ashore near Adloun during the night. They were looking for 'terrorists'. They saw the lights of the two cars approaching and they fired anti-tank rockets at the occupants. No time to check who they were. Who but 'terrorists' would be driving on this road? I was still carrying that AFP report in my pocket. Israeli forces, Weizman had said, had been told to 'do their best ... to avoid losses among the civilian population.'

We drove east towards Nabatieh, almost totally deserted save for some Palestinians under the cover of trees, holding rocket-launchers and rifles. An abandoned jeep stood in the main street, unguarded, its machine-gun hanging limply on its tripod at the back, a torn Palestinian flag attached to the front window.

Qaaqaiet al-Jisr. We scribbled names like this into our notebooks with little idea where we were. No time to look at the map. Back home in Beirut later, we would study the minuscule contours above the Litani to discover where we had been. We could hear the planes again. They had been howling and wailing above us, high and unseen in the glare of the sun, for almost five minutes. Then the first great explosions bloomed among the houses just across the valley. A Palestinian boy in a combat jacket and carrying a rifle – was he 14? No, younger – had been standing next to us. He had been wondering aloud if it was the village we were in or the one across the valley that was to be destroyed by the Israeli pilots.

We had stood on the roadway and stared across the valley at the village of Aadchit. I could see the rows of houses over the wadi and the mosque sweltering in the sun, and I was looking right at it when the sound of power-diving grew into a rising whine like the noise of a steam kettle coming to the boil. Then Aadchit was bathed in orange fire that rippled across the streets in less than five seconds. Two towers of black smoke had already begun to build their way above the hills when the blast came rumbling over to Qaaqaiet al-Jisr. It shook the road and the walls and rattled the iron window gratings of the houses around us until the bars banged against the glass. The Palestinian boy grinned and started to laugh as the village over the valley went on erupting. They had not bombed Qaaqaiet al-Jisr, not this time. He was safe.

Tyre was now populated by Palestinian gunmen, the only ones left south of the Litani River. The river bridge still held but it was sometimes difficult to know which army represented the greater danger. On 18 March, at a crossroads beside the Tyre waterfront, a gunman in black approached our car. Vartan was driving again and Dear was in the front passenger seat as usual. The man pointed a small black pistol through the window at Vartan. 'Take us to the north. If you don't do as I say, I will shoot the brains out of your head.' The man was deserting. Not only did he want to put one of his colleagues in the back with us, he wanted to tie a mobile anti-aircraft gun to the back of our car. Dear had not seen the pistol. 'Tell him to piss off,' he instructed Vartan. Then he saw the gun. 'Do whatever he wants.' Three guerrillas came running towards us from the other side. One pointed a rifle towards the man with the pistol. 'Leave the *sahafi* alone. You cannot run away. You stay here and fight and die with us.'

The old city was being shelled around the clock. Journalists found refuge at the International Red Cross centre in a disused hotel on the beach. Israeli shells fell on the lane leading to the building and smashed into the nearest apartment blocks. The Israelis had now set off a war that was wreaking a terrible retribution upon the Lebanese. Up to 10,000 refugees were on the roads every day. We passed them every morning and evening, many of them farm workers driving their tractors and machinery that still carried the dirt of the fields.

Could one blame them for such single-minded determination to escape the gunfire to the south? At least 100,000 civilians had already driven or begged their way to Beirut to settle in the slums of the southern suburbs or around Ouzai. The Lebanese government were later to estimate the total refugee population at 285,000 – three quarters of them Lebanese – representing half the population living in the area now occupied by Israel.

One evening, returning through Damour, I found that the Syrian army had blocked the road north and were ordering the refugees to return to the battle zone, to stay put in their homes. 'In Palestine, the Israelis claim they found a land without people,' a Syrian officer explained to us. 'Now they will take southern Lebanon and claim they have found another land without people if these refugees do not return.' As the refugees pressed on, physically pushing the Syrians aside, several soldiers began smashing the windscreens of the first cars with their rifle butts.

After almost a week, we could count the impact marks of 30 shells in the girders of the Litani River bridge and on the surface of the road on either side of it. Because the bridge was so badly damaged, we had to drive across it at 3 mph, watched by the Israelis on the hill to the south-east. We could actually see them standing there, watching us. Seconds after we began crossing the bridge, there would come the sound of the first incoming shells.

There was only one way to outwit the Israelis: to drive up to the edge of the bridge from the north at 70 or 80 mph, to jam on the brakes, to creep across as the Israelis alerted their gunners, and then to career away on the other side as the first shells hit the roadway. The same process had to be followed when travelling in the opposite direction. The place stank of cordite, and the remains of those civilians who had not worked out their own version of our plan could be seen lying in the ditches beside the highway. One old Volkswagen car had received a direct hit on the southern side of the bridge and remained in the middle of the road there for three days, the stench of its contents growing more hideous each time we inched past.

In Tyre itself, we could find only around 300 Lebanese civilians now. There had been 60,000 there before the invasion. Some of the civilians had erected small, symbolic walls of stones. They were only two or three feet high. They wanted the message to go out: that the Palestinians must leave and that the Israelis had no reason to go on shelling their city. Palestinians were withdrawing from Tyre but not in large numbers. To the north of Nabatieh, they were being resupplied by the Iraqis; Iraqi army trucks were observed by reporters being escorted south from Beirut by the Syrian army.

This was the day after we accidentally drove right through the Palestinian lines outside Tyre, past the gunmen sitting beside their mortars among the trees and up the friendly little road past the stone Phoenician sarcophagus which is supposed to contain the remains of King Hiram of Tyre, the man who sent the cedars of Lebanon to King Solomon to build the temple of Jerusalem. The Israeli tank that shelled us as we lay in the field below Qana must have done so routinely. Who but 'terrorists' would be on the road? David Hirst, the Middle East correspondent of the London *Guardian*, was almost killed the following day when an Israeli tank shelled him and his colleagues in a neighbouring village. They had sought shelter in a school building; the Israelis who later came across them and sent them off to Jerusalem explained that they assumed the journalists must have been 'terrorists'; like the civilians on the coast road north of Tyre or the inhabitants of Aadchit and so many other villages in the south of Lebanon.

This ugly obsession with 'terrorists', which reduced anyone – *anyone* – in the war zone to the level of an animal, was responsible for at least one war crime committed by the Israelis. Near a south Lebanese village occupied by Israeli troops, Lieutenant Daniel Pinto, the acting commander of an Israeli infantry company, strangled four Lebanese peasants whose bodies, tied hand and foot, were later found in a well. Another Israeli officer, Lieutenant-Colonel Arye Sadeh, ordered the execution of one of his battalion's prisoners during the first days of the advance into Lebanon. Pinto was court-martialled for his atrocity but the Israeli chief of staff, General Rafael Eitan, reduced the sentence to two years and then ordered Pinto's release. Sadeh received two and a half years' imprisonment and reduction in rank to major, a sentence that was later raised by an appeals court to five years and reduction to private. Eitan restored the original sentence. His specific orders to the Israeli army in 'Operation Litani' were 'to annihilate the terrorists and their infrastructure'. But who were the 'terrorists'? And who were the Israelis really fighting in this latest war?

The people of Tyre thought that their war was over by the morning of 21 March. 'I heard it on the BBC,' an old man with a slight limp and a torn jacket said as he approached us in the old part of the town. 'Ceasefire,' he shouted. 'The Israelis have called a ceasefire.' It was as well we had not told him about the ceasefire conditions.

For sharp on nine o'clock, with bureaucratic precision, the Israelis' guns across the olive groves just to the south of Tyre began to fire with a dreary booming sound and their shells crashed into some modern, blue-painted blocks of apartments near the Red Cross centre. They hit the roofs and the walls and then their shells began exploding inside the Roman stadium of ancient Tyre just to the south. The sixth-floor apartment balconies came down first, with all the windows. Israeli intelligence must have discovered that there had been a Palestinian office in the building. But the intelligence was not quite good enough. The PLO had left the office four days earlier. Now only the civilians would lose their homes. Even when the smoke cleared, we could still see some washing hanging from the only balcony to survive. At two in the afternoon, after a bombardment that was sometimes running at one shell every ten seconds or less, we heard Israeli radio announce that the south of Lebanon was 'relatively peaceful'.

Relative to what? The Israelis occupied all but this narrow strip of territory below the Litani. But they were now coming under rocket fire from Palestinian positions *north* of the river. The Israeli–Palestinian line had merely moved a few miles north – at a cost of up to 2,000 Lebanese and Palestinian lives and 20 Israelis. The Americans had agreed to support a United Nations force in southern Lebanon, an international army which was to carry the acronym UNIFIL. This stood for United Nations Interim Force in Lebanon. The catch, of course, was the word 'interim'.

It was true that the Israelis had pushed the PLO back from their frontier. But PLO men remained inside Beaufort Castle, from where they could still fire Katyushas into Galilee. So why did Israel invade? William Rees-Mogg, who was then editor of *The Times*, had told me he would never send a reporter to cover a war unless the journalist was absolutely certain that he knew what the war was about. It took us a few years to realise that we would only discover the true reasons for a war long after it had ended. Thus I was never able to meet Rees-Mogg's criteria; like the Lebanese, reporters had to wait until the war was over. And in Lebanon, of course, it never was. It was to be four years before the real meaning of this bloody little adventure became clear to us.

On 22 March, we took a short drive out of Tyre through some olive groves and came across an Israeli roadblock. '*Shalom,*' we chorused to the blonde Russian-born soldier who approached our car. Twenty-four hours earlier, we would have been 'terrorists'. Now the soldier asked if we were tourists. 'We did not think we would go so far,' he said. 'The terrorists have not fought us very much. Most of the terrorists did not fight hard — some of them, but very few. Nearly all the terrorists escaped.'

He gazed around at the gentle hills of southern Lebanon, at the distant hulk of Beaufort through the heat haze. Then he added something quite extraordinary. 'This sure is a beautiful country,' he said.

He had been bitten by the dragonfly. And he had not even felt its sting.

5 The Gentleman from Marjayoun

> I got a call from an Israeli officer ... to warn me that the
> Christians were likely to fire in our direction. He ... came
> on the radio, made his excuses and shouted: 'The Christians
> are going to fire in about six seconds – five – four – three
> – two – one.' And a couple of seconds later, shells started
> landing behind the United Nations lines. How was he so
> accurate? ... He was doing the shooting.
>
> Dutch UN battalion officer, Haris village,
> southern Lebanon
> *May 1980*

On 23 March 1978, the French returned to Lebanon. In their blue UN
helmets, they drove down the coast road from Beirut in 14 white-
painted trucks, across the wreckage of the Litani River bridge and into
Tyre. Some of the men and women in the poorer Shia villages shouted
encouragement to the young soldiers on board. A few of the older men
shouted '*Vive la France*', a gesture which was regarded with satisfaction
by Colonel Jean Germain Salvan. To his battalion of French Paratroopers
had fallen the honour of forming part of the advance guard of the new
United Nations army.

Down through the orange orchards and past those long rows of pine
trees they travelled, sitting in their open-top lorries, representatives of
another foreign army coming to save Lebanon. Only when they entered
Tyre did they see the Palestinian fedayeen in the streets, still heavily
armed and unbeaten, guerrillas who had refused to retreat before the
Israelis and who were even less likely to withdraw now that the French
had arrived. Some of the Palestinians raised their Kalashnikov rifles
over their heads in greeting. It was the kind of welcome that young
soldiers like to see in someone else's country. The French soldiers
waved back at the Palestinians, aware that Tyre would soon be under
the exclusive control of the UN. That was, after all, the implication of
their mandate, UN Security Council Resolution 425.

It was a document that combined morality, naivety and folly in about
equal proportions. The UN army, it announced, would 'confirm the
withdrawal of Israeli forces, restore international peace and security and
assist the Government of Lebanon in ensuring the return of its effective
authority in the area.' It would also 'use its best efforts to prevent the
recurrence of fighting and to ensure that its area of operation is not

utilized for hostile activities of any kind.' This was, to say the least, an ambitious undertaking. It required not only blindness to assume that the Israelis were going to stage a complete withdrawal but a willing suspension of disbelief to regard the 'Government of Lebanon' as anything but a powerless bureaucracy. The 'effective authority' of that government had not existed in southern Lebanon for many years, and it was unlikely that the exotic combination of international battalions about to take up residence in the region would be able to change that.

UNIFIL, according to its mandate, would have 'weapons of a defensive character'. These might have permitted the UN to perform its duties – perhaps even enabling them to carry out a little peace-*enforcing* in southern Lebanon – if the soldiers did not have to rely on the Israelis and the Palestinians to help them. But, sure enough, the mandate loftily explained that UNIFIL would 'proceed on the assumption that the parties to the conflict will take all the necessary steps for compliance with the decisions of the Security Council.' How many miles was it from that tall, glass-fronted building on the East River to the hills of southern Lebanon? No shell had ever swept past the UN headquarters or devastated the secretary general's staff. The mandate had been constructed on the arrogant assumption that the UN was so august a body that no one – least of all the militias of Lebanon or their regional superpower allies – would dare contradict it. And just after 10 am on 23 March, at the old Lebanese Hassan Borro barracks south of Tyre, the French Paratroop battalion received the first intimation that this was untrue.

The Lebanese Arab Army, the dissident Muslim faction of the national army, had occupied the barracks until the Israeli invasion, at which point they discreetly and very wisely deserted, leaving the Palestinians to defend the fort under Israeli shellfire. The local Palestinian commander, Abu Saif, was therefore the first to offer to hand over the barracks to Colonel Salvan. Only minutes after he had done so, however, two cars pulled up at the gates of the *caserne*. Three men emerged. The first identified himself as an officer in the Lebanese Arab Army, the second as an official from the Lebanese Ministry of Defence, a representative of the 'new' national army. The third man was his bodyguard. Both soldiers announced that they had come to reclaim their barracks. There was a roar of disapproval from the Palestinian guerrillas at the gate.

One of them, in a grey and white *kuffiah*, pulled a pistol from his belt and accused the Defence Ministry official of being a Phalangist. The bodyguard drew his gun. Another Palestinian at the gate fitted a projectile into his anti-tank rocket-launcher. At which point US Navy Lieutenant Conway Ziegler claimed a brief moment in Lebanese history. Temporarily attached to the UN force because he could speak Arabic – which the French could not – he strode between the men at the gate and pleaded with them to put down their weapons. An uneasy formula was reached, the first of thousands of UN-sponsored compromises. The Defence Ministry man was detained by the Palestinians and driven away in a car, while the Lebanese Arab Army officer sought the protection of the French. The bodyguard vanished.

The French troops relaxed, sitting under their trucks and cooking cans of beans on little stoves until more shouting came from the main gate. A group of heavily armed and dishevelled Palestinian guerrillas pushed their way past the UN guard and came clanking onto the parade ground, one of the Palestinians screaming abuse at a French Paratrooper who stood facing him with fixed bayonet. UN troops set up a light machine-gun beside the trees on the south side of the barracks. An Irish Army Air Corps officer, Captain Martin Egan, recalled his own country's bloody UN experience in the Congo. Could this be the same, he asked us? It would prove to be far worse. By nightfall, there were still Palestinians inside the French base. It would be weeks before UN – PLO relations were formally established.

Yassir Arafat's radical opponents within the PLO initially showed no inclination to accept the UN's presence in southern Lebanon, certainly not in the city which they had clung on to under Israeli gunfire. Ignoring the PLO chairman's orders to cooperate with the French UN battalion, the PFLP, DFLP and the pro-Iraqi Arab Liberation Front all harassed the French troops. In some incidents, the French – successors of the same army which had controlled Lebanon under the mandate – forgot that they were supposed to negotiate an end to the fighting and threatened the Palestinians instead. In early May, Salvan was driving in a jeep belonging to Fatah when dissident PLO gunmen opened fire on his vehicle, severely wounding him in both legs and killing a French soldier and Salvan's Palestinian driver. Arafat denounced the assassination attempt as a crime, adding, of course, that it was also 'a plot against the Palestinian revolution'.

But it was the Israelis who destroyed any opportunity the UN might have had of fulfilling its mandate. Even while his army was still in the process of invading Lebanon in March 1978 – before the UN force existed – General Mordechai Gur, Eitan's predecessor as Israeli chief of staff, had announced that it was his intention to 'pull back to the Christian enclaves between the Mediterranean and Mount Hermon to form a security belt along the Israeli-Lebanese frontier.' In one form or another, this 'security belt' – often one of the most *insecure* and dangerous areas of the country – was to become a permanent feature of southern Lebanon. Although actually under Israeli military orders, its nominal masters were the Christian militiamen who had been fighting the Palestinians and leftists for the previous four years, a murderous collection of Phalangist gunmen, renegade soldiers from the national army and local thugs who had distinguished themselves during the 1978 invasion by a particularly frightful massacre.

They had forced a large group of Shia men, women and children into a mosque in the village of Khiam and, under the eyes of Israeli officers, machine-gunned all of them to death. Only the persistence of Jonathan Randal of *The Washington Post* brought this slaughter – a real act of 'terrorism' if ever there was one – to light. Yet it made no difference to the Israelis. They publicly praised the Christian gunmen as outstanding patriots who alone had stood firm against Palestinian 'terrorists'. And Israel placed its faith – publicly at least – in a cashiered Lebanese army major called Saad Haddad. He was to be the ruler of what the Israelis now decided to call 'Free Lebanon', that strip of Lebanese territory that lay along Israel's border, 'cleansed' now of Palestinians and unwanted Shia opponents.

It was a unique kind of fiefdom. When you visited Haddad's little realm with its Israeli-made roads, its Israeli beer for sale in the shops, its Israeli food and Israeli-registered cars and Hebrew road-signs, its Israeli-armed militiamen and its complement of Israeli soldiers, it was occasionally possible to believe that this was Israel rather than Lebanon. It may have been 'free' in the eyes of the Israeli government press office in Jerusalem. But it was not going to be open to the United Nations, as Major-General Emmanuel Alexander Erskine, the Ghanaian commander of the UN army, quickly discovered. Marching his blue-helmeted men across a small bridge some three miles north of the Israeli frontier, Erskine was stopped in his tracks by an Israeli soldier who placed his rifle across the UN commander's ample chest. That would be as far as the UN would go. Except in one small corner of Haddad's empire; a place called Naqqoura.

So much, then, for the mandate which ordered the UN to 'confirm the withdrawal of Israeli forces' from southern Lebanon. So much for restoring the 'effective authority' of the Lebanese government in the area. So much for the 'compliance' of all parties to the conflict. The mandate was illusory. The UN estimated an initial six-month budget of 68 million dollars for its international army. More than 6,000 men would come under the UN flag at any one time. Battalions would be contributed by France, Ireland, Norway, Senegal, Nigeria, Holland, Finland, Fiji, Nepal, Ghana and, in the very early days, by the Shah's Iranian army. Helicopter and medical units would come from Italy and Sweden. At least four of the participating nations were NATO powers. The Dutch even brought TOW anti-tank missiles with them. But UNIFIL never reached the Israeli border, never restored the land to the authority of the Lebanese government and never received the full compliance of the parties to the conflict. Indeed, the Palestinians and Haddad's militia –

the latter with the full connivance of Israel – proceeded to attack and on several occasions kill UN soldiers.

From the start, the Palestinians were not unhappy with Israel's intransigence. If Haddad's men refused to allow the UN into their enclave, why should the PLO permit the UN into Tyre or the salient of territory that ran south from the Litani River bridge? So they stayed put. When the ceasefire had taken effect, two Palestinian combat units south of the Litani – one east of Tyre, the other south of Hasbaya – were still holding out. When Erskine's army moved in, the PLO insisted that these two areas should also remain in Palestinian hands *within* the UN zone.

Another foreign army had now entered Lebanon. Its soldiers had been cheered and feted on their way south. They found the Mediterranean beaches unspoiled, the weather ideal for sunbathing, the drink cheap and the people overwhelmingly friendly. Most of the people. The UN established its headquarters staff in the old Lebanon–Palestine customs post at Naqqoura, a Christian village with a long strand of dark green sea to the west and a ridge of low hills to the east. UN officers had turned down two other options for their headquarters – in Tyre and at the Zahrani refinery – because the former was in PLO-held territory and the latter was partly occupied by Syrian troops.

So magnificent was the landscape, so clear-cut the terms of the mandate, so highly moral its purpose, that the UN apparently saw nothing inept in its decision to turn Naqqoura into its base, even though Naqqoura was deep inside Haddad's enclave. Nor did the Israelis or Haddad object. His gunmen could cut off Naqqoura whenever they wished; and they did, laying siege to hundreds of UN troops, destroying one of their helicopters and shooting up Major-General Erskine's quarters for good measure. At midnight on 19 April 1978, UNIFIL headquarters was attacked with mortars, rocket-propelled grenades and heavy machine-guns; six Irish and two Dutch soldiers were wounded. The UN were forced to ask the Israelis to intervene with Haddad.

A series of important lessons had been learned. Haddad had proved to the UN that he had muscle and was prepared to use it; the Israelis ordered Haddad to raise the siege, thus demonstrating that they ultimately controlled his militia. And the UN realised that it was going to have to deal with the Israelis inside Lebanon. UN officers cynical enough to suspect – and later to confirm – that three Israeli officers had directed the attack on the Naqqoura headquarters concluded that their mission was likely to involve blood and fire as well as sunbathing. They were right.

Within weeks, Lebanon had begun to impose its own exclusive restraints upon the United Nations. The Norwegians maintained a cordon of troops around the 12 PLO men who refused to leave their hundred square yards of land south of Hasbaya. The Palestinians could not take their weapons out of the position and they could not bring ammunition into it. If a PLO guerrilla chose to leave, he could be replaced – but neither man would be permitted to travel under arms. The same rules applied to the 140 or so Palestinians surrounded by the Dutch battalion in what the UN called the 'Iron Triangle' east of Tyre.

Norwegian, Irish and Dutch soldiers would find themselves involved in interminable discussions with Haddad or Haddad's deputies over imaginary attempts by Shia Muslim villagers to cut off the Christian enclave's water or electricity supplies. The UN adopted a whole lexicon to take account of the enemies they dared not admit to having. Palestinians were logged on UN ops room situation reports as 'armed elements'. Haddad's men were 'de facto forces'. Neither term represented the whole truth, for even the UN was now finding that Lebanon distorted its sense of reality. When they confronted Haddad's men, Norwegian and Dutch troops, both drawn from NATO armies, found that they faced armour which had been supplied to the militia by Israel – which had in turn received the equipment from the United States. The weapons of one NATO power were thus directed against two other NATO powers in Lebanon.

The Palestinians outside the UN zone were still receiving ammunition and supplies from Iraq and also from Libya – via Jumblatt's Druze militia in the Chouf – while Syria was now openly allying itself with the PLO's cause in southern Lebanon. Syrian money and arms were also being channelled to Amal, the growing Shia militia in the south of the country, which was itself the product of the 'Movement of the Deprived' founded by Imam Mousa Sadr. Sadr's political organisation had been established to fight for Shia political rights which the Lebanese government had traditionally neglected; the Amal militia was, in Lebanon, the natural offspring of such a movement. In Beirut, the Sunni Mourabitoun also received weapons from Damascus.

In this manner, civil war combatants were re-armed by Syria, the very nation which had sworn to disarm them – under the pretext that militias *outside* Syrian control were being equipped by other sources. And this was indeed the case. The Phalangists in Beirut received their own shipments of Sherman tanks from the Israelis and boxes of M-16 rifles were brought ashore for the Phalange from Israeli vessels near Jounieh. Syrian arms had originally come from the Soviet Union. Most of the weapons that came from Israel were manufactured in the United States.

Such developments provided further evidence for those who believed that Lebanon was the victim of a superpower conspiracy, The Plot. The country was certainly being divided along old colonialist principles. Just as the French had used their proxies in Lebanon at the time of the mandate, so now the Israelis were using Lebanese gangs to control the far south of Lebanon and east Beirut while the Syrians employed equally disreputable militiamen to coerce west Beirut and central Lebanon.

Chamoun made no secret of his own predisposition towards the various nations now involving themselves in his country. 'We want to know if Lebanon is a sovereign state or a whorehouse,' he complained in March of 1978. 'We are told about Libyan, Iraqi and other forces coming to Lebanon under the pretext of liberating the south. If they really mean that, then we say that the Jews are much nicer.'

Chamoun's remarks were in keeping with the deteriorating relations between the Maronites and the Syrians. Although they initially cooperated with Syria, the Christian militias had become increasingly uncomfortable with their exigent Muslim allies in Damascus. In the rearguard of the Syrian troops who arrived in Beirut, as behind every army, had come the *mukhabarrat*, the intelligence services, young Syrians in plain clothes with pistols in their hip pockets, who became a law unto themselves. While Syrian troops did prevent hundreds of kidnaps and save thousands of lives, the presence of the *mukhabarrat* added an ominous element to the humanitarian assistance received from 'sister Syria'. Christian and Muslim Lebanese militia officers were arrested at night and taken to prison in Damascus.

The Gemayels and Chamouns were now seeing the Syrians as a threat, a foreign force as disturbing – possibly even more dangerous – than the Palestinians. Syrian troops were asked, then told and finally ordered to leave east Beirut by the Phalange. Fighting broke out between the militias, and Syrian tanks were moved down to the overgrown railway yards at Ein al-Rumaneh to shell the Christian area of Ashrafieh. Chamoun sat out the bombardment in the bunker beneath his Ashrafieh apartment, emerging during the inevitable ceasefires to warn the Lebanese government that if it sought a renewal of the Arab League mandate for the Syrian army in Lebanon, then the Cabinet ministers would be 'traitors'. The threat was a simple one: if Sarkis was deprived of Phalangist and Chamounist support and recognition, he might be forced to resign. Syria would then have to soldier on in Lebanon without the formal – and legally essential – permission of a Lebanese president.

From Israel came a familiar refrain. Israel could not 'stand idly by' while the Christians of east Beirut were annihilated. An even louder noise came from two Israeli jets which broke the sound barrier as they flew at low level over west Beirut, shattering the shop-front window panes on Hamra Street with their sonic booms. The Syrians understood this message and the artillery bombardment eased. Another red line had been drawn on the map of Lebanon.

In one sense, the daily fighting between Christians and Syrians was essential to the Maronite belief that they were struggling to save Lebanon's national integrity. When the Syrians opened fire on east Beirut, it was held up as proof that Damascus, far from being a peace-keeper, was repressing Lebanese freedom. Chamoun, who was a better publicist than politician, walked through the damaged streets of Ashrafieh for the local television cameras, extolling the courage of his militiamen. 'It is absolutely wrong to say that we are fighting because we are Christians,' he told me as we stood amid the rubble below Sassine Square in September of 1978. 'It *happens* that those who are fighting for the freedom of Lebanon are the Christians. The others are perhaps too weak or do not have the courage to fight. But it is not because we are of the Christian faith — it is because we want to defend our freedom and our dignity.'

And if the Syrians left? Would there not be another civil war? 'There will be one less enemy, first of all. Secondly, there will be nobody to start intriguing for a war. The Palestinians do not want war. We Lebanese do not want war among ourselves in Lebanon. We are ready to deal with all our differences and to find ways and means to live in peace together as we have done for fifty years. It is blackmail — Syrian blackmail — when they say that if they leave, there will be civil war in five minutes. That's blackmail.'

But it was also the truth, Chamoun's 50 years of peace was a lie. And only a second Syrian military advance into Beirut in 1987 was to save the city from a civil war even more bloody than that which had occurred in 1975 and 1976. Nor was Chamoun as forthcoming about the Israeli military support which the Maronites were receiving. When I asked him about this assistance, he replied: 'God is great, and he will provide us with ways and means to get the material aid and the equipment we need.' God clearly had powerful friends. Yet Chamoun was old and it was Bashir Gemayel who was negotiating with the Israelis for arms and political support.

Chamoun's was the voice still heard by Syria. While east Beirut was enveloped in the grey smoke of shell-bursts one day in October 1978, I stopped my car on the mountain road to Damascus for a Syrian army sergeant who was trying to hitch-hike home on leave. He was on the Syrian headquarters staff in Lebanon, a 37-year-old refugee from Golan in the 1967 war whose family now lived in Aleppo. After we had gone through the essential preliminaries of greeting each other, explaining our family background and deploring war in a generalised way, I asked him why the Syrians were besieging east Beirut. 'What makes you think we want to kill Christians?' he asked. 'If we wanted to murder Christians, we would have killed the Christians in Syria — but they are happy. I think that every time Camille Chamoun speaks, he wants to start a war.'

In Damascus, Syrian families would privately express to us their resentment that the country's soldiers should be risking their lives to keep two hostile communities from each other's throats. Damascus newspapers — all of them mouthpieces for Assad's regime — would praise the patience and restraint of Syrian troops in Beirut. The parallels with the British army in Northern Ireland were obvious, even if they were highly misleading.

But sometimes the Syrian soldiers did not believe all they were told. Steve Hindy of the Associated Press gave a lift to another Syrian soldier who was returning for a weekend's leave in Damascus. When they reached the Syrian capital, Hindy dutifully drove the soldier home and was invited to tea by his family. Did they believe that Syria would win the next war against Israel? he asked. The mother and the soldier's brothers all professed their belief Syria would win. 'We have wonderful new weapons,' one of the brothers said. But when Hindy turned to the soldier and asked him if Syria would be victorious in a war with Israel, the young man looked at the ground. Then he shook his head. 'No,' he said. 'We would not win.'

The Lebanese conflict continued to preoccupy the Syrians. Their troops in Lebanon were peace-keepers, were they not, authorised by the Arab League? Families in Damascus would talk of their desire to 'bring the boys home'. But the Maronites, who had come to represent a peculiarly European movement in the Levant, traditionally viewed the Muslim world with suspicion. They regarded the comparatively new nation of Israel with something akin to admiration. When the prospects of a Jewish state began to look more promising in the 1930s, Lebanese Christians — far from fearing the commencement of a Middle East conflict — felt that it would be advantageous to have another strong minority on the periphery of the Arab world. When President Emile Edde and the Patriarch of the Maronite Church met the Zionist leader Chaim Weizmann in Paris in 1937 — as Damascus radio reminded its listeners that autumn of 1978 — Edde went so far as to state publicly that he hoped that a new Jewish state's first treaty of friendship with a foreign nation would be with Lebanon. In Christian eyes, Maronites and Israelis were together holding back an encroaching Muslim world. The West sympathised with this scenario, which is why so many nations demanded a ceasefire in Beirut. No statesman was so forceful in his appeal as President Jimmy Carter.

Israel's first peace treaty was not with Lebanon but with Egypt. President Sadat's agreement at Camp David in September of 1978 to recognise Israel and its right to security in return for an Israeli withdrawal from occupied Sinai left Assad vulnerable and exposed. The Palestinians were even more bereft. The provision guaranteeing them the right to 'participate in the determination of their own future' was understandably regarded by Arafat and the PLO as an Arab betrayal. The Palestinians wanted to *decide* their future, not participate in its determination.

Nationalist anger in Beirut was a unifying element between Syrians, Palestinians and Lebanese Muslims, all of whom believed that Nasser's successor had committed an act of treason by visiting Jerusalem in 1977. From now on, the Syrians and the Palestinians would coordinate their policy on southern Lebanon. Who but they stood against the Israeli army now that Egypt had capitulated?

Sadat relied upon dramatic gestures to take the place of serious political argument. Philip Habib, who was to be President Ronald Reagan's special envoy to the Middle East, told me how he sat with the Egyptian leader in the garden of his Cairo home just before the 1977 Jerusalem visit. Sadat had asked Assad and King Husain whether they would be prepared to accompany him on his journey to Israel. They had refused. 'I am tired of the dwarfs,' Sadat suddenly shouted at Habib. 'If they won't come, I'll go alone.'

Sadat's decision led directly to his grave. In the Knesset, Sadat listened in silence as Menachem Begin evoked the old story of Israel's birth, of David and Goliath, of the tiny state fighting giants for its survival. If silence gave consent — whatever the parliamentary courtesies may have demanded — then Sadat was seen in the rest of the Arab world to have acquiesced in Jewish statehood. 'He has spoken to the world from his enemy's parliament,' I wrote then in *The Irish Times*. 'But he has not said whether, in sitting down with the Israelis, he believes he has also signed his death warrant.'

It was perhaps easier to comprehend this possibility in Beirut. When Sadat was eventually assassinated by one of his own Egyptian army officers four years later, the Palestinian guerrillas in the Beirut camps lit up the night sky with tracer in celebration. For hours their gunfire echoed out of the camps. Treachery and betrayal was easier to understand in Lebanon. The Lebanese and Palestinians there became adept at stripping away the substratum of good intentions from all such treaties.

Living in Beirut in the late 1970s, one was both intensely conscious of the changes in the neighbouring world — in Egypt and then in Iran and ultimately in Afghanistan — yet curiously isolated from these events. Another of those yellow-tinted clippings in my files shows that on 13 September 1978 I recorded 'the mysterious disappearance' of Imam Mousa Sadr, the Iranian-born Shia leader from southern Lebanon. Beirut newspapers variously speculated that he had been kidnapped by Savak, the Shah's secret police, or that he had himself been involved with the Libyan intelligence service. Sadr's disappearance — and presumed murder in Libya — were to have immense consequences in southern Lebanon, providing both a focus and an inspiration to the resistance guerrillas who would drive the Israelis out of the country. Yet amid the fighting in east Beirut I found time to file only five paragraphs to *The Times*. It was printed below the fold on the back page.

By mid-October of 1978, the Syrians realised they had to leave east Beirut. It was a blow to their prestige that was made even more humiliating by the necessity of stationing non-Syrian troops of the Arab League force – in this case, the Saudis – in the Christian sector of Beirut. Syrian–Christian relations were so hostile that the Maronites now entrusted their fate not to 'sister Syria', who had entered Lebanon at the request of a Lebanese Christian president just over two years earlier, but to the army of King Fahd, whose antipathy towards the Christian religion was such that not one church could be built in all Saudi Arabia.

The Syrian withdrawal came in return for a complex if almost facetious agreement reached between Sarkis, the Syrians and the foreign ministers of four other Arab nations. They had met in the Chouf mountains, in the magnificent Hall of Justice of the nineteenth-century Beit Eddine palace of the Emir Bashir II, predecessor of the Ottoman satrap whose failure to reconcile Christians and Druze had led to the first European involvement in Lebanon in 1842. The solemn Beit Eddine accord served notice that 'armed manifestations must be eliminated, guns must be collected and illegal possession of weapons must be prohibited.' More important – but even more impossible to impose – was a clause insisting that the Christians of Lebanon would no longer be permitted to deal with Israel.

Suleiman Franjieh, who had by now broken with the Gemayels and Chamouns, was prompted to demand a 'Lebanese–Arab treason court' to try Christian militia officers. Sarkis himself was deeply distressed when he saw the banners which had been hung – with Syrian permission – outside the palace at Beit Eddine. They called the Maronites fascists and demanded that Lebanon join the struggle against the Camp David 'surrender'. The enmity between Chamoun and Assad was in any case now a personal one, exacerbated by Chamoun's decision to publicise a damaging 40-year-old letter written by Syrian Alawites to Léon Blum, informing the prewar French prime minister that Syria was 'not yet ready' for freedom from colonial rule. One of the signatories was allegedly a Latakia peasant named Assad, the father of the man who now claimed to be the author of real Syrian independence.

The Phalange cared nothing for the Beit Eddine accord. The Christian militiamen went out of their way to mock it. They gleefully spray-painted the Star of David on the walls of the damaged apartment blocks in Ashrafieh, inking the word 'Israel' in Biro onto their khaki shirts and green dungarees. A few had even stencilled the Star of David onto their rifle butts, alongside idealised portraits of the Virgin. At least 700 Christians, most of them civilians, had died in Syria's indiscriminate bombardment and the Syrians suffered for their own intransigence. A surgeon at the Barbir hospital in west Beirut admitted privately that more than 120 Syrian soldiers had died under his care alone during the fighting.

A crowd of Phalangist militiamen, one of them wearing a black cowboy hat, allowed us to pick our way down the boulevard that led to the Rizk tower where the Syrians had been surrounded by the Christians for four weeks. A group of unshaven, tired and unsmiling Syrian paratroopers were loading hundreds of boxes of ammunition onto army lorries and piling dirty bedding in the road. Several soldiers gingerly emerged from the building with a series of large, evil-smelling sacks which were placed without much ceremony aboard the trucks. Presumably their contents would be buried in Syrian soil.

These were strange times for the Lebanese, months in which political patterns merged and then parted as if in a kaleidoscope, the symmetry of each new act of hostility, of threat and settlement, fused into a new dimension. This evolution was somehow made more acceptable by the radio voices which competed for the attention of the Lebanese. Beirutis had only to twist the medium wave dial on their transistors to hear the brassy Hollywood theme music of *Quo Vadis*, that creaky religious epic of the 1950s which converted Robert Taylor into a Christian along the Appian Way. The same music which once ushered the heroic Taylor into the forum of ancient Rome had been stolen by the Phalange, whose 'Voice of Lebanon' expounded an exclusively Maronite version of the daily news to its Christian listeners. Across the city in Corniche Mazraa, listeners who tuned to 240 metres medium wave were hourly blasted by the music of 'Allah Akhbar', the old Nasserite marching song of the 1967 Arab−Israeli war. It was the signal for another anti-isolationist news bulletin from the 'Voice of Arab Lebanon.'

Napoleon once said that he feared three newspapers more than one hundred thousand bayonets. The Beirut censors still mutilated the copy in the Beirut papers, but they could not control the radios, and Sarkis had reason to fear four of the illegal Lebanese stations more than all the surviving militias in Beirut. For while the civil war sputtered on only intermittently, the radio war was as vituperative, biased and venomous as ever. The four stations, which also included the Christian 'Voice of Unified Lebanon' and Bashir Gemayel's 'Voice of Free Lebanon', were factually unreliable and totally illegal. They would later be joined by the Druze 'Voice of the Mountain' and other broadcasting outlets.

On the Phalangist station, disc jockeys played pop records newly imported from Paris, interrupting their programmes for open-line telephone discussions with listeners. There was even a grotesque mutation of the BBC's 'Any Questions' programme in which the iniquities of leftists, communists and their fellow travellers were damned in bloodthirsty terms. Every day, 'Gemayel's daily disc' − a ten-minute lecture

on the integrity of Lebanon by Sheikh Pierre, the father of the Phalange –
would be transmitted. The 'Voice of Arab Lebanon' provided a mixture
of pan-Arab sentiment and invective against the 'isolationist – Zionist
conspiracy', longhand for the Israeli – Maronite alliance. To commemorate Nasser's revolution – an event which still served, so listeners were
informed, to 'bind Lebanon to the Arab nation' – only Arab music was
played.

Bashir Gemayel's 'Voice of Free Lebanon' occasionally transmitted
his military communiqués, always played French martial music and
often promised to rid Lebanon of 'aliens', an expression which certainly
included all Palestinians and possibly all Lebanese leftists as well. The
stations could appear harmless enough with their popular music and
'doctor's advice' spots, but during street battles – if they were not
shelled off the air – they would broadcast vivid descriptions of the
'animal' behaviour of their opponents. During the Christian – Syrian
fighting, Bashir Gemayel's broadcasts repeatedly spoke of pan-Arab
plans for a massacre of Christians. Their casualty claim of 1,500 dead
Maronites proved to be more than double the true figure.

The Lebanese government had only itself to blame for these illegal
stations. Beirut's official radio was heavily censored; sectarian killings
and ceasefire violations went unreported. Demands for the closure of the
private transmitters were met by the Phalangists with declarations that
they possessed a legal broadcasting licence, issued years before by a left-
wing government minister. Ibrahim Koleilat, the Mourabitoun commander, claimed that his station could not be categorised as private
since it belonged to the 'masses'.

In the wreckage of central Beirut that autumn of 1978, as many as 15
civilians were killed in a series of nightly artillery battles which started
when two rival militias attempted to loot the same ruined office block.
One Sunday night, a group of Phalangists crossed Beshara al-Khoury
Street intent on taking desks, typewriters and other equipment from the
office showroom. They literally walked into a gang of Saiqa guerrillas
who were emptying the contents of the building. Both Phalangists and
Saiqa called for artillery support before wiping each other out in a gun
battle inside the ruins. The subsequent bombardment continued for
several nights, killing the civilians.

Throughout this period, the small foreign community in Beirut remained comparatively unaffected. The British Embassy held its annual
Christmas carol service in the ambassador's Levantine residence in
Kantari. In Ein al-Mreisse, the Norwegian Embassy staff dispensed
champagne to Sunni politicians, PLO officials, Lebanese and foreign
journalists, economists, academics from the American University and to
a multitude of beautiful Lebanese women. A foreigner newly arrived in

Beirut might be frightened of the sound of gunfire or upset by the militia checkpoints near his home. But he would not feel personally threatened. Not yet.

The signs of failing international confidence in Lebanon were there nonetheless. At the end of 1978, the British Foreign Office decided to close its Arabic language school at Shemlan, an *alma mater* and second home to a generation of British ambassadors and spies. The Middle East Centre for Arabic Studies had been an honourable contribution to Arab learning even if one of its students was among the most prominent of British traitors. When I visited Shemlan that cold autumn, I found that Kim Philby was still remembered in the village as a friendly man of great charm whose atrocious Arabic had been further marred by a severe stutter. While Philby was only a visitor to the school, it was that other spy, George Blake, who really gave Shemlan its bad name. For Blake was a full-time student at the school with diplomatic status. He apparently spent part of his career there under the eyes of the British secret service, the Lebanese deuxième bureau and several other Arab security organs.

Julian Walker, the last Foreign Office director at Shemlan, who did not know Blake, suggested that the spy spoke poor Arabic, was only a temporary student and was probably farmed out to Shemlan by the Foreign Office because he was already under suspicion. This, however, had not prevented Kamal Jumblatt from regularly demanding the closure of what he called the 'spy school' at Shemlan. Whenever in the coming days I derided the idea that foreigners in Lebanon were secret agents, I would always be reminded of the two Britons — one a journalist and the other a diplomat — who very definitely were spies.

The British had tried to maintain the veneer of civilised life up at Shemlan. The notice-board still carried stern instructions on the 'correct manner' of dress upon which its former director, Sir Donald Maitland, had insisted. In one of the empty classrooms overlooking the sea, a pile of photographs which had curled in the sun showed how Her Majesty's servants relaxed in their salad days. There they were, the future Arabists of the Foreign Office, in stiff collars and bow-ties, waltzing around dance floors or at table, their faces young but already wearing an expression of diplomatic concern, in earnest conversation with vivacious ladies.

Beirut was still not an intrinsically dangerous place for visitors, although foreign diplomats were advised to stay away from the Palestinian camps. When Cyrus Vance, President Carter's secretary of state, visited the city in the autumn of 1977 to hear the Lebanese government's views on the future of the Palestinians, his motorcade back to the airport took a long, circuitous route that added an extra mile to the journey. His diversion, the US Embassy said later, had avoided the security risks of driving in the vicinity of the slums of Sabra and Chatila. Vance had succeeded in bypassing the very people whose future he had come to the Middle East to discuss.

The banality of the rhetoric with which the PLO in Lebanon denounced the subsequent Camp David accord misled us, made it almost possible to forget the volcanic anger that lay there, just beneath the crust. I remember watching a Palestinian in Beirut in September of 1978 as he read an Associated Press report coming over the wire from Tel Aviv. 'The great unresolved issue of the Camp David Mid-East summit,' the AP correspondent in Israel had written, 'is the future of about one hundred Jewish settlements on occupied Arab land.' The Palestinian looked at this sentence for some seconds, nodding at the sheet of paper in a confirmatory way. Then his face became contorted with anger. 'Who do the Americans think we are?' he exploded. 'Why don't they just say what they mean — that the least important question is the fate of two million Palestinian refugees?'

The Palestinians of Lebanon had reason to be worried. The more they studied the Camp David agreement, the more treacherous it appeared to be. What was to happen to the Palestinians of Lebanon? What role would *they* have in deciding their own future? Was southern Lebanon supposed to be the new Palestine for them? And if Israel was as expansionist as Assad and the PLO repeatedly claimed, where would it strike next? The Egyptian army had been neutered by the Camp David accord and the Americans and Israelis were trying to entice King Husain to enter negotiations, so where better for the Israeli army to concentrate its strength than against its enemies in Syria and Lebanon? Attacking Syria could be a costly affair. But Lebanon was a soft underbelly, a 'confrontation' state without a government, a divided house whose feuding tribes could be turned into enemies or allies.

Southern Lebanon became a catalyst, a hot, treacherous place of unexpected death and savage retaliation. Yet it was also a nirvana made all the more credible by the presence of the international army which had settled itself across the scrubland and hills between the sea and Mount Hermon. Ibl al-Saqi, that dangerous little village from which Abu Meyad had pointed out the Israeli tanks to me in 1977, was now transformed into the Norwegian battalion headquarters with an officers' mess, a library of Norwegian books and a sauna. Palestinian and Israeli shells passed literally over the heads of the Norwegian soldiers who occupied the village.

In May of 1980, the PLO regularly fired at Haddad's toytown 'capital' of Marjayoun. I spent one morning sitting with the Norwegians in the dusty square at Ibl al-Saqi as they watched the bombardment, viewing it much as they might have observed a remote ski competition or a sailing regatta. Small clouds of blue-grey smoke drifted lazily up from the red roofs of Marjayoun followed two seconds later by the distant sound of explosions. The Norwegians viewed it dispassionately, hands on hips, blue berets at a rakish angle, rifles slung nonchalantly over their shoulders.

All day it went on. At dusk, a reggae band from the newly arrived Ghanaian UN troops – who were to take up positions to the west of the Norwegians – tuned up their instruments next to the ruined church. For the children of Ibl al-Saqi, a Norwegian soldier produced an old-fashioned projector and began beaming Woody Woodpecker films onto the wall of a smashed house. On the roof of the officers' mess, a Nepalese colonel insisted on explaining to me how King Birendra's environmental wisdom had saved the architecture of old Kathmandu. Just to the north, three flares rose majestically as a Norwegian platoon tried to find a group of Palestinian infiltrators near the Hasbani River. A fire was still burning in Marjayoun.

The Norwegians had become dangerously addicted to Haddad's radio station, the 'Voice of Hope'. It was funded by an American hot-gospel religious foundation and emitted, in English and Arabic, a series of Biblical readings, country and western music and savage threats against the UN and the local Muslim population. An officer turned on the radio. 'My son,' came an American voice, 'give me thine heart and let thine eyes obscure my ways. For a whore is a deep ditch and a strange woman is a narrow pit.' What on earth did this mean? To whom was it addressed? To everyone, even the Norwegians. Why, Haddad had even obtained – from the Israelis, no doubt – a selection of Norwegian pop songs to entertain his local UN battalion.

Driving through southern Lebanon, we would listen to Haddad's radio in the car. An angry outburst from the major against the population of a village whom he accused of sheltering 'terrorists' would bring a gale of shells onto the nearest roads. It was essential listening. When the results of Ronald Reagan's first presidential election victory were announced, I was in the village of Qana, which was under the control of the UN's Fijian battalion. That morning, however, a different mood manifested itself over the air-waves. A few Biblical home truths were imparted ('For the drunken and glutton shall come to poverty, and drowsiness shall clothe a man with rags') and there were several reminders of filial duty which presumably appealed to Haddad the family man ('Hearken unto thy father that begat thee and despise not thy mother when she is old'). A mid-Atlantic voice announced a song. But there was no song.

Over the air came the sound of a door, a wooden door creaking slowly open. 'But wait a moment,' the announcer interrupted. There was a metallic sound as someone bumped into a microphone. The announcer's voice became hushed, awed. 'Ladies and gentlemen, today we have a special privilege for you. Major Haddad himself has just come into our studio . . .' A long pause. I looked out of the car window to the nearest UN post where two Fijians and a French officer were bent over their own radio, a look of almost palpable distress on their faces. Then Haddad, husky, roaring his words over the air. 'President Reagan. Congratulations. We welcome President Reagan to be president of America. America is our friend.' The UN soldiers turned off their radio, relaxed, grinning at each other. Safe for another day. Haddad was happy, was he not? Did he not *sound* happy?

There was something mesmeric about it all. Admirers of Coppola's Vietnam epic *Apocalypse Now* would have understood it well. The distant, burning town, the reggae band, the flares, Woody Woodpecker and this constant, monstrous radio station. The scenes were dreamlike, difficult to recall in sequence because of their gentle absurdity, impossible to forget because they epitomised so cruelly the impotence of the United Nations' crippled mission to Lebanon.

There were those who said that, given a little more political good will from the parties concerned, the United Nations would be able to move south to the Israeli–Lebanese frontier. They talked of tampering with the mandate, changing the emphasis from peace-keeping to peace-enforcement, ignoring the unpleasant truth that UN soldiers were in no strength to fight a pitched battle with Lebanon's private armies. Even more ignobly, UN officials outside Lebanon would point to the little United Nations flags that dotted the Lebanese Christian enclave on their maps. In one sense the UN were already in the enclave, they would tell you. But they did not say that the flags marked only isolated UN positions in which the Norwegian and Dutch troops were hostages to Major Haddad's gunmen.

And one had only to visit the UN units to understand the morose effect that the major's threats had upon UNIFIL. Within minutes of arrival at any battalion headquarters, an officer would be anxious to convey news of Haddad's latest intimidation. There followed one of a familiar series of warnings: that Haddad's gunners would shell a village if the Palestinians who were allegedly there did not leave it; that Haddad's men would kill another Irish soldier if his militia were harassed; that his artillery would destroy some mountain hamlet in UN territory if the local authorities did not return his water supply and let him take a bath. *Take a bath.*

These threats, however unreasonable – even crazy – created within the UN army in Lebanon an unhealthy obsession with Haddad's every personal mood. For the UN soldiers, Haddad had become King Lear, threatening the terrors of the earth from his little Ruritania, a hobgoblin monarch whose voice – when it came deep and booming over the United Nations' radio telephones – was greeted with moments of stunned silence by the young officers in the operations room. Major Haddad was of course no sprite; nor was he as insane as his detractors believed. The danger he represented lay not so much in his own militia, killers though they had proved to be, but in his Israeli mentors. And there lay the mystery of UNIFIL.

For no one in UNIFIL would claim to have any idea why the Israelis permitted Haddad to harass the UN lines. What, for example, was Lieutenant-Colonel Yoram Hamizrahi of Israeli military intelligence doing all the time in the south Lebanese village of Bent Jbail? Why was Lieutenant-Colonel Gary Gal of the Israeli army so frequently liaising with Haddad's gunmen in the Lebanese Christian enclave? And what was the shadowy figure of Major Haim – one of the most feared Israeli Shin Bet operatives – doing so often in Marjayoun?

Even when the Lebanese army sent a battalion to southern Lebanon to supoort UNIFIL, the Israelis allowed their Christian militia to shell it. Yet were these Lebanese soldiers not the representatives of the sovereign government whose authority was supposed to extend all the way to the Lebanese – Israeli border? Israel had itself agreed to the original UN mandate which called for the restoration of this sovereignty, which would – in theory – have put an end to Palestinian incursions into Israel.

The UN quickly discovered that the Israelis were physically present at Haddad's artillery positions during bombardments, presumably to help the militiamen with their coordinates. Cynicism replaced pride. 'I got a call from an Israeli officer over the radio,' a Dutch officer in Haris told me. 'He wanted to warn me that the Christians were likely to fire in our direction. He wanted me to know that it wouldn't be Israel's fault because they were trying to warn us. The Israeli came on the radio, made his excuses and shouted: "The Christians are going to fire in about six seconds–five–four–three–two–one." And a couple of seconds later, shells started landing behind the United Nations lines. How was he so accurate? He wanted me to know he was next to the artillery battery. He was doing the shooting.'

Major-General Erskine repeatedly expressed his astonishment at Israel's continued support of Haddad's gunmen but members of Erskine's head-quarters staff took a less sanguine view. They recalled that an old Zionist plan submitted to the 1919 peace conference at Versailles showed a proposed Israeli state running almost as far north as the Lebanese city of Sidon. They believed that the Israelis wanted instability in southern Lebanon and theorised that the Israeli army's Northern Command in Galilee wanted to re-occupy the area. And they nursed still darker suspicions that had their genesis in the murder by Haddad's men of two young Irish UN soldiers in April of 1980.

Privates Derek Smallhorn, Thomas Barrett and John O'Mahony were escorting two UN observers on 18 April inside Haddad's enclave. They were ambushed by Christian gunmen and taken to Bent Jbail where Smallhorn and Barrett were beaten up. O'Mahony was shot in the back, thigh and foot, but managed to escape. One of the UN observers – an American army officer – and an Associated Press correspondent who was travelling with the group later saw Smallhorn and Barrett, white-faced with fear, being bundled into a car and driven away to an unknown destination. About an hour later, both men were murdered with a single shot in the back of the neck. The assassinations took place inside Haddad's zone, in an area controlled by the Israelis.

Almost at once, the Israelis denied any knowledge of the killings. Haddad said that he had not ordered the murders which, he claimed, had been committed in revenge for the fatal shooting by UN troops of a militiaman at the village of At-Tiri. An immediate investigation by the United Nations and by the Garda Siochana, the Irish police force, concluded that the executions had been carried out by two brothers of the dead man – whose name was Barzi and who lived in the village of Blida. The Israelis did not make these two men available for interview. Israel, the self-declared scourge of 'terrorists', felt itself unable to condemn *these* men as 'terrorists'; indeed, it later assisted both of them to leave Lebanon – via Israel – to take up residence in Detroit. What infuriated officers of the Irish 46th Infantry Battalion, however, was intelligence information which suggested that a Shin Bet officer had actually been present at the murders and had stood by to witness the shots being fired into the necks of Barrett and Smallhorn. All that was known of the Israeli's identity was his code name, 'Abu Shawki'. His real name has never been published.

Of much more long-term significance was the reaction of the Israeli government. Shlomo Argov, the Israeli ambassador to Britain, who was also accredited to Ireland, condemned the killings of Smallhorn and Barrett as a 'dastardly act', but in an interview on Irish radio on 20 April he petulantly lectured the Irish on their Christian duties in Lebanon. '... if you will permit me to say so,' he said, 'you sit there all so smugly up in Dublin and just pass judgement on things that are happening on the other side of the moon, on the other side of the world, without any real feel for the situation ... To be quite honest with you, I should have expected a Christian nation to have a little sensitivity for people who are trying, among other things, in addition to preserving life and limb, also to preserve themselves as Christians ... I find it really incredulous [sic] that people in Dublin, of all places, should be so insensitive to the plight of a Christian minority. What is the world coming to?'*

The Irish felt that Argov had accused the wrong party of insensitivity,

* Shlomo Argov interviewed by Shane Kenny on Radio Telefis Eireann, Dublin 20 April 1980.

particularly when the ambassador asserted that Israel had lent its support to Haddad because he was 'a gentleman who is trying to prevent genocide from being inflicted on his people'. Only two days earlier, gunmen working for this 'gentleman' — militiamen who were paid, armed and uniformed by Israel — had shot dead another young Irish soldier during a battle in the village of At-Tiri. Private Stephen Griffin was only 21, and as his coffin, with his blue UN beret lying on the lid, was taken from St Joseph's church in Galway, Irish officers among the mourners spoke angrily of Israel's 'complicity' in the killings.

His grave was a long way from Lebanon. I had suggested to Charles Douglas-Home, who was then my foreign editor at *The Times*, that I should attend Griffin's funeral. It was a windy, cold, forbidding little cemetery of bleak low stone walls. His ten brothers and sisters stood around the grave and wept as the Irish army bugler played the Last Post. Far away to the west, it was just possible to see the thin white line of the Atlantic surf. But around the cemetery, the hills were broken up with great grey boulders that ran in lines towards the sea. When the sun shone briefly through the low clouds, they might almost have been the hills of southern Lebanon.

The Irish ambassador to Greece, who was accredited to Israel, demanded an explanation for the murders of Smallhorn and Barrett from Menachem Begin, the Israeli prime minister. Instead of an explanation, he was treated to another lecture, this time on the principles of the blood feud which — according to Begin — governed the militias of Lebanon. Did the ambassador not realise that the death of a Lebanese militiaman was likely to result in a revenge killing against the dead man's enemies? Two years later, faced with accusations of responsibility for a militia massacre on a vast scale at Sabra and Chatila, Begin would forget this little homily and claim that he could never have foreseen that Israel's Lebanese allies would participate in a blood feud.

Nor did the murders of Smallhorn and Barrett produce much sympathy for the Irish in Israel itself. In early May 1980, the *Jerusalem Post* carried a long article on Irish attitudes towards the Jews, recalling a 1905 Limerick pogrom in which a Jew was killed, and the brief popularity of the Irish Blueshirts — the Irish equivalent of the Nazi Brownshirts — in the years before the Second World War. The Lebanese Phalange and their Brownshirt past were not mentioned. In the Second World War, the article claimed, Ireland had been 'a hive of German espionage activity'. While this allegation had long ago been disproven, the *Jerusalem Post* accurately reminded its readers of Eamon de Valera's 1945 offer of condolence to the German envoy in Dublin on the death of Hitler.

The important paragraph, however, came towards the end. 'The pro-Palestinian bias of the ordinary soldiers in Ireland's UN force has been no secret.' it stated. 'The Irish press has repeatedly carried accounts of the identification that Ireland's UNIFIL men feel with those they believe to be sons of the soil, similar to themselves, only uprooted from their land by Israel.' The paper concluded that the Vatican wanted 'an internationalised Jerusalem' and could therefore be 'sure of particularly warm support from devoutly Catholic Ireland'.

An examination of Irish newspapers of this period proves only that Irish troops expressed their sympathy with the *Lebanese* — not the Palestinians — whom they were trying to protect from Haddad's wrath. But what had really angered the Israeli government was a statement made in Bahrain in February of 1980 by the Irish foreign minister, Brian Lenihan, acknowledging 'the role of the Palestine Liberation Organisation in representing the Palestinian people'. The Palestinians, he said, had the right to self-determination and to the establishment of an independent state in Palestine. From that moment, the Irish had been singled out for vilification by the Israelis. Journalists working out of Jerusalem were treated to long and supposedly humorous discourses on the whiskey-drinking Irish, or the 'Johnny Walker Irish' as the Israelis and their militia allies dubbed the UN battalion, with scant regard for geography.

Haddad himself dispatched a letter to *The Times* — a letter which he later admitted to me had been written by an Israeli liaison officer — in which he protested at the killing of 'a Lebanese boy of 15' (the dead militiaman) and stated that he had personally saved the lives of Irish soldiers who had been 'threatened with death' by relatives of the dead man. He accused the official UN spokesman of being a Palestinian — he was in fact Turkish — and signed himself 'Commander of Free Lebanon'. *The Times* published the letter, also allowing Haddad to give his address as 'Free Lebanon', a place which existed only in the imagination of the Israeli government press office. In a separate letter — which was at least the work of the man who sent it — Argov condemned my 'tendentious journalism', which he summarised as a collection of 'malicious insinuations' and 'barrack-room gossip'.* The vituperative nature of this correspondence was important. To report what UN officers suspected — in itself a matter of the gravest importance in any investigation of events in southern Lebanon — was to invite personal condemnation and reproach from Israel. Merely to suggest that the Israelis were behaving deceitfully in their relations with the United Nations — which their publicly acknowledged military support for Haddad more than adequately proved —

---

* See *The Times* of 3 and 7 June 1980. In another letter in the paper, the Dutch UN battalion's officer-interpreter described how UNIFIL had been forced to negotiate with the Israelis over the disposition of Haddad's 'own' tanks. My reports, he said, were 'more accurate than any despatches I have hitherto read that dealt with the same subjects'.

was unacceptable. Reporters who did so were denounced and even accused of being anti-semitic.

The constant Israeli description of Palestinians as 'terrorists' sometimes had the desired effect. Foreign correspondents based in Israel began to use the word even when reporting on PLO activities which bore no relation to anything that could be described as terrorism. Guerrillas became 'terrorists' and thus Lebanon was 'terrorist-infested'. A close colleague of mine in Jerusalem unthinkingly used the term while being interviewed on the BBC World Service about an Israeli air raid on Lebanon. Two Palestinian friends who heard him called me on the telephone in Beirut to express their rage. 'If we are terrorists, why are Haddad's men not terrorists?' they wanted to know.

The issue was of critical importance, as we would discover in 1982. Even *The Times* failed to resist the word. In May 1980, I had written an innocuous report about the UN's problems with Palestinian guerrillas. But the headline referred to the 'UN's ironic task of keeping peace with terrorists in its territory'. At no point in my report did the word 'terrorist' appear. I wrote a memorandum to Douglas-Home, pointing out that 'when we refer to PLO guerrillas in southern Lebanon as terrorists, we are, it seems to me, automatically aligning ourselves with Israel's position.' Major Haddad's militia was then indulging in far more violence than the Palestinians against civilians in southern Lebanon, yet *The Times* was not calling *his* gunmen 'terrorists'. If the word was to be used, it should apply to the terrorists on Israel's side as well as to Palestinian terrorists. Some days earlier, I told Douglas-Home, Israeli shells had landed less than 200 yards from my car on the main Tyre–Beirut road, but Moshe Brilliant, our stringer in Tel Aviv, had reported that day that an Israeli gunboat had shelled 'terrorist targets' in Lebanon. There was no other traffic in sight and my car, humming up the coastal highway, was presumably Brilliant's 'terrorist target'. Brilliant had not intended such an end for me. But Douglas-Home understood the point and banned the word 'terrorist' from all *Times* reports on the Middle East unless the word was used in direct speech.

None of this should have suggested that the Palestinians were playing anything but a selfish and often violent role in southern Lebanon. Their continued rocket attacks on the Christian enclave and occasionally against Israel itself were intended to provoke retaliation. On several occasions, Palestinian guerrillas had shot and killed Fijian soldiers who were trying to prevent their infiltration into the UN zone. In 1981, an Irish soldier was killed and another kidnapped, almost certainly by a PLO faction that wanted to embarrass Arafat's good relations with UNIFIL. The missing Irishman was never seen again. Fruitless inquiries by Irish diplomats in Lebanon suggested that the soldier – a farmer's son from the Aran Islands off the far west coast of Ireland – had been imprisoned in an underground cell beneath the Ein Helweh Palestinian camp at Sidon but had been killed there when an Israeli air raid destroyed the bunker. Later, the Irish army would be told that he was taken not to Sidon but to Beirut where, after months of lonely imprisonment underground, he was coldly executed just prior to the 1982 Israeli invasion.

Yet the UN's role in Lebanon was not dishonourable. The UN soldiers could — up to a point — protect the Shia villagers who lived in their zone. Perhaps because many of them came from rural backgrounds, the Norwegians and the Irish understood these people far more intimately than the Lebanese government could ever have done. The Norwegian battalion held annual dinners for the *mukhtars*, the village leaders, in their area and the officers were in no doubt of the UN's popularity. Their presence persuaded the villagers that it was safe to return home. The tobacco fields and olive groves were tended for the first time in more than four years.

In 1980, I sat with Norwegian UN officers at Ibl al-Saqi as they held a ceremonial dinner for the villagers in the makeshift officers' mess. The *mukhtar* of Ibl al-Saqi stood up to address the assembled guests in the old village house, its beams blackened with fire. There was a group of Norwegian diplomats there, together with the senior officers of the Norwegian battalion.

The old man stood a little unsteadily — this was before the days when the Shia clergy banned alcohol in their areas of southern Lebanon — but he appreciated the formality of the occasion. The meal was over and it was his turn to thank his Norwegian hosts. He looked towards Colonel Ole Roenning, the Norwegian battalion commander, then said softly and in Arabic: 'You are our parents and we are your children.' There were a few moments of silence and then a burst of applause from the other *mukhtars*. It had been a genuine, moving sentiment from the traditional village elder of Ibl al-Saqi's 200 men and women. The obligation was a difficult one to accept. What if the parents were forced by circumstances to abandon their responsibilities? It was better not to reply at all. Colonel Roenning, a balding man with a head like an eagle and with sharp, watchful eyes, beamed back at the old man and ordered that the glasses of aquavit be refilled.

Inevitably, the private army which so assiduously tried to damage the UN's cause came to be hated by the United Nations soldiers. Haddad's men began to encroach into the UN zone, not to infiltrate like the Palestinians but to set up military positions actually inside the UN's area of operations. It was a flagrant breach of all the agreements between the UN and the Israelis and it served only to undermine the morale and authority of the United Nations. The UN attempted to talk its way out of each crisis; but in Lebanon, compromise proved to be an untrustworthy weapon. It was perceived as a sign of weakness; which, in a way, it was.

Rashaf was as good a place as any to discover this. Like so many strategic villages in war, it was deserted. The place was in ruins, its houses and villas crumpled in on themselves since the Israeli air force raided it during the 1978 invasion. Except for the occasional foot patrol of Irish UN soldiers, the rubble had until May of 1980 been left to the lizards and the three-foot snakes that lay sunning themselves on the hot, broken tarmac of the country lanes. Not any more, however.

For in the spring of 1980, the Israelis helped Haddad's militia to build a road to the ruins. The militia then drove an Israeli-supplied Sherman tank up this road and parked it in the wreckage of the village. Rashaf was on a hill, a soft green hog's back of wild flowers and long grass from which it was just possible to see both the Irish battalion headquarters at Tibnin and the Dutch battalion headquarters at Haris. When the Sherman first appeared, the Irish noticed that its barrel was pointing towards Tibnin. Every few days, its crew would traverse the barrel towards Haris. And every few weeks, it would fire off a shell or two towards the UN compounds.

From time to time, I would visit the base of this little hill and sit with the Irish troops on the opposite, lower ridge to the north. They would show me their military maps, great laminated charts with the contours of southern Lebanon twisting in ever-decreasing circles like snailshells, the lines coiled so thickly into the wadis and climbing so sharply up the stony bluffs above them that Lebanon itself seemed to have been obscured. Yet the maps were as lamentable as Haddad's incursions. They showed the UN front line as a thick blue cordon running at least a mile *south* of Rashaf, south of the village of At-Tiri, and almost two miles south of the hamlet of Beit Yahoun.

Haddad now had his men on the edge of At-Tiri and another tank on the *northern* side of Beit Yahoun, having inexplicably also acquired permission to drive his military vehicles through two Irish UN checkpoints. And, of course, he now had Rashaf. When I asked the United Nations why their maps were so misleading, I was told that the thick blue line marked the southernmost point of United Nations operations, not the northernmost positions of Major Haddad's militia. But the lost ground − like the whole southern Lebanese Christian enclave of which the United Nations failed to take control − was no longer an operational area. It was effectively closed to UN troops. The maps were lying. And which Irish troops would attempt to prove them wrong by entering the enclave, now that Begin himself had warned that a 'blood feud' had been initiated against them?

Soul-searching was not one of the UN's strong points. General Erskine would let me travel with him as he toured the UN zone in southern Lebanon and it was easy to see how uncomfortable truths could be accommodated, how mandates could be discussed rather than fulfilled. Peace-keeping in southern Lebanon was about Making the Best of a Bad Job, the doctrine of the Brave Face. Sometimes the truth was only evident at the end of the journey.

I watched Erskine one spring day as he visited his Dutch battalion. It was a fine morning. Two companies of troops had paraded in their blue berets on the village square at Haris and Erskine inspected the soldiers while an elderly gramophone cranked out some tinny martial music. In the midday heat, a Dutch soldier had collapsed, his rifle clattering beside him. There was orange juice in the mess, a minute's car ride to the chopper pad, a salute to the Dutch commanding officer and Erskine climbed nimbly into his vibrating Bell helicopter, settling himself like a cat in the window seat, his tall frame bent towards the Perspex, his general's baton beside him.

Helicopters provide their occupants with an Olympian view of reality, and the general stared down at the folded hills of southern Lebanon, sheathed in stones and boulders, each topped by a shabby village and a minaret and a small United Nations post. Ten minutes later, the helicopter was over the coast, crossing the neat lines of olive groves beside the tough little French logistics unit. The UN headquarters at Naqqoura was due south, scarcely three miles away. But then the general's helicopter flew out to sea.

Indeed, it flew almost a mile out over the Mediterranean before the pilot turned the machine south and raced down to Naqqoura just above the waves. The tiny strip of land between the French and Naqqoura was controlled by Haddad's militia, who liked to shoot at helicopters. So the general was forced to take a circuitous flight path every time he returned to his base. Naqqoura was cut off as surely as any fortress can be amputated from its supporting army. Erskine would remain unmoved by this. He would sit in his office and play with the themes of peace-keeping. 'Changing our mandate to that of peace-enforcement,' he said one evening, 'would need the concurrence of the contributing nations and in the sort of situation in which we find ourselves here, I feel that any change to that effect would be counter-productive ...'

As Erskine spoke, there was a rumble of heavy artillery fire from outside the window of his office followed by the sound of detonations. He briefly asked an aide to find out what was happening. 'Even now our present posture may not be fully satisfactory ... we have the better of two evils. This is a very difficult, complex political issue and in the interests of our mission, of the United Nations, of the governments in the area, some serious efforts should be made to find a political solution to it.' This was the stuff of Lebanon. Unsatisfactory postures, complex political issues, possible solutions. Erskine was trapped. There was another roar of gunfire outside, louder this time, and the window began to rattle with the blast.

The general's dapper young ADC came into the room. 'Tyre is taking a hammering, Sir,' he said. So the general walked through his outer office, through his kitchen, and the three of us stood on the cramped balcony above the Mediterranean, watching the ancient Alexandrian city of Tyre come under shellfire from Israeli and militia artillery.

Erskine contemplated the flares for a time, candelabras of fire that dripped into the Mediterranean, lighting up the beach and the nearby hills and the faces of the operations room officers as they crunched across the gravel below us. 'People will start evacuating Tyre tonight,' the general said. But of course there was nothing he could do. It was an oft heard truism that Naqqoura was a prisoner of Haddad and the Israelis, just as the United Nations was a prisoner of Lebanon.

6 Let Them Come!

You cannot say that things will get worse now, or
tomorrow, or next week. But one day there must be a
resolution. Sooner or later, we will have to fight a war of
liberation.

Bashir Gemayel *10 August 1980*

In Beirut, they said the cedars of Lebanon were dying. In that winter of
1980 it was suggested that the trees, some of them 1,500 years old,
might have succumbed to a virus, might now be as incurably ill as the
body politic of the nation for which they had so long been a symbol.

Lamartine had called the cedars 'the most famous natural monuments
in the world', but like a schoolboy he could not resist carving his name
on one massive trunk. In Biblical times, an immense forest of these trees
lay across Mount Lebanon, the Cedars of the Lord which were used to
build the Temple of Jerusalem. Only at Bsharre and on the heights of
Barouk above the Chouf mountains did a few of the very ancient trees
remain. The Lebanese Ministry of Agriculture claimed it had discovered
a grey mould on the Bsharre trees and there was talk of giving the trees
an injection of chemicals. But the old guidebooks said that there were
also cedars clustered around a ravine high above Masser es Chouf. The
tourist buses that used to go there had long ago been used as street
barricades in Beirut: the guides had departed.

Christmas of 1980 was cold and the first snow had appeared on
Sannine. The highway south of Beirut was misted in sea spray; dark
clouds covered the roads in the lower Chouf. There had been flooding
near the deserted palace of the Emir Bashir at Beit Eddine. But near the
village of Barouk high in the Lebanon range, we caught just a glimpse
of something, a dark smudge of green on the bare, cold hills 6,000 feet
above sea level. There were three rusting signposts beside the main
road, each directing its complement of ghostly tourists towards the
cedars. Up one lane, three rotting huts – once serving beer to holidaymakers – stood forlornly beside a small forest, crude paintings of cedar
trees inscribed upon their damp walls. The grove here contained a few
young cedars, some brown with death, but the real cedars, as the
villagers told us without much enthusiasm, were much higher up the
mountains, almost inaccessible to visitors.

They were right about the height but wrong about the inaccessibility. Just outside Masser es Chouf, a village of impeccable Druze antecedents whose noble houses spoke of a more profitable and bygone age, a number of young men guarded a roadblock. They wore the khaki and green uniform of Jumblatt's militia and held automatic weapons. They shook their wrist at us by way of enquiry. We wanted to see the cedars of Lebanon. They smiled faintly and waved us through. A narrow road led upwards from their checkpoint, snaking past hilltop vineyards and neglected orange groves, turning back on itself up into the rocks of the Barouk mountains. After 1,000 feet, there were potholes and the road thinned to the width of a single vehicle. Hairpin bends built by long-dead French construction gangs had left their own toll of broken cars on the slopes beneath.

After 3,000 feet, the trees had vanished, although high above it was just possible to make out that smudge of green, a thick cluster of undergrowth clinging to the mountain top. The guidebook said that the last 2,000 feet had to be negotiated by mule track, but the old road snaked on upwards. At 4,500 feet, it was growing so cold that there were patches of frost and ice on the rocks. There was another militiaman to pass but he seemed out of touch, an old man with a stubble beard and a hard, lined face. He stood beside the road, his coat scarcely keeping the wind from his bones, his rifle lying on the stones beside him. He was more interested in gathering old wood for his winter fire, piling it into the boot of a battered white car. 'The cedars?' he asked, peering through the car window at us. He said nothing, but pointed upwards.

At 5,000 feet, the unmaintained road had broken apart after five civil war winters of ice and snow. Our car moved slowly, squeaking and bumping over big stones. The air was getting rarer and the steering column of the car increasingly hard to turn. I was out of breath. At over 5,900 feet, the track turned on itself again, the wheels of the car sending stones clicking and skidding down the ravine to the left and there, just on the skyline, was a thick, dark green canopy, appearing almost man-made. The road twisted once more and we were surrounded by the cedars.

They were neither sick nor dying. Their trunks were gnarled by centuries of wind, but their branches were firm, thick with age, waving slowly and hypnotically in the frozen breeze. The wind hissed and thrashed through them as if it was alive. To the south, above the cloud line, the mountains stretched away into what was once Phoenicia and Palestine, to the ancient kingdom of Syria in the east. One might still have built a temple of the trees, high above the cities and militias of Lebanon, where there were no gunmen, no *zaim*, no armies, mandates or covenants. The cedars, Lamartine suspected, 'know the history of the earth better than history itself.' If this was so, it was little wonder that they had clung to life only here, up in these high altitudes where the mountains, ice and wind ensured that the Lebanese who so often took the name of the cedars in vain would rarely appear.

If these trees had spirits, they could scarcely have experienced affection for those who claimed to be inspired by their eternal presence. The cedar, which had been used as the emblem of Lebanon – sandwiched uncomfortably between the inverted red and white tricolour of the Lebanese flag, stamped onto passports and work permits, painted onto the tails of the national airline's ageing fleet of Boeing 707s – had been purloined, transformed and corrupted by the militias. In west Beirut, the trees drooped on the party banners, their branches weighed down by the frost of hopeless political demands. For its insignia in the east of the city, the Phalange squeezed the great tree into a triangle, a simple mathematical formula in which all the ruggedness and creaking wood had been destroyed, a triangle within a circle, a symbol without life.

Only because they were both exploited and neglected did the cedars now provide a true symbol – disturbing and ironic – of the country in which they had their roots. Up at Bsharre some months later, a woman in a store offered me an ashtray of cedarwood. 'We are only allowed to make these from the dead branches that have fallen from the trees,' she said. 'It is against the law to damage the trees.' Yet even here the law was flouted. A few minutes later, amid the snow that lay around the cedar grove, I watched a group of young men systematically tearing the lowest branches from a massive cedar. 'You have your Lebanon and I have mine,' Khalil Gibran had written. 'Yours is political Lebanon and her problems; mine is natural Lebanon in all her beauty.' No longer. Gibran's grave lay less than a mile from the Bsharre cedar grove.

How strange that for a journalist living in Beirut at the turn of that decade, Lebanon could provide a sense of balance, an equilibrium that outsiders would never understand. For a Middle East correspondent reporting the upheavals in the remainder of the Arab world, in non-Arab Iran and Afghanistan as well as in Lebanon, the chaos and anarchy of Beirut possessed a special internal stability of its own. As the fault lines running through the country became more familiar, so one became less of a foreigner. It was as if an eccentric, even dangerous acquaintance had assumed characteristics that we eventually found endearing, even lovable. The more we learned in Beirut, the safer we felt; and thus we became more vulnerable.

It was not as if the physical dangers lay only in Lebanon; nor could there be any doubting the epic scale of the events going on outside its frontiers. When *The Times* closed down for 11 months in 1979, I spent weeks reporting the Iranian revolution for Canadian radio. How could one compare one of the great developments of twentieth-century history with Lebanon's little wars? I watched Ayatollah Khomeini one day – I sat a few feet from him – lecturing us on the evils of America, the necessity of returning the Shah to Iran for trial and the eternal nature of the Islamic Republic. He stared at the floor as he spoke. Only at the ground; at a tiny spot of light that fell onto the poorly carpeted floor of this crowded room at his home in Qom. Not once did he take his eyes off the emanation. It must have been produced by a crack in the window or a reflection from a mirror, but it was half an hour before it dawned upon us that he would not look at a single human being in the room, not even at his interpreter, Sadeq Qotbzadeh, in whose execution he would later calmly acquiesce.

Khomeini could condone the imprisonment of American diplomats in Tehran – the inhabitants of the 'spy nest' – and effortlessly prove the United States to be a paper tiger. He could shatter the self-confidence of some of the wealthiest Arab nations in the Gulf. There were no Khomeinis in Lebanon, no one with such awesome moral certainty in his own spiritual role. Nor were there revolutions on the titanic scale of Iran's. Day after day, I travelled by rail across the great deserts of Persia, to Isfahan and Shiraz and Tabriz; the windows of the carriages were broken, the compartment walls covered in posters of Khomeini. At Qom, I watched a warrant officer in the Shah's army defending himself before a religious court on charges of shooting civilians, pitifully relying on standards of justice that did not exist under the Islamic revolution. Iran's history had become a morality play in which Khomeini appeared, as heavenly, ethereal; in which the Shah's crown was held in place by two large white horns. Good and evil were juxtaposed in Iran in a simple, unarguable way. God was with Iran. America was the Great Satan.

Compared to *this*, one thought, Lebanon was stable, recognisable, a framework for one's existence. And always, we would fly back to Beirut between assignments, back to the familiar grubby airport with its shell-damaged terminal and overgrown boulevard, back to homes above the sea and picnics in the Chouf or dinner in Broumana; back to the Lebanese who could effortlessly make a telex or telephone connection to the remotest village in Ireland, who could book a flight to Kabul or arrange a weekend holiday opposite the temples of Baalbek. Their artistic taste could be impeccable or kitsch, but they were talented people in the most literal sense of the word. When I arrived in Beirut from Europe, I felt the oppressive, damp heat, saw the unkempt palm trees and smelt the Arabic coffee, the fruit stalls and the over-spiced meat. It was the beginning of the Orient. And when I flew back to Beirut from Iran, I could pick up the British papers, ask for a gin and tonic at any bar, choose a French, Italian or German restaurant for dinner. It was the beginning of the West. All things to all people, the Lebanese rarely questioned their own identity.

Pleading for seats on over-booked airliners, fighting for visas in filthy consular offices, so hot that the perspiration crept in streams through one's hair, it was easy to overlook the meaning of the events that we witnessed at such close quarters. We were, as Douglas-Home used to say, at 'the coal face', chiselling away with notebooks and Biros, searching for a symbol here, a quotation there, a form of words that captured the smell as well as the significance of an event, a small diamond buried deep in the shaft that might illuminate the history we were trying to report.

One would return to Beirut with images and impressions rather than conclusions: of a Soviet army colonel silently handing me a rifle to defend myself in the snow as Afghan guerrillas with knives surrounded a Russian army truck in the foothills of the Hindu Kush; of a young Iranian revolutionary guard standing under Iraqi shellfire at the battle of the Fish Lake in south-western Iran, his head bare to the shrapnel, holding a Koran tightly to his chest, smiling as if he had seen paradise; of an Iranian father sitting on the earth beside his son's grave in north Tehran, reading the headstone which said 'Do not weep for me father' and then watching the old man fall on top of the grave and cry uncontrollably; of a line of blindfolded Egyptian fundamentalists awaiting their turn for interrogation after Sadat's assassination, the prisoners unaware that the investigating policemen were holding razor blades; above all, of corpses. Iraqi bodies lying out in the sun at the battle of Dezful, the stench of their decomposition gusting into our helicopter; the bodies of Iranian boy soldiers outside Basra, torn in half as they ran through the minefields before the Shatt al-Arab river; of an Iraqi soldier, rotting into his sandbags in the swamps of Fao, on one finger of his black, dead hand a glistening, bright gold wedding ring.

The emerging political patterns were obvious. Sadat's death, the fall of the Shah, the Soviet invasion of Afghanistan all spoke of American weakness, of a loss of United States power and international prestige. By the same token, it was evident that the fundamentalist motivation behind Sadat's assassination, the inspiration of Khomeini's revolution, the strength of the Afghan resistance contained an even graver lesson. The new self-confidence, the emerging spirit of protest in the Islamic world — particularly within the Shia faith — would touch every nation in the region, even Lebanon.

Yet Lebanon's continued internal disintegration seemed isolated from all this, more comprehensible perhaps, certainly more consistent. And each time we returned home to Beirut, each time we queued for air connections at Dubai, Abu Dhabi, Amman or Cairo, we would feel affection for the old Lebanese 707 that moved up to the airport stand with its familiar, friendly cedar tree on the tail, thick, heavy green branches balanced on a bright brown trunk. Even when I flew back to

Lebanon to find that Bashir Gemayel had at last resolved to destroy Camille Chamoun's 'Tigers', the event appeared part of an insulated, confined war. Gemayel had grown tired of sharing Maronite power – and especially illegally acquired taxes – with Chamoun's National Liberal Party. In a 36-hour purge, the Phalange stormed into all the barracks and offices occupied by the 'Tigers', murdered several hundred civilians and then declared east Beirut 'cleansed' of the bandits who had 'terrorised' its citizens.

In west Beirut, Syrian pro-consulship had manifested itself in equally brutal form against the one institution that continued to deny the myths and lies in which the Lebanese were supposed to believe. Selim al-Lawzi was one of the most intelligent and prolific of Lebanese journalists, the author of two political novels and the founder of *Al Hawadess* magazine, whose sophistication was matched by its courage. While he was by no means popular with his journalist colleagues in Lebanon, who resented his abrasive style of writing and realised that his magazine's political reporting was often inaccurate, al-Lawzi's willingness to criticise the corrupt aspects of Syrian rule made him the subject of journalistic envy and of Syrian hatred.

He edited *Al Hawadess* from the safety of London but had made what was supposed to be a brief visit to Beirut at the beginning of 1980. On his way back to the airport on 24 February, he was kidnapped not far from a Syrian army checkpoint. On 5 March, a Lebanese shepherd came across his corpse, half preserved beneath a light covering of snow in the woods of Aramoun south of Beirut. His feet had been tied and he had been shot twice in the back of the neck. Much more horrific – and significant – were the signs of torture on his corpse. The flesh on his right hand – his writing hand – had been sloughed off with knives or burned off with acid. Here was a warning that Lebanese journalists might be expected to take to heart. Officially, he was the victim of Beirut's infamous Unidentified Gunmen. Unofficially, it was assumed that he had – like Kamal Jumblatt – paid the price for impugning the dignity of Damascus.

Nor was al-Lawzi the only press martyr. Riad Taha, the president of the Lebanese journalists' union, was also assassinated. The Lebanese government condemned these crimes, expressing ignorance as to the identity of the culprits. The funerals of both men were solemnly guarded by Syrian troops, an irony which was not lost on the mourners. But Syria's anger could also embrace the foreign press. Berndt Debussman, the Reuters bureau chief in Beirut, was the victim of an assassination attempt by two gunmen in west Beirut. At the time, the Syrian regime was suffering a series of guerrilla attacks by Muslim fundamentalists in Hama and Aleppo. On one occasion, hostile demonstrators had been shot down in the streets of Aleppo and Reuters agency carried reports out of Beirut suggesting that the disturbances were growing worse.

The thrust of these dispatches — that Assad's rule was in danger — was undoubtedly correct, although some of the reports, based upon the evidence of unidentified 'travellers from Syria', exaggerated the extent of the unrest. None of this excused the hatred with which the Syrians then privately condemned Reuters. Such persistent and untrue reports, they claimed, must be part of a conspiracy against Assad. The Plot. So the Unidentified Gunmen appeared and shot Debussman in the back. After treatment at the American University hospital — where he was guarded by Fatah guerrillas — he was flown out of Lebanon, never to return. A BBC staff reporter, Tim Llewellyn, and a British stringer working for the same news organisation later said that they too felt threatened and fled Lebanon.

It was hardly surprising that the Phalange tried to take advantage of these events. Journalists lived in west Beirut because this was the sector in which most of the embassies, the communications facilities and the international news agencies found themselves when the civil war front line took on its final, permanent form in 1976. Foreign correspondents were now invited by the Phalange to set up offices in east Beirut, an offer that was politely turned down. To stay in west Beirut might be dangerous but to move to east Beirut would be a political act. Those of us who stayed had reported the murders of al-Lawzi and Taha and suggested the probable culprits; we travelled to Aleppo to investigate the agitation against Assad's regime and filed our dispatches from west Beirut. We wrote about the gunmen who tried to kill Debussman and we waited to see what would happen next.

The first result was a publicity blitz by Gemayel. If the reporters would not flee west Beirut for the safety of Christian protection, they would at least be taken into Bashir Gemayel's confidence. Bashir no longer wished to project himself as a militia leader. Now he was a thinker, a politician, perhaps a statesman. A series of sumptuous buffet lunches were held in the hills above east Beirut, at which Gemayel could make friends with the journalists who had often portrayed him as a thug or gangster. But somehow, he was never able to shake off his former image. Some of us wondered as we made our way up the twisting mountain highway to lunch at Ain Saade if he really wanted to do so in the first place.

Looking around the sitting room, it would have been difficult to imagine a more relaxed group of luncheon guests. There in the armchair was the elderly, fragile, chain-smoking figure of Tewfiq Awad, perhaps Lebanon's most prestigious living author,* while across the high-pile

---

* Awad was to die on 16 April 1989 when a shell exploded in the home of his son-in-law, the Spanish ambassador to the Lebanon, who was also killed.

Persian rugs sat the Lebanese playwright Raymond Gebara, sipping ice-cold beer from a blue glass tankard and laughing at a stream of jokes. There were books about Japanese art on the sideboard, framed pictures of Gloucestershire villages above the staircase and records of Puccini's *Madame Butterfly*, of Schoenberg and of Beethoven's piano sonatas 30 and 31 stacked idly on a table. The only guest who looked a little out of place was the slightly paunchy figure pacing the balcony outside the french windows, staring moodily through green-tinted sun-glasses down towards the heat haze over east Beirut and the Mediterranean.

When Bashir Gemayel entered the room we all watched his every movement, and when he temporarily removed his shades, the large eyes surveyed us with the unhappy intensity of a hit-and-run victim trying to identify the man who had knocked him down. We were all guilty.

He had changed of late, his frame a little plumper than it had been when he led the Phalange militia during the civil war, his voice colder, more toneless and with a special note of disinterest when he might have been expected to show warmth or affection. His humourless gaze reflected nothing; his eyes were dead. Doll's eyes.

Perhaps this was not surprising. At 32, Bashir had emerged as leader of the most powerful private army in Christian Lebanon, a position he had consolidated with characteristic decisiveness when he ordered the slaughter of Dany Chamoun's 'Tigers'. The way Gemayel told it, this droll circumstance came to pass only because both sides had taken to using tanks in order to sort out their domestic arguments, firing rocket-launchers at each other in order to settle scores over a motoring accident or a minor territorial dispute. The 'Lebanese Forces', the hygienic title under which both militias had voluntarily combined themselves, had lost public support. If we in our cynicism, said Gemayel, wished to regard the subsequent battle as a power struggle between gangsters, well . . . and he shrugged his shoulders so expressively that we knew he did not want us to think that at all.

'The trouble was that anyone who controlled three or four tanks looked upon these weapons as a measure of his political importance,' he said. 'With three tanks, a man thought he could become a minister and that with five tanks he could become minister of agriculture – and with five tanks and five thousand men, he thought perhaps he could become minister of interior. I am talking about myself, about my brother, about Dany – about a lot of us. But for someone who had a vision of the Lebanese cause, which is six thousand years old, I did not think that we could justify our importance by the number of tanks we had in our gardens.'

Bashir Gemayel's voice continued in the same loud, expressionless monotone, only growing quieter for a moment when he admitted that he personally took the decision to 'solve' the divisions within the Christian military command – although he made no reference to the casualties of this solution. He never dropped his pretence of altruism, allowing just a hint of sadness – of the schoolmaster's 'This hurts me more than you' variety – when talking about his relations with Dany Chamoun. 'My relatiòns with him may be good but his relations with me are very bad,' he said. 'But it's not a matter of liking someone, and sooner or later Dany will realise that what was done was to his advantage and maybe to the advantage of the cause.'

Upon this note of selflessness, Bashir Gemayel repaired to lunch. Sweetmeats, skewered roast beef and salads were heaped on clay dishes and Gemayel was invited to fill his plate first. He did so enthusiastically, then turned with a small bow and handed his plate to the prettiest young woman among the guests. It was quintessential Gemayel, the chivalry of the most powerful knight in the Maronite court. He sat uneasily at a small table, the Mediterranean shimmering behind him and the occasional noise of country traffic rumbling up out of the little village of Ain Saade. The breeze came down out of the mountains and the cicadas rasped away in the olive trees. Gemayel sipped at a glass of iced water. Then suddenly, the anger showed through.

Lebanon's problems, he said, had begun when Suleiman Franjieh spoke on behalf of the Palestinians at the United Nations. Why was it that only Lebanon allowed the Palestinians to hold more power than the national army? Did the West not realise that it must stand firm against 'terrorism' and against its own enemies? 'You in the West have lost Iran,' he said, 'and soon you will lose Saudi Arabia and Kuwait ... People ask us to condemn the Israelis – but why should we? If we do that, people will want us to condemn the United States and then they will want us to condemn the Vatican. Condemnations are a sign of weakness.'

Bashir Gemayel picked up a knife from the table and began to stab a piece of bread with the tip of the blade. 'What makes you think we want a partitioned Lebanon?' he asked. 'It is the Palestinians who would like a partitioned Lebanon – already they control two thirds of the country.' Gemayel was pricking and prodding the bread until it danced on the table-top. 'You cannot say that things will get worse now, or tomorrow, or next week. But one day there must be a resolution. Sooner or later, we will have to fight a war of liberation.'

He looked around to observe the reaction to this doom-laden state-ment. There was silence, for we all knew what he meant: that the new Phalange believed they were powerful enough to drive the Palestinians from Lebanon. 'And now, there is internal dissent in Syria – what do you think is going to happen? Some people cannot say. Even now, some of you are under threat. Selim al-Lawzi was murdered and so was Riad Taha. Tim Llewellyn of the BBC has been threatened out of Beirut. But you cannot print these things ... The Lebanese government exists between four walls at Baabda palace, around a green card table. I am not a politician — because I never learnt to play cards.'

But Gemayel was in every way a politician, representing Maronite liberties under a real or imagined threat of Arab vengefulness, fighting for a minority that identified itself historically — and militarily — with the Jewish state less than a hundred miles to the south. And if the Phalangist army really did wage its war of 'liberation', it seemed clear that it was Bashir Gemayel who intended to play cards at Baabda.

Certainly Gemayel's goals were more likely to be fulfilled than those of the Palestinians whom he now seemed so intent on evicting. By late 1980, the Syrian military presence in Beirut had been corrupted; officers became involved in drug-dealing and protection rackets and large areas of the western, largely Muslim sector of the city fell once more into the hands of the Lebanese militias. Arafat's Fatah guerrillas also ran their own security police, a force that often proved more effective than the Syrian army and that did at least provide genuine protection — at a price — to some of the larger hotels in west Beirut. The Fakhani district where Yassir Arafat and the other PLO leaders maintained offices and homes had now become an extension of the Sabra camp, controlled and guarded by Fatah gunmen.

Weapons continued to pour into Lebanon. Crates of ammunition from Damascus were sent by road to southern Lebanon to nurture the growing power of the Shia Amal movement. Libyan shells were brought across the Syrian border to the Chouf mountains for Walid Jumblatt's Druze while Israeli boats moored at night off the Aquamarina just north of Jounieh to unload tank munitions for the Phalange. PLO anti-aircraft guns and ammunition arrived by air from Warsaw, sometimes packed into boxes in the cargo holds of passenger jets belonging to LOT, the Polish national airline.*

To investigate this traffic in arms and supplies was to tear away the thin fabric of political respectability with which the militias liked to surround themselves. Scarcely had I begun inquiries into the sale of German-made military trucks to the PLO in late 1980, for example, than I fell upon a story of faithless arms dealers, unexplained kidnappings near Beirut airport, a group of neo-Nazis who trained at a tumbledown castle in the German countryside and a possible link between the PLO and Gemayel's Phalange. True to the character of Lebanon, this mass of detail led to more questions than conclusions.

The affair revolved around the gloomy figure of Karl Heinz Hoffman,

---

* When Solidarity supporters among airline staff employed by LOT went on strike in 1981, they publicly complained that they had been forced to carry arms into Beirut airport on civil airliners.

the leader of the German 'Military Sport Group', whose 400 members were active in Heidelberg, Ingolstadt and Frankfurt. Hoffman's group had been banned in 1980 by Gerhard Baum, the West German interior minister, because he said it aimed at the overthrow of democracy; Hoffman was in the habit of equipping his 'sportsmen' with Second World War German helmets and jackboots in which they trooped around the grounds of a Teutonic castle near Erlangen. In short, they were not the sort of people with whom any self-respecting Lebanese militia would wish to be publicly associated.

But the Phalange – forgetting their own 1936 roots – became interested in Hoffman's activities in Beirut where, they claimed, he had been selling second-hand West German army lorries to the PLO. A Phalangist lawyer insisted to me that Hoffman and four colleagues from the 'Military Sport Group' had stayed with Fatah guerrillas in a west Beirut camp in August of 1980. According to the lawyer – whose knowledge of Hoffman's movements was remarkable given the Phalange claim that it had nothing to do with him – Hoffman travelled around Beirut in a red Leyland car bearing registration plates with the letters 'Fo-Ru'. The Phalangist said that Hoffman had told the PLO that he was fighting 'against Zionism and Judaism' and received in return a promise from the PLO that members of his 'Sport Group' could receive real-life battle training with Palestinian guerrillas in southern Lebanon.

The PLO, needless to say, denied any knowledge of Hoffman. Mahmoud Labadi, Arafat's official spokesman, said that he had heard of the German's presence in Beirut but that Hoffman was working for the Phalange in the east of the city. For their part, the Phalangists said that Hoffman had returned to west Beirut, flying into Lebanon on a Middle East Airlines flight from Zurich on 6 October 1981, in the company of his chauffeur, a man by the name of Klinger.

Diplomats at the West German embassy in Beirut at first washed their hands of the whole affair. They said that they knew nothing about any sale of second-hand army lorries to the PLO. Yet it remained a fact – and we could see this with our own eyes every time we drove around the guerrilla bases in southern Lebanon – that almost every PLO lorry on the roads of the country was a West German Mercedes military vehicle. The PLO said that the trucks could be purchased legally and that they would never deal with the likes of Hoffman. 'The most elegant, liberal, nice people come here to sell us things every day,' Labadi said softly. 'Why should we bother with a man of Hoffman's reputation?'

But someone clearly was dealing with Hoffman in Beirut. This became evident when news of a strange multiple kidnapping was broadcast by the Christian Phalangist radio station in September. According to the 'Voice of Lebanon', the four members of Hoffman's organisation who had arrived during the summer disappeared on 24 September while driving to the airport to fly home to Germany. The Phalange could even name the four men — Stephen Dupper from Karlsruhe, Peter Hamburger from Munich, Obfried Hepp from Aachen and Kep-Uwe Bergmann from Hamburg — adding that they had been staying along the old front line in the commercial district of west Beirut on 20 September when they had refused to participate in an attack against Phalangists in east Beirut.

Back copies of the Beirut daily newspapers showed that at around that date, four men called Dupper, Hamburger, Hepp and Bergmann had reported to the Lebanese police that gunmen had stolen their passports and money in central Beirut. The West German Embassy now confirmed that it had subsequently received a call from the four men, asking for new passports and money to take them home to Germany. The Federal German government privately agreed that it was aware the four had links with Hoffman, although the Embassy claimed it did not know this. The diplomats' ignorance continued while the four who had 'lost' their money spent three nights at the Commodore Hotel in Beirut after the alleged theft took place; and the Commodore Hotel was an institution known for its pecuniary finesse. One of the four spent $85 on room service.

On the morning of 24 September, the West German Embassy furnished all of them with travel papers and air tickets to Frankfurt. The four then set off for the airport — but they never reached it. Nor had they been seen since. The Phalangists, whose continuing knowledge of the affair now bordered on the miraculous, stated categorically that the four were kidnapped from their taxi by armed men travelling in two cars, a yellow Japanese saloon and a black limousine with a radio antenna. Even more amazingly, the Phalange possessed passport photographs of the four, the numbers of the Embassy travel papers which had been issued in confidence to the men on the morning of their disappearance, and details of their 'stolen' identification cards. They even knew the exact location of Hamburger's home in the Karl Marx Allee in Munich. The four men were now in the hands of the Palestinians, said the Phalange. They were in the custody of the Phalange, said the PLO. The Embassy again evinced ignorance.

In Bonn, the West German authorities were well aware of Hoffman's interest in second-hand army lorries. Members of his organisation had been turned back at the German—Austrian frontier while trying to drive Mercedes trucks across the border, vehicles apparently destined for the Middle East. But no further information was forthcoming. How did the Phalange demonstrate such extraordinary knowledge about Hoffman and the 'stolen' documents that belonged to the four men? How *did* those Mercedes army trucks reach the PLO in Beirut? Did they come from the West German army or from some other nation's armed forces? Were the four Germans really kidnapped? Or did they reach the airport and fly elsewhere on their original passports?

Several weeks later, we noticed a new fleet of Mercedes trucks on the roads of southern Lebanon, their paintwork so shiny that the Palestinians had smeared mud on the sides to prevent their identification from the air. But we also observed some new and identical vehicles in Phalangist areas north of Beirut. And word reached us that the four men had left Lebanon a month after their kidnap. The reader – as they used to say at the end of television serials – will have to make his own judgement. That was what Lebanon was like. You could amass facts, interview militia representatives, demand explanations from foreign embassies, but the moment you tried to draw a conclusion you were left with questions.

It was rather like interviewing Yassir Arafat. To arrange a meeting with him was in itself a trial of patience and journalistic commitment. Not just one but several visits to Labadi's office in Fakhani were obligatory. Why did one want to see the PLO chairman now? What did one want to talk about? A general chat about topics of current Middle East interest. Fine, Labadi would see what he could do. Beirut's crippled telephone system could make no connection to Fakhani. Another visit. Labadi is not there, just a gunman at the door and two young men reading magazines. Coffee, perhaps – or tea? Hours of waiting and Labadi would return. Yes, the request had been passed on, he would be in touch. A week later, another visit to Fakhani. Labadi would be on the telephone to his American wife. 'Robert, come in, come in. I have told the chairman of your request.' I thought you said that last time. 'Yes, yes, but I think it will be OK.' Sometimes Labadi's suggestion that Arafat would see you was like a doctor assuring a cancer patient that his tumour was benign.

Another week would pass. Then, at around ten o'clock at night, Labadi would track you down to a restaurant. 'Robert, are you free tonight? Do you remember your request?' Yes, yes, YES, I remember the request. 'Can you be at the Commodore in an hour?' At one o'clock in the morning, Labadi would bound into the lobby of the Commodore Hotel. 'Robert, are you ready?' The car would speed through the night-time Beirut streets, so fast that it was necessary to grip the seat or the door handle so as not to lose balance. Labadi would sit nervously in the back, glancing repeatedly at his watch. It was always the same: hour after squandered hour, week after week of requests, and then the PLO would discover time, so short, so pressing that for Arafat's acolytes a half minute could make the difference between favour and disgrace.

If only the Israelis had witnessed all this, could they ever again have denounced Arafat's 'well-oiled propaganda machine'? The car would clear the armed checkpoints at Fakhani, pull up at a darkened, shabby apartment block and gunmen would emerge from the shadows, youths with tense, nervous eyes and web ammunition pouches strapped to their chests. Labadi would identify himself. We had come to see the chairman; there was a smoothness that came over Labadi on such occasions. He would clasp his hands together in front of him, not deferentially but like a priest joining his fingertips at some approaching moment of reverence. He would smile at you in a powerful, slightly condescending way, the same glint of satisfaction he would adopt, no doubt, if he one day became personal private secretary to the President of Palestine. That look of ultimate sponsorship would not leave his face even when an aide showed us into a grubby office with cracked plastic seats and served tea. Yes, the chairman was a little tied up just now. But we would see him. Don't worry.

The elevator was cramped and dirty and when the door opened there was a doorway in which many people were standing. Only when we had pushed our way through did I realise how small Arafat was. A slightly plump, beady, tough little man whose *kuffiah* curled round the back of his head and the right side of his neck in a self-conscious way. I am Yassir Arafat, it declared. He touched it repeatedly, constantly readjusting its balance on his head and shoulder.

Arafat had a face that was both charming and yet somehow scandalous. He had large expressive eyes and a rough moustache. There was a slight — the very faintest — trace of Jean-Paul Belmondo, but the three-day growth of beard was disturbing. It spoke of laxity and failure, like a man who had spent the night underneath Waterloo Bridge with a gin bottle or sleeping on a subway grille on the lower East Side. Arafat did not drink and the stubble was to hide a persistent rash, but the impression was difficult to shake off. There was no youth or flamboyance. No teenager would ever pin this man's picture on a wall next to Che Guevara. There was no inspiration in the face, no power. It was easy to understand why his enemies mocked him: revolution gone to seed.

He was middle-aged, watchful, and his eyes seemed to grow larger and more agitated the longer you looked at him. They danced across Labadi's countenance and the faces of other men in the room for any hint of concern while his mouth puckered in a friendly, almost feminine way. The eyes never stopped moving or questioning your presence. What I wanted to say was: 'Mr Arafat, what big EYES you have.' But of course, what I actually said was: 'Good evening, Mr Arafat. It was very kind of you to see me.' For this was a formal business, a journalist visiting an Arab leader.

He was smiling, formally polite and insisted upon speaking English, a language upon which he was to work hard and successfully in the years to come. At that time, in 1981, he spoke it with just enough difficulty to make a visitor feel sorry for him. Labadi shrewdly realised that this could be an attractive, useful asset and thus sometimes allowed Arafat to talk away in barely comprehensible English to no apparent purpose. Labadi liked conversations with the chairman to run smoothly. He liked journalists to ask questions which were, to use his own disconcerting word, 'responsible'. It was never made clear to whom they were supposed to be responsible.

Arafat embarked on an inconsequential *tour d'horizon*. He was concerned about the situation in Afghanistan and was prepared to be a mediator if this would help to bring about a ceasefire between the Soviets and the guerrillas. He said he was astonished that Reagan had recently condemned the PLO as 'terrorists'; the PLO representative at the United Nations had been instructed to protest about this to the UN secretary general, Kurt Waldheim — who, as we were later to discover, was himself something of an expert on 'terrorism' and guerrilla warfare.

A principal theme was that of betrayal. 'I still remember what happened with Carter,' Arafat said. 'On the first day he came to power, he gave his famous slogan about "a homeland for the Palestinians". At first we said: "OK, let us wait and see." And as chairman of the PLO, I said that I appreciated what had been said. But I appreciated this too much . . . and what was the result?' Camp David had been 'a conspiracy of self-rule' and after Sadat's visit to Jerusalem, Carter's national security adviser, Zbigniew Brzezinski, had given an interview in which he had said 'Bye-bye PLO.' Arafat enjoyed repeating Brzezinski's words, spitting them out contemptuously. 'So we are not looking for what the Americans are saying now. We prefer to wait and see. I hope that the American government and the American administration [*sic*] will recognise the legal rights of the Palestinian people which have been accepted by the United Nations.'

It was at around this moment that Arafat's mood began to undergo startling changes. One moment, he would be outlining with great care and in a quiet voice his relationship with King Husain, the next almost choking with anger, shouting his condemnation of the 'terrorist military junta' that governed Israel. He gave the impression of a man caught between emotion and rhetoric, one who — had he observed his audience carefully enough — might have been able to decide which of the two would have the more productive effect. The problem was that his anger was real.

There were certain well-rehearsed lines that he had obviously polished and honed for every foreigner. 'We are four million people and we have been living in this tragedy for thirty-two years,' he said. 'Sixty per cent of our people have been kicked out of their homelands and are stateless . . . The Americans have a moral and an historical responsibility over the Palestinians.' But ask him about the suffering caused by Palestinian guerrilla raids into Israel, and Arafat became a good deal more agitated.

Indeed, once I began to cross-question him about this, he would interrupt, waving his finger in front of his face, shouting and banging his fist on the table while Labadi sat motionless and unhappy in the corner of the room.

In other wars, I said, the various armies of guerrillas, insurgents, rebels, call them what you will, seemed to be able to confine most of their attacks – not always but usually – to military and industrial targets. But Palestinians often appeared to end up killing Israeli children and women.

The fist slammed onto the table.

'Babies. Only babies. Yes? Only babies and children. Do you believe them [the Israelis]? ... another big lie. What is going on in the south of Lebanon?'

The fist slammed down mightily again.

'Who are suffering from the Phantoms and from F–15s and F–16 aircraft and from cluster bombs and fragmentation shells, even forbidden weapons? ... but the Israelis have the "right" to use very up-to-date and sophisticated weapons and I have not the right to use my armies to defend my people and to defend my small children.'

Arafat started muttering about 'rumours'. He wanted to say lies but the word kept coming out as 'rumours'.

Would he not agree that Israeli civilians were killed?

'Rumours.'

But children had been killed in a recent Palestinian attack.

'Another big rumour!' Arafat was shouting. Labadi began to lean forward across the table in case his carefully arranged interview got out of hand.

Did the Palestinians not have difficulty in justifying certain attacks?

'Always they [the Israelis] are preparing communiqués about small children and old women.'

But such attacks *did* happen, did they not?

'It doesn't! They don't! Definite!' Arafat's eyes were running round the room, to Labadi, to three advisers who were sitting to his right in business suits and who had listened coldly and unmoved at this exchange. The eyes swung back to me.

'Why do you ask these questions?'

Arafat was reaching out, I realised at once, for the reason, for some clue as to why things were going wrong. The Plot. Someone must have told me to ask these questions. He did not say this but I knew that is what he was thinking.

'Definitely I have the right to resist. Let them withdraw from my homeland, from *our* homeland ...'

I was recording the conversation, and on the tape Arafat's voice now grew so loud that it was impossible to control the sound level. His shouting made the needle in my recorder jump frighteningly, flicking again and again into the area of the dial marked red for warning.

Then Arafat's knee began to bounce up and down, shaking the table. Eighteen months later, Pierre Gemayel's foot would tap in agitation in a similar way in his high-ceilinged office. Perhaps there was some kind of dangerous signal in Lebanon which I was missing, some message that was the political equivalent of the Palestinian gunman putting a bullet in the breech of his Kalashnikov on the road to Tyre, a discreet, more sophisticated version of CLACK-CLICK.

Arafat was waiting to see if I would continue.

Well there might be some people, I began again, who would agree with Arafat's criticisms, yet when women and babies were killed . . .

'I am against it.'

Silence.

'But you have to ask these citizens [sic] why they are living in my homeland.'

Such incidents were a mistake?

'A mistake.'

They were a mistake.

'Yes.' He was not shouting now. His voice was almost inaudible.

'Yes. I am against it. But you have to ask these citizens why they are living in my homeland. They are participating in this tragedy.' The voice was rising again. 'They are participating in this crime with their government, the Israeli military junta, they have to stop it . . .'

Arafat's English began to collapse under the immense weight of his fury, the verbs and tenses snapping and breaking apart under the strain. He was literally out of breath. Labadi stood up and hurriedly ordered tea. Like a patient in a dentist's surgery, he was worried that there might be another painful cavity to fill.

Asking about a future Palestinian state was like applying cloves to the aching tooth. Arafat's fury was transformed almost at once into sentiment, into a long, cloying résumé of his personal dreams. Palestine would be 'a democratic oasis in the Middle East', it would be 'a liberal democracy'. Democracy – the word if not the political system–seemed to obsess him.

'We are proud of our democracy in the revolution,' he said. 'It is the hardest and most difficult kind of democracy – because it is democracy among the guns. But we have succeeded in creating a democracy and those freedom fighters who have been given a democracy will continue to have democracy in their independent state.' Democracy, democracy, democracy. The word seemed to have the same effect on Arafat as 'terrorism' had for the Israelis. If you went on saying it often enough, anything could be justified. Better still, you might end up believing in it.

Arafat fumbled in the pocket of his combat jacket and produced an old, wrinkled pale blue banknote. 'You see? You see?' He was smiling now. This was obviously another routine, like the pocket history of Palestinians with which we had started. 'This is a Palestine one pound note. It was issued by you British. You are British? This was one of your notes. And you see? It is in Arabic and it is in Hebrew. It is from before 1948. The Arab and the Jew, they were together in one Palestine.'

It seemed almost cruel to remind Arafat that the British mandate in Palestine was not a period of Arab–Jewish friendship. Nor was it a democracy in *any* sense of the word. It was a version of a system he claimed to despise: colonialism. The Arabs and Jews did not rule Palestine during the mandate. The British did. Could Arafat not see that this sad little banknote bore the legend 'Anglo-Palestine Bank', and that the word 'Anglo' preceded the word 'Palestine'?

But the PLO chairman was oblivious to this, happy now in his mythmaking. There would be a Palestinian state in his lifetime, yes, definitely, a Palestinian state in which Jews and Arabs shared equal citizenship with equal rights. Had the PLO not proposed in 1969 that there should be a joint Jewish–Christian–Muslim state of Palestine? This had been proof, so he said, that the Palestinians could come up with their own solutions.

But would Jews living in homes that had once belonged to Palestinians be forced to leave their houses? Arafat's face creased in benevolence towards these future Jewish citizens of his. 'No, no,' he said. 'We can deal with this matter. We can arrange it. We can find a solution. But they have to accept our right to return back.' Arafat did not involve himself in complexities. The Israelis had some very strong suspicions about what Arafat's 'solution' might entail and it would take seven years of failure and defeat and further tragedy for the Palestinians before the PLO chairman abandoned his dream of an Arab–Jewish state, accepted the partition of Palestine and acknowledged Israel's right to exist.

He still had much to learn in 1981. If Palestine came into existence, I said, if it was created – in whatever form – would Arafat give me a multiple re-entry visa? His face lit up with generosity. 'Why not? Why not?' Then one of the unsmiling aides spoke in his ear and Arafat added quickly: 'Yes, why not? – but that is if *I* am the president.' He had been reminded of that word 'democracy'. As for Lebanon, the PLO chairman had few words. He would continue the struggle for his home-land 'so as to leave Lebanon and to thank them for their hospitality'. The Lebanese, he said, were 'suffering too much'. Here at least was something upon which both Gemayel and he could agree, although this was not the only way in which the two men complemented each other. Gemayel was disturbing because he appeared to threaten you; Arafat was frightening because he wanted to be your friend.

Both, too, had to live in close, sometimes suffocating proximity to the Syrians. Here were friends whose sensitivities had to be regarded with the utmost care and circumspection. While the brutality of the regime could be and sometimes was exaggerated — by comparison to the rival Baathist regime in Iraq, for instance, Syria was indeed a 'liberal democracy' — Assad ruled with the help of some of the most repressive secret police apparatus in the Arab world. By the early 1980s, it had proved possible to identify at least eight security organisations functioning in Damascus, at least one of them run by the president's brother Rifaat.

Hafez al-Assad was not the intrinsically evil man that his domestic enemies portrayed him to be; his private life was beyond reproach and his patriotism real if self-centred. His understanding of the functioning of political power and his knowledge of human weakness was outstanding. He had given Syria the first prolonged period of stability since its independence and he naturally identified himself with this achievement. Any serious opposition to his leadership was thus an act of treachery, a betrayal of the Arab Socialist Baath Party, of the Syrian leadership and the Syrian people. Yes, The Plot also lived in Damascus. Indeed, the xenophobia that the Syrians so often displayed suggested that the international conspiracy so venerated in Lebanon had here become an article of political faith. Only a mild heart-attack in 1983 had warned Assad of human mutability. All other manifestations of opposition to his continued rule were ruthlessly crushed.

As long ago as 1974, Amnesty International had been reporting on torture in Syria, and the details of the systematic ill-treatment of prisoners in Damascus and other locations — including cities under Syrian control in Lebanon — had become a constant theme of their reports. Beating on the soles of the feet, caning, whipping with steel cables, sexual assault, suspension by the wrists, the breaking of bones and secret executions were repeatedly catalogued. Some prisoners had been incarcerated since 1963.

An Aleppo student who was imprisoned from July 1979 to March 1980 told Amnesty that the torture room in the military security prison in Aleppo was a sound-proofed booth built inside a room where torture instruments included 'a Russian tool for ripping out fingernails, pincers and scissors for plucking flesh and an apparatus called *al-Abd al-Aswad* [the black slave] on which they force the torture victim to sit. When switched on, a very hot and sharp metal skewer enters the rear, burning its way until it reaches the intestines, then returns only to be reinserted.'*

---

* For early examples of ill-treatment, see, for example, Amnesty's report of a mission to Israel and Syria to investigate allegations of torture 10–24 October 1974. Among the most comprehensive documentation is Amnesty's report to the Syrian government of 16 November 1983, which also named 192 lawyers, engineers and other professional people detained without trial for the previous three years. Since 1977, Israel had also been regularly accused of torturing

By 1984, one branch of the *mukhabarrat* had acquired a machine known as the 'German chair', which slowly broke the vertebrae of the victim strapped into it. It had allegedly been manufactured in East Germany, although there was later a less refined instrument which was locally produced and thus called the 'Syrian chair'. This broke backbones more quickly.

Syria's torturers were not without their tutors, and one of the earliest of them was still living in George Haddad Street, a quiet, tree-lined thoroughfare not far from the British Embassy. He was an Austrian pensioner of 71, a reticent old man known to his neighbours as George Fischer, an apparently harmless eccentric who kept pet rabbits on the roof of his apartment. Every day at ten o'clock, he took a constitutional walk outside his home and once a week he visited the Hamadiyeh souq next to the Umayyad mosque to buy vegetables. All that distinguished him from other visitors to the market were his blue eyes, four missing fingers and the two *mukhabarrat* gunmen who always accompanied him to the souk, Kalashnikovs in their hands.

A visit to George Haddad Street confirmed that Fischer was no ordinary retired expatriate. He lived on the third floor of a yellow-painted apartment building but his name did not appear beside any of the doorbells that were screwed onto the wall next to the tall wrought-iron double gate. Fischer's exclusivity was doubly emphasised by the young man who stood, day and night, opposite this gate, dressed in a black leather zip-up jacket with a pistol in his belt. At each end of the street, there stood two more Syrian security men, one resting a submachine-gun on his shoulder.

Certainly, Fischer had need of protection. In 1981, a parcel arrived for him with a Vienna postmark franked on the paper. It contained explosives and blew off four of his fingers. He had told a neighbour − a diplomat from the Swedish Embassy − that once, long ago, he used to train German shepherd dogs for the Syrian army. And one night, when he was very drunk, he told a friend that, before President Assad's 'corrective' revolution, he had instructed the Syrian security apparatus in the use of an ingenious interrogation machine. It was a wheel upon which prisoners could be strapped and beaten with electric cable. Every few minutes, an automatic pump would spray water through the wheel to open the prisoners' wounds, whereupon the whippings could start again.

prisoners. On 19 June 1977, *The Sunday Times* published details of the torture and ill-treatment of 22 named Arab prisoners after a five-month investigation by its reporters. Beatings and the use of electrodes on prisoners' sexual organs by Israeli security officials and their agents inside Israel and in Israeli-occupied territories − including Lebanon − have been widely documented. Both Syria and Israel insist that their security police meet only the highest standards of humanitarian behaviour.

If old Fischer was therefore an unconventional pensioner, his pedigree suggested an even more chilling career. For to his friend, he had confided that George Fischer was in fact Alois Brunner, SS *Obersturm-bannführer*, senior officer in the *Sonderkommando der Sicherheitspolizei für Judenangelegenheiten*, responsible for the deportation of tens of thousands of Jews from the Greek city of Salonika in 1943. Born in the Austrian village of Rohrbrunn in 1912, Brunner joined the Nazi Party in 1931 and entered the police school in Graz a year later. He assisted Adolf Eichmann in the arrest and deportation of Jews from Vienna in 1938 and was posted in 1943 to Salonika where, under the command of Maximilian Merten, he signed the orders for 46,091 Jews to be deported to Auschwitz and other extermination camps. Greek survivors of the Jewish Holocaust recall that he would whip uncooperative prisoners or threaten them while holding a revolver in each hand. He was subsequently transferred to command the French transit camp at Drancy, whence he deported a further 24,000 Jews to the camps in eastern Europe.

Then he disappeared. In the 1950s he was seen in Cairo, where he was allegedly helping Nasser to train the Egyptian security police in interrogation techniques. During the period of the United Arab Republic — the political union of Egypt and Syria — he travelled to Damascus, where he was still working, helping the Syrian secret service, when the Egyptian–Syrian alliance fell apart. In 1960, he advised on the purchase of 2,000 items of bugging equipment from East Germany, but his usefulness apparently ended. When Assad came to power in 1971, he 'inherited' Brunner who was, so the Syrians privately acknowledged, an embarrassment, an unsavoury throwback to the bad old days of reactionary Arab politics. Brunner was pensioned off after promising to remain silent. In return for keeping his mouth very firmly shut, he could stay in Damascus.

The Syrians did not want to take responsibility for him. But they had a problem. If a police torturer could be employed by one regime but then disowned and deported by another, how could the authorities ever trust their security men? If it became known that a trusted government servant — a dedicated murderer like Brunner, for example — could be thrown out of Syria at the convenience of a new government, how could future public servants be assured that they too might not one day have to account for their deeds? In short, if a secret policeman suspected that he might have to pay for his crimes, he would be more likely to negotiate with Syria's domestic opponents than arrest them. So Brunner was a kept man.

After vainly ringing Brunner's doorbell in Damascus in 1983, I made a formal request to the Syrian government's information ministry. Would they confirm that Brunner — or Fischer if they preferred — was living in the city? After two days, I received a telephone call from Adel

Zaaboub, the head of the foreign press relations department at the ministry. 'I have made enquiries and we have no such man in Syria,' he said. Then he added at once: 'I think you want to keep good relations with Syria.' Asked if this last comment was a threat to persuade me not to write about Brunner, Zaaboub replied: 'No, it is not a threat. We do not threaten people. I just think you want good relations to continue.'*

Through Brunner's Swedish neighbour, I then passed on a message to the elderly Austrian war criminal. Would he meet me to talk about his career during the Second World War? Back came the Swede with Brunner's reply: 'No. I cannot do so. I have signed an agreement with the Syrian government never to give interviews.' Brunner, it seemed, was something of an expert at signing documents.

If Brunner was a liability to the Syrians, however, Assad showed not the slightest political embarrassment when he had to deal with armed insurrection. Throughout 1980 and 1981, the Muslim Brotherhood, the Sunni fundamentalist movement in Syria, had staged a series of bomb attacks and assassinations against government buildings and officials. Their demands appeared in anonymous wall posters; in Aleppo in 1980, for example, the 'Organisation of Ulemas of Aleppo' demanded a 'commitment to *Sharia* [Islamic] law in all legislation', an end to the state of emergency in Syria, the release of all detainees, the reinstatement of all university teachers who had lost their jobs because of their political views, an end to 'misleading propaganda' and 'total freedom'. The Syrians suspected that the Israelis or the Phalange – or both – were involved in creating these militant groups, although weapons captured in Aleppo appeared to have come from across the Turkish border where Alparslan Turkes' 'Grey Wolves' militia was demanding that the Ankara government adopt Islamic laws. Mass arrests were made in Aleppo and in Hama, historically the most recalcitrant of Syrian cities.

Hama was an attractive old city on the Orontes River – about 120 miles from Beirut – whose ancient stone walls and creaking wooden water wheels, the *nourrias* of Hama, had been preserved with great care by its overwhelmingly Sunni population. Local families would spend their weekends picnicking beside the river, cooling giant watermelons in the waters of the Orontes as the huge wooden wheels whined on their iron axles. I had visited the city on at least six occasions over the previous two years, sometimes lunching beside the river and watching the children of Hama as they balanced precariously on the *nourrias*, climbing the blades and throwing themselves off into the river.

But like so many of the towns and cities across the border from Lebanon, appearances in Hama could be deceptive. When I spent a

---

* *The Times* carried my dispatch on Brunner across four columns on 17 March 1983. The Syrians made no response and 'good relations' continued.

night in the autumn of 1981 in the town's only hotel, a dingy place of cement corridors that served wine the colour and consistency of paraffin, the hours of darkness were broken by the sound of constant automatic gunfire. A visit to the homes of three very frightened foreign aid workers – two Australians and an Indian – confirmed a popular rumour in Damascus: that Hama was in a state of near-revolt against Assad's Baathist regime.

Dozens of senior Baath party members had been murdered in their homes – some, though not all of them, Alawites – and in many cases their wives and children had been killed with them. In revenge, Colonel Rifaat Assad's special forces and *mukhabarrat* agents working for the same units were now executing, torturing or beating up large numbers of Hama citizens accused of collaboration with the Brotherhood, the *ikhwan*.

Their targets usually included doctors and engineers. The deputy manager of the local steel factory had been beaten up in the street by special forces troops. A man called Shisakhli, who was thought to be prominent in the *ikhwan*, had been found on waste ground outside Hama, his eyes gouged out, his face covered in acid burns, and castrated. In the previous six weeks, eleven young men had been shot in the back of the neck beside the Orontes. The three foreigners had been told that 200 executions had taken place since the previous Easter. Of the city's population of 100,000, around 10,000 were Christians and they too suffered at the hands of Rifaat Assad's soldiers. In many cases, the victims were related to wanted men; if an *ikhwan* member fled, then his father or brother would be murdered. One of Rifaat Assad's military officers – a colonel who had been born near Hama – had been so sickened by his duties that he had requested a transfer to the Syrian army in Lebanon. One week after his arrival there, he was assassinated in west Beirut along with several of his colleagues. The Brotherhood had a long arm.

Although the *ikhwan* were Sunni Muslims, their inspiration clearly lay in the Iranian revolution. When I walked round the streets that autumn morning in 1981, heavily armed *mukhabarrat* men were tearing down posters which had been pasted to the walls overnight. Each had been signed by 'The Leadership of the Islamic Revolution in Syria' and listed a series of attacks allegedly carried out by *ikhwan* guerrillas against government buildings in Damascus. They included the 'Amiriya building and the air force secret service', the 'military secret service headquarters', the 'Russian secret service building', 'headquarters of defence and combat troops (Saraya) and the special units' and 'other interrogation and secret service buildings ...' The posters – each of which bore the Koranic inscription 'In the name of Allah, the beneficent, the merciful' – proclaimed that the attacks were 'solely directed against the criminals of the government.' Assad's regime would react to the forthcoming rebellion with a ferocity born of fear.

When the revolt broke out in Hama in February 1982, the Syrians immediately cut all telephone and road communication with the city. Foreign journalists could travel to Damascus – where they found that the Syrian government was now discovering the advantages of accusing its enemies of 'terrorism' – but were told that anyone attempting to visit Hama would be in a 'life-threatening situation'. The government, they were informed, would not guarantee their safety if they tried to go to the city; which was seen, not unreasonably, as a threat rather than as friendly advice. Rifaat Assad's military units were not going to treat journalists kindly.

By chance, two Irish friends of mine were then living in Aleppo, and on 17 February I set off in a taxi to the northern Syrian city – knowing full well, of course, that the main highway to Aleppo passed through Hama. Surely a foreigner travelling to the far north of the country could hardly be arrested because Hama lay on his route? On the journey to Aleppo, the police ordered the driver to make a wide detour around Hama and there was therefore little reason to believe I would be any more successful on the return trip to Damascus the following day. Western embassy diplomats in Damascus – those infamous 'usually reliable sources' that haunt reporters' dispatches from police states – were talking about thousands of dead in Hama after more than two weeks of fighting; still no reporters had been allowed to go there and it was unlikely that any foreigner would be able to talk his way into the city now.

Next morning, on the national highway to Damascus about 12 miles from Hama, it was possible to see a rim of smoke on the horizon, a flat brown sheen that lay over a four or five miles wide area. Further down the road, a policeman stopped the taxi. We were ordered to take another diversion, this time on a road that would take us to the east of the city. But then two soldiers approached the car. They looked at me then asked the driver if he would drive them back to their units in Hama. The driver looked at me. 'Take them to Hama,' I said. Lebanon had long ago taught me that if you have a Syrian soldier in your car, you can go where no one else can travel.

They were very young – perhaps no more than 18 – and they were unhappy at having to return from leave. 'The fighting has gone on for sixteen days – and there's no sign that it's going to finish,' one of them said. Both chain-smoked as we drove into the outskirts of Hama. There were modern apartment blocks, undamaged but with soldiers sitting on the roadway outside the buildings, some brewing tea on portable stoves. 'Where are you from?' England. 'England good.' I had been through this before. I did not say I was a journalist. Did these two young men not think it a little strange to be taking an Englishman into the closed city of Hama? They did not, of course, because if was *they* who had asked *us* to go to Hama.

Through the windows of the taxi there came a low rumbling sound that seemed to be continuous, and as the car pulled out of a road intersection the old city of Hama crept into view from behind some trees. It had been burning for a long time; a dense cloud of brown and grey smoke was steaming up from the walls and the narrow laneways beyond the Orontes. There was still street fighting going on because we could hear rifle fire crackling from inside the city. To the south, the graceful blue cupola of a mosque had been punctured by an explosion. A column of white smoke poured up through the hole.

Parked on the banks of the Orontes was a line of Syrian T-62 tanks, part of Rifaat's collection of armour from Damascus. Every minute or so, one of the barrels would shake, the tank would pitch backwards with the vibration and a shell would go hissing out over the river and explode amid the walls. It was now that the soldiers told the driver to stop. We stood by the car looking at the curtain of smoke that climbed steadily from the other bank. One of the vast wooden *nourrias* stood incongruously between us and the old city, most of its wooden blades smashed away by a shell.

One of our two soldiers came walking back to us with cups of tea. He was accompanied by several of his colleagues in grimy pale pink camouflage smocks, unshaven, their eyes bloodshot with lack of sleep. Half a mile to the west, two shells burst around a cluster of buildings and a trickle of brown smoke began to pour from the window of a blue-painted house. The soldiers shook hands in a tired, limp way and stared at us. Then they walked over to a tank and lay down to rest against the tracks of the vehicle.

The *mukhabarrat* appeared to be everywhere, even beside the tank crews, watching them, looking across the river in a harsh, unnerving way. Behind us, a group of women in black robes, several in veils, stood looking at the smoke. A little tongue of flame crept over a roof and then died away in the city. One of the security men began to look at us suspiciously. The driver and I made a great show of shaking hands with the soldiers again and one of them talked to the *mukhabarrat* man, hopefully telling him that we had been innocently brought into the city to give the soldiers a lift.

'We've got to go — now,' the driver said. He was a Christian from Damascus and he had developed an acute sense of danger over the past day and a half. He did not like the special interest that the *mukhabarrat* man was showing in us. '*Hala* — now, we go!' he said again urgently. We climbed into the car and drove up from the river bank as another tank fired. A policeman begged a ride and the driver took him aboard. Then a girl in her twenties ran into the road in front of us, a blue scarf protecting her round, peasant face. Her hands were pressed tightly together in appeal. 'Take me out, take me out.' She climbed in the back seat beside me. 'I went to look for my brother,' she said quietly. 'His house was on fire. He was not there. I went to the cemetery. There were more than a hundred bodies laid out but I could not find his. God be merciful.'

There was another rumbling explosion across the ghost-like city followed by a peppering of rifle shots that sounded thin and unreal down one of the streets, as if someone had dropped a pack of cards on a wooden table. Smoke had begun to blossom out of the buildings now, drifting down the streets in a brown mist. Another mosque, this time with a silver dome, its thin eggshell exterior smashed by another artillery round that had left a thick black stain on the tiles. Another woman in black in front of the car, this time carrying a child. 'In God's mercy,' she pleaded.

She sat in the back between me and the young woman, holding her little boy, crying and dirty, on her knees. The child and the woman stank as if they had not bathed for a week. 'I have been here days, I have been to the cemeteries for my family. They have laid out the bodies, and they watch us to see if we claim a body that they say is a *mujahed*. I have not eaten.' I remembered that I had in my pocket a Mars bar that I had bought the previous day in Damascus and I gave it to the little boy. His mother snatched it from him, tore off the paper and began to eat it herself, ravenously, terrified that her son might snatch it back. The child began to scream.

We stopped at a Baath Party militia checkpoint. Every few minutes, an armoured jeep would pull up beside us with a clutch of female refugees in the back; they were being brought out of the city after more than two weeks and they asked for water the moment they stepped onto the road. The seriousness of the fighting was evident from the words of an army officer who now took the place of the policeman in our car. A middle-aged man whose features were made deathly white by a fine dust that covered his face and shoulders, he sat in silence for a few minutes as we tried to negotiate one of Hama's main boulevards. There were shell-holes in the houses; lamp standards and glass lay across the streets; every few seconds the soldier would urge us to drive faster across streets that rang with sniper fire.

'Some of our people, our soldiers have gone over to the other side,' he said. The enormity of this statement caused him to remain silent for another minute. 'We are fighting our own people. Do you know that we have to fight underground?' The woman with the child pulled on my arm. Did I have more food? I did not. I told the driver to stop if he saw any kind of food stall that was open. There were none. The army officer went on talking. 'Those fanatics are fighting us in cellars with rockets and yesterday we found an underground hospital. There are girls fighting with the *ikhwan*. One of them was wounded last night and when we went to capture her, she set off a grenade against her stomach and killed twenty of my friends.'

The officer fell into silence again. It was as if we were carrying the tensions of his battle in our car. The checkpoints came every few hundred yards now, manned by gangs of Baathist militiamen, improbably dressed in flared white trousers and tight-fitting black shirts. Another officer begged a lift. 'Why don't they let us fight on Golan instead of this?' he asked his colleague. The two men knew each other – both had their homes in Hama. A convoy of ambulances drove past a road junction, red lights flashing, setting up a storm of dust along the half-ruined street. There were more tanks and howitzers attached to trucks. Some soldiers sat beside their tanks, covered in sweat and dirt. One of them had his arm in a sling but a dark red patch was beginning to show through it.

Hama was built on two levels, the lower inner city on the Orontes which was in the hands of the Brotherhood, and a higher lip of land where new apartments and small bungalows had received some shell and mortar fire. There was a road that ran around this lip and when we reached it, driving fast, for a few seconds we could see little smoke storms moving upwards from the streets beside the river. Rows of women – almost all in those long black robes – stood beside the road here, gazing at the scene like spectators at a nineteenth-century battle. A few were crying, others pleading for room in taxis. A policeman was trying to control the military traffic; motorcycle messengers, trucks, armoured personnel carriers, each mounted with machine-guns at front and rear. A flat, dun-coloured cloud hung over Hama as we drove out of the city.

I was, so far, the only Western eye-witness to the siege of Hama. It had been only the most cursory, the briefest of visits but it was enough to prove that the fighting was still going on, that it was on a huge scale – involving at least a division of troops – and that casualties must have been enormous. Something terrible was going on there. The Syrians would claim only that fatalities were in the hundreds. We later estimated them to be as high as 10,000. Some figures were to put the deaths at 20,000, higher even than the total fatalities of Israel's invasion of Lebanon four months later. Certainly, when we visited Hama in 1983, the old city – the walls, the narrow streets, the Beit Azem museum – had simply disappeared, the ancient ruins flattened and turned into a massive car park. In Damascus, I needed a comment from the information minister, Iskander Ahmed Iskander, an intelligent, cigar-smoking senior member of the Baath who had slyly invited the international press to Damascus without the slightest intention of permitting them to visit

Hama. As I was setting off on the ten-minute journey to the ministry in the Mezze suburb of the city, there was a terrific explosion and a mushroom cloud of smoke rose into the air over the building. The *ikhwan* had just bombed the ministry with a ton of explosives. Iskander Ahmed Iskander survived with a few scratches but there was no point in trying to reach him now. I filed my dispatch by telephone and headed by road for Beirut.

Two days later, Syrian state radio condemned my 'mischievous lies'. Fisk had never been to Hama, the broadcast said. Thus he could have seen nothing of the fighting. And so, of course, the starving people, the indiscriminate shelling, the defection of army units to the insurgents, all these had been fabrications too. *The Times* immediately said that it stood by my story, explained how I had entered the city and expressed its surprise that Syrian radio should have denied the veracity of my dispatch. The Syrians were in an ugly mood but it seemed better to confront them and demand an apology rather than lie low. I telephoned Iskander's office from Beirut and insisted on returning to see the minister. Surprisingly, a new visa was immediately granted and I drove back to find Iskander, slightly bandaged but sitting now in the safety of his second office at the national radio building. He formally disputed the facts of my report – though not my presence in the city. Did he intend to go on claiming that I was a liar? 'Robert, I have never said you were a liar.' But the radio said that. 'The radio? I have not heard this broadcast.' Iskander smiled, offered me a large Havana and said: 'Robert, Robert, only true friends can have this kind of argument.' Sister Syria had smiled upon me.

Given Syria's ruthless reputation, any conflict between Damascus and the Christians of Lebanon was bound to have international consequences. It was one thing for the West to express its concern at the repression that had been going on in Hama and Aleppo since 1980, but Syria's domestic enemies – the Muslim Brotherhood with their demand for an Islamic revolution – were not going to be friends of America or Europe if they ever came to power. The Christians of Lebanon were a different matter.

Since the summer of 1976, the Syrians had controlled the Bekaa Valley. The headquarters of their 'Arab Deterrent Force' was at the Bekaa market town of Chtaura and their troops were billeted all the way up the valley, around the Greek Orthodox town of Zahle – where Cody and I had seen the Syrians and Phalangists cooperating in 1976 – at the airbase at Rayak, in Baalbek and Hermel. When the Syrians pulled back from the Christian mountains above Beirut, however, there had been an understanding with the Maronites that the Phalange would not take military advantage of the Sannine Heights, the plateau of ice and snow that glistens amid the cloud layers high above central Lebanon. The

Syrians held most of the mountain ridges but Sannine was regarded as a neutral zone. If Syrian troops were positioned there, the Christians would regard them as a threat to the Maronites of east Beirut, which was just visible across the valleys and mountains to the south-west. If the Phalange were to claim the heights, the Syrians would regard them as a threat to their military hold on the Bekaa — which could also be seen far to the east in the heat haze from the top of Sannine.

Like all such cosy arrangements in Lebanon, this one collapsed because of political ambition. Bashir Gemayel, hitherto a publicly proclaimed friend of Syria, decided that the Christians of Zahle had to be protected, in the same way as the Maronites of east Beirut were guarded by the Phalange. The fact that Zahle's Christians had little time for Gemayel or the Phalangists — who were Maronite rather than Greek Orthodox — did not daunt Bashir's humanitarian concern. A road would have to be built to Zahle for the convenience of the local Christians who were, he assured his supporters, frightened of travelling through Syrian-controlled territory. In fact, little pretence was made of the intention to use the road to provide military reinforcements to the Phalangists who were living in Zahle. The road was immediately put under construction and began to snake its way alarmingly up the western slopes of Sannine.

In Damascus, this stone highway was viewed with understandably deep suspicion. The Phalangists still boasted of their friendship with Israel and Israeli arms were still regularly coming ashore at the Christian port of Jounieh. If the Phalangists were allowed to complete their road — if the Syrians were to stand back and allow it to run down the eastern side of Sannine into Zahle — then who was to say that their Israeli friends might not one day drive down it too? A sudden surprise attack by Israeli armour over the mountains could slice through the Syrian army in the Bekaa and then conceivably head north towards the Syrian frontier near Homs and cut Syria in half as well. For this reason, Gemayel's road had to be stopped.

There had already been fighting in Zahle, a pleasant town with an old stone hotel, a pretty river through its main boulevard and a claim to fame as the birthplace of the film actor Omar Sharif. Bashir Gemayel — who by late 1980 wished to present himself as the leader of Christian and not just Maronite Lebanon — unashamedly encouraged the Phalangists inside the town to attack the Syrians. By the spring of 1981, Zahle was effectively under Syrian siege. It was nothing like as brutal as the subsequent siege of Hama but the town came under regular tank fire, its civilian population suffering dozens of casualties as the fighting continued. The Israelis began to express their concern that the Syrians wished to commit 'genocide' against the Christians of Lebanon, a view that Gemayel did nothing to contradict. East Beirut came under Syrian artillery fire and the Phalange dug into the permafrost on the heights of Sannine, firing mortars across the snow at the nearest Syrian positions.

The battle of the Sannine Heights was presented to the world – and especially to Israel – as a struggle of immense political and even religious importance. Here in their mountain eyries, the Christians were once more fighting the masses of Islam who were intent on the destruction – the genocide – of this brave Lebanese minority. The struggle was thus calculated to appeal to Israelis, Americans, Western churches, Christian religious institutions and newspaper editors. In reality, it was a miserable affair. Even the banks of unmelted snow on the Sannine ridge had a soiled look about them, a faint brown sheen of dirt that stretched across to the narrow military road that the Phalange were still doggedly building through the ice.

Israel spoke in defence of the Christians. Israel, it was announced in Jerusalem, would 'not stand idly by' if the 'massacre' of Christians in Zahle continued. Gemayel had told the Israelis that if Zahle and Sannine fell, the Syrians would secure hegemony over all of Lebanon. It looked like a Phalangist trap to draw the Israelis into Lebanon; certainly that is how it was regarded by Major-General Yehoshua Saguy, the Israeli army chief of intelligence.* But Lieutenant-General Rafael Eitan, the Israeli chief of staff, proposed an air strike against the helicopters that were providing support to the Syrian troops on Sannine.

These helicopters – which the Syrians later maintained were used only for cargo flights – had been used in a surprise attack against the Phalangists on Sannine. On 28 April, the Israelis sent F-15 and F-16 fighter-bombers to attack the helicopters and shot two of them down near Rayak. The raid did nothing for the Phalangists who remained locked into their rear positions.

In mid-May of 1981, I found the Christian militia were holding a dirty, sandbagged mortar position at Wadih, 7,500 feet up Sannine, so high that the Phalangists were forced to hug their flasks to their chests to unfreeze their drinking water. They crouched there in their steel-hard frosted trench as a Syrian tank a mile away sent lonely, purposeless shells rushing over their heads. In the thin mountain air and sub-zero temperature, it was even a little difficult to breathe. After a few minutes' exertion, I was panting like an animal, gulping down frozen air that stung the inside of my lungs and made me cough.

The Phalangists welcomed us to their isolated little post with the enthusiasm of old men wondering why their nearest relatives have forgotten them late in life. They scurried around their nest, firing off mortar rounds and shouting with a weird combination of fear and excitement when the Syrians banged off a round in the other direction.

* See Schiff and Ya'ari, *Israel's Lebanon War*, p. 33.

It was, as the Francophile Phalangist lieutenant put it when we ran cowering behind his sandbags, *une guerre triste*, a dreary war; and it was one which neither side had at present much interest in winning.

The Syrians had prevented the Phalangists from completing their road to Zahle and the Phalangists had prevented the Syrians from reaching the Christian ski resort of Faraya and the metalled road down to the Mediterranean. The Syrians were actually on the highest peaks but the Christians were scarcely 50 feet below them, a geographical hierarchy with which both sides seemed to be temporarily content.

Up on Sannine, however, it was easy to see why both were frightened of each other's power. 'Look over the edge of the sandbags,' the Phalangist lieutenant said. 'Look just a little over the edge and see the Bekaa.' I did as he suggested. And there, through eyes almost immediately misted by the frozen wind, I could see the soft, green valley of the Bekaa, basking in the heat a world away to the east. Beyond it, just visible, were the mountains along the Syrian frontier.

I clambered along part of the military road; for military it undoubtedly was, with its mortar positions and Israeli-supplied Sherman tanks dug into revetments beside the hairpin bends and snow-covered crevasses. According to the local Phalangist commanders – young men, for the most part, with degrees in business studies, impeccable French and an interest in war and weapons that bordered on the maniacal – the Syrians had started the mountain battles on 2 April. On 21 April, they said, Syrian special forces troops were landed by helicopter on one of the Sannine peaks, and on 27 April the Syrians captured the old French fort with its bunkers just to the south, also with the use of helicopters. It was this that had prompted the Israeli attack on the following day.

The Phalangists claimed they were still being assaulted by Syrian air power, principally by missile-firing Gazelle helicopters. On 16 May, they said, a Mig jet had been used to fire rockets at them. Yet the results were impossible to see and the Phalangists seemed suspiciously unconcerned about another attack. There was, too, an amateurish quality about their tiny campaign in the mountains. At Wadih, the mortar sergeant stood and stared for more than half a minute when his artillery piece failed to fire. Then, very cautiously, he peered down the barrel. When he did retrieve the projectile, he placed it back in the mortar again; and when it fired correctly, it showered him – and us – with fine, wafer-thin pieces of jagged metal. After a few rounds had been sent off towards the Syrian tank a mile away, we saw the tank's barrel traverse to fire at us and a 24-year-old Phalangist lieutenant with a plastic left hand – replacing an original blown off in Beirut by a rocket-propelled grenade – shouted: 'They are going to fire back at us now.' He was right. The Syrian shells came whizzing back across the snow and exploded behind us.

When we tried to leave this absurd and fearful place, the German army lorry in which we were travelling – a Mercedes just like those in the PLO's fleet of trucks – blew a tyre and we found that there were no replacements. So we slogged our way nine miles down the mountains to Faraya, sliding on snowdrifts and ice and stumbling into cold, stony wadis while mortar rounds and tank shells swished back and forth above us. The gunfire could still be heard at Faraya, where the Mzaar Hotel had been turned into a barracks of broken windows, coffee pots, two-way radios and items of Israeli army clothing. The Phalangists here were dressed from boot to helmet in Israeli clothes. Some even greeted us with the word *Shalom* and short lectures on the battle for world freedom which the Phalangists were allegedly waging on the slopes of Mount Sannine. They all assured us that there were no real Israelis among them – not yet.

Israel's failure to sit idly by had meanwhile produced a new and much more serious crisis. The Syrians, the United Nations, almost all the Western diplomats in Damascus and Beirut – and even, privately, the Israelis themselves – had all along maintained that Israel and Syria were parties to an unwritten agreement not to attack each other's forces inside Lebanon. The Israelis had broken that accord when they attacked the Syrian helicopters on 28 April. So at dawn on 29 April, the Syrians had brought batteries of SAM-6 ground-to-air missiles into the Bekaa. There was no secrecy about this.

Within hours, I was watching the Syrians installing the rockets in fields just east of the Rayak–Masnaa road and on a low plateau of land behind some orchards north of the Beirut–Damascus highway. About 18 feet in length, painted a brilliant clean white with polished silver warheads and mounted in racks of three, they were distributed in patterns across the terrain – another battery was dug into earthworks south-west of Chtaura – and the Syrians clearly intended them to be seen. Israeli high-altitude reconnaissance jets photographed them and Western journalists based in Beirut travelled the roads of the Bekaa to take photographs of the missiles.

The Syrians did not like to see too much interest taken in their rockets. Bill Foley of AP was manhandled onto an army truck and had several of his high-definition lenses confiscated (and stolen) by special forces troops when he parked outside a Lebanese café opposite a missile base. Foley explained later that he had been waiting for an opportunity to film an Israeli air strike, an attack which – given his proximity to the batteries and Israel's penchant for destroying everything in a quarter-mile vicinity of a target – would have wiped out Foley and all his cameras had it then taken place. Driving past the same battery some days earlier, I too had been waylaid by two Syrian *mukhabarrat* gunmen who ordered the two women travelling in my car to climb into their own vehicle. When I refused to allow this, one of the men insisted on sitting in the back of my car with a gun in his hand and ordered me to drive to Syrian intelligence headquarters in Chtaura. I promised to do as I was told but drove him instead into the local Lebanese police station and complained that we were being kidnapped. Sister Syria apologised again.

But the Syrians *wanted* the pictures to go round the world. Those batteries must have been among the most photographed military installations in the Middle East. By Warsaw Pact standards, they were out of date. They were air-defence weapons; they could not possibly fly beyond the Lebanese frontier and threaten towns as the Israelis were later to claim. They were a deliberate *political* provocation. Their appearance in that abundant corner of the Bekaa prompted Alexander Haig, the American secretary of state, to appeal for help to the Soviets. By the end of that week, Menachem Begin, the Israeli prime minister, was publicly claiming ignorance of the missiles, even though his air force had furnished detailed pictures of the batteries' positions to the Israeli government. The Israeli guarantee of non-aggression in Lebanon had been broken and the Israelis did not want to acknowledge the results. The SAM-6s did not threaten Israel, but they were a danger to Israeli aircraft flying over the Bekaa. Israel had therefore, for the moment at least, lost air supremacy over north-eastern Lebanon. This was the price of taking on the self-appointed role of protector of the Christians. Only later would Begin decide that the SAM-6s constituted a 'national threat' to Israel.

The siege of Zahle had sensibly petered out by the beginning of July; this was, after all, a conflict between regional superpowers, not between Syria and the Phalange. As usual, it had been the civilians who had suffered for this fraudulent little war. When I entered the town on 1 July, a Phalangist officer wanted to show me around. 'You want to see the graves?' His arms were draped over the butt and barrel of an M-16 that was hanging round his neck. 'Look behind you.' Amid the heaps of sand and dirt and garbage, there were thin wooden crosses, some dead flowers and a drab band of pink tape to delineate the borders of a trash-heap cemetery.

'There are thirty-five bodies here,' the gunman said. 'We had no chance to give them funerals in the shelling. Half of them are civilians and there are children among them.' He wiped the perspiration from his face. It was midday and the flies played around our faces. A hot breeze tugged at a piece of paper tied with wire to one of the crosses. 'George,' it said in Arabic. A bulldozer was parked beside the graves, ready to plough out another corner of the burial ground if the shelling started again. The Phalange said that 300 people had died and that 3,000 had been wounded.

On one side of the derelict railway tracks was a ruined five-storey warehouse that collapsed on 38 civilians who were sheltering in the basement after bombardment by Rifaat Assad's tank gunners. Only a child was left alive – with her legs torn off. The tank which did the deed – by blowing off the concrete supports of the building – was still standing guiltily in a hay field, its muzzle pointed towards us. Around us, the houses yawned with shell-holes, fissures stained with smoke and buttressed with sandbags. Zahle had taken on the crushed, haunted appearance that Beirut had acquired five years earlier.

The ceasefire had been arranged by Reagan's special Middle East envoy, Philip Habib, a career diplomat of Lebanese ancestry, who had agreed with the Syrians that the Phalangists would leave Zahle before the withdrawal of the SAM-6 missiles. Like so much American policy in the Middle East, the accord was all-embracing. The missiles had no immediate connection with the siege of Zahle; they had been brought into Lebanon in response to the Israeli attack on the two helicopters. Only 95 Phalangist militiamen in fact withdrew from Zahle, and then only because their homes were in Beirut. The rest of Gemayel's gunmen lived in the town and stayed there.

America had now become involved in Lebanon and Reagan was staking a considerable amount of prestige on Washington's 'honest broker' role in the Middle East; Assad, of course, was aware that while the broker might be honest, he was certainly not neutral. Nor was it in Syria's interest to remove the new inhibitions which had been placed upon Israeli air power in eastern Lebanon. The Phalangists had not withdrawn the majority of their men from Zahle. So the Syrians did not withdraw their missiles.

Several small-scale Palestinian raids into Israel and the occasional mine explosion in Haddad's territory – which may not have been the PLO's work – had meanwhile produced threats of a full-scale Israeli invasion of Lebanon. Habib cemented over this crisis, too, using the United Nations and its new Irish commander, Lieutenant-General William Callaghan, to create another *de facto* – but unwritten – ceasefire agreement between the PLO and the Israelis.

The UN's role had not been entirely altruistic. Haddad's militias had been maintaining their harassment of United Nations forces and in March of 1981 several artillery shells were targeted onto a Nigerian UN position north of the Irish battalion area, killing two Nigerian soldiers. Callaghan believed the shells had been fired from Israeli – not Haddad's – artillery and he spoke of his 'outrage' at the 'barbaric circumstances' of the Nigerian deaths. Eitan later expressed his 'deep sorrow' at the deaths, according to a speech made to Irish UN troops by Callaghan on 17 March. The UN commander said that Eitan's 'intervention' calmed the situation after the Nigerian deaths but added: 'It is never open to me to negotiate under threat of fire or fire and it is not my intention ever to do so.' It was a statement he might later have regretted. Callaghan told me on 19 April that he had warned Major-General Avigdor Ben-Gal, the Israeli northern army commander, that UNIFIL would not go on tolerating harassment by Israeli forces. 'Ben-Gal and I get on very, very well — very well indeed,' Callaghan said. 'He told me UNIFIL couldn't push Israel around and I said: "Come on now, you know there was never any question of that." But I told him it was too much to have Israeli shells being fired at UN troops — fired by Israeli gunners actually inside southern Lebanon — and then accuse us of letting Palestinian infiltrators through our area of operations.'*

The Israeli—PLO truce was not an easy one. Palestinian forces in southern Lebanon largely adhered to it and showed considerable discipline in doing so; Arafat repeatedly reminded them that the Israelis would like to find an excuse to re-enter Lebanon in force. Palestinians on the Israeli-occupied West Bank were involved in armed attacks on Israelis and Arab gunmen attacked Israeli targets in Europe. The Israelis claimed that this was a violation of the south Lebanon ceasefire agreement. The Palestinians in turn said that Israeli overflights of southern Lebanon were also truce violations.

The PLO were sorely tested. Arafat was to say later that he was well aware that the Israelis were deepening their alliance with the Phalange and that this had grave long-term implications for Lebanon and especially for the Palestinians. In March of 1982, the DFLP in Beirut had claimed responsibility for a fatal grenade attack on Israeli troops in the Gaza Strip. Complete with references to 'heroic guerrillas', the communiqué was an extremely serious development. Arafat's officers berated the DFLP for putting out such a statement in Lebanon when the organisation could anyway not possibly have mounted an attack so far away. The meretricious claim was mere bravado. But it was duly noted by the Israelis.

Then on 22 April 1982 an Israeli air raid was staged against Damour, killing at least 19 Palestinians. The Israelis had claimed a truce violation: an Israeli soldier had been killed in southern Lebanon. The Israelis did not say what the soldier had been doing, although when I travelled to southern Lebanon later, I discovered that he had been visiting one of Haddad's artillery positions and that the mine could have been laid as

---

* During the same conversation with me, Callaghan said that some Israelis were also trying to slander him. They had been claiming, he said, that on taking over command of UNIFIL, he had told his troops: 'I'm not a monkey down out of the trees,' supposedly a reference to his Ghanaian predecessor, Erskine. 'You know,' Callaghan said, 'I'm meeting Begin on Tuesday and I'm going to tell him what I think about the Israeli statements about me. It is totally untrue that I said this. I don't say things like that.' The Israelis regularly tried to impugn the character of UN officers. Western correspondents were present at an Israeli army briefing after the 1982 invasion at which an Israeli officer told journalists that the Fijian battalion was responsible for spreading syphilis among Shia women in southern Lebanon.

long ago as 1978, perhaps even by the Israelis themselves or their own militiamen. But it had been enough.

For more than two hours, the Israeli aircraft swept in from the Mediterranean. I had driven down the highway with Cody and several other colleagues when the raid began; it was to be a foretaste of the coming invasion. When the Israeli bombs hit the hillside just off the seafront highway, they did so with a long, roaring explosion that bubbled out in a ball of fire 50 feet in height. Crouched by the roadside, we could see the Israeli jets quite clearly as they flew in pairs, turning over the runways of Beirut airport and losing altitude at frightening speed. Each aircraft would drop phosphorus to mislead any heat-seeking missiles fired by the Palestinians. Then the planes would rear upwards and the hillside above Damour would be washed in an orange and crimson fire.

A tiny brick hut in a banana grove – which the Israelis would later identify as a 'terrorist naval base' – disintegrated under one bomb only seconds after we had passed it. The Palestinians fired back wildly and uselessly. A truck carrying a heavy gun overtook me on the highway past Damour, its brass cartridge cases pinging off the road and clanging onto the roof of my car. The gunner, a bearded youth with a bandanna round his forehead, dropped the ammunition belt and live rounds sprayed over the road. My car skidded sideways on the metal cases, bumping into the truck. The gunner looked at me as if I had personally struck him. 'I'm sorry, I'm very sorry,' I shouted, reversed and drove on. In my rear view, I caught just the briefest glimpse, a frozen frame, of the young man stooping on the tarmac, collecting armfuls of anti-aircraft ammunition as a jet flew the length of the highway.

Arafat spent much of that night with his advisers in Fakhani, debating whether the PLO should respond to the attack. He regarded the raid not just with anger but with cynicism, coming as it did only an hour after the Israelis had announced that they would withdraw from the remainder of the Egyptian Sinai peninsula on schedule under the terms of the Camp David agreement. Was this attack meant to deflect Israeli attention from the Jewish settlers who were refusing to leave their last settlements in the Sinai?

The Americans vaguely threatened to suspend military or economic aid to the Israelis if they invaded Lebanon. And when Yaacov Bar-Simantov, an Israeli diplomat in Paris, was assassinated in April, the US government told the Israelis that it did not regard this as the 'high provocation' which would constitute a ceasefire violation. But most of us realised it was only a matter of time before the Israelis invaded. There was talk within the Phalange of a coming Israeli 'initiative'. An American television network had broadcast a news programme which gave precise details of a military invasion of Lebanon which, it said, might 'go all the way to Beirut'. Begin declared that while the settlers had to leave Sinai, they would never leave Eretz Israel — which according to him and his Likud Party included the West Bank, or Judaea and Samaria as the Israelis called it. One last, massive blow against the PLO in Lebanon would surely smash forever the dream of those Palestinians living in the occupied West Bank that they would ever have a state of their own. But if there was to be an invasion, the Syrians would surely become involved.

That spring, I had travelled down through the lower Bekaa and the Arkoub for what I thought might be the last time before the coming war. I wanted to see where the war would be fought. The poppies were blooming all across those groined and rocky hills where the Palestinians had sat through the last of the winter rains in their leaky tents. A blaze of red and pink spring flowers had spread up the meadows towards Hasbaya. The old Roman bridge over the Hasbani had been repaved for the local shepherds. Just south of Deir al-Ahmar — a village of chickens, puddles and concrete bungalows — Syrian tanks were dug into the fields, a bunch of dirty-fleeced sheep leaning elegiacally against their gun muzzles. A mile or two from the nearest UN checkpoint in the south, a solitary Fatah truck stood in a desolate orchard with a Katyusha rocket battery mounted next to the tailboard. To the east, the snows of Golan — silver in the morning sunlight — smothered the Israelis' high-altitude bunkers.

The Palestinians had brought more ammunition south but few weapons. The Israelis claimed the PLO had modern battle tanks but all I ever saw, north of the Litani, were a few museum-piece Russian T-34s, bought on the cheap from Indian army surplus after service in Russia in 1942. The Syrians had put some big ZSU 23−4 anti-aircraft guns south of the Damascus highway, squat tracked vehicles with a radar dish mounted behind four machine-guns. The Syrians evidently believed the Israelis would stage air strikes across the Bekaa.

As the months grew warmer, there were other ominous signs. The SAM-6 missiles, which had been taken off their launchers, had been restored. UN officers — ignoring Callaghan's conviction that the 'force of international opinion' would prevent the Israelis driving through UN lines — told us privately that they had confidential orders to get into their bunkers and stay there if the Israeli army invaded. Confronted by journalists one evening in Fakhani, Arafat had been asked if the Israelis would invade. 'Let them come!' he said cheerfully.

Every one of my journalistic assignments outside Lebanon that spring would be hurriedly curtailed. A threat by Arafat to end the ceasefire, a claim by Israel that the truce was valueless, would have me pleading at Bahrain or Dubai airports for an MEA seat to Beirut. In Damascus, I would receive urgent calls from Ivan Barnes, my foreign editor at *The Times*, suggesting that I should return immediately to Lebanon. I was in

Cairo on 3 June when the Israeli foreign minister Yitzhak Shamir — the boy who was taught by old Szymon Datner at the Jewish Gymnasium at Bialystok — called for the elimination of the PLO in order to 'advance' the Camp David peace process. That night, Shlomo Argov, the Israeli ambassador to Britain, was shot outside a Kensington hotel.

The would-be killers — for Argov survived the attack though gravely wounded — were all from Abu Nidal's gang of hired Palestinian assassins. At the time, their leadership was in Baghdad, where the Iraqis were happy to think that their Syrian enemies might become involved in a war with Israel. Arafat condemned the attempted killing of the ambassador, but on 4 June the Israeli air force bombed both southern Lebanon and west Beirut.

Israel had decided that the truce was at an end. How a ceasefire in southern Lebanon could apply to the streets of Kensington — which are a very long way from the Middle East — was never explained. In the Mena House Hotel beside the Pyramids that night, I watched the agency tape playing across the hotel television screen. A French cameraman whom I knew had been killed while filming a raid on a PLO ammunition dump inside the old Chamoun sports stadium near Fakhani. He had arrived to cover the results of the first air strike and was caught in the second. His sound recordist told friends later that he simply disappeared, blown away from her by shrapnel and pieces of rubble. She was left holding the broken camera lead. The Palestinians claimed 50 dead. The Lebanese authorities said that 210 civilians had died. A Palestinian children's hospital outside the Sabra camp was struck by one bomb. Sixty bodies were later taken from it.

There was no flight that evening from Cairo to Beirut. On the morning of 5 June, the air raids started again; there were to be 50 separate strikes throughout the day. Tom Baldwin, an AP staff reporter in Beirut, saw the results of the bombing of the coast road as he travelled up from Sidon during the morning. His copy came up on the hotel's television news channel at midday, a dreadful tale of civilians burned alive in their cars, liquefied by the bombs that were dropped by the Israelis north of Damour. I begged and cajoled the hotel switchboard to put a call through to Beirut. After more than two hours, a crackling line connected me to the AP bureau. Earleen Tatro, one of the senior staffers, answered the phone. Was this the invasion? Earleen was not a woman to suffer fools gladly. 'I've been so damned busy, Fisk, I haven't the slightest idea, but it looks like you should be here. Don't waste my time — talk to Baldwin.'

Baldwin's voice came hollowly down the line. Was it the invasion? 'Read the wire,' he said. He sounded shocked. 'I've seen some terrible things today.' But was this the beginning of an invasion? 'Read the wire,' he said again. Then the line cut. I waited until the story came round again on the television screen. I waited a long time. There were reports on the Falklands war, which was now at its height. British forces were in action against the Argentinians. But what was happening in Lebanon was to be of far greater consequence. Then on the screen I read once more about the civilians roasted in their cars. There was a 'bulletin' insert on Palestinian rocket attacks into Galilee in retaliation for the Israeli raids. A Katyusha had killed an Israeli driving in his car near a kibbutz.

I ordered a taxi and drove to Cairo airport. The evening MEA 747 for Beirut had already left the stand but the Lebanese station manager promised me a flight in the morning. I did not sleep. I watched the AP wire flicking over the screen and listened hourly to the BBC World Service. I called Barnes, the foreign editor, at his home – it was Saturday – and told him I had to return. 'I hope you're not wasting your time again,' he said, then laughed. I was at the airport by five o'clock next morning. The 707 had arrived from Beirut, its friendly old cedar tree standing out on the tail of the aircraft in the hot early morning sun. The MEA airline staff grinned at me. 'You see? Do the Lebanese ever let you down?' Last flight to Beirut.

7   No White Flags

Listen, I know you are recording this but personally I
would like to see them all dead ... I would like to see all
the Palestinians dead because they are a sickness
everywhere they go.

Israeli army lieutenant, Baabda, Lebanon *16 June 1982*

'Just find out how many — ask Timur how many he's seen!' The dark
brown wooden door of the Associated Press bureau in west Beirut could
not smother Earleen Tatro's voice. 'How many? How many?' I could
hear Baldwin shouting down a telephone to Timur Göksel, the United
Nations spokesman in southern Lebanon. 'How many tanks?' he kept
yelling. I pushed the door open. Here were the friends and colleagues
with whom I would share the next four dangerous months.

Farouk Nassar was sitting at his desk by the window, his typewriter
in front of him, talking over his shoulder to Earleen. 'How many,
Earleen?' It was a foolish question. 'How in God's name do I know?
Baldwin hasn't found out.' Nassar stood up and turned slowly, in
almost savage desperation. 'How can I write the nighter if I don't know
where the Israelis are?' Nassar saw me at the door. '*Habibi*, you made
it!'

Palestinian by birth but Lebanese by citizenship, Nassar had a family
link with *The Times*; his father had been a stringer for the paper in Haifa
during the last days of the Palestine mandate. No one could turn out an
agency night lead faster, estimate a militia's strength with more subtlety
or coin a phrase with greater shrewdness than Nassar. He loved horses
and never failed to lose his money at the Beirut race-track. He was a
generous, tough man with the air of a playboy, who drank fifteen-year-
old Scotch and smoked Churchill cigars. He possessed the one quality
which would have ensured his survival in any news agency: dependability.

The power was down, the air-conditioning had failed, Nassar's shirt
was blotchy with sweat, the perspiration running down his face from
his thin, white hair, making small detours around his severe brown
moustache. His beefy little arms swept wide. 'Fisky, how did you get
here? The Israelis have invaded, they are bombing all across southern
Lebanon.' He announced this with appropriate *gravitas*, like a preacher
telling his flock that their sins were about to be punished, just as he had

always said they would be. Earleen Tatro was back in the room, an imposing and bespectacled Indiana lady who had been 14 years with the AP, a woman of intense energy and the commendable cynicism which we all developed in order to stay alive in Lebanon. 'You took your time, Fisk. Now don't waste ours. The Israelis have invaded. They've gone right through the UN lines. Arafat wanted another ceasefire this morning but it didn't work.' The AP bureau chief, Nick Tatro, Earleen's husband, was not there. 'He's stuck in south Yemen. He can't get a plane back. Cody's with him.' I had a momentary impression of Cody's face, his eyes half closed with that special despair which he always demonstrated when the Middle East crushed his plans and ambitions. Cody now worked for *The Washington Post*. He should never have gone to Yemen at a time like this.

Earleen's face was lined with tiredness. 'Look, Fisk, write your story, do whatever you want — but keep out of my way. We've no power, the generator's broken, François is not here to mend it, and we can't get our nighter out. Leave the staff alone. Go write your essays out back somewhere.' We all loved Earleen. When the computer line to London and New York returned, she would sandwich my copy into the system between individual pages of AP copy. When the Israelis drew closer to Beirut — so close that their shells were smashing into the buildings around the AP office — I would sit beside Earleen Tatro at the telex machines, punching wire copy for the AP, an instant honorary unpaid member of the AP staff. There were times, in the coming weeks, when I suspect my loyalty to these people outweighed my allegiance to *The Times*.

The incoming wire was still operating, a long series of 'bulletins' on what was clearly a massive Israeli military strike into southern Lebanon. The messages clicked away on Earleen Tatro's desk, each preceded by a little mechanical bell to warn of their urgency. The datelines were Tel Aviv or Jerusalem — it was still too early for any international reaction — and the figures were vague. Up to 25,000 Israeli troops had entered Lebanon on three axes; up the coast road past the UN headquarters at Naqqoura — where Timur Göksel was actually watching columns of Merkava tanks driving past his office — through Tibnin where the Irish battalion had their headquarters, and across Ibl al-Saqi where I had spent so many days with the Norwegian soldiers over the past four years.

Was this to be a repeat performance of the 1978 invasion? Certainly, this operation was on a much more impressive scale. The Israelis were already approaching Tyre; Ahmed Mantash, AP's stringer in Sidon, came through on the phone to say that Israeli gunboats and aircraft were shelling his city as well. The bells on Earleen's desk went on ringing. AP's staff in Tel Aviv had been told about the 'limited aims' of the invasion which were – so they said – to push the PLO and its artillery out of range of the frontier and the northern Galilee area of Israel. This was no war of aggression, we were informed, merely a preventive action to secure peace. War and peace; how easily the Israelis associated these two words. The invasion now had a name. It was to be called 'Operation Peace for Galilee'. That is what the AP told us that Sunday morning, although it was not the invasion's real name. The operation was in fact called *Snowball*. And snowballs, we all knew, could be rolled along the ground, growing larger and larger the further they were pushed. Another bell. A Norwegian UN soldier had been killed in 'cross-fire' as Israelis and Palestinians opened an artillery bombardment from opposite sides of Ibl al-Saqi. So much for General William Callaghan's trust in the 'force of international opinion'.

Most of the AP copy running out of Israel was still accompanied by bells, but it also routinely carried a sentence at the top of each dispatch to the effect that the report had been submitted to the Israeli military censor. In some cases, the agency said that the censor had ordered material deleted. All of us realised that this was going to be an unprecedented war. There was no censorship in Beirut. For the very first time, the Western press would be operating on *both* sides of the front line in an Arab–Israeli war – and the foreign journalists in Beirut would have more freedom to tell the truth than their colleagues in Israel. In past conflicts, correspondents in Jerusalem and Tel Aviv had been given conducted tours of the war zone by Israeli army press officers. Journalists had watched the war from Israel's side while their opposite numbers in Arab capitals – in Egypt or Syria–were treated like spies, locked into luxury hotels on a diet of dishonest government statements. No more. No overseas press censor sat in any government office in Beirut. When I wanted to write a dispatch, I had to contend only with the power cuts, the line failures and the fickleness of François' generator.

The AP bureau was a microcosm of Lebanon's own religious matrix. Samir Ghattas, a member of the local AP staff, and his father François, the chief technician, were Greek Catholics. Farouk was a Palestinian Sunni. Charles Assi, the office manager, was a Maronite. The photographic staff included a Sunni editor, a Shia and an Armenian – Zavem Vartan. Scheherezade Faramarzi was an Iranian, taken onto the staff by Tatro when the Iran – Iraq war broke out. For AP Beirut was still the news agency's principal Middle East bureau.

The bureau itself was a labyrinth of tiny offices wedged into a decaying apartment block, a place of dirty white walls and heavy battleship-grey metal desks with glass tops and iron typewriters. A telex machine and a computer line thumped away in an adjoining room whose walls were draped with telex tapes which had already been used to send copy. A massive, evil-tempered generator stood on the balcony, its fuel stored in canisters beside the machine by Assi. At least half the bureau reeked of benzine. François Ghattas' home-made laboratory of soldering irons and radio communications equipment was stored in an opposite corner. The bureau thus acquired some of the properties of a car repair shop, an atmosphere that was only emphasised when Assi appeared each morning, clothed only in swimming trunks, to wash the bathrooms and the tile floors of the balconies.

Language both united and divided the bureau. Nick Tatro spoke Egyptian Arabic but most of the American staffers who worked here – Baldwin and the visiting 'firemen' who were to fly in from Rome and Paris during the invasion and the subsequent siege of Beirut – spoke no Arabic at all. The local staff spoke Arabic to each other but English to us. Earleen and Baldwin, for example, relied upon Nassar to translate the headlines of the Beirut newspapers, upon Samir Ghattas or Faramarzi – who spoke fluent Arabic as well as Farsi and English – to explain the local news broadcasts. What passed between these locally hired staffers remained a mystery to most of the Western AP reporters, with the exception of Tatro. Their concerns and fears remained unknown unless they chose to talk about them in English.

A curious symbiosis had thus developed: the Arabic-speaking staff, with families and lifelong friends in Beirut, depended upon the Westerners for their employment; yet the Westerners were almost totally reliant upon their Lebanese, Palestinian and Iranian colleagues for their knowledge of events. Farouk Nassar and Faramarzi or Ghattas could open the window through which the Americans saw Lebanon; or, if they thought the events outside unimportant, they could keep it shut. The shapes outside might still be visible but they would lack meaning. The understanding that governed this relationship said a lot about Lebanon. The AP bureau worked – unlike much of the country – because there was a mutuality of interest, trust and friendship. The journalists there had to depend upon each other; there was no other way. Perhaps it was not by chance that the AP functioned so harmoniously; it was the only office I ever entered in Lebanon where almost every religious community was represented.

At midday, the outgoing wire returned. Nassar's night lead began to click its way through the computer transmitter, an old model 15 teletype machine that was screwed onto the table like a vice. In 1982, news agencies in the Middle East were not yet equipped with computer screens; it would be two more years before we had instantaneous transmission. The siege of Beirut was therefore going to be reported on equipment that had changed little since the Second World War; the iron beast through which we filed at AP was based on an American army teletype system used in Korea. It took time; and if the power broke in the middle of transmission, the tape had to be re-coded and re-sent in its entirety.

The frustrations of journalism are never apparent to those who view the craft through romantic eyes. In Hitchcock's *Foreign Correspondent* — a film which persuaded me in my schooldays that I would like to be a reporter — Joel McCrea played a journalist who outwitted Nazi agents, won the most beautiful girl in the movie, filed scoop after scoop to his New York head office and survived in the Atlantic when his airliner was shot down by a German pocket battleship. To send his stories, he simply dictated his copy over the telephone. If only journalism had been that easy! In Beirut, making an international telephone connection could take six or seven hours. The telex often garbled copy and the computer line was dependent on the city's electrical power, the land-line that ran out to sea through the devastated port, and the abilities of François' generator.*

I knew that Barnes, my foreign editor, would be expecting a centre page feature to explain the background of the invasion, a lead for the front page and any further developments for later editions. These rigorous, necessary constraints governed my working life in Lebanon. And on this first dramatic day of the Israeli invasion, I realised at once that I would have no chance to leave the AP office. If I travelled to the south of Lebanon, I would not be able to return in time to file my dispatch to *The Times*. On the road from the airport that morning, I had seen the first of the refugee cars reaching the southern suburbs, a ghostly replay of those long columns of refugees fleeing the Israelis which I had witnessed in southern Lebanon four years earlier. PLO anti-aircraft guns were parked beside the shattered Chamoun stadium. The Syrian army's brigade in Beirut had degenerated through idleness and corruption; Lebanese army officers who acted in cooperation with what was still officially called the 'Arab Deterrent Force' said that the Syrian brigade did not even have an order of battle. Yet that morning, Syrian troops had appeared in the streets in battledress, wearing steel helmets and positioning artillery on the cliffs along Raouche.

Were the Syrians to become involved in the war, then the invasion would provoke a crisis between the Soviet Union and the United States; for while Moscow had always been irritated by Assad's habit of consulting his Soviet allies *after* rather than before taking military action, the Treaty of Friendship between the Soviet Union and Syria was regarded

* *The Times*, unlike most of its competitors, was printed only in London and had to be transported by train to the north of England and to Scotland. This necessitated early edition times. All my reports had to complete transmission to London during the afternoon — the latest by 4 pm Beirut time — which meant that I usually started to send copy over the AP wire at around 2.30 pm in Beirut. Combat reporting, which involved long car journeys through front lines and checkpoints, would have to be undertaken in the mornings.

as inviolable. Any threat against Syria would immediately involve Moscow. So how far would the Israelis go? I sent a computer line message to Barnes in London, telling him I had safely returned to west Beirut and warning him that 'if Israelis move up Bekaa, they are going to meet the Syrians, after which this conflict could get bigger very suddenly.' I advised him to arrange a Syrian visa for a London-based correspondent who would be ready to fly to Damascus.

The telex bell began to ring. Irish radio wanted a two-way interview. Canadian radio came on the telex immediately afterwards. Both wanted to know one question: how far would the Israelis go? I typed out the first lines of my radio report for Canada. '... Israeli troops were pouring into the country at midday local time today in what appeared to be a full-scale invasion of the south of the country ... Whether this invasion — for that is what it now appears to be — was premeditated long before the attempted assassination of Israel's ambassador to London, [which is] the ostensible reason the Israelis have given for the carnage in Lebanon over the past three days, is open to question. It looked in Lebanon today as if the Israelis had been planning this military operation for a long time ... The Israelis — if reports from Israel are to be believed over the past few days — are now intent on wiping out Palestinian guerrillas from Lebanon.'

Newspaper readers — like generals — need maps in time of war. Nothing is more confusing for a foreigner than a series of apparently unpronounceable names with no reference to their geographical or military importance. In the spring of 1982, I had sent to the graphics department of *The Times* a series of maps of Lebanon, each marked with the front lines in Beirut, the areas controlled by the militias, the Syrian army, the United Nations battalions and the government army. I kept an identical series of maps in my drawer in the AP bureau in Beirut. So once the invasion began, all I had to do was telex to my paper the changes in the contours, filing the coordinates of new military positions or known advances once they were established. But so fast was the triple Israeli thrust into the country that I found myself constantly updating the map details, changing the coordinates, pushing the Israelis deeper into the soft, dark terrain of Lebanon. By mid-afternoon, I was signalling a column of Israeli tanks approaching Nabatieh and the air bombing of Beaufort Castle — the great crusader keep in which I had sat under artillery fire with the Palestinians on that windy afternoon five years before.

I sat in Nick Tatro's back office, pouring onto a typewriter all that I remembered of this lovely countryside, of the UN's weakness, of the inevitability of an Israeli invasion, including the clues and cynicism which I had heard expressed about the invasion's planning. Could Argov's attempted assassination outside the Dorchester in London truly be the reason for this onslaught? 'How could a truce agreement along the Litani river ... possibly cover the pavement outside the Dorchester Hotel?' I typed. I suggested that Abu Nidal's faction had tried to kill Argov – the subsequent trial of the Palestinian gunmen proved this suspicion correct – but I also recalled the strange, dangerous fatalism of the Palestinians and Lebanese. 'It was, in a terrible sort of way, a relief. Lebanon has lived under the threat of an Israeli invasion for so long that its eventual fulfilment was something which the guerrilla fighters and the Lebanese themselves almost craved.'

Outside in the streets, gunmen had appeared, Fatah men, PFLP guerrillas, Mourabitoun militiamen and Druze fighters. I left the office briefly to see Kemal Salibi, one of the finest modern Lebanese historians and an old friend. He sat on the balcony of his Ottoman house in Manara and predicted that the Israelis were more interested in destroying the PLO than merely limiting its activities. 'They could come here,' he said. To Beirut? 'Why not?' To Salibi, the US administration did not appear to be a restraining influence. Alexander Haig had given a 'green light' to the Israelis. Had we not understood the significance of Menachem Begin's most recent visit to Washington? Salibi was a scholar of ancient Hebrew, a gentle, carefully groomed man with a very soft voice. It was unnerving to hear so urbane a man speaking with such foreboding. 'This could be a very terrible situation for all of us,' he said quietly. 'I fear the very worst.'

From the AP, I called a Palestinian, an officer in the Democratic Front for the Liberation of Palestine. He was in the Sabra camp and I could hear anti-aircraft guns firing at the other end of the line. No, he would predict nothing, only confusion. There could be no reliance upon Syria. This was his only comment. I began typing again. It was a conflict that held no dividends for the Americans. 'Their credibility in the Middle East,' I wrote, 'will suffer severely from this new invasion. They thought they could exercise increased "leverage" over Israel if they increased their military liaison in a strategic agreement and if they increased their military commitment. Yet it was American F-16 fighter bombers that were attacking over southern Lebanon ... The way is open for increased Soviet commitments to President Assad of Syria; the Russians gain a greater foothold in the region with every Israeli advance through Lebanon ...'

By early evening, the Israelis had cut off Tyre. Their aircraft showered the civilian inhabitants with leaflets, warning them that the invading army would blow up their homes if they sheltered PLO 'terrorists' and ordering them to display white flags on their windows and balconies. The UN reported that Israeli tanks were firing into buildings in which PLO men were thought to be hiding. Hundreds of terrified refugees stormed into the UN's positions inside the Lebanese army's Hassan

Borro barracks for safety, but the *caserne* itself then came under fire as Israelis and Palestinians fought within the city. Israeli objectives appeared to include the capture of Tyre and the salient up to the Litani River bridge – the area they had specifically failed to take in the 1978 invasion – and the seizure of Beaufort Castle, Nabatieh and part of the lower Arkoub Valley. These were the objectives which I included in my dispatch to London that evening; certainly, this is what most of the Israeli tank crews thought. Days later, they would tell us how even they were surprised when they were ordered to drive on. The only known Israeli casualty that day had been a lone pilot whose Skyhawk had been struck by a shoulder-held ground-to-air missile as he bombed the land around Nabatieh. He had baled out of his jet and was said to have been captured by the PLO.

It was after dark when Faramarzi received a phone call from the PLO. 'They say they're going to produce the pilot,' she shouted. We drove down to Sabra. The street lamps were out and there was shooting near Fakhani. Gunmen stopped us repeatedly on the roads, demanding to know our identity. In a hospital basement at Sabra, the Palestinians produced their prisoner. Captain Ahiaz Aharon was led into the floodlit room in a medical gown. It was stuffy and hot. At least 20 PLO men holding automatic weapons stood round Aharon. He was sweating too, sometimes holding his hands clasped in front of him, smiling vaguely at the television cameras. The PLO said he would make a statement. Aharon spoke in English, slowly, having obviously thought carefully about the words he would use. 'I came to bomb an artillery target and Beaufort Castle,' he said. 'I didn't find my target and my jet was hit. I landed [by parachute] in a village and there was a problem there because the farmers were angry. But when the people of the PLO came along, they took me and there was no more trouble.'

The villagers, who had been under air attack for three days, had tried to lynch Aharon. He was being beaten on the back when PLO gunmen had rescued him. But the PLO wanted no more descriptions. 'No questions,' one of the Palestinian officials screamed. We tried to continue talking to Aharon as he stood there in his white medical gown, a farcical combination of potential martyr and Dr Kildare. 'I have been treated well,' he said as television crews and gunmen began to push and shove each other in front of him. 'I am more than ever ...' A PLO man shouted at Aharon to stop. But as we were physically pushed away from him, Aharon smiled broadly at the cameras and shouted: 'I come from Herzelia. Regards to my family, my wife and daughter and sister – I hope to see them again ...' He was disappearing out of the rear door of the basement but wanted to complete his sentence. 'Soon,' he shouted.

That night, the Israelis started shooting at the Syrians. Damascus radio announced that Syrian troops in Lebanon were 'in direct contact' with the invading army somewhere south of Sidon. The telephone lines from Beirut to Tyre had collapsed in the late afternoon but AP stringers were still calling in from Sidon. Mantash said that he had heard the Israelis opened artillery fire on Syrian positions in the lower Chouf, just north of the Bisri River, and that Syrian troops had been seen evacuating the area under cover of darkness as their forward positions exploded behind them.

Before dawn next morning, I set off for the Bekaa with Karsten Tveit of Norwegian radio. Tveit was an enormous man with straw-coloured hair, very pale blue eyes and an insatiable, dangerous appetite to see everything in Lebanon at first hand. It was Cody who had taught me six years earlier that a journalist had to travel to a battle if he wanted to report it. Describing it at second hand from a bar, rewriting the agency tapes – which themselves contained second-hand information – was no way to report the Lebanon. But Tveit took Cody's journalistic precepts to extremes. Most people I knew fled when they came under shellfire. Tveit would stop only if the road came under fire. One thus doubted his wisdom rather than his courage, and it was a matter of perpetual amazement to me that Tveit did not die in Lebanon. But he always came back from his assignments intact. He was a survivor, and I made it a rule to travel only with survivors.

The Damascus highway across Mount Lebanon was still open. The road sweeps up through the Druze town of Aley and through Bhamdoun, the resort town in which I had stood with the Palestinians opposite the Syrian front line six years before. Syrian military traffic was moving on the highway but the mountain ridges were washed with their familiar colours of grey stone and bright green grass, the pine trees beside the road heavy with scent. With the car windows open, we could hear the whisper of jets high in the pale dawn sky, but only beyond the ruined ski lifts of Dahr al-Baidar did we begin to feel that worm of danger inside ourselves, that special agitation which always arrived when we were driving into a combat zone. Several truckloads of Syrian troops were moving down towards Chtaura.

When we turned south off the highway, on the road to the Arkoub – towards the advancing Israelis – the people of the lower Bekaa were standing outside their shops and villas, staring at the sky, squinting up into the sun with their hands protecting their eyes from the light. The population of entire villages were standing in their narrow streets doing the same thing, all looking to the sky with their hands to their heads as if engaged in some long, heavenly salute. Only when we arrived in the Druze village of Rashaya did we notice that the sound of the aircraft had grown louder, that the whisper had turned to a high-pitched howl interspersed with long, low rumblings from far away.

The village was old and so were its inhabitants: stooped women in long, coloured dresses, the men in black baggy trousers with fluffy white beards and nervous eyes. They wanted to leave because they thought the Israelis were sure to come. There were gunmen — Druze militiamen — on the furrowed streets and they exhibited the sort of sharp enthusiasm that usually afflicts young men in fear. The warriors of the Progressive Socialist Party held their rifles at the ready, but their movements, their voices — even the way they stared at us — had an uncomfortable edge about them. 'Everything is quiet here, there is no trouble,' we were told by a young, khaki-clad youth. He pointed down through the heat haze to where the valley of the Arkoub narrowed below Hasbaya. 'The next village is held by Fatah and after that are the Israelis,' he said. It was his way of saying that all that lay between Rachaya and Hasbaya — where Israeli tanks were now moving north — were a few of the Palestinian guerrillas whom the Israelis had vowed to wipe out. He did not say what everyone was thinking: that Rashaya might receive the same treatment as Nabatieh and the other towns across southern Lebanon, that it would be blitzed from the air.

It was then, just after eleven o'clock, that the Syrians on the valley floor below us fired their first shot at the Israelis, a long-range shell that left its gun with a curiously hollow explosion and hissed off over the foothills of the Arkoub towards the Israeli armour around Kaoukaba. A thin haze of blue cordite smoke rose from the artillery piece, a big old Russian 130mm gun that lay dug into the hard red earth below the little road that led up to Rachaya. A minute later, another round was fired from a gun further up the valley, its explosion echoing and re-echoing in the same empty fashion across the beautiful, stony little hills beneath Mount Hermon.

Only then did the villagers begin to show signs of panic, climbing into their cars or begging drivers for lifts out of the meandering valley. Tveit and I took an elderly couple to their son's home on a neighbouring road, and now we saw the movement in the fields. The Syrians were emerging from foxholes and trenches dug at right angles to ditches and laneways, some of them looking to the south through field-glasses, others staring into the sky.

It was hot, and there lay across the land that sort of warm expectancy that presages high summer rather than war. Perhaps the Syrians felt this too, for there was an almost lazy quality to their hostilities. They fired one round every bleak minute from field guns so newly entrenched in the soil that no one had bothered even to throw a tarpaulin over their shining, 22-foot barrels. Across the fields and beside the vineyards and up the sides of the little hills, hundreds of Syrian soldiers were digging their trenches and unloading boxes of ammunition in an orderly, routine way as if they were on manoeuvres. It was a restrained, almost gentlemanly conflict that we were watching there in the lower Bekaa.

But in the other tiny Druze villages, red-roofed in the midday sun, the inhabitants were demonstrating the same anxiety as the people of Rachaya. The refugees — for that is what the people had become the moment the first Syrian gun fired without considering their new status — piled their belongings into ancient buses and began their journey north. Some of the women were Shia and wore white scarves; all clutched boxes or babies.

On the roads they were passed by less well-dressed travellers, by Syrian troops in battered trucks and by young Palestinian guerrillas in cars and vans, their roofs — even their windscreens — smeared with mud to prevent a glimmer of sunlight betraying them to the Israeli pilots far above them. Down the road from Chtaura, too, came Katyusha rocket-launchers. There were lorryloads of shells in the orchards and, further north as we drove home, the Syrians were driving tracked mobile anti-aircraft guns through the fields. The guns still sounded, one shot a minute, as perspiring Syrian logistics men hooked up roadside cables and ground-lines, connecting unnamed battalions who were digging in beside villages with names like Sultan Yacoub, Mhaidse, Rafid and Khirbet Rouha, little names on those dense, contour-crowded maps which we would study with ever greater anxiety each passing day.

There was no need for a map when we descended the western slope of Mount Lebanon. A black tower of smoke was rising from the Palestinian camps and drifting northwards across the city; the Israelis had raided Fakhani and their planes were still circling above. We could see them clearly, infinitesimally small silver fish that moved slowly and with great patience over the city, circling gently, high over the column of smoke.

Tveit turned on the Phalangist 'Voice of Lebanon' radio. Beaufort Castle had been captured by Israeli commandos, it announced. Israeli troops had landed north of Sidon. '*North* of Sidon!' Tveit could not believe it. 'They are coming to Beirut.' We parked our car south of Kahhale on the mountain highway and watched the raid on Fakhani. One of the Israeli planes moved out of its circle in an indolent way and began to descend, picking up speed, nose down; it disappeared behind the smoke. A new column of smoke shot out from the haze, sideways, a dirty brown colour. Four seconds later, the sound reached us, a low thump whose vibration could be felt through the car. If the Israelis were north of Sidon, then they intended to capture the city and the Ein-Helweh camp. They would attack Damour. It was clear in Rachaya that the Druze did not want to fight the Israelis. So the roads through the Chouf, past Jumblatt's palace at Moukhtara, would be open to them. They could — it seemed inconceivable — but they could encircle Beirut.

The AP bureau was in satisfying uproar. Samir Ghattas was clutching a telephone to his ear and shouting to Nassar. 'The Israelis are approaching Damour.' Nassar rose from his typewriter. 'Impossible. They cannot have reached Damour.' When he saw Tveit and me, Nassar held out a hand, a kind of unspoken invitation. 'Tell me quickly – *quickly* – what did you see?' The Syrians are firing at the Israelis in the Bekaa. '*Habibi*, are you *sure*?' Farouk, we *saw* them. We were there. What about Fakhani? Earleen Tatro appeared. 'You're wasting our time again, Fisk. While you've been picnicking in the Bekaa, we've been covering an air raid. Read the damned wire.' The telex bell was ringing. 'Please onpass soonest to Robert Fisk of *The Times* c/o AP Beirut: Outlook World Service BBC interested historic stroke (strike) strategic two way on Beaufort Castle for broadcast today, what chance possible you ring us ...' The telephone lines had been down for hours. But it had not taken long for the capture of Beaufort to become 'historic'. François Ghattas was in the office, large, bulky, amiable, infinitely reliable François. Is the outgoing AP wire up? There was a cigarette on the lower right-hand edge of François' lip that spilled ash onto the floor. 'I am your right hand,' he said. François said that to everyone. It meant that the lines were working. I sent a computer message to *The Times*, telling Barnes that the Syrians were now involved in the fighting and concluding: 'There [is a] rumour that Israelis going for Damour just south of Beirut and Israeli ships can now be seen off the Beirut seafront. There are Israeli planes all over the sky right now but no bombing at moment – just anti-aircraft fire.'

The guns were not Syrian but Palestinian, four-barrelled artillery of Russian origin and Second World War vintage that could do no harm to a high-altitude supersonic jet. The PLO fraudulently claimed that they could destroy Israeli aircraft with their museum pieces but the most the weapons could do was scatter shrapnel over the streets. If they had any use at all, it was to raise the morale of the Palestinians, to give them the feeling that they were fighting back. The Lebanese who lived in west Beirut did not take such comfort from these guns.

The crack of their detonation shook the walls as well as the windows of the AP bureau. A group of PLO men had driven an anti-aircraft gun to one end of Nahme Yafet Street and were firing ceaselessly into the air. 'They will melt their barrels,' Nassar commented contemptuously. From the roof of the building – four floors above the AP offices – we watched the shell-bursts flecking the pale evening sky, a wasteful, purposeless exercise. There was not a plane within a mile of the explosions. The shrapnel clicked down around us, spinning off the sides of the apartment blocks and the Commodore Hotel across the road.

Then, just after four-thirty in the afternoon, a series of jets which we had seen twisting around the sky above west Beirut suddenly power-dived across the city, sweeping in a crescendo of sound over the rooftops of apartment blocks, scattering phosphorus balloons to protect themselves from heat-seeking missiles. From Fakhani, there now rose an even larger tower of smoke than we had seen from the hillside on our way back from the Bekaa. A pink flickering passed across the underside of this smoke, followed by five tremendous explosions so powerful that streets and buildings three miles away literally shook with the blast. For one extraordinary moment, the sky was filled with sharply outlined, bright green fires as the PLO's anti-aircraft shells burst vainly behind the retreating planes. The Israelis were now demolishing whole apartment blocks in their raids, their bombs exploding deep inside the buildings around Fakhani and pancaking thousands of tons of concrete floors, balconies and stairways onto their inhabitants.

By nightfall, Israeli troops were outside Sidon and controlled most of the land south of the Zahrani River. On a conservative estimate, this meant that up to 400 square miles of Lebanon — a tenth of the entire country — was now in Israeli hands. Göksel's office reported that UN soldiers were observing hundreds of Israeli tank reinforcements moving across the frontier into Lebanon; UN headquarters estimated that by nightfall the Israelis had put 45,000 men into Lebanon.

To say that Israel's war against the Palestinians was turning into a dangerous and also a very brutal conflict is to understate the political realities of her military adventure into Lebanon. A powerful anti-American sentiment was building up in even the most moderate Middle East states as a result of the war, a feeling of anger that manifested itself in physical terms in Beirut that same afternoon when the US Embassy on the Corniche was besieged by demonstrators and then came under fire from rocket-propelled grenades. Even President Hosni Mubarak of Egypt, who had every reason to maintain good relations with Washington now that the Israelis had evacuated the remainder of Sinai, described the invasion as 'outrageous'. The government-controlled Damascus press blamed Alexander Haig, asserting that he had prior knowledge of Begin's plan for an invasion and connived at it in the hope that Washington could gain strategic advantage from the annihilation of the PLO.

Yet it seemed that no restraint could be imposed upon the Israelis. Sidon was that night under heavy shellfire and air bombardment. Thousands of refugees from southern Lebanon had fled to Sidon on 4 and 5 June on the assumption that the city — 25 miles north of the battleground — would provide some protection. They were tragically mistaken. Night air attacks were now being made against buildings near the city centre. In Tyre, more than 1,000 refugees took shelter in the Red Cross centre, in the same beach hotel where we had taken cover in the first Israeli invasion four years earlier.

Although the Israelis were still at least 12 miles from the capital, Beirut already felt as if it were under siege. All MEA flights into the city had been cancelled; the last flight from Cairo, on which I had travelled, turned around in Beirut and took off empty for Larnaca in Cyprus.

Shortly afterwards, an MEA controller had allowed a flight from Paris to land in Beirut. The 707 never got off the ground again. It was still standing on the apron days later, its passenger door open, its crew long departed, when an Israeli shell hit one of its fuel tanks and blew up the aircraft. Travellers to Lebanon now had to fly to Damascus and drive across the Bekaa or take a plane to Cyprus and then the ferry boat to the Christian port of Jounieh. In the city, supplies of fruit and vegetables – traditionally grown in the south – suddenly ran out. Gasoline could now only be obtained with bribes. International communications were collapsing. It was as if one only had to shake the delicate structure of Beirut's economy for it to fall to pieces.*

That morning, forward Israeli tank crews were at Saadiyat, just south of Damour on the coastal highway between Beirut and Sidon. Why? In retrospect, it was obvious that Tveit and I had understood Israeli military strategy as we watched the Fakhani air raid from the hills above Beirut the previous day. But we could not understand the political motivation behind such an operation. Even if the Israelis chose to surround Beirut, would they then try to batter their way into the west of the city? Did they really want to destroy the PLO in Lebanon, actually to kill or take prisoner the thousands of guerrillas who were now retreating into the city? Or did they merely wish to consummate their alliance with the Phalange? And, if so, to what end? Did the Israelis believe – did the Americans believe – that the Phalange might be able to control Lebanon on their own? Was Bashir Gemayel to be their man, leading a new pro-Western state on the Mediterranean?

The road south of Beirut was now a nightmare. Terrified gunmen drove in both directions through the junction at Khalde south of the airport, where the remains of the civilians killed in the Israeli air strikes of 5 June still adhered to their burned-out cars. Puffs of white smoke drifted down from Aramoun where Israeli shells were landing. On the road we passed Mohamed Salam, who worked for the Kuwaiti News Agency. He talked to us through his car window as he drove – a familiar Lebanese habit – and said that he was trying, like us, to reach Saadiyat. We wanted to see the Israelis, to observe them in the flesh; in an as yet undefined way, we wanted to ask them why they were here.

We turned left at Khalde and headed into the lower Chouf hills. In

* A computer line message which I sent to *The Times* at 6.45 am on 8 June gives something of the flavour of the problems that confronted journalists: 'FYI (for your information), communications are beginning to collapse. Phone lines almost gone and AP wire is now faltering. Please place calls to me by phone starting at two pm your time this afternoon ... Please also ask Comcen [*Times* communications centre] to telex me at four your time on Lebanon 20636 if you don't get thru on phone. Electric power is now out for more than twelve hours a day and generators not working all the time. Informatively, I still operating from AP and ... [am] in my apartment on the seafront to stop refugees moving in in my absence. My power is out there but my home phone is working ...'

the orchards on both sides of the road, elements of a Syrian armoured unit had deployed. Several T-54 tanks were parked under the trees to the north of the highway and sandbags had been piled around revetments in the fields. A radio communications truck — a decrepit old vehicle that looked like a gypsy caravan with a thin, tall chimney on top — was standing on the road. These objects we passed quickly, driving at speed, knowing the Israeli air force's predilection for such targets.

We realised the coastal highway was under shellfire and we knew Damour was under air attack. But if we could travel east of Damour, we might be able to find the Israelis in Saadiyat. We drove on through narrow roads overhung with bushes, beneath walls dripping with large, honey-coloured flowers. In the small Druze villages, we found that the inhabitants had not fled, that the local gunmen had told their people not to leave their homes. Somehow, the word had got around that the Israelis would spare these Druze locations. We would later learn that Israeli Druze soldiers had already established that the Lebanese Druze had no intention of fighting the invading army. When we reached Baaouerta, we found the people there sitting in the porches of their homes drinking coffee and smoking, listening under the shade of their vines to the approaching sounds of war.

The families there offered us the protection of their small homes as the battle moved steadily towards them. At five-thirty that morning, the Israelis had bombed a valley just to the north, spraying the houses with red-hot shrapnel, but they had not attacked the village and the people there attributed this beneficence to the absence of Palestinian bases around their homes. Baaouerta shook to the noise of explosions but it was still undamaged. Damour lay to the west, hidden by a conical-shaped hill, but an anti-aircraft gun was firing away, puncturing the dark blue Mediterranean sky with fatuous white smoke puffs. An officer in Jumblatt's PSP militia — inappropriately dressed in cowboy boots, a white belt and stained fatigues — stood with us on the roof of a bungalow, watching the conical hill through binoculars to make sure the Palestinians did not try to enter Baaouerta. The villagers were not unsympathetic to the Palestinian cause but they intended to safeguard their precious hilltop neutrality.

Looking out over the Mediterranean, it was not difficult to see why. Less than a mile out to sea, two Israeli warships, grey against the blue water with strips of white foam behind them, were shelling the coastal road south of Damour, their projectiles landing on the dual carriageway with a high-pitched roar, sending up clouds of white dust. Just to the south, through the haze, lay Saadiyat where the leading Israeli Centurion tanks were dug into the roadside.

We had stood idly on the roof for perhaps an hour in the company of the militiaman and an old man, the grandfather of the family. It was just after midday when a little girl in a bright blue dress and pigtails climbed the concrete stairs to the roof, carrying a tray of delicately painted china cups and a jug of steaming coffee. She gave us a big smile; her parents wanted to show their kindness to the foreigners who had unexpectedly arrived at their home. We had just taken the cups and were holding them out to be filled when from immediately above us there came the sound of a jet aircraft power-diving.

The first Israeli aircraft came out of the sky so quickly that we had scarcely heard its whisper-thin jet engine high above us than it was sweeping at supersonic speed over the hills, spraying fire behind it and dropping nine or ten small dark objects into a little valley to the south. As the fighter-bomber pulled upwards, twisting in the sunlight, the earth seemed to heave near the wadi and eight massive fingers of thick black smoke sprang upwards. The walls and floor – the very air – of the little building where we stood, shook as the blast waves came cascading across the land towards us. Even before the jet was out of sight, we heard the next one coming.

It howled in from the east this time, turning hard over the dried-up bed of the Damour River and dropped its high explosives at the seaside end of the wadi. If the Palestinian guerrillas sheltering in the trees beyond that fold of hills survived just those two attacks, they must have had some deity on their side. The third aircraft came from above our heads. Perhaps the pilot feared a ground-to-air missile attack, for he brought his plane down in a sharp twisting dive that made us all catch our breath. From his aircraft there emerged a number of balloons that exploded behind the jet in a blaze of phosphorus. The balloons spilled out of the plane in its crazy dive, tracing the pattern of its descent in a spiral staircase of green light and fire that trailed down the summer sky. Through the field-glasses I caught a momentary image of the F-16 – drab-brown camouflage on its wings and the sun-glint sparkle of the cockpit canopy – before the blast waves came banging round us. From that fearsome wadi there came a ripple of explosions that spread along the river bed and sent those dark fingers of smoke jabbing upwards again, like a dead hand rising from the ground.

We watched all this with the nervousness of theatre-goers who fear that the ceiling might fall on them during the performance. It was the terrible beauty of it all that kept us silent. Then, after a minute or so, the old man sitting on the roof turned to us and said: 'What is to become of our country?' We did not reply. The militiaman in the cowboy hat reminded us gently of the recent history of the Middle East, of the Palestine mandate and of the creation of the state of Israel. The old man listened to this and then said: 'Your country helped to create Israel. You are deciding our future.'

There was an embarrassed silence, a moment which the militia officer and even the young girl understood. 'It is not just Israel,' the gunman remarked at last. 'We need a new Lebanon. We want to get rid of what this country used to be. We want a proper president, an independent leader, not someone who does what Syria tells him to do.' It was a strangely elliptical comment, for the planes that were burning the landscape around us were Israeli, not Syrian.

Yet there was no doubt that these two nations were deciding Lebanon's immediate future. We found the Syrians again an hour later, their armour and anti-aircraft guns heavily camouflaged now beneath trees and netting, spread out in a line through the laneways east of Khalde. They were not preparing an attack; they were there to let the Israelis know that Damascus did not intend to yield Beirut. This was Syria's 'red line'. As we passed their tanks, the soldiers by the roadside looked at us and I noticed that their eyes seemed unusually large. They gazed at us in an uncomprehending way and they repeatedly looked around them, at the hills above, at the sky, towards the sea. They were frightened.

And by nightfall, most of them were dead. The Israelis attacked the tanks in the late afternoon and destroyed them all. When I drove down the road four days later, all that was left of the armour was the wreckage of the communications truck that looked like a gypsy caravan, lying on its side in a ditch, its silly chimney crushed flat on the roadway by Israeli tank tracks. In the end, the Israelis devastated what was left of Damour with tank fire and drove into the ruins, right up to the broken church where I had watched the Palestinian children learning to be little guerrillas under the eyes of their unpleasantly avuncular commander six years before.

On the evening of 8 June 1982, the Israeli tanks were shelling the Khalde crossroads at the bottom of Beirut airport's 1–8 runway and their line troops could see the Lebanese capital with the naked eye. Up in the Chouf, the Druze had watched the arrival of Israeli armoured columns with complete docility. At Beit Eddine, where the palace of the Emir Bashir the Second stood on its plateau above the valley of the Hammam River, almost 100 Israeli tanks drove up the road from Baaqlin, blasting the town's two Syrian sentry-boxes on the highway – and their occupants – into the valley. On the heights of the Barouk mountains, where those ancient cedars had hitherto lived aloof from Lebanon's wars, Israeli paratroops arrived to set up a radio communications and listening base. From these cold mountain tops, they could look across the entire Bekaa, beyond Baalbek, and see the long grey slopes of the Anti-Lebanon range that marked the Lebanese–Syrian frontier. Far below lay the Beirut–Damascus highway.

The sheer speed and depth of the mass Israeli invasion stunned both the Palestinians and the Syrians. In Beirut that night, the PLO leaders spoke savagely of the moral cowardice of their fellow Arabs, of the so-called 'radical' nations that had broadcast appeals to 'mobilise the masses' on the Palestinians' behalf but failed to send either men or arms to support the cause for which they had ostensibly fought four wars with Israel. Salah Khalaf, whose *nom de guerre* was Abu Iyad, was the first to articulate the PLO's anger. As head of Fatah's security apparatus, the administration of west Beirut's defence would fall heavily upon his shoulders. 'The Arab nations with their existing regimes are as still as the grave,' he said. 'They accept the Israeli blows only with written or verbal condemnation.'

In southern Lebanon, PLO resistance had continued in Tyre and Sidon. The Israelis were reducing the Ein Helweh camp to ruins with most of its civilian population still inside. The Palestinians began to talk about Stalingrad, about a 'last stand', about victory in defeat. 'Land is not the only important thing,' Khalaf said. 'What is equally important is the will to fight, and we shall fight the Israelis from street to street.' Beirut, it seemed, was to be the Palestinians' Stalingrad. But if Beirut was to be Stalingrad, the Palestinians wished to play the role of the heroic Soviet defenders of the city in the Second World War. Yet it was the Germans not the Russians who were eventually surrounded at Stalingrad. And it was the Palestinians who were about to be trapped in Beirut.

That night, as the generator roared on the balcony of the AP bureau and the lights dimmed beside the telex machine, I punched out a news dispatch to *The Times*, and then filed a last, late paragraph. 'Shortly after dark,' I wrote, '. . . it looked as though the Israelis were planning to push northwards from the Chouf mountains and cut the main Beirut—Damascus highway on the hilltops near Bhamdoun, thus severing the Syrian army in Beirut from its forces in the Bekaa Valley. If the Israelis are working on such a strategy, then they could soon join up with the still quiescent forces of the right-wing Christian Phalange, the militia . . . whose enthusiasm for Israel has never been denied — or disguised — in Lebanon.' The paragraph was a prediction, but within 48 hours the Israelis would overtake all such assumptions and turn them into fact.

West Beirut was now flooded with thousands of refugees who camped out in the streets, squatted in the hallways of apartment blocks and in public parks. At my apartment that night, there was a knock on my door. It was my landlord, a Druze, a kind, good man who treated me and my friends as members of his own family. He had the same wide eyes as the Syrians I had seen earlier in the day. He too was frightened. Several of his family were already refugees from the fighting in east Beirut in 1975 and now they were thinking of fleeing once again. He knew that if he left, gunmen and squatters would move into the building. I packed my files and the most important documents belonging to

The Times and drove back to the AP bureau to store them in Tatro's office, warning my paper in a further message that I would be unable to prevent militiamen from looting my home if the landlord left. At least the AP office would not have to be abandoned; or so we hoped.

There was something surreal about Beirut for those of us lucky enough to be foreigners. A huge international press corps had now arrived in Lebanon. Hundreds of Israel-based reporters and camera crews moved north behind the Israeli army while hundreds more arrived by sea to join the resident correspondents in Beirut. The former were subject to censorship, the latter were not. Many journalists stayed in the comparative safety of east Beirut but most of the new arrivals came to join the reporters who lived in the west of the city. The wealthy Palestinian owner of the Commodore Hotel, Yussef Nazzal, now played host to some of the biggest names on the American television news shows. To sit at dinner with him in the sepulchral gloom of the Commodore's expensive restaurant was rather like dining at the captain's table on a great liner. The hotel's generator — long ago liberated from a shipwreck near Sidon — would thump away in the darkness while Nazzal ordered champagne and air-cooled Scotch beef, looking over his guests with a creditor's concern.

But the Commmodore was itself a trap. If it was a safe haven from the war — for the moment, at least — it also served to isolate the press from the world outside its doors. The American network crews, the resident journalists who had homes in the city, the wire service reporters and many of the newly arrived correspondents travelled daily around the country. But the hotel also contained a breed of journalistic lounge lizard, reporters who rarely left the building — or the downstairs bar — and who culled their information from the wire machines in the lobby. Virtually the only Lebanese to whom they spoke were the hotel staff, the cleaners and waiters and barmen. Their 'well informed sources' were the decreasing band of diplomats who visited the hotel. Inevitably, they began writing about the hotel, about the other reporters, about the parrot that imitated the sound of incoming shells and sang the first bars of the 'Marseillaise' and Beethoven's Fifth Symphony.

The Commodore put an unhealthy gloss on the story of Beirut; it was an unreal world that sometimes provided us with the illusion that we were watching a staged drama, a theatre, as if the tragedy taking place outside was a daily television serial in which we could indulge ourselves without harm. We all ate and drank at the Commodore; it was a meeting-place, a press club, a conference centre, in whose soiled corridors or dirty rooms we could plan our journeys and make our emergency filing arrangements. Why shouldn't we be allowed to relax after driving under shellfire or risking our lives in an air raid? But the hotel also turned us into voyeurs, arriving tired and anxious each evening to be met by smiling barmen, attentive waiters and a pianist. So things weren't so bad after all.

It was this claustrophobia, this insulation, that produced a sense of real shock among those journalists who rarely left the Commodore when a tank shell later smashed into the hotel and exploded in one of the bedrooms. That projectile not only broke through the wall of the Commodore; it punctured the surface of the goldfish bowl, as if Beirut had at last lost patience with the sleek, well-groomed creatures whom it saw through the glass doors.

Scarcely any computer messages were now arriving at the AP; the incoming wire service only worked for an hour a day but even those messages which did arrive seemed to bear little relation to the environment in which we lived. Each afternoon, the 'urgent' bells on the incoming wire would ring as AP's headquarters in New York reminded Earleen Tatro and her colleagues that they had still not sent their routine daily weather report. Was it sunny or overcast in Lebanon today? Or was there a hint of rain? Should one report light shellfire, heavy raids or intermittent bombardments?

On 9 June, *The Times* managed to file several memoranda to me, one of which asked if I would file future messages in shorter pages because 'by the time they are cut up here they sometimes get rather jumbled'. Another message announced that a friend of mine from Finland, Christina Joelsson, was due to arrive in Lebanon on holiday. *On holiday.* 'Keep work up and head down,' announced another message from London.

On the morning of 9 June, the Israelis began to cut the Beirut–Damascus highway. Tveit of Norwegian radio, Ane-Karine Arveson from the Norwegian Embassy and I had driven up past Kahhale at dawn as the air raids started over Beirut, but even the clean mountain air and the fir trees on the slopes could not lessen our anxiety now. If humiliation is a principal characteristic of Middle East wars, it was evident on the heights of Mount Lebanon. For up in the passes, teenage Syrian tank crews were desperately and vainly trying to hold open the only Syrian supply route to the Lebanese capital with tanks so hastily positioned on the mountainsides that they had not even had time to throw camouflage nets over their vehicles.

Syrian armour was across the road at Dahr al-Baidur and along the road down to Chtaura – the same road upon which Cody and I had been stopped by that bored Syrian soldier in the summer of 1976, exactly six years and five days before. Now, instead of the vanguard of a powerful Syrian army, we found the pathetic remnants of an armoured brigade whose crews were staring in fear at the skies. They concentrated on their binoculars, apprehensively searching for Israeli jets, but when they came under fire it was not from the air but from the ground. The first shells seemed to come as a shock to them, whizzing across the peaks from the Israeli tanks in Aazzouniye and exploding on the rocky hillsides to the north. It took the Syrians all of two minutes to return the fire, swinging their gun barrels across the highway and shooting back at targets they could not even see.

Tveit sat in the front of the car with a hired Lebanese driver, calculating the number of seconds between each shell-burst. 'They are hoping the Syrians will pack up and leave — this is not serious,' he said. To the north, we could see the Israeli shells bursting amid the scree, the sound of the explosions crackling and echoing down the mountainside. Several rounds landed on a smaller road to the south, on a laneway that led to Aley. When we took this southern road, we were stopped by a Syrian T-54 tank whose crew were sitting on the turret, trying to read a map and find out their location, arguing among themselves about the source of the Israeli gunfire. When we reached the opposite ridge above Aley, the cloud came down.

The high, bright sun was suddenly obscured by a thick mist that clung to the mountainside. Beneath this canopy — safe from the eyes of the Israeli bomber pilots — the Syrians were retreating, pulling as much of their armour and artillery out of the upper Chouf as they could save. Trucks towing anti-aircraft guns, lorries loaded down with mortars and shell cases drove wildly through the streets of Aley, the soldiers clinging to the sides and yelling at civilian motorists to clear the road. The heavy, muffled sound of gunfire came through the clouds and at one point a low-flying aircraft raced — sightless and unseen — over the town. As the fog closed in, these fleeing soldiers seemed to be victims of their own imagination as much as of their enemies. If ever ignorant armies clashed by night, they did so on this mountain ridge. On the other side of Aley — and we could have been no more than a mile from the nearest Israelis — a line of figures appeared out of the gloom, grey shapes tramping north in single file along the road.

They were Fatah men, using the cloud cover to retreat, gaunt, haggard guerrillas, unshaven and racked with fatigue. When we stopped the car to speak to them, they went on marching past us as if we were not there. There must have been 30 men and we tried to talk to them. I asked one where he was going but he walked past me in the fog like a ghost. Tveit was lost in his own thoughts. Then he said: 'They are asleep.'

After fighting for three days under constant air attack, these Palestinians were simply walking away from the war guided by the most basic of human instincts. They had abandoned victory — even martyrdom — for survival. Several were wounded; blood congealed through bandages on their arms. One man walked with his rifle over his shoulder and a great swathe of crimson gauze around his forehead. But all of them wore *kuffiahs*, not loosely around their necks but around their heads, as

Palestinian fighters did in the propaganda posters which the PLO published down in Beirut. They were soldiers now. Every man had kept his weapon. The Palestinians were fighting for Palestine again; and as usual, they were marching in the wrong direction. We stood there beside the road in silence as the sleepwalkers disappeared into the fog.

There were more Palestinians on the Beirut–Damascus highway, almost as tired as the men we had just seen. They had parked their jeeps and pick-up trucks on the grass verge of the road west of Chtaura after escaping the débâcle in southern Lebanon. On some of the lorries were Katyusha rocket-launchers, the thin missiles lodged in their racks ready for firing. Several Palestinians lay beside the trucks, fast asleep on the grass. The Syrians – who had fought these same men on this same highway six years earlier – now regarded the guerrillas as allies. Perhaps this was what President Assad had meant when he talked that same week about 'sharing the same trench as the Palestinians'. On the slopes of Mount Lebanon, it seemed that his army was about to share the same humiliation.

All along the mountain highway, the Syrians were bringing up more armour. There were Syrian tanks down the rough tracks off the main road now, driven into the long grass and wild flowers by crews who had no idea the Israelis were so close. All across the ridges, from Bhamdoun to Aley, the Syrians were frantically placing their armour, painfully exposed to potential air attack, a branch torn from a tree or a soldier's mattress the only pretence at camouflage. The Israeli shells arrived with awe-inspiring explosions, the echoes of each detonation clattering and clapping against the mountain walls for 15 seconds afterwards. Syria's lifeline to its army in Beirut was being strangled.

The Israelis were trying to nudge the Syrians into retreat with only four shells a minute, refusing to honour them with a war. Upon this extraordinary scene came a series of spectators. Most of them were civilians, men and women, driving fiercely along the highway towards Damascus to escape from Beirut, foot on the accelerator and faces fixed on the road ahead. There were more truckloads of Palestinian guerrillas, packed like cattle into dirty lorries that had brought them up from the fighting in the southern Bekaa. They were also unshaven but they waved at the frightened motorists and made victory signs, as if they were heading for military success rather than disaster.

Up the road, too, came a mud-spattered blue car containing the small khaki-clad figure of Bassam Abu Sharif, the official and usually highly informative spokesman for the Popular Front for the Liberation of Palestine. He had just come from the Arkoub where the Israelis were now advancing northwards. But he seemed less generous with his information on the highway to Beirut. Yes, he told us, he had just come from the battles in the south. 'Everything is going fine,' he said, and grinned meekly. *Everything*, we asked? 'Yes, everything,' and he smiled, not at us but in the direction of his steering wheel. He went on looking at the wheel as he said: 'Things are going very well for us — very well.' And with this fabrication, he drove off, waving a hand from the window. The Israeli shells went on hitting the ridges above the road, a cruel response to such untruthfulness.

The road down the other side of the mountain to Beirut was a wretched scene. Smoke covered much of the city but the Syrians on the highway paid no attention to it. Many of their checkpoints had now been abandoned and in the fields Syrian soldiers were loading ammunition onto lorries. In west Beirut, we watched Syrian *mukhabarrat* agents piling furniture into a fleet of dark green Range Rovers. Theirs was a retreat that the Lebanese would not mourn. The Syrian army now looked as though it was preparing to leave the Lebanese capital it had entered in such triumph and good order six years earlier. That lone piper on the tank that led the army into Beirut — the Pied Piper of Damascus — could never have foreseen this dismal departure.

Across the floor of the Bekaa Valley, Syria's military plight was far worse. During the afternoon, the Israelis staged air strikes against every Syrian SAM-6 missile battery between Mount Lebanon and the Anti-Lebanon mountains. With their avionics jammed by a high-altitude Israeli Boeing 707, the rockets never moved from their racks when the Israeli air force arrived in strength over the Bekaa, flying in from the Mediterranean and bombing the batteries along the Beirut–Damascus highway. The Syrians scrambled their own air force and lost more than 20 Mig jet fighters, destroyed by the Israeli air force's Sidewinder missiles. Within three days they were to lose a total of 79 aircraft in a series of vain sorties against the Israelis. An American television crew was taking tea in the garden of the Palmyra Hotel in Baalbek when one of the Syrian Migs fell out of the sky, narrowly missing the Roman Temple of Bacchus and exploding just to the south of the ruins. The only Syrian jet to attack the Israelis appeared over the coastal highway near Sidon, dropped a single bomb harmlessly on the beach and then fled away eastwards at low level over the Chouf.

The Syrians announced the 'greatest air combat' since the 1973 Middle East war — which was one way of describing defeat — and exaggerated the scale of the ground fighting between themselves and the Israelis. This was itself a paradox, since the Syrians were trying to avoid serious combat. It was for this reason that Philip Habib, who was in Tel Aviv vainly trying to secure another ceasefire, was now invited to Syria. The Syrians had no intention of sacrificing their country for the Palestinians. Damascus claimed that it had lost only three aircraft over the Bekaa, which was a palpable untruth as anyone visiting the Bekaa immediately realised. Yet mendacity was by no means confined to Syria. The Israelis were now claiming that all fighting had ceased in Tyre and Sidon. This was a lie; in both cities – especially inside the Ein Helweh camp in Sidon – the PLO was still holding out. From Sidon, too, came terrible reports of civilian casualties, of hundreds of refugees slaughtered by a night-time Israeli air attack on a school, of several Palestinian and Lebanese prisoners beaten or starved to death by Israeli soldiers. Subsequent investigation by Western journalists would prove that these reports were true.

There were times when both sides contrived to deny the truth. On the following afternoon, for example, Christina Joelsson arrived in Beirut for her holiday, having flown to Syria and persuaded a Damascus taxi driver to journey all the way across the Bekaa and through the tiny strip of territory that still connected the Syrian army with Beirut. As she was leaving Damascus, she had seen an Israeli jet fly low and at speed over the suburb of Mezze and drop a bomb on an apartment block. 'I saw it – there was a lot of smoke went up from a building – I saw the plane drop the bomb,' she told us in the AP bureau that night. Louis Faris, who was AP's stringer in Damascus – a man with the charm and personality of the old film star Peter Lorre – said the Syrians categorically denied Joelsson's account. So did the Israelis. But I ran a report of the bombing in my late file to London. Joelsson, who was employed by the Scandinavian airline SAS but also worked as a stringer for a Finnish newspaper, had visited Lebanon and witnessed air strikes before. She would not have made a mistake.

Only ten hours later did the Syrians and Israelis admit the truth. The Israeli plane, it transpired, was being pursued by a Syrian Mig and the pilot released his bomb-load to lighten his aircraft and escape. As a result, eight civilians were killed and 50 wounded. The Israelis had not wanted to admit that they bombed civilians in Damascus. The Syrians had not wanted to admit that the Israelis *could* bomb civilians in Damascus.

But Joelsson's extraordinary journey across the Bekaa revealed more than just a military accident over Damascus. She had travelled with a Swedish journalist and had been struck by the amount of Syrian armour along the roadside. She was tired, but we insisted on hearing every detail of her journey. How many tanks had she seen, we asked her. 'I don't know – maybe forty.' Where were they travelling? 'They were stationary.' Why? How could the Syrians park their tanks along the main road when the Israelis were attacking the missile batteries? 'They *couldn't* move,' Joelsson said impatiently. 'Don't you understand? – They couldn't move because they were all on fire.' It was then that AP's stringer in Baalbek succeeded in reaching the office by telephone from the Bekaa. The Syrians had sent a tank column over the Lebanese frontier north of Baalbek, he said. The tanks had become snarled up in a traffic jam of fleeing refugees who had in panic driven close to the tanks for protection when Israeli jets arrived overhead. The pilots must have seen the dozens of civilian cars but still they went ahead and bombed the armoured column, destroying every tank and killing every refugee. Up to 100 civilians were burned alive in their cars.

From the other side of the Israeli front line, reports still came to us of refugee deaths. *The Times* correspondent in Jerusalem, Christopher Walker, had been taken by the Israelis on a carefully chaperoned visit to Beaufort Castle – a disconcerting message from Barnes on the afternoon of 9 June told me he had been 'picknicking' (*sic*) beside the ruins – but still we had not found a way of getting through the Israeli line from Beirut. We wanted to travel inside Israel's occupation area unencumbered by press officers and censorship to assess what price the Israelis intended to exact for a ceasefire.

That night I filed a short paragraph at the end of my daily news dispatch which raised the same question. In return for a truce, I wrote, 'it seems likely that the Israelis would want to exert their influence over the forthcoming [Lebanese] presidential elections and it is not beyond the realms of possibility that Mr Beshir [*sic*] Gemayel, the Phalangist military leader, might attract the interest of the Israeli government as a possible contender for the highest office. For six years, Syria has exercised her own prerogative in Lebanon, deciding who shall be president and using Lebanon as a security buffer for herself. Perhaps now it will be Israel's turn.' I remembered that lunch with Gemayel but I also recalled something that Gemayel had said to me as we drank coffee afterwards, a sentence I unaccountably forgot to include in my dispatch to London two years before. 'We'll take help from the Israelis,' he had told me then. 'But you have to realise that the Israelis will only help you if you are of use to them. They don't do anything for nothing.'

Nor could their word be trusted. Early on the morning of 10 June, an Israeli plane had flown slowly but at high altitude over west Beirut. We were standing on the roof of the AP building at the time and watched as a cloud of rectangular yellow papers floated down from the aircraft. There must have been tens of thousands of leaflets drifting down on the warm early morning breeze, a lunatic confetti that settled on the roofs of apartment blocks, in the streets, in back gardens and on the surface of the Mediterranean along the Corniche. They were not addressed to the Lebanese but to the Syrian troops still in the city, specifically to Lieutenant-Colonel Omar Halal, the commander of what was left of the Syrian brigade in west Beirut. They were signed by Brigadier-General Amir Drori, the commander of Israel's northern invasion front. It was a curious way for one army officer to address another, albeit an enemy, an open letter delivered from 10,000 feet that told Colonel Halal that his days were numbered.

'We shall capture the city in a short period,' Drori's note said in

Arabic. 'We have committed a large part of our air, naval and ground forces for the area of Beirut city ... these forces outnumber and outgun all your forces. As an experienced general who lacks no wisdom, you surely know that any attempt to throw your forces against the [Israeli] Defence Force is tantamount to suicide.' While this letter obligingly set out Israel's military objectives for the Syrians – to capture the city, the Israelis would clearly have to cut the Beirut–Damascus highway – it also contained a trap. It was a smooth little note – that patronising reference to the Syrian general who 'lacks no wisdom' would not have been lost on Halal – but it also provided the Syrians with what was claimed to be a road to safety. For on the back of Drori's letter was a map of west Beirut and marked upon it was a safe passage out of the city. If the Syrians took this road to the Bekaa, they would not be bombed. The directions, indicated by a thick black line, led out of west Beirut, across the front line at Galerie Semaan and on to the Damascus highway at Hazmiyeh, then up to the road junction at Mdeirej ridge on the slopes of Mount Lebanon.

Gunmen in the streets of west Beirut immediately understood the danger implicit in this letter. They announced that the leaflet was 'poisoned' and we saw several militiamen dutifully folding the note inside old newspapers and hurling them onto garbage tips. And yet, of course, the leaflets *were* a subtle form of poison, chastening those Syrian troops who thought they should remain in Beirut.

Among the AP journalists now arriving in west Beirut was Bill Foley, a kind, courageous, but impatient photographer who had developed a chronic case of almost permanent ill-temper while on assignment amid the bureaucracy of Egypt. It was Foley who had been arrested by the Syrians beside the SAM-6 missile batteries the previous year. He and I both decided to take the Israelis' 'safe passage' out of Beirut to see how many Syrians fled the city. Near Galerie Semaan in the Chiyah district of west Beirut, we found trucks being loaded with shell boxes and near Hazmiyeh two Syrian soldiers – young men with moustaches, their faces running in perspiration – begged us for a lift to the other side of the mountain. They climbed into the back of our car, and sat there in silence, refusing to talk, looking in agitation out of the windows.

The Syrian checkpoints on the main road were almost deserted. On the mountain highway above Kahhale, however, the two soldiers suddenly demanded to get out. They had noticed a great pall of black smoke rising from the mountainsides. We drove on without them, past mobile artillery and jeeps. The towns of Aley and Bhamdoun still contained Syrian armour, but Syrian officers were evacuating the yellow stone bungalows at Sofar which had been requisitioned when the Syrian army entered Lebanon six years before. Foley and I both became worried at the same moment. We heard above the noise of our car engine a deep 'thump' and felt a burst of air through the window of the vehicle.

A huge explosion blasted round the corner of the mountainside, from the crossroads at Mdeirej ridge, the intersection marked on the maps that the Israelis had dropped over Beirut. In a dark brown cloud of smoke, we could see pieces of debris hurled hundreds of feet into the air, but Foley jammed his foot onto the brake when we saw two Syrian army trucks that had been thrown into a sloping field beside the road. Cars lay smashed beside them, either in a series of large bomb craters or smouldering beside the gorge to our left. 'Bill, they're being bombed. For Christ's sake get out of here!' There was another devastating explosion. Afterwards, we were to recall our exact words. The most mundane expressions become memorable when they are uttered in panic. I kept on shouting to Foley: 'Turn the car round, for Christ's sake' and Foley screamed back: 'What the fuck do you think I'm doing, you asshole?'

We raced back down the highway away from Mdeirej, Foley muttering 'Fuck me' over and over again, ramming the car's gear shift from second into third and back again as he fought the hairpin bends, banging his fist against the stick as if the car itself had tried to betray us. So this was Israel's 'safe passage' out of Beirut. The Syrians had driven into an ambush. No wonder those two terrified soldiers had left our car above Kahhale. No wonder Colonel Halal decided to keep what was left of his brigade in Beirut and chance his luck under siege.

We did not stop until we reached Hazmiyeh. There, in the afternoon sun, we parked the car by the highway and looked over all of Beirut. The southern and western edges of the city were an inferno. The air raids had started again, with a ferocity we had not seen before. Above the roadway that led through the pine forests east of the airport, across the west of the city to Fakhani, the shanty towns of Sabra and Chatila and beyond, black smoke hung in curtains across the sky, climbing ever higher as the jets fuelled the fires beneath it. Even where we were standing, three miles away in Hazmiyeh, shrapnel was tinkling onto the roadway and rooftops, the blast of the explosions slamming against the houses where the Christian families of east Beirut had gathered to watch the decimation of the Palestinians in the west.

Israel's vengeance against them was a fearful affair, a thing of unending explosions and bubbles of flame that ran back and forth across the far west of the city. The Israelis were telling the press in Tel Aviv and Jerusalem that they were helping to destroy 'terrorism'. The Palestinian radio station beside Fakhani was talking of the 'martyrdom' of the Palestinians. Watching it all from this gently sloping hillside at Hazmiyeh, one felt somehow crude, detached, voyeuristic, like the journalists who never left the Commodore Hotel but wrote about the tragedy of Lebanon. Foley and I even took photographs of each other leaning against the balcony of a house where a Christian family gave us coffee. The pictures are still there in my old files. Fisk and Foley smile while Beirut burns. Stupid smiles covered in sweat, risible, self-congratulatory smiles because we had almost been killed on the mountain but were now sipping coffee in the comfort of a family home.

Behind us, far across the haze, a coil of white smoke sprang up from the Palestinian camp in Bourj al-Barajneh, a column of dust and fumes that turned suddenly dark and began to mushroom outwards in fresh explosions. The same thing happened further to the west where the PLO and the Syrians had put their anti-aircraft guns below the airport. Each smoke column joined with others, each one propelled upwards by new explosions which appeared, to us three miles away, as pinpricks of light. From the sky, the Israeli jets kept power-diving, their cannon fire reaching us like the sound of tearing paper. Fifteen minutes later, they turned their attention to the ruins of the Cité Sportif, the stadium where the PLO had kept much of their ammunition and which had been pulverised by Israeli bombs in the 4 June raid. There must have been some munitions left, for there was a gulf of brilliant yellow flame and a bulb of fire shot into the sky.

It was impossible not to be moved by this, touched by the distance that separated violence on such a scale from the little rose gardens and bougainvillaea that blossomed beneath the houses of Hazmiyeh. It was a warm day and, despite the crash of explosions from the panorama before us, sparrows flitted between the rooftops, clinging to the branches of the fir trees up the road where women were now hanging out their washing in the sun.

It was clear that we were watching history, a Palestinian tragedy or defeat. But those fires demanded the answers to important questions, not just about the civilian casualties – although this was the supremely important moral issue – but about whether guerrilla armies can really be smashed by violence, their political or national aspirations burned out with high explosives.

The Christian family had joined us on the balcony, a middle-aged textile importer, his wife and teenage son, a baccalaureate student who was anxious to return to his afternoon classes. The Palestinian camps were now cowled in brown smoke clouds but from this darkness there occasionally leaped a missile, fired from a Palestinian's shoulder amid all the destruction, a vivid pink flame that would arc upwards through the smoke and then lose itself in the sunshine.

The teenager beside us had talked in a mature way about the war, its effect on the economy, on education, on his own studies. The Palestinians, he thought, had used Lebanon. There seemed no malice in his voice. Yet when we asked what he thought of the fires of west Beirut, he looked at us as if the question was unnecessary. 'It is good,' he said.

The Israelis were having a far easier time in their air offensive than on the ground. On the beaches around Khalde that afternoon, their forward tanks ran into concentrated mortar, Katyusha and small-arms fire from PLO guerrillas who had now allied themselves with Amal militiamen. Few people managed to witness these battles. When the French photographer Catherine Leroy, a journalist veteran of the Vietnam war, reached the beaches, she found DFLP men fighting from foxholes, firing rocket-propelled grenades at the Israeli armour. French colleagues who accompanied her said later that they had seen Leroy throw herself onto the beach seconds before their car was hit in an Israeli air strike. The vehicle blew up as an Israeli tank advanced down the main road through the gunfire. They returned to Beirut fearing that Leroy had died. Hours later, covered in dust and sand, Leroy arrived at the Commodore Hotel; she had been sheltered by Palestinian gunmen, she said. 'They were fighting the Israelis and holding them off – they were very professional.'*

Leroy was right. The joint forces of Palestinians and Amal were giving the Israelis their first experience of serious ground opposition in the advance on Beirut. At the time we attributed this to chance, although, down at Khalde, a remarkable phenomenon had taken shape. The Shia militiamen were running on foot into the Israeli gunfire to launch grenades at the Israeli armour, actually moving to within 20 feet of the tanks to open fire at them.

Some of the Shia fighters had torn off pieces of their shirts and wrapped them around their heads as bands of martyrdom as the Iranian revolutionary guards had begun doing a year before when they staged their first mass attacks against the Iraqis in the Gulf War a thousand miles to the east. When they set fire to one Israeli armoured vehicle, the gunmen were emboldened to advance further. None of us, I think, realised the critical importance of the events of Khalde that night. The Lebanese Shia were learning the principles of martyrdom and putting them into practice. Never before had we seen these men wear headbands like this; we thought it was another militia affectation but it was not. It was the beginning of a legend which also contained a strong element of truth. The Shia were now the Lebanese resistance, nationalist no doubt but also inspired by their religion. The party of God – in Arabic, the *Hezbollah* – were on the beaches of Khalde that night.

The crew of an Israeli armoured personnel carrier abandoned their vehicle and retreated with the remnants of an infantry company into a

---

* It was a further sign of the surreal character of the war that after Leroy's disappearance, I was able to send a message to Walker in Jerusalem through *The Times* in London, asking our Jerusalem correspondent to warn the Israeli army at Khalde that Leroy was missing and that they should try to help her on the beach if they overran the Palestinian line.

smashed school building at Medina Zahra at the bottom of the Aramoun hill. Many weeks later, Israeli troops in east Beirut told me that Shia gunmen had captured a Centurion tank and its Israeli crew. The prisoners were then shot in the back, he said.* Certainly two Israeli tanks could later be seen smouldering on the roadside. Late the same evening, Shia gunmen wearing those same strips of white material around their foreheads drove their captured Israeli armoured personnel carrier into Beirut. Its message was simple: the Israelis were not invincible after all.

As if taking revenge for their military débâcle at Khalde, the Israelis turned again upon the camps by air that night. Only hours after Reagan had appealed to Begin to call an immediate ceasefire in Lebanon, dozens of Israeli jets returned to drop thousands of tons of high explosives onto the Palestinian enclaves in west Beirut. Gunboats sailed close to the coast to shell the beaches at Khalde. In the AP bureau, we listened to an hysterical announcer broadcasting from the PLO's radio station at Fakhani. 'The enemy is bombing our camps, our women, our children,' he shrieked. The man was so overcome with anger that his voice became indistinct. 'We shall fight, fight, fight,' he screamed.

The Israeli encirclement of Beirut was almost complete. In the late afternoon, they had reached the hill town of Aley; a tank column drove right up to the gates of the Lebanese army barracks, whence emerged a local civilian dignitary who was ostensibly empowered to negotiate the surrender of the occupants on behalf of the Lebanese commander. The latter then ordered his men to lay down their arms, telling the few reporters present that 'the war is over and we are glad to see the Israelis.' The Palestinians, of course, said quite the opposite. Abu Sharif, the PFLP factotum who had claimed that everything was 'fine' in the Arkoub as the Israelis shelled the Beirut–Damascus highway, announced that night that the PLO had destroyed 150 Israeli armoured vehicles. It was an absurd lie. But he did say that the Palestinians had held back six Israeli attacks at Khalde, which was true. And he added that 'Begin will be defeated and he will find his defeat here – Beirut will be his graveyard.'

Philip Habib's peregrinations between Tel Aviv and Damascus eventually produced a 'ceasefire'. We fell into the habit of putting quotation marks around the word because only the final truce in Beirut – which was itself to be the prelude to the Sabra and Chatila massacre – lasted more than two days. Most of the ceasefires were called by Israel. And, as we found out ourselves when we stood on the west Beirut perimeter line, most of the ceasefires were also broken by Israel. The PLO claimed

---

* When I questioned an Israeli officer about this incident, he said that he would 'prefer not to comment'. If Israeli soldiers had in fact been murdered, it would have been natural to expect the Israelis to publicise the fact. But at this stage, the Israelis were in no mood to acknowledge that Beirut gunmen could capture a battle tank from their army.

that these self-declared truces were used by the Israelis to consolidate
their military positions. It was true that they usually ended in the same
manner: an Israeli unit would advance beyond its ceasefire line in order
to take more ground, the PLO would claim that this was a breach of the
truce and open fire, and the Israelis would announce that the Palestinians
had broken the ceasefire. Israeli artillery would then resume firing into
west Beirut. There were to be about 60 such 'ceasefires' over the coming
two months, all as illusory as the victories that both Israelis and
Palestinians claimed they were about to achieve.

The Syrians, who in the long term could only lose, nevertheless
achieved one vitally important military success; they prevented the
Israelis from capturing the highest point on the Beirut—Damascus highway. At a little-known battle in a village called Ain Dara, they fought
off Israeli tank attacks while under repeated Israeli air strikes. Without
air cover — and the predominant feature of the war was the vulnerability
of ground forces to the Israeli air force — the Syrians bled, quite
literally, to keep their enemy from the Mdeirej ridge, the same devastated
road intersection at which Foley and I had nearly been killed the
previous day.

When we reached the village of Ain Dara two hours after the Habib
ceasefire came into effect, the Syrian tanks were still burning fiercely
beside the narrow village road, their wounded and dead crews lying in
the fields, soaked in blood. Ain Dara itself had been wrecked, its houses
smashed open by Israeli shellfire; many were still on fire. Down the
road, the occupants of a lunatic asylum, long deserted by their nurses,
wailed from the roof of their shattered home. When we first arrived, a
Syrian soldier walked up to my driver holding the headless body of his
officer. He was crying, choking on his tears, pleading with us to put the
corpse in the trunk of our car and take it to Damascus. Four tanks in
the main street had been hit from the air; flames were still licking
around their tracks and ammunition lockers, scoring the rocks black
around them. A lorry had been flattened by bombs in a small wadi while
an armoured vehicle, burnt out, lay on the edge of a 400-foot precipice.

Through the orchards, mingled with the dark green foliage, a score of
bright golden fires burnt out of control, incinerated tanks whose crews
had already been burned alive. The orchards had borne bitter fruit in Ain
Dara that summer. In the centre of the village street a Syrian truck
stood intact, its cargo of corpses and wounded heaped in together, the
blood of the living running onto the bodies of their comrades. A soldier
sat on the back, the top of his head broken open and some kind of white
liquid mixing with the blood that poured in a torrent down his face. He
too was weeping, and his lips were moving slowly in what might have
been a prayer.

Ain Dara had been a mountain village, a small section of descending road which curved back on itself, lined on both sides with pleasant shambling villas, many of them now burning. From their ruins came other soldiers, some with bandages around their heads or arms, but still holding their rifles and wearing their steel helmets. They had fought off the Israelis for almost two days and the proof of their victory could just be seen at the corner of the village road. Across the valley, amid the pine trees, columns of blue smoke rose from burning Israeli tanks. They had been ambushed, not only by the Syrian armour that had just been destroyed from the air, but by Syrian troops firing Sagger missiles out of Ain Dara and the surrounding forest. The invincible army had again been brought to a halt.*

The Syrians we met in Ain Dara had the same dazed expression as the Fatah men we had seen sleepwalking their way through the clouds above Aley. But their exhaustion was less desolate. They greeted us, complete strangers, with offers of tea in their smashed outposts. An officer — one of Rifaat Assad's special forces — shook hands with us.

I had tied my handkerchief to the radio aerial of our car to make a flimsy white flag. It was supposed to show the Syrians that we were neutrals, that we meant no harm. We also thought that — if by some mischance we drove unwittingly through the Israeli lines — it might prevent the Israelis from firing at us. Given the extent of the Israeli defeat, it is unlikely that it would have saved our lives. But the handkerchief, flapping pathetically in front of the driver's side of the front window, caught the attention of a Syrian tank crew outside Ain Dara. The men were eating their lunch on the grass beside their vehicle and one of them stood up, a tall man with sandy hair showing beneath his helmet. He walked to our car, not vindictively but with a great sense of purpose, clutched my handkerchief and tore it from the aerial. He then handed it to me. 'No white flags,' he said.

By the night of 11 June, the ceasefire between the Syrians and the Israelis was holding; this was the most important part of the truce for the Israelis, who could no more afford an all-out war with Syria than Syria could with Israel. But AP dispatches on the wire from Tel Aviv indicated that the Israelis did not regard the PLO as a party to the truce. The fighting thus continued along the Beirut perimeter with another vain Israeli tank thrust against the Palestinians at Khalde. The Israelis also began to shell Lebanese residential areas of west Beirut.

Israeli warships had already fired rockets into the seafront apartment blocks the previous day, but on the late afternoon of 11 June their bombardment became more intense. Many of their shells fell in the

---

* There is a graphic description of this battle from the Israeli side in Schiff and Ya'ari, *Israel's Lebanon War*, pp. 161–2. The Israelis called it the battle of Ain Zhalta, the name of the next village down the road from Ain Dara.

Hamra district. As usual, the Israeli radio news announced that 'terrorist targets' were under attack in west Beirut — but this was untrue. That evening, I watched the bodies of a civilian youth and a schoolboy driven away from their shelled-out home near the Protestant College, their corpses bouncing in the back of an open-topped truck that took them to the mortuary.

The Israelis now occupied a quarter of Lebanon. For the people of west Beirut, the country's southern frontier now ran in a crooked line just below the number two runway at Beirut airport, a place of fire and desolation where hundreds of Palestinian and Lebanese Shia militiamen had died over the previous three days to prevent the new border moving still further northwards towards the city. The Lebanese leftists — the backbone of Kamal Jumblatt's old 1975–6 military alliance — had taken off their uniforms. The Druze had chosen not to defend the Chouf. Only the PLO and Amal were fighting.

For the Palestinians, there could be no future if they did not continue their battle. If they allowed themselves to be overwhelmed, the PLO would be smashed, its leadership killed or scattered, its existence no longer regarded as of any political significance. The Reagan administration would not worry if the PLO was destroyed. The Israelis would be delighted. The Syrians would claim that they had fought for the Palestinian cause in Lebanon, but the PLO's disappearance would not be totally unwelcome in Damascus. Syria's army had moved into Lebanon six years earlier in order to control the Palestinians. Now Israel's armies were doing the same thing, albeit far more savagely. Nor would other Arab states have cared unduly if the PLO's influence was shredded. In the Gulf, there were many who regarded the Palestinians as the only surviving expression of Arab militancy, but most of the rulers there saw this as a threat to their pro-Western regimes. They did not want another Middle East war and they wanted peace for themselves rather than sovereignty for the Palestinians. So did the Israelis.

What made the invasion more understandable, however, was the Israelis' belief that they could never control the occupied Palestinian West Bank and Gaza — captured in the 1967 war — as long as the PLO remained alive. The Israelis believed, correctly, that the people of the occupied territories drew their political will from the PLO. If the Israeli government wanted to increase the number of illegal Jewish settlements in the West Bank, even to annex the area, it could never do so unless the Palestinians in Beirut were neutralised. If the Israelis did not crush the PLO, then the Palestinians in the West Bank and Gaza might one day rise up against them. The PLO therefore had to be finished off.

But there was more to the invasion than this. The largely Muslim Lebanese population of west Beirut was now asking what Israel wanted to do to their sector of the city. Did the Israelis wish to conquer it or divert their constantly changing frontier around the west Beirut perimeter to the Christian Phalangists in east Beirut, turning Lebanon into a vassal state, cleansed of Palestinians and owing allegiance to Tel Aviv, the new Sublime Porte of the Levant? Even the Phalangists were now worried that this might be the case. Bashir Gemayel, who had accepted Israeli arms and support, remained uncharacteristically silent.

He could scarcely have praised the Israelis after they had killed so many of the Lebanese civilians who were citizens of the nation over which he wished to rule as president. At least 8,000 people – 2,000 of them in Sidon alone – had died since the invasion began and well over 400 people, almost all of them Lebanese civilians and most of them women and children, had been blasted to death in their apartment blocks by Israeli air strikes on 12 and 13 June. The Israelis were later to dispute these statistics, to claim that those who used them were dupes of the PLO or even – and this was becoming a reflex accusation against the press – anti-semitic.

But it was the Israelis who were lying about the figures, as their officers and government officials well knew. Hundreds of corpses were buried in just one mass grave in Sidon in the first week of the war. Their burial place, now known as Martyrs' Square, was at the road intersection at the bottom of Riad Solh Street which is today planted with carefully maintained palm trees and shrubs that grow in abundance above the gruesomely fertilised soil.

The daily newspapers in Beirut filled columns of their back pages with the names of the dead. There were more than 200 listed from a single Israeli air strike in Beirut on 5 June alone – the day before the invasion began – the details collected from the hospitals to which the bodies had been taken by the Red Cross and civil defence forces.

So enormous were the casualty tolls that the continued carnage even pushed news of the Falklands war into second place in British newspapers. Most of the dead in the capital were Muslims, although there were a few Christian Maronites who lived in west Beirut among the victims. On the edge of Sabra, the Muslim cemetery was now so crowded with dead from the Israeli raids that corpses were being buried 30 deep in mass graves, one on top of the other.

Tens of thousands of refugees, including many foreigners, were now trying to leave Lebanon through the Christian port of Jounieh. But the Israelis, whose gunboats patrolled the coastline, refused to let the boats leave. On the night of 14 June, the French and Italians were both planning to send warships to force the Israeli blockade and escort their nationals out of the country. The Phalange allowed most Lebanese Muslims through their lines, although only the wealthiest of Palestinians with connections in the Maronite community would have crossed to east

Beirut. The majority of the Palestinians were left to their fate in the west.

On the afternoon of 13 June, while Israeli jets flew through the skies above west Beirut to attack the Palestinian camps again, I walked from the AP bureau down to Kemal Salibi's home. Salibi sat in his galabia robe on his Ottoman balcony, a sad prophet who had decided to stay on in the chaos of west Beirut because it was here, he believed, that a real Arab culture still flowered. 'The *Kata'ib* [Phalange] wanted to turn Lebanon into a little Christian banana state,' he said. 'They wanted a third-rate beach club and skiing resort. But what sort of Lebanon is that? This is not the sort of country that I would care to identify with. A country has to stand for something. At least the Palestinians stand for something — for what remains of the Arab conscience. But the *Kata'ib* missed their opportunity for creating an *entente cordiale* with the PLO.' If the Israelis crushed the Palestinians — who were traditionally allied to the Muslim leftists in Lebanon — then the Phalange would *always* be the enemy of the Muslims; and the Muslims now comprised the majority of the Lebanese population.

That night, I filed a dispatch to *The Times* which concluded that 'the Lebanese ... take predictably cynical comfort from a basic fact of military life here: that Lebanon takes its own peculiar revenge on visiting men-at-arms. For every army that has entered Lebanon — the Palestinians, the Libyans, the Syrians, the Iraqis, even the United Nations — have found themselves bogged down in a political and military quagmire, humiliated before their enemies. There is no historical reason why Israel should not join this list.' As my copy clicked over the teletype computer wire from the AP bureau that evening, Ariel Sharon, the Israeli defence minister, was leading his army along that path of humiliation, a shell-cratered road of rice, rose water, bunting and cheers which would lead, inevitably, to bloodshed and tragedy.

For Sharon — who according to ministerial colleagues had all along misled the Israeli Cabinet about the real military and political objectives of the invasion — forced a passage for his armour through the foothills around Shweifat, a suburban village at the far southern edge of Beirut. And just before midnight, he and his forward Israeli line troops reached Baabda, the seat of the Lebanese government, where the glass and concrete palace of President Elias Sarkis stood on an escarpment above Beirut.

Before dawn the next morning, we found a taxi driver to take us across the front line, talked our way past the sleepy Palestinians on the last barricade, travelled across the rubble of Galerie Semaan and stopped just beyond Hazmiyeh in the Christian sector of east Beirut. There was an air of expectation. Families had gathered on their balconies, holding rice and rose water, talking quietly among themselves, many of them with radio sets to their ears. They were the same families I had watched blowing kisses to the Syrian army six years earlier. Now another army was coming. There was no apprehension, rather a sense of relief, almost merriment, combined with the sort of suspense that accompanies a meeting with a potential lover. Yet again, it was to be the end of the war, the end of Lebanon's grief. Here, once again, came an army that was supposed to represent renewal and political renaissance. For the Christians, victory over the Palestinians now seemed certain, and with it a genuine independence. For had not the Israeli government repeatedly stated since the invasion began eight days earlier that its army would not stay an hour — *not a minute* — longer than necessary?

A magnificent dawn spread across west Beirut, piercing the smoke haze over the city, flame-coloured across the windows of thousands of apartment blocks and illuminating the great arc of sea beyond the peninsula. West Beirut was surrounded in the morning glory. Then from up the tree-lined road came the sound of armoured tracks as if chains were being dragged along its surface. The Christians on the balconies craned forward. Our driver, a Sunni Muslim, abandoned us in terror, ran to his car and drove away in the direction of west Beirut. So we stood there on our own, our eyes fixed on the corner of the road where a lilac tree swayed in the breeze. We too had waited long to see the Israelis, tried hard to make our way through their lines to ask why they had invaded; and now they were coming to us.

There has to be a first tank. All invading armies, if you think about it, are likely to be led by a tank. But when it came down the road from Hadeth towards Hazmiyeh, a group of Israeli soldiers clinging to the armour around its improbably long gun barrel, it was still impossible to believe. The Israelis had arrived right here on the very outskirts of Beirut and the local Christian families ran into the street, some of them crying with happiness, their faces wreathed in smiles.

The soldiers did not look so happy. They were dirty and tired, their faces stained with boot polish to camouflage them through the darkness of the previous night, a slick of perspiration beneath their helmets. Several glanced across at the smoke haze over Beirut and just a few looked up the hill to where Lebanon's impotent president must have been counting the hours to his political demise. When we walked up the road, we found the Israelis actually debating what Elias Sarkis would do now that he controlled only 200 yards of Lebanon. Most of them were Ashkenazi Jews, many with blue eyes, some with New York accents, young men, almost boys, friendly, full of confidence.

Could this truly be the same army that was terrorising the population of west Beirut, that had killed so many thousands of Palestinians, whose air force used such awesome, murderous power against soldier and civilian alike? But how *could* one dislike these young men? They were educated, they talked about peace, some of them disagreed with each other over the aims of the war. No Syrian, no Palestinian would dare do that. It was difficult not to feel a kinship with these Europeans, to search, however vainly, for ways to excuse the terrible deeds that were being committed in their name and by their army and air force. These were Israelis, the invincible people with the invincible army, the children of the Holocaust, the people of the Exodus, the survivors who had emerged from the nadir of their race to flourish in a new state which they had fought and died to defend. This was the army that spoke, repeatedly, about the need to avoid civilian casualties, that talked of 'purity of arms', whose civilian-soldiers had — according to popular Hollywood legend — made the desert bloom.

A young medical orderly from Ashqelon, his bright red hair so long it almost touched his flak jacket, was pondering the political possibilities of Lebanon. 'Do you think the president is watching us from up there?' he asked, and he jerked his head in the direction of the palace high above us in the pine trees. 'I think Philip Habib should fly in here, take Sarkis over to the palace window and point out that we've arrived.'

The Israelis had indeed arrived, parking their tanks and armoured personnel carriers on a small bluff beside the main road that conveniently overlooked the Palestinian camp at Bourj al-Barajneh, escorted by a jubilant group of Lebanese Phalangist gunmen who were only too happy to sort out the tank jam on the road behind them. The Israelis were standing on the grass, smoking cigarettes, sipping from cans of Lebanese beer. After watching the ferocity of their air strikes and tank fire for more than a week, we had half expected to see giants, but of course the Israelis were, like most off-duty soldiers, instantaneously generous, politically naïve and just a little puzzled by their complex and bloody campaign in Lebanon.

Sitting inside an armoured vehicle, a soldier with a black moustache and flawless English — a corporal from Natanya — held out to me a handful of dark, crimson cherries. Had we had breakfast? Would we like a beer? It was served to us chilled. A group of junior officers gathered round the truck, listening to our conversation. They had all come ashore at Damour and had fought their way round Aley to reach this cool spot in the hills above Beirut where the Maronite community afforded them the first hospitality they had been shown since setting foot in Lebanon. A soldier from Jerusalem asked what the Palestinians were like, which was surprising since Jerusalem is also a Palestinian city and he had been fighting Palestinians all week. What did *he* think they were like, we asked?

'The Palestinians did not fight too well,' he said. 'We took some wounded and killed some. It is easy for them to fire a rocket-propelled grenade at us then run away. You don't have to be a good soldier to do that. The Syrians were better. Some of the Syrians were security men of Rifaat al-Assad and they fought too.' We sipped some beer and ate more cherries. Did the Israelis want to stay in Lebanon? No, the same soldier replied. They did not want to stay: they wanted to bring peace. We looked at him carefully with his rifle on his shoulder and grenades by his belt, but he meant what he said and the other soldiers all nodded. 'We wouldn't fight the Palestinians if they didn't fight us,' he said.

Across the road, a Lebanese girl was waving at an Israeli tank crew. A few families had driven up the gentle slope, tourists in a war, to gaze at this alien army in a foreign land. These were the same people who had thrown rose water at the Syrians. Now they were shouting 'Shalom' to the Israelis. But something was troubling the corporal from Ashqelon. 'What is it like in west Beirut?' he asked.

The other soldiers drew closer. It was a question that had clearly been on their minds. So we told them, slowly and without exaggeration, what west Beirut was like now, about the thousands of refugees who had poured into the city in advance of the invading army. We talked about the armed squatters who were stealing other people's homes and about the new and more malevolent breed of gunmen who had emerged on the streets. And we told them of the Israeli bombing raids, the hundreds of civilians who had died in them around Corniche Mazraa and Sabra, more than half of them women and children who were not — and could not have been — criminals or 'terrorists' or any other kind of enemy.

The soldiers listened carefully as we gave them the casualty figures. When we stopped speaking, they were silent. So we asked why they thought civilian areas had been bombed. It was the soldier from Natanya — the one with the black moustache — who responded first. He shrugged slightly. 'That is a political question,' he said. 'And we are soldiers.' His comrades clearly sensed the unsatisfactory nature of this reply. Then a captain leant forward and said: 'We have killed fewer people than your country has killed in the Falklands.' The other soldiers smiled at this statistical nonsense. Finally, the medical orderly spoke. 'We want peace and we came here to bring peace,' he said. 'We came to stop killings.'

If this was a *non sequitur* after so much bloodshed in Lebanon over the preceding eight days, the first Israelis to enter the outskirts of Beirut failed to realise it. Nor did they bring peace. Having personally led the armoured thrust that encircled west Beirut, Sharon travelled to the east of the city to consolidate his alliance with the Phalange during a series of meetings with Maronite leaders. Hundreds of Phalangist gunmen were immediately permitted into Israel's new area of occupation in the upper Chouf, to set up Christian militia checkpoints around Maronite villages which had hitherto remained immune from harm even though they were located in territory traditionally controlled by the Druze. The Syrians had never permitted the Phalange to enter these villages; Damascus had guaranteed the security of these Christians and — with the one terrible exception of the bloodletting that followed Kamal Jumblatt's murder — the safety of this minority in the Chouf had never been a political issue.

By introducing their Christian militia allies into the area, the Israelis overnight turned the Maronite villagers into associates of the Phalange, even though most of the inhabitants showed no enthusiasm for such 'protection'. Within hours, the Israelis had upset the delicate balance of trust that had previously existed between the communities in the mountains; for the Druze interpreted the arrival of the Phalange as a sign that the villagers intended to collaborate with their enemies. The seeds of another tragedy were thus sown on the night Sharon arrived to bring 'peace' to Beirut.

Encouraged by the willingness of the Israelis to cooperate with them, the Phalangists now appeared on the streets of east Beirut and up in the Christian hills around Baabda, setting up their own 'military police' checkpoints; the Christian gunmen at these roadblocks pasted strips of red tape around their helmets upon the front of which they painted the letters 'MP'. The Phalangists also brought their artillery up into the hills above the city and the Israelis made not the slightest attempt to stop them. Israeli troops in their turn drove into east Beirut and were welcomed as liberators. Israeli officers dined in the best restaurants while their soldiers went on shopping sprees through east Beirut's well-stocked supermarkets.

Israeli jeeps and trucks were jammed into the city's narrow streets, halting obediently at traffic lights as if this were Tel Aviv or Haifa. Across these streets, however, hung the triangular cedar symbol of the Phalange and upon the walls of houses there were pasted giant portraits of Bashir Gemayel and of his father Pierre. The latter was depicted not as an old man of 77 but as a youth leader with a small black tie. For the portrait was a copy of one that had been distributed to Phalangist offices back in 1936, shortly after Gemayel had returned from his seminal visit to Nazi Germany. Christian women waved at the conquering Israeli troops; within four weeks, the Israeli press would announce the betrothal of an Israeli soldier to a Maronite girl, the first since the invasion.

From west Beirut, Sunni Muslim families now turned up by the carload in the hills above the city, not as refugees but as tourists intent on seeing for themselves the new arrivals in Lebanon. Some of them picnicked beside the Israeli troop compounds at Baabda and invited Israeli soldiers to pose for snapshots with their families. The Sunnis did not regard the Israelis as their enemies.

The Lebanese possessed an exclusive quality of forgiveness based upon an intuitive calculation that weighed the sins of the past against the potential benefits of the future. The Israelis were winning, they had surrounded west Beirut, they promised peace and the eviction of the Palestinians and they said that they had no designs on Lebanon. So the Lebanese families who drove across from west Beirut disregarded the carnage of the past week and smiled upon the latest young soldiers to occupy their land.

They could see – as we could see when we travelled back and forth across the front line – that the Israelis were bringing hundreds of Merkava battle tanks and long-range artillery up to the west Beirut perimeter. Up in the Chouf, around Beit Eddine and Baaqlin and Deir al-Amar, we found the Israelis building concrete gun platforms for massive M107 self-propelled guns. In some cases, five-man crews had already installed the artillery and we noticed that their 33-foot barrels were always pointed high above the mountain ridges towards Beirut. At Baabda, the Lebanese watched a column of tracked M108 Howitzers grinding down towards Hadeth. The Lebanese Muslim picnickers saw this, yet still they smiled. Then they bundled their children back into their family cars and returned to west Beirut.

The Palestinians' leftist militia allies deserted the PLO on 14 June and Sarkis announced a 'Government of National Salvation' which would include Walid Jumblatt, Nabih Berri and, more importantly, Bashir Gemayel. Even Berri, the Amal leader, ordered his men to lay down their arms. Near the airport that evening, I found a group of Amal men throwing their guns into a ditch and tearing up their identity cards for fear that the Israelis would invade west Beirut the following day and take revenge for the battles at Khalde. On that evening of the 14th, I saw sheets and towels hanging from rooftop aerials and apartment balconies in the Hamra district of west Beirut; white flags of surrender. But the Palestinians were now surrounded and they had only west Beirut in which to fight. George Habash, the PFLP leader, promised again to turn Beirut into 'a new Stalingrad'.

Nor could the Syrians accept that the city they had sworn to protect should fall into Israeli hands. Habib wanted to assist Sarkis in the formation of his 'national salvation' Cabinet, but without Syria's support it was impossible to create a new *status quo* in Lebanon. On the 15th, the Syrian regime insisted that its troops in the city were there under the peace-keeping mandate which they had been given by the Arab League. The Syrian soldiers surrounded with the Palestinians in west Beirut were there, according to a statement read over Damascus radio, 'by virtue of an Arab decision and at the request of the legitimate Lebanese authorities'. Syrian troops 'would therefore carry out their duty to defend with all their strength the legitimate authority of the Lebanese government, as well as Lebanese territory and the Lebanese and Palestinian people.'

The most recent ceasefire did not hold. It was never intended to. The truce broke down a day later with a bombardment of Palestinians by Phalangist artillery on the hills around Baabda. Most of the Christian militia fire was directed towards a unit of PFLP men who had positioned themselves inside the science faculty of the Lebanese University, a rectangular, modern building of steel and plate glass that stood in a small grass campus below Hadeth, on the very edge of the west Beirut perimeter. The Israelis, who were billeting a company of infantry in a school building below the artillery batteries, made no attempt to intervene. Indeed, when we found them that morning the Israelis were sitting on a concrete wall to the south of the empty classrooms, watching the artillery rounds exploding in grey puffs on the campus.

Many of the Israelis here were Sephardic Jews, and they chatted in Arabic with the Phalangist gunmen who wandered down from the batteries on the hill above. Several of the officers were Ashkenazis like those we had seen two days earlier. Yet something had changed. It was not just the absence of the Muslim picnickers nor even the arrogance which the Phalangists now betrayed towards us in front of the Israelis, snatching our press cards from our hands, ordering us back to west Beirut and pointing their rifles at us when we protested. It had something to do with the casual way in which the Israelis asked them to leave us alone. The Israelis' automatic acceptance that the Phalange – a militia which had such dark political antecedents in the Europe of the Thirties – had a right to participate in this war, was frightening. Did they not realise that the very word 'Phalange' spoke of dictatorship and European anti-semitism? Did they not know that many of these Phalangist militia-men regarded the Palestinians as sub-humans worthy only of extermination, with exactly the same sentiments the Nazis had expressed towards the Jews?

The Israeli lieutenant who approached us was a young man whose curly hair and silver-framed glasses gave him a gentle, almost ascetic appearance. He seemed at first quite out of keeping with the tanks and troop-carriers on the hill above the battlefield. The Phalangist guns had been banging away from beside the Maronite church on the hill to our left when the soldier walked up to us with a quiet 'Shalom', volunteering like an academic that the artillery was 155 millimetre. Below us, on the narrow plain that separated the hills from the sea and the deserted airport, shells were exploding across the science annex, points of flame that moved along the side of the silvery building.

'There are terrorists down there and in the camp on the right,' the young soldier said, waving his hand in the general direction of west Beirut. He had lived in France for most of his youth, emigrating to Israel only six years earlier, and he spoke English with a strong French accent. In the autumn, he was due to commence his first term at law college in Jerusalem. But now he was a soldier, he had fought his way up from southern Lebanon through Tyre and evidently knew that not everyone approved of what his army had done in the past ten days. He had seen the ruins of Sidon.

'It was not really beautiful, I guess,' he said. 'But one has to do one's job. You know, you journalists must never forget what the villages in Galilee look like when they have been bombed.' We looked together down at the shellfire in Hadeth as the Phalangist gunners traversed their artillery to the right, sending clouds of grey smoke up from the edge of the Bourj al-Barajneh camp. But did he not think, we asked, that perhaps the destruction and slaughter in Lebanon these past days – almost 10,000 people were now estimated to have been killed – had been somewhat out of proportion to that wrought on northern Israel?

His response was immediate. 'It is not the difference between one dead and a thousand dead,' he said. 'It hurts as much. Seeing dead children and women here is not really nice but everyone is involved in this kind of war – the women too – so we can't always punish exactly the right people because otherwise it would cost us a lot of deaths. And for us, I guess – I hope you understand this – the death of one Israeli soldier is more important than the death of even several hundred Palestinians. We don't play football. I mean it's not the quantity of deaths – it's what we are trying to do. I hope there is going to be peace in Lebanon and if it costs a lot of lives, well that's it.'

The young man seemed unaware of any contradiction in this argument. Israel, he said, was trying to find a solution for future years, 'maybe having a peace, a Christian government or even with the Muslims having some arrangement where at least one of our neighbours would be at peace with us.' He did not regard Egypt as being at peace with Israel – he refused to say why – but he spoke of Israel as a country with a mission.

'Here we really have a chance for lasting peace because the people need us,' he said. 'We need them as peaceful neighbours but they need us because we are stronger, we are more organised, we can help them. We may like or not like the people but we need them because it's in our interest.' There was something over-zealous about this soldier, something messianic about his reasons for being here. We felt uncomfortable, unnerved by his words. I was recording our conversation for Canadian radio but he seemed quite unconcerned by the microphone I was holding in front of him. The Phalangist guns above us fired again and once more the flames erupted across the university building below us. There was a sustained pattering of machine-guns, strength made manifest through fire.

And what, we asked, about the Palestinians? The Israeli soldier sighed slightly, as if he knew the question had been coming all along. 'Listen,' he said. 'I know you are recording this but personally I would like to see them all dead. You may send this anywhere you like: I would like to see all the Palestinians dead because they are a sickness everywhere they go.'

Is not that, we asked, exactly what Hitler said about the Jews? 'It is, but there is a slight difference,' he replied, 'because the Palestinians receive help and they have so many countries around here that are ready to support them and to help them. But it's hypocrisy, you know. The Arab countries help them only in order to destroy Israel. They are not interested in welfare. I know it is a bit hard to put because maybe I'm a bit emotional about it. Personally, I wouldn't mind seeing the Palestinians all dead and helping to do it.'

Something deeply disturbing was exploding inside this young soldier, some phobia as powerful as the artillery above us. It was as if the lieutenant had suddenly and unaccountably decided that his morality should be sacrificed to the power of a far more sinister emotion. Perhaps it was my microphone that then caused the young lieutenant to hesitate. 'I know it doesn't sound very nice, and ...' He paused for several seconds as if he was trying to catch hold of his own thoughts, to control things that had come adrift during his expressions of hatred. There was a swish of shells over our heads and the thump of their explosion below a few seconds later. 'You were talking about Hitler. I know the argument that the Jews have suffered from Hitler and that nobody else has to suffer from the tyranny of the Jews. But I don't understand it. Our foremost interest is to live in peace and to flourish in our country, and if somebody disturbs us and tries to destroy us, there is no reason why we shouldn't destroy him first. You know, they said this in the Bible too.'

The shooting was growing more intense on the plain below and it seemed to influence the Israeli, whose right hand had come to rest on his rifle barrel. 'I don't say "Kill everyone." It's a wish, you see. Personally, I don't think our government would take the responsibility for massacring a lot of Palestinians. But anyway the least we can do is destroy their military capacity and diplomatic organisation.'

The soldier's mind returned to the question of Israel's power. 'But we are strong,' he said. 'There is no doubt about it. And we are strong enough to make the choices ... If we don't go now into west Beirut itself, it's not that we can't – it's because we don't want it. But now we are in a position of pressure. I hope the Palestinians will never go back to the south. Unless there is going to be a real force here – and I hope it's not going to be an Israeli force, rather an American or United Nations one – unless this force exists, the Palestinians will go back in a few years and all this will be for nothing.'

Even now, when I listen to my cassette recording of that extraordinary interview – the tape jarring as the Phalangist shells are fired over our heads – I can hear my own voice rising in incredulity at some of the soldier's words. Today, I realise that his was a statement of terrifying prescience. Then, it was merely another sign of things to come, an example of the moral slippage that would turn the invasion into Israel's first military defeat.

We said our farewells politely enough and the young lieutenant even flipped his right hand to his head in a friendly sort of salute. We looked again down onto the plain where the smoke from the university building had now formed a plateau of dark clouds across the west of the city, a rim of grime above the sea that merged imperceptibly with the heat haze. Peace was going to go on costing lives.

8   The Gravedigger's Diary

125 people inside, mostly children, women. Sheltering
from bombs in the basement. All dead. All of them had
burned. Flesh mostly burnt. Collected the bones of 125
people, also bags of gold rings, jewellery. Could only check
number of people from evidence of seven survivors who
were outside building at the time. Took bones to cemetery.
My decision to bury bodies there.

From the June 1982 report of Mahmoud Khadra,
director of the south Lebanon civil defence service,
on the Israeli bombing of a civilian apartment
block in Sidon.

The young man wanted to help us. The Israelis had bombed the elementary school around the corner, he said, and there were 120 dead
civilians still lying in the basement. It seemed hard to believe but there
was in the air a fine and terrible smell that told us he might be telling
the truth. Then when we had walked around the corner, the flies came
and clustered around us, settling on our faces and lips.

A younger man took us into the little school, its churned-up earthen
playground and basketball pitch littered with broken concrete, black-
boards and chairs. 'Be careful when you get to the bottom of the stairs,'
he said, and just where the banister ended there was a corpse, cut in
half, its arms thrown back as if in despair. 'Now look down to your
left,' the man said, and through the broken roof of the basement, we
saw them.

The bodies lay on top of each other to a depth of perhaps six feet,
their arms and legs wrapped round each other, congealed in death in a
strangely unnatural mass. So many hundreds of civilians were killed by
the Israeli air raids on Sidon that the local Red Cross had not yet had
time to bury all the dead. So at the little elementary school off the
Jezzine road, they had sprinkled the corpses with a powder of lime, a
benevolent white dust that somehow softened this evil place, turning the
bodies of the men, women and children into statues, like the carbonised
residents of ancient Pompeii when the ash of Vesuvius fell upon them.

An almost equal catastrophe appeared to have fallen upon Sidon, for
there were even more ghastly basements around the city, and there were
several mass graves where the governor, the *mohafez*, in despair ordered
the unclaimed dead to be interred. One such, containing 40 dead, lay on

a traffic island, half covered in garbage and rubble. In one hospital, we found a doctor so scarred by the number of casualties and corpses that had been brought to him over the past five days that he could not bring himself to describe what he had seen without breaking down. In several cellars, we found the bodies in pieces, heads and arms, toes and slit-open torsos tangled together. Everywhere – in the streets, in the houses, even on the seafront – we smelled death. It had a high, sweet odour. No animal but a human could reek like this, a special mixture of sweat, intestines and faeces, of people whose stomachs had been blown out of their bodies, of corpses rotting under the hot sun.

The Israeli air attacks were – until then, at least – the most ferocious ever delivered upon a Lebanese city. In the southern sector of Sidon, it looked as if a tornado had torn through the residential buildings and apartments, ripping off balconies and roof supports, tearing down massive walls and collapsing whole blocks inwards upon their occupants. Many of the dead were sandwiched inside these ruins. In the streets, where Israeli bulldozers had swept away the rubble with military briskness, the people of Sidon walked in a daze. They did not respond to the usual greetings and they stared at the surviving buildings because their city had never looked like this before.

Was it surprising that the Israelis did not want Sidon's affairs to be reported by Western correspondents based in Lebanon? Journalists arriving there from Israel were under military escort and submitted their dispatches to Israeli censorship. Besides, the reporters who drove up from Tel Aviv and Jerusalem were taken only to the seafront at Sidon, to the crusader castle, to an area near the souk which had remained undamaged by bombing and, later, to the flattened Ein Helweh camp. But no reporters from Beirut were to be permitted into Israel's occupation zone.

The Israeli major who stopped Jonathan Randal of *The Washington Post* and myself on the road south of Khalde had been quite blunt about it. A plump man with greying brown hair and modest English, he leaned on the roof of our car and looked through the window at us, shaking his head vigorously from side to side. 'I am under orders not to permit any correspondent from Beirut to go south from here,' he said. 'You must go back.' Randal explained, slowly and patiently, that while we were reporters – and we volunteered our press cards to the major – we were also travelling to Sidon to find out if the wife and daughter of a Lebanese journalist colleague of ours had survived the invasion. We had money to take to her from her husband. 'No way,' the major said. 'I'm sorry,' Randal replied. 'You clearly don't understand. We are going to Sidon to look for the family of one of our colleagues. That is why you must let us through.'

The road around us was in chaos. Military trucks carrying line troops, armoured personnel carriers and lorry-towed artillery pieces were trying to squeeze between our car and a shell-hole that had blown three feet out of the highway. A salvo of Katyusha rockets fired by the PLO from behind Beirut airport shrieked overhead and exploded on a bluff above us. The major was angry. So was Randal. He climbed out of the car. He was a thin, wiry man with a journalist's fixation for detail and a frightening temper. 'Now look here, my friend,' — Randal always called people 'my friend' when he was nervous or angry — 'my friend, I've already told you we've got to go through. You have no option but to let us go to Sidon. We are on a humanitarian mission.' The major wagged his finger in Randal's face. 'I don't care,' he shouted.

Randal raised his glasses to his forehead — this was always a dangerous sign — and strode into the road in front of another troop carrier. Behind it was a Merkava tank, its huge barrel pointing north towards the airport. Randal walked up to it, followed by the major. 'You see that tank?' he asked. The major looked at it. 'Well, I pay my damned taxes so you can have these damned toys — so you damned well let us through.' Another man joined the two men, a younger officer who spoke in Hebrew to the major. 'I'm not moving my damned car off the road until you let me through.' The major held up a warning hand. 'I mean what I say. You want to damn well order an American off this road, well I'm damned well not going to move when I have to pay my dollars to support your damned wars.' The younger officer nodded at Randal. 'You can go,' he said. Which is how we reached Sidon.

The coast road was a scene of devastation. Damour was in rubble, the stench of corpses drifting down from the town onto the two-lane highway. On the other side of the road, a Palestinian's body had been crushed flat, driven over repeatedly by vehicles which were on their way to Beirut, pressed into the tarmac until the corpse and the red pulp that spread from its stomach was only two or three inches thick.

From every house down the highway flew a white sheet or a towel, from television aerials, balconies, from flagpoles crudely erected on rooftops and garages. Between the road and the sea, along the beaches, the Israelis had built military camps above which dozens of blue and white Israeli flags floated in the summer breeze. At the Awali River, there were gunmen from Haddad's militia and an Israeli military police-man who demanded our passports and wanted to mark the pages with a rubber stamp bearing a Star of David. We refused to allow him to do this, pointing out that his checkpoint did not mark the northern frontier of Israel.

Both Randal and I knew Sidon well — we had been going there since 1976 — but the square where the municipal offices and the fire brigade had their headquarters was almost unrecognisable. The roadway was a dustbowl of craters and pieces of jagged iron, the buildings scorched and tottering, the city offices blasted open by a bomb which had evidently dropped through the front of the building, for there was a 15-foot cleavage cut into the stone above the front door. At the offices of the Lebanese Red Cross, a female doctor told us that up to 2,000 people had died.

'Be careful,' she said. 'The people here are frightened. The Israelis took everyone between the ages of sixteen and sixty to the beach and then hooded men arrived, escorted by Israeli plain-clothes police. When the men with the hoods pointed at a prisoner the Israelis took the prisoner away. There were tens of thousands on the beach and the Israelis have taken hundreds of them. The men with hoods pointed at Lebanese men who had never carried guns. The hooded men were collaborators. They pointed at men who hated the Palestinians but these men were taken away. Go up the Jezzine road, there you will find the dead. Go to the school and the Djad building and all the buildings round there. They were all hit.' As we were leaving, the woman ran after us and grabbed me by the arm. 'Do not make people say things that may incriminate them,' she said. 'Please remember, we have to be careful because we are under occupation now.'

On the Jezzine road, a tracked Israeli vehicle was parked beside a ruined house, the soldiers sitting on the back eating oranges. Men and women passed without looking at the soldiers, staring towards the city centre, walking through the clouds of dust in distraction. The road was a yellow fog through which permeated that dreadful smell. Our reaction to death − to the reality of dead bodies and mutilation − tended to be businesslike. It had to be.

Journalists who report wars have to be as dispassionate as doctors about the physical aspects of mortality. We needed the psychological strength to convince ourselves that gruesome detail was also scientific fact; we had to interpret the smell of human decomposition not as something disgusting but as a process of chemical change that was natural if unpleasant. Yet all this is easier said than done. Death *is* frightening. If nothing else, the dead of Lebanon − the repeated experience of seeing bodies lying like sacks in roadways, ditches and cellars − were a constant reminder to us of how easy it is to be killed. It is a necessary lesson. Just one little step across a very fine line, the slightest misjudgement over when to cross a road, when to smile or look serious in front of a gunman, could mean the difference between life and death.

But bodies in decay *are* disgusting. The smell of human remains in 100 degrees of heat is nauseating. It contradicts our most deeply held values: love, beauty, gentleness, health, cleanliness, hygiene, life. Both physically and mentally, that stench was the manifestation of our fear and revulsion. When we first walked down the stairs of the Sidon elementary school, we faced the old, familiar desire to retch. The smell of those men, women and children, sickly and thick, swamped us, tried to drive out of our minds and bodies the questions which we had to ask. Why did they die here? How could such an abomination have taken place? If 'terrorism' was a Katyusha attack on Galilee that killed one, five, even ten people, what did this charnel house represent? In reply, the flies ambushed us on the stairwell, settling voraciously on our lips and round our eyes, bringing the corruption of the corpses to our faces.

The first question – why? – was easy to answer. The school, according to neighbours, had been bombed at night, at two o'clock in the morning of 7 June, the second day of the invasion. The refugees in the basement had been both Palestinians and Lebanese who had fled the city of Tyre in the hope that they would find safety in Sidon. They had been allowed to take sanctuary in the elementary school for the night. But we had already found, outside the school, in a crooked, narrow street that connected the building to the Jezzine road, the mangled, charred remains of an anti-aircraft gun, its barrels absurdly twisted, on top of the wreckage of a jeep.

At some point in the night, we guessed, a PLO guerrilla had driven that anti-aircraft gun here and fired at the Israeli planes that were roaming the dark skies above the city. He may have been unaware that the school contained more than 100 refugees, although this is highly unlikely. His disregard was criminal, like that of the Israeli who killed him. For an Israeli pilot had presumably seen the gun flashes and decided to bomb the artillery. The Israeli could not have seen what he was aiming at; he could have had no idea how many civilians were in the area. Nor could he have cared. For if the Israelis were really worried about civilian casualties, they would never have dropped ordnance at night into a densely populated city. But the pilot was fighting 'terrorists'.

In the roof of the school there was a jagged hole, like the one we had seen earlier above the door of the municipality building, made by the Israeli bomb. It had not exploded on contact with the roof. The bomb had been designed to detonate only when it could no longer penetrate the hard surfaces that it struck. So it passed through three floors of the building right into the darkened cellar where the refugees were huddled in terror and only then, when it came into contact with the firm, immovable floor, did it blow up.

The bodies lay in a giant heap that had left the children on top and the women beneath them. The bomb must have somehow lifted the huddled mass of refugees and sucked the heaviest of them into its vortex. The white lime dust lay more thickly over some parts of the pile than others, leaving the children exposed, their legs splayed open, heads down. Randal stood beside me, scribbling in his notebook. Then he put the notebook into his pocket and just looked at the great heap of bodies. I saw tears in his eyes. 'Dear God,' he said. 'Those poor, poor people.'

An Israeli officer attached to his army's 'press liaison unit' in east Beirut was to tell me next day that the story of unburied bodies in Sidon was 'PLO propaganda', that anyone who had died in Sidon was a 'terrorist' or − at worst − a civilian who had died at the hands of 'terrorists'. The claim that more than 100 people, including children, had died in that school basement was 'utter rubbish'. He instructed me to 'check my facts' before I wrote slanderous articles to the contrary. When I told him I had visited the school and seen the corpses with my own eyes, he told me I had received no permission to visit Sidon, that I should have travelled there with an Israeli escort officer and that I should not visit the city again.

Outside the school that hot afternoon, the Israeli soldiers on the armoured vehicle had finished their oranges. They must have smelled the stench of the bodies but they betrayed no curiosity. It was 11 days since these scores of people had been killed yet still they lay unburied. How many in the meantime had been taken from other cellars?

It was two and a half years before I met the headmaster of the Sidon elementary school. A quiet, thoughtful man, Habib Zeidan took me into his school one cold afternoon in February 1985. The building had been repaired. The holes in the roof had been plastered over and the staircase painted green. The broken classroom windows had been replaced and the earth playground that doubled as a basketball pitch now had a smart concrete surface. The posts at each end held two new nets and a basketball lay at the foot of the post at the far end of the pitch. The wall of the basement had been rebuilt.

'I let them in that day, you know,' Zeidan said. He was a Christian with a thick tousle of brown hair over his forehead. 'You cannot imagine what Sidon was like. They came to me on the evening of the sixth, a hundred and twenty of them, mostly women and children, some old people, maybe three young men with guns. They had walked all day from Tyre. They were sick and tired and they begged me for shelter so I got the key of the basement and opened the school for them. I let them in. I sent them down there. They walked past me that evening, down the staircase. The children were so tired, they were asleep on their mothers' shoulders.'

Zeidan said he had been told the Palestinians fired an anti-aircraft gun from the road outside the school. 'Would you believe they could do that? And would you believe the Israelis could bomb a city like this at night in this way?' What happened to the bodies? 'Well, the children came − the children who are pupils here − and they saw what had happened and they became very frightened of the bodies. We had most of them taken away and they were buried at "Martyrs' Square". They had no identification cards but most of them were from Tyre. They were just put in the ground with the rest of the victims. About sixty of them were left here so I had them buried under the playground – down there.'

So that was why the pitch was now covered in concrete. The dead lay under the far post, beneath the spot where the basketball rested. 'I told the children later that they had all been buried in the cemetery. But of course, there are sixty beneath the playground. The children have never been told. There is nothing to show that the bodies are there.'

Across the street from the school stood the Djad building, an apartment block whose southern walls had been sheared off with enormous force leaving the tables, beds and chairs of the inside apartments leaning precariously over the edge of the open floors. Randal and I went there too. It was dark and we had matches. It too contained a basement of horror, a place of such heat and stench that our gorges rose at the prospect of entering it in the half-light. Pieces of human remains were visible and a kind of dried, liquefied fat lay on parts of the floor. Years later, I discovered its grim story.

It fell to Mahmoud Khadra, the director of the south Lebanon civil defence service, to enter this particular charnel house. In 1985, he pulled out his files of June 1982 for me and read his report, written in the immediate aftermath of the bombing. 'Djad building,' it said. '125 people inside, mostly children, women. Sheltering from bombs in the basement. All dead. All of them had burned. Flesh mostly burnt. Collected the bones of 125 people, also bags of gold rings, jewellery. Could only check number of people from evidence of seven survivors who were outside building at the time. Took bones to cemetery. My decision to bury bodies there.'

It was a strange sensation to talk about this slaughter to Khadra in February of 1985, when the Israeli army was about to *leave* Sidon, when armed Lebanese guerrillas were appearing on the streets of the city and attacking the retreating Israelis with rocket-propelled grenades. Even while we were studying that 2½ year-old report, an explosion boomed across Sidon as an Israeli tank came under attack near Ein Helweh. It was as if events in Lebanon moved too quickly for any serious historical research.

Khadra had talked at length to the seven survivors of the Djad building, men who had been in the street when the Israeli bomb killed their families in the basement on 7 June 1982. 'There was one man – his name was Ahmed Shamseddin – and he lost his wife, four children, his sister and her five children, his brother-in-law and mother. An Israeli plane dropped the bomb and crushed half the building. He was knocked unconscious by the explosions but he always believed his family had escaped.'

Khadra smiled sorrowfully as he told his story. 'Shamseddin was about forty-five or forty-six but he went a bit mad because of what happened. He walked day after day round the hospitals asking for his wife and children and telling everyone their names. He would go up to the Israeli soldiers in their trucks and climb onto the lorries and ask them to find his wife and children. He went to see the Israeli commanders in the governor's office. Some wounded people from Sidon were taken to hospitals in Israel and the Israelis let him go there. He went there three times and he did the same as he did in Sidon, he walked on foot round the hospitals in Nahariya and kept telling everyone the names of his family. Of course, he never found them.'

The fate of the 125 civilians in the Djad building had been sealed for the same reason as that of the 120 people in the basement of the elementary school. 'The Israelis just bombed any buildings where there were fighters,' Khadra said. 'They did not care who was in the buildings or who they killed. They bombed the Djad because there were fighters with anti-aircraft guns outside the building. When the invasion started, I went to meet with representatives of all the groups of fighters in Sidon. I gave them instructions to be far from the buildings which had families living in them. But they did not all obey me.'

Randal and I had been told the same thing that day in 1982 when we first saw what had happened to Sidon. Several residents told us that the Palestinians had brought death to both themselves and the civilians around them. We at last found the wife of the Lebanese journalist, a middle-class Sunni woman. 'When the Israelis came,' she told us, 'the Palestinian fighters took their guns and placed them next to our homes, next to apartment blocks and hospitals and schools. They thought this would protect them. We pleaded with them to take their guns away but they refused. So when they fired at the Israelis, the planes came and bombed our homes.'

A doctor – no one wanted to be named in Sidon that day – told us that the Palestinians had positioned guns on the roof of the Lebanese government hospital beside the Ein Helweh camp. 'The guerrillas knew what would happen. The Israeli planes came and bombed the hospital. Everyone there died – the sick, the wounded, the fighters with them.' He was right. Khadra's files showed long afterwards how the hospital was destroyed. The Israelis knew it was a hospital but because the PLO fired at them from the roof, they bombed it to the ground. Khadra's report on the incident read: '5 sick children in beds, others sick or wounded adults. All 90 occupants dead. All corpses dismembered by the bombing.'

But in other parts of Sidon, Israeli bombs destroyed houses and their occupants haphazardly. A family died in their home in the Sabagh district. Twenty civilians were burned to death in the basement of the Baba building, their corpses thrown from the cellar and scattered onto the roadway by the bomb that killed them. The Israelis were to claim later that they had dropped leaflets over the town ordering the civilians to collect on the beach to escape the bombing. They had done this in Tyre. But the people of Sidon told us that day – and the Israelis privately admitted the same to me later – that the warnings did not come in time. The leaflets were dropped. But only *after* the bombing; by which time the *mohafez* was already ordering the construction of the first mass grave at the square at the end of Riad Solh Street.

The place was clouded with sand and dust. Fires still burned in Sidon and the days and nights of aerial bombing had so pulverised Ein Helweh camp that the air was filled with the particles of hundreds of shattered homes. It was several hours before we realised why so many of the younger men wore that wide-eyed expression. They were stunned by the events of the past week but they were also terrified of being arrested. Even then, rumours had begun to circulate in Sidon that prisoners had been starved and beaten to death by Israeli soldiers.

Most of the hundreds of men who were removed from the beach were blindfolded and taken to one of two locations: the Sisters of St Joseph's school or the Safa fruit canning factory on the southern outskirts of Sidon. It was here that at least ten men were reported to have died of thirst after being beaten by Israeli guards. Randal and I found a Lebanese Red Cross worker who had been held with these prisoners.

'They held us for four days, almost all the time out in the open,' he said. 'They gave us water but no food and ten men died near me. I saw one man – I think he was a Palestinian – and he asked for food. A soldier hit him in the stomach with his rifle and the man started coughing blood. He choked on it, on the blood, and then he collapsed and died. I do not know why the Israelis do this. Many of us hated the Palestinians and are pleased the Israelis have come. But now they have taken hundreds of people, including a man of sixty-two.'

These descriptions were to become more commonplace every day. The Israelis denied their veracity, claiming that those who gave such evidence were 'terrorist suspects'. Since only those arrested by the Israelis could be witnesses to this brutality – and since anyone arrested by them was deemed a 'terrorist suspect' – any journalist who took the accounts seriously would be a dupe or a victim of 'PLO propaganda'. But the stories were true. Israeli officers later wrote about this persistent cruelty* and 18 months later, after weeks of investigation in Sidon, I

---

* See, for example, *My War Diary: Israel in Lebanon* by Lieutenant-Colonel Dov Yermiya (London, Pluto Press, 1983), especially pp. 27–8, 67 and 109–15. Yermiya gives several testaments of repeated beatings with clubs, administered by Israeli troops to blindfolded men. The author also says that the hooded informers – who were known to the Israelis as 'monkeys' – 'pointed to innocent residents as if they were terrorists, and ... helped their friends pass through the lineup without being caught' (p. 28). As a result of his account, Lt-Col. Yermiya was struck off the Israeli army reserve list.

found the graves of seven men who had died in Israeli captivity and been brought to the local cemetery by an Israeli officer for secret burial on the night of 11 June – a week before Randal and I arrived in Sidon.*

Israeli occupation was evidently going to be a harsh, often deadly affair, although Israeli Shin Bet agents were already moving into Sidon – just as the Syrian *mukhabarrat* agents moved behind the Syrian army – to institute a system of identification papers that would categorise the civilian population of the city into reliable, neutral or hostile citizens. That afternoon, 18 June, several Lebanese – including an old man of 70 – showed me their passports, each of which had been stamped by the Israelis. All bore the figure 0507 but some of the stamps were rectangular in shape, some oblong and some circular. All carried within them the Star of David. But the Lebanese who owned the passports had not been told into which category they fell. The old man had a circular stamp in his passport. So was he regarded as a law-abiding citizen? Or was he supposed to be a 'terrorist suspect'?

Randal and I found that plain-clothes Israeli agents with Uzi submachine-guns began to look at us suspiciously as we talked to Lebanese in the streets of Sidon. After I had spoken to a woman, I saw her taken to one side by one of these Israeli gunmen and questioned. We were in the southernmost square of the city a few yards from the mass grave; displaced and homeless Palestinians stood by the roadside amid the dust of buses and Israeli tanks. We dared not risk incriminating them by asking more questions. But through the crowd towards us came the small, blond figure of a European girl in a long blue dress, perhaps no more than 17 years old.

When she came nearer, she looked twice her age. Her eyes were bloodshot and she walked with a slight stoop. A man beside her was pushing a cart with clothes inside it. We stopped her and asked who she was. 'I am German but I am married to a Palestinian,' she said. 'He was taken away by the Israelis. I don't know where he is. I am going to the camp to see if our home survived.' The girl was tired and her head hung to one side. She would say no more and set off into the crowd again. But then she stopped and turned to us. 'I have been here six months,' she said. 'I have lived through it all.' Then she disappeared.

Randal and I drove out of Sidon in silence. We were both asking ourselves the same question. If this was what the Israelis did to Sidon – if so many hundreds of civilians could be killed by the Israelis here in so short a period of time – how many would they kill in Beirut, where at least half a million people were living crowded into the encircled western sector of the city?

South of Damour, we ran into a convoy that gave us reason to fear the

* See pp. 423–8.

worst. In fact, it was not a convoy but a juggernaut, a 15-mile-long column of Merkava and Centurion tanks – three tanks abreast – moving at 15 mph up the coast road towards Beirut. It was as if the entire Israeli army was advancing on the city as one giant armoured centipede, the tracks of the Merkavas and Centurions tearing up the tarmac surface of the highway, scything through the long grass on the central reservation, bathing the landscape in a fog of blue exhaust smoke.

We threaded through this legion of armour, hooting our way past personnel carriers, petrol tankers, troop transporters, jeeps and ammunition lorries. Convoys of tanks had already been parked on the hillside further up the road and dug into revetments above Kfarshima and Hadeth. So much equipment were the Israelis sending up to Beirut that the beaches and banana plantations between the coastal highway and the sea were covered with tanks and heavy artillery for a distance of 20 miles. At times, Randal and I had to veer sharply to avoid colliding with the barrels of the Merkavas which were traversing right and left as they moved.

At Khalde, Israeli policemen were trying to move the tank columns into single file for the narrow road around west Beirut, a track now littered with rubble, broken boxes of ammunition and thousands of empty shell cases. There must have been an entire military division on the move with all its armour and artillery. Israeli mortars as well as artillery were now positioned to the east of Khalde overlooking the airport and the southern tip of the Beirut perimeter. Most of the tanks were British-made Centurions with extra armour-plating around the base of their turrets. Heavy artillery had been placed under the highway motorway bridges. Short of transport lorries, the Israeli army had even commandeered their own commercial *Eged* buses – the Jerusalem and Haifa advertisements still plastered to the back – to ferry troop re-inforcements up from the Israeli frontier.

It was impressive, and it inspired both respect and fear. It was awesome and crude, power in its most blatant form. But what was really troubling about it was the idea – difficult to shake off – that this vision was so out of all proportion to the natural world, so powerful, that it seemed to be a *creative* force. Dodging between these goliaths in our tiny car, Randal and I were affected by it all. In spite of what we had just seen in Sidon, we felt a kind of elation at this astonishing military display. Was it because we were both doing what we loved – reporting history as it happened, witnessing history at first hand – or was it something less easily defined, a newness, a sense that things would never be the same again? It was exciting to watch a nation create new facts; and creating facts was something the Israelis enjoyed doing.

They had changed the political geography of the Sinai peninsula when they captured the desert in 1967. They had done the same with the West Bank and Gaza and with east Jerusalem and Golan. Never mind the cost. That is what this great machinery was saying to us; never mind the cost. Here was a phenomenon that took no account of emotion, that changed landscape, lives, even geography without hesitating for an instant. It represented strength, the same strength that the Israeli lieutenant had talked of with such pride on the hill at Baabda.

It had so little to do with the smell of corpses which had infected our noses and eyes in Sidon just an hour before. One of the comforts of firing a big gun during a siege must be the satisfaction of watching the results at long range. Inside a tank or behind an M107, a smudge of smoke against a building can be marked off against a map coordinate. The blood and shattered bones at the other end of the trajectory have no physical contact with the gun. But Randal and I were driving towards the other end of the trajectory, back to west Beirut, where the casualty statistics marked the other side of the concave mirror through which armies fight their wars.

Just as the Israelis had killed thousands of civilians in the first week and a half of their invasion of Lebanon, so their army's publicity machine now tried to bring the victims back to life. The international outcry that had greeted the heavy civilian casualty toll made this task imperative. On paper, this was easy. Israeli soldiers, we were told *ad nauseam*, risked their own safety to protect the lives of civilians. So a 66-page document was produced for the international press by the spokesman for the Israel Defence Force in Tel Aviv, a brochure of such bias and factual inaccuracy and containing so many untruthful statements that even the Israelis were later to express their embarrassment at its publication.*

It claimed that only ten civilians died in the fierce fighting around Nabatieh, that only 50 were killed in Tyre and 'approximately 400' in Sidon. Despite the evidence of the slaughter in Sidon and the savagery of the shelling and aerial bombing of Ein Helweh camp with its thousands of civilian inhabitants, despite the horrendous fatality lists from the air strikes against apartment blocks in west Beirut, this mendacious document stated that the Israeli army and air force 'took extraordinary measures to avoid inflicting casualties on the civilian population.' .

Even when it attempted to prove that Palestinian guerrillas had sited gun positions near apartment blocks and hospitals, it used my own report from Sidon of 18 June − but only those paragraphs in which I quoted residents who complained that the PLO had placed civilian lives at risk. The document printed a photograph of this part of my dispatch but totally deleted the first 531 words of the report which recorded the

* *Operation Peace for Galilee: the Lebanese Border*, published 21 June 1982.

savagery of the air raids, the 100 or more corpses in the basement of the elementary school and the Red Cross estimate of between 1,500 and 2,000 civilian fatalities.

The cynicism of the Israeli army publication may be judged from its treatment of just one paragraph from my dispatch, the second half of which was cut out from the photograph printed in the document:

At their own Ein el-Helweh camp, the Palestinians actually put their guns on the roof of the hospital. *As another doctor put it: 'The guerrillas knew what would happen. The Israeli planes came and bombed the hospital. Everyone there died — the sick, the wounded, the fighters with them.'*

The italicised section of this paragraph was missing from the Israeli report, obviously cut because it stated the unpalatable truth: that if the Palestinians put guns on a hospital, the Israelis would go ahead and bomb the hospital anyway, killing all the patients inside. This, after all, contradicted an Israeli statement in the document which said that Israeli troops were 'constantly reminded to avoid civilian casualties ...' For the same reason, the final 585 words of my report — which covered the Israelis' brutal treatment of their prisoners in Sidon — were also deleted.*

By the end of the second week of the Israeli invasion, however, this crude rewriting of history collapsed under the weight of evidence, collected in west Beirut and across the Israeli-occupied areas of Lebanon, that up to 14,000 people — the vast majority civilians — had been killed, and another 20,000 wounded. Red Cross and Lebanese police figures, sometimes collected by personnel who were not unsympathetic to the new political 'facts' created by the Israeli invasion, showed that by the end of the first week (14 June), 9,583 people had died and 16,608 had been wounded throughout Lebanon. There was no breakdown between men, women and children but the police said that most had died in Israeli air attacks.

The highest casualty toll outside Beirut was in Sidon, where the local police — who were now cooperating with the Israeli occupation authorities — reported 1,109 people dead in the city itself and 3,681 wounded. But a further 1,167 people had died in the Sidon Palestinian camps of Ein Helweh and Mieh Mieh where 1,859 were wounded. A total of 1,200 men, women and children were reported killed in Tyre, most of them in the Palestinian camps at Rashidiyeh, Bourj al-Shemali and al-Bass. The wounded in Tyre totalled 2,018.

Earleen Tatro in the AP bureau spent hours collating these figures from the Red Cross, newspaper reports, lists of air-raid victims filed at Beirut hospitals and from AP's stringers outside the Lebanese capital. The fighting on the outskirts of Beirut near the international airport took a heavy toll. In just the small section of highway that encompasses

* For the full report, see *The Times*, 19 June 1982.

Khalde, Ouzai, Al Zahra and St Simon, 518 people died and 619 were wounded. Many of these were Palestinian and Shia guerrillas; a year later, when the US contingent of the multinational force occupied part of this area, I saw US Marines uncovering a body on the beach from the June 1982 fighting. The Americans discovered the corpses of the Palestinian defenders – or parts of their remains – at an average rate of one torso every week; all were reburied. In the Beirut suburbs near the airport roundabout, a further 165 people died and 215 people were wounded.

But the most horrific toll of casualties was in west Beirut. Here, no fewer than 2,461 had been killed by Israeli air strikes, by artillery fire from the land and by Israeli naval vessels. Most of them died in Sabra and Chatila – where two of the Palestinian camps were located – the Arab University area around Fakhani, the district near the UNESCO offices, Bir Hassan, Bir al-Abed, Abu Shaker, Basta (the last four districts all containing substantial Shia populations), Treik Jdeide and Mseitbeh. In these areas, 3,574 people were also wounded.

Hundreds of people died in the villages of southern Lebanon, especially along the Litani River. Hospital and civil defence figures showed that 768 were killed in Adloun, Sarafand, Arnoun, Jbaa, Arab Selim, Maghdousheh, Jezzine, Fitouli, Ghame, Ghassamieh, Al-Ghazieh, Harouf, Room and Nabatieh. The wounded in these locations amounted to 2,834. The Jezzine deaths included Syrians belonging to an armoured unit who were bombed in a mountain forest and whose corpses were left where they died for more than two weeks before local villagers complained of the smell and the Phalangists doused the remains in burning petrol. In several of these places, Palestinian guerrillas were obviously prominent among the casualties. The town of Nabatieh, for example, was a PLO stronghold and the village of Sarafand – the Biblical *Sarepta*, famous for the miracles of the Prophet Elijah – had contained a large PLO military base. Arnoun was beside the Palestinian positions at Beaufort Castle. But many of the other villages had little or no military significance.*

---

* Other casualty figures included Damour, Naameh, Haret al-Naameh, Baskinta and Ain Drafil (399 dead and 212 wounded), and villages south of Damour, including Saadiyat (269 dead). A substantial proportion of the Damour dead were probably Palestinian guerrillas but 487 people, almost all civilians, died at Ain Dara, Ain Zhalta and Al Barouk – the scene of intense fighting between Israeli and Syrian troops – and in scattered shelling that involved the villages and towns of Beit Eddine, Baaqlin and Moukhtara. A further 257 died at Aley, Kfar Hata, Abieh, ain Ksour, Al Banieh, Ghaber Chamoun, Aramoun, Shemlan, Ein Aab, Soukh al-Gharb, Keifoun, Baissour, Jamhour, Dar al-Wahesh, Sous and Kahhale. In the Bekaa Valley, where Syrian and Israeli tanks fought artillery duels and Israeli planes bombed the Syrian SAM-6 batteries, 368 people died, mostly in Hasbaya, Ghlieh, Sohmor, Yohmor, Chtaura, along the Beirut–Damascus highway near Masnaa and on the main road between Baalbek and the Syrian frontier near Homs. Nearly all of the latter were civilians, many of them motorists trying to flee the country for the safety of Syria.

Israeli attempts to deny these casualty figures varied according to the degree of international criticism Israel received. It quickly became evident that Israel's own figures for civilian casualties – a total of 460 in all of Lebanon between 4 and 21 June – were so preposterous as to be counter-productive. It was ridiculous for the Israelis to assert in their briefing papers that 'Lebanese civilian casualties were minor in comparison with the exaggerated [sic] figures printed in the foreign press.'* What had happened to the other 13,000 dead? Israel's public relations apparatus could not expect the world to believe in mass resurrection on this scale.

So a new tactic was adopted. Israel issued casualty figures for its own losses but no longer offered figures for the invasion death toll among Lebanese and Palestinians. Instead, its spokesman and supporters claimed that the statistics in Lebanon had come from the PLO – from 'terrorists' – and that the international press, whom it had hitherto counted on for fairly unanimous support, had been tricked by Yassir Arafat and his infamous 'well-oiled terrorist propaganda machine'. In fact, not one serious statistic ever came from the PLO. Arafat's only attempt to estimate casualties – he claimed that there were 'thirty thousand dead and wounded' – was so meaningless that I decided not to give any credence to his words in *The Times*. The wounded had to be separated from the fatalities to give any idea of the seriousness of the casualties.

Similarly, the Israelis accused the press of swallowing PLO figures for homeless civilians, alleging that Fathi Arafat, the PLO chairman's brother, who was head of the Palestinian Red Crescent, had said that 600,000 people were driven from their homes by the Israeli invasion. Fathi Arafat did indeed give a press conference at the Commodore Hotel, but of such vacuity that I did not even bother to report it. The figure – which was in fact a grotesque exaggeration – was made public on 13 June, not by the PLO but by Francesco Noseda, the head of the Lebanese committee of the International Red Cross. I and other journalists who later visited southern Lebanon were able to disprove the ICRC figure – and published this fact in our newspapers – but we could scarcely disagree with Noseda's other words. He said that conditions for civilians in Lebanon had become 'unbearable' and that he feared 'the horrors the city of Beirut will face unless there is a solution'.

We did not have to wait long to find out what this meant. That mass of armour in which Randal and I had become caught up on our way back to Beirut from Sidon was now employed to shell the Muslim western sector of the city. The PLO must surrender, the Israelis announced. And to that end, early on the morning of 21 June, they began a long and bloody bombardment of west Beirut. Their shells fell right

* *Operation Peace for Galilee: the Lebanese Border*, p. 56.

across the city, on apartment blocks, streets, on the public parks where the refugees were camping, on the Palestinian hovels of Bourj al-Barajneh, on Fakhani where the PLO had its offices, and on hospitals.

The Palestinians drove some of their guns out of the camps and into the residential Hamra district. If this was a war about 'terrorism', then for the people of west Beirut, two groups of terrorists now threatened their lives. One of them was the Palestinian guerrilla movement which shamelessly drove its anti-aircraft guns and rocket-launchers in among the apartment blocks for protection; the other group were the men of the Israeli army who with equal deliberation fired shells at the rate of one a minute into the residential quarters of west Beirut.

It started before dawn. The outgoing Palestinian shells — fired at the Israeli lines across Baabda and Khalde — echoed across the city with a faint thumping sound. The incoming projectiles arrived with a vengeful clap of sound that had the ambulances wailing through the streets within minutes. It was scarcely daylight when an Israeli heavy artillery round came hissing over west Beirut and smashed into a first-floor flat in the rue Emile Edde, a dusty residential thoroughfare of old apartments and garbage heaps behind the AP bureau. The shell tore into the building, slicing off the balcony and spraying fire onto a small black Volkswagen that was driving down the road.

I ran down the street from the AP office to find that the car had exploded. Almost at once, a bloodied woman was brought out of the flat, her right hand missing, the bone projecting through the gristle of her wrist. Gunmen gathered, as they always did on such occasions, screaming at people to clear the streets, firing automatic rifles in the air to emphasise their words. From a neighbouring doorway, there emerged a tall woman in a long, pink cloak, perhaps a nightgown, who held aloft the tiny, swaddled figure of a baby as if she was offering up the child for sacrifice. She was crying in a high-pitched ululating voice, as people in Lebanon do in the ritual of lamentation.

Only then did we see the trickle of blood on the child's face, and a gunman wearing a cowboy hat took the baby from the woman, gently but in horror, and thrust it through the open window of a mud-coloured ambulance. Beirut's day of terror-shelling had just begun. Memories of the 1975–6 civil war helped to save lives. People in west Beirut had learned to stay inside their homes under bombardment, retreating indoors as other men and women might take cover from a shower of rain. And so the streets around Corniche Mazraa and the formerly graceful seafront of Ramlet al-Baida were deserted as the shells fell across them.

Grey and white puffs of smoke emerged from the roofs of apartments and amid the Muslim slums nearer to Sabra. The shells cut down all before them. Often they arrived in salvoes of four or five, smashing down walls, telegraph poles, balconies, trees, advertisement hoardings, roofs, and staircases. At one point, the artillery fire was so intense that the streets reeked of cordite.

Lebanese state radio broadcast warnings to the 600,000 or so civilians still in west Beirut to go to their basements, which — given the evidence we had seen with our own eyes in Sidon — did not seem an entirely safe place to hide. By nightfall, Fatah guerrillas could be seen parking their truck-mounted recoilless rifles beside hotels and apartment blocks, inviting destruction upon the civilian population. Several Palestinian officers did their best to organise relief services, guiding ambulances through the streets from the American University hospital. Others behaved less heroically, threatening civilians with their rifles and harassing the few Western correspondents who ventured onto the streets.

The Israelis tried once more on the following day to capture the highest point on the Beirut–Damascus highway with a tank attack against the Syrians outside Aley. The gunfire in the mountains — the end of the latest Israeli–Syrian truce — could clearly be heard in Beirut and boomed even more loudly around the presidential palace at Baabda where Sarkis was trying to persuade Muslim and Christian politicians to produce a formula that would end the war. For the first time, Philip Habib, Reagan's envoy, was invited to join these discussions, thus bringing American influence to bear directly upon the Lebanese. Jumblatt, Berri and Bashir Gemayel — who had all met together at Baabda — had already agreed that the PLO should leave west Beirut. But how?

The day after the Israelis invaded Lebanon and drove unmolested through the UN lines in the south of the country, Yassir Arafat had summoned Samir Sambar, the UN's Beirut spokesman, to his headquarters in Fakhani. There — in a state of fury and shouting in a high-pitched voice — Arafat raged at the unfortunate United Nations official about the UN's ineffectiveness and its 'connivance' with the Israeli invaders. He had even unkinder words for Callaghan, the UN's Irish commander in Lebanon. Within a week, however, Arafat became a more reasonable man.

Sambar's jovial and plump figure returned three times to Arafat's office, where he was welcomed by the PLO chairman as one of several men who might be able to save the Palestinian guerrilla movement from physical extinction. Lebanese ministers for whom Arafat had shown scant regard in the past suddenly found themselves courted by the man whose guerrillas were now trapped in Beirut. Would the Lebanese army, he asked, like to take control of the west of the city? Would the United States like to talk to the PLO if the Palestinians formally renounced all violence against Israel?

So far, a declaration of non-belligerency — a laying-down of arms — was as far as Arafat was prepared to go. Habib had made it clear to

Chafiq Wazzan, Sarkis' prime minister – to whom Arafat was talking – that this was not enough. The Americans wanted the PLO to recognise Israel but Arafat knew that to concede this now would break up the structure of the Palestinian guerrilla movement as irrevocably as its military structure in southern Lebanon had already been smashed by Israeli firepower. Arafat hoped that the Soviets might have some influence, although Leonid Brezhnev had done no more than condemn the Israeli invasion. New Soviet equipment was already arriving in Syria to replace the matériel destroyed by the Israelis.

Bassam Abu Sharif, the PFLP spokesman who had spoken with such false optimism on the mountain highway, was prepared to acknowledge the PLO's predicament while revealing its political tactics. 'We are in Beirut and we are surrounded,' he said one night by the Commodore Hotel's empty swimming pool. 'The PLO is in a difficult position. But it is not so difficult as some people imagine. As the hours go by, other parties are going to become involved – the Arab nations, the Soviet Union – and there will be many changes.'

Many of Arafat's advisers now believed that Israel's invasion was merely a prelude to the annexation of the West Bank and Gaza, something that could not be achieved while Palestinian nationalists in the occupied territories still had a focus for their political aspirations in Beirut. If this was true, then the Israelis would not be prepared to allow the PLO to survive in anything like its present form. But while the Israelis might be prepared to tolerate an international outcry over further civilian casualties of the war, they would not wish to fight their way into west Beirut with the large number of *Israeli* dead and wounded that such a project would entail.

If the Israelis did not wish to commit their ground forces, however, could not their air force reduce west Beirut to submission? On the afternoon of 22 June, an ominous event took place. Six Israeli Skyhawk and Kfir fighter-bombers dived at low level over residential districts near the sea, releasing those fiery balloons to distract any SAM-7 ground-to-air missiles but then flying off over the Mediterranean without releasing any bombs. I watched the planes that afternoon, sweeping over the rooftops in the bright sunlight, their pilots sometimes silhouetted in their cockpits. Perhaps it was a little psychological warfare, an attempt to show the PLO that no square metre of Beirut air space was off limits to the Israeli air force. But I remembered that residents of Sidon had told me how Israeli planes performed similarly harmless aerobatics before they bombed the city, leaving more than a thousand dead.

That night, I sent a message to *The Times*, telling Barnes that 'unless Israeli jets overhead [are] having fun, I suspect some grim hours may lie ahead here.' The next day, I asked what Walker in Jerusalem made of these unusual aerobatics. 'Quite a lot of journalists in west Beirut have pulled out to east [Beirut] for safety,' I told Barnes. 'Those of us who intend to stay ... would naturally like any warning we can get of an attack. After seeing Sidon, some of us are conscious that the same thing could happen here (I for one plan to steer clear of basements).' Barnes' reply came back on the AP computer wire within an hour. Walker in Jerusalem had told him that press visits to Lebanon on the coastal highway for Israeli-based reporters had been cancelled for the 23rd. 'Twould seem to be a good day to visit Jounieh to see how the evacuation is going ...' Barnes advised. 'But not repeat not a good day for basements. Regards.'

That evening, another message arrived from Barnes. 'Informatively,' it read, 'Chris [Walker] hearing that although his people [sic] still saying they do not wish to take over city, they stressing they not repeat not ruling out commando and air activities against specific targets.' I replied to *The Times* foreign desk that 'I plan stay thru it all here and watch.' Late that night, a car bomb exploded next to a PLO ammunition dump on the Muslim side of the old front line. It was an enormous bomb that blew a 45-foot crater in the road and brought down an entire block of apartments. The building collapsed like a concertina, crushing more than 50 of its occupants to death, most of them Shia refugees from southern Lebanon. Syrian troops in west Beirut found two other car bombs and captured three Lebanese Shia men who had been driving in one of them.

Under brutal interrogation by the PLO, they said that a Shin Bet officer based in Damour had rigged the bombs. One of the men said his brother had been arrested by the Israelis who had threatened to kill him if he did not help plant the bomb. The explosives – which we saw the following day – all had printed Hebrew words on them. The PLO later took the three men to the crater where, watched by the relatives of those who had died in the apartment block, they were shot with automatic rifles. Their bodies were doused with petrol and burned. The crowd then buried them by kicking rubble and dust into the crater.

The 24th of June was as bad as we feared it would be. As we breakfasted, the sound of jets came sweeping down the morning skies towards the Palestinian camps and the window panes shook with the explosions that followed. Then just before lunchtime, one of those small Israeli gunboats appeared mischievously off the seafront. I watched it from the balcony of my home. There was a pinpoint of light from its decks and then, clearly visible, a missile came slithering and skimming across the waves towards the Corniche. The first rocket hit the sea 100 yards from the shore and blew up in an explosion of green water and spray. But the second missile – a rocket trailing black smoke – passed over the seafront and smashed straight into the unfinished hotel block that served as local headquarters for the Druze militia.

A rain of shells fell across west Beirut, setting fire to an apartment block near the coast and crashing onto the streets around Hamra and the coast road at Ramlet al-Baida. They hit shops and flats owned by Lebanese families, by embassy personnel and foreign newspaper correspondents. All telephone communication between east and west Beirut was now cut. The shelling had broken the underground water pipes and there was an acute water shortage in the west of the city. Electricity was rationed to four hours a day. The Israelis offered another 'ceasefire' but the PLO rejected the terms as constituting 'total surrender'.*

Israel now had 100,000 soldiers in Lebanon, with 1,300 tanks, the same number of personnel carriers and 12,000 troops and supply lorries. The figures had to be accurate because they came from Timur Göksel, the UN spokesman in Naqqoura. His information came from the UN troops through whose check-points the Israelis daily drove with such disregard for international opinion on their way up from the frontier. Seven hundred of those tanks were now positioned around Beirut. Alongside them were two hundred and ten 155mm and 175mm guns. In the early hours of 25 June, a small Israeli raiding party landed on the rocks just below my apartment, firing at the nearest buildings — two of their bullets hit my balcony wall — in order to test the strength of the defenders. Druze and Palestinian gunmen shot back at them and the Israelis disappeared into the darkness. What were they planning?

The Muslim Lebanese were now the subject of repeated exhortations from the Israelis. They should leave the west of the city and flee their homes if they valued the lives of their families. In leaflets dropped from the air, in Arabic-language radio broadcasts, it was a recurring, insistent motif. But the Muslims did not want to abandon their homes. Tens of thousands of them were too poor to move elsewhere and those with possessions were not inclined to leave their houses to gunmen and looters. Besides, west Beirut was their *home*, the place where they were born, educated, married, had children.

In these initial days of the siege, many Lebanese in the west of the city discovered how much they loved Beirut. In opposing the Israeli demands, they discovered something within themselves that they had never before perceived — that there was more to being a citizen than enriching one's family. They wanted the Palestinians to leave west Beirut and they knew that they were powerless to force the PLO from the city. But the Lebanese of west Beirut debated their own future endlessly in the columns of *An Nahar* and *As Safir*, the two leading

---

* The Israeli demands were: (1) no PLO or other Palestinian military presence in Lebanon — guerrillas would have to surrender their arms but could leave for another country if they wished; (2) no Palestinian 'extra-territorial enclaves' (i.e. no PLO control of the camps) in Lebanon; (3) all Palestinians in Lebanon would have to be under Lebanese government authority; (4) the Lebanese army would be deployed throughout Lebanon.

newpapers, over Beirut radio, and at long, candle-lit meetings with friends and distant family members whom they had lost the habit of visiting.

Resilience was the best word to describe this new quality. My landlord appeared at the front door when I returned home for breakfast one morning after reporting a series of dawn air raids. He was holding a net full of fish. 'Mr Robert, see what I have here?' he shouted. 'Fish. I caught them. I went down there to the rocks and I caught the fish. We have no electricity, we have no gas, we have no water, we have no telephones but we can live. See? See?' And he held the net of lugubrious, grey fish in front of my face. He had learned that he could look after himself, that he did not have to leave west Beirut just because the Israelis had told him to. It would be easy to exaggerate the effect of the siege on the people of west Beirut. Their sad mixture of hospitality, suspicion and cynicism was in some ways strengthened. But they acquired a new sense of identity which was to sustain them through the terrible years to come.

So, too, did the Palestinians. But their new self-respect was to undergo an ordeal by fire. The Palestinians of the camps would die in their hundreds over the coming weeks while the PLO prevaricated, fought, negotiated, cajoled and threatened on their behalf. But fight the PLO would, with great courage, against hopeless odds, until the world began to realise that perhaps the Palestinians were playing the role of David against an Israeli Goliath.

It was perfectly true that the PLO had no choice; and Arafat's eventual decision to retreat from Beirut would tear his guerrilla movement apart. But in the ruins of Sabra, Chatila and Bourj al-Barajneh that summer, the Palestinians also learned that they did not have to surrender. After one heavy air raid on Chatila, I watched them come out of their air-raid shelters, shouting and screaming abuse at the aircraft still wheeling high above them. They were not doing this for the television cameras. I was the only Westerner there and they had not noticed me. Fires were burning in one corner of the camp and thick, acrid smoke drifted through the hovels. But there they were, children, women, gunmen, hugging each other and laughing. They were intoxicated with their own survival. The rhetoric of no surrender worked; or so it seemed.

It also had its selfish side. Arafat made a long and militant broadcast over the PLO's radio station on the evening of 25 June, praising the 'heroic resistance' of his guerrillas, promising them that by their actions they would 'determine the dignity of the coming generation and will ensure that the children of Palestine and the entire Arab world will live in freedom with their heads held high.' He told his audience to 'stand fast in Beirut'. But at no point in his broadcast did Arafat suggest that Beirut did not belong to the Palestinians at all, but to the Lebanese.

The Israeli air raids intensified. The anxiety, even panic, of Lebanese Muslim leaders sometimes transformed itself into a type of hysteria. Walid Jumblatt, who liked melodrama, had been trying to negotiate with Sarkis for a PLO surrender and a demilitarisation of west Beirut. His efforts were never going to succeed; Arafat was not going to consign the safety of the PLO to the good offices of the Druze. But on the morning of the 25th, Jumblatt called a press conference in the Lebanese Ministry of Information in west Beirut to announce that he was calling off his negotiations. Israeli jets were swarming through the skies above the city, their engines screaming through the windows of the building, as Jumblatt banged his hand on the table and shouted: 'Let the PLO be terrorist.'

Bomb explosions vibrated through the building as Jumblatt, in a voice rising steadily in intensity and emotion, said that the PLO had been prepared for an honourable surrender. 'But I don't think Israel will give it to them,' he said. 'They [the Israelis] just want to kill them and kill the Lebanese with them.' A more radical PLO would emerge from the ruins of the defeated organisation, Jumblatt said, hammering his hand on the table again, his voice rising unnervingly. Then, finally losing control of his emotions and with sweat pouring down his face, he shrieked: 'I would like to see the PLO go terrorist, first against Arab leaders and secondly against Israel ... because we have to face American terrorism, Israeli terrorism.' Beirut, he concluded, was going to be destroyed.

Behind him, Chafiq Wazzan, the Lebanese prime minister, stood in silence, his normally smiling face set in a mask of contempt, not for what Jumblatt was saying but for the Israelis whose aircraft almost drowned out the press conference. Another great rumble of explosions shook the building. Wazzan stepped towards the table. 'Every time we reach some kind of understanding [about a PLO surrender], we run into a new escalation, as if it is designed to pressure us,' he said in a voice shaking with anger. 'I have informed President Sarkis that I cannot continue shouldering my responsibility under this blackmail and escalation.'

The Israeli air force hit another apartment block that morning and killed everyone inside it. The pilots presumably meant to drop their bombs on the scruffy Mourabitoun militia office on Corniche Mazraa, but they missed. Instead, their handiwork was spread in fire and rubble half the length of Abu Chaker Street, and the people of this miserable little lane — those who survived, that is — could not grasp what had happened to them.

It would be a cliché to say that the street looked like the wartime newsreels of European cities, because all aerial bombing of civilian areas tends to create the same effect. Abu Chaker Street was in ruins, its collapsed apartment blocks still smoking, some of the dead still in their pancaked apartments, between hundreds of tons of concrete. Across the road lay the detritus of their lives: mattresses, broken paintings, pieces of a wooden chair with a child's carving on them, old food, smashed toys and small, unthinkable puddles where the flies had congregated.

The perspiring ambulance crews had so far counted 32 dead, most of them men and women who were hiding in their flats when an Israeli bomb exploded on the roof of their block and tore down half the building. A sofa still hung precariously over one floor, there were pictures askew on two walls; and on the fifth floor, a ghostly halo amid the dust, there hung a chandelier, its lights still burning from some maverick power line that the bombs had failed to disconnect.

Foley was there and so was Alex Eftyvoulos, the AP Cyprus correspondent who had been brought in to reinforce the Beirut bureau, a half-Russian Greek Cypriot with a nine-inch black beard that made him look like Rasputin. Foley was taking pictures at the end of the street and I noticed that he was repeatedly looking at the sky. The jets were coming back. Eftyvoulos seemed unconcerned. I walked instinctively into the shadow of the ruined flats where a little boy was standing, watching the sky. There were six jets at around 7,000 feet, racing unconcerned above a thin layer of anti-aircraft fire. They headed south; they were not bothered about us now.

Two women pulled some clothes from beneath shards of concrete just down the street and an old man, a butcher who gave his name as Shehadi Denowi, walked up to us while we were inspecting the flames which still licked around someone's kitchen. His daughter had been taken to hospital, he said. And he described briefly, almost without emotion, how her stomach had been torn out by shrapnel from the Israeli bomb. An unshaven man with deep, bloodshot eyes, Denowi was still in a state of shock. He was shaking slightly but he spoke slowly, coherently and with care. 'This was a civilian area,' he said. 'The planes are terrorising us. This is no way for soldiers to fight.' Then we heard the jets again.

We ran into the doorways of buildings so cracked by the earlier bombings that a mere vibration might have brought them down. This time, the Israeli planes were lower, diving towards Bourj al-Barajneh, but the tremor of explosions that followed created its own peculiar panic in Abu Chaker Street. A woman, too terrified to move, stood in the road weeping, heedless of the shouts of her friends.

'Shall we find out where the jets are going?' It was Eftyvoulos, smiling in a kindly, dangerous way. His desire to drive into, rather than out of, danger was familiar, disconcerting and shaming. Sure, why not? Foley wanted to come. So through some inclination that reality should have corrected, we followed the jets and drove the wide, empty road towards Bourj al-Barajneh, a fearful highway where teenagers were firing museum-piece anti-aircraft guns at the supersonic jets and tremendous explosions shook the ground.

At the northern end of the airport road, Foley wanted to leave the car to take pictures. In retrospect, memory speeds up such events, running them faster and faster like an old silent movie so that the images blur into each other and become less distinct. I did not like the car. Jets bombed cars, especially here. The landscape was a wilderness of burned-out trucks, bomb craters and smoke. A building across the deserted overpass was burning out of control, a great torch of fire that twisted like a whirlwind. Down the road, shells were coming, whizzing at hip-height and exploding in the trees behind us.

I stood by a ditch, a ridiculous figure with my hands hanging at my sides, watching Foley taking pictures of the fire, the smoke round the neighbouring buildings, the burned-out cars. He looked across at Eftyvoulos. 'There's nothing to take pictures of here,' he complained. 'Let's go further down.' Further down? Efty, I think we should head back. There was a shattering explosion that made Foley crouch on the ground. 'Why?' It was Eftyvoulos. 'Why go now when things are happening?' Eftyvoulos was not foolhardy. Like all of us, he calculated risks. The Israelis could not see us here. If we were hit, it was bad luck, not miscalculation on our part.

Brown smoke enveloped us. The ground smelled of sewage and I realised I was standing next to a river of slime that was making its way cautiously across the road. Two Palestinian gunmen walked past us. 'Hi there!' one of them called cheerfully and held his rifle in the air by way of greeting. They were tired, bored, heading back up to their positions inside the ruins of the Cité Sportif that we could just see through the smoke.

We climbed back in the car and drove on up the road. I started making long, complicated explanations about my edition times to Eftyvoulos. I had to file my first dispatch within an hour. We really should go back to the office now. Foley and Eftyvoulos ignored my protests. They knew my editions were not that early. We reached the end of the highway near the Kuwaiti Embassy and here we stood by the road again, watching the planes as they worked on the camps, their piercing engines almost drowning the sound of the bombs.

It was difficult to see the jets before they dived because they approached from above us, out of the sun over the Mediterranean, but I did catch sight of just one plane, a lone aircraft streaking down the sky like Tennyson's eagle. Was it like this for the pilot as he flew in over the Mediterranean and prepared to bomb the ash pits of the camps? 'The wrinkled sea beneath him crawls ... And like a thunderbolt he falls.' Those familiar dead fingers of brown smoke shot up out of the slums followed by a detonation so loud that even Eftyvoulos hunched his shoulders.

I could hear the sound of Foley's motor-drive whirring beside me. But there was one abiding image of this lunatic front line, something which was to make me ashamed of my own abject fear. For just there, under shellfire in a little park of dust and ammunition boxes, stood a Syrian tank, an old T-54 with a few branches of dried-up leaves thrown over it for camouflage. We always recognised the T-54s by the position of the sleeve on the gun barrel. On the T-54, the sleeve was at the end of the muzzle, on the T-62, it was halfway down. Through a mist of anxiety, I noted this dull, pointless fact. Somehow the jets must have missed the thing, or were saving it up for later. But it would be bombed. Tanks are bombed. These Israelis would pick off this little morsel today. We had to leave.

It was then that I saw them, two Syrian soldiers, steel helmets on their heads, rifles in their hands, shoulder-deep in their foxholes 100 yards from the tank. Normally, they would have asked our business but they stood up and waved despite the shellfire. 'Hallo, you guys!' one of them shouted across at us, and we felt sorry for him because we knew he was going to die. '*Shlonak*? How's it going?' It was the other Syrian. They were both on the other side of the road. He took off his helmet in the heat and smiled. 'Hi there!' he shouted again, and climbed out of his foxhole, waiting for me to cross the road to him. I knew what he was thinking. He was frightened and he knew he was going to die. He wanted some human contact, to find some person whose momentary presence might assuage his justified fear. *Mahaba*! Hi! That would be enough.

I wanted to leave him. Another jet screamed down the sky above us followed by the thunder of its bombs. The other soldier beckoned to me. I could not cross the road. Yes, I thought these two young men were going to die. But I would not wait 30 seconds to give them that human contact they needed because I feared that I too might die.

'Let's get the fuck out of here.' It was Foley. Now there was no time to cross the road to talk to the two Syrian teenagers in their ill-fitting uniforms, standing up to their waists in the muck in front of that stupid tank. I looked across at them for the last time and they both nodded, sharing their secret with me. Then the second soldier turned round in an indifferent way and climbed back into his foxhole. That is how we left them, surrounded in west Beirut, hopelessly cut off from the rest of their army, waiting with a soldier's patience for the air attack that would incinerate them both.

We drove back to Spinney's broken old supermarket — looted back in the 1975 war — and paused to watch the funeral towers of black smoke over Ouzai and the airport, until a gunboat almost invisible in the haze over the sea fired shells around us, the projectiles flying over our heads. We fled; towards Raouche where the fish restaurants were smouldering from an earlier bombardment, down the cliff road towards the Corniche where the gunboat fired another round — at us, at our tiny car racing along the seafront — and there it was again, the same whizzing sound, a tremendous crack and part of the road exploded 20 yards behind us. We scuttled back to the office, to Earleen Tatro's hectoring and the old iron wire machine.*

I went back a day later, during one of Beirut's 'ceasefires', a grubby little window of opportunity in which I crept shamefully out towards the airport in my car, to the spot where those two Syrian soldiers had called to me. When I saw the turret of one of the tanks lying on its side in a ditch, I knew what had happened. I peered gingerly into one of the foxholes and there was the slightest trace of carbonised human remains.

The end of these latest raids came almost magically. Exactly three minutes after Alexander Haig resigned as US secretary of state, the shelling and bombing stopped, as if someone had turned off a switch. Philip Habib called up Saeb Salam, a former Lebanese prime minister and another of the Muslim politicians whom Arafat was using to negotiate with the Americans, and announced that a new ceasefire was in progress, a truce that was, as Salam put it, 'definite and total'. Thus, it seemed, did a change in American foreign policy bring instantaneous silence to the darkened city of Beirut. The political power that could produce such a transition, so suddenly, was astounding.

Haig had given tacit approval for the Israeli invasion; his 'green light', according to the Israelis, was his friendly response to Sharon on 20 May when the Israeli defence minister first disclosed his plans for the attack on Lebanon. Haig had never disguised his pro-Israeli sympathies and State Department officials would later confide that he had seen political 'opportunities' for the United States in a pacified, pro-Western Lebanon.

While remaining outwardly calm, the Saudis, however, had sent a series of urgent messages to Washington, imploring Reagan to put pressure on the Israelis to halt their invasion. Reagan did not receive these initial warnings; Haig apparently blocked them at the State Department. Only when the besieging Israeli army seemed on the point of smashing its way into west Beirut did the Saudis threaten to pull a switch of their own. According to Saudi diplomats in Beirut, King Fahd

---

* A foreign correspondent's life can contain elements of futility. In London, an industrial dispute involving the electricians' union was disrupting publication of *The Times*. The paper was not printed that night and so my report of the air raids could not be published. 'No paper, Bob, agen tonite,' the telex operator typed through to me in Beirut. My reply ('OK mate, Jesus Christ, you can imagine what I feel like') was met sympathetically by the operator with the words: 'Yes, it is bloody, particularly for u, bloody awful and ungrateful. But electricians ... we'll say no more.'

of Saudi Arabia warned that his country would withdraw all its invest-
ments from the United States at once and impose oil sanctions against
the West within hours if the Israeli army was not brought under control.
Reagan was at last made aware of the gravity of the crisis and Haig –
who has always denied that he gave Israel a 'green light' – resigned.
Lebanon had claimed another victim.

Few of us really thought this would offer anything more than a
temporary respite from the Israeli siege. 'Please note,' I messaged Barnes at
The Times next morning, 'there little hope here that ceasefire will hold
for more than couple days and would be unwise to think the shooting is
over.' AP had brought more staff into west Beirut. Nick Tatro – the
bureau chief, Earleen's husband – had struggled back from Yemen via
Damascus a week after the invasion began. He combined toughness and
sensitivity in a way that appealed to the Lebanese AP staff whom he
understood better than most of his colleagues; he, after all, spoke
Arabic. He was also a company man who watched the wire with the
pride of an executive while ensuring that the AP's good name was
upheld by the unbiased reporting of his journalists. He displayed a
somewhat brutal attitude towards the war – regarding it, I suspected, as
a natural phenomenon provoked by the psyche of the Lebanese. When
he disagreed with my assessment of the situation, he would bellow:
'Come off it, Fisky,' as if I were peddling quack medicine. When he
agreed, he would shout: 'Fucking A, man.'

Into Tatro's bureau there also walked one afternoon a tall ex-Marine
with thick-lensed spectacles that made his eyes look like pebbles, an
immensely resilient, kind man who was AP's Johannesburg correspondent. Terry Anderson was overweight and he talked in small gasps
like a football coach who insists on running round the field while talking
to his team. The AP had sent him to help its Tel Aviv bureau and
Anderson had travelled up to Lebanon with an Israeli army escort
officer. He abandoned the man in east Beirut and walked across the line
to the Muslim west of the city. 'I just couldn't stand listening to any
more of their lies,' Anderson told us when he arrived in the office.

To say that Anderson was fearless might be an overstatement. Foolhardy, certainly. He also developed the strange habit of falling asleep at
odd moments of the day, lying on the coffee-stained office floor to doze
during an air raid but then suddenly driving onto the streets during a
heavy artillery bombardment. He had a businesslike way of dealing with
Israeli complaints about the press bias. 'All they've gotta do is understand
one thing,' he announced. 'That when you do bad things, people are
going to say bad things about you.'

On Sunday, 27 June, there was another leaflet raid. The jets that flew
over west Beirut this time dropped leaflets crudely printed on slips of
pink and green paper in slightly ungrammatical Arabic, all addressed to

the Lebanese population whose safety — after the past week of largely indiscriminate bombardment — had once more supposedly become of concern to the Israelis. Its text left no doubt that the truce was only temporary:

> The latest Israeli Defence Force is continuing its war against the terrorists and has not used its full force yet. The IDF is concerned not to hurt innocent citizens and anyone who does not fight against it.
>
> Residents of Beirut, make use of the ceasefire and save your lives ...
> Save your life and those of your beloved ones.
>
> The Commander of the IDF.

This was a disconcerting letter to fall on anyone's home. It was a matter of considerable debate, however, whether this message was really designed to save lives — and thus rid Israel of some of the opprobrium heaped upon it for the thousands of civilian casualties in Lebanon — or whether it merely constituted further pressure upon the PLO to surrender. Arafat responded directly over his radio station, once more promising to 'fight to defend Beirut ... and exact a heavy, very heavy price from the enemy for any attempt to storm the city.'

These martial words belied the acrimonious discussions that were even then going on among the senior officers of the PLO. The latest Israeli surrender terms had been forwarded by the Americans through Saeb Salam, and they now included a new demand that every guerrilla leave the capital. Khalil Wazzir, who was Arafat's second-in-command and was to be murdered by the Israelis in Tunis in 1988, emerged from one meeting to tell reporters that the ceasefire demands were 'a humiliating solution'. The PLO, he said, would refuse to give up its arms and surrender.

Most of the PLO leadership acknowledged that the Palestinians were on the verge of military defeat. Arafat and his colleagues were demanding some kind of honourable surrender, a laying down of arms that would permit the PLO to survive in political form. If Arafat and his comrades took up the Israeli offer of safe passage out of Beirut while their guerrillas were evicted from the capital, then they believed that the prestige of the PLO as a resistance movement would be broken forever, and this would in turn also destroy the will of the Palestinians in the West bank and Gaza to oppose Israeli occupation. The Israelis were well aware of this argument and thought that it was correct. That is why the Palestinians were so stubborn in their refusal to leave west Beirut.

Arafat met Chafiq Wazzan in the latter's office that night for further talks. As the two men conversed, a car bomb exploded 500 yards from the prime minister's office, killing four pedestrians. Who was planting these bombs? Why had that last unexploded car bomb been found to contain Israeli-manufactured detonators? That night, the Red Cross, hospital and police figures for total fatalities since the Israeli invasion came to 10,112. Most were civilians, 250 of them in the air raids which Foley, Eftyvoulos and I had witnessed two days earlier.

The last hopes for peace now appeared to rest upon Salam. In any other country, he might have been called an 'elder statesman' but so many of Lebanon's political leaders were already of such antiquity that the phrase seemed meaningless. He had twice been Lebanon's prime minister and his family political background went back to his father's membership of the Ottoman parliament. Salam, who was 77 but looked 60 and smoked Churchill cigars, kept his father's Turkish parliamentary pass framed on the bookshelf of his west Beirut office, a faded green card containing a tiny photograph of a gruff-looking young man with a moustache, and a fez perched on top of his head.

But it would have been a mistake to think that Salam was overwhelmed by the political burden laid upon him. He positively enjoyed it. He would sit in his little office, gesticulating with a thin marble letter-opener, evidently delighted to be the centre of international attention, a Lebanese statesman with the reputation, assiduously cultivated, of being politically uncontaminated. He was the principal mediator between the Americans and the PLO and the trusted confidant of Arafat and Bashir Gemayel, the one man — so he thought — who might be able to save west Beirut from destruction.

It was Salam's contention that the PLO would have to surrender its arms, that it should be allowed to do so with honour, that it had fought a 'glorious war' but must now come to terms with political and military reality. This, at least, is what Salam said although the 'glory' of the Palestinian war was not a virtue he had chosen to praise before. Peace was something he regarded as a slippery object.

'It is like the tantalising apple that you almost reach and then it escapes you,' he told me towards the end of June, tapping his letter-opener on the back of his left hand. 'You get flexibility on one side and then a hardening on the other.' The Israelis and the Palestinians were now creating problems of nomenclature that made even the tantalising apple seem to be hanging from a very high branch. The Israelis were talking about 'adjustment of lines' in west Beirut; the Palestinians referred to 'disengagement'. Salam shrugged. 'Maybe you know better how to tell the difference between these two.' He liked to address his audience — especially journalists — with such suggestions, sometimes rising from his chair in his natty white suit, his white eyebrows rising and falling with political concern.

He had twice been Lebanon's prime minister, under Fouad Chehab in 1960 and then under Suleiman Franjieh ten years later. He boycotted the Sarkis elections and so deftly avoided Syrian contamination. His decision stood him in good stead. Now he had been able to arrange for Arafat to visit his three-storey home and to telephone from there to

Bashir Gemayel in east Beirut. If these two men could agree on the nature of a Palestinian surrender, then surely the Israelis would have no reason to attack west Beirut again.

Salam's job had been made more difficult by administrative confusion in the State Department in Washington. 'At one point last week,' Salam said, 'the Saudis told the PLO that they had got assurances from William Clark [the US national security adviser] that there would be a disengagement. But the State Department was working on another line, saying there would be an adjustment of [military] lines.' It was the latter message that had been handed to Habib and this, Salam somehow conjectured, lay behind Haig's resignation.

Salam seemed quite unconcerned by the fall of such worldly figures. He had created for himself a comforting niche in his country's modern history, reflected perhaps in the Levantine elegance of his own home with its oil paintings and Persian carpets and crystal chandeliers. The white rooms were tall and cool, the bookshelves lined with leather volumes in English, French and Arabic. A coloured portrait of King Faisal of Saudi Arabia at prayer hung on one wall while outside, beyond the climbing plants by the doorway, a mosque sweltered in the heat.

So far, the PLO had agreed in its talks with Salam that it would cease to be a military force in Lebanon and that it would place its camps and men under Lebanese control. The Israelis, however, still wanted the Palestinian leadership exiled from Lebanon. 'Everybody has the feeling,' Salam said, 'that time is running out, that time is very precious.' And suddenly, that letter-opener was banging down hard on the back of Salam's left hand, faster and faster like a pendulum with a faulty spring. Time was moving for Salam as well. For President Sarkis needed a new prime minister and Salam could yet be the broker that he – and even his possible successor, Bashir Gemayel – were looking for.

The one player in the Lebanon war to whom Salam was definitely not talking was Syria. President Assad's soldiers in Beirut now appeared doomed and his army in the mountains had suffered serious reverses on the mountain highway. Although they had not lost the ridge at Mdeirej, Syrian armoured units closer to Beirut had been attacked by Israeli paratroopers and pushed back to a new front line beyond Bhamdoun. The Israeli assault so surprised the Syrians – who were adhering to the latest ceasefire – that several Syrian tanks were destroyed by Israeli infantry.

All the way up the highway from Kahhale, I found evidence of the ignominious Syrian retreat: tanks abandoned in the fields, heavy machine-guns left intact on rooftops, Syrian troops lying dead beside the road, shot in the back as they ran away. One soldier's body was sprawled across the central reservation until a Lebanese Christian poured petrol over it and set the corpse on fire. As it lay there afterwards, blackened and shrivelled, a passing Lebanese motorist travelling down the mountain with his family stopped his car on the other side of the road. I watched him calmly climb from the vehicle with a pocket camera in his hand, walk over to the remains, take a snapshot and return smiling to the car. One for the family album. There were times when the Lebanese mind seemed truly impenetrable.

Some of the Syrian armour was smashed and scalded. Other bodies lay in the undergrowth of the roadside ditches; the smell on the highway told us they were still there. The burned-out tanks stood beside the roadway, their turrets twisted sideways, their paint melted off in the explosions that killed their crews. In Bhamdoun itself, Syrian transport lorries had been crushed on the pavements, some gutted, others abandoned even as their occupants were loading blankets and supplies in a vain attempt to retreat in good order.

The Israeli front line on the mountains above Beirut was now a ten-foot-high barricade of rubble and earth pushed across the dual carriageway, a solitary revetment behind which stood a cluster of Israeli army jeeps, radio aerials swinging in the cold wind, their drivers studying the terrain up the road through field-glasses. Two miles up the hill, the Syrian army was withdrawing, pulling what was left of its armour and trucks out of Sofar.

The Israelis at the barricade did not know this. But when we drove down a country lane to the right of the barricade, up a crumbling track between tobacco plantations and through a village shaded by tall trees, we found ourselves near the old casino in Sofar and there was a solitary Syrian paratrooper. Further along the road, his comrades were loading the last Syrian lorry in the town with mattresses and a stove. In anticipation of another Israeli advance, the Syrians were ready to leave.

But their preparations were unnecessary. The Israelis portrayed the Syrian retreat from Bhamdoun as a rout. The Phalangists, whom the Israelis had once again brought into their newly acquired area of occupation, commandeered the abandoned tanks which were still in working order. The Israeli officers in Bhamdoun, easygoing men with Ray-Ban sun-glasses who talked with their hands in their pockets, claimed that the Syrians had good equipment but no fighting spirit. But it was not quite that simple. Much of that equipment − the T-54 tanks, for example − was more than 15 years old, and the heavy casualties later admitted by the Israelis suggested that at least some of Assad's battalions died holding their ground. If this was not the case, then why did the Israelis, with their Centurion tanks, halt just below Sofar, in such a tactically disadvantageous position?

Yet the real purpose of the Israeli push across the mountains and of the Israeli armour now massed below Sofar was to prevent the Syrians returning to west Beirut and breaking the encirclement of the city. If either Syrian troops or Palestinian guerrillas still inside the capital were to travel the mountain road to Damascus, it would be only through Israel's good grace.

Although they constituted only a tiny proportion of the 600,000 population, hundreds of residents of west Beirut were now leaving the besieged sector of the city, some of them taking truckloads of household furniture. It was the Phalange, not the Israelis, who searched their vehicles when they crossed into east Beirut. The Israeli army would make increasing use of the Phalangists in the coming weeks, refusing to interfere when the Christian gunmen threatened motorists or stole food from Muslim families, even when this was done under the eyes of Israeli troops.

The Israelis showed no embarrassment at this but they did follow one consistent practice: they never called the Phalange by its real name. They called it the 'Lebanese Forces', which was the notional title of the old Gemayel–Chamoun alliance, a coalition that had no real meaning now that the Phalangist alliance with Israel had been consecrated around west Beirut. If the Israelis had called their allies Phalangists, of course, it would have raised awkward questions. Thoughts would have travelled not forward into the future of the prosperous friendship of Jew and Christian Maronite, but backwards to 1936, to those young men in their dark shirts who had paraded for their youth leader at Ein al-Rumaneh. Any repeated mention of the Phalange would have evoked memories of Franco, of Fascism and of Nazism.

Israeli radio fell in step with this short circuit around history. Listeners were always told of the rapturous welcome given to the Israelis by the 'Lebanese Forces'. Foreign correspondents working from Israel – many of them unfamiliar with Lebanese history – fell into the same habit. The *Jerusalem Post* only started investigating historical links between the Israelis and the Phalangists more than a year after the invasion. Until then, they were the 'Lebanese Forces'.

It was a convenient phrase. It sounded apolitical and official. It gave the impression that the Phalange, far from being just another murderous Lebanese militia, were a disciplined army with legal status, that they worked not for Bashir Gemayel but for the president of Lebanon. Indeed, the Israelis hoped that Bashir Gemayel *would* be the president of Lebanon. In which case, the 'Lebanese Forces' might turn out to possess the authority that the Israelis already pretended they had.

On the morning of 28 June, the leaflets fluttered down again upon west Beirut, an unseasonal autumn of green and yellow paper that now carried a special urgency, words of warning so coarse and inelegant that they reminded one of the threats which medieval barons would send to the occupants of a besieged castle. 'You in west Beirut should remember today that time is running out and with every delay the risk to your dear ones increases . . .' the leaflets said. The Israelis did not wish to harm innocent civilians. 'Hurry up. Save the lives of your dear ones before it is too late.' Most of the papers were dropped over Corniche Mazraa, where several hundred civilians had already died in Israeli air attacks.

The Israelis now put pressure on the Western press in Beirut. To correspondents in the east of the city, the Israelis privately acknowledged that journalists in the western sector were, as one of them put it, 'a thorn in our side'. Reports from west Beirut were biased in favour of the 'terrorists', the Israelis claimed. After a news conference in east Beirut, an Israeli officer said that reporters in the Muslim area should leave at once, 'for safety reasons'.

I sent a message to Barnes recounting an incident in which another Israeli officer 'suggested to me that I may not be able to move around in occupied areas in future as I was not subject to military censorship. Earlier, he had asked me if I had seen Syrian troops in Sofar and requested their dispositions. I refused to give this information, just as I would refuse any Syrian request for intelligence about the Israelis. I told [the] Israeli officer that any suggestion that I was unable to travel around Lebanon was "unacceptable" and that I would continue to do my job as [a] journalist in the country.' This message was passed to Charles Douglas-Home, the editor of *The Times*, who insisted that I continue to operate in all areas of Lebanon, whether the Israelis liked it or not. There was little doubt, however, why the Israelis wanted us out of west Beirut: we were now among the very few independent witnesses to the horrifying results of their increasingly indiscriminate air raids and bombardments.

The consistent and accurate reporting of this human suffering was our most important journalistic duty now that the earlier battles and the movement of great armies had frozen along the front lines around the west Beirut perimeter. Earleen Tatro had assiduously collected the lists of casualties from hospitals and from the Red Cross. Now Nick Tatro and I wanted to check the cemeteries. The Israelis still claimed that the casualty figures were lies, that the information came from the PLO rather than from our own investigations. Not once did they ever produce evidence to the contrary: the dead do not rise from their graves. But if the Israelis were prepared to go on denying the truth, what did the gravediggers of Beirut say about all this?

Tatro and I drove to a little cemetery on the corner of Sabra, perhaps only half a mile from the front line where many of the pine trees had been torn apart by Israeli shellfire. The cicadas hissed and crackled so loudly in the surviving evergreen trees that the cemetery seemed alive with sound. But Abu Tayeb was oblivious to them. 'I have never seen so many dead as this last month,' he said, and led us down a dirt path where we walked carefully over his gravedigger's shovels and trowels.

There were small communal graves beneath the trees, the earth still fresh on them and a carpet of flies that lay upon the ground. Under shellfire, Abu Tayeb did not have time to bury the bodies deep.

They were the victims of the Israeli air raids, civilians for the most part but guerrillas as well, thrown in panic into these earthen pits as the bombardment swept over Sabra. Their graves were unmarked but Abu Tayeb kept a grubby, brown-covered diary, its pages sometimes stained with earth, in which he had recorded their names and a few details of their role in life. He pointed to a square of brown clay to our left. 'In here,' he said, 'are the following fifteen people.' And he read through their dead identities like a preacher in a pulpit: 'Jamal Mohamed Ibrahim, an old man, Mohamed Ahmed Bakru, a Syrian soldier, Ashraf Mohamed Acca, a nine-year-old boy . . .'

Abu Tayeb was a middle-aged man in a dirty cardigan whose teeth appeared to have been worked over in vain by a score of dentists. He smiled occasionally, especially when he failed to understand why the statistics of civilian deaths were politically important. Only a Palestinian official who stood beneath the trees realised this, which is why he stepped forward briefly and suggested to Abu Tayeb in Arabic that he need not bother to tell us that Ghabi Hussein, whose corpse also lay beneath us, was a member of the Popular Front for the Liberation of Palestine.

But most of the newly buried dead there were civilians. Abu Tayeb had interred 250 since the Israelis invaded Lebanon on 6 June, fourteen of them in a communal earthen tomb on 13 June, thirty in another mass grave on the following day, fifteen more bodies buried together on 22 June. 'Some of them were women and many were children,' he said. Abu Tayeb's own four children — the two teenage boys were gravediggers themselves — listened to all this with the wisdom of great age.

Abu Tayeb had dug most of the 1,800 graves there since he arrived in Beirut in 1970. There were rows of Palestinian 'martyrs' there too, guerrillas who died in the civil war of 1975—6 and in the factional fighting that followed. Photographs of their faces, shielded from the sun by plastic and steel frames, stood above each tomb, usually with a map of mandate Palestine attached to the picture. Other graves carried the photographs of young women or children in shiny white dresses. Some of the 300 Lebanese and Palestinians who were killed in an Israeli air raid on Beirut in 1981 also lay there. But if just this small corner of Sabra contained 250 casualties from the last months of fighting, there had to be thousands of dead scattered across west Beirut's eight much larger cemeteries. We already had the names of 270 men, women and children who died on just the second day of Israeli bombing in Beirut in June.

From beneath our feet came a sharp smell to remind us of the shallowness of those new graves. Across the trees, in a corner of the cemetery, some Israeli shells had fallen – probably aimed at a Palestinian guerrilla position 400 yards away – and the gravestones there had been smashed to shards, the marble and plastic flowers and photographs strewn across the earth. Abu Tayeb had dug three more communal graves in anticipation that the ceasefire would not last. After that, he said, his little graveyard would be full.

As if the casualty figures were not embarrassing enough for the Israelis, there now emerged growing evidence that they were using cluster bombs against west Beirut. These weapons had been purchased by Israel from the United States on the strict condition that they would never be employed against civilians. President Reagan had already spoken of his concern at the use of cluster bombs during the invasion of Lebanon but the Israelis, it now transpired, had not only dropped these bombs on tanks and smaller vehicles – for which they were designed – but had employed them as anti-personnel weapons in civilian areas. Tatro and Randal and I had discovered several of the weapons unexploded in and around the Palestinian camps in Beirut and a number of the plastic bomb casings – still clearly marked with the code and date of American manufacture – had been found in the capital and in other parts of Lebanon.

What made the cluster bomb so fearful was its indiscriminate nature. It killed by showering anyone close to its detonation with clouds of steel balls and metal fragments. Used in a residential area, it was a murderous weapon. Two types of cluster bombs had been sold by the United States to Israel, both under specific restrictions which the Americans curiously refused to make public. It was their discovery inside the Palestinian camps that caused such concern in Washington, for many of those injured by the bombs were civilians.

One type of cluster bomb which I had seen and examined consisted of a set of triangular metal caskets, each of which contained a cylindrical pellet of explosive of a white powdery chemical. I found dozens of these unexploded caskets in Chatila in the alleyways between the ruined concrete hovels not far from the Kuwaiti Embassy. So adamant were the Israelis that they had not used these weapons on the camps that I actually took a bag of caskets to my home and reassembled them on a table in my living room. It looked like a bomb known in the United States as a CBU-58, which is specifically designed for use against jeeps, mobile radar sets and other lightly armed equipment. Randal and other journalists had come across identical caskets in Corniche Mazraa, an area heavily populated by Shia and Sunni Muslims.

Another type of bomb, which appeared similar to the 'Rockeye' anti-tank cluster bomb, contained a number of small, heavy 'bomblets' crudely made in three parts, each about three inches in diameter.

Several of these caskets, which looked at first sight like large, thick arrowheads, fell unexploded on roads near Ouzai, at the southern end of the Beirut seafront. Most of the casings were about three metres long and made of a light, plastic-like substance which broke into two parts after the bombs had been released. The PLO, which had its own propaganda reasons for publicising the Israelis' use of the weapon, found several of these casings around Beirut over the preceding three weeks.*

We found children in the Barbir hospital who had been wounded by the bomblets. In some cases, they had been hurt because they had found them lying in the streets outside their homes, had failed to recognise their significance and had played with them until they exploded in their hands. We made notes on all this, hundreds of pages of notes. We were continually visiting hospitals, talking to the International Red Cross, driving — sometimes running on foot — to apartment blocks that had been bombed by Israeli planes. Amid the muck and the human remains, we scribbled away on jotters and pieces of paper. In a sense, each of our notebooks became a gravedigger's diary.

With such sophisticated weaponry now being used against west Beirut, the mournful exodus of citizens continued, their family cars caparisoned with beds, mattresses and stoves. In some areas of west Beirut, Lebanese gunmen fought with each other for possession of abandoned homes, but the seafront south of Raouche was now deserted except for wandering groups of guerrilla fighters, rifles in hand, transistor radios in the other. The radio had become a lifeline for civilian and militiaman alike. Of all Beirut's sieges — by the crusaders, by Saladin in the twelfth century, by the Anglo-Turkish fleet in 1840 — none were on such a scale as the city's twentieth-century encirclement by the Israeli army. Almost all the Western embassies — including the British — had now left west Beirut. The Norwegians and the Canadians bravely stayed on, although the Canadian ambassador was shortly to be bombed out of his residence by an Israeli air raid.

The PLO had formally announced that it would leave the city — Salam publicised the fact on 30 June — but this brought little hope of relief for west Beirut. The method of the PLO's departure and the date of its evacuation — even details of how many guerrillas should leave — had yet to be decided and there were those within the PLO leadership who were doing their best to prolong the negotiations and thus force

---

* I wrote a long report for *The Times* on the use of cluster bombs in Lebanon and the paper published the technical data and serial numbers which I had seen stencilled on the weapons. Most were clearly marked 'anti-tank bomb cluster'. Some bore the words 'US Navy'. Several appeared to have been radar-guided. A complex electronic device containing a timing mechanism was found in one bomb at Ouzai bearing the abbreviated name of the American company — 'Gen Time Corp.' — that manufactured it. See *The Times* of 2 July 1982.

Israel to continue the siege. Ariel Sharon was on hand to provide the assurance that Israel's patience could become exhausted.

He turned up for lunch at the Alexandre Hotel in east Beirut on 2 July, escorted by armed Israeli bodyguards, and announced to reporters in the dining room that 'our only reason for being here is to destroy the terrorist PLO . . .' Sharon was an obese man who sweated profusely in the midday heat but smiled expansively as he sat down in his bright blue shirt and told the assembled journalists – how familiar were those words – that his army had 'no intention of keeping one square inch of Lebanese territory'. The Israelis were not fighting the Lebanese or the 'Palestinian people' but the PLO.

Two hours later, Bashir Gemayel returned to east Beirut from Saudi Arabia where he had been told that several Arab nations might support his candidature for the Lebanese presidency if the PLO was allowed to keep some tangible presence in Beirut. Gemayel had rejected the offer. He went immediately to the presidential palace for a meeting with Habib, Sarkis and Wazzan and then re-emerged on the steps to tell the waiting correspondents that the PLO had no intention of leaving west Beirut. He said this in a matter-of-fact way but his face was hard, his eyes searching as always through the faces in front of him. The PLO had said they would leave. 'They are lying,' he said softly, speaking in a form of Arabic slang. 'They lied to Habib, to Sarkis, to Wazzan. They lied all round.' This lie, he said, risked the 'total obliteration' of west Beirut.

The planes came back. Before dawn, they dropped aerial percussion bombs above west Beirut. It sounded as if the whole city was collapsing. The jets flew at low level, firing cascades of flares over the rooftops, a string of fire that produced a fantasy of yellow light over the city. On the front line at the museum, Israeli loudspeakers urged civilians to leave the west. On the other side, Palestinian tannoys informed the families who were walking between the sand embankments and earthworks that their womenfolk would be raped by the Phalange.

In a 200-mile round-trip into southern Lebanon, Eftyvoulos and I found that the Israelis were now installing their Phalangist allies around Sidon, beside the rubble of the Palestinian camp at Ein Helweh and up in the mountain town of Jezzine. Israelis and Phalangists manned joint checkpoints together, often beneath that drawing of the young Pierre Gemayel staring fixedly at his new political dawn. In some southern Shia villages, Shia militiamen had been allowed to bear arms again, to join a 'national guard' loyal to Israel. And Haddad's gunmen, the scourge of those same southern villages, had now turned up at Sidon, guarding the Awali River bridge alongside the Israelis.

On the road back to Beirut, we saw the Israelis transporting back to Israel the ancient tanks which they had captured from the PLO, T-34s of 1944 vintage. A truckload of captured AK-47 rifles drove past us, hundreds of weapons bouncing up and down in the back of the lorry like gifts to be distributed at a children's party. They were shared out, too, among Haddad's gunmen. But therein lay the recurring political problem behind the moral issues of this war.

If the Palestinian guerrillas were an army — if they were a military force with an impressive and threatening armoury, as the Israelis made out — then how could the Israelis also call them 'terrorists'? The British once regarded the Jews and Arabs who opposed them in Palestine as 'terrorists'. Menachem Begin had been a 'terrorist' leader who had blown up the King David Hotel in Jerusalem, at that time the ninth most savage act of 'terrorism' this century, at least according to the British.

In east Beirut, the Israeli army officers — even the Israeli journalists who now travelled regularly up from Tel Aviv — used the word 'terrorism' loosely, giving the war a moral flavour which it did not in reality possess. Terrorism, terrorism, terrorism. Never before had its use become so all-pervasive, so ominous and dangerous. In one sense, it was the most frightening aspect of the war. For who *were* the 'terrorists' in Beirut? The Palestinian guerrilla fighters who had slaughtered their Christian opponents in the civil war? The Phalangist gunmen who had slaughtered so many Palestinian civilians and who were now allied to the Israelis? The Israeli soldiers and pilots who killed thousands of innocent people while pursuing the ghost of 'international terrorism'?

If an Israeli regarded a Palestinian guerrilla as a terrorist, then what of his brother who kept his gun or his sister who cleaned his combat jacket or his parents who believed he was fighting, however ruthlessly, for a cause: the right to a country? There was an equal lack of semantic care in the PLO's own appreciation of itself. Arafat talked of defiance yet failed to realise — or care — that many Lebanese hated him for his arrogance and past violence. The Palestinians refused to examine their rhetoric now that they were trapped in Beirut. The Muslim population was their only protection and they were ready to sacrifice those civilian lives in their own Armageddon.

On the morning of 5 July, the Israelis switched off the electrical power circuits to west Beirut and cut the water supply. No more food was to be allowed in. In the last moments of the latest 'ceasefire', I watched Israeli troops grabbing baskets of food from Muslim women crossing to the west and throwing them into a ditch. At the museum crossing point, we observed Israelis carrying out their new duties with such enthusiasm that they confiscated two sandwiches from a policeman who was walking from east to west Beirut. I saw a Phalangist militiaman at Galerie Semaan grab two bottles of water from an old woman who had heard that the water supply had been cut and was hoping to take them to the west. He smashed them on the roadway in front of four Israeli soldiers. 'Fuck your sister,' the Phalangist shouted at the old woman, and the four Israelis laughed.

She must have been 65, maybe 70. She had a white scarf round her head. She was overweight, fat, and she was perspiring with fear as much as with the heat. Why were they doing this? It was puzzling to me, standing there near the woman, that the Israelis did not intervene. The Phalangist was screaming at the woman now. 'You whore. Were you taking this water to the terrorists?' The Israelis were still laughing.

It was like a contagion. It had something to do with that word 'terrorists'; the Phalangist had used the Arabic word *muharabin* and the Israelis had understood him. It seemed as if all the compassion which the Israelis might normally have felt for the old woman had suddenly dried up. Was this the word, 'terrorist', that came into their minds when they thought of the civilians of west Beirut? Terrorist. Like an instruction on a computer screen, it was a code, it gave permission for something, a dispensation, a blessing upon future action. Would the Israeli army bomb west Beirut to the ground?

When I approached the gunman and asked why he was shouting at the old woman, he turned like a tiger, pulled back the bolt on his M-16 and pointed it at my stomach. 'Fuck your sister.' CLACK-CLICK. Then he pointed his rifle at the woman's stomach. The Israelis were only ten feet away but they did nothing. I knew the gunman would not fire. Other journalists were walking down the road towards us. But the old woman was terrified. She put her hands in front of her, clasped them together, imploring. She could think of nothing to say. So she put her head on one side, looked at the Phalangist and said: 'Oh God, please.'

9   Surgical Precision

> I had to take the babies and put them in buckets of water
> to put out the flames. When I took them out half an hour
> later, they were still burning. Even in the mortuary, they
> smouldered for hours.
>
> Dr Amal Shamaa of the Barbir hospital, after Israeli
> phosphorus shells had been fired into West Beirut
> *29 July 1982*

Alia Abu Said lay on her side in the hospital ward, coughing repeatedly into a stained handkerchief. 'She has phosphorus in her lungs,' the doctor said. 'She gave birth prematurely this morning. I don't know if we can save the baby. The problem is that it is also coughing. The baby has a form of phosphorus poisoning as well.' There was a muttering of middle-aged women at the door where Alia's female relatives, with their tight headscarves and lined Palestinian faces, were waiting to see her. She looked at them and tried to smile. Three of her five children were already dead.

Terry Anderson and I were to get to know this hospital well. What we saw here we would not easily forget. Visiting the Barbir hospital was to see what gunfire does to flesh, to exorcise the mysticism of those great guns that Randal and I had seen on our way back from Sidon.

Alia Abu Said could not remember much about the Israeli phosphorus shell that hit her two-storey shack in the Bourj al-Barajneh camp on 29 July. It was painful even to ask her about it, for she wheezed her replies, coughing and choking into that stained handkerchief. She lay on her right side because the skin on her left arm and leg and the left side of her face had been partially burned away. 'My husband put me downstairs in the house for safety when the shelling started,' she said. 'But the bomb came in downstairs. The smoke was white.'

When Alia Abu Said and 11 other members of her family arrived at the Barbir hospital, they were still on fire. The phosphorus had burnt into their skin and set light to their hair. Dr Amal Shamaa had to smother them in blankets and shave off their burning hair before picking out the white phosphorus from their flesh. In another room a few yards away, Alia's sister lay beside her husband, Hussain Baitam. Both were badly burned and could hardly speak because the moment they attempted to do so, they suffered fits of coughing. Hussain was 53 but looked chillingly younger with his hair missing and his burned face a terrible bright pink. He stared towards the window, irritating his deep bronchial cough with a cigarette. Few of the doctors of west Beirut had treated phosphorus wounds before, and most resorted to a burn cream which coloured the skin a bright red after it was applied. On admission, both Hussain and his wife had been taken to a maternity unit so that the doctors could bathe them repeatedly in tubs of water.

The medical staff at the Barbir hospital were shocked by these wounds. When the family was brought into the emergency room at the end of July, Dr Shamaa found that two five-day-old twins had already died. But they were still on fire.

Shamaa's story was a dreadful one and her voice broke as she told it. 'I had to take the babies and put them in buckets of water to put out the flames,' she said. 'When I took them out half an hour later, they were still burning. Even in the mortuary, they smouldered for hours.' Next morning, Amal Shamaa took the tiny corpses out of the mortuary for burial. To her horror, they again burst into flames.

Alia Abu Said's 4½-year-old son Aham lay in the children's ward moaning. Nurses were dressing his wounds again and although his face was almost free of burns, his legs and arms were terribly disfigured. He was coughing and spitting and the male doctor in the ward, a kindly, balding man with tired eyes, kept talking to the little boy, trying to explain to him that he would get better. In private, he was less confident. The boy would recover, he said, unless he suffered a pulmonary infection. Dr Shamaa had already watched another of Alia's children die the previous day of a perforated lung.

But neither the Baitams nor the Abu Saids knew what phosphorus was, nor did they know why it was used against them by the Israelis. Many of their friends in the Palestinian camps had been taken to hospital with shrapnel wounds. Shamaa had counted 19 cases of phosphorus burns between 6 June and 29 July. One of the victims was a Palestinian guerrilla. The rest were civilians. Eight of them had died and three of these were Sabah's children.

Anderson and I had spent a lot of time at the Barbir hospital, which lay at the western end of the museum crossing point along the old front line. It had quickly become apparent to us that the tragedy of west Beirut's civilians was contained not just in the lists of dead, in the mortuary files and the gravediggers' records but in the wards of Beirut's ever more vulnerable hospitals. They had all been hit now by Israeli artillery fire; the Barbir — the top floor of which had been wrecked by Israeli shells — and the Makassed and American University hospitals. The home for orphaned children near Chatila was blown open by an Israeli salvo and the infants there abandoned by their nurses; journalists found them crying, sitting in their own excreta in the wreckage of the orphanage.

Anderson and I had been on the streets of west Beirut under some of the worst Israeli bombardments of July, 'time-on-target' salvoes from Israeli guns that laid 50 shells at a time across a narrow street, slaughtering everyone within a 500-yard radius of the explosions. Anderson had stood on the AP bureau roof with me for an entire afternoon as phosphorus shells crashed onto the buildings round us, the gentle, fluffy white clouds from the explosions drifting off across the apartments as if they were no more than smoke from a garden bonfire. One had plopped onto the roof of the headquarters of the International Red Cross. We saw it explode just behind the huge Red Cross flag that was strapped to the roof to prevent air attack. We reported it. The International Red Cross complained. The Israelis then denied that they had ever shelled the Red Cross.

Anderson at least knew what phosphorus was from his own training as a Marine in Vietnam. Dr Shamaa asked me if I could discover the chemical composition of phosphorus shells so that she could prepare more efficient antidotes to the appalling burn cases that she was receiving. I asked *The Times* for help and Michael Horsnell, one of the paper's London-based reporters, sent back a frightening message on 30 July. He wrote:

> White phosphorus has been used to fill mortar and artillery shells and grenades since the First World War. It was used to start the Hamburg fire storms in World War Two ... white phosphorus shells are manufactured in UK, US and West Germany, have a high-explosive squash head and are fired from the M109 155 mm howitzer ... not believed to be supplied to Israel by US under any special conditions, and is regarded as 'routine ammunition'. Almost certainly not covered by international convention ... however it is regarded as 'very useful in house clearing' – the smoke hangs around for a long time and burns. Victims should have their burns smothered quickly and then doused with oceans of water. During the fire storms in Hamburg the police would patrol in boats, shooting victims to put them out of their misery ...

We were beginning to understand why. On the afternoon of 29 July, Anderson had returned to the office from the Barbir in a state of suppressed fury. He had just watched Ahmed Baitam die. I had thought Dr Shamaa would be able to save the three-year-old child despite the awful burns on his face. I had left Anderson at the hospital and returned to cover the Israeli artillery bombardment of Ramlet al-Baida. Anderson sat down at his typewriter in front of the coffee stand, threaded a sheet of copy paper into the machine, looked up at me and said: 'I watched him die.' He was crying. 'Why did that have to happen? For Christ's sake, why?' Anderson had a seven-year-old daughter and loved children. All his Marine toughness had been blown out of him. He attacked the typewriter as if it were the cause of the child's death and began one of the most moving reports of the war:

Three-year-old Ahmed Baitam, his face and part of his chest covered with severe burns, was tied to the bed with soft bandages. As Dr Amal Shamaa leaned over to point out the injuries caused by burning phosphorus, his heart stopped.

The doctor bent over his body and put her stethoscope on his chest, then called to a nurse and medical orderly, 'Arrest.'

The slim, intense pediatrician began pushing hard on the wounded chest, while the orderly started breathing into his mouth. The nurse ran for heart needles and an electro-shock machine. Dr Shamaa ... leaned against a wall. 'It was respiratory damage. They inhale the phosphorus,' she said ...

When I returned to the hospital, it was under fire, the shells landing in the streets on both sides of the building. The one child out of danger was Alia's daughter Amira, who now sat on a bed with a small tent pitched over her burnt legs, smiling at her unexpected English visitor. Just once she cast her eyes over to the next bed where a tiny child lay like a flower, a little girl with her leg almost torn off, dwarfed by the sheets upon which she lay. Alia's husband walked into the ward. Unlike his family, he could never be described as a civilian. He wore the green battledress of a Palestinian guerrilla and his bearded face showed no emotion. 'He came to see his wife and he understands that three of his children are dead,' Dr Shamaa whispered to me. 'When we told him the news, he just wanted to say goodbye to them.'

The Barbir itself had been in the firing line for almost three weeks. When I first met Shamaa on 12 July, I found the institution in chaos, with glass and small pieces of concrete across the floors of wards and corridors. A two-foot-wide trail of blood ran from the children's ward to the third floor of the hospital. Between the shards of glass and broken fittings, it snaked across the tiled floor to the stairs. An Israeli shell had burst 20 feet from the windows and in some places the blood was darker than usual, as if an abstract artist had run amok with a tin of light brown paint. Dr Shamaa had been anxious to account for it all. 'This was a visitor to the hospital,' she said in the clinical voice that surgeons use when they are very tired. 'When the shell hit the roof of the building across the road, he was standing next to the bed. He lost a lot of tissue. He may have to lose his leg.'

It was an impersonal account of the night's shellfire that only made Amal Shamaa's feelings – when they emerged – all the more shocking. She was a small woman with dark hair and large eyes and a doctor's strong hands. Israeli shells had fallen around her hospital for four hours and two of them had caused substantial damage to the upper floors.

'This was deliberate. The Israelis know this hospital is here. I mean, even someone who's shelling from the sea or from the mountains can be more accurate than this. The nearest military target is ...' And Dr Shamaa paused for a long time while she contemplated the difference between emotion and truth. 'It is quite a distance away,' she finished.

But it was not. Just below the hospital, perhaps 18 yards across the road, there stood a T-34 tank, an absurd old leviathan that the Mourabitoun, the Nasserite Sunni militia, had positioned behind an embankment of sand and earth above the classical museum. The crossing point between east and west Beirut lay half a mile from the Barbir and the streets around it were guarded by Palestinian guerrillas and Syrian troops. There were gunmen and uniformed militias walking in and out of the hospital. A young man holding a rocket-propelled grenade and with a pocket full of white-finned projectiles leaned against a marble column by the outpatients' department.

It was, of course, a fact of life in Beirut. In a city that was an armed camp, hospitals were not going to escape the contamination of their patients' politics. Thirty per cent of the wounded crammed into the beds and floors of the Barbir's lower rooms were guerrillas, sometimes still in their torn khaki battledress or stripped beneath bloodstained sheets, their faces bandaged beneath a tangle of drip-feeds and glucose bottles. Their comrades sat with them, their rifles beside the beds, holding hands, half-shaven, embarrassed amid the whitewashed walls and the smell of disinfectant.

But many of the Barbir's patients had had to be transferred to other hospitals after the shellfire damaged the building; more than half the 40 who remained were civilians. Of the 21 brought in during the latest bombardment, most were suffering from shrapnel wounds. There were six casualties from the shells *inside* the hospital. The Barbir received 200 dead between 4 June and 10 July and on one occasion there were 20 corpses in a mortuary that had been designed for only six. Dr Shamaa, who was trained at Johns Hopkins and Duke universities in the United States, could not hide her revulsion at the memory. 'The hospital staff could not leave the building because of air attacks and shellfire,' she said. 'The whole place smelled of death for four or five days. Then we managed to go out and we put them in a communal grave. We still don't know who they were.'

If the Israeli artillerymen did not mean to shell the Barbir hospital, they paid precious little attention to its presence. Every locally produced map of Beirut clearly marked the building as a hospital. The road outside was pitted with craters and shell-holes that had in every case missed the sandbagged military positions nearer to the front line. The Israeli gunners up at Baabda — for that is where the shellfire came from — chose a very promiscuous trajectory down which to fire.

Even now, however, the Israelis still tried to censor accounts of the suffering of west Beirut's civilians. On the morning of 25 June, for example, an American television crew from the National Broadcasting Company had driven to the Barbir hospital to film some of the victims of that day's shelling in Bourj al-Barajneh. What they found there upset them deeply. Many of the wounded turned out to be not guerrillas but children, infants less than a year old, their bodies gashed and lacerated by shrapnel, older children bleeding so profusely that they could never survive. One of the crew, heartbroken at the screaming and pain around him, broke down and wept, just as Anderson was to do when Ahmed Baitam died.

The work of the hospital was duly filmed, including a harrowing 20-second sequence of the wounded children. The recording was promptly sent across the front lines to east Beirut and was then driven at speed down to the Israeli frontier and to Tel Aviv for transmission by satellite to New York. But even though the report was not filmed in an area under Israeli military control, the Israeli censor in Tel Aviv insisted on vetting the film. The Israelis were constantly telling the Americans that they were not responsible for such civilian casualties. And the hospital sequence of the wounded children was too much for him. So – for 'security reasons' – he cut it from the film, and the United States public was spared the horror of the Barbir hospital.

It was not the first time that the Israelis had interfered with the work of the three American television networks, nor was it to be the last. Repeatedly, film shipped from west Beirut to Tel Aviv – with the encouragement as well as the permission of the Israeli censors – had been tampered with by Israeli officials. Film of Israeli air strikes on civilian areas of Beirut – sometimes taken with great courage and at enormous personal risk by the camera crews – was ruthlessly excised. Infuriated by the Israeli interference, television producers in New York blacked out the screen for the same number of seconds or minutes as the duration of the censored material, telling American viewers that this section of their report had been excised by the Israeli military authorities. Then the networks began shipping film to Damascus. The Syrians insisted on seeing the film but they did not cut it.*

What had happened, of course, was that for the first time since the foundation of the Jewish state, Western journalists had found themselves free to travel and report on a major Middle East conflict from the other side of Israel's front line. Television crews and newspaper correspondents

* On one occasion, when the international telecommunications authority refused to permit Syria to use the satellite because the Damascus government refused to pay its recent bills, the three American networks underwrote Syria's debts and restored the satellite. So the Israeli censors were – at great cost – partially defeated. As the siege continued and both Israelis and Syrians exhibited sensitivity about journalists' coverage of the battle, it became clear that Syrian sensitivity was often disturbed by the commentaries; the Israelis were taking exception to the pictures. David Phillips, one of NBC's most efficient field producers, then sent his video-tapes to Damascus for transmission without sound and his soundtracks to Tel Aviv for transmission without pictures. The pictures and sound would be married up only when both had been received in New York.

based in Beirut had been driving all over Lebanon, talking to Palestinian guerrillas as well as Israeli troops and, most serious of all for the Israelis, describing the civilian casualties of the Israeli invasion. Crouching in ditches or bunkers during Israeli air strikes, driving through Israeli shellfire, the press in Beirut — and particularly the American press — had been recording the results of this military adventure with a detail and accuracy that the Israelis would have preferred the world not to hear about.

The Israeli view of this had been summed up adequately in their 21 June publication which stated baldly that '"Operation Peace for Galilee" was not directed against the Lebanese or Palestinian peoples ... The terrorists are responsible for any civilian casualties since they were the ones who had placed their headquarters and installations in populated civilian areas and held Lebanese men, women and children captive.'

But the people of west Beirut were *not* captives. For four hours one evening in July, the Palestinians had closed their line to civilians wishing to leave the city, but this was in response to a Phalangist statement that the east Beirut side of the line had been shut; after which, the only thing that prevented the inhabitants of west Beirut from leaving their homes was their own unwillingness to do so even under Israeli shellfire. Up to 100,000 civilians did eventually leave the west of the city, many after the fighting stopped in August, but half a million remained.

As usual, it was the poor and the refugees who came to Beirut from southern Lebanon at the height of the invasion who suffered most. They camped out in office blocks, cinemas, the lobbies of apartments, the foyers of shopping arcades and in tents in the streets. In one abandoned multi-storey commercial building in early July, I found dozens of refugees eating and sleeping on bare floors, their children urinating against the walls, the rooms swarming with flies. Without electricity to work the pumps, they were now going to lose their water supply and the only three lavatory systems available to them.

On 5 July, the United States had given its support to a UN Security Council resolution calling for the restoration of water and electricity to the 600,000 people in west Beirut. This prompted an immediate reply from an Israeli military spokesman in Tel Aviv who issued a communiqué categorically denying that the Israelis had cut off power and water from the west of the city. Early the next day, however, Mahmoud Ammar, the Lebanese minister of hydroelectric resources — who was by chance a strong opponent of the Palestinian guerrillas trapped in west Beirut — announced that the Israelis had turned off the main tap at the water distribution centre in Ashrafieh in east Beirut, thus depriving the population of west Beirut of water. He condemned the Israeli action as 'inhuman'.

Several hours later, a group of Western correspondents, including

Baldwin of the AP, discovered Israeli soldiers actually inside the switching station which controlled water supplies to the west of the city. The troops were in the sub-station, surrounded by sleeping bags and cookers. Weapons were lying around the building. According to Ammar, they had forced their way into the station with automatic rifles, shut the valves and dismantled the wheel controlling the pipes to west Beirut. 'Without the wheel, we cannot get water to west Beirut,' Ammar said. 'It is like a key and the Israelis have it.'

It then transpired that the Israelis had interfered with the Beirut electric power lines in the third week of June; Israeli army electricians had severed the cables at the Hazmiyeh electric sub-station. They were thus able to trim the current into west Beirut but they had finally cut it altogether in early July when Israeli officers arrived at the headquarters of the electricity company in east Beirut with their own maps of the city's grid system. Only hours after that, more Israeli soldiers entered the three-storey sub-station at Karantina not far from the port in east Beirut and ordered the Lebanese employees to switch off all power to west Beirut.

The Israelis now denied their denial. Yes, it was true that the electricity and water supplies to west Beirut had been cut. No explanation was given for what had clearly been a plain, old-fashioned lie. Instead, Colonel Paul Kedar of the Israeli army's press liaison bureau in east Beirut appeared at a press conference to claim that the Israelis were not really trying to hurt civilians. 'We are not aiming at them,' he said. 'I would agree they are suffering. I don't know to what degree. Look, they are not starving yet. They are not thirsty yet ... whatever is being done [sic] is being done to further a certain aim. This is to get the PLO out of Beirut.'

But as Ammar himself told us, the Palestinian guerrillas had water and generators of their own. 'They have been at war for years and they have supplies.' He was right. The PLO suffered no serious shortages. Their generators could be heard roaring away during the night around Fakhani. When foreign correspondents were invited to a PLO press conference in the first week of July, we were shown into a book-lined, air-conditioned bunker and served chilled pineapple juice and hot coffee. The PLO might be hardest hit by shellfire, but food blockades were unlikely to hurt it; the Palestinian camps had stores of food to last them several weeks of siege.

We tried to visit Fakhani between air raids or during the short, illusory ceasefires. The briefest visit, however, was enough to confirm the PLO's arrogance. 'Why didn't you get this pass renewed two days ago?' one of their more diminutive officials shouted at me in mid-July. We carried press credentials from all the militias and armies in and around Beirut — the Druze, the Mourabitoun, Fatah, Amal, the

Phalange, the Syrian government and the Israeli army. This was not a concession to their supposed authority, merely proof that could be offered to gunmen and soldiers that their own officers had vouchsafed our identity as genuine. The Israelis eagerly participated in the system; they, too, wanted to ensure that only *bona fide* reporters could pass through their checkpoints.

The PLO official was objecting to my failure to have my pass brought up to date. This was supposed to be done every four days. In theory, it was for bureaucratic reasons. In practice, it was an attempt to force correspondents to pay at least one visit to the PLO's offices each week. I was two days late. 'Well – what's your reason for being late?' the PLO official asked. 'Haven't you been on the streets?' I told him, gently, that journalists in west Beirut sometimes had other things to do than wait outside Palestinian offices for pieces of paper. 'Don't do it again,' the man snapped. 'You could get in trouble for this.' But surely, I ventured, this was Lebanon; the Palestinians did not actually own west Beirut.

The man drew in his breath with a hiss. 'I'm not going to waste my time arguing with you.' Yet the trouble in west Beirut over the previous seven years was that many Palestinians had acted as if they *did* own this sector of the city. Arafat was now on the PLO's radio station praising the 'Lebanese masses' who were defending 'proud, encircled Beirut'. But there *were* no Lebanese 'masses'. Only a very few of the 600,000 civilians in west Beirut gave wholehearted support to the Palestinian cause. Most would have been as happy as the Israelis to see the PLO leave, providing the guerrillas were not replaced by Phalangist militiamen from east Beirut.

There was still, even now, an inability within the PLO to admit that the Palestinian presence in Lebanon had contributed to the nation's agony. Arafat and his colleagues blithely continued to associate the Phalangists with the forces of 'imperialism', as part of the international conspiracy with which the Arab regimes had always been obsessed. This only helped to encourage the political and religious division of Lebanon. True, the Phalangists were now collaborating with the Israelis, but the contempt with which the Palestinian guerrillas had treated the Lebanese was almost subconscious and long preceded the 1982 invasion. Even before 1978, in the village of Bent Jbail in southern Lebanon, a PLO officer had been explaining to me how Lebanese civilians had always been free to move around the area. But when I asked if this included Maronites from the north, he had become angry. 'Oh no, we don't want foreigners here,' he had said.

Even the PLO's alliance with Amal had virtually collapsed before the invasion. The Shia villagers of the south had been armed by the Palestinians but in several areas east of Tyre, Amal militiamen had ordered Palestinians to leave and opened fire on them when they had

refused. Just three weeks before the invasion, Palestinians had fought a
nine-hour gun battle in the streets of Sidon against the local Lebanese
Sunni militia. Two civilians had been killed, 17 had been wounded and
part of the old souk burned to the ground at a cost of 16 million dollars.
Was it any wonder that the Sunni population of Sidon turned against
the defeated Palestinians after their city was bombed, rather than against
the nation which had just caused so much destruction?

And so now, in west Beirut, the tragedy was waiting to be played out
again. The roadblocks around the Muslim sector were manned by
Palestinians, the armed men wandering along the closed shops in Hamra
Street were Palestinians. There was even a young man who spent two
weeks in the newsroom of *An Nahar,* censoring dispatches that he
deemed unfavourable to the PLO. He too was a Palestinian.

The Lebanese militiamen who did still patrol the streets were now
telling the Palestinians to stay out of certain areas of west Beirut. They
had good reason to give such instructions. In mid-July, I had come
across an armed Palestinian in Nahme Yafet Street, an intelligent, brave
man whom I had known for some years. He was troubled by reports of a
PLO withdrawal plan. 'We will never withdraw,' he said firmly. 'And if
the Israelis come into west Beirut, we shall destroy it all with them. If
necessary, we shall destroy all Lebanon.' The capacity to do that had
gone; there were fewer than 12,000 Palestinian guerrillas in all west
Beirut. But there was no doubt about the man's emotion. As usual, the
state of Lebanon turned out to be worth less than the unborn state of
Palestine.

Arafat himself started performing for the cameras. He could be seen
receiving the Israeli journalist Uri Avneri. We saw him greeting five
polite, over-enthusiastic, naïve but not entirely gullible members of the
US Congress. Arafat now preferred to be photographed filling sandbags
on the west Beirut front line. Holding Palestinian babies or cuddling
young guerrilla 'cubs' was definitely *passé.* This was why he now sported a
dapper Afrika Korps-type forage cap in keeping, presumably, with the
daring days through which he imagined he was living. But in private, he
was encountering one problem that he did not choose to talk about to
the journalists who questioned him. We were uncertain then as to how
serious this problem might be, but in a dispatch to *The Times* on 26
July I referred to 'a challenge to his authority that is potentially more
dangerous to him than the Israelis'.

It was difficult to define the nature of this challenge, although we
occasionally saw evidence of it. Palestinian guerrillas on the west Beirut
perimeter began talking of their refusal to follow any order for an
evacuation, expressing their concern for the vulnerable Palestinian families
whom they would have to leave behind in the camps. This dissatisfaction
with the PLO leadership was exacerbated when Arafat decided that US

recognition of the PLO should be a condition for a Palestinian departure from west Beirut. Whatever political satisfaction could be gained from such recognition – even if it were forthcoming – it would still mean that Arafat had been reduced to political rather than military struggle. It showed the guerrillas that their battle was almost over.

The PFLP was among the most reluctant to leave. Ever since the Israelis had surrounded Beirut, George Habash had seen advantage in the siege. In the past, he told his supporters, the Palestinians had to fight their way into Israel to attack the Israelis. Now the Israeli tanks were only yards from their homes and they could at last fight their enemy at close quarters. Nayef Hawatmeh took the line of least resistance. In the third week of west Beirut's encirclement, I had gone to his underground headquarters to find the normally radical leader of the Democratic Front for the Liberation of Palestine looking for an honourable agreement to end the fighting.

Pale and unsmiling, at times apparently shaking from fatigue, Hawatmeh talked now not of resistance but of surrender, of a Palestinian agreement to leave Beirut. His sudden demonstration of apathy was not surprising. We had watched Hawatmeh a few days earlier as he paid an official call on the Soviet Embassy in west Beirut. The Soviet Union had consistently supported its DFLP allies within the PLO and had condemned the Israeli invasion of Lebanon in harsh terms, warning that the conflagration could involve the superpowers. Hawatmeh had sent a personal message to Leonid Brezhnev, asking for Soviet military support and proposing that the Syrian air force send new Soviet-made anti-aircraft missiles to the Palestinians in an air-drop over west Beirut.

Israeli shells were landing at the upper end of Corniche Mazraa when Hawatmeh arrived at the Soviet Embassy escorted by two carloads of bodyguards. He was in the building for only five minutes. When he emerged, he seemed not even to hear the explosions a few hundred yards away. His face was grey. When I asked him if he had received any message from Moscow, he could hardly control his fury. 'Comrade Brezhnev', he said, spitting out the words, 'has sent the Palestinian people his fraternal greetings and support in their heroic struggle.' Then he climbed into his limousine and drove away in a cloud of dust followed by his bodyguards. There was to be no air-drop.

The Soviets were not going to waste their time with the Palestinians when they had far more important friends to protect. Between 20 and 25 June, several dozen batteries of SAM-8 surface-to-air missiles were delivered to the Syrians. The missiles, with a speed of Mach 2, were far more effective than the SAM-6s that the Israelis had destroyed on the floor of the Bekaa and could almost equal the 1,450 mph speed of an Israeli Phantom fighter-bomber. The Israelis destroyed three of the new missile batteries in air strikes on 20 June but the Syrians shot down an Israeli jet. Soviet journalists in west Beirut told us that Moscow was also shipping substantial new supplies of Mig-21 and Mig-23 fighter aircraft to the Syrian port of Latakia to replace the 80 jets that Assad's air force had lost in their battles against Israeli planes over Lebanon. Phalangist radio stations north of Beirut now reported that Soviet military personnel had been brought into Syria to calibrate the new missiles. Bassam Abu Sharif had been right in the early days of the siege; the Soviets *were* becoming involved.

Such developments seemed to have no meaning in west Beirut. After a month under siege and under repeated bombardment and air attack, it had become a place of anxiety and filth. It smelled dirty. Even when the city was not under fire, clouds of smoke drifted through the streets from piles of burning garbage. The streets around Hamra reeked of faeces, for now that the Israelis had cut the water supply, the residents and refugees emptied their ordure in the gutters just as the inhabitants of medieval cities had done.

We noticed children suffering from scabies and women coughing as they walked each morning to the basements of apartments where gunmen had forced the owners to open up long-disused natural wells. Sea water was used for washing, a trickle of liquid that splashed from showers and taps and left our bodies with a thin covering of grease and salt. Compared to the thousands of civilians around us, journalists led a privileged life. We had money, we could buy food at exorbitant prices, we could leave if we wished. By walking across the front line between bombardments, we could take a taxi to Jounieh, a boat to Cyprus and within 36 hours we could be in Switzerland or France. We could not complain about hardship or danger if we chose to stay.

The press corps was dwindling. Several reporters discovered that sudden and unexpected vacations were due to them and quietly left their homes or the Commodore Hotel. Others crossed the line to work permanently out of east Beirut, asking us to take messages back to their colleagues in the west when we crossed and re-crossed the lines on one-day journeys to the east. We became touchy about people leaving. We placed an unkind interpretation upon the departure of Western diplomats. Most of them − including the British − fled at the first whiff of cordite. The British Embassy staff had lectured us over the years about our 'irresponsible reporting'. Now, when west Beirut faced destruction, it was the 'irresponsible' press that stayed behind to record the fate of its inhabitants.

Those of us who stayed developed stomach complaints accompanied by permanent diarrhoea. I was tormented by a skin rash that started on my wrists and worked its way up my arms to my neck and chest. At night, we experienced bizarre, absurd dreams. I woke up in my seafront apartment at dawn one morning literally shaking with fear. I had seen an Israeli jet — an F-16 whose outline I had quite clearly recognised — fly at speed through the three-foot window at the left-hand side of my bedroom, pass one foot above the bed and exit through the French windows to the right with a shriek of jet engines. What was this miniature fighter-bomber doing in my bedroom? Why had its one-inch pilot flown past my bed?

West Beirut also existed in a kind of sleep. It was the place where time stopped on 6 June. In July and August, when I walked into the Librairie Antoine, my favourite bookshop in Hamra Street, the latest airmail editions of the foreign newspapers were all dated 6 June. When we visited the airport terminal which now lay between the Palestinian and Israeli front lines, the green and red boarding cards were still piled on the check-in desks for the outbound flights to Europe that never left on 6 June. Until an Israeli shell destroyed it, the 6 June MEA flight to Paris stood on the apron, its catering pallets containing the rotting food that was to have been consumed on the flight to France. On the road to the airport was a city bus, deserted at a bus stop on 6 June when the driver decided on his own initiative that normal services should be suspended.

One became affected by this sense of timelessness, sealed into west Beirut like a bacillus from the new Lebanon outside. Down at the American University, founded by the stern Daniel Bliss in 1866, students could still research through Ottoman newspapers or play tennis on the hard courts. Beside the main hall, the trunks of Roman columns baked in the sun beneath red and pink creepers. Only now there was an anti-aircraft gun at the bottom of the lawns.

In a greenhouse behind the faculty of agriculture, Professor John Ryan from Dublin could be found, studying his experimental serial plants, each pot fertilised to varying intensity to assess the potential grain yield of unplanted Lebanese harvests. In the greenhouse, the generator pumped a mean trickle of water across the plants, turning the warmth into a clammy heat relieved only by the thin breeze that insinuated its way through a jagged hole in the roof. There were a few diamond shards of glass clustering the roots of one plant, evidence of the shell splinter that intruded from the real world outside.

But where was the real world? You could look for it, if you wished, in Fakhani where the streets had a demented look about them; the buildings windowless and doorless, the pavements piled with glass, a block or two crumpled, a sandwich of concrete, curtains, metal stanchions, human remains and wire. Behind one sandbagged portico, there stood a hallway with an improbable ceiling of pseudo-Regency stucco design. And beyond this was a stuffy office wherein laboured Mahmoud Labadi, the PLO spokesman, the man for whom time rarely used to matter.

He had changed since the invasion. There was a trace of cynicism behind the moustache and the spectacles with the thin, dark frames. The salon socialist had given way to the man of action, but the transformation was not convincing. Perhaps it was the flared trousers that gave him away. Or the little revolver firmly buttoned into its holster. Labadi was no gunman. He talked about the difficulties of the siege, the complexities of the discussions at Baabda between Salam and Sarkis and Habib, about the PLO's refusal to compromise on principle. The word 'evacuation' never crossed his lips.

On the walls of his office, there were posters of young Palestinian girls holding rifles, of the fedayeen marching through the poppy fields of southern Lebanon, of martyred guerrillas staring soullessly upon superimposed photographs of Jerusalem. No hint here that Jerusalem had never been so far away, that it was the Israelis who now enjoyed the poppy fields. Outside the office was a row of unexploded Israeli bombs, lined up in order of size, green and white and yellow with small fins like toys, an artistic composition to define the violence of the west Beirut siege.

But was it a siege when most civilians could come and go between artillery rounds? Down at the museum crossing point, six armies protected their barricades against enemies who never materialised at the other end of the street. I spent a morning down there in mid-July. There was an Amal militiaman wearing a plastic pendant of Ayatollah Khomeini, a Palestinian guerrilla who turned out to be Burmese – the PLO had its share of Third World military trainees – and Nasserite Sunni gunmen who had placed atop an earthen revetment a neo-classical portrait of Nasser. Beyond this dubious symbol of pan-Arabism, there stood a Lebanese army sentry, and beyond him, at the eastern end of the road, an Israeli soldier and beside him a Phalangist officer.

All six armies were pretending the others were not there. Even the police played the same game. In my car, I almost collided with a truck outside the museum, between the Israelis and the Palestinians, and from within a rusting bus shelter emerged a traffic cop, helmet on his head, goggles around his neck. And there on the world's most famous front line, he cautioned me that I had committed a traffic offence.

In the AP bureau, Nick Tatro's cursing as the telex line collapsed, the smell of Nassar's Churchill cigars, Charles Assi's willingness to make coffee even as shells hit the neighbouring buildings, provided a comforting routine. With accurate if unnerving instinct, animals sought shelter from the streets. Two cats and a dog made their way uninvited to the AP bureau to be looked after by Earleen Tatro, whose affection for intelligent animals balanced her contempt for dumb reporters. When the computer line failed for three consecutive days, François Ghattas, the AP's engineer, discovered that the PTT batteries had run down because the Israelis had cut the power. So he rigged a line from the AP bureau to the PTT telecommunications centre — which was itself down on the front line — and used the AP's generator to feed electricity *into* the PTT in the hope of restoring the line. Two hours later, the computer message system began to click away in the AP bureau again.

Tatro and I were still worried that our communications could be destroyed by shelling or that lack of fuel would close down the office generator. Mona Es-Said, a journalist on the Lebanese English-language magazine *Monday Morning*, had told me that her brother Fuad was a radio ham. Fuad Es-Said duly arrived at the office in August to set up a ham radio link with friends in England. Barnes at *The Times* talked to the operators at his end while Es-Said tuned an old AP transmitter — bought but never used during the 1975–6 civil war — to the agreed wavelength. If all communications in Beirut failed, Tatro and I would still be in business.

But this was Lebanon, where the end never really came. By the third month of the siege, we found fresh fruit on sale in west Beirut. Some of it was in boxes with Hebrew writing. The Lebanese were buying it, for thousands of dollars, from the Israelis. We scrounged fuel too, sometimes directly from the Israeli army. The Lebanese had discovered that this was easy, and they were right. We did not have to plead for it. We paid for it, bribed for it with dollar bills. One news agency was said to have drained the entire fuel reserve of a Merkava tank with the connivance of its Israeli crew, four soldiers of Russian-Jewish extraction who openly announced that the war was a farce. I watched money being exchanged down by the port, an Israeli soldier warmly shaking hands with a Lebanese taxi driver after selling him a box of army rations and allowing him to drive back to west Beirut. The driver would make handsome profits. The soldier had money to spend. The Israelis were being corrupted by Lebanon, as surely as the Syrians had been corrupted before them.

The battle of Beirut — for that is what the siege had now become — was therefore not a simple conflict in which one foreign army surrounded another. Both sides became contaminated by the immoral consequences of their own political and strategic aims. Arafat had long ago acknowledged that the PLO would have to leave Beirut but he sought political advantage as well as guarantees of security by delaying any evacuation. The Israelis knew that the PLO *would* leave Beirut, but feared that delay would wipe out the political advantages which Israel stood to achieve. While Israel therefore declared and broke unilateral ceasefires by using each truce to gain tactical advantage on the ground, the PLO promised to evacuate Beirut but then found cause to continue negotiations in order to dilute Israel's military victory. Every Israeli air raid, every Israeli artillery bombardment helped to achieve Arafat's end, for it showed the bloody lengths to which his enemies were prepared to go in pursuit of their goals.

Arafat had already let it be known that he would not accept American military protection for the evacuation of his 11,000 or more guerrillas from Beirut. The PLO could not be seen to hide behind the United States in order to escape from the Israelis. He was fearful that this might happen. Yet he was even more fearful that the Americans might *not* afford their protection to the PLO. For without the presence of Israel's American allies in Beirut, the Israelis might renege on any promises of safe passage for the PLO and either attack the guerrillas during their evacuation or kill the Palestinian civilians left behind once the PLO had left. Therefore Arafat was prepared to allow his men to depart under the auspices of a multinational force that included not only US Marines but French and Italian troops. If anything went wrong with this arrangement, the blame would fall on the Europeans as well as the Americans.

There were other issues to be resolved, however, and Arafat procrastinated yet again. On the morning of 29 July 1982, for example, he visited Saeb Salam once more for further discussions about a PLO evacuation. The Israelis had given him 24 hours to give a final decision, something that Arafat could not do; for to yield to an Israeli ultimatum would be to acknowledge defeat. He did not even look perturbed; a trifle gaunt and tired, perhaps, slimmer, too, for his pot-belly had disappeared during the siege. But when he strode briskly out of Salam's mansion, he was the very model of a modern guerrilla general, from his German-style forage cap, uncreased green battledress and clean webbed belt down to his black army boots. He had not worn his *kuffiah* scarf for weeks.

Yet we felt there was just the slightest hint — a mere suggestion in the words he used — that there really might be some agreement in the offing, unsigned and definitely undelivered, but one which could be relayed to Philip Habib's office up at Baabda. Arafat had, he said, received no 'official proposals' from Habib. And when I asked Arafat if it was true that Habib had demanded an 'unequivocal response' from the PLO within the next 12 hours, Arafat glared back angrily at me. 'Are you Mr Habib's official spokesman?' he shouted. 'I am sorry but I have to deal officially with His Excellency, not with you.'

The key word was 'official' and it came up again later. He would discuss the evacuation with the rest of the PLO leadership — with Salah Khalaf and Khalil Wazzir (Abu Jihad), with Hawatmeh and Habash, he said — but he had yet to receive 'any official message' concerning direct talks between President Reagan and the PLO. Arafat was still holding out for US recognition of the PLO in return for its withdrawal from Beirut. He was working on the principle that Reagan's growing embarrassment at the Israeli siege would overcome America's refusal to talk to the PLO until it acknowledged Israel's right to exist and renounced 'terrorism'.*

As usual, the options, concessions, demands and rejections of Israel and the PLO were discussed by Sarkis and Habib up at Baabda against the roar of gunfire and incoming shells. The Israelis were already finding that the continuation of the war was proving costly in more than political terms. In the vain battle against the Syrians to reach Bhamdoun, the Israelis had suffered 27 fatalities.

On 10 July, an Israeli officer at Baabda – presumably seeking to impress the Palestinians with the weight of firepower that was to be used against them – obligingly let local Beirut newspaper photographers take pictures of the principal Israeli ammunition supply dump on a small hill not far from the presidential palace. The PLO, which often had little to do but study the morning papers, launched dozens of Katyushas at the hill on the evening of 11 July and hit it within seconds. I was standing on the roof of a building in Kantari in west Beirut when the dump blew up; even there, five miles from the explosion, I felt the blast as the Israelis' ammunition exploded in a sheet of flame and black smoke more than a mile high. Then on 4 August, Palestinian and Syrian shellfire hit two Israeli positions near the airport, killing 13 Israelis, wounding 19 and incapacitating another six with shell-shock. Israeli officers blamed Sharon directly for a policy of 'tightening the noose' around west Beirut that led directly to the killing of Israeli soldiers.†

These casualties, of course, bore no relation to the catastrophe that had befallen thousands of Lebanese and Palestinian civilians. Even Israel's final military casualty toll of more than 500 fatalities equalled only about 3.5 per cent of the total Lebanese and Palestinian dead, although Israel's own losses would increase as its occupation dragged on for another three years. But Israeli casualties helped to fuel a growing

---

* The basis of the final evacuation plan had in fact been agreed at Arafat's meeting with Salam on 29 July. It involved, at that stage, the withdrawal of all PLO guerrillas from Beirut and their dispersal to Syria, Jordan, Iraq, Algeria, South Yemen, Kuwait and the United Arab Emirates. It also called for a multinational force that would deploy in West Beirut to safeguard the PLO evacuation under the framework of a United Nations resolution that would permit the PLO to recognise Israel on a reciprocal basis, followed by direct talks between the PLO and the US government. Following a 'stable and lasting ceasefire' in Lebanon – and here was truly eccentric optimism – a timetable would be drawn up for the 'total withdrawal' of both Syrian and Israeli armies from Lebanon.

† The contempt felt by Israeli officers towards Sharon over these incidents only became known in 1984 when five reserve officers, including three colonels, demanded a commission of inquiry into the soldiers' deaths. See *The Jerusalem Post* of 13 April 1984 ('IDF silent on colonel's "I accuse".'); of 9 May 1984 ('Officers demand inquiry into Sharon's role in 1982 battles'); and of 10 May 1984 ('Sharon critics question casualties.')

anti-war movement in Israel that was to reach its height after the massacres at Sabra and Chatila.

The Muslim Lebanese militias certainly intended that a final Israeli assault on west Beirut should be as localised as possible. The Druze erected earth ramparts around Ein al-Mreisse – one massive embankment of clay and sand was built below my own apartment – to prevent PLO guerrillas fortifying the local houses to fight the Israelis. Residents of Ramlet al-Baida who found that PLO men had stored ammunition in their basements chose to sleep at the Commodore or Bristol hotels.

We heard, too, intriguing though unverifiable rumours that not only the PLO was encircled in Beirut. Information from Palestinian friends, for example, suggested that a group of men from the Basque ETA movement had been receiving training from radical Palestinian groups in Lebanon and had become trapped in west Beirut, together with several Soviet 'advisers'. Another report had it that the man who brought the ETA members into Lebanon was called 'Ramirez' and was wanted by the French police after a bombing in France. Could this, we wondered, be the Carlos Ramirez who was known as 'the Jackal', who had kidnapped the OPEC leaders from their meeting in Vienna in 1975 and who had just been accused by the French police of bombing a train?

The Israelis had often accused the PLO of training 'European terrorists' and the PFLP had certainly encouraged members of the Japanese Red Army Faction to visit Lebanon. According to the Israelis, IRA members also received regular assistance from the PLO. In all my visits to southern Lebanon, I had seen Bangladeshi, Iranian, Burmese and Pakistani PLO volunteers but never Irishmen. I had been *The Times* correspondent in Belfast from 1972 to 1975 and was now a constant visitor to the Irish UN battalions in southern Lebanon. If any IRA men had been there, I would have heard of it.

But one evening in west Beirut that summer, after a car bomb had exploded outside the offices of the Palestine Research Institute, I took shelter from the shelling in the lobby of an office block. Leaning against the wall in combat fatigues and holding an AK-47 rifle was a tall young European man with blue eyes and brown, almost red hair. He told me he was a Canadian who had chosen to fight for the PLO. But I recognised him. I had last seen him in Londonderry in 1972, holding a rifle in the Bogside. He was an IRA man. I even remembered his first name. He was friendly and talked, in his Northern Ireland accent, about his fear that he might not survive the siege of Beirut. 'Watch out for the shells, Bob,' he said as I left. I never saw him again.

Yet it was not difficult to leave Beirut. Neither ETA nor IRA members would be caught by the Israelis. Penetrating the Israeli lines was easy. Phalangists were bribed to assist in the evacuation of some Palestinian families. And somehow, during the siege that summer, a group of kidnappers managed to smuggle an American academic – perhaps the best-known university figure in the Lebanese capital – out of his campus in west Beirut, all the way to Iran.

Amid the fighting, the kidnapping of David Dodge, the acting president of the American University, on 19 July was a mere footnote; four paragraphs were all I filed to *The Times*, recording the fear of Lebanese colleagues that 'some anti-American group' might be responsible for Dodge's abduction, but noting that the PLO had ordered its guerrillas to search for the missing man.

None of us knew then how important Dodge's kidnap really was. We had still not heard of *Al-Jihad Al-Islami* – Islamic Jihad, or Holy War – and we had no idea that the Iranian revolution had penetrated so deeply into the aspirations of the Shia population in west Beirut. We had not connected the extraordinarily brave resistance of the Shia militiamen at Khalde with anything other than hatred of the invading Israelis.

Had we been told then that Islamic Jihad had arranged Dodge's disappearance, we could only have expressed our ignorance. According to a Palestinian student who witnessed the kidnap, two gunmen in a Renault estate wagon pulled up next to Dodge as he was walking past the university's west hall. When the American refused to get into the car, one of the men leapt from the vehicle and hit him on the back of the head with the butt of his pistol.

A routine kidnap surely, something that would quickly be explained, almost as swiftly as we would witness his release; or so we thought. Two days earlier, Samir Sambar, the UN Beirut representative, had taken Dodge and myself to lunch at the Bristol Hotel. Dodge had been full of humour, mocking the American diplomats who told him to leave west Beirut, insisting that the American University had to remain open despite the Israeli invasion.

It would be a year before he was released – with Syrian help – and he would then be under an oath of silence not to speak of his experiences. In the minds of many Westerners, kidnapping would eclipse, and outlast, Israel's invasion of Lebanon. In three years' time, we would be afraid of Islamic Jihad. It would take Terry Anderson away from his family and friends and colleagues. It would threaten us all. But, like the disappearance of the Imam Mousa Sadr, we missed the significance of the incident. The seeds of the next war were never so obvious – and never so ignored – as when the war which sowed them was still in progress.

And this conflict now contained the elements of fantasy as well as death. In the morning, we could talk to the Palestinian defenders of west Beirut. In the afternoon, we could take tea with the army that wished to destroy them. Which I did in mid-July. Captain Maher and Lieutenant Sharon faced each other across a quarter of a mile of barricades, mined streets and one runway of Beirut airport. They had never met, although their fields of fire covered the same broken buildings and smouldering garbage heaps, the same desolate airport road along the west Beirut front line.

Captain Maher was a father of two children, a thoughtful, slightly mannered man who smoked cigarettes through a holder and talked in slow, carefully constructed phrases as if he feared some political ambush. Lieutenant Sharon was younger, a 23-year-old from a middle-class family with a tousle of brown hair that fell over his forehead and a soldier's directness that burst into his conversation from time to time like shellfire. Captain Maher was a company commander in the Democratic Front for the Liberation of Palestine. Lieutenant Sharon was a company commander in the Israeli army. Both were to survive the war, although each would have been content if the other had died.

To find Maher, I had to drive through the ruined camps of Sabra and Chatila, around several dozen revetments of sand and earth, along a narrow, sewage-washed road, past a mobile anti-aircraft gun and into the garage of a shrapnel-splashed villa where the crackle of rifle fire from the other side of a field of rubble was a measure of the latest ceasefire violation. Maher was a tall man with a thin moustache and a goatee beard who sat on a half-painted wooden chair, swatting a cloud of flies away, from his broken-handled cup of scalding hot coffee. As a DFLP officer, he wore on his battledress tunic a small, golden badge of Palestine with a red star beside it. His pockets were filled with ammunition clips and a string of grenades were tied around his waist.

Maher wanted to talk politics rather than soldiering and he made no secret of his motivation. He learned English on a BA correspondence course, but his years at a Soviet military academy had added a rhetorical touch to his fluency. 'The Israelis want to liquidate us,' he said slowly. 'My emotion is the emotion of a Palestinian fighter who wants to confront an invasion. I want to liquidate the soldier who wants to liquidate me. I think it's a just feeling that one should want to liquidate such a person. I feel here that I'm facing a real enemy. We have faced Israeli officers, we have faced their soldiers and we have confronted them and pushed them back and inflicted big losses on them.'

Liquidation and confrontation. How often the Palestinians used these bypass words. Maher could not bring himself to say kill and fight. He had to say liquidate and confront. He was trapped by his rhetoric as surely as he was trapped by the Israelis; but he had also taught himself to understand his motives in this way, to channel them through the language of dogma and ideology. In the past, Western correspondents in Beirut had despaired of ever reporting the real thoughts of Palestinian guerrillas because they were so often couched in florid, impossible language.

I had once conducted a long interview with a PLO officer in southern Lebanon, a courageous man with at least a thousand men under his command. But all he would talk of was confrontation. 'We shall stand in the same ditch in confronting the Zionist death wagon,' he had announced to me. I could not persuade him to break out of this jargon and talk to me in the ordinary language which he used with his own men. How could I report this nonsense? What reader of *The Times* would not be insulted by it? I could not include such vacuous propaganda in my dispatches, even in quotation marks.

Only later did I learn to 'confront' the jargon, to challenge this language directly when it was used. I sensed the need to do this with Maher. He had paused after his first words, aware perhaps of how oddly they conflicted with the desperate position in which the Palestinians now found themselves in west Beirut. Despite all his talk of 'pushing back' the Israelis, his enemies were moving inexorably *forward*, not back.

'We are not trapped,' he said suddenly. 'Yes, it's true that on the military level we are surrounded by the Israeli forces, but on the other hand they will fall into a trap themselves if they try to advance. They would suffer so many casualties. They might be capable of advancing some metres but they could not retreat from this trap.' His words were translated into Arabic for the five guerrillas who had walked up to listen, and they all nodded their agreement, though without quite the same degree of confidence that Captain Maher wished to express.

But was this not in reality a trap for the Palestinians? Was their revolution not coming to an end in the midden of west Beirut? Maher was becoming more aware of his audience. Such an idea, he said, was being expressed by 'Arab reactionary regimes'. Saudi Arabia, Jordan and Egypt were saying these things. 'We are not surprised to hear this because the Israeli invasion was part of the Camp David accords with which they helped the Americans in the Middle East. That is why this will be a trap for the Arab reactionaries as well as the Israelis.' Maher was straying again into rhetoric, into the world of superpower conspiracies. The Plot. I had to interrupt him.

He did not resent this. Yes, he agreed, the PLO had made certain agreements with the Lebanese government 'concerning some withdrawal from Beirut' but this would not be at the expense of Palestinian principles. Then he asked: 'Have you talked to the Israelis here? What do they say about us?' So I told Captain Maher that the Israelis thought of him as a terrorist and of the PLO as a terrorist organisation. I told him, too, that the Israelis claimed the PLO had deliberately placed its guns in civilian areas. And I waited for Maher's reaction.

At first, there was none. But was it not true that the Palestinians used civilian areas of Beirut as cover, I asked? Captain Maher gave a very slight smile at the predicament in which this question had placed him.

'Yes, it's true,' he replied. And he went on to admit that Soviet weapons had proved less reliable than the Palestinians might have wished. But something else was bothering him. The Palestinians were not terrorists, he said.

'I am a human being. The Israeli soldier opposite me, he is a human being, too. Reagan and Begin are human beings like my daughter who comes under shellfire every day. All are human beings. But one human is different from another. The human who comes under shelling and invasion and oppression is better than the human who comes to invade and liquidate civilians. When I think of my opposite number over there' — and Captain Maher pointed to the other side of the airport where the Israeli front line lay — 'I feel he is my enemy.'

Maher looked for some kind of response, some sympathy perhaps. Had *he* met Israelis, I asked? 'No,' he replied. 'I spoke to them through my gun.' This might have been mere rhetoric were it not for the troubled expression that crossed Maher's face. He did not need to be prompted to continue. 'I have been a soldier for six years. Before that I was in the political section but I began to feel the military thing was more important, that to be a soldier was something necessary for me.' And almost at once, I suspected that Maher's struggle was within himself, that there was some conflict going on between political belief and reality and that he was trying to resolve it here, amid the flies and garbage heaps and smashed roads and the evident danger of the west Beirut perimeter.

Not so Lieutenant Sharon. His own paratroop headquarters was just over half a mile away on the other side of the airport but to reach him, I had to drive across west Beirut, negotiate my way through Palestinian and leftist roadblocks near the museum and show my passport to an Israeli soldier 400 yards down the road. Below the rim of hills that stood over west Beirut, Lieutenant Sharon was resting. It was the Jewish Sabbath and he was playing table tennis with his fellow officers in a wrecked building, still in his creased battledress blouse but wearing shorts and running shoes, half soldier, half holidaymaker.

He was a shy man whose uncombed hair gave him a schoolboy appearance. His home was at Holon near Tel Aviv. He had a girl friend there but no planned future when he finished his five years in the army in the autumn. It was, he thought, a surrealistic war. 'The first weeks were a real war,' he said. 'You know, you shoot and run and act like a soldier. But after that, it was like a visit to Lebanon. We talk to the civilians now and lead an almost normal life. When there is time to think and rethink those early weeks, I would not like to go through it again. But if tomorrow I have to, I'll do it good, like I did yesterday.'

It was all said with the enthusiasm of youth. There was no pause for hesitation, no talk of confrontation and liquidation. In the early weeks of the Israeli invasion, both Lieutenant Sharon and Captain Maher had fought around Aley — they just might have seen each other there — although Sharon did not know the name of the Palestinian company commander on the other side of the airport. 'Sure he's a human being,' he said. 'I look on him and the Palestinians as people just like me. I would live beside a Palestinian in Israel or any other place. But if we have to fight, we fight.'

There were no instant ideological commitments to trammel up Lieutenant Sharon's flow of words. If he had sought out the reasons for this war, he seemed content with what he had found. 'It's quite clear in my mind that what we are fighting for is the defence of Israel, certainly the defence of the northern border areas of the country to make sure they are not continuously attacked. This whole business of saying we'd go as far as forty kilometres or sixty kilometres is just a big confusion. Maybe nobody should have said forty kilometres. But this is not a matter of exact kilometres. We have to make sure that the enemy cannot continue to harass. What we have to be sure of is that they don't have the arms and the ability to continue.'

Lieutenant Sharon may have been taking the same view as his government, but in one significant way his language deviated from that of official Israeli spokesmen. He did not refer to the Palestinians as 'terrorists'. Did he think of Captain Maher and his men in these terms? 'Now, yes I do,' he said. 'The guerrillas fight, shoot and kill Israeli soldiers here. So now we fight them because they are terrorists. But maybe tomorrow they will put their guns down and come and talk and go away from Beirut. I look at them as terrorists because I know they are responsible for all the terrorist actions that have been going on over the last seven, eight, ten years.'

But Sharon did not use the word 'terrorist' again. He seemed unsure of why the Palestinians were still fighting. 'There is obviously political motivation, particularly in the leadership, but you shouldn't forget that a large proportion of them are mercenaries, foreigners, Europeans, Bangladeshis, people who may be here for different ideologies of their own or because they are being paid. But I don't deny that overall there is political motivation.' There were indeed a few hundred foreigners fighting with the PLO, although Sharon's view of their strength was a gross exaggeration. Yet something was troubling Sharon, just as Maher had been disturbed by his own thoughts of shared humanity.

'A few days ago, we saw some Palestinians,' Sharon said. 'They walked out in front of their positions, yes, right in front of us down here. They had pictures of Yassir Arafat and they waved them in the air and danced up and down and shouted at us. We didn't know what to do. We don't know why they did that, right in front of us. No, we didn't shoot them. They waved the pictures, then they went back to their positions and we didn't see them again. No, I don't want to go into the Palestinian issue. It starts way back ... they must have a solution, otherwise it will never finish. And the fact that nobody wants to take them is a sign of how big the problem is.' Would he perhaps have accepted the idea — one day — of a Palestinian state? There was silence. He could not reply, he said, because 'an officer cannot answer a political question.'

Lieutenant Sharon and Captain Maher faced each other across the airport, the first a soldier who would not dwell upon politics, the second a guerrilla who could not separate politics from his every military word and deed. Through Sharon's field glasses, I looked across no-man's-land and could just see Maher's villa, although the Israelis did not know where it was. Sharon watched me squint through the binoculars. 'The only definite thing,' he said with less youthful emphasis, 'is that when we leave here, there won't be any Palestinian forces left in Beirut.'

At the end of July, they bombed almost every day, flight after flight of them, hour after hour, those silvery fish circling in the high, bright sky and then falling across the firmament towards the camps, towards the Corniche, the apartment blocks of west Beirut. On 22 July, after Palestinian guerrillas had ambushed an Israeli patrol deep inside occupied southern Lebanon, killing five of the soldiers, the Israelis took their revenge with an attack on west Beirut by swarms of Kfir and F-16 fighter-bombers. As usual, the Israeli retaliation was out of all proportion to the original attack. On the roof of the AP bureau, Earleen Tatro, Anderson and I stood in awe of the planes as they turned and pounced on the camps.

Those brown, dead tunnels of smoke would sprout out of the buildings at enormous speed, sometimes followed by so many explosions that the ground shook continuously for more than a minute. That afternoon, the sky around us was filled with aircraft, exploding anti-aircraft shells and missile tracks. We would not go to the basement. After Sidon, none of us would go to the basement. Several journalists stayed in the cellars of the Commodore, but we avoided the place, not through courage but cowardice. We thought you had to be brave to stay in a basement. So we stood on the roof with the shrapnel raining out of the sky, sometimes cowering beside the shed which housed the elevator engines, sometimes crouching beside the three-foot concrete wall that surrounded the roof.

No one had expected the raids to go on this long. The Israelis announced a seventh 'ceasefire'. The following day, they came back again. The truce had been broken, the Israelis claimed. I was driving down the Corniche towards my home when the planes came in, low over the Mediterranean, black like distant seabirds until they were racing across the seafront. An anti-aircraft missile soared up, a glint of silver and a rope of white smoke that thundered between the apartments, missed the jets and fell impotently into the Mediterranean.

We were awed by it. We could find no other word for it. The air raids were awesome. They inspired the most basic fear; of total, sudden, inescapable annihilation. Often we never saw the planes because they flew too fast. In the sweaty mornings, with the smell of burning garbage drifting over the city, we heard them coming in a crescendo of sound. Hardly ever did we see the bombs they dropped. Who *were* these people? Not the Israelis whom we met and re-met every day on the front lines, but the pilots who inflicted this savagery upon west Beirut. Were they not told — did they not know — that they were killing thousands of civilians, smashing families between the walls, floors and furniture of their homes with such total violence that their corpses often emerged from the rubble flattened into huge shadows, their bodies only an inch or two thick, their heads broken open like eggs?

We wondered what those pilots thought as they soared in over the sea. Didn't Beirut look like Haifa or Tel Aviv? Had that word 'terrorist' drugged the pilots as well as the soldiers? I telexed *The Times* to ask Walker in Jerusalem if he could interview one of these 'warriors of the air'. Back came the reply: the Israelis would allow no press interviews with their pilots. Israeli propaganda had it that theirs was one of the world's most sophisticated air forces, whose pilots picked off their enemies with pin-point accuracy. 'Surgical precision' was the word the Israelis used about their air strikes, a tired cliché that quickly found its way into the dispatches filed by Israeli-based foreign correspondents. The Israelis said the same about artillery bombardments. So what was happening? Did the Israelis *think* that they were hitting 'terrorists' but were merely mistaking their targets, killing innocents in error? Or were they indeed as accurate as they claimed — in which case, one could only conclude that they intended to slaughter so many people? The equation seemed obvious to the Lebanese and Palestinians: the Israelis were either bunglers or murderers. Many times, we were asked which was true. We could never reply. Certainly, the Israelis could not have it both ways.

On the 27th, I actually saw the bomb. For a brief half second, it hurtled down like a meteorite between two blocks of apartments at Raouche and the explosion felt as if it was coming out of the back of my head. I was covered in the fog of brown smoke and swirling dust that swept down the suburban hill, and only then did I hear the sound of the departing Israeli jet.

Ten minutes was all we reckoned we had. The planes usually came back after ten minutes. To finish off the survivors? To catch the rescuers out in the open? We never knew. When Nick Tatro and I reached Iskandar Street, half a building had been blown away, an eight-storey apartment block that had crumpled into a ten-foot-high pile of compacted concrete. Nine minutes. There were flames washing up the side of the Canadian ambassador's residence across the road. And from the doorway of one gutted flat, two men carried a filthy sheet, heavy with liquid, some soiled clothes and a blackened foot hanging from one end. Eight minutes. The rubble of stones and wire and hunks of concrete three feet thick had sprayed down the street and some shrapnel had attacked a building up the hill, blasting a ten-foot hole in the wall to expose the elevator shaft. There were gunmen – teenagers with automatic rifles and older men with pistols at their hips – directing the screaming ambulances, and there was a young Red Cross girl with streaming brown hair climbing over an earthen barricade in a long white coat, her face transfixed with excitement and fear. Seven minutes.

The detritus of the bomb attack was typical and pathetic; a pile of curtains, telephone lines and a complete set of Collins' blue-covered Illustrated Encyclopaedia, riven into shreds beside the ruined houses. Six minutes. At the bottom of the street stood a middle-aged man with a moustache, whose perspiration streamed down his grubby shirt. 'There was nothing here to hit, only civilians,' he said. 'There was a building one block away where the Palestinians had a gun but they didn't hit it.' He was right; the nearest tank – a Syrian T-54 – also stood untouched in its little park almost a quarter of a mile away. Five minutes. We used to say this was half-time.

'Why the fuck did they do that?' Tatro asked. The question was directed at me. If the Israelis intended to hit Iskandar Street, it was difficult to find the reason. A lawyer colleague of Walid Jumblatt was rumoured to live in the crushed apartment building. A family – a husband, wife and two young daughters – died in the bombing. I had met them once; they were friends of the Canadian ambassador. Four minutes. We were growing nervous. A group of Palestinian gunmen had been guarding a block around the corner where several hundred refugees – most of them Palestinians – were living. The road, like most of the seafront streets in Raouche, had been mined two weeks earlier. But the people of Iskandar Street were civilians. The most prominent residents – some of whom had lost their homes – had been the ambassadors of Canada, Switzerland, Yugoslavia and Greece, who could scarcely be regarded as military targets. Three minutes.

One of west Beirut's three surviving fire engines turned up at rue d'Australie at the upper end of Iskandar Street and we watched its ill-clad crew pumping a miserable trickle of water through a rubber hose up to a burning flat. The fire crew were looking at the sky, holding their wretched hose, a lunatic cameo of those old photographs of the London Blitz. Two minutes. 'Come on Fisky, let's leave.' Tatro was even-headed. We tried to walk, not run, back to the car. We could hear the planes and the Red Cross girl was running away. 'OK, let's go, let's go.'

Natanya, Israel, 14 April 1987

The pavements were overflowing with azaleas, the flowers flourishing across the walls so thickly that it was sometimes impossible to see the neat, single-storey homes behind the bushes. There was a lilac tree at one end of the street. And Brigadier-General Specter was in his garden, just as he said he would be, in shorts and sandals, pulling weeds out of a flower bed, a tall, tanned man with a large, gentle face. 'So you found us,' he shouted across the fence. 'Come along in. Shall we have some tea out here? It's a *wonderful* afternoon.'

I followed him across the lawn. His wife Aliza smiled in a shy, kind way. There was a teenage son in the house. Through the open living room doors came the sound of Bach's Mass in B minor. Specter sat down on a metal-framed garden chair. 'So how can I help you?' He was friendly, courteous, intelligent, a lively man who talked about morality and the purity of arms. And he was one of the pilots. This man with the big, thoughtful eyes and the attractive wife with the pleasant smile and Bach on the tape deck had flown the eagle down the firmament five years before. His was one of the planes we had watched with such fear and awe.

On the telephone from Jerusalem, I had told Specter what I was trying to find out. How did it happen? Why did he and his colleagues do what they did? Specter understood why I asked these questions. He wanted to talk. At the beginning, he often looked at his feet, at his sandals, as he spoke. Then he would glance at me, to see if I understood what he was saying. His English was not perfect but he spoke with great care, pausing over words to ensure that they accurately reflected what he wanted to say. He had commanded an airbase in Galilee, but yes, he had flown missions over Beirut with his squadron.

'The feeling we had was not of attacking a fully civilian area,' he said. '... It was hitting given points in the city. This was not area bombing. We were not flying bombers like in World War Two. We were flying fighters. The points we attacked were designated. The points were always in connection with fighting on the ground. We could see this from the air. We were in support. It took some time for us to understand that there were things that were not the same in this war.'

Did he not visit Beirut later, when the Israelis had occupied the city, to see what his pilots had done? 'None of us visited the ground places. These were missions in a war. You go, you come back and land. Then you go back and attack again. The pilots were briefed and debriefed for ten or fifteen minutes. We were making two or three missions a day.'

But did none of the pilots object? Did none of them *know* what was happening, what they were hitting? 'Some people among us were sensitive from the beginning. Some said: "Look, we are bombing in civilian areas." I must say one important thing. This sensitiveness went all along the line. General Ivri [Major-General David Ivri, commander of the Israeli air force] was the most sensitive person to this. There was considerable discussion about this at every briefing.'

Specter was more confident now, nodding towards me to emphasise his points, smiling when he thought I had understood exactly what he wanted to say. 'There were rules; firstly, if we did not find the designated target, it was absolutely forbidden for us to throw bombs in a non-target area. Secondly, targets of "opportunity" were only those targets which shot at us. We were only allowed to attack them if they were three miles out of a built-up area. If a terrorist fired at us in a built-up area, we were absolutely forbidden to touch the target ...'

Did all the pilots obey this rule? 'People like myself, we gave briefings as well as flew. I knew that we thought about the rules in every echelon but there were intelligence officers explaining why a target was important, why the timing of the target was important. We sometimes could not find the target. We often dropped bombs in the sea off Beirut if this happened. We personally did not have ways to check our targets. We did not have our own sources.'

So who were the intelligence officers? Where did their information come from? Specter moved his right hand from left to right in a dismissive motion. 'I cannot answer that.' Did the pilots believe the intelligence officers who were designating 'targets'? 'I would say that at this time, the country itself became sensitive ... We thought there was probably too much bombing, that it would not lead to anything. Our people were asking questions, yes. There were always connotations of ghettoes for us Israelis, considering our own background. But the terrorists were there who were a few weeks before killing our Israelis in Kiryat Shmona and Ma'alot.'

Most of the time, Specter said, his pilots believed that the intelligence officers had placed targets correctly. 'But attacking in built-up areas like the suburbs of Beirut, it gave the terrorists an opportunity to change places, to move around. Or am I mistaken?'

I turned to a clean page in my notebook and drew on it a crude but recognisable picture of the west Beirut peninsula, of the Corniche, Pigeon Rocks and Raouche, and I drew, very carefully, the outline of Iskandar Street. And near the bottom of Iskandar Street, I drew a square and told Specter that this building — this building packed with innocent people — had been bombed on 27 July and that almost a hundred of those innocent people had been killed in this building. Was he perhaps flying on 27 July? Did he remember this raid? He did not remember – he was telling the truth – but he did not like the question.

'There could be reasons for this. Firstly, that somebody did this mischievously because he had some reasons.' Did Specter mean intelligence officers? He nodded. 'Secondly, it could be a pilot was given another target and made a mistake – these are part of the dangers of war. But the question should be statistical. How many mistakes do Israeli pilots make? How many mistakes do Israeli intelligence make? Or was our timing wrong? Had the terrorists left the building?'

But the casualties. Did the pilots not *read* about what they had done? Did they not see the newspapers? 'We read the newspapers, yes. But you saw Begin's attitude, that if Hitler was in a house and there were innocent people in that house, he would bomb it.' Specter watched to see my reaction to this remark but he seemed uneasy, as if he himself did not accept the premise that lay behind Begin's morality.

'But there were some weeks towards the end when there were questions. We knew we were hitting places innocent people lived. In the beginning, probably our feeling was "We hit a few [buildings] and they will leave." Nobody, I think, actually used these words. But as time passed, we felt we were hitting more of these buildings. Our normal education which we had from our teaching at school took over. This sensitivity began at first with our commanders. We would say to our pilots: "Look, gentlemen, at times you are going to be directed at targets which are very problematic ..." I remember General Ivri saying: "We will end with a peace with Lebanon – we are not here to ruin this place."'

But surely there were many mistakes? Specter was still sitting in his metal-framed chair, basking in the sunlight that filtered through the leaves of the tree. Aliza brought tea and cakes and put them on the table beneath the tree. Tea and cakes with the fighter pilot. Bach had finished on the tape deck. 'Sometimes in war, you kill people,' Specter said. 'This is what war is all about. Yes, human awareness is there. We relied on intelligence very, very much. This was not an article of faith. But our country relies on intelligence even in peacetime. In the one case where it failed, we paid for it – in the Yom Kippur war.'

But surely the intelligence was wrong? Thousands of civilians died in Lebanon. Whole apartment blocks were destroyed by the Israeli planes. Israeli intelligence had to have been wrong, surely? Specter was still reluctant to talk about the intelligence briefings at his Galilee airbase. But he also recognised that the issues were not being addressed.

'I will tell you this. There would be a briefing. There would be a map. The intelligence people would say: "This house has been located as a centre for terrorists. There are 'X' number of terrorists in this house – ten, fifteen, twenty, five, a given number – and the timing that this building is to be hit is such-and-such a time in the day or night or whatever." This meant that somebody knew the habits of the terrorists and that at this given time, there is a good possibility of them being there.'

Somebody? What somebody? What is a 'good possibility'? Anyone who had been in west Beirut in 1982 would realise this was rubbish. 'I must say I don't think even now that there was somebody there [in west Beirut] with a map, "X-ing" house after house. No. Our intelligence tried to get some of the terrorists killed — it turned out to be a very ineffective way of doing it. You see, we believed at that time that when terrorists took over a building, most [sic] of the innocent people were driven out; that the terrorists took over the buildings, that they were using the innocent people as hostages to cover themselves ... We believed the target was what we call "militarised".'

When did the pilots realise this was all wrong?

'The Sabra and Chatila massacre was the cornerstone of everything, that what we were doing was not just a mistake but was wrong. The strain, the tension of some of our people was real. Pilots came again and again and asked: "Can we be sure about the targets? Are they alright?"'

Specter could not stop talking now. The reticence was gone. 'Look, there is a problem. The Yom Kippur war was a war of life and death for our state. But some of our pilots turned out to be pacifists at the wrong time ... In the middle of the war, they found they were pacifists. Now to be a pacifist is probably a nice thing to be most of the year — but not when you are at war. In other words, we told our pilots: "If you want to refuse orders, deal with your ideology before you begin your flying course." In the Lebanon war, the officers were telling the pilots: "We are not making area [indiscriminate] attacks — is this clear?" The pilots would say "Yes." The officers would ask if they realised the intelligence was good and the pilots would say "Yes." They were told the reason for the war — the terrorists. The officers told the pilots to remember: "You do not live in Kiryat Shmona — you live in the safety of Tel Aviv."

'But things changed very quickly. The mood turned very quickly among us when we realised that there was real uncertainty about the war. At the start, we would come back from attacks and the intelligence people would ask: "Did you hit the target well?" If you did, the intelligence people would show pictures and tell you the number of people killed who were terrorists.'

Terrorists. Specter was using the word more and more. When I asked him why he mentioned the word so often, he stopped using it. Tell me, I said, tell me what it felt like to bomb west Beirut. What was it like to be up there in the jet and know you were going to bomb Beirut? What did Beirut *look* like?

'A bit like Haifa.' Specter raised his eyebrows to see if I understood. Haifa lies on a peninsula, like Beirut. It has high-rise apartment blocks.

There are hills behind it. 'It reminded me of Haifa. It was very much like Haifa, you know, the countryside outside, the sea, the peninsula.' I realised suddenly what this meant; that Specter and the other pilots must have practised their raids over Haifa, that the Israeli port of Haifa had been the 'dummy' for the real onslaught up the coast on Beirut.

Specter was intense now, remembering what it was like. He sat upright in the metal-framed chair, in his garden cockpit. He uncrossed his legs because he was in a little cramped fuselage on the lawn. 'In the very moment you are over Beirut, in the seconds, in the moment of flying into an attack, in this moment you do not think of more general questions. But you come back from the mission, you return a human being and you behave the way you are brought up and educated. When doing a technical job, you are very concentrated ...'

But if it was so technical, why were all the 'mistakes' made? After all, it was a computer, was it not, that aligned the target? Didn't the computer mean that the building that was hit was always the one that the Israelis intended to hit?

'It is not like that. We use our eyes, we compare our intelligence with what we see on the ground in Beirut. The computer helps us, yes, it helps us with the timing. The pilot's problem is not just to find the target but to hit it. The computer calculates the precise moment of delivery but the computer does not find the target.'

What does?

'We do.'

How?

'Well, we have photographs. You see we are given photographs of the target, a building, say. We have to find it.'

How?

'With our eyes. We fly over and look for it.'

Aren't the photographs locked onto the computer system?

'No. We hold the photographs in our hand.' Specter held up his left hand, his right hand holding a set of ghostly controls. 'We held the photographs in our hand, you see. Then we looked at the pictures and tried to find the buildings on the ground ...'

West Beirut, 5 August 1982

As usual, we did not hear the planes until afterwards. The explosions were muffled, the old Beirut sound of doors slamming deep beneath the earth. But when we reached rue Aussi, it looked as though an earthquake had hit the street. The bombs had levelled two five-storey apartment blocks and beneath the 30 feet of pancaked concrete there were — according to the woman who screamed at us from her ruined home over the road — more than 100 people.

There was a corpse or two, spread-eagled across the road, and there were some frantic men in khaki denims digging with their hands at a pile of iron stanchions and girders, rubble too heavy for any man to lift. There was a man weeping amid a small pile of smashed wooden shutters, crying into his cupped hands and then gesticulating with upraised palms in that peculiar way that is meant to beseech both God and passers-by. His wife was in there somewhere. Nine minutes.

Next to the rubble was a jeep upon which was mounted a recoilless rifle manned by three young men. It was undamaged and could not have been there when the Israeli jets struck. For some months now, this little street had been cordoned off by Yassir Arafat's Squad 17 security organisation, and somewhere in the narrow thoroughfare there had been a PLO office. Eight minutes. Someone told us that Arafat himself had held a meeting in one of the two buildings but had left only minutes before the planes arrived. Here indeed, someone was 'X-ing' houses.

The civilians, of course, had outnumbered the guerrillas in rue Aussi. As usual, the Israelis had cut down the civilians. Beneath one of the blocks of flats, there had been a car repair shop. In the basement. And many of the people in rue Aussi had of course fled to the basement when they heard the planes. The building collapsed on top of them. A middle-aged man ran from his house across the street. 'Take pictures,' he shouted at us. 'Take pictures. This is what your bombs have done.' Seven minutes.

The young men from the Red Crescent had arrived but they had none of the equipment needed to lift the tons of masonry off the dead and wounded. So we all stared at this tomb in utter helplessness. Most of the occupants had been squatters from the devastated camps at Sabra and Chatila or from southern Lebanon. Then someone shouted '*Tiara, tiara.*' We had all grown used to that word now. It means 'aircraft'. So we turned our backs and fled down the road, towards the Sanaya park. Six minutes.

Terry Anderson arrived, dripping perspiration, drawing in his breath quickly. Sam Koo was with him, a Korean-born AP staffer from the Rome bureau. Terry, be careful, it's been five minutes already. Anderson looked at the silver shapes moving distantly in the heavens above us. 'They're not bombing, Fisky. They're just doing reconnaissance.' I wasn't so sure. There was a fat, pregnant woman shrieking up the road. Her husband was entombed in the bombed building. The planes were still there, gliding like fish in the sky above us, so slowly, watching.

I left Anderson. Koo went to talk to the shrieking woman. I wanted to leave. Four minutes. I did not like the look of those planes. The Red Crescent men were clawing at the rubble. The recoilless rifle had been taken away. There was a car parked between the rubble and the Sanaya park. A haze of dust and smoke rose steadily from the building. Three minutes. The planes still circled. What were they waiting for? I drove away. The crowds of rescue workers in the street had pulled out 11 bodies. Wounded people were emerging from apartments on the opposite side of the road. Then the explosion cut them down. Ten minutes were up. It wasn't the planes. It was the car — the car parked halfway up rue Aussi. Koo was talking to the woman at the moment of detonation. She was beheaded in a shower of blood, right there in front of him as he was filling his notebook with her words, dead the moment Koo was blown off his feet. Anderson was thrown into the ruins of the bombed building. The planes still circled, watching. A reconnaissance mission, yes. But a *car bomb*. We hadn't thought of that.

SVC PROFNE EXFISK BEIRUT: THINK YOU SHOULD KNOW SOONEST THAT ISRAELI TANK SALVOS ARE NOW HITTING ALL THE BUILDINGS ROUND HERE, INCLUDING COMMODORE HOTEL WHICH TAKEN THREE 75MM ROUNDS IN BEDROOMS FROM TANKS ... HOUSE JUST GOT HIT NEXT TO HOSPITAL (AMERICAN UNIVERSITY) BY FOUR SALVOS. ALL CASUALTIES CIVILIANS (ONE DEAD MAN SEEN, ONE DEAD BABY). WOULD BE GRATEFUL YOU ASK WALKER TO ASK HIS PEOPLE ABOUT THE QUESTION OF MILITARY TARGETS, ETC. AS I SHALL BE REPORTING ALL THIS AT LENGTH, WOULD LIKE TO HAVE HIS QUOTE FOR USE IN STORY. CIVILIAN TARGETS ARE NOT MILITARY TARGETS — SO WHAT OF PINPOINT ACCURACY, ETC ... AP STILL OPERATING ... AND I STILL WITH THEM. THEREFORE YOU CAN STILL GET ME ON DIRECT LINE TELEX APBEY 20636LE.

Barnes had come back at once, his message distorted by the line breaks and the varying pitch of François' generator.

CONCENTRATE ON GETTING SOME AEEE EARLY COPY TO US N CASE LINESGO STOP FOR GODDSAKE DONT GETYOURSELF SHOT ... EVEN FOR EARLY COPY OVER.

On the streets, his message was meaningless. With an NBC television crew, I had crept down to the Corniche to find the shells landing across the athletics track, blasting the glass windows out of the Geffinor tower where Middle East Airlines maintained its city headquarters. The Israeli fire was falling across all of west Beirut. A shell hit the prime minister's office, four shells hit the back of the Bristol Hotel, three hit the Commodore, two hit a cinema in the Piccadilly district, six hit the house opposite the American University hospital. Anderson and I actually saw the salvo explode in a huge golden flame only seconds before another round smashed into the roof of the hospital.

They fell at the rate of one shell every ten seconds. Phosphorus shells exploded down Hamra Street, blasting through the walls of the offices of *L'Orient Le Jour* and devastating the American United Press International bureau. To call the gunfire indiscriminate was an understatement. It would also have been a lie. The Israeli bombardment of 4 August was, we realised, later, *discriminate*. It targeted every civilian area, every institution, in west Beirut — hospitals, schools, apartments, shops, newspaper offices, hotels, the prime minister's office and the parks. Incredibly, the Israeli shells even blew part of the roof off the city's synagogue in Wadi Abu Jamil where the remnants of Beirut's tiny Jewish community still lived.

At the height of the shelling, I ran from house to house like a frightened cat, scampering between doorways, all the way from the AP bureau to the American University hospital. There was blood everywhere. In the emergency wards, I found at least a hundred men, women and children lying in their own blood on the floor or moaning on trolleys in the corridors. There was vomit and blood on the walls. An old half-naked woman was lying on a stretcher, whimpering and crying with her breasts lolling off the stretcher, in other people's blood on the floor.

I ran across to the mortuary. Limbs and arms — dozens of them — had been stacked against a wall. There were several dead babies lying in plastic bags on the floor, neatly packaged up, the cellophane stapled above the tiny heads, as if they were being sent back to a manufacturer for repairs. Human entrails lay across the pathway outside. Someone had been trying to piece bodies together. They had found a leg, a torso, but three arms lay next to the torso. The place was slippery, it reeked of people's stomachs. A three-armed man, I kept saying to myself. *A three-armed man.* Someone that morning had managed to create a three-armed man.

The refugees in Sanaya park did not stand a chance. They had no concrete protection. They had tents. By the time I reached Sanaya, there were women standing among the trees, wailing and shrieking like animals, covered head to toe in blood or wandering through the cordite smoke in a dream. The older they were, the more bloody they appeared to be. I had only just realised this. The elderly would look terrible, torn apart by the shells, the younger people would be swamped in blood but the dead children always looked as if they were sleeping, only a hairline of blood showing that they were dead.

Ditchley, England, 26 September 1987

Philip Habib is a big gruff man with giant spectacles and an enormous appetite, sitting at the end of the dinner table. He has spent the morning lecturing the American, Israeli and Lebanese delegates to the annual symposium on the Middle East. The autumn sunlight filters into the dining room, glinting on the surface of the oil paintings, shining a bright, cheerful red through the wine glasses on the table. Habib is munching popadums. He never talked to us in Beirut. He does not want to talk now. But I sit next to him and ask him, again and again, about that day. He was there. He was President Reagan's representative, his special envoy. He could talk to the Israelis. Why didn't he stop the bloodshed?

'I was at Baabda. I could see it. I told the Israelis they were destroying the city, that they were firing non-stop. They just said they weren't. They said they weren't doing that. I called Sharon on the phone. He said it wasn't true. That damned man said to me on the phone that what I saw happening wasn't happening. So I held the telephone out of the window so he could hear the explosions. Then he said to me: "What kind of conversation is this where you hold a telephone out of a window?"'

West Beirut, 4 August 1982

Waves of Israeli fighters raced across the city at dusk, swooping amid a blaze of anti-aircraft fire to bomb the camps and then turning away into the evening sky for Galilee and home. The Israelis announced later that they were merely 'tightening' the siege of west Beirut. There was, a spokesman announced in Tel Aviv, no question of 'an all-out attempt to conquer the city'. But there was. The Israelis had driven Merkavas across the front line at the museum and had almost passed the Barbir when Syrian troops ambushed the armour, destroyed the fifth tank and turned on the crews of the four tanks trapped in front of it. The battle of Beirut had become a war of no quarter.

The few diplomats left in west Beirut were becoming outspoken in their condemnation of Israel. Theodore Arcand, the Canadian ambassador, who had known families killed in the Iskandar Street bombing, found it 'truly unbelievable' that civilians could be immolated in this way. 'Eighty people were killed — so much for "pin-point bombing",' he said. '... I always had an enormous admiration for the Israelis, their musicians, their men of science, which I try to think of despite my travels in southern Lebanon ... and I wonder where the Israel I knew has gone. And I am sure many Israelis are wondering.'

Yet the Israelis seemed unperturbed by the furore that their bombardment had provoked. How could the press compare this with the Second World War, the Israelis asked? How could journalists suggest that this was like Dresden? I never met a reporter who had described Beirut in these terms. It could *not* be compared to the Second World War. To draw a parallel with Dresden would be a gross exaggeration. West Beirut was simply a disgrace, a place of rubble and desolation and houses ripped apart so savagely and with such speed that rescue workers had not yet even begun to dig through the floors and debris.

What would be the result of all this? Not now or in a few days or even when the PLO had gone. But what would happen in a year or in five years' time to a people who were subjected to this unprecedented military onslaught, bombed and shelled by outsiders with munitions made in America, France, Britain and eastern Europe? Anderson and I talked then about this, about whether Lebanon might not hold some frightful revenge for these powers, the invaders, the visitors, the foreigners.

Nick Tatro and I asked ourselves the same question as we drove down the old coast road to Ouzai after Israel had announced another unilateral 'ceasefire'. There was not a house — not one small shop — undamaged. Perhaps 80 per cent of the buildings in the four square miles of those southern suburbs — apartment blocks, embassies, stores and offices — had been gouged with shell-holes, set on fire or totally destroyed. The Israeli bombs had hit everything, from residential houses to clinics, laneways and graveyards. Even the local fire station had been torn to pieces.

We drove down the main road at only 10 mph, for the highway was pitted with shell-holes, the tarmac surface strewn with live ammunition, bomb casings and debris. There were just a few people left there; a young gunman in braces and a white shirt near the airport road and five old Kurds in white headdresses carrying some dirty mattresses and pans down the centre of the broken boulevard, looking straight in front of them as if to turn their heads would reawaken something they did not wish to remember.

There had been a line of Arab embassies along this road. They were in ruins now, their windows stained with fire and their walls broken by shells. The Summerland Hotel with its swimming pool and barbecue restaurants and shopping centre was partially burnt out. The houses stretching right up through Bir Hassan towards the airport had been smashed, mostly by shells fired from the sea. In some cases, the projectiles had passed right through the buildings, entering the sitting room, plunging through corridors and blasting their way out of the back kitchens.

Down at Ouzai, we could go no further than a sand barricade across the road just below the landing lights of the airport runways. Two hundred yards further on were the first Israeli tanks. So few were the Palestinian positions between Ouzai and Raouche that the Israelis could probably have driven on into west Beirut, but the crews would have had little to look at on the way save the desolation wrought by their own army.

It became worse as we drove east. The old sports stadium near the airport — one of the few genuinely military targets to be hit — had been cut open, its terraces fractured and blown down in jagged hunks of concrete. Behind it, the apartments of Sabra had been bombed out. In some cases, ten-storey blocks had collapsed under the air bombing. In others, half the building had given way, floors buckling like the edges of a heavily dog-eared book. Half the rooms remained intact with their sofas and chairs and brass lamps in their conventional setting but with the carpets spilling out into space.

Near Fakhani, where the PLO had its offices, several of the apartment buildings were still on fire, the flames curling around the ruins, un-hindered by the Beirut fire brigade. Little wonder it was, for Israeli shells had crashed down on the fire station beside the Arab university and damaged the two vehicles there beyond repair. Twelve of west Beirut's 50 firemen had been wounded in the preceding two months but there was now so little water pressure in the mains that the brigade's activities had become purely symbolic. They 'attended' fires but could not put them out; which is why 25 fires were still smouldering that morning.

The Barbir hospital had been hit by two Israeli shells — for the third time in two weeks — and tank fire had ignited the trees around the Sabra cemetery where the branches gave off an eerie blue smoke above the graves. In Bourj al-Barajneh, not one hut or building appeared to have escaped the air strikes. Even the small militia hospital there had been hit; a bomb had exploded against the red cross painted on the roof. Downstairs we found an old Palestinian woman with tattoos on her face. She had fled to the camp two months earlier to escape the air raids on southern Lebanon. Her husband and son had already died in west Beirut.

The Syrians and Palestinians had fought back. Several Syrian tanks could be seen, charred and smoking, near Bourj al-Barajneh, and a Syrian artillery position had been wiped out by shells from an Israeli gunboat. At one end of Corniche Mazraa, three guerrillas had spent eight hours firing vainly at the jets as the buildings round them were gutted by bombs. They went on firing, courageously and pointlessly, amid the shrapnel until a shell brought down a tree on top of them and broke the barrels of their gun.

Each evening, the dust and smoke from west Beirut would drift far out over the Mediterranean. Even the crews of the American warships 20 miles beyond the horizon could smell it. In the city, the evenings arrived prematurely, the sun disappearing not into the sea but behind a growing crimson veil. More than a hundred miles away, in Haifa, the Israelis noticed the same unfamiliar effect upon the distant skyline, the creeping darkness that west Beirut's destruction now placed across the setting sun. From Tripoli and the mountains of the ancient cedars to the land that was Palestine, the sky glowed hot and blood-red.

10 Dawn at Midnight

> We are now on the eve of achieving what we set forth to
> accomplish: an end to the bloodshed in Beirut ...
>
> President Ronald Reagan *1 September 1982*
> fifteen days before the Sabra and Chatila massacre

As Safir was the sort of paper that believed in preparing for news stories
long in advance. Weeks before the Israelis invaded Lebanon, Bassem
Sabbagh, the editor, ordered enough newsprint and generator fuel to go
on publishing during a siege. And at the beginning of August 1982, he
asked the paper's cartoonist, Naj al-Ali, to draw a picture to run on the
back page the day the Palestinians would begin their evacuation from
Beirut.

It took al-Ali four days to produce the cartoon and it now lay on
Sabbagh's desk, an eight-inch-square drawing of a Palestinian guerrilla
cowled in a *kuffiah* with a rifle over his shoulder, turning with outstretched hand to a Lebanese leftist militiaman. 'Well, it's goodbye
then,' the Palestinian was saying. And the Lebanese was replying: 'Are
you really sure about that?' It was a careful, ambiguous cartoon, confirming the departure of the Palestinians while apparently insisting upon
the friendship of the Muslims of west Beirut who had suffered so much
through the PLO's presence. It did not reflect the truth but it represented a
version of reality, just as the Beirut press had always done.

As Safir was a brave little paper, its circulation now reduced from a
'peacetime' 45,000 to around 7,000. But Sabbagh made no secret of the
leftist, political motives of his journalism. *As Safir*'s daily sales in Lebanon
generated only 2,000 dollars a day, it carried few advertisements, four of
its reporters had been killed in the early days of the 1975–6 civil war
and three of its photographers were badly wounded in the Israeli invasion.
One of them had been hit in the back by shrapnel at Khalde. The paper
sent its editions to left-wing Arab nations like Syria and Libya on a basis
of sale and no return; the Arab governments paid a block subscription.
This was a subsidy under another name, which was why *As Safir* rarely
criticised Libya or Syria.

Yet when the Lebanese publisher Selim al-Lawzi was murdered in
1980 – almost certainly on Syrian orders – *As Safir* courageously

reported the killing in an eight-column headline across the top of its front page. The newspaper's survival under Israeli shells was itself a political act. During the bloodiest bombardment, a few of its 45 staff members brought out a four-page special edition with 21 photographs of the destruction and a cartoon which showed a small boy holding a flower up to a tired young woman in a ruined house and saying to her: 'Good morning, Lebanon.'

For it was an essentially *Lebanese* paper. 'We have no choice but to go on printing,' Sabbagh told me, 'because if *As Safir* stops, that means Beirut is dead, and we want to keep it alive.' It was this pride, this city-patriotism, that had persuaded the staff to go on working during the siege, curling up on mattresses next to the telex machines.* The printers slept beside their Goss offset machines in the basement, safe from the shrapnel that fell daily around the building. Here was a paper that represented the old spirit of pan-Arabism, the voice of the Lebanese who opposed the French creation of Greater Syria. Sabbagh saw himself as the mouthpiece of the Lebanese 'National Movement', which was why he would go on publishing 'until the Israelis come'.

Until the Israelis come? The Israelis were not going to come. They had agreed to stay out of west Beirut if the PLO left. Sabbagh was not so sure. I sensed that The Plot might be affecting his judgement. The Israelis had promised the Americans that they would not enter west Beirut. But Sabbagh suspected that promises and ambitions were always in conflict. He also believed that politics and journalism should be indistinguishable. 'We cannot work as journalists without politics,' he said. 'They are inseparable, especially in Lebanon. We are in a situation of war – the Israelis are not far away from us. We have to play politics now because we want our people to stay here. But we want the Palestinians to go now because it is the only way to save Beirut. The Palestinians know that we have no other choice. We are sorry to say that but it is the truth.'

Off the coast of Beirut each night, we could now see the lights of two big ships, advance vessels of the US Sixth Fleet whose Marine contingent would land, alongside French and Italian troops, to escort the Palestinians out of the city, by sea to South and North Yemen, Tunisia, Sudan and Egypt, by land to Syria, Jordan and Iraq. The lights winked at us through the darkness, friendly little fireflies that conveyed a special

---

* *As Safir*'s staff included not only Lebanese and Palestinians but Egyptians, Tunisians and Syrians, each of whom wrote in his own distinctive linguistic style. Past contributors had included Selim al-Hoss, who became Chafiq Wazzan's successor as Lebanese prime minister, Mohamed Heikal, the distinguished Egyptian journalist, Kamal Jumblatt and even Lord Carrington – before he became British foreign secretary – as well as leading members of the PLO and the Syrian Baath Party.

message to the Lebanese and the Palestinians. The West was coming. The Americans were coming. Lebanon's future was assured.

Yet every time that our assumptions became locked in stone, the Israelis broke them open. On 10 August, Christopher Walker, *The Times* correspondent in Jerusalem, asked Barnes to tell me that 'a lot of heavy material [is] moving in your direction.' What did this mean? Nick Tatro dismissed the message. This was surely a routine Israeli troop transfer, fresh soldiers relieving the line troops around the Beirut perimeter. But if this was the case, why were they bringing more 'material'? The tanks were already in position around Beirut. Why did they need more?

An official from Hawatmeh's Democratic Front for the Liberation of Palestine, a man called Jamil who affected Maher's habit of smoking cigarettes through a holder, turned up at the Commodore Hotel to tell journalists that his organisation was committed to the PLO's evacuation. The Palestinian camps would be left unarmed, he said. Only civilians would remain there, mostly women and children but a number of old men too. Those who had been squatting in apartment blocks would return to the camps before the PLO left. They would be safe. There were American guarantees, promises from Habib that these people would not be harmed. Arafat was to receive from Habib a written assurance to this effect.

I had argued about this with Ane-Karine Arveson, the Norwegian Embassy's second secretary, who had travelled with Tveit and myself during the early days of the invasion. As a diplomat, she believed in assurances, especially when they were underwritten by the superpowers. I was not so sure. Perhaps because I was now very tired, I had developed a simplistic formula, based on experience, which I applied consistently to the participants in this war; whatever they said, whatever they promised, they could be relied upon to break their word.

When the Israelis said they would only advance 40 kilometres into Lebanon, they had gone all the way to Beirut. They had lied about the civilian casualties, they had lied about turning off the electricity and water supplies to west Beirut. The PLO had said it was ready to leave west Beirut when it clearly intended to prevaricate. When Arafat's officials said they would never leave, they were lying. The Israelis had denied using cluster bombs and phosphorus shells on civilian areas. They were lying. Now they had promised that they would not enter Beirut. Every political instinct said they would keep their word. Every journalistic instinct said they would not.

At the end of his press conference, I asked Jamil what he could do to protect the Palestinian civilians in the camps — in Sabra and Chatila and Bourj al-Barajneh — if the Israelis *did* break their promise and enter west Beirut. 'Nothing,' he said. For years afterwards, he would recall my question and his answer, always asking me why neither of us had realised the significance of our brief exchange at the time.

Perhaps it was because we both had other things on our minds. On 12 August, without warning – certainly without military provocation – dozens of Israeli fighter-bombers appeared over west Beirut just after dawn and raced at low level over the city. We had never seen them so low, only a few hundred feet over the rooftops, so close to us as we stood on the roof of the AP bureau that we could make out the Star of David painted on the fuselage of the planes. One jet turned above the roofs and banked over the office and I saw the pilot's head move in the cockpit as if he was searching for a target.

He knew what he was aiming for: the camps. For nine hours, the Israelis bombed them, unloading hundreds of tons of high explosives onto Sabra and Chatila. The bombs fell together, three or four jets dropping them at the same time with a sound like sheets being torn in half. There was no resistance, no anti-aircraft fire, no missiles, which is why the Israelis could fly so low. Massive clouds of dust and ash funnelled into the air over the camps and from the southern suburbs.

Why? The Israelis never told us. Sarkis and Wazzan appealed to Reagan and to King Fahd of Saudi Arabia to intervene. But the Americans seemed powerless – or unwilling – to control the Israeli firepower that was being used on the city. 'If the Israelis want to kill us all, let them do it and let's get it over and done with,' Wazzan shouted on the steps of the presidential palace, waving his arms at the jets that were screeching through the sky above him. 'We have offered all the concessions requested from us for the PLO evacuation and we have even reached the stage of defining the PLO's departure routes. Then we have this. What's the meaning of all these thousands of destructive explosives? Why?'

Over Corniche Mazraa, I noticed Israeli jets dropping projectiles that exploded at 50-foot intervals down the sky in black clouds of smoke, detonating eight or nine times before they reached the ground. The Israelis were using anti-tank cluster bombs again on the apartment blocks of west Beirut. Around the city, the new Israeli armour arrived – the tanks and guns which Walker had warned me about – and Israeli soldiers could also be seen erecting dozens of searchlights on the hills above Hadeth and Shweifat. The whole city could now be lit up at night. But why?

That night, Colonel Yehiel Ben-Zvi, the official spokesman for the Israeli army command at Baabda, partly answered this question. 'We have finished a very intensive build-up in and around Beirut as part of a large operation . . . if and when we have to attack,' he said. At the time, his comments seemed absurd, inappropriate. He was not referring to the air raids, but to the possibility of an Israeli advance into west Beirut. But the Israelis had agreed they would not do that. They were going to leave once the PLO had evacuated the city. The war was over. The death toll for Beirut alone now stood at 3,983. In Lebanon, 11,492 people had been killed since the start of the invasion. This, however, underestimated the true figure. There were so many dismembered bodies brought into the mortuaries on the afternoon of 12 August that the doctors we spoke to would only say that 'several hundred' had died.

It was a period of flux. The Lebanese spoke of renewal, the Palestinians of victory — which meant defeat. In the slums of west Beirut, the people grew poorer. For them, the strategic implications of the war, the political opportunities, the moral claims, had no relevance. To talk to these people was to realise that our long essays on the principles of war, on Israeli ambition, American leverage, Palestinian contempt, in no way touched upon the lives of those who suffered most during the siege.

On 10 August, for example, Salma Sherif arrived at her local bakery in Wadi Abu Jamil at four in the morning and left six hours later with just ten pieces of flat Arabic bread. Menachem Begin would never have heard of Salma Sherif. Not even her local militia rulers from the Amal movement would have known her name. She counted among the half million civilians who had stayed in west Beirut. As long as she did not speak or seek influence, she did not matter. Her life involved a constant search for cheap food to feed too many children. She had paid one dollar fifty for the bread which would have to last her six children and seven nephews for two days. Only 60 dollars was left in the family savings. When that ran out, they would begin to starve. Already they were drinking salt water.

Salma was a beautiful woman with dark eyes and the sort of smile that Renaissance artists gave to Madonnas. But she was prematurely old for her 29 years, weighed down by a seventh pregnancy, her greying hair pulled back tightly beneath a pale blue scarf. She wore a long flowing dress, an awful leopard-skin print whose tastelessness was somehow lost in the miserable circumstances in which she lived. The Sherif family ate and slept in a disused, vandalised hospital, about 600 yards from the Israeli tanks in Beirut port, cooking rice in a bathroom and sleeping on the floor of what was once a ward. There were flies on the walls, on the floor, on the faces of Salma, her husband and six children. The place smelled of urine.

Perhaps that was why Hussein Sherif dragged constantly on a cigarette, a precious packet of cheap Lebanese-made Marlboros that he offered to us with the sort of expression that made us turn down his generosity. He was a street vegetable seller. But the Israelis were again refusing to allow fresh fruit and vegetables into west Beirut and Hussein was out of work. The family were of Turkish origin and Salma used to wear gold necklaces and earrings, but she sold them all for 800 dollars when the Israeli siege began in June and nearly all of the money had been spent on food. Her six children were not yet showing signs of malnutrition but they were thin. Mohamed, who was five and wandered on his own around the old hospital corridors, was suffering from acute diarrhoea.

Salma smiled a lot when she talked. Her story was quintessentially Lebanese, a combination of bad luck, fortitude, fear and distrust. 'We have been in difficulties before, but never as bad as this,' she said. 'We were in Tel al-Za'atar where the Palestinians had a camp during the civil war and we were forced to move here seven years ago. But we were safe and my husband sometimes earned a hundred lira [17 dollars] a day. Now from one day to the next, we don't know what will happen. The UNICEF people came here two days ago and gave us some fresh water but the rest of the time we drink salt water. I am frightened to go to the bakery in case the Israelis bomb us and I never see my children again.'

She was not exaggerating her fear. When the Israelis shelled the civilian areas of west Beirut the previous week, three pieces of jagged shrapnel had come smashing through the windows of Salma's makeshift kitchen, ricocheting around the room between her and her 13-year-old daughter Nadia. The glass was still fractured and Salma showed it off as if it was a family heirloom, as precious as the old treadle Singer sewing machine that gathered dust on the bedroom floor.

Why did they stay in west Beirut rather than leave for the comparative safety of Israeli-occupied southern Lebanon? Salma's reply was both moving and shocking. 'We live here because it is the most beautiful place. We have our roots here and our emotions. We thought this was the freest place to live.'

Hussein interrupted, grudging and irritated. 'There was too much freedom,' he muttered. Salma became more pragmatic. 'Look at the price,' she said. 'It cost twice what is left of my savings to take a taxi to the other side of Beirut. We cannot afford to leave.' She remained wistful, almost indifferent to her plight. Then her eyes moved to the window and to the narrow street outside where some barefoot children were playing beside a garbage dump.

'It is Begin I blame,' she said. 'Do you know this used to be the Jewish area of Beirut? But only the old Jews remain now and they will stay here until they die. Why do the Israelis do this?' She was aware suddenly of what she had said, of the dark side of her feelings. 'Look,' she said, 'we want to live in peace with everyone and we do not know why there is this war.'

Several of the old Jews — at least four — would indeed stay until they died; because within three years, they would be kidnapped and murdered, their bodies left a few hundred yards from Wadi Abu Jamil. A few of the survivors claimed that this was an indirect result of the savagery of Israel's invasion and its effect upon the Shia Muslims. Yet the Jewish community itself suffered from Menachem Begin's military adventure in

Lebanon. Only 300 yards down the road from Salma Sherif's home, an Israeli shell had smashed the roof of the synagogue. The Israeli gunfire had swept over Wadi Abu Jamil and forced most of the 50 elderly Jews who lived there to flee to east Beirut and to Jounieh. Only 15 now remained.

The pretty synagogue of yellow and white stone had already lost its windows when a car bomb exploded a quarter of a mile away. Two Israeli shells punched holes in the roof of the building some days later. One of the few Jews to stay in Wadi Abu Jamil, Jacob Eskenazi, said that the projectiles were fired from the sea and that the same Israeli vessel later shelled the houses around the synagogue.

Several other shells hit the grounds of the building and damaged the women's bathing room beside the forecourt of the synagogue. It had been built in 1926 by Moise Abraham Sassoon of Calcutta – according to the marble plaques in Hebrew and French on the façade – in memory of his father, Abraham Eliahou Sassoon 'who died in Beirut on the first day of Adar Cheni 5657,' the Jewish calendar date for March 1898. Most of Beirut's Jews had left Lebanon after the Second World War and there had been a further exodus after the 1967 Middle East war, although there was no evidence then of anti-Jewish sentiment in the city. When the PLO controlled the area in the 1975–6 conflict, they even placed guards on the synagogue. But now it was in ruins. The last ten families to worship there padlocked the door after the Israeli shells came through the roof.

Muslim and Christian refugees now lived behind the synagogue, cooking their meals in a side yard. One of them brought a ladder and placed it against a broken window so that I could see the damage. The metal roof frame had collapsed and rubble had cascaded down onto the chairs along the north side of the building, scattering debris and stones across the pulpit. As is the custom in Sephardic synagogues of the Middle East, the pulpit was in the centre of the building, surrounded by a rectangle of chairs. At the back, the Torah ark appeared to be untouched, although glass shards hung from the chandeliers.

But two marble tablets representing the Ten Commandments had been broken by one shell, spraying half the commandments in marble chips across the courtyard. In front of the synagogue, I also found a marble Star of David. It had been slashed in half by shrapnel. Eskenazi, a balding man with wispy dark hair, did not understand why the area was bombarded. He made no comment or condemnation, save to take my notebook quietly and write something inside it. When I looked at it later, I found that he had written: 'I have a son in Tel Aviv.'

In Bourj al-Barajneh, unlike Wadi Abu Jamil, it was difficult to find anything still standing. When we used to visit the camp, we found that after climbing over so many walls, underneath so many dangling parapets, the place began to affect our sense of dimension; a township made into a moonscape where we walked on roads of crushed roofs. Every few minutes, our Palestinian guide would point to a pile of broken breeze-blocks and list the number of people who had died underneath.

The Palestinians realised the importance of taking visitors around Bourj al-Barajneh because most of it had been destroyed in the Israeli air raids. Even now, there were PLO officials who felt it necessary to inject a political message into this desolation. In mid-August, a plump man in an ill-fitting blue suit, who must have been a PLO official, stopped me on the edge of the camp and felt compelled to deliver an unnecessary, futile lecture on the history of the Palestinians, emphasising again and again that he wanted the Israelis to stay in Israel but would like to share a democratic state with them. He used the word democracy too often and the Palestinians standing around him did not understand.

What made his words truly irrelevant was the wasteland around him. Street after street, laneway after crushed laneway was in ruins, and when I walked around the camp with a teenage guerrilla we could hear only the sound of our own footsteps on the crushed glass and powdered concrete. There were no birds, and almost no people. 'This was a house of fourteen people,' the teenager said. He had a sprouting black moustache and carried his automatic rifle over his shoulder in an easy, familiar manner. The indifferent way in which he spoke was impressive, setting him apart from the blue-suited propagandist who needed this devastation to prove his point.

We were standing next to three walls under which lay a roof of thick concrete that had been broken up and cracked like a jigsaw puzzle. On one wall, there was a crude oil painting of a river with a barge sailing upstream, the sort of vessel the Iraqi marsh people use on the Shatt al-Arab waterway. On another wall, there was a coloured photograph of a young man in a smart uniform beneath a Palestinian flag. He stared out at us, smiling and stupid, from the picture frame. 'The fourteen people all died here,' the Palestinian said, and pointed to the jigsaw of the roof.

We walked around the corner where some water pipes were bubbling amid a sewer and there stood two storeys of what was once a house. On the half of the upper floor that was still intact, there was a wooden table with a pile of brightly coloured clothes on it. And next to the clothes there stood a sewing machine, a big black and gold machine that was silhouetted against the sky like some kind of monument. 'A mother and her three children died here,' the guerrilla said. It was like this all the way. We would clamber over concrete and then we would stop and the gunman with the moustache would announce another small casualty list, as if we were pausing at shrines rather than ruins. I might have been able to disbelieve him, were it not for the smells that seeped from the buildings.

There were huge, wicked pieces of shell-casing and bomb shrapnel lying everywhere, hunks of heavy metal with razor-sharp edges that could cut their way through 20 men and women and still kill others, and small brass filings that glinted gold in the sunshine. We turned another corner and there were two people, sitting beside a house with no roof.

They were very old women, birdlike creatures with wizened skin who could not hear us; they had been deafened by age or bombs, bemused old ladies who played with three kittens. One of the women, when she saw the guerrilla beside me, raised her right hand, her two fingers splayed in a 'V' for victory, a gesture that was at the same time both pathetic and terrible, for she could not possibly comprehend any victory in these ruins. We asked them, very slowly and loudly, where they came from, and their faces lit up. 'Nazareth,' they chorused and began cackling to each other, frightening the cats away. There was a child standing on the corner, a little girl of perhaps two with long, unwashed brown hair. She was barefoot, standing in a sewer; she ran away when we called to her.

A few hundred yards away, I discovered an old underground car park and down there amid the dust was an emergency clinic where a Belgian surgeon was examining some people lying on beds. He was a sensitive, intelligent man who talked in the same way as the guerrilla, apparently indifferent to the political implications of what he said. 'You know, when you first see these air raids, they are exciting and you somehow enjoy watching the planes diving and the explosions. But you should see the results.'

The doctor moved along the beds as he talked, watching his patients with something akin to suspicion, as if they might die without giving him sufficient notice. 'There was a shelter near here with thirty people inside,' he said. 'Most of them were civilians although there were three or four fighters there. The shelter took a direct hit and the roof came down and they all suffered massive brain injuries. Two men came in here with the top of their heads missing down to their eyes. I don't know how they were still able to breathe. I laid them on beds where they could die in comfort.'

We came to the bed of a man so badly burned that he was swathed from his head to his toes in bandages two or three inches thick. He looked like the Michelin Man, save for the dribble of pale, half-red liquid which, somewhere about his middle, seeped from the bandages. He was evidently in dreadful pain but we greeted him in Arabic and his head moved slightly, his charred mouth moving into a dark circle like an undersea plant. He was constantly warmed by blankets; badly burned people freeze at night. He would probably die soon.

Was he burned by phosphorus? I asked. No, the surgeon replied. 'He was a man whose house caught fire in the raids and then collapsed on top of him. He was trapped in the flames and roasted. These are just ordinary burns.'

Fatigue permeated the camps, and all of west Beirut, even the Israeli lines where we would see the soldiers lying in the grass by the race track, their weapons and military radios beside them. Across from the Israelis, the Palestinians exhibited the same nonchalant, distracted air. Abu Rusian was only 40 yards from the Israeli line in Ouzai when I found him on 16 August, tucking into his lunch like a tourist. There was a plate of beans, a small mountain of rice, cheese and a saucer of large, slippery olives on the table, and the other guerrillas were shovelling the food onto their plates with knives. 'We have not been told we are leaving,' he said, wiping his mouth on a large and dirty handkerchief. 'Maybe the French will come here, maybe the Italians. We have been told nothing. But it's quiet. Do you want some olives, some cheese?'

Abu Rusian did not even know where he would be sent, to Algeria, to South Yemen, to Syria. A young gunman brought us glass mugs of steaming tea which we sipped in the shade of Abu Rusian's headquarters, a ruined five-storey apartment block whose balconies had draped themselves down the wall. There were flies around the table and across the road a rooster crowed. The war was almost over. Abu Rusian knew that. We felt it everywhere we went in west Beirut. It had a strange effect on the Palestinian guerrillas. One of them galloped a horse down Hamra Street with a rifle on his back and a cowboy hat on his head. Three Syrian soldiers stood on the Avenue de Paris on the seafront, firing pistols at fish. On the shore near the American Embassy, Palestinians wandered among crowds of bathers, some in bathing trunks and with only their Kalashnikovs to distinguish them from the Lebanese. If it was not yet peace, it was certainly not war.

The Lebanese government formally submitted written requests on 19 August for the arrival of the multinational 'disengagement' force. Fouad Boutros, the Lebanese foreign minister, handed the letters to the ambassadors of the United States, France and Italy at a meeting at Sarkis' presidential palace. The Lebanese were inviting more foreigners to visit them − for a limited period only of course − solely to escort the Palestinians, those other foreigners, out of Beirut.

The Americans and French and Italians had no territorial or political ambitions. They were just helping to solve a problem, staying for a few days as honoured and welcome guests while this little matter of the PLO was finally brought to a close. This was no invasion, no act of intimidation. Lebanon was sending out the invitations, having forgotten that it was the Israeli invasion that had made them necessary in the first place. But then, how many Lebanese wanted the PLO to stay? Had not the Israelis done them all a favour? Even in west Beirut, we heard this question asked. Lebanon needed a strong new leader, someone with guts, who could rid Lebanon of all its foreigners. Everyone knew this was true.

Presidential elections would be held on 23 August. Bashir Gemayel would be elected. Everyone knew this too. Just as the Syrians had ensured the vote for Sarkis, so now the Israelis would guarantee Gemayel's victory. The PLO evacuation agreement included a clause that demanded the departure of all foreign armies from Lebanon. Here was a policy to which every Lebanese could give his or her support.

On Hamra Street, the Palestinians were buying suitcases, big brown plastic bags for their clothes and papers and for the photographs of the families they were leaving behind in Sabra and Chatila and Bourj al-Barajneh. The Lebanese thought they understood what this meant. If the PLO left, their problems would be over. How often had the Lebanese been told that the arrival of the Palestinian guerrillas from Jordan in 1970 – not those earlier, more civilised refugees from Palestine in 1948 – had destroyed their country?

The government ordered the renovation of the temporary parliament building at Villa Mansour on the front line opposite the museum. The parliament itself looked a little like Lebanese democracy. The doors had been smashed, the windows lay in pieces across the floors and the great mirrors in the conference room were cracked and shattered beyond repair. The floor was littered with glass, and in the parliamentary chamber three bullet holes had punctured the wall behind the speaker's chair. Only a pseudo-baroque tapestry – a cameo of a young Regency buck carrying an overdressed maiden across an icy stream – remained untouched.

Nevertheless, democracy – or at least the spirit of that elusive state of affairs – wrought some marvellous changes in Beirut. In anticipation of the arrival of the Americans, French and Italians, the Israeli army abandoned their positions inside the international airport terminal and removed their soldiers from the museum. A convoy of lorries carrying fruit and vegetables down the old airport road heralded the end of the Israeli food blockade. The PLO announced that it would free Ahiaz Aharon, the Israeli pilot who had been captured on the first day of the invasion and whom we had last seen in the hospital basement at Sabra.

The Lebanese army reappeared. Lebanese soldiers arrived at the airport terminal. They set up their cots inside the national museum. To see them there, in the halls once dedicated to the glories of Phoenicia, was itself a lesson in Lebanese history. They patrolled the deserted museum galleries like strangers, thin young men with carefully groomed moustaches and grubby tunics, peering at the sarcophagi that had been entombed in protective concrete since the start of the 1975–6 civil war. Their boots crunched over six-inch shards of priceless Phoenician jars, all of them smashed by shellfire. Beneath graffiti scribbled on the walls by Syrian soldiers, lay the remains of a magnificent Roman mosaic floor. A 20-foot map in marble was embedded on an upper wall, a cartographer's tribute to the Phoenician cultural and commercial ideal that stretched from Morocco to Persia. Lebanon's heritage stood before these young Lebanese soldiers but they looked at it vacantly, drawing heavily on their Marlboros. The museum had become another barracks.

The Palestinians thought a lot about their own fate. How many times had we heard them say that if the PLO left Beirut, it would mean the end of the Palestinian struggle? I filed a long dispatch to *The Times* on 20 August, suggesting again that the PLO might tear itself apart in the aftermath of evacuation. I wrote about one of the Palestinian gunmen I had met during an air raid, how he had banged his coffee cup down on the table in front of him in fury. He would not contemplate evacuation. 'Do you know what that would mean?' he had asked. 'It would be the end of the PLO, the end of the Palestinians as a people. If Abu Ammar [Arafat] tells us to get out of here, do you think everyone is going to obey him and allow those people up there to win?' There was an air raid in progress as we spoke, punctuating his speech with machine-gun fire and explosions, and the man jerked his thumb contemptuously upwards towards the unseen jets. 'It is better to die here.'

He was a young man who had clearly discussed his views with his comrades, deeply dispirited at the talk of evacuation and at hints of corruption which he had heard about the PLO's leadership. Had I heard, he wanted to know, that the PLO commander in Sidon had run away when the Israelis invaded, had deserted his post in the face of the enemy? Did I know that money had been filched from the PLO youth movement's accounts? Was I aware that PLO officers had taken their wives and children to Damascus but had failed to return to fight the Israelis? Yet it was a measure of the PLO's surviving powers of leadership that this same man was now preparing to leave Lebanon in deference to Arafat's instructions.

For a week now, he and the other thousands of PLO guerrillas in west Beirut had been told that they had won a great victory, that their suffering over the previous two months had been a feat of arms unparalleled in Arab history since 1948. For two months, according to Arafat, his guerrillas had held off the full might of the Israeli army and air force. No nation of the Arab world had done this before.

I filed three reports to *The Times* on 20 August of which the shortest − and the one upon which I spent least time − touched by chance upon the future tragedy of the Palestinians. After their evacuation, I wrote:

the guerrillas of the Palestine Liberation Organisation will be at the mercy of Arab regimes which have no love for revolutionary instability and which were thus content to leave the PLO to its doom when the Israelis encircled Beirut. For a week or so, the capitals of the Arab world will fete Mr Arafat's guerrillas ... But it will not last long. Having received no real military assistance from Jordan, Iraq, Egypt, South Yemen, Algeria or Tunisia, Mr Arafat is now consigning his men to

those comatose nations, handing them over, in fact, to the security
services of a whole series of largely repressive regimes.

Arafat was well aware of this, I wrote. Why else would he choose to base
himself in Tunisia, the only state in the region likely to give him some
independence of thought and action? There was a price to pay, too, for
it was after all difficult to travel much further from Jerusalem than the
coffee shops of Tunis. What kind of control could he exercise from
there upon the guerrillas who would be watched and cultivated and
bullied hundreds of miles away in the hands of competing Arab nations?

Yet even then, in 1982, in the very moment of military defeat, the
idea of a Palestinian uprising on the West Bank was being talked about.
I had quite forgotten this was the case until I rediscovered my own
report of the 20 August which suggested that the creation of this new
diaspora of guerrillas from Lebanon was the reason why:

> the PLO has vowed to concentrate its attention now upon the occupied
> West Bank and Gaza, to provoke greater resistance among the Palestinian
> population there. If Israel attacked the PLO in Lebanon to clear the way
> for annexation of the West Bank and Gaza — as the PLO suspect — then
> the logical reaction of the Palestinians will be to revolutionise the occupied
> territories so that annexation is an irrelevancy.

The Palestinians would try to build upon two victories which the
PLO had achieved. Firstly, it had sucked Israel into the morass of
Lebanon where, like the Arab nations which had interfered there before,
Israel would find her military and economic strength sapped by civil war
and the hardships of occupying a foreign country. Controlling Lebanon
was going to be a far more bloody business than controlling the West
Bank and Gaza, as Israel was already discovering. Secondly, the world — or
more specifically, the United States — had seen a new face of the Middle
East in which the Israelis shelled civilians while the Palestinians appeared
more like soldiers than 'terrorists'.

Arafat's own official farewell to Beirut was obviously written for
posterity, since its message bore neither truth nor relevance to the
present. The siege of Beirut had been heroic, historic, bloody, glorious.
The Lebanese and Palestinians had been 'united under the hell of
hundreds of thousands of bombs'. Beirut had recorded 'a miracle of
heroism', it had become 'a symbol which will go down in our history'. If
this speech had been addressed to the Palestinians, it might have been
understandable, even if it arrogantly avoided any reference to the truth.
There was no reference to the hundreds of thousands of Lebanese
Muslims who had no desire for their city to be turned into a battlefield,
nor to the 'fraternal' Lebanese Muslim militias who had prepared to
defend their areas not *with* the PLO, but *against* it.

But Arafat's message of 29 August was specifically directed to the
'Lebanese masses' whose sacrifice in the PLO's war against the Israelis

had supposedly created new and eternal bonds of brotherhood. 'The fountain of Lebanese—Palestinian blood which gushed from the dust, destruction and rubble, from the massacres and tragedies, from the processions of martyrs, has affirmed the glory of steadfastness, the will to confront and the miracle of sacrifice.' At only one point did Arafat address 'those Lebanese brethren with whom we have had differences in the past', but he failed to identify these groups. Perhaps he was referring to the Shia Muslims of the south who turned against the PLO in the weeks before the Israeli invasion. Surely he was not talking about the Phalange, who could never have accepted his assurance that the Palestinians had been martyred 'in defence of Lebanon'.

The Israelis would later talk of dying for Lebanon as well as for Galilee. The Americans and the French would talk about their sacrifice for the people of Lebanon. Sacrifice was also the word used by the Syrian government when it referred to its own losses 'on behalf of sister Lebanon'. All these foreign nations had sworn — or would swear — that their young men had died *for* rather than *in* Lebanon. Rarely if ever did they ask why.

For Arafat, the issues were simple if not simplistic. Palestinians and Lebanese had died in defence of a land that would 'remain Arab through and through'. His was the path of the sleepwalker, the believer in the blood sacrifice. Those who had been steadfast in battle against the Israelis would know how to transform their 'new revolutionary awakening' into 'a beam of light and victory on the long road of pains, the road of Golgotha, towards liberated Palestine and to our noble Jerusalem'.* But Arafat was not going to Jerusalem. He was leaving Beirut on a Greek cruise ship for exile in Tunisia.

His rhetoric was an essential element in the myth that had to be established for the Palestinians as they entered the dark days of introspection and recrimination that followed their evacuation from Beirut. For in the heat of Aden and in the desert encampments south of Tunis, they would have time enough to dwell upon the consequences of their mistakes in Lebanon and to examine the nature of their betrayal — by some of their own leaders as well as by the rest of the Arab world. Military strength would soon be turned into frustration. United Nations resolutions and speeches in favour of Palestinian autonomy would mean little to men whose lives were wasting away in the camps of Syria and South Yemen.

Appropriately, the Palestinians' departure from Beirut was preceded by a symbol of death, of nine coffins bouncing in the back of a grey Red

* For Arafat's full speech to the Lebanese, see the Palestinian news agency *WAFA*, report No. 174/82, item 5 of 29 August 1982.

Cross lorry which drove at speed along the deserted, ruined quaysides of Beirut harbour. The PLO was returning Israel's dead both from this war and from earlier encounters. Four of the coffins were old. They had been stored in a building which was bombed in an Israeli air raid in July, according to PLO officials, and guerrillas had spent hours searching through the rubble for traces of the caskets. The other coffins were new, bright mahogany boxes with big brass handles, newly purchased from a west Beirut undertaker.

Accompanying the Red Cross lorry with its dead men, was a dark blue Peugeot car containing two living Israelis, Ahiaz Aharon, the pilot captured on 6 June, and an Israeli soldier who had been taken prisoner on the west Beirut perimeter during the last week of fighting. They were escorted by jeeploads of PLO 'military police' with Palestinian flags crudely painted on their white helmets. I saw Aharon at the moment of his release at Fakhani, white-faced, tired, nervous, his face breaking into a smile of relief when he caught sight of the television cameras outside the PLO's offices in Fakhani. The other Israeli prisoner looked stunned, his eyes continually straying towards the ruins of two large apartment blocks on the corner of the street which had been bombed two weeks earlier.

Aharon seemed almost unable to speak. 'I was treated very well during the whole two and one half months,' he said. When we asked him what he thought about the war, he replied with care. 'War is always a very great tragedy and I hope there will not be any more war,' he said. '. . . I always heard what happened. I had a radio. I heard Israel [radio]. I heard the BBC.' Colonel Abu Zaim, a PLO 'security' officer with close Syrian connections, put his arm around Aharon's shoulders. 'We have been taking him from place to place in order to save his life,' he announced. 'We have treated him as a human being. He has felt during his stay with us that his guards were not his guards but his friends.'

Friends? Another lie. The truth was that the PLO had always understood the importance of using prisoners as bargaining counters, knowing that Israel always tried to recover its captured soldiers and airmen. The Israelis used Palestinian and Lebanese prisoners in precisely the same way. In this case, the prisoners and the corpses were being exchanged for free passage out of Beirut, an evacuation in which the PLO had been 'allowed' by Menachem Begin to carry their personal arms with them. There was little the Israelis could do to prevent the Palestinian guerrillas carrying their rifles on their shoulders when they left. Since the Israelis did not want to fight them hand-to-hand, they had no option but to let the Palestinians leave as soldiers. Nevertheless, Begin portrayed this as an act of chivalry on his part. The PLO would be permitted to leave with honour.

Within 15 days, well over 10,000 Palestinian guerrillas and Syrian troops would be evacuated from west Beirut, guarded by American Marines, French Foreign Legionnaires and Italian Bersaglieri. Their departure was, of course, predicated on guarantees of protection for the tens of thousands of Palestinian civilians who would be left behind in Sabra, Chatila and Bourj al-Barajneh camps, assurances that had been underwritten, personally, by Philip Habib. If these promises were to be broken, then America's word — and Europe's — would be proved worthless.

Yet the sight of the first multinational force unit, a contingent of 350 French Paratroopers whose warship steered past the carcasses of half-sunken ships in Beirut port, was meant to inspire confidence in both Palestinians and Lebanese. Washington, Paris and Rome were placing their good name upon this operation. As the first Palestinians moved down to Beirut port for embarkation on 21 August, the Palestinian state-within-a-state — 12 years of semi-autonomy and often-abused freedom within the frontiers of Lebanon — came to an end.

The 400 Palestinian guerrillas provided a mind-numbing, almost grotesque demonstration of firepower as they left, shooting rifles, anti-tank rockets and mortars into the air as they passed through the Beirut streets towards the waterfront. The siege of west Beirut appeared to have ended as, once again, a major Middle East power — this time Israel — tried to prop up the Lebanese government and return it to some form of sovereignty. But this would no more be the product of Lebanese democracy than Sarkis' election back in 1976. This was to be a creation of the new *pax Israeliana*, symbolised by the installation of Bashir Gemayel.

Did we guess then what this might mean? In the weeks to come, I would look back through my notes and tape-recordings, through the video-tapes of the Palestinian departure and of Gemayel's election, running through recorded interviews and my own messages to *The Times*. Did we not understand then that the final act of the tragedy had yet to take place?

There were hints. I found that on 22 August, the second day of the PLO evacuation, the fourth sentence of my news dispatch to London included the observation that 'in the Muslim sector of Beirut, tens of thousands of Lebanese and Palestinian civilians now fear that the Lebanese Christian Phalangists — their old enemies from the civil war of 1975–6 — will turn upon their defenceless homes and take over the whole of the capital within a matter of weeks.'

Why did I write that? When, four weeks later, even these words proved to have been a totally inadequate prediction of the horrors that were to take place, I could not clearly recall why I had written them with such apparent conviction. This tell-tale but undeveloped sentence had its genesis in the scenes of grief and incomprehension that I had witnessed in west Beirut that morning as Palestinian women and children took their leave of the husbands, fathers, sons, lovers who were going into exile.

It was as if they knew something which I could not accept; that while I could transmit their knowledge, I could do so only by relating their fears — sourcing the remark to *their* analysis of the future, rather than my own. They knew something, instinctively, which I did not. In a sense, I must have known this too, but I believed — as the PLO obviously did — that an American guarantee was a promise that was meant to be kept. I prepared to go on holiday to Ireland. I had not grasped the significance of what I had written.

Perhaps we were also overwhelmed by the physical drama that was now unfolding before us. For hours every day through the hot afternoons of late August 1982, we would watch the Palestinian farewell to arms as thousands of PLO men drove in convoys of Lebanese army trucks down to the harbour. Arafat's Fatah guerrillas left in brand-new khaki uniform and *kuffiahs*, their faces cowled, rocket-propelled grenade-launchers on their backs. Begin had compared his gesture of 'allowing' the PLO to take their light arms with them to the honour afforded a defeated army in the Middle Ages. The Palestinians did their best to leave as soldiers.

But of course, they refused — outwardly — to regard themselves as vanquished. As the guerrillas journeyed slowly through the streets of west Beirut, Lebanese militiamen fired tens of thousands of rounds of ammunition into the sky, a roar that swept over the city like thunder. It was another of those historic Beirut moments, as both the Lebanese and Palestinians knew, for the PLO could scarcely return to Beirut in its present form and its guerrillas would now be scattered — as Israel always wanted them to be — across the Arab world. Many Palestinian women screamed and wept as they draped their arms around husbands and brothers who were leaving. Did *they* have some intimation of the future? Why did several guerrillas take their children with them on the boats?

Many of these men spoke of returning to Beirut, insisting that their revolution was not dead, that they had created history by holding off the Israelis. But as the lorries reached the port, the Palestinians on board smiled less. They still shouted 'Palestine Palestine' and gave the two-fingered victory sign at the last Palestinian checkpoint, a building on the dockside whence PLO snipers emerged from behind broken walls to shout their support. But round the corner at the broken gates of the harbour stood troops of the French Foreign Legion, in battledress and green berets, unsmiling, apparently indifferent to the importance of the Palestinian exodus.

The French quickly escorted the lorries across the bleak landscape of the deserted harbour to a large warehouse. From there, the Palestinians walked to the Greek Cypriot ferry boat that was to take them into exile. They were given no opportunity for last-minute gestures of defiance. Hurried onto the ship, they stood along the decks, gazing at the skyline of the great city which they had helped to ruin.

From the roof of a dockyard building almost half a mile away, Israeli troops watched the evacuation through binoculars. For them, this was not a military evacuation but the 'expulsion of terrorists'. Ariel Sharon had returned to Beirut to reaffirm that the PLO had lost the battle and that the guerrillas were leaving as defeated men. Although the port was supposed to be under exclusively French military control, several Israeli armoured vehicles remained inside the harbour area.

The Lebanese army were supposed to participate in the French security operation, but had been prevented from doing so by the Israelis. And there at the very end of my own report on 22 August was another indication that things were not quite as they seemed. When the multi-national force left Beirut, I wrote, 'the civilians of west Beirut will have only the Lebanese army to protect them ... It is not the sort of army upon which the people of the Muslim sector of the city are likely to place much reliance.'

Yet none of us, so far as I recall, even discussed the corollary of these suspicions, that the civilians of west Beirut – particularly the Palestinians – had never been so vulnerable and might therefore pay for their vulnerability with their lives. Political and journalistic instincts again came into conflict. There were the clues *in my very own words* at the time. Yet again I ignored them. Once more, political instinct prevailed over journalistic instinct.

None of my friends and colleagues on the AP could later remember any defined sense of unease at that time about what was to happen. Earleen and Nick Tatro set off for a holiday in Scotland. The war was over. I decided to leave for Ireland when the last Palestinians boarded the last boat out of Beirut. Gerry Labelle, an AP Washington staffer who had been drafted into Beirut just before the evacuation began, was to say later that it was only at the very end, when the multinational force contingents left earlier than scheduled, that he felt something might be amiss.

But Labelle himself had only been abroad twice before in his life; he had hitherto been employed covering the work of the Nuclear and Consumer Products Safety Commissions in Washington. He was 40 and his moustache showed signs of grey, yet he was wide-eyed with innocence and enthusiasm at his new responsibility of reporting the 'end' of the Lebanon war. A New Yorker who grew up in Arizona, he enjoyed gin and tonic and cigarettes, the latter being the worse of his two failings since he also suffered from chronic asthma. Labelle was a brave, gentle soul who would entertain and bore his friends with ceaseless repetition of the words of H. L. Mencken, the turn-of-the-century American journalist and magazine editor. Many of Labelle's comments were preceded by the phrase 'as my old friend H. L. Mencken would say ...' and his favourite quotation involved Mencken's premise that two things were impossible in life; just one drink, and an honest politician. We all of us should have paid more heed to Mencken's second proposition.

Day after day, we watched the Palestinians leave in the same chaotic, dismal, illusory journey to the docks. I knew some of them. But when I found them in the lines of men – emotional, afraid to talk lest they broke down – they were different people, less anxious to describe the future, mouthing words they had heard rather than thought about. There was Mustapha, the PLO man who had taken me to the school for little guerrillas in Damour six long years before, thinner now, less arrogant, leading his two small boys to the lorry that would take them to Beirut port. They were seven and eight years old, dressed in khaki, weighed down by the automatic weapons that Mustapha had slung over their shoulders. They were not to be allowed to forget this day. Mustapha smiled in an embarrassed way. Yes, he was sad. No, he did not know what would happen in the future. Of course the PLO would survive. He was glad to be asked no more questions.

Maher was less deferential. He was not the same Maher that I remembered from our meeting five weeks earlier. Then he had sat on a small stool in Ouzai, smoking cigarettes through his holder as he explained the principles of revolution, of 'confrontation' and 'liquidation'. Now he was perspiring under a steel helmet, a protection I never saw him wear under fire. A new black and white *kuffiah* scarf was round his neck, and he seemed to feel he was on stage, an actor in a tragedy in which he should really have had no part. Yes, there would be a Palestine, he said. The struggle would go on. But I could tell he doubted this because he spoke with hesitation and weariness, stunned by what was at last happening to the PLO.

He seemed to be on the verge of tears. Others went beyond this; not just the Palestinian women and girls who cried as they kissed their husbands farewell, but the Lebanese who came to watch their departure, men and women who had – unlike most other Muslims in west Beirut – felt some deep sympathy for the Palestinian cause, partly because it was to them an essentially *Arab* cause. I discovered an old friend, a restaurant waiter who had adopted seven Palestinian orphans, wandering aimlessly between the lorries as the guerrillas climbed aboard. He was well, he said. All his family had survived the bombardments.

He was looking at something over my shoulder where a garbage tip was burning, and when I turned round I saw a guerrilla a few yards away kissing a small baby, its mother with her head in her hands, an older woman raising her arms towards the man's face, an El Greco of beseeching eyes and hands. And when I turned back, my friend was weeping uncontrollably. He was not lamenting an individual's fate.

There was something far deeper than that at stake in the bomb-damaged sports field where the PLO men gathered, its floor littered with Israeli shrapnel and its rubbish heaps stinking in the heat. The emotional speeches played some part in it, for they spoke of Palestine and Jerusalem and listed the Palestinian camps in Lebanon that had been destroyed, from the days of the civil war until the air raids of the past weeks which finally broke Sabra, Chatila and Bourj al-Barajneh. The speeches were not just about the endurance of the Palestinians; they were about Arabism, about being an Arab, which is why no one there spoke with any bitterness about the Arab countries which refused to help them but to which the Palestinian guerrillas were now going into exile.

Perhaps that is why the Palestinians did not leave Beirut as soldiers, much as they obviously wished to do so. Despite their new uniforms, their steel helmets, the fresh webbing on their rifles, these men left as guerrillas, exulting in the discharge of rifle fire that spread across Beirut in farewell. They passed down the streets of Fakhani, of Corniche Mazraa, of Kantari, like men in a dream, enveloped in sound as thousands of teenagers – gunmen, soldiers, militiamen, 'terrorists', by whatever name their friends and enemies chose to call them – fired into the air as if in defiance of one last, heavenly air strike.

It was meant to be an epic departure but somehow it failed to be. Driving down to the port, amid the truckloads of guerrillas, one felt it had more in common with Fellini or Coppola, a passage through a place of ruins, of gunfire so loud it made our heads sing, of ever-burning garbage tips and flies. One gunman loosed off a stream of bullets that cut through one of the PLO lorries, hitting a guerrilla on board, blasting through his chin and blowing his brains onto the street. Near Kantari, a black limousine pulled level with my car and from it emerged Walid Jumblatt. Before I even had time to speak to him, he was out of his car, waving an automatic rifle over his head and firing off round after round above an apartment block, his eyes focused on the sky, his mouth framed into an open, endless smile. Round the corner stood George Habash; he too was smiling, pumping the hands of gunmen who wandered up to him, dodging the cascades of rice – that traditional form of greeting and farewell – as they fell like hailstones around us.

It was at one and the same time both sad and monstrous that gunfire should always – even now – be the most familiar voice of the Palestinians. There were children with huge pistols, firing them at walls, there were militiamen blazing away with short-range anti-aircraft shells that made the ground shake and the air momentarily heavy. Young guerrillas took pictures from beside the road. How many of them would have stayed to die had they been given the choice, how many understood what was happening, how many had done terrible things in Lebanon these past seven years since the civil war gave the Palestinians such power?

At the port entrance, Lebanese guerrillas in pink and blue and yellow battledress and camouflage smocks ran onto the rubbish dumps that lined the seafront, firing rocket-launchers and throwing hand grenades into the sea as the bullets skittered up the walls. A girl, a lovely, small, delicate figure in a cowboy hat, shrieked with laughter at a man who had collapsed with a rifle in his hands. Was it for all this that so many men and women and children had died so terribly since June?

On the other side of the port, in east Beirut, the Maronites saw logic in these events. On 23 August, they celebrated the fruit of their alliance with Israel, the election of Bashir Gemayel as president of Lebanon. There was no surprise. By now, his elevation was assured. He was Israel's man. The election was held in the Lebanese army's military academy at Fayadiye on the hills above east Beirut, and most of the assembly members acquiesced in the pre-ordained parts which they were expected to play. Generally clad in glistening white suits, the deputies arrived in dark Cadillacs surrounded by squads of bodyguards carrying automatic rifles, pistols, grenades and rocket-launchers.

Camille Chamoun had made a faint effort to oppose the Phalangist candidate by publicly suggesting to potential prime ministers that Bashir Gemayel might not be quite the sort of man they would wish to serve. But throughout the parliamentary session, he sat next to the emaciated figure of Pierre Gemayel, the proud father, the Phalangist founder who was at last able to enjoy the fulfilment of his life. At times like these, the *zaim* understood the meaning of national unity.

It was a quintessentially Lebanese affair. Most of the parliament members who had turned up were Maronites and Shia Muslims, but when they discovered that they had failed to achieve the 62-man quorum for their meeting, hurried telephone calls were made to some of the 30 deputies who had somehow forgotten the election. At lunchtime, therefore, long after the session should have been concluded, four elderly MPs arrived at the barracks, physically assisted into the building by large and extremely well-armed men. Security officials screamed at journalists that they should not take pictures of the members being hustled so unceremoniously into the chamber. Such scenes might be misunderstood outside Lebanon.*

Having thus been duly reminded of their democratic duties, the deputies gave the session a quorum, and on the second vote Bashir

---

* The subtleties – or otherwise – of Lebanon's unicameral parliament could not disguise the fact that many Sunni members of the assembly had boycotted the sitting. Of those members who did attend, three left their voting slips blank during the first round of voting and a fourth submitted the name of Raymond Edde, a liberal Maronite who lived in self-imposed exile in Paris and who was not even a candidate. In the aftermath of Gemayel's election, Lebanese gunmen in west Beirut set fire to the homes of eleven of the assembly members who had voted for him, killing a 15-year-old boy after mistaking him for the son of a deputy.

Gemayel, gunman, militia leader, controller of the largest private army in Lebanon, the man who had stared so moodily and with such longing down upon Beirut on that hot August day back in 1980, was elected president of his country. One day, he had told me then, there would have to be a resolution. 'Sooner or later, we will have to fight a war of liberation.' But now there was no need for such a war. The Israelis had won the war for the Phalange. Now there would be no partition. Now Lebanon could be united. Bashir Gemayel would be in the palace at Baabda, sitting around the 'card table' to which he had so sarcastically referred at that hilltop luncheon two years earlier.

If power conferred respectability, the Lebanese took this formula to their hearts. Even Saeb Salam, we now heard, was prepared to consider the prime ministership under Gemayel. In west Beirut that very day, Gemayel's picture appeared in the streets. There was Bashir, the people's leader, smiling benevolently down upon Hamra Street. Shopkeepers pasted his portrait on their windows.

Scarcely had Kamel Asaad, the parliament speaker, announced Gemayel's victory than machine-gun fire could be heard through the windows of the chamber. Outside, several Phalangists in white shirts were firing a heavy-calibre machine-gun from the top of a jeep, loud enough to drown out the words of the deputies. A few minutes later, seven Israeli Merkava tanks slithered and cut their way up the road towards Baabda from east Beirut; pasted to the turrets of each one was a newly printed poster of President-elect Gemayel, pictures of a slightly chubby, charming young man in a sober suit and tie. A diplomat and statesman, no longer a gunman, courtesy of the Israeli army.

Yet Bashir Gemayel's relations with the Israelis were at best cautious, at worst permeated with deepest suspicion. Many times he had said that every square kilometre of Lebanon should be free of foreign domination and he now made it clear that this included the Israelis. On a secret visit to Israel, he was confronted by Begin and Sharon, both of whom demanded a formal peace treaty between Lebanon and Israel before the end of the year. So this was why Lebanon had been invaded.

Gemayel believed that the two men were bullying him. Begin thought that having established the Phalange in political power, it was time to call in Israel's debts, unaware that in Lebanon it is always the *Lebanese* who decide on the payment. One of Gemayel's lieutenants was later to tell me how Bashir had returned from the meeting in Israel, denouncing Begin as a trickster. 'The way he spoke to me was as if I was a vassal,' the Phalangist quoted Gemayel as saying. 'Begin called me "boy", but I am the president of Lebanon.'*

---

* A remarkably similar Israeli version of the encounter between Gemayel and Begin appears in Schiff and Ya'ari, *Israel's Lebanon War*, pp. 234–6, where Gemayel is quoted as later telling his father Pierre that Begin 'treated me like a child!'

Nor was Gemayel going to allow the Israelis to propel him into a war against the Syrians. Two days after his election, Damascus radio stated that Syrian troops would only be withdrawn from Lebanon when the last Israeli soldier left the country, while a military official in Damascus was quoted as saying that if 'Sheikh Bashir Gemayel' — a polite term of address which the Syrians did not usually apply to the Phalangist leader — concluded a peace agreement with the Israelis, 'Syria will consider herself to be in a state of war with him.'

The Americans at least gave Bashir Gemayel their blessing. If he was Israel's candidate, then he would be America's too. He had talked often in the past of the 'internationalisation' of Beirut, of securing the help of the major Western powers to restore Lebanese sovereignty. Now it seemed as if that support was forthcoming. On 25 August, American Marines landed in Lebanon for the first time since 1958 and within seven hours were shepherding PLO guerrillas onto the evacuation ships which were to take them north to the Syrian port of Tartous. Seven warships of the US Sixth Fleet rode at anchor off Beirut port while the French Foreign Legionnaires deployed through the ruins of the front line to the museum and newly arrived Italian troops took up position along the west Beirut perimeter at Galerie Semaan. Here was Arafat's 'disengagement force' in action.

It was just after five in the morning that the first of 800 men from the 32nd Marine Amphibious Unit came ashore by landing craft at the port. Colonel James Mead, a former fighter-bomber pilot in Vietnam, stood before his men under a red and gold banner 300 yards from the Palestinian front line, surrounded by photographers and correspondents.

A few minutes later, Captain Robert Johnstone, a Scottish-born US Marine officer, walked casually across the lines to the western side of the port where he saluted and shook hands with Lieutenant-Colonel Basagh Zarab of the Palestine Liberation Army. The two men stood shoulder to shoulder, answering questions from journalists, Johnstone emphasising that he was there as part of an international force but innocently insisting that his meeting with the Palestinian officer was a good thing if it helped to bring a settlement to Lebanon. Zarab, in battledress and red beret with PLO flashes on his sleeve, suggested that America would be doing Israel's job in Beirut even if the United States was part of the disengagement force. But he also said that he never thought he would see the day in which he would shake hands with an American Marine officer. It was the nearest the United States would come in 1982 to recognising the PLO.

Johnstone became a celebrity; Zarab was forgotten. But next morning, I returned to see Zarab, down in the cavernous ruins of the old front line. Labelle came too because he had never before seen this place of darkness that defined so much about Lebanon and its suffering. The US Marines

were to move up the line in a few hours but Zarab was still there with
his guerrillas, ritually holding his positions until the Americans arrived.
He laughed at us because he did not understand why we wanted to talk
to him rather than the Americans.

'Why do you not have a gun?' he asked. I took out my pen. This is
my gun. Zarab chuckled. He produced a small black pistol from his belt
and pointed it at my head. 'Which is more powerful?' The gun. Joke.
Then he told us to follow him up the street.

How well I knew this place. There was the top of the Fattal building
and rue Trablos where the gunboy had treated me with disdain as he sat
on his twisted office chair in 1976. I walked past the front of the
malodorous back entrance to the postal sorting office through which I
had padded so long before. Zarab took us into a tottering ruin upon
whose bullet-scarred façade were the words 'Opera Cinema'. 'Come with
me,' he said. It seemed to be our fate in Lebanon, following gunmen
who said 'Come with me' and then clambering deeper and deeper into
muck and rubble.

In the gloom of the interior, we could make out the faces of other
Palestinians, sitting on mattresses on the floor. But Zarab took us
straight across to some very narrow wooden slits that had been built into
a mountain of rusting oildrums and sandbags at the far end of the
building. We were behind what would have been the cinema screen;
sunlight streamed through the wooden apertures. Through them, we
could see undergrowth, a forest of bushes and trees spreading far across
what had once been Martyrs' Square.

In the semi-darkness, Zarab turned to us and said slowly: 'No one has
been allowed to see inside this place before. We fought here. But the
war is over. Will you help me to destroy all this?' So together Zarab,
Labelle and I put our shoulders to the cement-filled oildrums and
sandbags and pushed for several seconds, hard, our feet scraping and
skidding on the rubbish that was strewn on the floor. It began to shift,
ponderously, a grudging movement in which the whole mass of heavy
drums and bags of sand, congealed together by the years, swayed away
and then moved back towards us, resisting our pressure.

But the second time we pushed, it moved away and hung at a slight
angle for a few more seconds until with a roar, the whole machine-gun
nest – built by the Palestinians in fear and hatred four years earlier –
suddenly gave way, collapsing forward and spilling over into the square.
We coughed in the muck and dust that poured through the cavern of
light that we had opened up. There before us was the moonscape plaza
into which no one had dared walk since 1978. And beyond, through the
dust, dangled the triangular cedar tree flag of the Phalange.

We stared at each other, not quite sure what would happen. But there
were no shots from the other side of Martyrs' Square. The war really

was over. Below us, in the sewage-smeared street, another Palestinian climbed onto a barricade and pushed the staff of a large Lebanese flag between the sandbags on the top, to symbolise that the PLO were indeed handing back Lebanon's sovereignty. It had been intended as a private occasion, witnessed only by the Palestinians themselves, so Zarab watched to see if we understood the significance of the ceremony.

In 1976, I had also stood here, watching the Palestinians emerge from the ruins across this road, embracing the Syrian soldiers who had arrived in Beirut, crying as they put their arms around the army of 'peace-keepers' who had come to occupy the city. On that occasion, I had approached the line from the Phalangist side. Now I had watched its dismantling – participated in its destruction – alongside the Palestinians. Could I really have thought this *was* the end of the Lebanon war? I used those words in my report that night. 'The war really was over,' I said in my dispatch.

In a few hours, the American Marines would be here and Zarab would then leave on the overland evacuation to Damascus. He held out his hand. 'Find me when you come to Syria,' he said. 'I will not be returning here.' So he wrote down a telephone number in Syria and walked off to inspect a squad of his men who were piling their kitbags in the street. Almost 4,000 Palestinian guerrillas had now left Beirut.

A Red Cross ship, the *Flora*, had already put to sea, bound for Athens with hundreds of wounded Palestinians aboard, many of them without legs or arms. They had been taken through the streets of west Beirut in convoys of ambulances with sirens howling and were greeted – despite Red Cross appeals for silence – with volleys of gunfire from PLO men who had not yet left the city. Already, nine people had been killed and 27 wounded by stray bullets during the farewell shooting of the last five days.

Along their way to the harbour, the latest evacuees had passed along the seafront Corniche where their colleagues fired mortars into the Mediterranean. A convoy of French troops, travelling in the opposite direction, paused beside the road to watch the Palestinians go by. The PLO men had adorned their trucks with pictures of Arafat, Lenin, Marx and Lebanese socialist leaders of lesser repute. A French officer gave a two-finger victory sign at a truckload of DFLP men and received a *kuffiah* scarf by way of return. The Foreign Legionnaire tossed a box of cigars to the Palestinian.

It was the Italians who that day received another of those signals which, had we heeded them, might have made us more cautious about the 'end' of the war. The Italian contingent landed at the port and made their way through west Beirut to Galerie Semaan, where they set up a checkpoint at the roofless church of Saint Michel at Boulevard Ariss, the street on which Cody and I had watched the Syrians arrive back in 1976.*

No sooner had the Italians deployed at Galerie Semaan than the local PLO commander and his colleagues from the Shia Amal militia refused to withdraw their men from the Boulevard. It took the Italians five hours to talk them off the road, but even then the Shia gunmen would only allow the Italians to enter one building on the corner of the street. Captain Corrado Cantatore, the Italian military attaché who was also a UN officer, refused to accept this. 'Excuse me,' he told the bearded Palestinian officer, 'but the rules are quite clear. You must be at least two hundred metres from us. You will have to ask Abu Walid [the PLO's chief of staff] and he will tell you.'

But the Palestinian would not be consoled. He walked to within six inches of Cantatore's face and shouted at him. *'There is going to be trouble,'* he said. *'Bashir Gemayel has just been made president and when the Italians go, his men will invade here. Why should the Lebanese militias retreat now and give him ground?'*

Again, I wrote down this man's words in my notepad. I even quoted him – in full – in my report, which was published prominently on the following day. But I also sent the paper details of my holiday plans and received a message back from John Grant, the managing editor, thanking me for my work 'now that the Lebanon war is virtually over'.

Another warning sign. On the 27th of August, I was standing at the roundabout at Hazmiyeh, waiting for the Syrian army's evacuation column to stream across from Galerie Semaan. An English woman from a British Zionist organisation approached me, holding a tape-recorder. Why had the Western press fabricated the reports of casualties during the Israeli siege of Beirut? she demanded to know. I explained, slowly and in detail, why the figures were correct; to no avail. Why was the press so anti-semitic? I told her, politely, that this was not true, that we could not ourselves falsify the number of casualties, making them lower than they actually were, just because the Israelis and their supporters might slander us with smears of anti-semitism if we did not.

* The Italians were to prove by far the most conscientious of the international troops in the multinational force but their initial arrival was inauspicious. When their first landing craft ground alongside the harbour wall, the doors of the vessel proved to be locked and for several minutes correspondents on the quayside could hear the luckless sharpshooters of the Governolo Regiment hammering on the doors to get out. When they did eventually emerge into the bright Mediterranean sunlight, they were rather surprisingly accoutred with white helmets decorated with large black feathers, and armoured vehicles that were also painted a virgin white. In retrospect, we would come to realise that the Italians did truly represent a peace-keeping force – that the white paint was genuinely representative of their intentions – while the Americans and French preferred to bring ashore trucks in camouflage paint filled with boxes of ammunition. The Italians brought with them two lorryloads of pasta so that their soldiers – in the imperishable words of their commanding officer, Lieutenant-Colonel Bruno Tosetti – would be 'completely self-supporting'.

Then the woman began to talk rather than ask questions. She spoke of her worries about the discipline of the Israeli army, of how some soldiers had been corrupted by the war, of how her cousin who was an Israeli soldier had been appalled to see his comrades looting a house. And she spoke about the Phalange. Her fear, she said, was that the Phalange might enter west Beirut once the PLO had left. 'I know they are the allies of Israel but I don't trust them,' she said. I said that I thought there would be bloodshed if they were permitted into the camps. She agreed.

But how did the Lebanese react to this epic of defeat? Above Bhamdoun, the Druze had gathered beneath the pine trees well before six o'clock in the morning to watch the procession. There were perhaps 400 villagers, young men and women, parents and a few grandmothers who sat on rugs on the hard ground, dressed in black and knitting with pure white wool. Some of the families had brought small stoves that hissed and sputtered beneath jugs of Arabic coffee while their children played around them, watching the dawn rise over the mountains as if it was a public holiday. Almost every family played a transistor radio, alert to the commentator's every word on the progress of the Syrian and Palestinian convoy from Beirut.

And when it could eventually be made out three miles away on the mountainside – an endless line of slow-moving trucks following two white jeeps – there was an air of strange anticipation among the Druze people of Bhamdoun. They stood and grasped their sacks of rice long before the first Italian soldiers in those jeeps led the convoy up the road past the pine forest. These Druze had never loved the Palestinians but they feared the Phalangists who had replaced the Syrians in their mountain town. The Israelis watched through field-glasses from behind the trees.

There was just the slightest reticence among the family groups at the sight of the first lorry, crowded with Syrian troops in full battledress, in steel helmets and with rifles raised above their heads, a moment of discretion that the Lebanese always observed when watched by a new army of occupation. But then it burst from them. 'Palestine–Assad, Palestine–Assad,' the men at the front chorused and the young Syrian troops, moving in military defeat through the territory of their conquerors, roared back 'Palestine, Palestine', as if they were on a victory parade.

There were photographs of President Hafez al-Assad on the first trucks but then the image changed, inevitably, to that of Yassir Arafat. The men aboard were now dressed in the green fatigues of the Palestine Liberation Army, the PLO's regular soldiers, their faces masks of excitement, chanting Arafat's name, screaming 'Victory for Palestine' as if they were travelling towards a homeland rather than moving into a second exile. As the lorries drew level with the forest, the people there threw handfuls of rice onto the soldiers and guerrillas. It was the same old salute to departing friends, albeit ones who had invited themselves into Lebanon and who had – many of them – treated it so cruelly those past seven years.

There were hundreds of them, one and a half thousand in all, driving up the mountains on vehicles laden with stores and boxes of ammunition and rocket-launchers, motorcycles and bedding, the lorries so decrepit that while some still showed the battalion markings of the Syrian army's 85th Brigade, they had to be towed by smaller vehicles. The Israelis chose to ignore them, their patrols driving between the evacuation trucks, their soldiers not raising their eyes to see the red, white, black and green Palestinian banners floating over them. When the guerrillas passed through Bhamdoun town, some of them caught sight of the blue and white Star of David flag hanging over the road and they turned and spat on the ground in front of it. This was not just an army leaving the enclave of west Beirut, but men who carried their hatred along with the memory of their own suffering in the city's ten-week siege.

Up the highway, enthusiasm for the Palestinians was less evident. An Israeli army officer in civilian clothes and a white floppy hat watched the convoy pass with distaste. 'I am glad they are leaving,' he said. What did he think of them leaving as self-assumed victors? 'What can we do about it?' he asked, and then we heard shooting round the corner where the troops on the Syrian forward line opposite the Israelis were welcoming their fellow soldiers from Beirut. 'Ah,' said the Israeli, 'they have started their fantasia.'

But there was not much reverie across that mountain front line. The Syrians stood along the roadway above the ravines, through Mdeirej and all the way down to Chtaura, firing their rifles in the air, but, driving alongside the convoy, I could watch the emotions changing. Palestinians who had bellowed their joy while travelling through occupied territory now relaxed into silence as they jolted down the twisting road to the Bekaa, their faces tired, washed out, trying to comprehend the new future which was at hand in Syria, even though many of them had been trained there.

Thousands of Palestinian guerrillas from all over the Bekaa had gathered in Chtaura to welcome the evacuees with rifle and anti-aircraft fire, a lunatic bawl of sound from a rabble of gunmen. But among the Syrian soldiers arriving from Beirut was General Mohamed Zahran, the Syrian army's deputy garrison commander in the Lebanese capital, grinning at his men from his Range Rover but then suddenly forgetting them as a Syrian government car drew up next to him and a little boy in a brown shirt – he could have been no more than five years old – stepped out next to him.

General Zahran seized his son in his arms and there among his men he broke down and wept, sobbing tears across the child's face and down his shirt, his shoulders shaking with relief. With the little boy in his arms, he led the remnants of his 85th Brigade back to Damascus, where the Syrian government had promised them the 'usual welcome' for victorious soldiers. A few days later, Assad disbanded the 85th Brigade in disgrace.

Another warning sign. On 29 August, there was a second overland evacuation. On this occasion, the Israelis drove much closer to the Palestinians and some of the PLO men made obscene gestures at the Israeli flags at Galerie Semaan. Others leaned over the side of the trucks and smiled at the Israelis; a number of Israeli soldiers cheerfully waved back at their Palestinian enemies. But that afternoon a new demand was reported to have come from the Israelis. General Rafael Eitan, the Israeli chief of staff, now wanted the Mourabitoun militia evacuated from west Beirut. Why?

They were not Palestinians but Lebanese Sunnis. Their withdrawal from the city was never part of Philip Habib's evacuation plan. How could Lebanese be evacuated from Lebanon — even if the Israelis felt no compunction about expelling Palestinians from the West Bank? Why did Eitan want the Sunni militia out of west Beirut? There were, after all, no plans to evacuate the Phalange from *east* Beirut. Later, it was explained, Eitan had been misquoted. He merely wanted the west Beirut Lebanese militias removed from the perimeter front line. Why?

Arafat left on 30 August, in the style to which he was accustomed: in chaos, emotion, semi-dignity and the sound of gunfire. Surrounded by guerrillas, camera crews, French Legionnaires, diplomats and American Marines, he was carried on a wave of hysteria through the streets to the port. No leave-taking was ever quite like it.

I perched on top of one of Zarab's abandoned concrete emplacements beside the harbour gate to watch him go. It was the only vantage point from which I could see Arafat. He had had at least a month to prepare for this final departure. It must have been morally as well as psychologically repugnant to him; he must have struggled hard to transform humiliation into celebration. Arafat was putting a brave face on the unthinkable. But he *had* to believe in the invincibility which he had created with words. In defeat, he had drawn the architecture of victory, and now he looked with reverence upon his construction. He had persuaded himself that what he wished to be true, was true. He was a dogged, stubborn man.

Arafat's face was glazed in an expression somewhere between ecstasy and fanaticism as he walked the few last, muddy yards to the harbour past an honour guard of PLO guerrillas, drawn up three deep, rifles at present-arms, in the rubble of what had been the PLO's front line. He saluted the two PLO banners lowered towards him and then, his *kuffiah* bobbing above the mob of gunmen, soldiers and reporters, he was crushed unceremoniously into a black limousine and driven to the quayside for his journey into exile – under escort by American Marines.

He had driven to the port in Chafiq Wazzan's black, bullet-proof car and stopped on his way to talk to Jumblatt at the Druze leader's town house at Mseitbeh. 'I am leaving to continue the struggle so that we can win,' he told a mob of journalists in Jumblatt's hallway. 'I am very proud because we had the honour to defend this part of Beirut ... I am leaving this city but my heart is here.' Asked to which Arab nation he was travelling, he replied: 'Palestine.'

Mahmoud Labadi was down at the port, still sporting his pistol and with a lieutenant's insignia on his khaki shirt; it had been sewn onto his lapel overnight by his American wife. 'We have to look smart,' he said. No worries now about public relations, about the presentation of Arafat's world view. History would take care of the next few minutes. 'Are we sad? Of course, we are sad. Abu Ammar [Arafat] is sad. What do you think we feel?'

The PLO announced that it was still looking for an Arab capital that would 'offer the same as Beirut', a statement that must have sent a chill through the citizens of any capital which Arafat and his colleagues deemed worthy of their presence. For if anything characterised the PLO leader's last journey through Beirut, it was the contrast between Arafat's exultant face and the destruction all around him. The PLO had helped to bring this upon the city. As he drove to the harbour, Arafat did not look at the ruins.

As he approached the French lines at the port, he was briefly distracted by several explosions low over the sea. A Lebanese militiaman was firing his grenade-launcher at the waves. The American Marines were in flak jackets and the French stood with machine-guns on top of the nearest warehouses. A few ambassadors – French, Greek, Italian and North Korean – arrived hurriedly to pay their respects to the departing PLO chairman, while 600 yards away the Israeli army, which still regarded Arafat as no more than a terrorist, studied his movements in silence from a factory roof.

Almost pushed off his feet by French camera crews, Arafat was quite unable to inspect the Palestinian honour parade. Lebanese militia officers who held their respective banners out to him were ignored.

It was perfectly in keeping with all that had gone before. This was drama of a kind which Arafat understood. It was as if he needed to play this role. As the Greek ferry *Atlantis*, carrying Arafat away from Beirut for the last time, cleared the lighthouse on the harbour wall, the vessel gave a low, two-minute blast on its horn. Arafat, standing on the foredeck with several hundred of his guerrillas, could be seen giving a two-finger victory sign towards the receding shoreline of Beirut but was then lost in the haze as the ship pulled out to the open sea, protected by the grey shapes of two American warships. By three in the afternoon, they were over the horizon, only a thin, dark smudge of smoke to mark their passage.

But Arafat understood something about Lebanon, perhaps even about his own lapse of responsibility in the country in which he had based himself for 12 years. For as the evening closed around the *Atlantis*, Arafat sat in a chair on the deck and read to the guerrillas lying on the wooden boards around him. In his hands he held not the Koran but the Bible, and the PLO leader read to his guerrillas from verse 17 of chapter 2 of the Old Testament Book of Habbakuk:

For the violence done to Lebanon shall sweep over you, the havoc done to its beasts shall break your own spirit, because of bloodshed and violence done to the land, to the city and all its inhabitants.

This, he felt, would now be the fate of the Israelis.

The mournful evacuations continued for two days after Arafat's departure. The last units of the Syrian 85th Brigade left by road on 30 August, a convoy of broken military vehicles and shrapnel-scratched armour that made its way through the Israeli lines at Galerie Semaan in silence with none of the festivities that had hitherto attended such events. There were ten old T-54 tanks on transporters – two of them apparently damaged beyond repair – and a score of armoured vehicles whose Syrian crews sat grim-faced aboard the vehicles as they passed the Israeli flags.

It was an ignominious passage of arms. The Syrians even had to face Major Haddad. The Israelis had brought him up to Beirut and he stood on the roundabout at Hazmiyeh watching the first Syrian flat-bed trucks moving slowly across the line from Galerie Semaan. Did he really think the Palestinians and Syrians were defeated, I asked him? He looked at me scornfully. 'I see the march of victory in the Syrian defeat,' he shouted. 'Why do you think they are withdrawing? They are not going for tourism purposes. This is part of our victory.'

And when the first tank was hauled past Haddad, one of the Syrian soldiers – mistaking him for an ordinary onlooker – waved his hand. Haddad stepped forward, pointed to the man, and then jerked the third finger of his right hand contemptuously towards the ground. Fuck you. He went on making obscene gestures at the Syrians, encouraging Lebanese soldiers to do the same. Many of them complied. When a Syrian truck loaded down with furniture passed the Christians up the road, there was a burst of slow, ironic applause. 'They have been looting even now,' Haddad said.

The PLO's heavy weapons – their field artillery and Katyushas – were supposed to have been handed over to the Lebanese army, but those same guns now appeared in the hands of Amal and the Mourabitoun. The militias were actively preparing to defend west Beirut from the

Israelis and the Phalange. Another sign. The last shipload of Palestinian guerrillas left Beirut port on the morning of 1 September, allowing Caspar Weinberger, the American defence secretary, to turn up in Beirut to claim an operational victory for the Marines.*

Surrounded by almost half the 800 US Marine contingent – for this was, of course, a photo-opportunity as well as a political message – the defence secretary announced that the mission of the multinational force in Beirut was 'practically speaking ... pretty well completed'. The Israeli army was supposed to have left the area of the harbour, but four Israeli armoured vehicles could be seen only 400 yards from Weinberger, their crews watching him through binoculars. They were not supposed to be there. Weinberger did not appear to notice them. US Defence Department officials could provide no explanation for the Israeli presence.

---

* Such was the chaos of the evacuation that the exact total of Palestinians and Syrian forces withdrawn from west Beirut has, typically, never been resolved. Precise statistics were also difficult to obtain because some PLO men took wives and friends with them on the boats, others delayed their scheduled departure and the multinational force refused to give the daily figures for evacuees. By 27 August, I calculated from information given to me privately by Italian officers that 6,764 guerrillas had left Beirut, and by the 29th that 9,100 had been evacuated. The final statistic included a further one thousand evacuees by sea and at least another thousand by land, totalling more than 11,100.

Randal puts the overall figure at 'more than eight thousand guerrillas, thirty-five hundred members of the regular Palestine Liberation Army, and twenty-seven hundred Syrians' (*The Tragedy of Lebanon*, p. 271), making a total of 14,200. Schiff and Ya 'ari provide a similar total of 14,398, including 664 women and children, of whom 8,144 left by sea, and 6,254 Syrian soldiers and members of the Palestine Liberation Army overland along the Beirut–Damascus highway (*Israel's Lebanon War*, p. 228). In *Reason Not the Need: Eyewitness Chronicles of Israel's War in Lebanon* (Spokesman books for the Bertrand Russell Peace Foundation, London, 1984), the total figure is given as only 8,185 (pp. 95–7). Contemporary reports spoke of plans for 15,000 Palestinian guerrillas and Syrian soldiers to be evacuated (see, for example, *Monday Morning* (Beirut), 30 August – 5 September 1982). Chafiq Wazzan, the Lebanese prime minister, corrected this figure to 12,000 (*Monday Morning*, 6–12 September 1982).

I reported the following evacuee figures: on 21 August, 262 members of the regular Palestine Liberation Army (Badr Brigade) by sea en route to Jordan and 135 members of the 'Arab Liberation Front' en route to Iraq; on 22 August, 800 members of the PLA's Ein Jallout Brigade, 200 members of the PFLP–GC and Fatah guerrillas taken by sea en route to Jordan, Iraq and Syria; on 23 August, 700 men of DFLP and PFLP, by sea en route to Tunisia, Iraq and South Yemen; on 24 August, 900 member of Fatah and DFLP by sea en route for Syria, South Yemen and Sudan; on 25 August, 1,160 members of DFLP, Saiqa and Fatah by sea to Syria and Sudan; on 26 August, 697 members of Fatah, PLA and DFLP, including wounded; on 27 August, 1,500 PLA (Hittin Brigade), Fatah guerrillas and troops of Syrian 85th Brigade overland to Damascus and 600 PLA and Fatah men by sea; on 28 August, 700 DFLP and PFLP guerrillas by sea to Tartous in Syria (including Habash, Hawatmeh, and Ahmed Jibril of the PFLP–GC); on 29 August, 2,400 PLO evacuees, of whom 1,200 were PLA (Qadisiyeh Brigade) who travelled overland to Syria and 700 Fatah, who left by sea.

This total of 10,054 was augmented by at least 600 Palestinians who left by sea with Arafat on 30 August, 1,200 Syrian troops who left overland on the same day, a further 1,000 PLO men on 31 August and approximately 600 more by sea on 1 September. This made a total of 12,254 evacuees, although figures for the last three days may have been exaggerated. At least 10,000 Palestinian guerrillas remained in eastern and northern Lebanon – especially around Tripoli – in those areas which still lay under Syrian military control.

Weinberger seemed to think that the problems of Lebanon could be solved with a political programme, mutual trust and a strong dose of common sense. This was what we used to call the American 'one—two—three' school of politics in the Middle East; military action, followed by political aims followed by a solution. Never a settlement, always a solution. In retrospect, Weinberger's press conference on the Beirut quayside was ironic, almost macabre.

Reagan had earlier suggested the basis of a new American peace plan for the Middle East, involving Palestinian self-government on the West Bank and in Gaza in association with Jordan, with Jerusalem undivided but its status open to negotiation. Begin had indignantly rejected the plan, suggesting that the US administration was trying to bring down the Israeli government as it had once brought down the Allende government in Chile. Weinberger appeared unaware of Begin's extraordinary response and a US Embassy official had to ask journalists to lend him news agency reports of Begin's reaction to show to the defence secretary.

'The President is discussing with Prime Minister Begin and others the way to solve the long-term problem because what we have just completed today is phase one,' Weinberger said. 'Phase two is getting all the foreign forces out of Lebanon and phase three is of course the solution — if it can be found and I'm confident it can — to the Palestinian problem as opposed to just the PLO, and I think that is something that is an absolute essential if we are to have anything like a permanent peace.'

One—two—three. Just like that. Even then, we were amazed at the naivety of Weinberger's words, let alone those of Reagan, whose message to the Marine unit in Beirut announced: 'We are now on the eve of achieving what we set forth to accomplish: an end to the bloodshed in Beirut and the re-establishment of Lebanese government sovereignty over their capital.' With the Israelis watching from within the port perimeter — in clear violation of the disengagement agreement — and with Lebanon's 40-strong military contingent in the harbour outnumbered by the Marines, such Lebanese sovereignty as might exist seemed very brittle indeed.

As usual, the Palestinians had been implicitly blamed for the Middle East conflict — Weinberger referred not to the Palestinian—Israeli problem but to 'the Palestinian problem' — and his conviction that peace would return to Lebanon was founded on two very dangerous contentions. 'The Syrians,' he said, 'have told many people that they wish to leave and go back home, as the Israelis have told us that they wish to leave and go home, that they do not covet or want a single inch of Lebanese territory.' Who were these 'people' to whom the Syrians had declared their desire to withdraw? And if the Israelis wished to go, why were they still in Beirut? Why were they watching this performance from 400 yards away, in total breach of their promises? Not a single inch of

Lebanese territory did they want. That is what the Syrians always claimed. Lebanon was beginning to cast its spell over the Americans too.

And us. Labelle promised he would call me in Ireland if he thought there was any need for me to return to Beirut. Next day, I took the boat to Cyprus from where I had a booking on a flight to Europe. Offshore, an Israeli gunboat forced the ferry to stop engines for two hours while the passengers sweated on the decks. 'Don't take pictures,' the passengers kept shouting at me. Almost all of them were Maronites, some of them Phalangists; and they were frightened of the Israelis.

It rained. Heavy, soft Irish rain that fell across Dublin and washed away the feel of perspiration. *The Irish Times* carried the headline 'Peace force starts to leave' on its front page on 11 September 1982, which seemed a little premature because the multinational troops were supposed to have stayed in Beirut for a month. They had only completed 17 days.

I set off for Donegal. In Belfast, I bought a copy of the *Daily Telegraph* in which Sharon was reported to have made 'a surprise visit to his troops' forward positions in the southern suburbs of Beirut'. Here, he claimed that '2,000 terrorists' had remained in the city after the PLO evacuation. It was as if Lebanon followed me around, as if it were impossible to shake off the events of the past three months.

In the Queen's University bookshop in Belfast, a young shop-assistant approached me. 'I heard you talking about Lebanon,' she said. She had read my reports on the air raids on west Beirut. Did I remember writing about the raid on Abu Chaker Street, where the sofa was hanging out of the apartment block after the Israeli bomb destroyed one of the buildings? Of course I did. 'I am Lebanese. It was my home. It was our sofa. My family all died there. I am the only one left.'

In Donegal, I found a hotel that sold Lebanese wine, the gentle Ksara red wine that came from the Bekaa. Who were these mysterious 'terrorists' whom Sharon had suddenly discovered in west Beirut? Why were they never mentioned before?

Labelle had called *The Times* with a message for me. He was puzzled that the American Marines had left so early. He dismissed Sharon's words as 'the usual bullshit' but was troubled by an incident in west Beirut in which a French UN officer had been shot in the chest and killed near an Israeli position. Officially, the French soldier was hit by stray bullets during a brief firefight between Israelis and Lebanese militiamen. Later, the UN told us that he was shot as he took photographs of Israeli troops advancing some hundred yards further towards the city. The Israelis were at their old game of 'salami-slicing', shaving off small pieces of west Beirut, gradually reducing the unoccupied area of the city. The UN could find no record of a gun battle at the time. The Israelis later admitted that their soldiers near the airport *had* moved forward but only, they claimed, 'to clear landmines'. Labelle thought it was 'a one-off thing' and told me to enjoy my holiday.

I drove slowly down the west coast of Ireland. It rained hard when I reached Westport in County Mayo, and I escaped to a run-down bar, a place of stained carpets, a breath-taking range of whiskey bottles and a massive colour television set at whose screen the customers glanced from time to time, even though the sound was inaudible above the conversation. I could just hear the Angelus bells at six o'clock. I looked up when the news started a minute later and felt my heart thump faster. Jerking across the screen was a fighter-bomber, the camera hand-held by someone who must have been afraid. I could see the spray of phosphorus balloons falling away from the plane, the pink flames drifting down above the bar.

The camera panned left and there were those familiar dead fingers of brown smoke and video-tape of wounded men. Syrian uniforms. I recognised a mountain in the background. The Bekaa. The Israelis were bombing the Syrians. I was nervous. What was going on back in Lebanon?

I called *The Times* collect from a pay-phone in the bar. Barnes was there, laughing at my concern. AP was reporting a single Israeli air raid on a Syrian missile battery in the Bekaa. There was no message from Labelle.

The sky cleared, and I travelled on beneath a great arc of Atlantic blue sky. The television film had aroused some sense of impending disaster. The road to Galway stretched in a straight line through the fields but I could not shake off the idea that I should be in Lebanon. It was 14 September, a late high summer's evening, and the farmers were burning the stubble off their fields, columns of dark smoke that tunnelled upwards.

That evening, the BBC said that there had been a bomb explosion at the Phalangist headquarters in east Beirut. I called *The Times* again from a Galway hotel. Bashir Gemayel had been in the building but had escaped unharmed. I slept badly. Before breakfast, the BBC broke the spell. Bashir Gemayel had been assassinated and the Israelis were invading west Beirut.

When the Israelis had invaded Lebanon, Tatro and Cody were in Aden. Now the Israelis were entering west Beirut and I was on the west coast of Ireland. It was just after nine in the morning. I had no breakfast. If I had a journalist's duty to report on Lebanon, what was I doing here? Why had I stayed on through the days of the siege to be away now, at the very final moment of the tragedy? What would happen to the Palestinian camps? This was not the first question I asked myself. Shaking off my sleep, I was trying to remember the first name of Bashir's brother, the direct telephone number of the AP bureau in west

Beirut, the time at which Ivan Barnes would arrive at *The Times* office in London.

I drove east, dangerously and fast, desperate to reach Dublin. From there, at least I could fly to Europe. Beirut airport had been closed since 6 June but I hoped Damascus would be open. I saw a bar that was advertising coffee and asked to use the telephone. I placed a call to Charles Douglas-Home, the editor of *The Times*. Charlie sounded relaxed, nonchalant. 'Bob, you really don't have to go back. The Israelis say they are going in to west Beirut to preserve law and order. By all means go if you like, but you don't have to break off your holiday.' I told him I thought the Israelis would take the Phalangists into west Beirut with them. He doubted this, adding that they would be kept under control by the Israelis, even if they were allowed into the west of the city.

It was impossible to believe this. I had talked to the Israelis, watched their aircraft and bombardment, listened to their constant, repeated obsession with 'terrorism'. Terrorists, terrorists, terrorists. After all that had happened in Lebanon since 6 June, I could not *imagine* that the Israelis would be able to enter west Beirut without a catastrophe. It was a journalist's instinct. I had to be right. And I was in Ireland.

I called Barnes from the same pay-phone. Telephone lines to Beirut had been cut, but Labelle had managed to telex *The Times* with a brief message for me. He thought I should return – quickly. The Lebanese leftist militias were fighting the Israelis. The Israelis had not managed to occupy all of west Beirut – they still had a long way to go. Then the telex line also cut.

Barnes wanted an analysis on the future of Lebanon and a feature article on Bashir Gemayel by three in the afternoon. They were written by hand. I still have copies of the two articles. I began the first story by recalling an Israeli colonel's warning to me just before I left Beirut. 'The colonel was not a cynical man,' I wrote,

> but he possessed the wisdom of forethought and there was a kind of tiredness in his voice when he turned to us and said: 'You know, it is not getting rid of the Palestinians that is going to be our big problem; our problem is going to be stopping the Phalange going in to west Beirut and settling old scores.'

I had not reported the colonel's words before. I had ignored them, just as I had formed a mental block against the other ominous signs. Despite all I had seen, only now did I begin to realise the true significance of what he had told me. Yet I knew nothing about the Phalangists entering west Beirut. That midday, as I drove to Dublin, the Phalangists were still in *east* Beirut. They had not yet crossed the line.

In Dublin, I found a phone booth at the airport and filed my two features. *The Times* used both. But the first paragraph of the analysis – the paragraph that included the warning by the Israeli colonel – was cut out. It was not a conspiracy. It was not excised for political reasons. I later met the sub-editor who made the mistake. He was sorry, but he had been short of space on the page and had room to focus only on my remarks about the *future* of Lebanon, not about what people had told me *in the past*. He, too, ignored the significance of what the colonel had said. He, too, had a mental block.

The woman at the Aer Lingus airline check-in desk was like a mother encouraging her child to pass his exams. 'Of *course* you must get to Beirut. The airport's closed, isn't it? We'll get you to Damascus, overnight via Geneva. Don't tell Swissair you don't have a visa for Syria or they won't let you aboard. You'll have to fight your way in when you get to Damascus. Good luck.'

I spent hours at Geneva as the Swissair flight was delayed. At dawn I was over the Alps; by early evening, my plane landed at Damascus. The immigration official was friendly, bought me a cup of tea but no, he was sorry, he needed permission from the Ministry of Information to allow me to transit by road to Beirut. I called Adel Zaaboub, the Ministry man, at his home. He would help – but only in the morning. The Ministry of Foreign Affairs would also have to give its permission, and the Ministry was closed for the night.

I pleaded – with Zaaboub, with the immigration officer, with the *mukhabarrat* gunmen guarding the airport. They were polite, they understood my urgency. But I would have to wait until the morning. It was the evening of 16 September. Here was a moment when the Syrians needed the international press to witness what was happening in Beirut, to report on Gemayel's death, on what must have seemed to them an appalling blow to Israel's strategic aspirations in Lebanon, and the best they could do was ask me to wait until morning because the officials of the Ministry of Foreign Affairs were asleep. No one there yet knew, of course, that the Phalange had entered west Beirut with the Israelis.

I did not sleep. I walked the floor of the arrivals lounge at Damascus International Airport and watched the sun rise, purple and hot, over the mountains. Then the friendly immigration official told me he had just received a telephone call. I could enter Syria. I had a visa. Would I like another cup of tea?

I took a taxi to the Sheraton Hotel in Damascus where I found a driver who would go to Lebanon – under normal circumstances, a three-hour drive. When we reached the border crossing at Masnaa, he refused to go further. A Lebanese taxi offered to take me to Beirut. I climbed in, but when he arrived at Chtaura on the western side of the Bekaa, he, too, pulled out of the deal. 'Beirut boom-boom,' he announced in English, and turned off the engine. I begged another driver, a young man with a miniature Koran dangling above the windscreen, to take me further.

'Come,' he said. On the mountain highway, the Syrians waved us through, past the spot where Cody and I had first seen the Syrian army in 1976, past the road junction at Mdeirej where Foley and I had almost been killed in the air strike. Just east of Bhamdoun, the driver stopped. I grabbed my hold-all and followed him across a field. He was walking quickly, following a line of cotton — yes, cotton — up a small wadi to the south of an earth revetment. I knew that the Israelis had positioned a tank behind the embrasure. 'Stay behind me, follow the cotton,' the young man said. 'We are in a minefield.'

A minefield. Thirty-six hours out of Dublin, forty-eight hours without sleep, and this youth was leading me through an Israeli minefield. I hardly breathed. I watched the cotton with more attention than those who escaped through the passages of the Minotaur. Over a bank of flowers, we found several cars and a man emerged from one of them, an older man who looked faintly like my brave teenage driver. 'This is my brother — he will take you to Beirut. Pay him for me when you get there.' I could have cried.

The brother drove at speed. And there below us lay Beirut in the heat haze, the great peninsula lunging into the Mediterranean, the high-rise apartment blocks, the devastation of the camps, the airport runways shimmering in the far distance. At the museum, a Phalangist officer refused to let us cross. I knew him. His name was Maxim. 'Robert, what are you doing? There is no story. The Israelis have gone in to preserve law and order.' Do you believe that? 'Why not?' Please let me cross. 'I'm sorry — it's not safe. There's been some shooting.' Law and order? Maxim smiled in a genuinely friendly way. 'No way, Robert.'

The driver took me to the Alexandre Hotel in east Beirut. I found another friend, a press spokesman for Dany Chamoun. He phoned a Maronite driver who was fearful but prepared to consider a trip to west Beirut if I paid him 500 dollars. We headed for the port. There had been no sign of the Israelis at the museum and I guessed they must be using the port as their supply line into west Beirut.

Just outside the harbour, I saw a tank heading west, a big Merkava with its barrel traversing right and left in a quick, frightened way. 'Follow him,' I said to the driver. He was a kindly soul with a little brown moustache. He wanted to help, he wanted 500 dollars. He followed the tank. Too close. I could hear shooting far away. 'Get back in case someone fires at him — give the tank some room. Forty metres.' The driver slowed. An Israeli army military policeman pointed at our car. I waved at him and pointed at the tank. It worked; the soldier thought I was an Israeli journalist. The driver slowed down. 'It's OK — go, go, go. He's letting us through.'

The tank lunged across the road, its iron tracks lashing into the old dock railway lines, squealing on the metal. We were halfway through the port. I could see the Geffinor building above the ruins. Round the next corner stood Zarab's concrete hut and the cinema where I had helped to push down the machine-gun nest.

The head and shoulders of one of the tank crew emerged from the turret, talking rapidly into a radio. The Merkava must have been moving at 40 mph. There was a distant explosion. My driver slowed. 'Follow the tank.' He kept on slowing, his courage seeping away. 'It's OK, it's all right, follow the tank.' His foot danced between the gas pedal and the brake and settled gently onto the brake. 'No. No. Just follow the tank. We're OK.' He touched the gas then took his foot off again.

'Follow the tank. Follow it. It's OK. Follow it. For Christ's sake, just do it! *FOLLOW THE FUCKING TANK!*'

The driver's fear of me outweighed his fear of the tank, just for a few seconds. And by then, we had crossed. He could see the ruined hotels and the lines of Israeli infantry along the sides of the road, the Israeli soldiers installing telephone land-lines, the Israeli jeeps parked along the Corniche. We went on following the Merkava along the seafront. It was a dream, more powerful, more incredible than any illusion. We followed the tank all the way to my own front door. And there was my landlord, waving to me from his tiny garden. 'Mr Robert, you have come back. Welcome.'

It was already evening. In the AP, Labelle was cursing beside the telex machine, long, unrepeatable oaths because all the lines were now collapsing. He was drawing on a cigarette and wheezing. He looked up at me with big, unsmiling red eyes. 'So you made it. About fucking time.'

I swayed as I walked. I needed to sleep, anywhere. There was shooting in the camps. In the Commodore Hotel, I found Loren Jenkins of *The Washington Post*, a bearded man with a huge head of black hair and an even fiercer temper than Randal's. He was a hard, tough man from Colorado who believed that all politicians were liars.

He was leaning across the reception desk, talking on the telephone. When he put the phone down, he turned to me without a word of greeting. It was 17 September. I had not seen him for weeks. 'Fisky, something's going on in the camps. The Israelis have brought the fucking Phalangists with them. I've just been down to Saeb Salam's place and this woman turned up and said she just saw some fucker cut her husband's throat in Chatila. Want to come with me in the morning?'

I found Karsten Tveit of Norwegian radio. 'Where *were* you?' he roared. He would come in the morning, too. I liked the idea of Tveit coming with us. Two tough survivors were good protection. I went home but could not sleep. From my window, I could see the cigarettes of the Israeli tank crews on the Corniche glowing in the darkness. I had travelled too far, too fast, for too long, to be able to lie down.

I stood on the balcony and heard jets, low flying fighter-bombers racing through the darkness above me. One of them dropped a flare, then another, and the opaqueness over the city cleared in a blossom of golden light that spread across the sky over the camps. It was bright daylight, silvery yellow. I could read a book on my balcony by the light. The flares sprayed down slowly, almost all of them over the Sabra–Chatila district, but one burned-out flare fell into my street, still attached to its tiny parachute, clacking against the metal fence and rolling down the roadway.

The Israeli tank crews along the Corniche seemed to have no idea why the flares were being dropped. I could see them now, looking around like children who had discovered dawn at midnight. The flares went on, floating across the sky, gently spreading their great golden light over west Beirut until the whole city was bathed in their luminescence. Dawn at midnight. As if some fundamental law of physics, governing both time and light, were being broken.

11 Terrorists

Pregnant women will give birth to terrorists; the children
when they grow up will be terrorists.

Phalangist involved in the Sabra and Chatila massacre,
when questioned by an Israeli tank crew, west Beirut
17 September 1982

We know, it's not to our liking, and don't interfere.

Message from an Israeli army battalion commander to his
men, on learning that Palestinians were being massacred
17 September 1982

It was the flies that told us. There were millions of them, their hum
almost as eloquent as the smell. Big as bluebottles, they covered us,
unaware at first of the difference between the living and the dead. If we
stood still, writing in our notebooks, they would settle like an army –
legions of them – on the white surface of our notebooks, hands, arms,
faces, always congregating around our eyes and mouths, moving from
body to body, from the many dead to the few living, from corpse to
reporter, their small green bodies panting with excitement as they found
new flesh upon which to settle and feast.

If we did not move quickly enough, they bit us. Mostly they stayed
around our heads in a grey cloud, waiting for us to assume the generous
stillness of the dead. They were obliging, these flies, forming our only
physical link with the victims who lay around us, reminding us that
there is life in death. Someone benefits. The flies were impartial. It
mattered not the slightest that the bodies here had been the victims of
mass murder. The flies would have performed in just this way for the
unburied dead of any community. Doubtless it was like this on hot
afternoons during the Great Plague.

At first, we did not use the word massacre. We said very little because
the flies would move unerringly for our mouths. We held handkerchiefs
over our mouths for this reason, then we clasped the material to our
noses as well because the flies moved over our faces. If the smell of the
dead in Sidon was nauseating, the stench in Chatila made us retch.
Through the thickest of handkerchiefs, we smelled them. After some
minutes, *we* began to smell of the dead.

They were everywhere, in the road, in laneways, in back yards and broken rooms, beneath crumpled masonry and across the top of garbage tips. The murderers — the Christian militiamen whom Israel had let into the camps to 'flush out terrorists' — had only just left. In some cases, the blood was still wet on the ground. When we had seen a hundred bodies, we stopped counting. Down every alleyway, there were corpses — women, young men, babies and grandparents — lying together in lazy and terrible profusion where they had been knifed or machine-gunned to death. Each corridor through the rubble produced more bodies. The patients at a Palestinian hospital had disappeared after gunmen ordered the doctors to leave. Everywhere, we found signs of hastily dug mass graves. Perhaps a thousand people were butchered; probably half that number again.

Even while we were there, amid the evidence of such savagery, we could see the Israelis watching us. From the top of the tower block to the west — the second building on the Avenue Camille Chamoun — we could see them staring at us through field-glasses, scanning back and forth across the streets of corpses, the lenses of the binoculars sometimes flashing in the sun as their gaze ranged through the camp. Loren Jenkins cursed a lot. I thought it was probably his way of controlling his feelings of nausea amid this terrible smell. All of us wanted to vomit. We were *breathing* death, inhaling the very putrescence of the bloated corpses around us. Jenkins immediately realised that the Israeli defence minister would have to bear some responsibility for this horror. '*Sharon!*' he shouted. 'That fucker Sharon! This is Deir Yassin all over again.'

What we found inside the Palestinian Chatila camp at ten o'clock on the morning of 18 September 1982 did not quite beggar description, although it would have been easier to re-tell in the cold prose of a medical examination. There had been massacres before in Lebanon, but rarely on this scale and never overlooked by a regular, supposedly disciplined army. In the panic and hatred of battle, tens of thousands had been killed in this country. But these people, hundreds of them, had been shot down unarmed. This was a mass killing, an incident — how easily we used the word 'incident' in Lebanon — that was also an atrocity. It went beyond even what the Israelis would have in other circumstances called a *terrorist* atrocity. It was a war crime.

Jenkins and Tveit and I were so overwhelmed by what we found in Chatila that at first we were unable to register our own shock. Bill Foley of AP had come with us. All he could say as he walked round was 'Jesus Christ!' over and over again. We might have accepted evidence of a few murders; even dozens of bodies, killed in the heat of combat. But there were women lying in houses with their skirts torn up to their waists and their legs wide apart, children with their throats cut, rows of young men shot in the back after being lined up at an execution wall. There were babies — blackened babies because they had been slaughtered more than

24 hours earlier and their small bodies were already in a state of decomposition — tossed into rubbish heaps alongside discarded US army ration tins, Israeli army medical equipment and empty bottles of whisky.

Where were the murderers? Or, to use the Israelis' vocabulary, where were the 'terrorists'? When we drove down to Chatila, we had seen the Israelis on the top of the apartments in the Avenue Camille Chamoun but they made no attempt to stop us. In fact, we had first driven to the Bourj al-Barajneh camp because someone told us that there was a massacre there. All we saw was a Lebanese soldier chasing a car thief down a street. It was only when we were driving back past the entrance to Chatila that Jenkins decided to stop the car. 'I don't like this,' he said. 'Where is everyone? What the fuck is that smell?'

Just inside the southern entrance to the camp, there used to be a number of single-storey concrete-walled houses. I had conducted many interviews inside these hovels in the late 1970s. When we walked across the muddy entrance of Chatila, we found that these buildings had all been dynamited to the ground. There were cartridge cases across the main road. I saw several Israeli flare canisters, still attached to their tiny parachutes. Clouds of flies moved across the rubble, raiding parties with a nose for victory.

Down a laneway to our right, no more than 50 yards from the entrance, there lay a pile of corpses. There were more than a dozen of them, young men whose arms and legs had been wrapped around each other in the agony of death. All had been shot at point-blank range through the cheek, the bullet tearing away a line of flesh up to the ear and entering the brain. Some had vivid crimson or black scars down the left side of their throats. One had been castrated, his trousers torn open and a settlement of flies throbbing over his torn intestines.

The eyes of these young men were all open. The youngest was only 12 or 13 years old. They were dressed in jeans and coloured shirts, the material absurdly tight over their flesh now that their bodies had begun to bloat in the heat. They had not been robbed. On one blackened wrist, a Swiss watch recorded the correct time, the second hand still ticking round uselessly, expending the last energies of its dead owner.

On the other side of the main road, up a track through the debris, we found the bodies of five women and several children. The women were middle-aged and their corpses lay draped over a pile of rubble. One lay on her back, her dress torn open and the head of a little girl emerging from behind her. The girl had short, dark curly hair, her eyes were staring at us and there was a frown on her face. She was dead.

Another child lay on the roadway like a discarded doll, her white dress stained with mud and dust. She could have been no more than three years old. The back of her head had been blown away by a bullet fired into her brain. One of the women also held a tiny baby to her body. The bullet that had passed through her breast had killed the baby too. Someone had slit open the woman's stomach, cutting sideways and then upwards, perhaps trying to kill her unborn child. Her eyes were wide open, her dark face frozen in horror.

Tveit tried to record all this on tape, speaking slowly and unemotionally in Norwegian. 'I have come to another body, that of a woman and her baby. They are dead. There are three other women. They are dead ...' From time to time, he would snap the 'pause' button and lean over to be sick, retching over the muck on the road. Foley and Jenkins and I explored one narrow avenue and heard the sound of a tracked vehicle. 'They're still here,' Jenkins said and looked hard at me. They were still there. The murderers were still there, in the camp. Foley's first concern was that the Christian militiamen might take his film, the only evidence − so far as he knew − of what had happened. He ran off down the laneway.

Jenkins and I had darker fears. If the murderers were still in the camp, it was the witnesses rather than the photographic evidence that they would wish to destroy. We saw a brown metal gate ajar; we pushed it open and ran into the yard, closing it quickly behind us. We heard the vehicle approaching down a neighbouring road, its tracks clanking against pieces of concrete. Jenkins and I looked at each other in fear and then knew that we were not alone. We *felt* the presence of another human. She lay just beside us, a young, pretty woman lying on her back.

She lay there as if she was sunbathing in the heat, and the blood running from her back was still wet. The murderers had just left. She just lay there, feet together, arms outspread, as if she had seen her saviour. Her face was peaceful, eyes closed, a beautiful woman whose head was now granted a strange halo. For a clothes line hung above her and there were children's trousers and some socks pegged to the line. Other clothes lay scattered on the ground. She must have been hanging out her family's clothes when the murderers came. As she fell, the clothes pegs in her hand sprayed over the yard and formed a small wooden circle round her head.

Only the insignificant hole in her breast and the growing stain across the yard told of her death. Even the flies had not yet found her. I thought Jenkins was praying but he was just cursing again and muttering 'Dear God' in between the curses. I felt so sorry for this woman. Perhaps it was easier to feel pity for someone so young, so innocent, someone whose body had not yet begun to rot. I kept looking at her face, the neat way she lay beneath the clothes line, almost expecting her to open her eyes.

She must have hidden in her home when she heard the shooting in the camp. She must have escaped the attention of the Israeli-backed gunmen until that very morning. She had walked into her yard, heard no shooting, assumed the trouble was over and gone about her daily chores. She could not have known what had happened. Then the yard door must have opened, as quickly as we had just opened it, and the murderers would have walked in and killed her. Just like that. They had left and we had arrived, perhaps only a minute or two later.

We stayed in the yard for several more minutes. Jenkins and I were very frightened. Like Tveit, who had temporarily disappeared, he was a survivor. I felt safe with Jenkins. The militiamen — the murderers of this girl — had raped and knifed the women in Chatila and shot the men but I rather suspected they would hesitate to kill Jenkins, an American who would try to talk them down. 'Let's get out of here,' he said, and we left. He peered into the street first, I followed, closing the door very slowly because I did not want to disturb the sleeping, dead woman with her halo of clothes pegs.

Foley was back in the street near the entrance to the camp. The tracked vehicle had gone, although I could still hear it moving on the main road outside, moving up towards the Israelis who were still watching us. Jenkins heard Tveit calling from behind a pile of bodies and I lost sight of him. We kept losing sight of each other behind piles of corpses. At one moment I would be talking to Jenkins, at the next I would turn to find that I was addressing a young man, bent backwards over the pillar of a house, his arms hanging behind his head.

I could hear Jenkins and Tveit perhaps a hundred yards away, on the other side of a high barricade covered with earth and sand that had been newly erected by a bulldozer. It was perhaps 12 feet high and I climbed with difficulty up one side of it, my feet slipping in the muck. Near the top, I lost my balance and for support grabbed a hunk of dark red stone that protruded from the earth. But it was no stone. It was clammy and hot and it stuck to my hand and when I looked down I saw that I was holding a human elbow that protruded, a triangle of flesh and bone, from the earth.

I let go of it in horror, wiping the dead flesh on my trousers, and staggered the last few feet to the top of the barricade. But the smell was appalling and at my feet a face was looking at me with half its mouth missing. A bullet or a knife had torn it away and what was left of the mouth was a nest of flies. I tried not to look at it. I could see, in the distance, Jenkins and Tveit standing by some more corpses in front of a wall but I could not shout to them for help because I knew I would be sick if I opened my mouth.

I walked on the top of the barricade, looking desperately for a place from which to jump all the way to the ground on the other side. But each time I took a step, the earth moved up towards me. The whole embankment of muck shifted and vibrated with my weight in a dreadful, springy way and, when I looked down again, I saw that the sand was only a light covering over more limbs and faces. A large stone turned out to be a stomach. I could see a man's head, a woman's naked breast, the feet of a child. I was walking on dozens of corpses which were moving beneath my feet.

The bodies had been buried by someone in panic. They had been bulldozed to the side of the laneway. Indeed, when I looked up, I could see a bulldozer — its driver's seat empty — standing guiltily just down the road.

I tried hard but vainly not to tread on the faces beneath me. We all of us felt a traditional respect for the dead, even here, now. I kept telling myself that these monstrous cadavers were not enemies, that these dead people would approve of my being here, would want Tveit and Jenkins and me to see all this and that therefore I should not be frightened. But I had never seen so many corpses before.

I jumped to the ground and ran towards Jenkins and Tveit. I think I was whimpering in a silly way because Jenkins looked around, surprised. But the moment I opened my mouth to speak, flies entered it. I spat them out. Tveit was being sick. He had been staring at what might have been sacks in front of a low stone wall. They formed a line, young men and boys, lying prostrate. They had been executed, shot in the back against the wall and they lay, at once pathetic and terrible, where they had fallen.

This wall and its huddle of corpses were reminiscent of something we had all seen before. Only afterwards did we realise how similar it was to those old photographs of executions in occupied Europe during the Second World War. There may have been 12 or 20 bodies there. Some lay beneath others. When I leaned down to look at them closely, I noticed the same dark scar on the left side of their throats. The murderers must have marked their prisoners for execution in this way. Cut a throat with a knife and it meant the man was doomed, a 'terrorist' to be executed at once.

As we stood there, we heard a shout in Arabic from across the ruins. 'They are coming back,' a man was screaming. So we ran in fear towards the road. I think, in retrospect, that it was probably anger that stopped us leaving, for we now waited near the entrance to the camp to glimpse the faces of the men who were responsible for all this. They must have been sent in here with Israeli permission. They must have been armed by the Israelis. Their handiwork had clearly been watched — closely observed — by the Israelis, by those same Israelis who were still watching us through their field-glasses.

Another armoured vehicle could be heard moving behind a wall to the west — perhaps it was Phalangist, perhaps Israeli — but no one appeared. So we walked on. It was always the same. Inside the ruins of the Chatila hovels, families had retreated to their bedrooms when the militiamen came through the front door and there they lay, slumped over the beds, pushed beneath chairs, hurled over cooking pots. Many of the women here had been raped, their clothes lying across the floor, their naked bodies thrown on top of their husbands or brothers, all now dark with death.

There was another laneway deeper inside the camp where another bulldozer had left its tracks in the mud. We followed these tracks until we came to a hundred square yards of newly ploughed earth. Flies carpeted the ground and there again was that familiar, fine, sweet terrible smell. We looked at this place, all of us suspecting what was indeed the truth, that this was a hastily dug mass grave. We noticed that our shoes began to sink into the soft earth, that it had a liquid, almost watery quality to it, and we stepped back in terror towards the track.

A Norwegian diplomat – one of Ane-Karina Arveson's colleagues – had driven down the road outside a few hours earlier and had seen a bulldozer with a dozen corpses in its scoop, arms and legs swaying from the vehicle's iron bucket. Who had dug this earth over with such efficiency? Who drove the bulldozer? There was only one certainty: that the Israelis knew the answer, that they had watched it happen, that their allies – Phalangists or Haddad militiamen – had been sent into Chatila and had committed this act of mass murder. Here was the gravest act of terrorism – the largest in scale and time carried out by individuals who could see and touch the innocent people they were murdering – in the recent history of the Middle East.

There were, remarkably, survivors. Three small children called to us from a roof to say they had hidden while the massacre took place. Some weeping women shouted at us that their men had been killed. All said Haddad's men and the Phalange were responsible and gave accurate descriptions of the different cedar tree badges of the two militias.

There were more bodies on the main road. 'That was my neighbour, Mr Nouri,' a woman shouted at me. 'He was ninety.' And there in a pile of garbage on the pavement beside her lay a very old man with a thin grey beard, a small woollen hat still on his head. Another old man lay by his front door in his pyjamas, slaughtered as he ran for safety a few hours earlier. Incredibly, there were dead horses, three of them, big white stallions which had been machine-gunned to death beside a hovel, one of them with its hoof on a wall, trying to leap to safety as the militiamen shot it.

There had been fighting inside the camp. The road near the Sabra mosque was slippery with cartridge cases and ammunition clips and some of the equipment was of the Soviet type used by the Palestinians. The few men here who still possessed weapons had tried to defend their families. Their stories would never be known. When did they realise that their people were being massacred? How could they fight with so few weapons? In the middle of the road outside the mosque, there lay a perfectly carved scale-model toy wooden Kalashnikov rifle, its barrel snapped in two.

We walked back and forth in the camp, on each journey finding more bodies, stuffed into ditches, thrown over walls, lined up and shot. We began to recognise the corpses that we had seen before. Up there is the woman with the little girl looking over her shoulder, there is Mr Nouri again, lying in the rubbish beside the road. On one occasion, I intentionally glanced at the woman with the child because I had half expected her to have moved, to have assumed a different position. The dead were becoming real to us.

Further north, in the Sabra section of the camp, women came up to us, crying with fear and appealing for help. Their men – sons, husbands, fathers – had been taken from their homes at the time of the massacre. A few had already been found at the execution walls but others were still missing. A Reuters correspondent had seen men being held under guard by Israeli troops in the ruins of the sports stadium. There were more journalists now, Lebanese newspaper photographers and diplomats. We found two Swiss delegates from the International Red Cross and told them where we had found mass graves. Swedish radio's correspondent was in the camp.

We found hundreds of the missing men in the stadium, just as the Reuters man had said. They were Lebanese for the most part – Lebanese as well as Palestinians lived in Sabra – and they were being taken away for 'interrogation' by militiamen. The whole western side of the ruined sports stadium was guarded by uniformed Israeli troops together with plain-clothes Shin Bet intelligence operatives, big, heavy-set men wearing Ray-Bans with Uzi machine-guns in their hands. There were also militiamen there, three of whom I saw leading a frightened man away from the stadium. The Israelis let them do this. They had agreed to this procedure. The Israelis themselves explained to us that this was a search for 'terrorists'. Terrorists.

The very word 'terrorists' now sounded obscene. It had become a murderous word, a word that had helped to bring about this atrocity. Jenkins and I saw hundreds of prisoners, squatting on their heels or lying in the dust beneath the stadium wall. I walked across to them, ignoring the Israelis who obviously thought that Jenkins and I were Shin Bet. I walked right into one of the underground stadium rooms which was being used as a cell. 'Help us,' one man said. An Israeli soldier appeared. Press, I said. 'Get out of here, these men are terrorists.'

But they were not. A few yards away, the Reuters correspondent found his own telex operator – a Lebanese man whose home was on Corniche Mazraa – sitting in one of the cells. We found an Israeli

officer. He was a *Tat Aluf*, a colonel. We told him we had found the
Reuters telex operator. He had to be released. After much pleading, the
man was given to us. The British Reuters reporter led him away, an arm
around his shoulders.

I walked into another of the 'cells'. 'They take us away, one by one,
for interrogation,' one of the prisoners said. 'They are Haddad men.
Usually they bring the people back after interrogation but not always.
Sometimes the people do not return.' Another Israeli colonel appeared,
pointed at me and ordered me to leave. I wanted to go on talking. The
prisoners were silent. Why could they not talk? 'They can talk if they
want,' the Israeli colonel said. 'But they have nothing to say.'

The nearest bodies lay only 500 yards away. The stench of the corpses
filled the air where these Israeli soldiers and Shin Bet men were standing.
But they were still talking about 'terrorists'. It was surreal, grotesque.
Jenkins found an officer whom he recognised. 'These people are being
held here for questioning – they are terrorist suspects,' the Israeli was
saying. It was irrelevant. Excuse me, excuse me for one moment, I
asked, but what has been happening here? There are bodies everywhere,
just over there – I pointed to the side of the stadium – there are piles
of them. 'I don't know about that.' But you can *smell* them. 'I'm sorry, I
have no information.'

I turned to the soldier. He was a tall man with short dark hair and a
tanned complexion, well-built, slightly plump. Look I said, forgive me
for saying it like this, but there are scenes in there that look like
something out of Treblinka. It was the first comparison I could think of
to what I had just witnessed. I had not said 'Treblinka' because Jews
were murdered there. Treblinka was an extermination camp. The Israeli
looked at me without emotion.

I was trying to make him understand the enormity of what had
happened, that this was not just a small excess but a massacre perpetrated
by Israel's allies under Israel's eyes. I was trying to make him understand.
Could he not *smell* the air? I asked him that. The Israeli should have
argued with me. He could at least have pointed out – correctly – that
there was no comparison in scale between what had happened in Chatila
and what happened in Treblinka. But he did not. He had to pretend
that he did not know what was in Chatila.

Jenkins was angry. 'Why don't you tell us what happened? There's
been mass murder here. What happened? Tell us. Did you let the
Christian militia in here yesterday?'

'I wasn't here yesterday. I only arrived this morning.'

Jenkins' eyes narrowed and he stepped back in fury. 'You're lying,'
he said. 'You *were* here yesterday. I saw you. You stopped my fucking
car when I wanted to go to Chatila. I spoke to you yesterday. You *were*
here. You're lying.' The Israeli obviously remembered Jenkins. He held

up his hand. 'I thought you were asking me something different. I don't remember. I have no idea what's been happening here.'

Along the main road, there was a line of Merkava tanks, their crews sitting on the turrets, smoking, watching the men being led from the stadium in ones and twos, some being set free, others being led away by Shin Bet men or by Lebanese men in drab khaki overalls.

We walked back towards the camp. A Palestinian woman walked up to me, smiling in a harsh, cruel way. 'Got some good pictures, have you?' she asked. 'Got some good things to write? Is everything all right for you? It's a nice day, isn't it?' I thought she was going to curse me but she just kept up her controlled sarcasm. 'You press people take good pictures. I hope everything is fine for you. Have a nice day here.'

Jenkins left to telex his office. Tveit drove to the Commodore Hotel to use the telephone. I walked back through the camp with my handkerchief over my face, past Mr Nouri and the other old man, to the left of the execution wall, below the barricade of corpses, the empty bulldozer, the dead horses, the woman with the child looking over her shoulder. Only when I was approaching the exit to Chatila, the track that led onto the main road between the Kuwaiti Embassy and Fakhani, did I realise that I was the only living soul in this part of the camp.

There was a roaring of engines from the road and above the breeze-block wall, beyond the trees, I could see an Israeli tank column. The disembodied voice of an Israeli officer came floating through the trees from a tannoy on an armoured personnel carrier. 'Stay off the streets,' he ordered. 'We are only looking for terrorists. Stay off the streets. We will shoot.'

This was more than grotesque. The Israelis were instructing the dead to stay off the streets. It was farcical, absurd, monstrous. I walked to the gate, my handkerchief still across my mouth and nose. The tank column was followed by two lines of Israeli infantry. They walked behind the camp wall and then, when they reached the entrance to Chatila, they sprinted across the opening, rifles at the ready, taking position at the other side, covering each other from the ghostly 'terrorists' inside.

I walked out into the street. 'Hey, you — get out of here.' A junior Israeli officer walked up to me. Press, I said. 'You are not permitted here. Get out of here.' I refused. I had simply seen too much. 'I'm ordering you to leave at once.' I just shook my head. I felt sick. My clothes stank. I smelled of dead people. But after what I had just seen, I was beyond obeying such instructions. And I was mesmerised by these soldiers. They were still running across the entrance to the camp to avoid the phantom 'terrorists'.

The officer walked up to me and glared in my face. There's no one there, I said. 'I've given you an order to leave here. Do as you're told,' the soldier shouted. You don't understand, I said. Everyone here is dead. They're all dead in there. There's no one there – only dead people. Three Israeli soldiers stood beside the officer, looking at me as if I was mad. I looked at the officer because I suspected he might himself be a little insane. No I won't leave.

One of the three soldiers put his hand on my arm. 'There are terrorists in the camp and you will be killed.' That's not true, I said. Everyone there is dead. Can't you *smell* them? The soldier looked at me in disbelief. Really, I said, women and children have been murdered in there. There are dead babies. The officer waved his hand at me dismissively. 'You'll be killed,' he said, and walked away.

I began to feel like one of those characters in a mystery film who call the police to report a murder only to be accused of fabricating the story. Perhaps if I walked back into Chatila now, the bodies would be gone, the streets cleaned up, the hovels reconstructed, their dead owners cooking lunch or sleeping off the hot early afternoon in those back bedrooms. I went across to one of the lines of infantry that were approaching the entrance to the camp and walked along beside a tall, friendly-looking soldier.

What is going on? 'I don't know. I'm not allowed to talk to you.' No, seriously, what is going on? The man smiled. I could tell he wanted to be friendly. His uniform was dirty and he held his Galil assault rifle in his hands with ease, a professional soldier who was tired and needed friends. Everyone was dead in the camp, I said. Women, children, all murdered. 'Why?' he asked. I was wondering if he knew. 'The Christians were there,' he said. Why? 'I don't know. It was nothing to do with me. I wasn't there.' We had come to the camp gate. He crouched down.

Even this likeable, friendly man was now ready to go into action against the ghosts. I walked into the entrance of Chatila, standing upright in the centre of the road. How obsessed were these young men? To my astonishment, they too began to crouch at one side of the entrance and then to run to the other side, a distance of perhaps 30 feet, bent double, scuttling past my feet with their rifles pointed into the camp. I thought they were mad. They, of course, thought I was mad. They believed – they were possessed of an absolute certainty and conviction – that 'terrorists' were in Chatila.

How could I explain to them that the terrorists had left, that the terrorists had worn Israeli uniforms, that the terrorists had been sent into Chatila by Israeli officers, that the victims of the terrorists were not Israelis but Palestinians and Lebanese? I tried. I walked alongside these soldiers and told them I was a journalist and asked their names. After some minutes, they grew used to my presence. So I met Moshe, Raphael, Benny, all carrying their heavy rifles down the road past Chatila, all fearful of terrorists. Terrorists, terrorists, terrorists. The word came up in every sentence, like a punctuation mark. It was as if no statement, no belief could be expressed without the presence of terrorists.

'There are terrorists everywhere,' Benny said. 'Be very careful.' Benny came from Ashqelon. He was married and he wanted to go home. He had only come to Lebanon to get rid of terrorists. When the terrorists had left Beirut, he would go home. But hadn't the PLO *left* Beirut? Had he not seen the evacuation or read about it in the papers? 'They didn't leave,' he said. 'Lots of them are still here. That is why we are here.'

But everyone in this area of Chatila was dead. 'I don't know about that. But there are terrorists everywhere here. This is a very dangerous place. Haven't you heard the shooting?' I explained that the Lebanese militias had been shooting at the Israelis only because the Israelis had invaded west Beirut, that some Palestinians had tried to defend themselves against the militias inside Chatila.

It was pointless. The columns of infantry marched all the way through the southern suburbs of Beirut to Galerie Semaan – opposite their own siege front line – and eventually, in the ruins of the line, someone, some 'terrorist' who chose to oppose this occupation army, opened fire with a rifle. From the sound of the shot, I suspected it came from a narrow street off Boulevard Ariss, but the Israelis were sure it came from a ruined building.

They threw themselves into the muck beside the road and I jumped into a ditch beside an Israeli major. An armoured personnel carrier drove up the road and its crew opened fire at the ruins with a Vulcan gun, a weapon which fired a continuous stream of metal at its target and blew pieces of the building into the air like confetti. The Israeli major and I lay huddled in our ditch for 15 minutes. He asked about Chatila, very innocently, and I told him what I had seen.

Then he said: 'I tell you this. The Haddad men were supposed to go in with us. We had to shoot two of them yesterday. We killed one and wounded another. Two more we took away. They were doing a bad thing. That is all I will tell you.'

Was this at Chatila, I asked? Had he been there himself? He would say no more. In the days to come, I would discover that the major's story was only partly true. Then his radio operator, who had been lying beside us in the mud, crawled up next to me. He was a young man. He pointed to his chest. 'We Israelis don't do that sort of thing,' he said. 'It was the Christians.'

So they *did* know what had happened in Chatila.

Did *we*? Even now, after all the warnings we had heard, after all the clues, after ignoring all our journalistic instincts – after seeing the very evidence of Chatila with our own eyes – we as reporters could still not comprehend exactly what had happened. When I returned to the AP office, I found that all telex, computer line and telephone communcations were down. Steve Hindy of AP's Cairo staff was running the bureau in

Tatro's absence on holiday. Hindy was arguing with Labelle and Foley about what they had seen.

'Are you sure it was a massacre?'

Foley was waving pictures in front of him. 'Look at them Steve, look at them. You haven't been there yet.'

'But how many dead are there?'

'What the fuck does it matter? It was a massacre.'

'Yes, but was it? People have been killed in Lebanon like this before.'

I sat in the corner of the room, listening to this. I smelled bad and I was tired. It was a Saturday. *The Times* would not be published until the Sunday night. I could go home if I wanted but the conversation was part of the same tragedy I had seen that morning. When does a killing become an outrage? When does an atrocity become a massacre? Or, put another way, how many killings make a massacre? Thirty? A hundred? Three hundred? When is a massacre not a massacre? When the figures are too low? Or when the massacre is carried out by Israel's friends rather than Israel's enemies?

That, I suspected, was what this argument was about. If Syrian troops had crossed into Israel, surrounded a kibbutz and allowed their Palestinian allies to slaughter the Jewish inhabitants, no Western news agency would waste its time afterwards arguing about whether or not it should be called a massacre.

But in Beirut, the victims were Palestinians. The guilty were certainly Christian militiamen – from which particular unit we were still unsure – but the Israelis were also guilty. If the Israelis had not taken part in the killings, they had certainly sent the militia into the camp. They had trained them, given them uniforms, handed them US army rations and Israeli medical equipment. Then they had watched the murderers in the camps, they had given them military assistance – the Israeli air force had dropped all those flares to help the men who were murdering the inhabitants of Sabra and Chatila – and they had established military liaison with the murderers in the camps.

All this we knew by late Saturday afternoon, but Hindy still debated whether this had been a massacre.

'Go and look for yourself,' Foley kept shouting. He held up picture after picture of corpses, the bodies locked in each other's arms. 'Look at this.' A picture of a baby with its brains missing. 'Look at this.' A woman with a bullet through her breast. 'And this, and this . . .' Foley was intense, passionate, like a man trying to sell dirty pictures to an unwilling customer at the seaside. 'For Christ's sake, Steve, it was a massacre, a *massacre!*'

I went home. I felt ill, sick because of the smell of my clothes, and I showered for more than an hour but could not shake off the stench. Four hours after I had gone to bed, I woke up sweating and nauseated, convinced that the corpses of Chatila were piled on the sheets and blankets round me, that I was actually lying between the bodies, that they were all in the room, even old Mr Nouri. I could *smell* them still, in my own home. In the morning, my cleaning lady Ayesha refused to wash my clothes. 'Please burn them, Mr Robert. They are not good.'

By the following day, Chatila had become infamous. It was peopled with reporters and camera crews and diplomats. For the first time since the massacre, the living outnumbered the dead. And as the bodies lay in the heat, they expanded, contorted into shapes beyond imagination, bloated so much that belts and the straps of wristwatches cut brutally into the decaying flesh. They bubbled, cooked in the sun noisily and emitted trails of black, oily liquid that ran from the execution walls. No one could publish pictures of this or describe the reality in a newspaper.

The AP computer line began functioning again at midday on Sunday. I filed a long dispatch to *The Times* on everything I had seen in Sabra and Chatila, on the Christian militias which were allied to Israel, on the ignominious withdrawal of Israeli troops from the perimeter of the camps, the collapse of Israel's 'law and order' mission to west Beirut. The Israelis now started blaming the Americans.

For once, just briefly, Palestinians and Israelis could share a common policy. Both blamed the United States. The Palestinians could at least do so with some justice. The PLO had been told by Philip Habib that the Israelis would not enter west Beirut if the guerrillas left. The US Marines had left early — after only 17 days in Beirut — and America's promise had been broken when the Israelis invaded west Beirut. So much for the guarantees.

Arafat was in Damascus when he was shown the video-tape of the bodies. He said that Philip Habib had personally signed a piece of paper guaranteeing protection to the Palestinians who remained in west Beirut. He was right.

At that dining room table near Oxford in the autumn of 1987, Habib admitted that Arafat was correct. 'What Arafat said is absolutely true,' he said. 'He was absolutely telling the truth. I signed this paper which guaranteed that these people [the Palestinians] in west Beirut would not be harmed. I got specific guarantees on this from Bashir and from the Israelis — from Sharon. I was sitting on my *terrasse* overlooking San Francisco Bay when I heard what happened. I was phoned about it. I called the president. I don't remember what I said or what the president said. What happened has never been a source of comfort to me. No, I didn't communicate with Arafat afterwards. I didn't need to. The Palestinians knew what I thought.'

The Palestinians principally blamed the Israelis, and not without reason. It was Israel which sent the murderers into the camps. But the Israeli authorities immediately blamed America. No less a figure than

General Rafael Eitan, the Israeli chief of staff, held a hurried news conference near the sports stadium where he accused Morris Draper, the American deputy assistant secretary of state for Near Eastern Affairs, of refusing to establish contact between the Israeli and Lebanese armies. Because the Americans would not facilitate talks between the Israelis and the Lebanese, the Israelis had been unable to ask the Lebanese army to enter west Beirut after Bashir Gemayel's death and thus had to get the Christian militias to do the job.

Even if anyone had taken this argument seriously, they could scarcely have overlooked the fact that the Israelis had commandeered numerous Lebanese army barracks over the previous three weeks and were therefore in rather intimate contact with the Lebanese military authorities without any help from the Americans. Indeed, Lebanese troops almost always saluted Israeli soldiers when the Israelis passed through their checkpoints.

During the Sunday afternoon, there was panic again in Chatila when survivors heard rumours that the Phalange and Major Haddad's militia were returning to the camp to complete their work. Hundreds of people fled to the exit of Chatila, leaving Red Cross officials standing at the newly opened mass graves. Several of the Palestinians even pleaded for the arrival of Israeli soldiers to protect them. They might have thought differently had they heard Eitan announce at the news conference that his army could not prevent Christian militiamen from entering the camps because 'they are Lebanese and this is Lebanon – they are free to move anywhere in their country.' This statement bore no examination. Israeli troops would never have permitted Muslim militias to enter east Beirut – though they too were Lebanese – and to suggest that the militias had the right to move into Chatila was turning a blind eye to murder.

Although civil defence workers who were recovering the bodies were now issued with oxygen masks to protect them from the smell of putrefaction, many men and women continued to search for relatives with nothing more than handkerchiefs to cover their faces. On 20 September, the Lebanese Red Cross uncovered two more mass graves and laid out the corpses of a further 120 victims of the massacre. The survivors continued to insist that Haddad's militia had played the principal role in the killings and when two of Haddad's armoured vehicles – given to them by the Israelis – drove down Hamra Street, another panic started among the remaining Palestinians.

We spent hours each day in the camps, counting the corpses, talking to more and more witnesses who had hidden during the massacre but who told horrifying stories of the butchery. Many spoke of hearing the militiamen addressing each other by Shia Muslim names. The Phalange is an almost exclusively Maronite force but Haddad's militia included many Shias – the Israelis claimed that a majority of his gunmen were

Shias — and the survivors described in precise detail the badges and emblems of Haddad's men on the uniforms of the murderers.

Tveit and I knew that Lebanese army units near the airport must have seen the militiamen moving around Sabra and Chatila between 16 and 18 September. On the 20th, four Lebanese army officers and one member of the Lebanese gendarmerie stationed in Hay al-Sellum, just north of the airport runways, told us that they had seen Lebanese militiamen arriving at Beirut airport on an Israeli air force Hercules transport aircraft 24 hours before the massacre began. The soldiers were frightened; they knew what their fate was likely to be if the Christian gunmen suspected them of disclosing such information.

At the airport terminal, Tveit and I were told that on the previous Thursday, 16 September, two Hercules C130s had landed on the number one runway and that jeeps and armed men emerged from the planes. The men were too far away to be identified by staff at the airport, although they noted that one of the aircraft took off almost at once and headed south. The other Hercules stayed on the tarmac for several hours. The Israelis proved unhelpful; an Israeli security officer at the military encampment beside the airport said he could not remember any planes arriving there on the 16th. But Tveit and I found five metal signposts running from the Israeli camp at the airport to the road junction at Kfarshima — on the back road to Chatila — with 'Phalange MP' written on each in Arabic.

An officer in the United Nations Truce Supervisory Organisation also saw armed men leaving the airport area on 16 September. He said that some were wearing Phalangist insignia while others were dressed in the uniform of Haddad's militia.* In the camp, we were told that the first killings took place on Thursday morning when armed men arrived in 30 lorries. The killers began to knife and cut the throats of women and children in Chatila and later began sniping with rifles at anyone who moved out of doors. But it was only on the Friday afternoon, they said, that the 'real' massacre began with mass killings.

I filed a dispatch to *The Times*, reporting that evidence was emerging 'that the Israeli army — far from being ignorant of the presence of right-

---

* The two militias were easily identifiable. The Phalangists wore a triangular cedar tree insignia with the Arabic words *Kata' ib Lubnaniya* on the tunic pocket. Haddad's men wore the sign of a golden sword superimposed upon a cedar tree — representative of a real tree as opposed to the Phalangists' symbolic triangle cedar — with the words 'Army of Free Lebanon' (*sic*) underneath. Lebanese newspapers suggested at the time that the Israelis had put Haddad men into Chatila in Phalangist uniform in order to contaminate the new Lebanese presidential candidate — Bashir Gemayel's weak and politically unreliable brother, Amin — and thus boost the chances of electoral success for Camille Chamoun, who had now emerged as Israel's political champion in Lebanon. The Plot was still alive.

wing militias during the Palestinian massacre at Chatila last week —
actually transported several hundred of Major Saad Haddad's gunmen
from southern Lebanon to Beirut last Thursday and permitted the
militias to control the entrance to Chatila camp for several hours before
the killings began ...' On the following day, the Israelis denounced my
report as 'malicious'; only later did they agree that two Hercules aircraft
had landed at Beirut on 16 September. But the planes, they said, carried
only Israeli troops.

Something very strange was occurring. The Israelis were now making
no secret of Phalangist responsibility for the massacre. The Phalangists
were trained and uniformed by the Israelis, just as were Haddad's
gunmen. They were armed with almost exactly the same weapons as
Haddad's men. They performed precisely the same brutal functions in
the Israeli-occupied areas of the Chouf, the Metn, and now in west
Beirut, as Haddad's men did in southern Lebanon. Indeed, the Phalangists
had been closer political allies than Haddad's men. The Israelis willingly
disclosed the Phalangist involvement in the massacre. Confidential Israeli
press briefings in Tel Aviv even named the Phalangist commander in
Chatila, a man called Elie Hobeika. But merely to mention the possibility
of Haddad's involvement incensed the Israelis. Why?

Why was Haddad's name so sacrosanct while the reputation of the
Phalange was so easy to sacrifice? We suspected at once that the
Phalangists had now outrun their usefulness to Israel. With Bashir
Gemayel murdered, the Phalangists might provide a useful auxiliary
force — for 'flushing out terrorists' in west Beirut, for example — but
were no longer politically important. Gemayel's death destroyed any
immediate Israeli hope of an Israeli–Lebanese peace treaty. Haddad's
ragtag army, however, was more important than ever. If Israel had to
abandon its adventure in Lebanon, then it would have to fall back upon
the Haddad militia to protect Galilee from guerrilla infiltration, even if
this itself was an admission that the entire invasion had failed in its
objectives.

I was determined to talk to Haddad, if possible without the presence
of the Israeli army officer who was always at the major's side when he
talked to the press. On 21 September, I set off to the very far south of
Lebanon, to Haddad's own village of Marjayoun, from where he used to
make such bloody threats against the United Nations soldiers and the
Shia Muslim villages to the north. In Beirut, they were still digging the
bodies out of the earth. But on the long car journey south, it was a
magnificent autumn day with high cumulus clouds moving slowly over
the mountains above Jezzine and a vale of blue mist settling into the
valleys at dusk. From Marjayoun, I could see the lights of the nearest
Israeli kibbutz and watch the trail of Israeli lorries and military vehicles
winding in convoy northwards up the Arkoub and the lower Bekaa.

Haddad's house stood on a narrow road guarded by a lone, chain-smoking gunman. I asked to see the major. Perhaps tomorrow, he said. I asked the man to go to Haddad for me and tell him I had travelled all the way from Beirut to see him. The gunman went down to the house and returned after two minutes. 'I am sorry,' he said, shrugging his shoulders. 'He is very tired.' I pulled out my notebook and wrote a short, miserable message to Haddad, of how I had gone to great trouble to see him, of how essential it was for him to clarify the involvement of his forces in the massacre now that his enemies were suggesting that he was behind the killings. I told him, too, that my editor would be angry with me if Haddad would not talk to me.

Then I sat down on a grass bank opposite the house, hugging my knees in the cold, and waited to see if the gentleman from Marjayoun, the demon of all the United Nations' worst dreams, would take the bait. Across the road in that dull, unprepossessing house was the man who would shell whole villages if his water supply ran out. In that building with cigarette stubs littering the steps, lived the man who – not long before the Israeli invasion – had fired three shells into Sidon on Easter Sunday, slaughtering every customer in the local coffee shop at the end of Riad Solh Street. When the door opened, another militiaman walked out, chain-smoking like the guard at the end of the road, a thin man in badly creased green fatigues with a tired expression on his face.

Only when he was ten yards away did I realise that it was Haddad. He seemed leaner than he had appeared at Galerie Semaan a month earlier when I had observed him making obscene gestures at the departing Syrian army 85th Brigade. 'What is it you want?' he asked. He did not say it in a friendly way but with a kind of growl. 'I am very tired.' There were bags under his eyes. He looked ill. I repeated what I had written in my note to him.

He walked back to the house but did not invite me inside. He sat on the steps outside, dragging greedily on his cigarette, out of breath but anxious to talk. A small girl with long, curly hair, Haddad's daughter, ran down the steps and began to play in the dust of the road. There was no Israeli army press 'minder' to direct Haddad's words and he spoke in a confident way as if it was unusual to have the opportunity to speak for himself. 'We are innocent people, we are peaceful people, we didn't hurt anybody,' he said. 'I am always frank and sincere. If I do something, I don't deny it and I say it without any fear. It kills me, this accusation that we took part in the killing. This is more than a crime – the accusation is worse than the crime itself.'

This was not a statement likely to commend itself to the Palestinian and Lebanese survivors of Sabra and Chatila. But I wanted to ask Haddad about his own movements, and about the intriguing comments made to me by the Israeli major as we cowered in the ditch at Galerie

Semaan while the Vulcan gun blew bits off the ruined building. Was it true that he was at Beirut airport on 17 September?

'Yes, I was at the airport,' he said. 'I was taken there in a helicopter, yes, an Israeli helicopter. But I was going to Bikfaya to pay my respects to the Gemayel family on the death of Bashir. It's just that I become a bit tired if I drive all the way. I arrived in Beirut at around nine o'clock on Friday morning and I left the airport at some time on Friday afternoon. I don't remember the exact time. But I was in Bikfaya, not in Beirut, in the time in between: there is a picture of me at the Gemayel home in the newspaper *Al Anwar*.'

There was indeed such a photograph on page three of the paper's edition of 18 September. But what about the accusation made by dozens of survivors that his men were in Chatila camp, in uniform, at that very moment, killing women and children? Haddad's careful recollections – the thoughts of a man with a cast-iron alibi – broke apart in a burst of anger. 'All of them, they are liars,' he growled. Here was the more familiar Haddad, the renegade major who inspired fear with just one warning over the radio. 'They are most of them paid by the PLO.'

But then he paused for a long time, controlling this outburst, spreading his hands in front of him and looking at them. 'Maybe they saw some of our badges because some of our people may have been serving with other forces in Beirut. Officially, I didn't have any men in Beirut. Besides, some people collect badges as souvenirs and they may have used them during the killings.' At this, Haddad tapped the sleeve of his uniform where a plastic insignia bearing the symbol of a golden sword upon a cedar tree flapped from his epaulette. 'Now these people claim that we have been using tanks and bulldozers in Beirut. But I have only one Caterpillar [vehicle] and it is now in Israel to be mended.'

But what about the Israeli major's evidence that at least one Haddad man had been shot by the Israelis themselves in Beirut? Haddad rubbed his eyes. 'Three of our men went to Beirut on Friday,' he said, 'because they heard of the killings and wanted to rescue some relatives in the Mseitbeh area. The men were from here in the south ... they had an argument with some members of the Lebanese Socialist Party in Beirut. One of my men was wounded and the other two sought refuge with the IDF.'

But if these men knew of the massacre on the Friday, was Haddad himself not aware of what was taking place? 'No. We did not know of it then. Neither Amin Gemayel nor I spoke about it. Listen, since seven years, we have been in a continual fight. I defy anybody to mention one mass killing committed by our people against Lebanese or non-Lebanese. Our war was against terrorists and against Syrians. The terrorists left Beirut. So we have no reason to go there and fight against Lebanese or Palestinians who are not armed. If we had the intention of menacing

Palestinians, there are more than a hundred thousand of them south of the Awali River where we are allowed to operate. You can ask them if any of their people were killed by our people ...'

According to Haddad, his militia could 'do nothing without the coordination of the Israeli army'. He repeated this several times. 'To make any individual action is not feasible. Every move we make has to be coordinated with the IDF [Israel Defence Force]. We have strict orders not to cross north of the Awali River.' While his words only bore out what the United Nations had long claimed – that the Israelis coordinated every violent act that Haddad's militia committed – they were also untrue in a more immediate sense. The Awali River runs just north of Sidon, yet on my way to see Haddad I had seen his militiamen, with sword-and-cedar badges on their uniforms – sitting next to Israeli troops ten miles north of the river.

But Haddad had an acute sense of his own importance in Lebanese history. 'I will tell you why people say these things about me,' he said towards the end of our meeting. 'There were two strong men in Lebanon – Bashir Gemayel and Haddad. They killed Bashir – now they try to burn Haddad. They are Lebanese who say these things. They do not like a patriot like me.'

Was he suggesting that the Phalange were accusing him of the massacre, that perhaps the Phalange had killed their own leader, Bashir Gemayel? 'I never once mentioned the word "Phalange",' he said. He stood up. I asked him, once more, how many of his men had really been in Beirut on 17 September. He had not expected to be asked this question again and his answer came promptly and revealingly. 'Perhaps ten served with other people there. Perhaps twenty ...' He stopped. 'But this business has nothing to do with me. Why, I wouldn't even know where to find Chatila.'

In several respects, Haddad's statements to me only raised new questions. Who were the 'twenty' men who might have 'served with other people' in Beirut on 17 September? Was Haddad trying to implicate elements of the Phalange in the murder of Gemayel? Why? Yet none of these questions touched upon the issue which was now occupying the minds of Tveit and myself.

We still wanted to know what actually happened in that crucial period between 16 and 18 September. Above all else, we were fascinated by *how* such a thing could occur. We were, of course, anxious to discover the identity of the culprits and the degree of culpability of the Israelis who sent the militiamen into the camps and then watched the massacre take place. But this touched upon the very point which most concerned us: how could an army which claimed 'purity of arms' in its wars, which loudly defended the morality of its men, which represented the children of the Holocaust, have allowed such an outrage to take place?

We visited every television crew which had filmed in the area of Chatila, just before or during the massacre. We talked to every diplomat and reporter who had been in the area of Chatila between 16 and 18 September. All were at the time ignorant of the slaughter going on inside the camp, but their evidence would surely yield some clues to the events which were taking place a few yards away.

James Pringle of *Newsweek*, for example, had arrived outside the entrance to Chatila at four o'clock on Friday afternoon and approached a militiaman whom he identified as a member of Haddad's forces. Asked what was going on inside the camp, the gunman, a thickset man with a moustache, replied simply and in English: 'We are slaughtering.' Pringle dismissed this at the time as a joke in bad taste. About 40 yards away, he came across an Israeli officer who identified himself as 'Colonel Eli' who said he was 53 and came from Tel Aviv. Pringle said that 'Eli' told him the Israelis were 'not going in to purify [*sic*] the area'. Asked what would happen if the Christian militiamen got out of hand, 'Eli' replied: 'I hope that will not happen.'

We collected all the Israeli press statements issued between 16 and 18 September, the most incriminating of which was timed 11.20 hours on the 16th and announced that 'the IDF is in control of all key points in Beirut. Refugee camps harbouring terrorist concentrations remained encircled and enclosed ... The IDF spokesman repeats and emphasises that contrary to the agreement [for the earlier PLO evacuation], a large number of terrorists remained in Beirut with mortars of various kinds in their possession in addition to their personal arms and anti-tank weapons.'

The 'terrorists' were the Lebanese militias, who specifically did *not* have to leave Beirut under the terms of the evacuation agreement. But the key words were '*encircled and enclosed*'. The Israelis controlled the camps. They admitted this. Therefore they had to take responsibility for what went on inside them. Yet this still did not answer the question: How could the massacre have been permitted to take place?

Tveit obtained hours of rough-cut television material, discarded tape and unused film which was left on the cutting-room floors in the Beirut bureaus of the various foreign television networks during the period of the massacre. At the time, of course, the crews had no idea of the significance of what they were filming. Footage of women on a truck being refused permission to leave Sabra and Chatila, a picture of a very old man with a grey beard and a woollen hat being ordered back into Chatila, held no significance for them. The film had never been transmitted and might have been thrown away altogether if Tveit had not asked to view it.

With the help of American network crews — and particularly of a courageous Danish television film unit — he patched together more than an hour of material that had been shot around Chatila during those crucial three days. We played through the tape on Tveit's video player. The images flicked crudely onto the screen — he had not yet edited the film — but were all the more powerful for this reason.

These were rough-cuts of history. A truckload of women emerges from the Chatila entrance and a militiaman — too far away for us to recognise his insignia — orders the truck to return to the camp. The women are shouting and crying but the soundtrack does not pick up their words. A Lebanese army jeep arrives at the entrance; Phalangists order the Lebanese soldiers to enter the camp with their hands in the air. A Phalangist gunman points his rifle to the camera and curses. The lens points to the ground then swings daringly back to the Phalangist and the jeep.

Tveit pushes the wind-back button again and again so that the jeep reappears on the frames, punching the pause button at the moment when the registration number of the vehicle is clear enough to read: '502493'. The tape cuts to an old man with a woollen hat and beard. I catch my breath. Tveit also recognises him at once. 'Mr Nouri,' we both say. Yes, it is Mr Nouri, whose body we saw on the 18th, lying in a pile of garbage, the 90-year-old Palestinian who was identified by his female neighbour as he lay there in the sun. We run the tape back. Nouri walks again into the camp. We wind the tape back further. Nouri makes some kind of appeal to the Phalangist at the camp entrance and the gunman points back towards the camp. Nouri will not be allowed to leave. He is doomed. The camera is not close enough to let us see the expression on his face. Does he know what is going on? We make him walk up to the Phalangist several more times. Over and over again, we make him walk back into the camp. He has returned briefly to life on this little screen.

The tape jerks again. There are Israeli troops, armed, near the stadium. It is the evening of the 16th, the Thursday. An elderly Palestinian woman in a flowered dress and a yellow scarf is crying and pleading to a soldier, a young Israeli lieutenant who is sitting on a chair outside a house. Both are speaking in Arabic.

Palestinian woman:	Who is the officer here?
Israeli soldier:	You can talk to me.
Woman:	They took my husband and my two sons and they smashed the teeth of one of my sons and they put us on the ground for a long time without water and food and we had also a small baby with us ... Didn't you come here to protect us?
Soldier:	Who did this? The *Kata'ib*? [Phalange]
Woman:	Yes. The *Kata'ib* came to Sabra—Chatila, and now we cannot go back to our homes.
Soldier:	... Where is Chatila?
Woman:	Over there. We accept your presence if you are here to help us.

Soldier:	If I saw the *Kata'ib*, I would have spoken to them. But I haven't seen anybody ... Some people told us that in this building there were not terrorists — but even in this house we found ten [of them] with weapons.
Woman:	But do you accept that the *Kata'ib* have killed four families? If you go to Chatila now, you will see the victims. Just go. We can show you the victims. They killed a child of nine months. Is that merciful? Please bring back my children.
Israeli:	Where are your children?
Woman:	With the *kata'ib*. They also killed old people, an old woman, an old man. They killed them before my eyes. I have seen it myself.
Israeli:	I do not know what I can do. Go back to your homes. Maybe the *Kata'ib* have left now.

The tape was made by an American cameraman for Visnews who did not speak Arabic. He had no idea what the woman and the soldier were saying. His tape would have been thrown away had Tveit not found it. The Israeli soldier on the tape does not seem to be disturbed by what he hears. He looks away. The clip ends. Then we see the outer wall of the camp, just above the stadium. Three Israeli soldiers in Israeli uniform are eating a lunch of cooked rations on the pavement. The camera pans left and two militiamen emerge through a hole in the wall, holding automatic rifles. They shout to the Israelis and the camera moves in close-up on the two men. These are the murderers of Chatila. They are around 30, slightly fat, and they are smirking. They have big, unpleasant smiles and they shout something unintelligible to the Israelis. Then they see the camera and the smiles vanish. One of the Israelis stands up and points to the camera and the tape ends.

Yes, the Israelis *knew*. By now some of the Israeli soldiers who were around Chatila — decent, honest men who could not accept the things which they had heard about or even witnessed — had been telling journalists, in confidence, that yes, they knew what was going on. In some cases, they admitted, they *saw* the killings. But they did nothing. It transpired that at 7.30 am on the morning of Friday, 17 September, Ze'ev Schiff, the military correspondent of the Israeli newspaper *Ha'aretz*, heard a report from a source in the Israeli army general staff in Tel Aviv that there was 'a slaughter' going on in the camps. He reported this to Mordechai Zippori, the Israeli minister of communications, who was an old friend of Schiff's. Zippori called Yitzhak Shamir, the Israeli foreign minister. Shamir did not act upon the call and never asked his staff to check the report of a massacre. But why did not Schiff at least call his colleagues in Beirut? If the international press corps in west Beirut could have been alerted to the massacre on the *Friday* morning —

instead of discovering it for themselves on Saturday morning – then perhaps the killings could have been stopped. But Schiff chose instead to go to his friend, the Israeli minister. So even the Israeli press failed in their responsibilities at this critical moment.

But Schiff did not actually *see* the massacres taking place. He could not be certain that the report was true. Other Israelis were *watching* the slaughter take place, some of them from beside the sports stadium, from the very positions which the Israelis used to watch us as we walked among the corpses on the Saturday morning.

One such man was Lieutenant Avi Grabowski, the deputy commander of the Israeli army tank company who subsequently testified to the Israeli commission of inquiry into the massacre that he had witnessed the murder of five women and children. Between eight and nine o'clock on the Friday morning, according to the commission's final report,* he saw two Phalangists hitting two young men in Chatila camp. 'The soldiers [*sic*] led the men back into the camp, after a short time he [Grabowski] heard a few shots and saw the two Phalangist soldiers coming out. At a later hour he ... saw that Phalangist soldiers had killed a group of five women and children.' The commission report went on to relate how:

> Lieutenant Grabowski wanted to report the event by communications set to his superiors, but the tank crew told him that they had already heard a communications report to the battalion commander that civilians were being killed, [and] the battalion commander had replied, 'We know, it's not to our liking, and don't interfere.' Lieutenant Grabowski saw another case in which a Phalangist killed a civilian.

In his evidence to the commission, Grabowski related how at noon on the Friday, his tank crew had asked a Phalangist why they were killing civilians. The Phalangist had replied: 'Pregnant women will give birth to terrorists; the children when they grow up will be terrorists.'†

Amid the protestations of moral decency that had become part of the Israeli army's propaganda defences, something had come adrift, something that was both dangerous and obsessive. What was it that Israeli lieutenant had told me on the hills above Beirut on 16 June? 'I would like to see them all dead ... I would like to see all the Palestinians dead because they are a sickness wherever they go ... Personally, I don't think our government would take the responsibility of massacring a lot of Palestinians.' He was right. Journalists who pointed out, with factual accuracy, that as an occupier, Israel was responsible for what went on inside the camps, were accused by Begin's government in Jerusalem of

---

* *The Commission of Inquiry into the Events at the Refugee Camps in Beirut*, 1983, final report by Yitzhak Kahan, President of the Israeli Supreme Court, Aharon Barak, Justice of the Supreme Court, and Yona Efrat, Reserve Major-General, IDF.

† *Jerusalem Post* 1 November 1982. 'IDF soldier saw women, children killed.'

committing a 'blood libel' against Jews. 'No one will preach to us moral values or respect for human life, on whose basis we were educated and will continue to educate generations of fighters in Israel,' the Israeli government portentously announced.

But Israeli moral values *were* at issue in this mass murder. The Israelis had watched their allies massacre innocents and had done nothing to prevent the atrocity. The Israelis would not have acted in so disgraceful a manner had the victims been Israeli civilians rather than Palestinians. Israel's 'respect' for human life evidently differentiated between the human life of Israelis and Palestinians. The former was sacrosanct. The latter expendable. The Palestinians whom that Israeli lieutenant had wished to see 'all dead' had indeed been murdered; the Israelis watched the cull through field-glasses – and did nothing. To them, the Palestinians were 'terrorists'.

Even the Kahan commission's 1983 report was a victim of Israel's savage obsession with 'terrorism'. The Israelis portrayed the document as powerful evidence that their democracy still shone like a beacon over the dictatorships of other Middle Eastern states. What Arab nation had ever published a report of this kind, a condemnation of both its army and its leaders? Where was the PLO's report into intimidation in southern Lebanon? Where was President Assad's report on the massacres at Hama in 1982?

But the Kahan commission report was a flawed document. The title of the inquiry – into 'the events at the refugee camps ...'. – managed to avoid the fatal, politically embarrassing word 'Palestinian'. Was this not in fact an inquiry into 'the events at the *Palestinian* refugee camps'? But that is not what it said. And why did the commission use the word 'events' when it meant 'massacre'?

There were repeated references in the commission's final report to Palestinian 'terrorists' in the camps – presumably the 2,000 strangely elusive and undiscovered 'terrorists' of whom Sharon had spoken in early September 1982 – but the judges provided not a single piece of evidence to substantiate the allegation that these 'terrorists' existed. Indeed, the only real terrorists in the camps – the Christian militiamen who were sent there by the Israelis – were respectfully described by the judges as Phalangists, or 'soldiers'. *Soldiers.*

Three foreign doctors, one of them Jewish, who had Palestinian sympathies and witnessed the start of the massacre, were rightly described by the commission as having no 'special sympathy for Israel'. Yet the evidence of Israelis – who could have had no 'special sympathy' for the Palestinians – was largely accepted at face value. Even the evidence of Haddad, whose cruel militia had taken dozens of innocent lives in southern Lebanon – including the murder of UN soldiers – was treated with respect. While the commission could not rule out 'the possibility ... that one [*sic*] of the men from Major Haddad's forces infiltrated into the camps', the judges nonetheless decided that 'no responsibility, either direct or indirect, is to be imputed to the commanders of Major Haddad's forces.' The commission did not point out that the 'commanders' of Haddad's militia were Israelis.

Begin, Sharon, Eitan, Drori and other Israeli officers were condemned with varying degrees of harshness. The commission wisely decided that it was 'unable to accept the position of the Prime Minister that no-one imagined that what happened was liable to happen'; the judges could not accept that Begin was 'absolutely unaware' of the danger of a massacre if the Phalangists were sent into the camps.

Indeed not. Was this not, after all, the same Begin who had lectured the Irish ambassador to Israel on the principles of the Lebanese blood feud after the murder of the two Irish UN soldiers, Smallhorn and Barrett, in 1978? This was not something the judges chose to recall.

The Kahan commission concluded that Sharon bore 'personal responsibility' for what happened in the camps and suggested that Begin remove him from office. It recommended that Major-General Yehoshua Saguy, the director of military intelligence, be fired, and it fixed considerable blame upon Drori 'without recourse to any further recommendation'.

Yet the Kahan report failed to address two intrinsically important factors in the massacre: the obsession with 'terrorism' and the extraordinary influence of the Second World War upon Begin and the actions of the Israelis during the Lebanon war. Even after the horror of Chatila, in the immediate aftermath of the massacre, it was clear that the Israelis had not learned their lesson. Until they left west Beirut, they would fire flares over the city every evening at seven o'clock. A cold yellow glow would bathe the buildings, the slums, ruins and Palestinian camps. A Hebrew voice over a crackling radio in a blacked-out street would issue orders to lonely, frightened soldiers. The Israelis were hunting for 'terrorists' again.

It had become not just an obsession but an amorphous military objective with neither end nor meaning. The Palestinian guerrillas were 'terrorists'. Then the Lebanese militias were 'terrorists', and then the Palestinian civilians of Chatila became 'terrorists', even when they were dead. Evening after evening, Foley and I would watch the Israeli patrols along Hamra Street. Israeli officers would shout down the street from the back of their armoured vehicles: 'We have come to cleanse your area of terrorists.' And the Lebanese would look on, uncomprehending, fearful of what might follow.

Sooner even than they could have predicted, Israeli soldiers became involved in a war of ambushes and attempted assassination on the streets of occupied west Beirut. A resistance movement began to form itself within the Shia militia. Scarcely had Israeli soldiers completed their fruitless search for a man who fired a rocket-propelled grenade at one of their patrols on 24 September than a gunman ran up to three Israeli officers drinking coffee at the Movenpick restaurant in Hamra Street in mid-afternoon and opened fire at them. By the time I reached the scene, Israeli plain-clothes gunmen were herding Lebanese men into the entrance of a boutique for questioning.

A witness told me that the gunman had run up to the Israeli officers at the café, screamed 'You are killing Lebanese' and fired a full clip of ammunition into them. When he ran away, the Lebanese in the street watched impassively. Every young man who had remained out of doors was arrested by the Israeli gunmen. 'We are looking for terrorists,' an Israeli officer shouted in Arabic through a tannoy from his vehicle. 'Help us find the man who shot our soldiers and we will take him to court. We want to clean the area of terrorists.' There was no movement from the apartment blocks around him in Hamra Street; nor were there any courts in Lebanon.

Nor were 'terrorists' taken to court. Families would approach reporters, cautiously, unsure whether we lived in Beirut or had arrived with the Israelis. They would produce photographs of young men and even women who had been taken from their homes. Could we find them? The parents of a young Palestinian woman came to see me. She had been taken from a taxi by Phalangist gunmen near Damour. Israeli soldiers had seen this happen. The parents hoped that since the Israelis had witnessed her detention, she could not have been harmed. But no one had seen her since a leering Phalangist had led her away and ordered the taxi driver to continue his journey to Sidon. She was never seen again.

A Shia girl who cleaned the flat of a Lebanese translator at an American television network bureau in west Beirut told me how her husband had been taken from their home in the ruined hotel district by uniformed Israeli soldiers and driven away in an Israeli army truck. Could I find him? I could elicit no information from the Israelis. The man was never seen again. What were we supposed to make of these disappearances?

Then Phalangist officers I knew in east Beirut told me that at least 2,000 'terrorists' – women as well as men – had been killed in Chatila. One Christian gunman told me he had seen dumper trucks filled with corpses being driven past Israeli troops outside Chatila on 17 September. Tveit was told by a Phalangist that 'you won't find out what happened to the others unless the government decides to build a subway line under Beirut.' I kept hearing rumours that there were a thousand bodies buried 'where you play sport' and thought at first that there must be an undiscovered mass grave under the ruined sports stadium beside Chatila. Only later was I told that the bodies had been buried beneath the golf course between Chatila and the airport. I went there afterwards and found large areas of newly dug earth and the tracks of bulldozers. But by then the Lebanese army controlled the area and refused to let the Red Cross carry out investigations. To this day, the graves remain unexcavated.

It was becoming clear that even after Chatila, Israel's 'terrorist' enemies were being liquidated in west Beirut. Who was perpetrating these murders? Were the Phalangists still in west Beirut? Or was Shin Bet involved in the killings? Certainly, death squads had been in existence in Haddad's area of southern Lebanon for years; they would reappear with increasing frequency in Israel's occupation area over the coming two years, just as Syrian death squads had performed their tasks in west Beirut in the past. The Israeli secret service Mossad, as the Kahan commission revealed in 1983, had a complex system of liaison with the Phalange in which Mossad operatives actually sat in Phalangist offices in Beirut alongside the men who carried out the Sabra and Chatila murders. The Lebanese swiftly concluded that Israelis as well as Phalangists were murdering 'terrorist' suspects.

The Israelis were moving ever deeper into a dark and purposeless world. Perhaps once, back in early June, the journey did not seem so impenetrable. The Israelis saw their mission then as a stabilising one, a battle against their enemies which would end in the security of a 25-mile-deep buffer zone along the Awali River. Then in the flush of victory they pushed on to Beirut, where there appeared to be other prizes: a friendly Maronite state with an even friendlier Maronite leader whose Phalangist army — however embarrassing its antecedents — could help in the subjugation of west Beirut.

That, of course, is where it all began to go wrong, for the Israelis had acquired two contradictory military and political aims: the destruction of 'terrorism' — a word used with ever more promiscuity and ever less thought — and the creation of a Christian-dominated Lebanon which would accept a peace treaty with Israel. The first aim had been fuelled by the PLO's presence and then proved understandable — at least in Israeli eyes — around Sidon.

Exactly what happened when the Israelis laid siege to the Palestinian camp of Ein Helweh just east of Sidon has never been fully revealed. But many Israeli soldiers — perhaps as many as 50 — died in the area in the second week of the war and there is some evidence that many of them were murdered by the PLO. The Israelis afterwards refused to discuss the affair but here is the account of a young Palestinian guerrilla who described it to me a month later:

> When the Israelis bombed the Ein Helweh camp, they killed hundreds of our civilians. They did not care about killing our people. They wanted to kill all of us. But then they staged a ground attack and the Palestinian fighters captured forty-three of them. Colonel Azami was there, he was

the Palestinian commander. He took these people prisoner and he tied the Israelis around a building and strapped explosives to their legs. He said that if the Israelis would not let our fighters leave the camp, he would blow up the prisoners. So they [the Israelis] let the fighters out. The Palestinians took some of the Israelis with them. Azami was magnificent. Our men got free. Then he got to the hills and he ordered all the Israeli prisoners to be got rid of. They were a difficulty. The explosives were still strapped to their legs and the Israelis were blown up. They were killed.

Was this part of the psychological background to the massacre at Chatila? There was no secondary confirmation of what the Palestinian told me but several Israeli soldiers later said that 'something terrible' happened in Sidon and that by the time the Israeli army surrounded Beirut, it was in no mood to attack the Palestinian camps with infantry. Thus when Israeli troops did move into the Muslim sector of the capital, they sent the Phalange into Chatila to kill the 'terrorists'.

The real terrorists turned out to be Israel's Christian allies. Israel had armed them, paid them, uniformed them, in some cases fed them. They were Israel's creatures. Referring to Jewish suffering abroad, the Kahan commission had itself stated that 'the Jewish public's stand has always been that the responsibility for such deeds falls not only on those who ... committed atrocities, but also on those who were responsible for safety and public order, who could have prevented the disturbances and did not fulfil their obligations in this respect.' The Israeli units around Chatila had not understood this. They were blind to it. They had forgotten the basic rule which all foreign armies invading Lebanon are forced to learn: that by making friends with one group of terrorists, you become a terrorist yourself.

Yet this still did not account for what happened at Chatila. The nature of Bashir Gemayel's militia leadership was there for all to see. His ascension to the presidency, so brutally cut short in September, was ominous. As early as June, Professor Yussef Ibish had compared Gemayel's putative rule with that of General Franco — 'With malice to all and charity to none, he will rule this place,' Ibish had said — and had predicted that the Israelis would use 'lists of names' which they would use in mass arrests and killings. 'They are going to shoot them — it is going to be a huge Tel al-Za'atar,' he said, referring to the Phalangist massacre of Palestinians in 1976. The man who did lead the Phalange into Chatila — Elie Hobeika — had once lived in Damour. His family were among those murdered there by the Palestinians. His fiancée was among the women butchered by the Palestinians in the town.

But the Israelis reserved the word 'terrorism' exclusively for their enemies, not their Phalangist friends, as the Kahan report demonstrated all too revealingly. Uri Avneri, the liberal Israeli journalist who interviewed

Arafat during the siege of west Beirut — Israeli Cabinet ministers later demanded that he should as a result be tried for treason — described the use of the term 'terrorists' as 'a media crime, an excuse for murder'. It was, he told me in Tel Aviv in 1986, 'a Nazi kind of method' to influence minds, 'a process of dehumanising people that was essential to prepare for war'.*

For the Israelis — for Sharon and Begin and their soldiers — 'terrorist' did not have the same connotation as it does elsewhere. In Europe and America, in many Asian countries, even in the Soviet Union, the word 'terrorism' evokes images of hijackings, bombs planted in restaurants or schools or airports, the murder of civilians on planes, buses, trains or ships. But in Israel, 'terrorist' means all Palestinian Arabs — and very often, all *Arabs* — who oppose Israel in word or deed. Loren Jenkins used to refer to 'the careless depreciation of meaning' that the Israelis imposed on the word, claiming that this distorted the reality of terrorism. But it was not 'careless'. It was deliberate. Like the Syrians, the Soviets, the Americans and the British, the Israelis drew a careful distinction between good terrorists and bad terrorists. In Israel's case, the former were sympathetic to Israel and were graced with various, less harmful epithets — 'militiamen', 'fighters', 'soldiers' — while the latter opposed Israel and were therefore terrorists pure and simple, guilty of the most heinous crimes, blood-soaked and mindless, the sort of people who should be 'cleansed' from society.

By labelling Palestinians as terrorists, the Israelis were describing their enemies as evil rather than hostile. If the Palestinians could be portrayed as mindless barbarians, surely no sane individual would dare regard their political claims as serious. Anyone who expressed sympathy for the Palestinians was evidently anti-semitic — and therefore not just anti-Israeli or anti-Jewish, but pro-Nazi — which no right-thinking individual would wish to be. Anyone who even suggested that the Israelis might be wrong in their war against the Palestinians could be castigated in the same way. Do you think Hitler was right? Do you agree with what happened at Auschwitz? No, of course not. If Israel called the PLO its enemy, then the Middle East dispute involved two hostile parties. But if the world believed that the Palestinians were *evil* — that they represented sin in its crudest form — then the dispute did not exist. The battle was between right and wrong, David and Goliath,

---

* According to Avneri, Sharon told him eight months before the war that he wanted to destroy the PLO in Lebanon, put the Phalangists in power 'as a kind of Christian protectorate' and get the Syrians out of Lebanon. 'He wanted to push the Palestinians into Syria in the hope that the Syrians would push them down to Jordan which would then be turned into a Palestinian state. Sharon had this Napoleonic idea. He wanted to have a Palestinian revolution in Jordan.' By contrast, the Israeli army 'didn't give a damn about the Palestinians because the PLO never was a military threat — it was the Syrians whom the army was worried about.'

Israel and the 'terrorists'. The tragedy of the Israelis was that they came to believe this myth.

The word 'terrorism', however, ran in tandem with constant reminders of the fate of the Jews in the Second World War. After the massacre at Sabra and Chatila, many nations asked themselves how a people who had suffered so terribly at Hitler's hands could permit such an atrocity to take place under their eyes. Throughout the siege of Beirut, the PLO accused Israel of employing the same tactics as Hitler used against the Jews. To survivors of the Holocaust, this Palestinian claim approached blasphemy. How could the Israeli army, fighting 'terrorists' to protect its citizens, taught from its inception that 'purity of arms' was to be its moral code, possibly be compared to the mass murderers of Nazi Germany?

The Sabra and Chatila massacre did not change these arguments. But it profoundly muddied them. The Israelis had watched the atrocities. No soldier in any occupation army could expect a court to absolve him of guilt because his militia allies had perpetrated such a crime.

Yet even after seeing the phosphorus burns that had turned those two babies into human torches in the Barbir hospital, we never spoke of the Israelis as Nazis. No Israeli government ever attempted the systematic elimination of an entire race of people. Three hundred and fifty thousand Israelis – ten per cent of the country's population – gathered in Tel Aviv to protest their revulsion at what had happened in Sabra and Chatila.

But it was still impossible to push away the parallels with that greatest of recent wars. The German army had allowed Croatian militiamen – every bit as brutal and 'Christian' as the Phalangists – to massacre the inhabitants of Serbian villages in Yugoslavia in 1942; the Yugoslavs later executed German officers for allowing the atrocities to take place.

Of course, the war in Lebanon bore no relation to the Second World War in scale. By 1988, the entire death toll of all Lebanon's 13 years of war – about 100,000 – did not even approach the 138,690 civilian victims of the atomic bomb blast at Hiroshima in 1945. Lebanon's dead were only just over twice the number of fatalities in the Hamburg firestorm raid in 1943. The Spanish Civil War, which lasted from 1936 to 1939, claimed more than five times the total dead of the Lebanese wars until now. The Soviet Union estimated that seven million of its civilians were killed between 1941 and 1945. The Khmer Rouge in Cambodia murdered an estimated three million people, most of them civilians. The Algerian authorities say that they lost a million people in their war against the French from 1954 to 1962.

Yet on the level of individual atrocities, the massacre at Sabra and Chatila stands alongside similar outrages in the Second World War. The number of bodies found at Sabra and Chatila and the growing list of 'missing' Palestinians and Lebanese civilians — as well as the evidence of Phalangist officers in the weeks that followed — suggested that well over a thousand people were murdered in the Beirut camps between 16 and 18 September 1982, quite possibly as many as two thousand. Even Israel's lowest estimate of fatalities in the massacre — 460 — is only nine fewer than the estimated number of victims who were murdered by the Nazis at the Czech village of Lidice in 1942 or subsequently transported to concentration camp.* The minimum Beirut massacre total given by the director of Israeli military intelligence — 700 — is 58 more than the total number of French civilians murdered by German SS troops at the village of Oradour-sur-Glane in 1944.

Merely to draw these comparisons is to outrage the sensibilities of Israelis, indeed of thousands of Jews throughout the world, many of them Holocaust survivors. Even if the parallels of scale could be entertained, Syria's murderous suppression of the Hama uprising would have much more in common with the behaviour of the Nazis in occupied Europe. And it is a fact — shamelessly ignored by many Arab nations — that the Israeli demonstration in Tel Aviv, held in protest at the massacre, was essentially an affirmation by Israelis that they were *not* prepared to allow their country to behave like Nazi Germany. One of their common themes was a demand for Begin's resignation.

Unwittingly, perhaps, the demonstrators focused upon the one man who did more than anyone else to draw a parallel between Israel's invasion of Lebanon and the Second World War. For it was Begin, a Holocaust survivor whose own family was murdered by the Nazis in Poland, who repeatedly — through the long summer weeks of the Beirut siege — drew comparisons between the Lebanon invasion and the 1939–45 war. It was he who portrayed himself in a letter to President Reagan that summer as marching to 'Berlin' in order to liquidate 'Hitler'. Arafat at the time was busy comparing his forces to the defenders of Stalingrad but it was Begin who returned, with puzzling consistency, to the Second World War.

So frequently did he refer to the Holocaust that one prominent Jewish historian of the Holocaust wrote personally to the Israeli prime minister, begging him to stop using the victims of Auschwitz to justify the Lebanon war. It was no use. For Begin, the Holocaust appeared to

---

* The Kahan commission prudently decided that it could not rely on either Lebanese or Palestinian statistics for the massacre, and put the minimum death toll at 460. But it admitted that 'it is possible that more bodies are lying ... in the graves that were dug by the assailants near the camps', presumably a reference to the corpses beneath the golf course. The commission's report stated that the director of Israeli military intelligence had testified to a figure of 'between 700 and 800' murdered at Chatila. The Lidice killings were carried out in revenge for the murder by Allied agents of Reinhard Heydrich, the Nazi 'protector' of Bohemia and Moravia. The Germans shot 173 male villagers and sent 198 women and 98 children to Ravensbrück concentration camp.

justify the unjustifiable. A 'Holocaust complex', according to Professor Nadav Safran of Harvard, had taken possession of Begin. 'He lives it, he thinks he has a monopoly over its antecedents, its consequences, its significance ...' But Begin also chose to draw upon other examples from the Hitler period.

In defence of his country's air raids over Beirut, he indignantly reminded the West of the Allied fire-bombing raid on Dresden when at least 35,000 Germans, mostly civilians, were killed in February 1945. When European nations continued to criticise the civilian casualty toll from Israeli air strikes against Beirut, Begin responded by recalling that the RAF had accidentally bombed a school house in Copenhagen during a raid on the local Gestapo headquarters in the Second World War.

Yet his parallel was disingenuous. The British had not bombed the school because of simple pilot error in targeting a military objective – which was presumably meant to be Begin's excuse for the Israeli air raids on civilian homes in Beirut. When the Copenhagen raid took place on 21 March 1945, one of the RAF Mosquito bombers flew so low that it clipped its wing on a railroad tower and crashed on the convent school. The aircraft's high-octane fuel set the building alight and five subsequent planes bombed the burning school on the assumption it must be the Gestapo headquarters. Eighty-three children, twenty nuns and three firemen were killed.

But no Israeli aircraft was lost over Beirut and no such incident ever occurred there. The civilians in Lebanon died, in their thousands, because the Israelis bombed their homes, repeatedly and from a great height, over a period of weeks. The Israelis did not fly low to identify their targets more clearly, as the RAF had done in its vain effort to avoid civilian casualties at Copenhagen.

By far the most revealing of Begin's analogies, however, came in an address he gave to the Israeli National Defence College on 8 August 1982, a speech that received little attention, either at the time or in the years that followed. His theme was the necessity of invading Lebanon even though this could not be regarded – like Israel's previous conflicts – as 'a war of no alternative'. Begin's opponents, both inside and outside Israel, had questioned the purpose of the Lebanon war with ever-growing suspicion as the Israeli army surrounded Beirut and placed Arafat under siege. Why had Israel started a war that it could have avoided? The existence of the Israeli state was not threatened, as it had been in 1948, 1967 and 1973. Now Begin wanted to challenge his critics with a new argument: that 'There is no divine mandate to go to war only if there is no alternative.'

A classic war of no alternative, he said, was the Second World War. On the eve of war, Britain stood helpless. The London and Paris governments had forced Czechoslovakia to 'bend its knee' before Hitler;

Ribbentrop and Molotov had signed the Soviet–German treaty. In September 1939, German forces attacked Poland. In June 1941, the Germans attacked the Soviet Union. It was, Begin said, 'a war of no alternative for Poland, a war without option for France and a war without choice for Russia. What price did humanity pay for this war of no alternative? Between 30 and 40 million ... among them six million Jews – the only people against whom the Nazis used gas ... This is the terrible consequence of a war of no alternative.'

Yet, Begin claimed, 'thanks to research and the facts known to us', there was no longer any doubt that the Second World War could have been prevented. 'On 7 March 1936, Hitler announced that he was abrogating the Treaty of Versailles ... he introduced two battalions of the German army into the demilitarized Rhineland. At that time, two French divisions would have sufficed to capture all the German soldiers who entered the Rhineland. As a result of that, Hitler would have fallen ...' Begin did not name the source of his 'research' for this simplistic view of history, but in an extraordinary passage he went on to make a direct connection between the results of the Second World War and Israel's desire to hold on to the occupied Palestinian West Bank, the territory which Begin includes in 'the land of Israel', *Eretz Yisra'el*:

> If this [French action against the Germans in the Rhineland] had happened, the Second World War would have been prevented, more than 30 million people would have remained alive, tens of millions of others would not have been wounded and the tragedy of Hiroshima would have been averted. Humanity would have looked different today. *The six million Jews slaughtered then would today be more than 12 million, and the whole of Eretz Yisra'el would be in our hands.**

The implications of this statement were far-reaching. Begin had concluded that the Nazi slaughter of six million Jews had prevented the fulfilment of the dream of *Eretz Yisra'el*. If Hitler had not murdered the Jews of Europe, they too would have helped found the state of Israel and would have outnumbered the indigenous Arab population. Begin did not allow the dubious historical accuracy of such a statement to invalidate his argument. Hitler had prevented the fulfilment of Begin's Jewish dream and now Arafat too wished to prevent it. Hitler and Arafat shared a common cause. No wonder Begin fantasised in his letter to Reagan that his advance upon Beirut was a march to Berlin, that Arafat was Hitler.

Here was the critical connection between the past and the present which had been enshrined at the Yad Vashem Holocaust memorial outside Jerusalem. Indeed Yad Vashem supplies the visual support for Begin's argument, a place of accusation against the Arabs of Palestine as

---

* My italics. The text of Begin's speech can be found in *The Jerusalem Post* of 20 August 1982.

well as the Nazis of Europe, even against the British of mandate Palestine who turned back Holocaust refugees. If Sheikh Haj Amin Al-Husseini, whose photograph is displayed at the memorial, was a war criminal for allying himself with the Nazis, then so was Arafat. The Arab Palestinians of the 1939–45 war looked to the Germans to prevent Jewish immigration to Palestine. Now Arafat was the enemy of the Jewish state. Begin's men had him surrounded in Berlin/Beirut, in his bunker.*

Begin told his audience that Israel had, through its invasion of Lebanon, 'destroyed the combat potential of 20,000 terrorists', destroyed 'the best tanks and planes the Syrians had' and 24 Syrian ground-to-air missile batteries. If Beirut was Berlin, southern Lebanon was evidently supposed to be the Rhineland which the French had allowed Hitler to occupy in 1936. Only this time – in Lebanon – a war of no alternative had been averted by a war of alternative.

Now Begin claimed that 'with the end of the fighting in Lebanon, we have ahead of us many years of establishing peace treaties and peaceful relations with the various Arab countries.' It would all prove to be untrue. There would be no peace treaties and no peaceful relations, not even with Lebanon. But Begin never betrayed any doubts. Israel 'will not initiate any attack against any Arab country,' he promised. Unless, presumably, it was to prevent war.

Avneri was deeply shocked by this speech. 'Begin had his own personal complexes and conscience,' he said. 'When Hitler came, he tried to escape from Poland to Romania but was arrested by the Soviets in Lithuania. He came here [to Israel] in 1942 under [the Polish General] Anders. He stayed in the Polish army until he was discharged ... the fact that he left his people and came here may have intensified his attitude towards the Holocaust. He was the demagogue *par excellence*. He addressed the deepest emotions of the people. Demagogues are generally sincere. They cannot be successful unless they believe what they say – at least while they are saying it. He did believe that Arafat was the second Hitler. Basically, he believed in it just as he believed that he was saving the Christians of Lebanon from a genocide.'

But still this did not answer the most pressing question. Even if the

---

* As late as 1989, Sharon was himself propagating the same dangerous, distorted historical analogy. In the late winter of 1988, the US State Department opened talks with the PLO in Tunis after Arafat renounced 'terrorism'. This, Sharon announced in an interview with *The Wall Street Journal* (10–11 February 1989), was worse than the British and French appeasement policies before the Second World War and the betrayal of Czechoslovakia to Hitler, when 'the world, to prevent war, sacrificed one of the democracies.' Arafat was 'like Hitler who wanted so much to negotiate with the Allies in the second half of the Second World War ... and the Allies said no. They said there are enemies with whom you don't talk. They pushed him to the bunker in Berlin where he found his death, and Arafat is the same kind of enemy, that with whom you don't talk. [He's] got too much blood on his hands.' The thrust of Sharon's argument was that the creation of a Palestinian state would mean a war in which 'the terrorists will be acting from behind a cordon of UN forces and observers.'

Palestinians could be equated with the Nazis, how could the Israelis, whose people were victims of the Nazis, have allowed the massacre to take place? Four years later, in 1986, Brigadier-General Specter, the Israeli pilot who flew bombing missions over west Beirut in the summer of 1982, grappled with what the Israelis had done in Lebanon.

'The first generation after the Holocaust were very, very aware of a possible degradation of our morals, of ourselves,' he said. 'We asked how this could happen to the Germans, how they could think of a "final solution" when human lives were involved. When I joined the air force, I was taught about when a pilot should not obey orders, that the designation [of a target] is in the soldier's soul. I believe that an operation [in Lebanon] was absolutely necessary at that time but I believe now that people in general, Sharon and Rafael [Eitan] had a final solution – a terrible phrase, I know. They wanted a war to end all wars ... They went too far, they did too much ... the important question is the way we fight the terrorists – are we doing more wrongs than rights?'

Avneri was more cynical. 'I will tell you something about the Holocaust,' he said. 'It would be nice to believe that people who have undergone suffering have been purified by suffering. But it's the opposite, it makes them worse. It corrupts. There is something in suffering that creates a kind of egoism. Herzog [the Israeli president] was speaking at the site of the concentration camp at Bergen-Belsen but he spoke only about the Jews. How could he not mention that others – many others – had suffered there? Sick people, when they are in pain, cannot speak about anyone but themselves. And when such monstrous things have happened to your people, you feel nothing can be compared to it. You get a moral power-of-attorney, a permit to do anything you want – because nothing can compare with what has happened to us. This is a moral immunity which is very clearly felt in Israel. Everyone is convinced that the IDF is more humane than any other army. "Purity of arms" was the slogan of the Haganah army in early '48. But it never was true at all.'

Politicians, according to Avneri, used the Holocaust as moral blackmail. 'But it's real, it's not invented – it's there. It produces an odd kind of schizophrenic attitude. The Israelis will say: "We'll never allow another Warsaw ghetto or Auschwitz to happen again." Then they'll tell you they can conquer the whole Middle East in forty-eight hours. No one feels any contradiction in this.'

Does this partly account for the curious way in which reasonable, thoughtful people – even men who suffered terribly – cannot bring themselves to criticise Israel when it is palpably obvious that the nation is at fault, that its army has behaved in a brutal, cruel way? At these times, normal standards of judgement seem to be suspended. Elie Wiesel, the Auschwitz survivor whose courage permeates his books on the Holocaust, failed dismally to speak out on the massacre of Palestinians at Sabra and Chatila, expressing 'sadness' but adding that this 'sadness' was 'with Israel, not against Israel' and concluding that 'after all, the Israeli soldiers did not kill.' As Noam Chomsky says of this startling remark, the Israelis 'had often killed [by bombing] at Sabra and Chatila in the preceding weeks, arousing no "sadness" on Wiesel's part ...'*

Similarly, Nathan Sharansky, the Soviet refusenik who spent years in Soviet prison camps before emigrating to Israel, could not bring himself to condemn brutal Israeli policies on the West Bank. Conor Cruise O'Brien, the distinguished Irish essayist and politician, wrote a book about Israel in which he preferred to see the Sabra and Chatila massacre in the context of a Lebanese war in which different communities had traditionally committed atrocities against one another. In *New Republic*, he wrote that 'most Lebanese – including Muslims and Druses, as well as Christians – were glad that Israel invaded Lebanon.'

Even Jane Fonda, who so enraged the American public by visiting Hanoi and expressing her sympathies with the suffering of the North Vietnamese during the Vietnam war, felt unable to criticise Israel during the Lebanon war. Far from it, she travelled to east Beirut to entertain Israeli troops during the siege, where she watched the west of the city being shelled and 'expressed her identification with Israel's struggle against Palestinian terror, and her understanding for the Israeli invasion in Lebanon ...'† In New York after the war, she 'announced her unqualified support for Israel and condemned the hypocrisy with regard to Israel in connection with the Lebanon war.' She attributed this to 'anti-Semitism'.‡ The historian Barbara Tuchman, whose brilliant analysis of the first days of the 1914–18 war, *The Guns of August*, is recognised as unsurpassed in its field, responded to the massacre only by noting that 'the complications of the Arab world are not such as the Israelis can control.' What concerned her was 'the survival and future of Israel and of Jews in the Diaspora – myself among them.'

By way of contrast, the Israeli novelist A. B. Yehoshua observed that 'even if I could believe that IDF soldiers who stood at a distance of 100 metres from the camps did not know what happened, then this would be the same lack of knowledge of the Germans who stood outside Buchenwald and Treblinka and did not know what was happening! We too did not want to know.'§

Chomsky, whose research into the Lebanon war goes deeper than any other contemporary work, quotes Professor Yeshayahu Leibovitz of the Hebrew University, the editor of *Encyclopedia Hebraica*, who wrote that:

* Chomsky, *Fateful Triangle*, pp. 386–7.
† ibid., p. 268, quoting *Yediot Ahronot*, 4 July 1982.
‡ ibid., p. 269, quoting *Al Hamishmar*, 5 December 1982.
§ ibid., p. 387.

the massacre was done by us. The Phalangists are our mercenaries, exactly as the Ukrainians and the Croatians and the Slovakians were the mercenaries of Hitler, who organised them as soldiers to do the work for him. Even so have we organised the assassins in Lebanon in order to murder the Palestinians.*

The answer to such accusations was always the same. As Yosef Burg, the Israeli minister of interior and religious affairs, said: 'Christians killed Muslims – how are the Jews guilty?' Begin's words to his own Cabinet were even more self-righteous. 'The *goyim* are killing the *goyim*,' he said. 'And they want to hang the Jews for it.'

The Israelis left west Beirut without warning or fanfare on 26 September 1982, driving their tanks out of town at speed, like an army that had done wrong and knew it. Even the Lebanese troops who had taken up position around the wreckage of Chatila had been unprepared for so hurried a departure. Many of the Israelis had moved out before dawn, driving their armour along the Corniche towards the port in the half-light. By nightfall, on the eve of Yom Kippur – a name that was once synonymous with Israeli military achievement – the Israelis had nearly all gone.

On the streets in their place stood the diminutive armoured vehicles of the Lebanese army and a few truckloads of French Paratroopers. For the multinational force had returned to the city, sent back by nations with a guilty conscience. The Americans, French and Italians understood that responsibility for the massacre touched them too. The French soldiers could even be seen, briefly, in Chatila, walking around the rubble, searching for mines, surgical masks over their faces to shield them from the stench of decomposition.

The Israelis left just in time. When they withdrew, there was an average of one assassination attempt against Israeli troops in west Beirut every five hours. Israeli soldiers were fast becoming involved in a guerrilla war with unidentified gunmen. We did not know then that a new Shia Muslim resistance movement was being born. On one evening alone, the Israelis were attacked with rocket-propelled grenades near Hamra Street, at Fakhani and along Corniche Mazraa.

Tveit and I tried to find Hobeika. We found the address of his young wife but he had apparently left east Beirut. Phalangist officers told us he had been Bashir Gemayel's personal bodyguard, a man whom the murdered president-elect had introduced to a number of foreign diplomats as a leading light in Maronite politics.

After two days of work, I eventually traced a Lebanese army intelligence officer who confirmed that the registration number of the Lebanese army Land-Rover which Tveit and I had seen on the rough-cut video-

---

* ibid.

tape taken outside Chatila corresponded to a jeep based at the Bir Hassan barracks of the Lebanese army near Chatila. The officer would say no more because, he said, the Israelis were 'fully involved' in the Chatila massacre. When I asked him what he meant, he replied: 'Our observation post there [at the barracks] saw them go into Chatila — Israelis, Phalange and Haddad together.' Then he asked me: 'Are you the one who said the Israelis flew Haddad's men into the airport on Thursday?' I was. 'You were right,' he said. 'We saw it and I have read it in our observation report.' I said the Israelis had denied my report. He said: 'Of course.'

Who killed Bashir Gemayel? Amid the corpses of Chatila, the question seemed irrelevant. Gemayel was a militia leader. He had enemies. The Phalange claimed they had arrested an Armenian who confessed to working for Syrian intelligence. Yes, the Syrians could well have arranged Gemayel's murder. There were rumours that the Palestinians had planned Gemayel's death. Why not? There were accounts to be squared in the aftermath of Karantina and Tel al-Za'atar. Lebanese newspapers suggested that Suleiman Franjieh could have plotted Gemayel's murder. An easy assumption: Franjieh had yet to revenge himself upon the man who ordered the slaughter of his son Tony, his daughter-in-law and grandchild in the cold hills of northern Lebanon in 1978. Later, the Phalange would suggest that Bashir Gemayel was killed by the Israelis because he had refused to give way to Begin's demand for a formal peace treaty with Israel. No Lebanese was likely to dismiss such an idea.

Not long before his brother's assassination, Amin Gemayel had unburdened himself of a few thoughts on the Lebanese presidency. 'It would serve no one's purpose,' he told a Lebanese magazine, 'to win the presidency and lose the Republic.' But this was to be his fate. With his large eyes and thick, slightly overlong hair parted down the middle, Amin Gemayel looked more like a dandy than a political baron. He had neither the military ruthlessness nor the capacity for hatred that characterised his dead brother — even though both men were lawyers by profession and supported each other during the 1975–6 civil war.

In an awful way, the shrapnel that rained down upon Beirut during Amin Gemayel's election was all too appropriate. Only the 21-gun salute smothered the drum-fire of sound from the Lebanese army's exploding ammunition depot almost three miles away. At the army barracks at Fayadiye, he assumed the highest office — with 77 out of 80 votes — to the thunder of massive explosions. Then, white-suited and standing beneath a portrait of his murdered brother, Amin Gemayel promised to bring peace to his country and stamp out 'the wars of others' in Lebanon, without actually naming the Israelis, Palestinians and Syrians. Unsmiling and hesitant, he drove off with his army intelligence officer to lunch with Philip Habib, who was in an ideal position to acquaint him with the realities of power.

These realities, of course, involved not the extent of Amin Gemayel's power but the restrictions placed upon it by the armies which occupied his country. He could not insult them because he would have to plead with them, treat with them, intrigue with them to achieve the goal which he announced — the same aim to which the returning multinational force would now publicly aspire: 'a strong, independent sovereign state capable of safeguarding public freedoms and bringing about a withdrawal of all foreign armies from the entire soil of the homeland.'

The bodies that were found in Chatila were buried in a plot of land just to the right of the entrance to the camp in a ceremony of great grief and nauseating stench. The corpses were placed in shrouds and laid at the bottom of a pit which was then filled in by a bulldozer.

One of the few Israelis to have kept a detailed diary of events at the time of the massacre was Bruce Kashdan, a bald Israeli Foreign Ministry official with an uncanny resemblance to Bill Foley, the AP photographer. The two men were sometimes confused with each other, to Kashdan's amusement and Foley's consternation. Kashdan was at Baabda at the time of the massacre, and he told the Kahan commission how on 17 September, Morris Draper, the US diplomat in east Beirut, telephoned him to warn that 'using the Phalange in west Beirut could have horrible results.' Kashdan said he was not told after Draper's call that the Phalange had entered the camps.

At ten o'clock on Saturday morning, however, he received another call from Draper, who said:

You must stop the massacres. They are obscene. I have an officer in the camp counting the bodies. You ought to be ashamed. The situation is rotten and terrible. They are killing children. You are in absolute control of the area and you are therefore responsible for that area.

Kashdan was later posted to the new Israeli 'liaison office' overlooking the Mediterranean north of Beirut, the embryonic diplomatic bureau which the Israelis — in their dreamlike optimism — still hoped to turn one day into a fully fledged embassy. I knew Kashdan and liked him. He had evidently been gravely upset by the massacres and I wondered what he felt about the responsibility for what had happened.

I sat in his office, the Israeli flag on its roof, and asked him what he thought the dead of the Holocaust might have said had they seen Chatila. What would Anne Frank have said? Her diary, which I first read at school as a 12-year-old, showed that she believed in the essential goodness of humans. She died of typhus at Bergen-Belsen in 1945, after being betrayed to the Nazis, like Szymon Datner's family in Bialystok. What would Anne Frank have said, I asked, if she had walked with me through the entrance of Chatila on the morning of 18 September and had seen what I saw there?

Kashdan thought about this for a long time. 'Well,' he said, 'I don't think she would have understood it. Lebanon is so complex a place.' We looked at each other. He must have known how unsatisfactory, how weak his answer was. Anne Frank had written with disgust of how the Germans planned to 'cleanse' Utrecht of Jews. 'As if the Jews were cockroaches,' she had written in her diary, employing the same word that General Rafael Eitan would use to describe the Palestinians of the West Bank shortly after his retirement.* No, I doubted very much if Anne Frank would have failed to understand what happened at Chatila. I had a shrewd suspicion what she might have said. And so, I think, did Kashdan.

Tveit and I continued our inquiries. We questioned the survivors again. We heard strange stories. Foley was told that an Israeli photographer believed one of the massacre victims had been a Jewish Holocaust survivor from Auschwitz. Could it be true? The woman had travelled to Palestine with other Jewish immigrants in 1946, the tale went, but had married an Arab, travelling into exile with him in 1948 and eventually settling in the slums of Chatila. Someone, so the story had it, had seen her Auschwitz number tattooed on her wrist. The Phalangists had taken her away on 17 September, shot her and thrown her in a mass grave. Foley did not see the photographer again. We could never confirm the story.

In the years after the massacre, we would return to the camp at each anniversary to talk to the survivors. Some would tell us that the Israelis were in the camp with the Phalange during the killing. Many elderly Palestinians can understand and speak Hebrew and claim that they talked in Hebrew to Israelis during the massacre. So were the Israelis in the camp?

As the years passed, there was more killing and destruction at Chatila. Shells would fall on the final mass grave of the hundreds of 1982 victims.

Scheherezade Faramarzi, AP's Iranian reporter, had formed a friendship with several Palestinian women and she would talk to them for hours about their memories, forcing them to repeat their experiences over and over to see if there was some detail, some minute fact that we had overlooked.

September 1984. Sawssan, aged 14: 'My wish is for a Phalange to come here so I could kill him with a knife and take my revenge. The

---

* Speaking to an Israeli Knesset committee in 1983, Eitan boasted that after Israel had further multiplied its West Bank settlements, 'all the Arabs will be able to do is scuttle around like drugged cockroaches in a bottle.' See *The Times*, 15 April 1983.

Kata'ib [Phalange] killed my three brothers, my grandfather, my two uncles.' Amneh Shehadeh, aged 40, born at Khasayer near Haifa: 'I wish I had seen the body of my son. I wish I had seen him dead and I wish I knew who killed him so I could commit this crime against his murderer. There were Jews here too. They had more mercy than the *Kata'ib*. If it hadn't been for the Jews who came in here, all the women, girls and children would have been killed. One Jew was here, yes, at the massacre, and he said: "Come on, come on *madame, madame*, baby this way." There was a *Kata'ib* man there with a mask and holes in it showing his eyes.'

The women spoke in a wail that turned to shrieks when they approached the moment of personal catastrophe. Um Hussein, aged 36. Her husband Hamid Mustafa Khalifeh, aged 39, was killed in the massacre. So were two of her sons. She has eight surviving children to care for. She has fine features and smiles at us when she speaks, as if to protect us from her own story.

Some people have pity for me and help me but it is difficult to accustom myself to this new life where I have nothing left. I am used to being treated like a lady, to be taken here and there, to have the door opened for me. Now my wings have been broken, shattered. My husband and the two boys were my columns, my support. You might say my house has collapsed. When I see people happy, I am sad. My son Mohamed keeps on calling for his father. He waits for him at the gate or at the window and stretches out his hands ... I am worn out, my hands tremble. I cannot work at home, can't clean up or sweep the house. I feel ever so lonely ... I try to avoid passing the spot where they were killed. I remember how Hussein's head, his body were thrown here and there. I have even moved my house to avoid the place. Every Monday and Thursday, I go to the graveyard to pray over their souls. I go whenever their faces come into my mind. It happened on the Thursday afternoon, at six o'clock, the black day. They took them and killed them. I pray when I go to the graveyard. I take a tape-recording of the Koran and play it to them. I cry. I take flowers with me and throw them when I enter the graveyard. I don't know where my husband and my boys are lying. I wish I knew where they are buried so I could put up their pictures and build a marble stone for them and wash the marble every now and then. But I know they are there. So when I go to the graveyard, I just throw the flowers and hope they land on the right places.

12 Pandora's Box

> We can go on like this — recreating and reflecting the
> existing images of each other, and reflecting these
> reflections — endlessly and hatefully — as in a hall of
> mirrors. The result will be that all of us — Israelis,
> Palestinians, Arabs — will be locked in endless and bloody
> agony in a hall of mirrors of our own creation and from
> which there is no exit.
>   Or we can begin by adopting a certain integrity — a
> certain generosity — in the use of language.
>   That's not too hard. It's the easiest of the hard things
> that must be done if we are ever to come to peace with one
> another, and so with ourselves.
>
> Israeli journalist Michael Elkins, in the Jerusalem Post,
13 November 1983

The week after the massacre at Sabra and Chatila, *Newsweek* magazine
decided that the most important event of the previous seven days had
been the death of Princess Grace of Monaco in a road accident. *Two*
weeks after the massacre — when the enormity of what had happened
had presumably penetrated its offices in New York — *Newsweek* was in
no doubt about its priorities. The magazine's cover story was headlined
'Israel in Torment' and carried a picture of a dead dove, an olive branch
in its beak, its blood staining the Star of David. One of the subsidiary
cover headlines recorded 'The Anguish of American Jews' while an
inside report dwelt upon 'The Troubled Soul of Israel'.

These expressions were instructive; anyone in west Beirut might have
concluded that it was the *Palestinians* — not the Israelis — who were in
'torment', and that it was the survivors of Sabra and Chatila — not
American Jews — who were chiefly experiencing 'anguish'. If Israel had
a 'troubled soul', then what were the feelings of the Palestinians who
had been betrayed by America's promise of protection for the civilians
left behind by the PLO?

The magazine's news coverage was less flawed than its headlines. It
attempted to give a chronological account of the massacre, it carried a
detailed opinion poll showing the drop in US public support for Israel as
a result of the murders, and it was harshly critical of both Begin and
Sharon. *Newsweek* reported that Israel had 'transformed itself from the
underdog to the overlord in the Middle East — but at what price to the

original sustaining dream of Zion?' Israel, one of its reports concluded, had 'moved steadily and perhaps irreversibly to the right'; as its isolation had increased, 'it has looked to its guns while its moral sense, normally one of the world's most acute, has often grown callous.'

Yet *Newsweek* showed its bias. One section of its report on the massacre referred to 'the festering Arab question', noting that 'the Arabs' blood hate has done more than anything else to corner Israel and turn it hard.' Here were the 'buzz' words the Israeli government itself might have used if invited to write *Newsweek's* report. The Arab question was 'festering' – dirty, unclean, unwashed – while Arab 'blood hate' – unreasoning, mindless, evil – was ultimately to blame for Israel's sins. For Israel's moral sense, as the magazine had reminded its readers, was 'normally one of the world's most acute'. *Newsweek* revealed no source for this sweeping generalisation.

No one in Beirut registered any surprise at this kind of coverage. Had the dead of Sabra and Chatila been Jews rather than Palestinians, Israelis rather than Arabs, would *Newsweek* still have thought the demise of Princess Grace the more important story?

The Wall Street Journal, whose sympathy for Israel has been the driving force behind its editorials on the Middle East, briskly dismissed the significance of the massacre at Sabra and Chatila in a leader on the first anniversary of the slaughter. While the 'assaults [*sic*] deserved the shocked response' which they received, the paper said, 'it's worth noting that ... the Sabra and Chatila casualties ... included only 15 women and 20 children. The rest of the 460 counted victims were males, including many Lebanese, Iranians and Syrians as well as Palestinians.' Quite apart from the untruthfulness of this statement – on the day the massacre ended, Jenkins and I saw scores of dead women and children – the tone and implication of the paper's words were themselves a disgrace.

What was the significance of claiming that so few women and children were killed? Was a total of 35 women and children not worthy of *The Wall Street Journal*'s compassion? Of course there were Lebanese among the dead; thousands of Lebanese poor, particularly from the Shia community, lived among the Palestinians in Sabra. And many Palestinians were born in Syria and thus carried Syrian identification documents. We never found any trace of dead Iranians. But what if we had? Was *The Wall Street Journal* suggesting that murdering an Iranian is less important than murdering a Lebanese, or that killing Syrians carries less moral opprobrium than slaughtering Palestinians? Or was it the other way round?

To understand the shameful nature of these editorials – for *The Wall Street Journal* was not alone in dismissing the significance of what happened in west Beirut – we in Lebanon used to reverse the circumstances of the deed. If, for example, 460 Israelis had been massacred, would the same paper have minimised the extent of the atrocity by pointing out that 'only' 35 of the slaughtered Jews were women and children? Had *The Wall Street Journal* done this, it would surely have been instantly accused of anti-semitism. And had it gone on to point out that of the Israeli men who were murdered, a substantial proportion had not even been born in Israel but were immigrants from, say, Yemen or Morocco – or from New York – would it not have been publicly condemned as both inflammatory and racist?

It has always been difficult to explain to Arabs why the Western press, with only a few exceptions, has been so consistently pro-Israeli in its editorial opinions and often in its reporting as well. To those of us working in Beirut, the inability of newspaper editors to see the Middle East as a harsh and uncompromising conflict between peoples was both vexing and provocative. Repeatedly, television as well as newspaper reporters would find that their head offices believed the Arab–Israeli dispute to be a battle of David and Goliath, between good and evil. The Israelis, of course, represented the side of good. The Arabs were mendacious, untrustworthy, capable of the most bestial cruelty. Thus newspaper cartoons in the West – even, from time to time, in *The Times* – would depict Arabs as hook-nosed, leering and unshaven. Had Israelis been portrayed with these same characteristics, the papers would have been condemned – rightly – as anti-semitic.

The Arabs have, of course, helped to create this bias. The cancer of dictatorship, repression and corruption has eaten deeply into the fabric of the Middle East nation-states which obtained their independence after the Second World War. Not even the most liberal or pro-Western Arab regimes have been able to create an electoral democracy like Israel's; and while Arab leaders may believe that Western-style democracy is unsuited to their societies, they cannot provide a similar excuse for the lack of personal and political freedom which fetters the lives of their subjects. Nor have they ever been able to explain why torture is so all-pervasive and essential a part of their security apparatus.

There is a wealth of evidence that Israel has practised – and still practises – torture against its Arab opponents. Anyone who suspects this is untrue should ask to inspect the Israeli security service's 'Russian Compound' in Jerusalem or demand to see the inmates of Khiam prison in Israel's occupation zone in southern Lebanon. Nor has Israel's democracy been extended to the Palestinians of the West Bank and the Gaza Strip. Democratically elected Palestinian mayors and officials have been deposed by the occupation authorities when they have opposed Israel's policies.

But the long Arab flirtation with east European socialism – and the weird cocktail of tribal loyalties, pan-Arab triumphalism and empty rhetoric that this produced — created distrust and sometimes downright hatred in the West. The impassioned demands for Arab unity and the contradictory but persistent proof that these regimes preferred to fight each other rather than Israel, further damaged the Arab cause. Only Lebanon, with its large Christian community, its unwritten 'democratic' covenant and its greedy fascination for all things Western, seemed remotely attractive amid these dictatorships.

There is a growing volume of research into the history of Western attitudes towards Palestine, of which Edward Said's *Orientalism* was the most seminal, but the Holocaust created the sympathy and guilt which the West felt towards the state of Israel. The idea that the Jews of Israel 'made the desert bloom' — even though there was ample evidence that Jews and Arabs in Palestine had been producing this effect for generations — held an extraordinary attraction for a postwar world whose cities had been laid waste and whose people had been slaughtered on a scale unprecedented in history. That this new state of Israel should have been created by the very race against whom the greatest and most evil of crimes had been committed, made it an irresistible symbol of human renewal.

While the British could not forget that the Jews of Palestine had waged a guerrilla war against them — a conflict that involved the Jews in a campaign of 'terrorism' just as murderous as the Arab 'terrorism' against which Israel later claimed to be fighting on the world's behalf — popular imagination in the West had been captured by the image of a small, vulnerable country rising from the ashes of Auschwitz to reassert the moral values which had been lost in two world wars. Even the Jewish massacre of Palestinians at Deir Yassin in 1948 failed to interrupt the message that Israeli power was based upon 'purity of arms'.

Jewish American support for Israel coincided with the official United States postwar policy of opposing the spread of communism, a struggle in which a friendly pro-American, pro-Western Israel was clearly an asset in the Middle East. It was not difficult for Israel to portray itself as a democratic oasis in a sea of hostile, potentially communist Arab states. Those in the West who dared to challenge this image were reminded of the Holocaust and of the collective guilt of the 'civilised' world which had turned its back upon the Jews of Europe when Hitler tried to destroy them.

At Yad Vashem, there is a large aerial photograph of the Auschwitz-Birkenau extermination camp, taken from a US aircraft during the Second World War. It shows not only the compounds, barracks and railhead, but even a party of Jews making their way from the selection ramp to the gas chambers for liquidation. Why did the Allies not even bomb the railway lines to Auschwitz? Why did they ignore Jewish appeals to bomb the gas chambers? That photograph at Yad Vashem draws the West into the circle of guilt as surely as the pictures of Sheikh Haj Amin Al-Husseini inspecting the Muslim SS units implicated the Palestinians. Why did Pius XII not appeal for the lives of the Jews? Why did Christianity not save the Jews of Europe?

Compared to these momentous questions, the fate of the Palestinians appeared irrelevant. In a world which was witnessing the mass resettlement of millions of European civilians, the displacement of around 500,000 Arabs for the people of the Holocaust was not going to damage many consciences in the West. Indeed, the sacrifice of those Palestinians was one way in which the West could avoid answering the terrible question: why was Hitler permitted to exterminate the Jews of Europe?

Anyone in Europe or America who dared to criticise Israel's behaviour in the coming decades was invariably attacked by the Israelis – or by Israel's supporters in other countries – with veiled or direct accusations of anti-semitism. For all but a few diplomats and writers, Israel acquired a moral immunity; its motives had to be regarded as unimpeachable, its enemies as barbaric, if less efficient, than the Nazis. Presidents, prime ministers, diplomats, politicians, churchmen, authors, actors, editors and journalists did not need to visit Yad Vashem to be reminded of this. The merest suggestion that Israel had done wrong in the Middle East would bring forth outraged protests not just from Israel but from within the nation where the criticism was originally made; for Israel's moral defences existed within every overseas Jewish community, the most powerful of which lived in the United States.

Thus there came into being a whole genre of uncritical pro-Israeli literature and films. The best-known popular example was Leon Uris' *Exodus*, an epic about the postwar Jewish immigration to Palestine and the foundation of the state of Israel. The story of the Jews *is* an epic of history, but the need to present Israel's story in a blameless light produced a defective, incomplete understanding of the Middle East. Israel's army was extolled in print and on the screen as invincible, its secret services as daring and infallible. At best, this provided a constant reminder to the Israelis of the high standards which they had set themselves before the world.

At worst, it produced material about the Arabs which was racist and – since the Arabs are also Semites – anti-semitic as well. In literature and on film, the Arabs were portrayed as Israel's propagandists would have wished; uneducated, dishonest, vicious, physically dirty and rapacious. In 1949, for example, Arthur Koestler felt able to write of the Palestinian exodus in *Promise and Fulfilment*:

The old ones will tie a mattress and a brass coffee-pot on the donkey, the old woman will walk ahead leading the donkey by the rein and the old man will ride on it, wrapped in his kuffiyeh, and sunk in solemn meditation about the lost opportunity of raping his youngest grandchild.*

By 1956, the American writer Edmund Wilson was able to describe the position of Arabs in Israel as:

rather like that of the Navahos in the American southwest; a once fierce but still picturesque, pathetically retarded people, cut off from the main community but presenting a recurrent problem. In a large Arab town like Acre, the squalor of the swarming streets inspires in an Israeli the same distaste that it does in a visiting Westerner. For the Jew, the spectacle of flocks of urchins, dirty, untaught, diseased, bawling and shrieking and begging, inspires even moral horror.†

This is the language of the Nazis, who described the Jews of the ghettos of eastern Europe in precisely the same terms, as a people deserving of 'moral horror'. In this case, of course, it is the Arabs who have produced the 'problem'.‡

While reporters rarely used language of this kind, Western news coverage of the Middle East was for many years based on Israel's own view of the conflict. Israel welcomed the foreign press and was rewarded with generally favourable reporting. American and other Western correspondents were often of Jewish origin and felt an immediate affinity to the nation they were sent to cover. The history, culture and people of Israel were familiar and the communications generally efficient; it was easy to sympathise with the Israelis and to ignore some of the more glaring contradictions in the line propagated by the government's public relations men. Israel, for instance, was regularly portrayed as a vulnerable, tiny nation of Holocaust survivors, hemmed in on three sides by ruthless and undemocratic Arab regimes who wished to finish Hitler's work by driving the Jews into the sea. Yet its powerful army was just as often depicted as an unconquerable force, without precedent in feats of arms and daring. The discrepancy between terrifying vulnerability and enormous military power was rarely explored.

The Arabs, on the other hand, were ordained to play the role of aggressors, either arrogantly demanding the liquidation of Israel or — after their defeat in the 1967 war — supporting the Palestinian 'terrorists'

---

* Promise and Fulfilment by Arthur Koestler (London, Macmillan, 1949), pp. 199–200, quoted in Gilmour, Dispossessed, p. 15.

† Black, Red, Blond and Olive by Edmund Wilson (New York, Oxford University Press, 1956), pp. 462–3.

‡ The commercial cinema has also denigrated Arabs. Ashanti, a feature film about the kidnapping of the wife of an English doctor by Arab slave-traders, for example, was made partly in Israel in the late 1970s and depicted Arabs as almost exclusively child-molesters, rapists, murderers, liars and thieves. The only 'honest' Arab is murdered at the end of the movie, in which the actors Michael Caine, Omar Sharif and Peter Ustinov appeared. Even the producers of the film of John Le Carré's novel The Little Drummer Girl, with its critical portrayal of the Mossad intelligence organisation, felt constrained to announce publicly that Le Carré was a supporter of Israel. In one of the film's final scenes, Israeli aircraft bomb Palestinian 'terrorists' in a refugee camp — killing not one innocent civilian.

who wanted to kill the Jews of Israel and take their homes. Newspapers often maintained two correspondents in the Middle East, one in Jerusalem — to report on Israel — and the other in Beirut to cover the rest of the Arab world. But this did not ensure that both sides were fairly represented. The Israelis deluged reporters with information and offers of assistance, while many Arab nations regarded Western journalists as spies, refusing to respond to the simplest of enquiries or to produce even the most junior of ministers for interviews.

In time of war, the Israelis would take journalists to the front — or at least to that part of the line from where the most politically advantageous reports might be written — while Arab nations would routinely confine Western reporters to their capitals, supplying them only with speeches of unquotable rhetoric and details of non-existent military successes. With rare exceptions, combat coverage of Middle East wars therefore came exclusively out of Israel — so long as Israel was fighting in Syria, Jordan or Egypt. If Israel ever went to war in Lebanon, however, a different situation would apply. For the Lebanese government was too weak and its security authorities too divided to impose censorship upon the Western journalists based in Beirut.

Israel's military operations in Lebanon therefore proved a critical turning point. Almost overnight, the traditional Jerusalem—Beirut newspaper system of covering the Middle East no longer operated in Israel's favour. Reporters travelling with Israeli troops were subject to severe restrictions on their movements and sometimes to censorship, but their opposite numbers in Beirut could travel freely and write whatever they wished. For the very first time, reporters had open access to the *Arab* side of a Middle East war and found that Israel's supposedly invincible army, with its moral high ground and clearly stated military objectives against 'terrorists', did not perform in the way that legend would have suggested. The Israelis acted brutally, they mistreated prisoners, killed thousands of civilians, lied about their activities and then watched their militia allies slaughter the occupants of a refugee camp. In fact, they behaved very much like the 'uncivilised' Arab armies whom they had so consistently denigrated over the preceding 30 years.

The reporting from Lebanon — first in 1978 during the first Israeli invasion, and then in 1982 — was a new and disturbing experience for the Israelis. They no longer had a monopoly on the truth. Israeli official statements were denied by journalists who had witnessed the suffering of civilians under indiscriminate bombardment. The old terminology — of 'pre-emptive strikes' against 'terrorists', of 'surgical precision' bombing, of 'pin-point accuracy' bombardments, of 'mopping-up' operations — was no longer accepted by reporters who could see for themselves what these phrases really meant.

The shattering of Israel's humanitarian image was a devastating moment in the country's history. The reporting of the siege of west Beirut — and particularly the television images of an all-powerful army shelling largely civilian areas — had an incalculable effect on Western opinion. Those who had, even subconsciously, felt that Israel was a guardian of moral values in an anarchic world were forced to reconsider long-held beliefs. It was scarcely surprising that foreign supporters of Israel — and especially the Jewish diaspora — would experience a deep sense of shock, even outrage, when confronted with such evidence.

It was thus with profound relief that they greeted Israel's own explanation for otherwise inexplicable phenomena: The Plot. Not a conspiracy according to the Arab definition, perhaps, but a distant cousin nonetheless, and one which would henceforth be introduced into every interview or discussion about the conduct of the Lebanon war. The journalists had lied.

Earleen Tatro of AP was among the first to understand the process of demonising the press. One morning in late August 1982, as the PLO were evacuating Beirut, she threw a thick file of papers onto my desk in the office. 'Take a look at that, Fisk,' she said. 'They're already rewriting history.' It was a translation of a long article in the Israeli newspaper *Maariv*, headlined 'The Media Sold Their Conscience to the PLO'. It quoted an anonymous 'tall, middle-aged journalist' of unspecified nationality as saying that foreign correspondents in Beirut 'sold their journalistic conscience, receiving bribes according to their importance and influence and paying with silence or sympathetic articles about the Palestinian struggle.' Other foreign correspondents, according to the same informant, 'did not have to be bribed' because they were intimidated into silence.

The same article went on to quote further anonymous journalists as giving 'great weight to the destructive role of the media in the anti-Lebanese conspiracy [*sic*]. They talk about the "total sale" of newspapers and radio and television networks to the terrorist organisations.' No evidence was provided for these accusations. But seven days later, *Maariv* published what it claimed was a detailed account of the 'physical liquidation' of journalists in Beirut, 'acts of terror perpetrated against the media until ... "PLO discipline" had been imposed on the press in west Beirut.' According to the paper, the 'terrorists' had 'liquidated ... Larry Buchman, correspondent of the ABC television network' and 'Sean Toolan, ABC correspondent'.

From beyond the grave, Buchman must have laughed at this sad, pathetically untruthful account of his demise. He had been a stringer not for television but for ABC radio, a cheerful, hard-working reporter with no axe to grind. But he was not killed by 'terrorists' in Beirut. He died in a plane crash in Jordan. He was flying out of Amman on a private jet hired by ABC when the aircraft went out of control and landed upside-down near the runway, killing Buchman, ABC producer David Jane and the plane's two-man crew. Buchman and Jane were carrying a videotaped interview with Arafat which had earlier been conducted in Beirut by Barbara Walters of ABC television; the tape had been taken to Amman for editing and satellite transmission to the United States. His end was tragic and unnecessary; the aircraft crashed not because of 'terrorism' but because the Jordanian pilot — despite previous warnings that he should not do so — had chosen to wear cowboy boots on the flight deck. On take-off, he caught his heel under the rudder and turned the plane over.

Toolan might have laughed even louder from the afterworld. An Irish-born stringer for *The Observer* of London as well as ABC radio, he had formed attachments to several married women in Beirut. One of them was the wife of a British Embassy official; another was a Palestinian girl whose jealous husband decided to stop the affair by hiring two gunmen to murder him. Walking home to Ein Mreisse in the early hours one morning in 1981 from the bar of the Commodore Hotel, Toolan was attacked by the men who hit him in the face with an ice-pick and then shot him in the back of the neck. They were said to have been paid 750 Lebanese pounds — about 60 US dollars at the current rate of exchange — to kill Toolan. We never found out if the gunmen were Palestinians or Lebanese; even in a more law-abiding Arab capital, Toolan might have suffered a similar fate for seducing an Arab's wife.

But the Israelis turned him into a victim of 'terrorism' and claimed later that Toolan had been deliberately killed because of an ABC television film which had attacked the PLO. *Maariv* also took up the case of Edouard Saab, the editor of *L'Orient Le Jour* who doubled as a correspondent for the French daily *Le Monde*. In 1976, the paper said, Saab had bitterly criticised the Palestinians and as a result, at a roadblock on the front line, 'a terrorist emptied a round into his head, and he slumped down into a pool of blood. An American friend, the Beirut correspondent for *Newsweek* was sitting beside him but came out unharmed.'* Saab was indeed shot on the line in 1976, but he was killed — like many hundreds of Lebanese — by a sniper who could not have known his identity. He was not at a roadblock; he was trying to drive his car round a shell-hole when the gunman fired from hundreds of yards away. Saab's friend was Henry Tanner of the *New York Times*, not a *Newsweek* correspondent.

The only Western journalist in Beirut whose death could be attributed without a shadow of doubt to Palestinian gunmen was Robert Pfeffer, a German reporter who had taken leave of absence from his magazine in 1977 to write a book about Palestinian gun-running. After valiantly

* See *Maariv*, 20 and 27 August 1982.

ignoring a series of telephoned warnings from anonymous callers that he should leave Beirut, he was murdered at the door of his home by at least three assassins firing automatic rifles, all of them believed to be members of the Popular Front for the Liberation of Palestine.

Here was a clear case of a journalist losing his life because of his pursuit of the truth. For apologists to claim — as they later did — that Pfeffer's death was the reaction of suspicious gunmen who feared for their own internal military security, rather than an attempt to intimidate journalists, was to miss the point. The PLO denied any involvement in the murder but the implication was that journalistic inquiries into gun-running were off-limits. Certainly, Douglas-Home and I talked about this when I was making my own inquiries into the connection between the PLO and the Hoffman group which was supplying arms to Beirut. I decided then that we could not allow The Times to be influenced by Pfeffer's fate. Either we told the truth about what went on in Beirut or we left Lebanon altogether. Douglas-Home agreed, and the results of my inquiries — which the PLO condemned as 'lies' — were published in the newspaper, prominently and uncut.

It was certainly true that journalists fell victim to the general lawlessness of Lebanon. In a preposterous incident in the spring of 1981, a group of five American journalists in Beirut, including Foley of AP and another photographer, set off at midnight — after an extremely long and liquid dinner — to investigate reports of an Israeli landing near Damour. Israeli jets had strafed the main road during the day and PFLP guerrillas on the coast road were stunned to see the five men, all dressed in jackets and ties, hurtling down the highway towards them in the early hours.

The Palestinians feared a raid by Israeli saboteurs, and here were five Westerners, all claiming to be journalists but none carrying press identification and one with no film in his camera. Their suspicions were further aroused when they found a bullet-proof vest in the trunk of the journalists' car. The five men were held for 20 hours, during which time they were strip-searched in an underground prison beneath Sabra camp and interrogated to find out whether they were Israeli agents. At least one of them was told to write a 'last letter' to a friend. The purpose, of course, was to find out if the prisoner, in extremis, broke down and wrote to a family in Israel. When Foley wrote a 'last letter' to Nick Tatro, apologising for making the AP look so ridiculous, it became obvious to the Palestinian captors that the five men were what they said they were: foolish journalists rather than reckless spies. Many coffees later, the embarrassed five were released.

The Israelis were to seize on this incident a year later to claim that the Beirut press corps were intimidated by 'terrorists'. Christopher Walker, The Times correspondent in Jerusalem, believed the Israeli allegation had been prompted by the showing in America of an ABC television documentary, *Under the Israeli Thumb*, which was highly critical of Israeli policies on the occupied West Bank. It did not dawn on us then, of course, that the claim might also be used to undermine the credibility of American journalists who would shortly be covering not a night-time Israeli raid but a full-scale Israeli invasion.

Within five months, the Israelis were telling the world of the martyrdom of Buchman and Toolan, and their stories were taken up by Jewish newspapers in the United States and Britain. Already the *Jerusalem Post* had told its readers of a 'conspiracy of silence' in Beirut, wherein journalists were 'intimidated and, in some cases, murdered by the PLO'. According to the paper, 'the PLO news service was so efficient that newsmen did not need to leave their hotel-bar in Beirut.'*

Mahmoud Labadi, Arafat's factotum in the PLO, was personally flattered by this description of his tiresome, ramshackle and hopelessly inefficient publicity organisation – until we told him that it was totally untrue. But the stories continued. Israeli press officers at their head-quarters below Baabda would assail journalists from west Beirut with a series of questions. Why had we not reported the 'truth' about the PLO? Why had we not recorded the murder of journalists by the 'terrorists'? Why had we not told our readers of the PLO's intimidation of villages in southern Lebanon? Why had we not described the way in which the PLO had positioned guns beside civilian apartment blocks in west Beirut? Why had we not – and this question came in the aftermath of the Sabra and Chatila massacre – why had we not reported the Syrian killings at Hama?

Day after day, I would explain that we had indeed reported the behaviour of the PLO in Beirut and southern Lebanon. I would tell Israeli officers that in dozens of trips to villages in the south of Lebanon, I had witnessed the PLO's arrogance and reported on its intimidation. I recounted the instances which I had personally witnessed.† I pointed out that we had reported the deaths of Lebanese and foreign journalists and suggested the identity of the culprits. I said that *The Times* had carried a series of dispatches under my by-line on the PLO's use of civilian 'cover' for their guns and that I had personally been to Hama during the suppression of the rebellion there.

It was useless. No sooner had I explained in detail to one Israeli that the 'conspiracy of silence' was an Israeli invention, than an Israeli foreign ministry official or an army officer from a different unit would demand answers to the same list of questions all over again. Why had I not had the courage to go to Hama when the Syrians were slaughtering

---

* *Jerusalem Post*, 14 July 1982.
† All the incidents involving the PLO recounted in chapters 3, 4, 6, 7, 8 and 9 of this book, for example, were recorded – most of them in far greater detail – in the pages of *The Times*, under my by-line, between 1976 and 1982.

the inhabitants? Why had I been cowed into silence by the PLO? Once more I would start to explain that I *had* been to Hama, that we were *not* cowed by the PLO, but to no avail.

'Israel has been getting a raw deal in international press coverage of Operation Peace for Galilee,' Major Yehuda Weinraub complained in the *IDF Journal*, the house magazine of the Israel military spokesman in Jerusalem. 'This coverage has been characterised by an inordinate number of factual errors as well as by unprofessional journalistic techniques such as quoting exclusively from one source, introducing value judgements [*sic*] into articles, withholding information and employing words charged with unsavory [*sic*] emotional connotations . . .'*

Any attempt at self-criticism on the part of the Israelis inevitably focused on the strict censorship which the Israeli military authorities enforced in the initial days of the Lebanon invasion. If Israel had failed in the public relations war, then it must have been due to some administrative error, some inadequate policy towards the media which would be rectified in future. Perhaps journalists should have been allowed into Lebanon from Israel at an earlier date. Perhaps the anonymous Israeli military 'spokesman' should have given more details of the extent of the operation in early June. But not once did these Israelis face the truth: that no amount of public relations effort could change the reality of the war in Lebanon, a conflict against 'terrorism' which turned into a bloodbath for thousands of civilians and culminated in a massacre in which the Israeli army bore at least indirect responsibility.

Most of the Israelis believed their own propaganda. They were convinced that the press had lied, just as they had no doubt that they were conducting a war against 'terrorism'. The journalists were to blame. Why else would Israel's name — hitherto treated with such respect by newspapers and television — suddenly find itself besmirched in Lebanon? Slowly, but with ever-increasing frequency, the Israelis suggested that we were anti-semitic. Like Hitler and Arafat.

The sheer volume of work — and danger — that journalists in Lebanon faced meant that we scarcely had time to notice these attacks. If the Israelis had decided to follow their bombardment of west Beirut by turning their guns on the press, we had to concentrate on our task of chronicling the deployment of the multinational force and the collapse of civil order in those areas of Lebanon under Israeli occupation. For the Druze were now at war with the Christian militiamen whom the Israelis had unwisely installed in the Chouf in the heady days of early June.

If ever there was a time for a foreign army to take stock of its actions in Lebanon, this was it. The Syrians had come to grief because they had

* *IDF Journal*, December 1982, vol. 1, no. 2.

failed to understand that their own long-term objectives were no longer
relevant. Now the Israelis resolutely refused to face any serious public
analysis of the hopeless political aims upon which they had embarked in
the same country. A unified – and pacified – Lebanon eluded the
Israelis as surely as it had the Syrians. And although the PLO had
evacuated Beirut, an estimated 16,000 Palestinian guerrillas remained
elsewhere in Lebanon, particularly in Tripoli and the Bekaa.

Yet the only public analysis upon which the Israelis saw fit to embark
in the following months – outside the deliberations of the Kahan
commission on the Sabra and Chatila massacre – was an expensive
'symposium' on 'War and the Press', organised by the *Jerusalem Post* as
part of the newspaper's fiftieth anniversary celebrations. Here, commen-
tators like Martin Peretz, editor of the pro-Israeli Washington weekly
New Republic, Dr Conor Cruise O'Brien and even Colonel Paul Kedar,
who had been the Israeli military spokesman in Beirut, took the opportunity to attack journalists for their coverage of the war.*

Peretz told his audience that the PLO in Lebanon 'censored photographs of weapons caches in civilian areas, resulting in the broadcasting
of TV pictures ... of Israeli shells being fired, but not of what they had
hit ...' O'Brien, whose articles in *The Observer* had proved so favourable
to Israel during the war that they were copied and distributed to visiting
journalists by Israeli military press officers, said that his paper's editor
had 'banished all his pieces [on Lebanon and the PLO] to obscure parts
of the paper' in 1981 but that after Israel invaded Lebanon, coverage of
Lebanon became '*à la mode*'.

Kedar, who back in July had been forced to admit that the Israelis
lied when they said they had not cut electricity and water supplies to
west Beirut but had expressed the belief that the civilian population
were 'not starving yet', condemned the 'abysmal ignorance' of journalists
in Lebanon who 'assumed the arrogant pose as the keepers of the world
conscience.' David Landau, the *Jerusalem Post*'s diplomatic correspondent, pointed out that the same reaction would have ensued had the
British army 'bombed Belfast's Bogside to get at the IRA, and accidentally
hit a school'.† O'Brien confronted the issue of Israel's morality, asking
why Jews, with their long history of persecution, should be expected to
'behave better' when logic would demand 'that those who were persecuted
should be forgiven poor behaviour.'

Yet all this avoided the real issue: Lebanon. Israel was in trouble not
because of the press but because it had invaded Lebanon. It had become

---

* See the *Jerusalem Post*, 5 December 1982.
† It was in keeping with the lamentable inaccuracies that occurred in all these discussions that
the *Jerusalem Post* should have thought the Catholic Bogside area of Londonderry was located
in Belfast.

trapped in the country by its own illusions – of fighting 'terrorism', of saving Christianity, of creating a pliant Lebanese state, even of avenging the Holocaust. These dreams lay behind the military adventures in Lebanon, but they were not addressed by the Israelis. Even Jewish newspapers in the diaspora chose to avoid these questions. In London, the *Jewish Chronicle*, with its long and honourable history – and with the financial resources to investigate what had gone wrong in the war by sending its own reporters to Lebanon – chose to print little more than the Israeli version of events, together with a few dissenting readers' letters.

By May of 1983, Israeli troops were facing a serious guerrilla war in Shia Muslim areas of Lebanon, amid the population that had supposedly welcomed the invading army less than a year before. Yet in London, the Institute of Jewish Affairs held a 'symposium' on 5 May, not on Israel and the Lebanon war but on 'The *Media* and the Lebanon War', at which the chairman opened the proceedings with remarks to the effect that there was 'unanimity' – later qualified to 'virtual unanimity' after objections from the floor – that the media of the world had 'vilified and distorted' Israeli actions in Lebanon.

By chance, I was in London on that day and sat at the back of the hall as Melvin Lasky, the editor of *Encounter* magazine, announced that journalists in west Beirut were 'censored by the Syrians although their copy did not say this'. This, of course, was untrue. Lasky said that the Jews 'have always been a story.' They were half the story of the Bible; they were a people, a culture. But his venom was reserved for 'the shallowness, the cheapness' of Western reporting. Reporters, he said, had talked of indiscriminate bombing. How did those reporters know what indiscriminate bombing was? 'The reporter doesn't know what the bomb hits – he's on the fourteenth floor of the Commodore Hotel.'

This nonsense was cheered by the largely Jewish audience. Lasky compared coverage of Lebanon to British press coverage of the Soviet Union in the 1930s, and of Germany in the late 1940s when, he said, Fleet Street constantly gave the impression that the Nazis were about to make a comeback. He mentioned my name and there was a growl of dislike from the audience. Robert Fisk was 'a charming and talented fellow', Lasky said. 'If my daughter at Oxford had written like him at the age of seventeen, I'd have been very proud. But if she'd written like him at twenty-two . . .' There were jeers and laughter from the audience. Fisk, Lasky said, had won a journalism award for his reporting of the Israeli invasion but this was 'one of the most irresponsible acts of journalism in our time'.

Watching all this from the back of the hall, I could only reflect on how far away these people were from Lebanon, how dismally incomplete was the account they were receiving of a war which even now was engulfing the army of the nation of which they were obviously so proud. Michael Pinto-Duschinsky, a Jewish academic from Oxford who attempted to defend American and British journalists in Lebanon, was howled down with contempt. Lasky became angry, raising his voice and shouting. 'But it *wasn't* "genocide", it *wasn't* "total war".' That night, I wrote to Charles Douglas-Home, the editor of *The Times*, describing what I had heard. 'Obviously,' I wrote, 'I was supposed to have used these words — "genocide" and "total war" — in my reports although of course I never did so. Again and again throughout the meeting, people kept quoting things I had never written — afterwards, people came up to me and accused me of writing the most extraordinary things, that the Israelis were all murderers . . .'

Donald Trelford, the editor of *The Observer*, and Jeremy Isaacs, then chief executive of Channel Four television, attempted to defend the press, but Lasky insisted that all journalists were intimidated in west Beirut. In my memorandum to Douglas-Home that night, I wrote that:

> there has always been (and is) an atmosphere of fear in Beirut but in general the press has stood up to it. When we started receiving warnings after I reported from Hama, you will recall that Horton* wanted me to 'go on holiday' but I refused. We talked tough to the Syrians, stood our ground and kept on reporting without being intimidated. This was our job — it was *my* job — and I would never have forgiven myself had I scuttled out of Beirut. Lasky of course does not know about this. Nor, I suspect, would he particularly care. His tone — that of a passionate, populist orator — almost exactly suited his audience. It was what they wanted to hear . . . The press, according to Lasky, is clearly intimidated, greedy for fame, sensationalist, potentially anti-semitic and lazy.

Pinto-Duschinsky attempted to defend me. A writer in the *Jewish Chronicle*, he said, had criticised Fisk's press award and condemned the 'fact' that Fisk had accepted Palestinian casualty figures. 'I looked up the paper and I found that what Fisk actually said was "I distrusted the Arab figures and I distrusted the Israeli figures." If you go back and have a look at the Western press, you'll find that these claims [of bias] are untrue.' Again, Pinto-Duschinsky was shouted down. Why, Lasky asked, did not journalists tell people about the PLO's state-within-a-state in the years before the Israeli invasion? 'Why didn't Robert Fisk, for one?'

It was difficult to feel angry with Lasky. What he said was so patently unfair that it was impossible to take it seriously. But one could only feel sorry for his audience. Throughout the evening, a middle-aged lady sat beside me. Two of her fingers were missing. They were amputated after she suffered frostbite in Dachau concentration camp. From her family,

---

* Brian Horton, a newly appointed but unpopular foreign editor of *The Times*.

only she and her husband had survived. She was now totally committed to Israel and obviously saw dark and sinister objectives in any criticism of the state or its actions. Only as I said goodbye to her did she ask my name, and when I told her she said: 'Well, our opinions will never agree.' I asked her what she thought my opinions were, and she said she did not know. I assumed she had merely read the *Jewish Chronicle*'s quotations from *The Times*.

I later received a letter from a Jewish woman who had attended the IJA meeting and who wrote that 'the paranoia and distrust of the Media and certain individual journalists and reporters is at times totally irrational and quite unbalanced and hysterical ... It is incapable of making rational judgements. Did you notice the average age of the audience? I would guess that at least ¾ were fifty plus – i.e. the Begin/Holocaust generation ... I feel terribly sorry that Jews are being force fed their own propaganda.' Most Jews, the writer concluded, were reluctant to accept the fact that Israel was now a superpower in the Middle East.

There was no lack of opportunity to reply to the attacks made upon the press in Lebanon. Like other journalists in Beirut, I was invited to address 'symposia', or even small private meetings of Israeli supporters. But the experience of my colleagues had not been encouraging. In attempting to defend their work, they were forced to recount the events of the Beirut siege and the enormous civilian casualties which had resulted. They were then accused of accepting PLO statistics and, by the same token, of defending the Palestinian cause. Instead of helping readers to understand what had actually happened, the correspondents were thus unwittingly tainted with the very reputation they wished to avoid. Henceforth, they would be referred to in the Israeli press as 'controversial' journalists. A controversy involved a dispute; and the word of a journalist who was in dispute over the facts could obviously not be taken at face value. He had become a participant in the events rather than a witness, and thus untrustworthy. This was a trap I wished to avoid.

This, however, did not mean that we should not answer readers' letters. I received more than a hundred in 1982 alone, either addressed to Douglas-Home and forwarded to Beirut or sent directly to me, at least 80 per cent of them hostile and most of them from Jewish readers. Although the letters were sometimes personally insulting, I replied to every one, and in some detail. It seemed to me that the only defence journalists could adopt to such attacks was the time-honoured and traditional one; to stand by their reports.

My files of the period 1981–5 show that both the volume of letters and the hostility of their contents increased in proportion to Israel's problems in Lebanon. After the initial Israeli military attack in June 1982, for example, I received not one critical letter about my reports.

Only after three months — when public opinion had been outraged by the bombardment of Beirut and the subsequent Sabra and Chatila massacre — did letters arrive at the rate of 15 or 20 a week, almost uniformly critical and almost all alleging that the Western press had been intimidated by 'terrorists'. As Israel retreated slowly and painfully out of Lebanon in the period 1983—5, the letters arrived at a steady rate, invariably more aggressive after reports that Israeli troops had killed Lebanese villagers or vandalised the homes of civilians or allowed their militia allies to torture prisoners.

It was as if the criticism that might have been levelled against the Israelis was transferred instead to the press. When I wrote thus of the Syrians — when, for example, I described the butchery of prisoners in Syrian hands in Beirut in February 1987 — not a letter arrived to criticise my reports. The Syrians were presumed to be brutal. The Israelis were supposed to be a civilised army upholding 'purity of arms'. In southern Lebanon, I would meet young Israeli soldiers who privately expressed their own horror at the tactics and behaviour of their comrades. Israel's supporters in Europe were not so attuned to reality.

'Fisk! You're as pathetic and immature as the Arabs you interview,' a reader wrote to me in April 1984, after I had spent two days researching killings in the southern Lebanese village of Jibchit. Several people, including a young woman, had been shot dead by militiamen sent into the village by Israeli troops to look for 'terrorists', a small-scale version of what happened at Sabra and Chatila.

Further reports on Israeli killings in the south of Lebanon — particularly the slaughter in Zrariyeh, where Israelis killed more than 30 people, driving over some of them in tanks and leaving the words 'this is the revenge of the Israeli army' in red paint on the wall of the village well* — provoked another flurry of letters, some of them deeply sarcastic in tone. 'Under the pretence of writing for "The Free Press", but obviously following the instructions of the Central Commissariat of Propaganda in the Foreign Office, you filed a report last week, claiming that Israel's Army was now behaving at what is considered below standards acceptable to other Western Armies,' a reader complained from London in March 1985. 'Is Israeli behaviour worse than U.S. behaviour in Mi-Lai [sic], Vietnam, worse than Nagasaki & Hiroshima? Is Israeli behaviour worse than ... handing millions of Jews to the Nazis ...?'†

---

* See pp. 581—2.
† I wrote a two-page reply to this question, recording that Israeli soldiers had themselves drawn my attention to what they regarded as 'indiscipline' within their army, that there were 'considerable and marked differences' between, say, the British army's anti-guerrilla operations in Northern Ireland and those of Israel in Lebanon. 'You suggest that incidents like "My Lai" were "acceptable" in other western armies,' I wrote. 'But surely the point is that My Lai was *not* acceptable — which is why the culprits were put on trial in the United States ...'

A number of Israeli supporters kept up a barrage of criticism over my coverage of the guerrilla war in southern Lebanon, all based on the premise that the Lebanese resistance movement in southern Lebanon was composed of 'terrorists' and that the tactics used against them − the killing of villagers and their sheikhs, the vandalisation and destruction of their homes in front of UN troops − were therefore in some way acceptable.

In some cases, readers produced a deluge of 'facts' to support their contention that *The Times* was biased in its coverage of Israel in Lebanon, every one of which would have to be proved untrue if the newspaper was to avoid the claim that it had failed to reply to searching questions. There then came the same familiar allegations: that the casualty figures of the 1982 invasion had been exaggerated because the statistics had been taken from the PLO, which had been intimidating the press in west Beirut. 'Prior to the Israeli invasion in 1982,' a reader declared in March 1986, 'over one hundred journalists were murdered in that country.' This, he wrote, accounted for the 'highly selective reporting' of Lebanon. Why had I failed to report 'one of the most brutal atrocities of the civil war, when the PLO massacred four thousand of Nabatieh's inhabitants'? Why had I not reported on the Syrian 'narcotics empire' in the Chouf? I had committed no fewer than 23 'distortions' in my reports from southern Lebanon; the reader gave no indication what they were.

Again, I replied in detail. The claim that a hundred journalists had been murdered before 1982 was untrue. We had reported fully on the handful of correspondents who had been murdered and we had named the possible killers, including the Syrians and the Phalange. I could not report on the 'massacre' of 4,000 civilians in Nabatieh because it never occurred. 'Indeed,' I wrote in my reply, 'most of the civilians killed in Nabatieh over the years − and they never numbered anything like four thousand − were the victims of shellfire from renegade Lebanese Army troops (and militiamen) led by Saad Haddad.' The Syrian narcotics 'empire' was in the upper Bekaa, not the Chouf, and I had reported on this in 1976 and 1977, giving details of how hashish was channelled through Damascus International Airport − long before the Israelis took any interest in the affair.

But the letters continued, often with the same untrue allegations, usually with a few new ones thrown in. Why, I wondered, were the mysterious 4,000 'dead' of Nabatieh suddenly discovered? There had been corpses enough in Lebanon over the past few years without *inventing* massacres. But of course, too many of the dead in recent years − according to the most detailed figures, almost 17,825 between 4 June and the end of September 1982 alone − were the result of Israeli action. Israeli responsibility for all this had to be expunged. The PLO was to blame, the Lebanese militias and the anti-semitic press were to blame.

Journalists lied. This was the underlying theme of almost all the critical correspondence about Lebanon received by *The Times*. In 1985, one reader was still angrily denying that civilians had died of phosphorus burns in west Beirut in 1982. 'May I draw your attention to the statement *"reporters* were watching a baby die of phosphorus poisoning."' I presume that Mr Robert Fisk did not see the baby itself and no other casualty from phosphorus poisoning is mentioned. Does not that seem strange?' What could one say to objections like these?

Dozens of readers complained about the casualty figures. Repeatedly, I would describe the cross-checking that we had done at the time, the evidence we had amassed with our own eyes, the corpses we had personally counted. By 1985, some readers were insisting that the figure was even lower than *Israel's* figure for the total deaths of the 1982 invasion. One reader who did not accept this told *The Times* that I was therefore 'an inveterate liar and a bigot', a statement which was both slanderous and actionable. I sent him two long pages of statistics and casualty details from the Lebanon invasion.

'We could go on with these statistics forever,' I told Barnes in a wire message from Beirut in June 1985. 'The more they are questioned, the more doubtful they are meant to appear, which is why a lot of people want to question them.' Years after the Israeli invasion, I found that I was still spending up to eight hours a week going back through notes and files for details of the casualties to send to readers who often ignored my previous letters and simply repeated their original accusation: that the PLO had manufactured the lists of dead, that the press were duped, bribed or intimidated by 'terrorists', that perhaps we were anti-semitic.

The sheer amount of time and effort that was needed to reply to these letters was prohibitive. Hours that could have been spent on news reporting were used up replying to readers whose letters contained the most factually detailed but totally inaccurate claims about events in Lebanon.* It would have been easier to ignore them. It would have been easier still not to have written the reports that provoked the correspondence – or to have written them in such a way that they reflected only Israel's version of events. 'These people are not looking for information,' Nick Tatro of AP told me one afternoon in Beirut as I

---

* In May 1981, for example, a reader sent a long and detailed letter to the editor of *The Times* about an Israeli air strike on Damour and took issue with my own account of the raid. My dispatch had thrown doubt on Israeli claims that Libyans were manning SAM-9 missiles in the area. The letter, however, included the most specific details about the arrival of Libyan troops in Lebanon, the deployment of missile batteries and four separate quotations from other newspapers which appeared to contradict my own report. But the dates of the Libyan arrival in Lebanon, the allegation that they had not been withdrawn, the technical details of the SAM-9 deployment, were all factually wrong. The quotations were from the reports of journalists who had not been to the scene – as I had. Yet it needed a reply of more than 2,000 words to refute categorically the contents of the reader's letter.

began to wade through another pile of letters. 'They are not trying to elicit information. They are trying to *inhibit* you from reporting information.' Were they?

Certainly, Middle East embassies in London did their best to bend Douglas-Home's ear. The Israelis repeatedly complained that I was writing untruthfully about the war in Lebanon, sometimes accusing me of lying. The Israeli ambassador asked Douglas-Home to withdraw me from the Middle East. The Iraqis once did the same — after I had reported that the wives of men who opposed Saddam Hussein's regime in Baghdad were gang-raped in front of their husbands. The Syrians, too, did their best to have me removed from Beirut, not just because I had reported from Hama but because — in the words of the Syrian ambassador in London — I had shown 'a contempt for Arabs in general'.

In October 1984, the Syrians were angered by my report that while Damascus and Amman were ostensibly edging towards military hostilities, President Assad of Syria had been receiving personal and friendly telephone calls from King Husain. This information had in fact been given to me by King Husain himself — much to Assad's discomfort — but the Syrians believed I was trying to demonstrate that the quarrel between the two countries was 'not serious'. More ominously, the Syrian ambassador complained to Edward Mortimer, a senior leader writer on *The Times*, that I should not have spent so much time and used up so much editorial space reporting the murder of a Jew in Lebanon when — in his words — 'killings in Lebanon were unfortunately such a commonplace affair these last ten years.'

But the Israelis went further and complained to the British Foreign Office about my reporting, as if they expected the British government to interfere with *The Times*' coverage of Lebanon. On a number of occasions, the Israeli ambassador suggested to Foreign Office officials that my reports from Beirut had been fabricated. These criticisms were not only made in Britain.

The Irish Times published my dispatches under a syndication arrangement with *The Times*, and Chaim Herzog, the Israeli president, chose to attack my reporting while on a state visit to Ireland in June of 1985. In Dublin, President Herzog spoke at length with Garret FitzGerald, the Irish Taoiseach (Prime Minister), about the conflict between Irish UN troops and the Israeli army in Lebanon. According to the confidential Irish government minutes of the conversation:

in a subsequent informal discussion about Lebanon, the President said that reporting from that country, especially Beirut, was unreliable. He said that no journalist who wished to stay objective could remain in that city — he would be killed. The Taoiseach asked about Robert Fisk the London *Times* reporter — and *Irish Times* stringer — in Beirut. President Herzog, in an uncharacteristically vicious response, said that Fisk was a virulent hater of Israel and was totally biased.

That the Israeli president, of all people, should have chosen to make such untruthful remarks about the journalists who worked in Beirut – that he should have made such libellous remarks to the prime minister of a foreign nation – contained its own message for the Irish authorities.

But it also demonstrated the degree to which the Israelis were prepared to go to suppress reporting of the events which had so profoundly changed the image of Israel. On the other side of the Atlantic, American newspaper and television correspondents faced a veritable campaign against their coverage of the Israeli invasion of Lebanon, an offensive that was to continue for at least seven more years. The Israelis drew up a hit-list of 48 American daily newspapers of which, they claimed, 31 had 'negative ratings' for their coverage of Israel. Just who drew up this list – and on what basis – was not disclosed. But its implication was obvious. A negative rating suggested that the paper was anti-Israeli. And to be anti-Israeli, in the eyes of the Israeli government, was akin to being anti-semitic. Moshe Arens, the Israeli ambassador in Washington and later to be Israeli defence minister, told editors of *The Washington Post* that their paper's columns were more 'negative' towards Israel than any other in the United States.*

Thomas Friedman, who was the *The New York Times* correspondent in Beirut during the siege, was condemned as a 'self-hating Jew' on Israeli army radio. Martin Peretz of *New Republic* assaulted the American media, while even magazines which normally demonstrated more interest in sex than in Israel, provided a platform for critics of the press.

In an article entitled 'The Media's Most Disgraceful Hour', Arnold Foster asked readers of *Penthouse* why 'American journalists enthusiastically joined the lynch mob against Israel'. He recounted how the head of the 'information service' of the Phalange militia (which he, of course, called the 'Lebanese Forces') had asked him in east Beirut why American journalists had not sought casualty figures 'when the terrorists were taking particular delight in counting the weekly number of Catholic nuns they'd raped ... why only now the overwhelming concern for a horde of human animals?' Foster claimed that the Israelis risked their lives to spare civilian lives; casualties of the invasion were only 'in the low hundreds' but 'influential newspapers and television networks devoted inordinate space and time rehashing again and again the alleged guilt of the Israelis.'†

Ariel Sharon sued *Time* magazine. He claimed they had falsely stated that he instigated the killings at Sabra and Chatila. In a decision without

---

* See *Jerusalem Post*, 11 November 1982.
† *Penthouse* February 1983. 'When Israelis came to a PLO attack point located in a multiple dwelling,' he wrote, 'no advance bombing to soften up the enemy was sanctioned. The order was for the area to be taken in hand-to-hand fighting lest non-combatants be hurt: costly in dead and injured Israeli soldiers, but this is the manner of Jewish warfare.' This was a pretty exclusive view of Israeli military tactics.

precedent, the judge went into secret session for 25 minutes, barring the press and public from court. Sharon won. All the old chestnuts were now roasted again. Ze'ev Chafets, the former director of the Israeli government press office in Jerusalem, published a book which said that Western journalists in Beirut had been 'terrorised' by bands of thugs and repeated the claim that Sean Toolan was murdered by Palestinians in reprisal for an anti-PLO programme on ABC television.* Chafets' thesis, as one American journalism magazine put it, was that 'the American press, by accident or design, is engaged in a conspiracy to defame Israel.'†

By 1988, the Center for Media and Public Affairs in Washington found 'negative spin', most of which was 'anti-Israeli', in stories which appeared in the *New York Times* and US television networks. A sentence quoted from a Palestinian who had been deported from the West Bank to Lebanon – 'I'm losing the most important thing in my life, my home' – was coded as 'negative'. So was a statement by a Canadian government minister who described the beating and maiming of prisoners by Israeli soldiers on the West Bank as 'totally unacceptable and in many cases illegal under international law'. A critical comment about Israeli military behaviour in the Israeli newspaper *Ha'aretz* was also coded 'negative' when it was quoted in the *New York Times*. As a result of this nonsense, Jeane Kirkpatrick, the former US delegate to the United Nations, felt able to claim that 'now, finally, there is evidence' about 'unfair reporting of Israel.'‡

The effect of Israel's attack on the press was not so evident in Britain, but it was there all the same. In the autumn of 1982, Charles Douglas-Home, the editor of *The Times*, was invited by the Israeli Embassy in London to visit Israel along with Rupert Murdoch, the newspaper's owner, who was a consistent supporter of Israel. Only after accepting did Douglas-Home discover that he and his employer would be travelling with a well-known Zionist fund-raiser from New York. Douglas-Home and Murdoch were taken into Lebanon by Israeli military helicopter in the company of David Kimche, the director of the Israeli Foreign Ministry. As they were flying over Sidon, according to Douglas-Home, Kimche pointed to the city and shouted: 'That's the place that your Robert Fisk said we razed to the ground.' Douglas-Home told him, correctly, that I had never said such a thing.

Douglas-Home sat beside Murdoch on the flight back to London from Tel Aviv. 'I knew Rupert was interested in what I was writing,' he

---

* *Double Vision: How America's Press Distorts Our View of the Middle East* by Ze'ev Chafets (New York, William Morrow, 1984).
† *Washington Journalism Review*, December 1984.
‡ See *International Herald Tribune* 18 June 1988, 'The Reality in Israel Is Not Neutral', by Anthony Lewis (reprinted from the *New York Times*).

told me later. 'He sort of waited for me to tell him what it was although he didn't demand it. I didn't show it to him.' In the past, Douglas-Home had angered the Israelis, not least because of a regular series of articles he contributed to the Saudi magazine *Al Majella*.* But he was influenced by his visit to Israel. His editorial portrayed the results of Israel's invasion of Lebanon in optimistic terms. He foresaw an arc of peace in the Levant, stretching from northern Lebanon to western Egypt. A later editorial would ignore the increasing evidence of collapse in Lebanon and the growing guerrilla resistance to the Israeli army in order to conclude that 'there is now no worthy Palestinian to whom the world can talk' and that 'perhaps at last the Palestinians on the West Bank and in the Gaza Strip will stop hoping that stage-strutters such as Mr Arafat can rescue them miraculously from doing business with the Israelis.'†

However much his own views on the Middle East had changed, Douglas-Home loyally stood by what I wrote in *The Times*. He replied, sometimes with great harshness, to Israeli government officials who condemned my work or demanded my withdrawal. He was, in that sense, a perfect boss whom I could always rely on for support. But in the spring of 1983 he exhibited just one sign of nervousness. It was over a report which I filed on the killing of Lebanese and Palestinian prisoners in Israeli custody in Sidon. It proved to be a sad case of how the system of investigative reporting — of scrupulously checking facts and interviewing eye-witnesses — could prove self-defeating, how the very framework upon which we worked as journalists could be used as an argument to prevent disclosure of information.

I had first heard of the prisoners' deaths in June 1982, and months later — when the siege of west Beirut was over and the PLO had been evacuated — I suggested to Douglas-Home that I should investigate the truth of these reports. In view of the seriousness of the allegations — and the implications for the Israelis if they proved to be true — we agreed that I should take as much time as necessary to research the deaths of at least seven young men who had been prisoners of the Israelis.

During the long, rainy winter of 1982–3, I travelled repeatedly down to Sidon. In all, I made 27 journeys to the city and gathered material for a long report which described how the corpses of seven men, found in Israeli detention in June of 1982 with nylon cords binding their hands, were taken under Israeli military escort to a Sidon cemetery where the local gravedigger was ordered to bury the unidentified corpses without ceremony.

* See, for example, *Al Majella* 6–12 March 1982: 'For Israel, the Big Question Is Palestine', by Charles Douglas-Home.
† *The Times* 23 July 1983.

My dispatch pointed out that allegations of cruelty and murder came from both sides in Sidon in the initial days of the invasion. I also described how thousands of civilians in Sidon had been ordered to parade on the beaches where hooded men selected hundreds of them for interrogation by Israeli intelligence officers.

I interviewed Ahmed Batrouni, a 50-year-old Lebanese cobbler who was detained in the Sidon convent school on 9 June and who said that he 'was blindfolded by the Israelis but could hear other prisoners begging for water in the midday heat. I could hear men falling to the ground. They kept asking for water but the Israelis would not give it to them. They were dying of thirst. Then on the next day, the Israelis beat these people and one of them fell on the ground near me. I could see through a corner of my blindfold and there were flies on his face. An Israeli doctor came − a very tall man − and wanted to know if the man was dead. He looked at him and said he was dead.'

Batrouni, who had a weal on his right wrist which he said was made by the cord which bound his hands, told me that an ambulance with a red cross on the side was then driven up to the school and that an Israeli officer removed his blindfold and told him to put the dead man − together with another body − into the vehicle.

I also spoke to an engineer at the Jiyeh power station ten miles from Sidon, a Christian with no love for the Palestinians, who was driving past the graveyard at around midday on 11 June 1982. A middle-aged man with a wife and family, he had been questioned by Israeli military investigators and pleaded with me not to publish his name lest he be mistaken for an informer. As he approached the cemetery, he said, he was stopped by a Lebanese police adjutant who knew him to be an engineer and by an Israeli military policeman who told him to cut open the cemetery gates with his engineering tools and help carry five of the seven bodies from two vehicles, one of them an Israeli car, the other a former Palestinian Red Crescent ambulance. The engineer named a Sidon taxi driver who had also been forced to carry the corpses. I traced the driver as well as the Lebanese policeman. I spoke to the local Sidon gravedigger, an old Syrian called Chehadi who had fought in the French army in the Second World War. All confirmed the events.

By the time I had made ten journeys to Sidon to investigate the deaths of the seven men, I noticed that the Israelis began to take an interest in my presence. Twice, I was trailed around the city by a carload of heavily armed men wearing Ray-Bans. Whenever I stopped, they pulled up a hundred yards behind me. They watched the houses I visited. Their Mercedes had Israeli registration plates. A week after I first asked the engineer's family for information, three armed Israelis − two in plain clothes and one in uniform − asked to see him. He refused to disclose what they had said to him but told me he was now reluctant to discuss the deaths.

Chehadi told me he left the corpses of the seven men at the open entrance to the cemetery for two days in the hope that relatives would identify them. He said that the men were in civilian clothes and that their hands were tied with nylon rope. 'There were bruises on the necks of two of them,' he said. 'After two days, the bodies began to smell in the heat so I had to bury them. I dug beneath an old family vault in the cemetery and put them there.' Chehadi showed me the vault in which he had buried the seven men and gave me the names of six of those he had been able to identify: Mohamed Akra, Aboud Abrousli, Yahya Musri, Samir Sabbagh and Mohamed Mansour, all of whom were Lebanese, and Mohamed Abu Sikini, a Palestinian. Chehadi never discovered the identity of the seventh man, who was Egyptian.

When I first approached the Israeli authorities about the seven deaths, they said they knew nothing about them. I then went to the Israeli military liaison and press office at Baabda and formally requested information about the seven men. I gave officials there the names of the six men whom Chehadi had buried, and told the Israelis that they had been taken into custody by Israeli armed forces in the first week of June 1982. Again, I was told that the Israeli authorities had no knowledge of their deaths. An official Israeli spokesman said categorically that no prisoners had died in Israeli custody in Sidon.

It was now early March of 1983. I had interviewed at least 20 people in Sidon who had been witnesses to the deaths of the men or had participated in the removal of their bodies or their burial. I spoke to Colonel Ali Ashur, the Lebanese police chief in Sidon, and he too confirmed that 'at least' six men died in Israeli custody in June 1982. Shortly after our first conversation, he told me he had been 'visited' by several Israeli officers and was no longer allowed to speak to me. In classic tradition, my witnesses were being 'nobbled'. On my last two trips to Sidon, I was followed all the way back to the outskirts of Beirut by gunmen. On the second occasion, their car had Israeli registration plates.

I called Ivan Barnes, my foreign editor, and asked him to give the names of the dead men to Walker in Jerusalem with a request to seek clarification from the authorities there. Walker was told by the Israelis that there was 'nothing to add to the previous statement' on the matter. Nothing was known of the deaths. In a wire message to me in Beirut on 1 March, Barnes commented that he found this 'a singularly unsatisfactory answer'. Douglas-Home had earlier suggested that he might call the Israeli Embassy in London for a response if none was forthcoming in Lebanon or Israel.

I now returned for the third time to the Israeli information office at Baabda and submitted a formal application in writing, requesting the whereabouts of the six named men. Within 24 hours, the official spokesman admitted that seven bodies had been 'found' at a temporary Israeli detention centre in Sidon when the prisoners there were being moved to a new 'holding centre' at the Safa fruit-packing factory in Sidon. But he said that he knew of no military investigation into the deaths and regarded the matter as closed.

I immediately telephoned Douglas-Home, who had kept in touch with me over the investigations throughout the winter months, to tell him that the Israelis themselves now confirmed the deaths in custody. I filed a detailed ten-page dispatch to *The Times* on the affair. But next morning, the report did not appear in the newspaper.

I called Douglas-Home. 'You've obviously done a lot of work, Bob,' he said. 'But this really needs a peg. I'm not sure how we're justified in running a story like this so long after the event. The Israelis will say that we are dredging things up.' It was one of the very few times that I expressed my exasperation with Douglas-Home. I could see no way out of this particular Catch-22 that he had constructed. If I had filed a report the previous autumn with neither names nor witnesses, the Israelis would have been able to dispute its authenticity. Indeed, they would have been able to level against *The Times* the very accusations of bias which we had always rejected. Yet when a thorough investigation proved that these men *had* died in Israeli custody − when the Israelis had been forced as a result to retract their statement of ignorance and admit that the men died − Douglas-Home believed that the very length of time which it had taken to verify the prisoners' fate now prevented the report being published.

These prisoners had died in Israeli custody. There was ample evidence that most of them had been killed, either through neglect or beatings. The International Red Cross itself privately referred to their deaths as murder. Our witnesses had been intimidated. I had myself been ostentatiously followed around Sidon by Shin Bet agents. And Douglas-Home had suddenly lost the will to print an investigation which he had all along encouraged. I called him back. I was angry.

Any editor who stands loyally by his reporter in the way that Douglas-Home had done for me over the years − in Northern Ireland as well as in Lebanon − creates an enormous reservoir of loyalty in a journalist. Charlie was one of my heroes. I understood that he wanted to ensure that we had no chink in our armour when our critics attacked *The Times*. I knew that he would have to defend me when the article was published. But this worked both ways. If a reporter takes the risk of being shot on a battlefield, an editor has to be prepared to suffer a whiff of grapeshot at cocktail parties on his reporter's behalf, even the occasional outraged letter from an ambassador or two. But there was an element of weakness here which troubled me.

'What could change your mind, Charlie?' I asked him. He thought about this. 'Well, are the Israelis setting up a military inquiry into the deaths?' he asked. This was hopeless. The Israelis had no intention of doing so. I knew that the military investigators had questioned Chehadi and other witnesses about the deaths of the prisoners, but the Israelis had themselves told me there would be no inquiry. They *might* announce an inquiry if *The Times* published details of the deaths in Israeli captivity, but this would be in response to my report. Douglas-Home asked me to call him back the next day.

Instead, I called the Israeli information office at Baabda again. I acted on a hunch. One of the officers at Baabda, a middle-aged army reservist who was born in Britain, had told me that he was personally angry when he heard of the deaths of the prisoners. I suspected that if *he* made it known to the Israeli authorities that my report *was* going to appear in the paper, the Israelis might issue a more definitive statement. I told him that I had filed my dispatch to London and wanted to know if the Israeli army wished to make any further comment. I asked whether, on reflection, the Israeli army might after all institute an inquiry into the deaths.

Half an hour later, the Israeli reservist called back. Yes, he said, there would be an inquiry. In fact, a full military inquiry was actually taking place at that very moment and the results would be made public. I thanked him for his information, then telephoned Douglas-Home and told him that the Israelis now said they were holding an inquiry.

I filed a new first paragraph to my original report, stating that 'Israeli military investigators are compiling a report on the mysterious deaths of seven young men whose bodies were found in an Israeli detention centre in Sidon shortly after Israel's invasion of Lebanon . . .' All the details of my original dispatch were included, together with the names of the dead men and the identity of most of the witnesses. On the evening of publication, I heard from Barnes that a deputy editor was asking for the report to be cut by two thirds. Douglas-Home was having a medical examination; although none of us knew it at the time, he was suffering from cancer. I called his secretary and asked her to pass a message to the editor: that while I accepted decisions made for editorial reasons, any cutting of my report at this stage would amount to a declaration of no confidence in my work by the newspaper and I would consider resigning. Douglas-Home called me back later to say the report was running in *The Times* at its full length.*

I now waited for the results of the Israeli inquiry. They were not

* See *The Times*, 19 March 1983.

forthcoming. Nor was I surprised. I suspected that in reality there *was* no inquiry, even though, when I called the Israeli army at Baabda, they insisted that there was. I requested Barnes to call Walker in Jerusalem and ask him to follow up my report in Israel. He replied that the Israeli Ministry of Defence in Tel Aviv could provide no further details.

By midsummer of 1983, there was still no news. It was a year since the men had died. By the autumn, the Israeli army, under increasing guerrilla attack, were withdrawing from the Chouf, pulling their line troops down to a new front just north of Sidon. It became more and more difficult for me to reach Israeli officers. In all, Walker made 13 separate requests for information on the results of the inquiry. But at last, on 4 March 1984 — 21 months after the seven corpses were taken to Chehadi's cemetery in Sidon — an Israeli spokesman issued a statement to Walker which announced that:

> a full military police investigation into the matter was held but no member of the Israeli Defence Forces was found to be involved or implicated in any way. We could not ascertain who was responsible for the killings [*sic*] but as it was found after extensive investigation that no IDF soldier had any connection with them, the file has now been closed.

Indeed it had.

I never learned the reason for Douglas-Home's uncharacteristic hesitation in running my report. Was it because he had been deeply influenced by his recent visit to Israel? Or was it because he was preoccupied with the cancer which was even then killing him? Although his staff were at first told that his ailment was the result of a riding accident, Douglas-Home must already have known that he was dying. Yet his doubts never manifested themselves again — even when I was confirming far more damaging allegations against the Israeli army in southern Lebanon.

The report itself, of course, had no palpable effect on events in Lebanon. The prisoners' deaths had anyway been overshadowed by far more dreadful events. Yet the killings were important; not just because of the cruel way in which the men had been done to death; not even because the Israelis had shown total disregard for prisoners who had been brutally murdered in their custody. They helped to provide the impetus for the fledgeling Lebanese resistance movement in Sidon. Five of the seven men were Lebanese — and it was the Lebanese whom the Israelis had allegedly arrived to 'liberate' from the Palestinian 'terrorists'. Even at the time, there was talk in Sidon of retaliation for those killings. They were a symbol of just how vengeful the Lebanese war would prove to be for the Israelis who had embarked upon it. They were yet one further reason why Lebanon would doom its occupiers.

It would, however, be unfair to suggest that dishonest governments and brutal armies, historical bias and editorial timidity, as well as the

actual physical danger, were solely responsible for the problems of reporting Lebanon, or of covering other Middle East nations. Journalists have
contributed to their own difficulties.

Over the years in Beirut, my colleagues and I often felt a sense of
anger, even disgust, at the way in which the events we witnessed were
recorded, at the matrix of words − finite and often inappropriate −
within which journalists chose to limit their reports. We would ask
ourselves why the events we witnessed, the city we lived in, the culture
of the place, its beauty and squalor − even the *smell* of Beirut − were all
too frequently homogenised into sterile, overused nomenclature.

To us, Beirut was *real*. In winter, I would stand on the balcony of my
home and watch the storms lash over the Mediterranean, hear the sea-
spray beating against my windows at night as forked lightning flickered
over the bedroom walls. On the coast road south, distraught, frightened
soldiers would stand guard at windy checkpoints, their rifles glistening
in the rain. In midsummer, the Lebanese would clog the roads to the
mountains, escaping the fumes and dangers of the city for the broken
ski resorts. In moments of great danger, we would find ourselves in
places of blood, stench and sweat. But we felt affection for this city and
came to respect the way in which its people could suffer such humiliation
and still cling to their homes.

How, therefore, should one react to the work of a reporter who
described Beirut in June 1982, in these words:

This is Beirut − bustling and boisterous, sparkling and splashing and
spicy Beirut, bumper to bumper concert hall for the mad music of the
Middle East ... this is the apocalypse, the harvest of the eight bloody
years of civil war, sectarian violence, religion against religion ...*

Was I alone in finding these words, like those in thousands of other
similar reports, both cheap and offensive? Or was it false moralising to
complain, when we ourselves acknowledged that Lebanon was a land of
betrayal and fear?

I knew Beirut's streets and buildings better than those of any other
city, better than London or Paris or New York. But when I read what
was written about Beirut, I often found myself a stranger there. After
most of the Western journalists had moved to Cyprus in 1985 and 1986
for fear of being kidnapped, the west Beirut in which I had my home
was transformed in newspapers and wire service reports into 'mainly
Muslim' west Beirut, or it became 'kidnap-plagued, mainly Muslim
west Beirut'. When I landed at Beirut on one of Middle East Airlines'
old 707s in 1987, I was supposed to believe that I was arriving at the
'hijack-plagued airport', even when there had been no hijacked aircraft
on its runways for two years. Sometimes, I would fly into the 'boycott-

---

* ABC reporter James Wooten on *This Week with David Brinkley*, 12 June 1982.

plagued airport', since President Reagan, in his wisdom, had chosen to persuade other airlines to cancel their services to Lebanon.

Indeed, it became difficult to find a Lebanon that had not become shackled to a cliché, to a deadening form of words that killed off Beirut and its people more assuredly than any Lebanese militia leader or occupying army could destroy the country. The drama and tragedy of the place were reduced to a series of code-words that were as facile as they were politically dangerous.

The art — or craft — of reporting in Lebanon was being debased by a style of writing that reduced complex and tragic events to a common denominator, which both insulted the victims and mocked their suffering. Television journalism, with its dependence on the image, its subordination of words to pictures, contributed to this process. So did radio journalism, especially in America where a 35-second time limit is normally imposed on each foreign report. The news agencies — which catered for radio and television as well as newspapers — helped to create the unreal world in which this crisis was framed. I began to suspect that the clichés that governed so many reports and headlines about Lebanon actively hindered our task of telling the truth about what was happening there.

In one sense, all this was harmless enough, even farcical, a sub-editor's paranoia in which the complex was rendered simple by the injection of a comfortable, meaningless but friendly platitude. Thus in Lebanon, the Druze people were usually transmogrified by the wire agencies into a 'hardy warrior race', its leaders invariably 'chieftains'. Weapons were similarly fitted into a verbal armchair. A rocket-launcher became 'multi-barrelled' and a Kalashnikov rifle, we were always re-minded, was 'Soviet-made'. Tanks never moved across an international frontier; they 'rolled'. Sometimes — if the Syrians were involved — 'Soviet-made' tanks 'rolled'. Syria is, after all, 'Soviet-backed'.

In purely literary terms, these phrases were just silly. Journalistically, they were a verbal killer. They comprised a dead language of easy parallels and simplistic allusions which helped neither the editor nor the reader to understand the tragedy that was still continuing in Lebanon. Language is supposed to give expression to thought, to liberate ideas, to give us freedom. But sub-editors and news agencies were — and in many cases, still are — using these words as a lazy and meaningless substitute. The language of clichés did not help to free our minds. The words imprisoned us.

Such words were doubly dangerous because they also killed truth. Not truth in the absolute sense, which is an unreachable objective pursued by journalists at their peril. It was Edward Mortimer who referred to 'the illusion . . . both outside journalism and to a lesser extent inside it, that reality is out there somewhere, ready-made, waiting to be found, like the treasure in a treasure-hunt, and that the journalist's task was simply to find it and bring it back undamaged to his public.'* But those clichés actively collaborated in a process of political bias. While Syrian tanks were 'Soviet-made', the fact that many Israeli tanks were 'American-made' was rarely deemed worthy of note. The 'Soviet' in 'Soviet-made' was a buzz word, warning the reader that the subject — the Syrian tank — was menacing. The Soviets controlled President Reagan's 'evil empire'. That a weapon made in the United States might be just as threatening — even more so — in the hands of the Israelis, did not occur to many reporters. And if Syria was 'Soviet-backed' — which it assuredly is — how often were readers reminded in a similar epithet that Israel was 'American-backed', as it is to an infinitely greater degree, both financially and militarily? Never on the wire services and rarely in radio or television reports. Separate reports might outline Israeli indebtedness to the United States and question the nature of American influence over Israel; but in a straight news dispatch, 'American-backed' was *never* used, presumably because it would spoil the image of vulnerable little Israel, a David confronting the Goliath of Soviet-backed Syria.

Examples of this news spin were legion. If Palestinians in Lebanon used 'Soviet-made' Kalashnikov rifles, we were rarely informed that the Phalangists used 'American-made' M-16s which they had acquired from Christian units of the Lebanese army — which in its turn had bought the weapons from the Americans — or from the Israelis who had donated American weapons to their brutal militia allies in Lebanon. United Nations soldiers in southern Lebanon were killed by shellfire from tanks manned by the South Lebanon Army militia. These tanks were Shermans, made in the United States. Yet only infrequently did the wire services make reference to this fact.

If editors could not be cured of their addiction to clichés, we used to ask, could they not at least be persuaded to use clichés fairly? If, for example, Palestinians carried out a raid into Israel, the wire services would often describe this as a 'sneak attack', which in itself was often a fair description. But what happened if Israel attacked an Iraqi nuclear plant? After the Israeli air strike against the Osiris reactor in Baghdad in 1981, we took bets in Beirut as to which news agency would be first to refer to the assault — in which a French technician was killed — as a 'daring raid'. The AP bureau in Tel Aviv used the phrase within 48 hours.

Palestinian attacks also earned the epithet 'cowardly'. When Palestinian guerrillas murdered civilians, the adjective was accurate enough. But in January 1988, at which point I was no longer covering Lebanon for *The Times*, the paper referred to a Palestinian assault on an Israeli *military*

---

* 'Islam and the Western Journalist' by Edward Mortimer, *Middle East Journal*, vol. 35, no. 4, Autumn 1981.

base as a 'cowardly' attack — because it had been carried out at night when the Israeli soldiers were slumbering in their guardhouses. In fact, the particular guerrilla attack to which the paper referred involved considerable courage on the part of the Palestinian involved. He travelled by hang-glider through the night over the mountains of southern Lebanon, landed undetected inside Israel and proceeded to attack a military rather than a civilian target until he was himself shot dead. In future, it seemed, guerrillas would only be able to avoid moral condemnation in *The Times* if they staged their hang-glider attacks in broad daylight.

But clichés moved into darker corners than this. In 1986, for example, a British reporter working for an American wire agency referred to the circumstances of the Lebanon war as 'Lebanon's seemingly endless lunacy'. A reader might even feel some sympathy for this expression. Yet historical tragedies of similar proportions have not been recorded in this way. The Spanish civil war, which claimed half a million lives, the European Thirty Years War, the English Wars of the Roses — with their *zaim* of Lancaster and York — have been rationalised by the West. They were explicable. So why not Lebanon?

The use of that word 'lunacy' — the buzz word for madness and the asylum — had disturbing overtones. The Lebanese, the phrase implied, were crazy, mad, perhaps not quite human. And if not human or sane — well then, can anyone blame other powers for invading their country or killing their people or referring to Lebanon — as George Shultz, the American secretary of state, did so arrogantly in February 1987 — as 'like a plague-infested place from the Middle Ages'?* There it was: a 'plague' — as in 'kidnap-plagued' or 'hijack-plagued' — the very cliché that had been used so often in the wire copy out of Beirut. Plagues have to be eradicated, wiped out. In Nazi terminology, countries have to be 'cleansed' of plagues.

Journalists did not plot this kind of writing. Often enough, it emerged on copy desks and sub-editor's tables through a process of tiredness, idleness or lack of thought. The fact that most Western journalists had by the mid-Eighties abandoned the dangers of Beirut for the comforts of Cyprus probably contributed to this process. Cyprus is a European island whose abundance of swimming-pools and fine beaches is not matched by its news value. Journalists who took up residence there propagated the idea that the island was a centre of information; the Associated Press actually claimed that its Nicosia bureau was 'AP's Middle East listening post',† as if Cyprus — which is not even an Arab country — performed the same function as Hong Kong during the Chinese cultural revolution, when mainland China was inaccessible. By

---

* *US News and World Report*, 2 February 1987.
† See AP's *Newsfeatures Report* of 27 October 1986.

this stage, Iran restricted visas for journalists. But the Arab world was *not* inaccessible.

Of course, by this time, Beirut had become extremely dangerous for Westerners. At one point in 1986, the four Western correspondents still based in Beirut were outnumbered by those journalists held hostage in the city. Married correspondents could not be asked to risk the lives of their families. But over the years, a Middle East posting in the Arab world had come to be regarded as a sinecure, a post with few risks because Arab governments would not permit journalists to enter a combat zone. Lebanon changed all that.

Some of the reporters who moved to Cyprus betrayed embarrassment at their decision to live there: BBC radio correspondents on the island routinely failed to 'dateline' their reports when they broadcast from Cyprus, only announcing their location – in Amman or Baghdad, for example – when they were in the Arab world. When journalists filed radio reports from Cyprus, BBC announcers would usually tell listeners only that their correspondent was 'in the Middle East', in itself a dubious assertion. The reporters were out of touch with Lebanon, and the longer they stayed away from west Beirut, the more dangerous it was for them to return.

It was all very well to go on living in west Beirut, as four of us did, aware each day of the changing political moods, the 'safe' streets, the checkpoints to avoid. But to visit a city with which one was no longer familiar required real courage. The ever-increasing Cyprus press corps therefore preferred to cover west Beirut from Nicosia. Keith Graves of BBC television – who had anyway moved to Cyprus from Israel, not from Lebanon – was a shining exception to this pattern, repeatedly flying into west Beirut to report from the city despite the obvious danger to himself. Few of his colleagues exhibited the same dedication.

Although only a hundred miles separate Lebanon from Cyprus, the distance reduced the sensitivity of reporters in Nicosia and immunised them against the realities of Lebanon. The Lebanese people, with whom they had in the past lived and worked, became of less account than the story. An unhappy example of this came in February of 1987 when Druze and Palestinian gunmen burst into the Commodore Hotel, looted the building and stole both money and passports belonging to the staff. Within days, Yussef Nazzal, the owner, closed the hotel and fired all but a handful of his employees. I found them in the lobby that day, cleaners, laundry-maids, barmen, reception clerks and waiters, many with large families to support, in desperate need of money. Some of them were crying.

The Cyprus journalists knew many of the hotel staff. For years, they had looked after these same reporters when they lived in Beirut, had joked with them, talked about their families, advised them on the wisdom of hazardous journeys. But now the reporters forgot the Lebanese. Instead, a British journalist in Nicosia – not Graves – publicly offered a 500-dollar reward for the return of the hotel parrot which had disappeared when the building was looted. The Lebanese hotel staff found this incomprehensible. How could the Westerners who had been their friends for so long now care more about a parrot than about human beings?

Certainly, no collection was ever made by journalists for their old Lebanese friends among the Commodore's staff. Nor was their plight mentioned in the news reports out of Nicosia. It was the story of the Commodore's missing parrot that went round the world. The Cyprus reporters saw to that.

This shabby, discreditable journalistic episode was a symbol of just how isolated many of these correspondents had become. Cyprus was even more of a trap than the Commodore itself had been during the 1982 Israeli invasion. Lebanon was viewed in simplistic terms; blood was no longer real, suffering was ignored. A death toll was now a scorecard. How to liven up such a story? Simple. Recall with affection the old Commodore Hotel and that parrot – 'Coco', wasn't that its name? – which used to imitate incoming shells. And then add clichés. Never before was Beirut more 'war-torn', its streets more 'kidnap-plagued', its population more riddled with 'fanatical' Muslim extremists.

The same process – caused partly, of course, by boredom – had taken hold among journalists in Belfast in the early 1970s. In those days, it was Northern Ireland's tragedy that was swallowed up by clichés. Who was it, I used to wonder then, who invented 'security chiefs', 'polarisation' and 'crackdown'? Who decided that Protestant Belfast was 'staunch' or 'loyal' while Catholic Belfast contained 'hard republican areas'? The Irish poet Seamus Heaney had written then of:

... the jottings and analyses
Of politicians and newspapermen
Who've scribbled down the long campaign from gas
And protest to gelignite and sten,

Who proved upon their pulses 'escalate'.
'Backlash' and 'crack down', 'the provisional wing',
'Polarization' and 'long-standing hate'.
Yet I live here, I live here too ...*

The 'voice of sanity', Heaney commented, was getting hoarse. It sometimes seemed the same to us in west Beirut when we talked and wrote of the Western hostages held in the city. And hostages they were, cruelly held, innocent, torn from their families and friends for political

---

* 'Whatever You Say, Say Nothing', in Seamus Heaney's *North* (London, Faber and Faber, 1975).

motives, prisoners without sentence, every bit as deserving of the sympathy of Amnesty International as the doomed men of the Middle East's state prisons. Terry Anderson, who had become the AP's bureau chief in Beirut in 1983, was the longest-held of all those hostages. When he was kidnapped in 1985, we had become close friends.

And yet − there should always be an 'and yet' in reporting the Middle East − why was it that Western hostages were called 'hostages' − which they were − while Lebanese Shia Muslim prisoners held in an Israeli-controlled jail in southern Lebanon were referred to by journalists simply as 'prisoners'? These Lebanese were also held illegally, without charge and − according to one of the militia leaders who controls their lives − as hostages for the good conduct of their fellow villagers in southern Lebanon. Both the International Red Cross and Amnesty International have expressed grave concern at the use of torture in this jail at the village of Khiam, torture against both men and women. I interviewed some of the released prisoners who spoke of the use of torture with electricity applied to their genitals. The freedom of these men and women in Khiam was said to be part of the price of the freedom of Western hostages in Beirut. Yet still we persisted in our reports in calling the Lebanese 'prisoners', the Westerners 'hostages'.

What's in a name? Not long before he was kidnapped − and he may have felt very differently in the months that followed − I remember Terry Anderson giving an instruction to his staff in Beirut. 'Don't use the word "terrorist",' he said. 'It is pejorative out here.' Anderson was right. That one word 'terrorist' has been used to justify more political and military action than any defined policy in the Middle East in the past decade.

Journalists have aided and abetted this process. I used the word myself when I first arrived in the Middle East, before I realised that it was as dangerous as it was misleading. Thereafter, it was the subject of a series of memoranda that I sent to *The Times* in an effort to maintain balance in our reporting from the region. 'As you know, both Arabs and Israelis accuse each other of employing terrorism,' I wrote to the paper's foreign editor in July 1981, and:

> there is ample evidence to demonstrate that both sides are right. Palestinian attacks on Israeli civilians are intended to terrorise Israelis, just as Israeli reprisal raids on Lebanese villages (often containing more Lebanese than Palestinians) are intended to terrorise the local population into ejecting the PLO men from their area.
>
> Once we use the word 'terrorism' in this context, however, we open a Pandora's box from which emerges either an Arab or an Israeli demanding to know why we don't describe the *other* side as terrorists ... If we are going to refer to terrorist attacks on Israel, then I think we have to start talking about Haddad's attacks on UNIFIL soldiers and on south Lebanese

towns as terrorism. What else, after all, was Haddad's order to shell Sidon last Easter Monday – civilian death toll 20 – when he said he only issued the instruction because his men were demanding back pay from the Lebanese government? We did not describe this as terrorism and we do not refer to 'Israeli-supported terrorists'. Nor should we refer, therefore, to Palestinian 'terrorists' ... I happen personally to believe that PLO men who kill Israeli women and babies *are* terrorists; just as I personally believe that right-wing gunmen who blow up houses over the heads of women and babies in UN areas of Lebanon are also terrorists. But ... in the Middle East especially, I believe we must avoid these pejorative terms unless we want to apply them across the board with all the acrimony that will cause among our readers.

Two and a half years later, when Lebanese guerrillas were deliberately killing themselves in bombing attacks in southern Lebanon, news agency reports out of Jerusalem and Tel Aviv were referring to them as 'terrorist' assaults. Even the UN troops regarded these attacks as part of a national resistance war against an occupying army. But some of the wire service copy found its way into *The Times*. In November 1983 I wrote to Tim Austin, the assistant foreign editor, reiterating the dangers of using a word that had become pejorative rather than descriptive, partly 'because the word implies a legitimacy on the part of those *attacked* which we have no right to use in a news report. An Afghan who sacrificed his life by bombing a Soviet occupation barracks in Kabul would never be described as a "terrorist" in *The Times*. However misguided the suicide bombers of Lebanon may be, it is equally unwise to refer to opponents of Israel's occupation who deliberately kill themselves as "terrorists" ... Equally, I notice that the word "outrage" is cropping up in reference to the attacks on the Israelis in Israeli-occupied southern Lebanon ... When the Israelis bomb a target in Lebanon causing heavy civilian casualties, we never refer to this as an "outrage".'

Many journalists working in the Middle East were troubled about the use of the word 'terrorist', although few could make their voice heard. In June 1986, for example, one of AP's Middle East staff – an American – sent a formal note to a colleague over the wire, complaining about a reference to Mohamed Abbas, whose Palestinian group had murdered an elderly Jewish passenger on board the Italian cruise liner *Achille Lauro*. 'It is racially offensive to many people in this part of the world, and to Arab-Americans in the United States, to sling about the cliché "Palestinian terrorist" or "Arab terrorist",' the reporter wrote. '... Abbas certainly has engaged in acts that most people in [the] States would consider terrorism ... but then, so have the Contras and Savimbi's folks in Angola, who are not automatically labelled terrorists in our copy. [Rabbi] Kahane has an American arrest record for conspiring to

manufacture explosives ... we do not routinely refer to him as a
terrorist ...' Back came the reply: 'Agree with you personally but fear
losing battle, especially with copy which comes from WX [Washington]
or NY [New York], where staffers influenced by administration propaganda, general anti-Arab climate, etc ...'

This double standard of reporting was not difficult to identify. If
attacks on the Israelis in southern Lebanon *were* the work of terrorists,
then why had we not used the same word for the Christian Phalangists
who bombed Syrian troops in Lebanon? Why, repeatedly, did copy
from Israel refer to Israelis killing 'Arabs' in Lebanon, gifting the
occupation army with a nationality (Israeli) while using a racial distinction
(Arab) about its enemies? Was this because a citizen of Lebanese
nationality or Palestinian birth did not count as much as an Israeli?

Similarly, when the Israelis forced ships in international waters to sail
to Haifa, where passengers were often taken away and imprisoned,
journalists in Israel went to extraordinary lengths to avoid any phrase
that might offend the Israelis. Had the Syrians or Palestinians forced a
boatload of Israelis into Tartous or Sidon, for instance, it would immediately have been labelled a 'terrorist hijacking'. Yet when the Israeli navy
stopped the Larnaca—Beirut ferry-boat in July 1984, the *Times* stringer
in Tel Aviv described how the ship had been 'diverted' to Haifa, where
some of its passengers had been 'detained'. Palestinian guerrillas did
sometimes hire their own vessels to travel to Lebanon. But the people
on board this ferry-boat were not gunmen — I often took the same ferry
myself — and a woman aboard the ship was subsequently imprisoned for
more than a year after being jailed in Haifa under a local *Israeli* law.
When I later referred to the incident as 'a hijacking' — which is what it
was — Charles Douglas-Home received the inevitable rebuke from the
Israelis. It was not an act of piracy, they claimed. It was an act of 'self-
defence'.

Thus the Israelis felt free to refer to their area of occupied southern
Lebanon as their 'security zone', a phrase enthusiastically taken up by
many news organisations, sometimes including the BBC, which only
later referred to it as a 'self-declared' or 'so-called' security zone. The
Israelis 'maintained' a 'security zone' in southern Lebanon to prevent
Palestinian infiltration into Israel. The phrase lent legitimacy to a military
occupation, a legitimacy which the press would not have granted if the
Syrians or Lebanese had occupied part of northern Israel and declared it
a 'security zone' to prevent infiltration by Israelis into Lebanon.

Journalists in Israel experienced difficulties when the Israelis kidnapped
Mordechai Vanunu, an Israeli citizen, from Rome to Tel Aviv to face
charges of betraying nuclear secrets to the London *Sunday Times*. Here
was a case of kidnapping that clearly breached the law — if not Israeli

law, then certainly Italian law. Israel need not have worried. Correspondents duly found a new phrase. Vanunu had been 'spirited away' from Italy.

Similarly, when Israeli soldiers were captured by Lebanese guerrillas, they were reported to have been 'kidnapped', as if the Israeli presence in Lebanon was in some way legitimate. Suspected resistance men in southern Lebanon, however, were 'captured' by Israeli troops.* When the Israelis forced a Syrian government aircraft to land at Tel Aviv in February 1986 this was described in reports in *The Times* as an 'interception' and a 'mid-air swoop', while a strap headline over a dispatch from the paper's new Jerusalem correspondent read: 'Terror suspects questioned.'† In fact, all those aboard the plane were Syrian government officials.

Even more complex verbal contortions had to be invented when Israeli gunmen and bombers began to carry out attacks — 'terrorist' attacks by any other yardstick — against Palestinians in the West Bank. If these men were 'terrorists', then the moral legitimacy of Israel's war against 'terrorism' would be undermined. So the 'terrorists' became 'Jewish extremists' or, on the AP and UPI wires, the 'Jewish underground'. 'Underground' was an interesting word to choose. It had connotations of the Second World War French underground, the Resistance, the *maquisards* who resisted Nazi rule, the Jewish underground movement in wartime Poland and the Polish underground who fought in the 1944 Warsaw uprising. It added an aura of legitimacy, even heroism, to the deeds of the Israelis who were blowing the legs off Palestinian mayors. Only after several months did journalists bring themselves to call these men 'terrorists', and even then with considerable reluctance.‡ An equivalent linguistic problem confronted the press when it became known that two Palestinian bus hijackers had been bludgeoned to death by Israeli plain-clothes agents after their arrest. Yitzhak Shamir, the Israeli prime minister, referred to the killings as 'a mishap' and journalists generally went along with this idea, referring to the 'deaths' of the Palestinians — who should have been brought before the courts — as if they were victims of heart failure or some other natural phenomenon. While reporting that the men had been beaten to death, in not one dispatch did foreign news agencies use the appropriate word for such an act: murder.

But it was the word 'terrorism' that acquired so strange and frightening a

* See, for example, AP's report from Tyre on the Israeli release of five Lebanese Shia Muslims on 6 December 1984.
† See *The Times*, 5 and 6 February 1986.
‡ See, for example, *The Times* of 20 December 1986 in which Ian Murray reported from Jerusalem that Israeli police were investigating the possible reappearance of 'the extremist Jewish underground gang'.

power, defining national enemies and political allies far outside the Middle East. International news organisations betrayed their own national and political sentiments by their use of the expression. By the mid-1980s, the AP used 'terrorist' about Arabs but rarely about the IRA in Northern Ireland, where the agreed word was 'guerrillas', presumably because AP serves a number of news outlets in the United States with a large Irish-American audience. The BBC, which increasingly referred to Arab 'terrorists', *always* referred to the IRA as 'terrorists' but scarcely ever called ANC bombers in South Africa 'terrorists', probably because the BBC, in its wisdom, had decided that the ANC's cause was more 'justified' than the Palestinians' or the IRA's.

Tass and *Pravda*, of course, referred to Afghan rebels as 'terrorists'. The Western press would never do this, even though the Afghan guerrillas – 'freedom fighters' or 'insurgents' were alternative descriptions – murdered the wives and children of Communist Party officials, burned down schools and fired rockets onto the civilian population of Kabul. A startling example of double standards occurred in September 1985, when a British newspaper reported that an airliner carrying civilian passengers had been 'downed by rebels'. Something wrong here, surely. *Terrorists* destroy civilian airliners. No one was in any doubt about that in 1988 when a bomb exploded aboard a Pan Am Boeing 747 over Scotland, killing all on board.

But no. For the newspaper – the London *Sunday Times* – was reporting the destruction of an *Afghan* civil airliner which belonged to the communist (and most assuredly 'Soviet-backed') government in Kabul. The 47 passengers and five crew were all killed.*

How did these terrorists become rebels? Can rebels just as easily become terrorists? How do you qualify for such a metamorphosis? Does it hurt less to be blown out of the sky by an American-made Stinger surface-to-air missile than it does by a Soviet-made SAM-7 surface-to-air missile? Does the killer's political affiliation mean that death comes more swiftly, perhaps more happily than would otherwise be the case? What on earth went on in the *Sunday Times* sub-editor's mind when he wrote that headline? It was not just a case of one man's terrorist being another man's freedom fighter. This in itself is a cliché. Either a terrorist is a terrorist, or he is not.

In the Israeli press, there was little debate on the subject. At the start of the Israeli invasion in 1982, the *Jerusalem Post* was busy tampering with AP's reports from Beirut, changing every reference to 'guerrilla' into 'terrorist', until the AP told the paper's editor to stop. In a short article in the *Jerusalem Post* entitled 'The Politics of Terror' – in which the author contrived to use the word 'terror' and 'terrorist' 31 times in

* *Sunday Times*, 8 September 1985.

19 paragraphs – Hirsh Goodman stated ominously that 'if the [Israeli] government wants to stymie the political message of terror, it has to deal with terror deep in the shadows, far from the eye of the camera ...'* Only rarely did an Israeli journalist question the received official view, as Michael Elkins did in 1983. Discussing a Lebanese suicide bomb attack on an Israeli barracks at Tyre, he wrote that the target was military and the intent was to kill Israeli military personnel, and thus:

> it is at least arguable that by the criteria we ourselves have demanded, supported by historic precedent, and despite the bleak and tragic impact upon us, what happened in Tyre may not be dismissed as terrorism, but was instead a guerrilla action.
>
> I come to this painfully ... I suggest that by calling the action in Tyre 'terrorist', we are demonstrating yet again our stubborn and increasingly pervasive refusal to see any slightest core of legitimacy in the Palestinian and Arab side of the conflict between us.

Elkins blamed the 'self-defeating obduracy' of Palestinians and Arab governments for denying Israel's right to legitimacy. Israel and its enemies could continue like this, he wrote, 'recreating and reflecting the existing images of each other, and reflecting these reflections – endlessly and hatefully – as in a hall of mirrors.' But the result, he concluded:

> will be that all of us – Israelis, Palestinians, Arabs – will be locked in endless and bloody agony in a hall of mirrors of our own creation and from which there is no exit.
>
> Or we can begin by adopting a certain integrity – a certain generosity – in the use of language.
>
> That's not too hard. It's the easiest of the hard things that must be done if we are ever to come to peace with one another, and so with ourselves.*

The issue, in the end, *is* about the integrity of words rather than the definition of terrorism. Every attempt at the latter has failed. George Shultz's effort in this direction was as weak as any other. 'Freedom fighters or revolutionaries don't blow up buses containing non-combatants – terrorist murderers do,' he said in Washington in June 1984, quoting Senator Henry 'Scoop' Jackson. 'Freedom fighters don't assassinate innocent businessmen or hijack innocent men, women and children – terrorist murderers do.' Yet Shultz knew very well that the Afghan 'freedom fighters' whom his government supported and the Contra 'freedom fighters' so close to President Reagan's heart did indeed kill non-combatants, including 'innocent men, women and children'.

An American State Department definition of 'international terrorism' in 1976 was an equally lamentable failure. International terrorism, it

---

* *Jerusalem Post*, 20 April 1984.
* *Jerusalem Post*, 13 November 1983.

said, could take the form of assassination, murder or kidnapping, it was politically motivated and transcended national boundaries.* This certainly includes a large number of Palestinian terrorist crimes. But it also includes terrorist crimes perpetrated or commissioned by Israelis. The murder of Khalil Wazzir (Abu Jihad), the PLO's second-in-command, by Israeli gunmen in Tunis in April 1988, for example, precisely fitted the State Department definition of international terrorism. But no department of the American government suggested that Israel was guilty of terrorism.

Even if Abu Jihad's combatant status made this act acceptable as a military operation, the acts of Israel's proxy militias in Lebanon – including both the Phalange and the 'South Lebanon Army' – certainly fall into the State Department's terrorism category. But never has the United States government denounced them as such. Even the Sabra and Chatila massacres – which brought the American marines back to Beirut – were never condemned in Washington as a *terrorist* crime.

No such hesitation followed the killing of the crippled Jewish passenger aboard the *Achille Lauro* by Mohamed Abbas's gunmen, the murder of a US navy diver aboard the hijacked TWA airliner at Beirut in 1985, the bomb placed aboard an American airliner which blew three passengers to their deaths high over Greece in 1986, the murder of passengers at Rome and Vienna airports or the destruction of the Pan Am 747 over Scotland in 1988. Nor should there have been hesitation. These were all terrorist crimes.

But 'terrorism' no longer means terrorism. It is not a definition; it is a political contrivance. 'Terrorists' are those who use violence against the side that is using the word. The only terrorists whom Israel acknowledges are those who oppose Israel. The only terrorists the United States acknowledges are those who oppose the United States or their allies. The only terrorists Palestinians acknowledge – for they too use the word – are those opposed to the Palestinians.

To adopt the word means that we have taken a side in the Middle East, not between right and wrong, good and evil, David and Goliath, but with one set of combatants against another. For journalists in the Middle East, the use of the word 'terrorism' is akin to carrying a gun.

* See statement by Robert A. Fearey, Special Assistant to the Secretary of State and 'Coordinator for Combatting Terrorism', before the Los Angeles World Affairs Council, 19 February 1976. For other contributions – of varying sanity – towards the definition of terrorism, see 'Who is a Terrorist?' by Charles Hoffman in the *Jerusalem Post*, 8 February 1984; 'One Man's Freedom Fighter is ...' by Sean Cronin in *The Irish Times*, 13 July 1985; '"Murder Inc." or Freedom Fighters?' by Neal Ascherson in *The Observer* (London) 14 July 1985; 'Double Standards on Terrorism' by Max Hastings in *The Sunday Times*, 29 December 1985; and 'Cruel Murderers, not Freedom Fighters' by Irving R. Kaufman in *International Herald Tribune*, 25 August 1986 (originally printed in the *New York Times*).

Unless the word is used about *all* acts of terrorism — which it is not — then its employment turns the reporter into a participant in the war. He becomes a belligerent. In Lebanon, it also means the journalist believes that the immensely powerful armies and militias in the country can be divided into 'good guys' and 'bad guys'. They cannot; in Lebanon, they are all bad.

This was the mistake the Americans made when they sent their Marines back to Beirut in September of 1982. Ignorant of Lebanon's history, convinced of their stabilising mission, believing in moral certainties which do not exist in the country, weaned on our clichés, they returned to inherit a killing-ground.

13 The 'Root'

We've come here to help our Lebanese friends. But what I
want to know is, what's going to happen to the
Palestinians? . . . We've got to do something for them.

> Colonel James Mead, commanding US 32nd Marine
> Amphibious Unit, Beirut *November 1982*

We want to guide and inform the people of Lebanon. Our
only goal is to Islamicise the place and, as the Imam
Khomeini says, we have to export the Islamic revolution to
the world. So like any other Muslims, we have come here
with the aim of saving the deprived Palestinians and the
deprived Lebanese.

> Iranian revolutionary guard, Baalbek *November 1982*

The winter rains came early in 1982. They started in the first week of
October, squalling over the Mediterranean and falling across Lebanon
in a storm of hail and thunder. The streets of Beirut, which had never
been able to cope with the downpours of winter, were awash with water
and sewage. It rained down on the soldiers of the multinational force,
the Americans, French and Italians huddled in their raincapes in doorways and dugouts. It drenched the Israeli tank crews just south of the
airport. And in the Chatila camp, it flooded the sunken mass grave of
the Palestinians murdered by Israel's Christian allies two weeks earlier.

It also washed through the homes of the survivors of that massacre,
through the huts of thousands of Palestinian civilians who now faced a
new and uncertain world in Lebanon. The storms were worse than the
inundation of 1976. In the Ein Helweh camp in Sidon, the Israelis had
completed their destruction by bulldozing the bombed-out ruins. So
there were no homes left. The Palestinians were given tents in which to
take shelter. Then the rains came.

In the burned-out pine forests around the museum, marines of the
8th French Parachute Regiment discovered that the storms had washed
the red earth from the corpses of Shia militiamen and Palestinians killed
along the west Beirut perimeter during the siege. The torrents tore the
mud from shallow graves in dirt parking lots. And as the rain penetrated
the great embankments of sand that had been thrown up as a protective
screen around Chiyah, it revealed that even in these defensive walls the
dead had been interred.

In the ruins of Chatila, the rains uncovered two more victims of the massacre, a young woman who had been knifed to death and the body of her unborn baby which had been torn from her womb and which lay in the same muddy grave. At Khalde, the Americans of the 32nd Marine Amphibious Unit found on the beaches that the rain separated sand from flesh, flesh from bone. Skulls and femurs, pieces of bombed human remains, were exhumed from the sediment by nature, the water running over, round, under the skeletons of the war. When the storms moved in off the sea, the lightning flashing over the deserted airport and the slums of Hay al-Sellum, it was as if Lebanon was giving up its dead, revealing its terrible secrets to the innocent young men of the multinational force.

What message did they read in the red soil of Beirut that wet autumn? The soldiers who arrived were decent men, motivated by a sense of moral purpose and national pride, unaware that Lebanon never rewarded its guests. In several streets, the US Marines and the French paratroopers were pelted with rose water and rice, just as the Israelis had been greeted in east Beirut, and just as the Syrians had been greeted before them. The tradition held fearful portents which were never understood by the recipients.

For it was a sense of guilt that brought the Americans, French and Italians back to Beirut less than two weeks after their premature departure. They did not return with any overt political purpose, although it did not take long for President Reagan to discover one. The decision to redeploy the international army in Beirut was taken by Reagan and Shultz on 18 and 19 September, the weekend the Sabra and Chatila massacre ended. It was, as one of Reagan's senior advisers would say later, 'an emotional ... response to a tragic event', a decision influenced 'by the feeling that the United States had assumed responsibility for the safety of the Palestinians and that our friends, the Israelis, had allowed the worst to happen.'*

This was a coy way of expressing both the shame and the political embarrassment which the massacre of the Palestinians imposed upon the Reagan administration. The Americans had guaranteed the safety of Palestinian civilians in west Beirut and had trusted their Israeli 'friends' to behave accordingly. But America's guarantee and trust had proved worthless at the very moment when Reagan's political proposals – for Palestinian self-government on the West Bank and Gaza in association with Jordan – called for Arab confidence in Washington. Begin had already briskly and insultingly rejected the plan. What did America's influence count for now?

* Geoffrey Kemp, who was Middle East specialist on the National Security Council staff in 1982, in his lecture *The American Peacekeeping Role in Lebanon: 1982–84* (Norwegian Institute of International Affairs, Oslo, 28 October 1985).

The bones of US strategy remained the same. The American 'one–two–three' school of politics which we in Beirut so derided – military action followed by political aims followed by a 'solution' – had been outlined in Weinberger's naïve address to the press on the Beirut quayside on 1 September. The evacuation of the PLO had been 'phase one' and the second stage was to be achieved by 'getting all the foreign forces out of Lebanon'. This would be followed, incredibly, by 'the solution to the Palestinian problem'.*

The French and Italians, who shared the same guilt as the Americans because they had repeated the same promises, heeded the Reagan administration's request to go back to Beirut. So dramatic was the moment – so urgent the need – that the political contradictions inherent in their redeployment were obscured, even to those who had most reason to comprehend them.

How were the 'foreign armies' to be persuaded to leave Lebanon? And how could America cajole the Syrians into withdrawing when one of the parties to the Lebanon war – Israel – was openly acknowledged to be America's 'friend'? If the international army was returning to protect the Muslims of west Beirut, and in particular, the Palestinians, how did this square with their obligations to the sovereign government of Lebanon which had originally invited the Americans, French and Italians to Beirut? Was this government truly democratic? Or did it represent only the Phalangists?

These fundamental questions were not addressed. For the return of the multinational force – or the 'MNF' as it inevitably became known – was in its very first days a humanitarian mission. And its military might seemed irresistible. We watched the multinational force transform west Beirut. The city was saved, even if its future remained in doubt. For its Lebanese inhabitants and for the Westerners who still lived there, west Beirut felt *safe*. How could it be otherwise when the greatest power on earth had invested its political prestige in protecting the city?

Those of us who had lived through the siege, witnessed the bombings and walked between the bodies of Sabra and Chatila, were awed by the evidence of such enormous military power. And so, of course, were the Lebanese. Wherever I drove in the city, I came across American or European troops. US Marines patrolled the airport road, Italian Bersaglieri stood guard round the edges of Sabra and Chatila, French Paratroopers controlled the front line. The engines of the US Marine helicopters thumped over the city day and night, carrying equipment and ammunition to the forward US lines below Hadeth.

The Americans' M-60 tanks were brought ashore on Green Beach, the

* See above, pp. 350–1.

seafront MNF landing zone above Khalde. I spent a whole day sitting on the beach with Foley, watching the Marines bring in wire-guided missiles, mortars and amphibious assault vehicles, 'proof positive', as I wrote in my dispatch that night, that the MNF's mission to Lebanon 'could turn into an extremely long, even dangerous, operation.'

Yet I found my own prediction difficult to believe. At sea, all around the peninsula of west Beirut, in the great arc of Beirut bay, lay one of the largest naval fleets in the world. American and French aircraft carriers, nuclear-powered destroyers and frigates, landing craft and patrol boats were spread across the Mediterranean. At night, from my bedroom balcony overlooking the sea, I could gaze across a whole city of winking, swaying lights far out into the darkness.

Here, surely, was a cliché made whole. Surely now, there really was 'light at the end of the tunnel', a chance of peace, the end of the war, the very last rebuilding of Beirut. This optimism was a drug more potent than any grown in the Bekaa Valley. At the eleventh hour, the Lebanese were to be given the chance of re-creating the happy, unified, strong Lebanon which had in fact never existed — except within their own imagination.

'Today, in Lebanon, men are awakening to the historical challenge that faces them,' Amin Gemayel told the UN General Assembly in October. 'They are a match to our mountains, and their aspirations are as high as our cedars. Give us peace, and we shall again astound the world.' Indeed they would, if not in quite the way that Amin Gemayel predicted.

These dreams acquired a power of their own which needed ever greater forces to sustain them. On a tour of America and Europe, the Lebanese president said he wanted the MNF's 3,800 troops to be increased to thirty thousand. *Thirty thousand.* Why not? He wanted troops to come from Britain as well, and from Canada, Australia, Belgium, Austria, even South Korea. Lebanon's dreams could surely be given substance by the enormous economic power of the West. Gemayel said he needed 12 billion dollars in long-term economic assistance. Malcolm Kerr, the president of the American University in Beirut, asked for an investment of 100 million dollars in his colleges. The United States promised Lebanon 105 million dollars by the end of 1982.

This lunatic optimism even infected the cynical confines of the AP bureau. The Lebanese staff planned holidays abroad. Terry Anderson arrived from South Africa with his wife and daughter to become a permanent member of AP's staff in Lebanon. As a Vietnam Marine veteran, he was immediately assigned to cover the US Marine contingent in west Beirut. Nick Tatro returned from holiday convinced that the reconstruction of the Lebanese army could save Lebanon. Only Farouk Nassar remained immune from the contagion. He would lean over the

AP balcony in the hot autumn afternoons and ruminate on the political possibilities. 'You know, Fisky, this could end up in a bloodbath,' he pronounced one day in late October. Why? 'Because Amin Gemayel is a Phalangist and his friends are in the government. The MNF will end up supporting the Phalange.'

If the logic of this was devastating, the evidence to support Nassar's contention did not yet exist. The MNF had been welcomed in west Beirut as saviours. They had not invaded Lebanon; they had arrived to save the people who lived there. The Italians shopped in Hamra Street, the French dined out in the *Spaghetteria* and *Quo Vadis* restaurants. Off-duty American Marine officers propped up the bar of the Commodore Hotel. To many of us – and to many of the MNF troops – Beirut now seemed to be a Western city. But of course, it was not.

Like the Lebanese, we saw what we wanted to see. Beirut's cafés were packed, its shops were again being rebuilt in the devastated commercial heart of the city. For the first time in seven years, Western airlines flew into Beirut. Pan Am opened a service to Lebanon – for some unfathomable reason, the Marines at the airport were ordered to salute every Pan Am jet taking off – and the port filled with commercial shipping. On the old front line, in those dank alleys through which we had wandered back in 1976, French bomb disposal officers now un-seeded the streets of mines. Beirut was performing a ritual act: it was returning to normal. We held parties and picnicked on the beach. It hardly dawned on the inhabitants that almost all the rest of their country lay under the military occupation of Israel and Syria.

For Beirut was itself an illusion, a mirror into which we and the Lebanese looked in order to see ourselves. When we smiled, Beirut smiled back. It had a strange effect. The Lebanese believed in happiness with the fervour of missionaries. If they believed hard enough in something, then it would come true. It was an affliction to which few sought a cure. No one wished to travel out of the city, across those front lines into the oppressed nation on the other side of the Beirut perimeter. Beirut had become an independent city state, a capital without a country.

On the maps which Tatro taped to the walls of the AP bureau, the MNF's deployment looked a straightforward, uncomplicated affair. The three contingents parcelled out west Beirut between them. The American Marines took over the airport and its perimeter down to Khalde, the very terrain upon which the French army had pitched its tents 122 years earlier when it came to Lebanon to rescue the Maronites after the Druze–Christian war. American Marines patrolled the Shia Muslim slums of the southern suburbs while French paratroopers occupied much of the commercial centre of west Beirut. The Italian area of operations included not just Sabra and Chatila but Bourj al-Barajneh and the adjacent Lebanese Shia districts as well. On the map of west

Beirut, the French were at the top, the Italians in the middle and the Americans at the bottom.

But it was not this simple. The MNF had not arrived as a bulwark between two sides. It had no mandate from the United Nations. Indeed, the Americans opposed UN participation, since they wished to prevent any Soviet involvement in Lebanon. Save for the evacuation of the PLO and the departure of the Israeli army from west Beirut − a withdrawal of only six or seven miles − the armies and militias of Lebanon remained frozen in the same positions they had occupied when the fighting stopped in August.

The Israeli front line now ran along the west Beirut perimeter from the crossroads at Khalde, up the old Sidon road to the east of Beirut airport's second runway, finishing at Galerie Semaan. This was precisely the same line the Israelis held during the siege. East Beirut was still occupied by Israeli troops and their Phalangist allies. French troops only began patrolling the Christian sector of the city with much trepidation in October. The Phalange had no love for the multinational force and jealously clung on to its own checkpoints and areas of control to the north of the capital and in the mountains to the east.

Along this ridge-line, the Syrian army now stood, from the coastline 20 miles north of Beirut, along the summit of Mount Lebanon to Sofar on the Beirut−Damascus highway and then east across the floor of the Bekaa Valley. To the south of the Syrians − and to the east of the MNF − lay the Chouf, where Druze and Maronite militias were now in a state of semi-war. The Israelis, who had brought the Phalange into the Chouf in June, were either unable or unwilling to bring this conflict to a halt, even though it was of their making. Further south, the Israeli occupation troops were fighting a Lebanese resistance movement that was daily growing more aggressive.

Nor had the Palestinians disappeared from Lebanon. Up to 10,000 guerrillas remained in the Bekaa and in the northern Lebanese city of Tripoli. In Baalbek, several hundred Iranian revolutionary guards dominated the city with the acquiescence of the Syrians. Syria was Iran's only Arab ally and had encouraged Iranian involvement in Lebanon. The cocktail of armies induced a special kind of weariness. After a visit to Baalbek in the autumn of 1982, I drove home through checkpoints successively manned by Iranians, Palestinians from the PFLP, regular Syrian troops, plain-clothes Syrian *mukhabarrat* agents, Syrian Special Forces units, Israelis, Phalangists, Lebanese soldiers, French Paratroopers and US Marines. There were, in all, at least 33 foreign armies and local militias in Lebanon when the MNF arrived.

Even inside the MNF's area of operations − within the dusty, choking, half-ruined streets patrolled by the Americans, French and Italians − there remained the Muslim militiamen who had fought the Israelis.

Although they temporarily hid their weapons when Lebanese government control was reimposed in west Beirut, these forces still existed. Shia Muslim groups were the most powerful; their extensive military and intelligence network continued to operate under the guise of political movements. Amal was the most prominent of these organisations, although a more fundamentalist faction, which had shown such courage in the battles around Khalde, drew its inspiration from Iran.

The MNF contingents had been deployed with considerable fore-thought. The Americans had been placed opposite the Israelis on the grounds that they would be able to control their Israeli 'friends'. The French had been stationed opposite the Phalange because the Christians were likely to be more amenable to the nation which had protected them for more than a century. Being a Mediterranean people, the Italians were likely to inspire sympathy among the Lebanese and Palestinian Muslim poor. They had therefore been deployed in Sabra, Chatila and Bourj al-Barajneh.

This was shrewd political planning but it rested on some very narrow assumptions. If the international army stayed for only a limited period — for three months, six at the most — then the Americans, French and Italians might be able to leave in good order after assisting the 'legitimate Lebanese authorities' to control all of Beirut and after persuading the Israelis and Syrians to withdraw from Lebanon. But the 'legitimate Lebanese authorities' — as Farouk Nassar of AP realised — were working for a Phalangist administration, specifically created with Israel's assistance. Furthermore, there was no assurance that the Syrians and Israelis would be obliging enough to leave Lebanon in so short a period of time, if at all.

If, in the meantime, the Lebanese government became involved in a civil war — especially a conflict involving the militia forces that still existed *within* the MNF's area of operations — then the partisanship of the international army would become evident and its stated role a mockery. Furthermore, Reagan had told Congress on 29 September 1988 that the MNF mission 'expressly rules out any combat responsibilities for the US forces.'

Logically, therefore, the MNF would have to leave in the event of renewed civil war. But it would not be able to leave. Armies do not admit failure. For the MNF's mission was not just burdened with the tragedy of Lebanon; it represented the prestige of a superpower and two of Europe's most powerful nations. Thus was set the stage for an epic catastrophe. All the elements of farce and tragedy — from *hubris* and delusion to final calamity — were to attend the multinational force's disastrous mission to Beirut. In 17 months, we were to witness the collapse of the West in Lebanon, with consequences as irreparable as they were terrifying.

Even before the international army had arrived in Lebanon, the ill omens were obvious. As usual, we reported them but did not understand how fatal they would prove to be. While the Israelis were still besieging west Beirut, a series of gruesome sectarian killings had started in the Chouf. Druze villagers were found in ditches near their homes, shot in the back of the head. Christians were discovered with their throats cut from ear to ear. The Druze regarded the Phalange rather than the Israelis as their oppressors. They would therefore identify the Phalangist president of Lebanon — Amin Gemayel — as their enemy rather than their friend. So how would they respond when the MNF tried to prop up Gemayel's administration?

The newly appointed Phalangists within Gemayel's government made no secret of their grandiose ambitions. Alfred Mady, the Lebanese president's special adviser in Washington, who was also the Phalange's US representative, proclaimed 'the birth of America's second ally' in the Middle East.* That was a dangerous fantasy. If Lebanon was to be Israel's equal in the Middle East, it would also have to be Israel's ally. Was it to foster such an alliance that the MNF had been sent back to Beirut? As journalists, we mocked such conspiracy theories. But the Lebanese took them seriously, and not — it transpired — without reason.

Covering the multinational force promised to be an easy assignment. Soldiers are usually told that they are on the side of the angels; only rarely do they believe it. News agency reports seemed to write themselves. When the main force of Marines came ashore at Ouzai, dozens of television crews recorded their every stumble. Seven warships stood off the coast as landing craft dipped through the waves to deposit their dripping jeeps and bulldozers on the sand. It was perhaps disconcerting for the Marines who ran up the beaches to find that Ouzai was not quite the golden strand they had imagined it to be.

The beaches were six feet deep in garbage and America's contingent to the multinational force had to wade through tons of rusting cans, old sacks and flotsam before they gained the security of dry land. Within days, Marines were offering baked beans from their mess tins to the Shia Muslim children of Bourj al-Barajneh; a fast-food chain in Dayton, Ohio, flew 3,000 hamburgers into Beirut for the 1,300 men of the Marine contingent. French troops bought sodas, beer and cigarettes from Lebanon's army of travelling grocers who set up shop around the MNF's battalion headquarters. These events were reported with academic diligence.

Our dispatches were filled with such nonsense. No activity was too unimportant, no ritual too slight to go unrecorded. When Lebanese

---

* *Monday Morning*, 25–31 October 1982.

troops were invited to join Marines at prayer in the American military chapel deep inside the headquarters of the US Battalion Landing Team – a half-ruined block that was once used to train pilots for the Lebanese national airline, MEA – scores of photographers turned up for the service. At Green Beach one Sunday in early October 1982, we heard the US navy's Catholic chaplain announce to his Marine worshippers at the seafront landing zone west of the airport that they would recite a rosary 'in honour of Our Lady of Mount Lebanon, the patron saint of the country we're being hosted in'. At the Protestant service down the beach, the Marines sang 'Amazing Grace' after asking God 'to grant this country a peace that will last'. The Lebanese, it seemed, were to receive divine as well as international assistance.

It was preferable to have an army arrive in Lebanon with prayers rather than surgical precision bombing. But the Americans landed with familiar illusions. They had come to bring peace, they used to tell us. The Syrians told us the same thing when they entered Lebanon in 1976. The Israelis used the same expression when they invaded the previous June. But now America was the 'honest broker' – another of our favourite clichés – intent on preventing further war between 'age-old antagonists'. The United States Marines supported the 'sovereignty' of Lebanon – whatever that was – and they wanted to see the withdrawal of 'all foreign forces' from Lebanon, just as Weinberger had said.

There was nothing immoral about these aspirations. Hearing them enunciated by the 'grunts', the American line troops, or by the earnest young Marine signallers on Green Beach, it was almost possible to believe that these vague aims could be achieved. The soldiers meant what they said. Goodwill was the word the Marines used most. Everything could be achieved with goodwill. So amorphous, intangible, necessary, was there not bound to be goodwill? In Beirut that autumn – in the 'Root', as the Marines called the city – every ton of ammunition landed at Green Beach was supplemented with a supply of goodwill. French illusions were created more by history than naïvety. They emphasised their century-old connection with the country, the unique understanding which their experience as a mandate power had supposedly given them in Lebanon. And of course, France had ambitions as a European superpower. It was not going to be left out of a project of such potential political significance, least of all when the Americans were involved. French officers dined at high table in their ambassador's ruined residence at the Forêt des Pins, their red wine served by liveried waiters, their table graced by attractive Lebanese girls. If the French army had scarcely won a war in more than 60 years, it was surely not going to lose a peace-keeping mission in Lebanon.

Only the Italians seemed to understand why they were there. Many of their soldiers were from poor families in the south of Italy, the

Mezzogiorno, and they instinctively sympathised with the slum-dwellers among whom they were billeted. They were humble men with none of the swagger and arrogance that American and French troops often unwittingly demonstrated towards the Lebanese. The Italians were ordered to defend Sabra and Chatila, and this they did with great dedication, refusing to be drawn into the later battles between the MNF and the Lebanese.

They set up a field hospital on the edge of Chatila. While the Marines watched imported movies — *Rambo 2* was their most popular entertainment — the Italians held classes in Arabic. General Franco Angioni, commanding the Italian contingent, distributed books on the history of Lebanon to his troops. Which was why, when we visited the Italian soldiers around Chatila, they spoke thoughtfully about the Palestinians, the Druze, the Maronites and the Shia Muslims. The Italians were not as optimistic as their colleagues.

Colonel James Mead, the Marine commander, had some notion of the tragedy. Mead held the Silver Star, America's third highest award for gallantry, which he earned directing a rescue operation for US Marines trapped in the jungle. He proved to be a forthright spokesman for the MNF: 'And you can quote me on that' would be his invariable sign-off to any pronouncement. 'We've come here to help our Lebanese friends,' he said one night in early November when the Marines laid on a barbecue for the press. 'But what I want to know is, what's going to happen to the Palestinians? Is anything being done for them? What can we do for these people? I've been in the camps. Have you seen them? Do you realise what they have been through? We've got to do something for them.'

Yet Mead's good sense could be deceptive. Just two days later, he was holding a briefing for correspondents in his battalion headquarters. Guerrillas were mounting a series of assaults against Israeli armour on the old Sidon road, the rutted narrow highway that curved round the Marine perimeter and which now served as a main supply route to the Israeli lines above Bhamdoun. These guerrillas, the Israelis claimed, were emerging from Bourj al-Barajneh — within the Marine area — and then returning to the American-protected zone after completing their attacks. Mead was sure this was not true. 'I can tell you this,' he told us. 'The terrorists attacking the Israelis did not come from our area, so far as we are aware. And you can quote me on that.'

Terrorists? *Terrorists?* Had the MNF already, after less than two weeks in Lebanon, decided that anyone attacking the Israelis must be a 'terrorist'? I asked Mead why he used the word. His senior officers laughed. 'Well, what should I call them?' Mead asked. 'If you don't like terrorists, I'll call them "outlaws". How's that? Outlaws. You're not supposed to go around shooting at people.'

Mead had missed the point. Even at this early stage of the MNF deployment, there obviously existed within the American contingent the idea that at least one of the foreign armies in Lebanon had some right to be there, or at least a right to expect immunity from attack. The Israelis were being shot at — and would go on being attacked — because they were invaders in a foreign land. Mead gave them legitimacy by referring to their enemies as 'terrorists' or 'outlaws'. The same lack of perspective attended the MNF's response to the initial actions of Gemayel's government.

No sooner had the MNF arrived in Beirut to support the Lebanese government than the powerless Lebanese army and the long-dormant deuxième bureau turned into petty tyrants. Aware that they were protected by three Western armies, weak and fearful officers whose normal docility often bordered on cowardice became bullies overnight. Under their command, Lebanese troops raided tens of thousands of homes all over west Beirut, confiscating weapons, arresting hundreds of young men and interrogating thousands of civilians. There were no such searches in east Beirut: a Phalangist administration was not going to harass Christians.

At dawn on 3 October, thousands of Lebanese soldiers cordoned off a quarter of the entire city. Anyone whose identity papers were not in order was immediately arrested. On the seafront Corniche outside my home, outside the AP bureau, in Hamra Street and in the suburbs, elderly Palestinians, Shia Muslims from southern Lebanon, Sudanese students, Turks and Kurds were loaded onto lorries, sometimes blindfolded with their own shirts, and taken to east Beirut for interrogation by the deuxième bureau. All this was done in the presence and under the protection of French and Italian troops of the multinational force.

Palestinian men who were living within the Italian military cordon around Chatila were arrested in the early hours by plain-clothes Lebanese agents who were themselves escorted by Italian troops. Not content with checking papers, many Lebanese army units blocked off whole districts of west Beirut, refusing to allow even the most legitimate Lebanese citizens to enter or leave the area. The banking system closed down for the day. Being a resourceful people, many Lebanese avoided the restrictions by walking through the front entrances of apartment blocks and leaving through rear doors still uncontrolled by the army. MNF troops presided over the whole charade.

By the Lebanese army's *Bain Militaire* club, I came across a French Paratroop sergeant watching an old Palestinian, his head in his hands, being ordered at rifle point into the back of a truck by Lebanese soldiers. 'We have nothing to do with this,' the Frenchman said to me. 'It's a political matter. We are only here to look after the Lebanese army.' The prisoner, unshaven and wearing faded blue jeans, pleaded to be released. When I climbed onto the truck to talk to him, he showed me his residence papers. He had lived in Lebanon since the exodus from Palestine in 1948, but the documents were out of date. He was taken away in the truck.

The MNF, who were supposed to be protecting the survivors of Sabra and Chatila, were watching Palestinians being taken away, sometimes violently, for interrogation in east Beirut by officials loyal to the very same militia which carried out the massacre. This was too much for the Italians. During a government raid into Chatila, they refused to allow Lebanese troops to take Palestinians from the camp. When the Lebanese refused to release their captives, the Italian Bersaglieri attacked the soldiers with rifle butts and forced them to free the Palestinians.

The thousands of arrested men were first taken to a Lebanese army barracks near the Museum and then — if the deuxième bureau expressed particular interest in a prisoner — to the basements of the Lebanese Defence Ministry not far from the president's palace at Baabda. Here, they were tied up and beaten by their interrogators before being transported in lorries to the Israeli–Syrian front line below Sofar and ordered to cross to the Syrian side.

Even more disturbing were the lists of prisoners who disappeared. The Italians believed that up to 100 men from their area of operations went missing after being arrested. They did not return to their homes and were never seen again. Whether they were handed to the Phalange militia or to the Israelis, we never discovered. MNF officers were in no doubt that they had been murdered. Ambassadors of the three nations in the MNF visited Gemayel to complain about the reports of torture and killings. According to one French diplomat, it was a 'mild and polite' expression of concern to the president. Gemayel, as the ambassadors remembered, had just returned from the United States where President Reagan had personally promised support for the Lebanese government.*

In the ruined Palestinian camp of Ein Helweh just east of Sidon, the Lebanese government's intentions were equally clear if less violently

* In the succeeding months, Westerners were also arrested and ordered to leave Lebanon. Among the foreigners deported was Paola Crociani, an Italian freelance photographer working for the Associated Press under Tatro in Beirut. Accused by the Phalange of maintaining a friendship with a Palestinian, she was held overnight in a prison where she heard other captives screaming with pain and then, without being allowed to contact her Embassy, was taken to Beirut airport and put on a flight to Rome.

Some weeks later, after the arrival in Beirut of a small British MNF contingent, the Phalangist who controlled the deuxième bureau temporarily refused to renew my residence permit and press card, claiming that my reports on the Phalange during the 1975–6 conflict had been 'distorted'. When I suggested to the Maronite official in charge of the Information Ministry that deporting a British journalist might be misunderstood by a British government which had just sent troops to support Gemayel's administration, she replied: 'You think we need your little army to help us? We can do without your country. Lebanon is strong again. It needs no one.' The latter was certainly true.

expressed. When Foley and I visited the camp in mid-November, my car sank up to its axles in the mud. The rains swept horizontally across the wreckage, turning the rubble into a thick, clay-like consistency that adhered to our shoes and made it difficult even to walk the runnels that passed for streets. A small river of mud and sewage washed past the broken walls where a clutch of Palestinian families watched our passage, the water matting their hair and soaking their clothes.

These people had suffered terribly in the Israeli invasion. Hundreds of men from Ein Helweh had been imprisoned in the new Israeli prison camp at Ansar for real or imagined participation in Palestinian guerrilla movements.* But now the inhabitants were afflicted with a special frustration. On a rectangle of broken stones and clay stood 15 dark green canvas tents, each floored with concrete breeze-blocks and all but one of them uninhabited. They were supposed to protect the refugees through the winter months and there were supposed to be 2,500 of them in all; but the refugees refused to live in them.

For the tents represented a political as well as a social problem. They were erected by the United Nations Relief and Works Agency (UNRWA) with the approval of the Lebanese authorities, who were prepared to shield the refugees from the harshness of winter providing the shield did not become too permanent. Put less diplomatically, the Lebanese government was none too keen to rebuild the stone shacks in which the Palestinians used to live – especially when it was trying to reconstruct all of Lebanon for the Lebanese – if by so doing the Palestinians would be encouraged to stay on in their country of adoption. The Lebanese wanted the Palestinians to go home – wherever 'home' might prove to be.

The Palestinians at Ein Helweh were well aware of the political significance of the tents, which is why they burned down the first canvas shelter that UNRWA put up on this miserable little square of land. This was in itself a potentially foolhardy gesture when the first towering cumulus clouds loomed over the Mediterranean, but the inhabitants of Ein Helweh appeared to have put their trust in the people who destroyed so much of their camp in the first place: the Israelis. For the Israeli government had announced that it would like to see the refugees housed in real buildings with concrete walls, and had even offered to send ten bags of cement to every homeless Palestinian in the camp. Part of the money for this project had already been donated by an American Jewish organisation. The Israelis publicised this humanitarian gesture although

---

* Between 4,000 and 4,500 Palestinians were held at Ansar. According to Dr Israel Shahak, chairman of the Israeli League for Human and Civil Rights, up to 20,000 prisoners – three quarters of them Lebanese – were in Israeli custody by the end of 1982. See Chomsky, *Fateful Triangle*, p. 391.

they were aware of its contradictions. They said they wanted to stabilise Lebanon. The more Palestinians who left, the more stable Lebanon would presumably be. But Israel could scarcely urge the Palestinians of Ein Helweh to go 'home' – since 'home', in most cases, would have meant Israel.

The refugees at Ein Helweh still had some shelter, even if shell-holes in roofs were stuffed with plastic sheeting to keep out the rain. Several hundred Palestinians lived in a series of ruined garages and smashed schools, which did not please the local Lebanese, some of whom owned land in Ein Helweh. They wanted their property back – at the expense of the Palestinians – and Gemayel's government was supporting their demand.

In Beirut, outside Chatila, we watched the Lebanese army destroying dozens of Palestinian shacks. The structures had been constructed illegally outside the walls of the camp, the Lebanese explained. They were therefore bulldozed into the ground. There were few buildings still standing inside Chatila – the Phalangists had seen to that during the massacre, dynamiting the hovels on top of many of the bodies – and now there were no homes outside the camp either. Again, the multinational force watched this development without interfering. One evening, the Lebanese army raided the Palestinian Gaza hospital in west Beirut, seizing newly arrived medical supplies, all of which had been donated by Italians and transported to Lebanon by the Italian *Bersaglieri*.

After his election as president, Bashir Gemayel had drawn up a plan to rid Lebanon of the Palestinians. A quarter of a million of them, he thought, could be deported. He discussed these proposals with Lebanese foreign ministry officials. Even now, more than a month after his death, the list of missing men, the deportations, the arrests and interrogations gave a chilling idea of what Bashir Gemayel's Lebanon would have been like. Amin Gemayel was trying to rebuild his country in his brother's image. Amin's Lebanon, too, would have been an ungenerous and brutal little dictatorship.

Yet Gemayel's Phalange had been hopelessly discredited. And the army which had put Gemayel in power was now entangled in the poisoned fruits of its own invasion. Every day the Israelis were attacked, at Galerie Semaan, on the old Sidon road opposite the Marines, on the coast road south, in the towns and cities which they had stormed and occupied in June. Shia gunmen ambushed an Israeli foot patrol on the edge of east Beirut and killed two soldiers. The Israelis gave no immediate confirmation, but when I reached Galerie Semaan I was just in time to see the legs of two dead Israelis dangling from the back of a departing armoured personnel carrier. Driving down to Sidon, Scheherezade Faramarzi of AP narrowly escaped being killed when a roadside bomb exploded near an Israeli patrol. The victims were a civilian family who were nearest the bomb. Faramarzi found the father sitting on the roadside, weeping and covered in blood.

In the Druze hill-town of Aley, gunmen – probably Palestinian – opened fire on an Israeli bus carrying troops to Beirut. They riddled the vehicle with automatic fire, killing six of the Israelis and wounding another 22. The Israelis were so confident of their military power that they had paid little heed to the danger of attack from *inside* their occupation zone. When we reached the scene, we discovered that the Israelis had been travelling with their rifles under their seats and had not managed to fire one shot at their attackers.

Israel's self-confidence in Lebanon was extraordinary. The Israelis erected a transmitter near Aley to beam Israeli television programmes into Beirut. Travelling branches of the Israeli Bank Leumi opened for business in the Chouf and east Beirut for any Lebanese wishing to exchange Lebanese pounds for shekels. In Sidon, a Lebanese travel agent was induced to act as an official agent for El Al, the Israeli airline.

When this tranquillity was disturbed by guerrilla attacks, the Israelis therefore hit back wildly. In retaliation for the Aley ambush, the Israeli air force bombed a Syrian missile battery on the slopes of Dahr al-Baidur. When they were ambushed on the old Sidon road, they brought a Merkava tank up from Khalde and shelled the building from which they claimed the shots had come. The first tank round exploded in the kitchen of an apartment, beheading the mother of a Lebanese army colonel. Israeli foot patrols on the same road fired thousand of rounds into the houses, bushes and trees beside them, wounding and sometimes killing householders, farmers or fruit-pickers. Many of their rounds passed dangerously close to the US Marine positions, prompting a series of formal complaints from Colonel Mead. 'Their tactics are ineffective and unprofessional,' he announced to us. Privately, he added an observation of his own. 'The Israelis think they are pretty good,' he said. 'But they are a fourth-rate army fighting a seventh-rate army.'

Yet the seventh-rate army – whether it was composed of Lebanese Shia Muslims or Palestinians – was clearly challenging the Israelis. Its effects were visible in the columns of the Israeli press which now referred to Lebanon not as a country to be liberated or as a future ally but as a 'quagmire', a 'bog', a place of ingratitude and faithlessness. The Phalange had let the Israelis do all the fighting around Beirut, Israeli editorials complained. The Phalange had besmirched Israel's name at Sabra and Chatila. The Lebanese Shia who had allegedly welcomed the Israelis so wholeheartedly in the south of the country were now assisting the 'terrorists' in attacking Israeli troops. The Lebanese were 'intimidated' by Syria. Israeli soldiers, it was now decided, were bravely acting as 'policemen' in Lebanon, preventing Druze and Christians from killing each other.

Rarely during this early period of the occupation of Lebanon did the Israelis blame themselves for their predicament. Now the Israelis announced — at press conferences and briefings for correspondents — that they were playing the role of policemen, even of 'peace-keepers', in the Chouf. So now there were supposed to be two sets of peace-keepers in Lebanon: the MNF in Beirut and the Israelis in the Chouf. The Lebanese Muslims did not accept this definition, although the parallel was a dangerous one for the MNF.

The first seismic tremor to hit the Israelis came in Tyre, the city they had conquered in the very first days of their invasion. They had established their military headquarters in the city inside an eight-storey apartment block just north of the main road junction which connected the port to the coastal highway. The structure was made of breeze-blocks and wire-mesh supports, just like the buildings which had invariably collapsed on their occupants under Israeli air attack. The Israeli headquarters contained operations rooms, billets for troops, a unit of plain-clothes Shin Bet operatives and a number of Palestinian and Lebanese prisoners awaiting interrogation. On 11 November 1982, a massive explosion tore through the block, bringing the whole building to the ground in less than ten seconds.

The Lebanese radio stations were first to report that Israelis had been killed in Tyre. A few minutes after Farouk Nassar had monitored the Phalange's 'Voice of Lebanon' dispatch, the bells on the AP wire machine rang in the Beirut bureau. We had not heard the 'urgent' bells for several weeks. The first dispatch came out of Tel Aviv, a brief, one-paragraph report of an explosion. There were casualties. Christina Joelsson, who had visited Beirut during the siege and reported for a Finnish newspaper, was back in Lebanon. We drove south, passed through the Israeli lines at Khalde but were stopped by Israeli military policemen outside the Zahrani oil terminal just south of Sidon. No one was allowed to travel to Tyre. All roads to the city were closed, the Israelis said. The military policemen were polite but they appeared shocked. 'We don't know how many died. It is very bad,' one of them said.

We drove east towards the Shia town of Nabatieh. Joelsson and I suspected that if we took the winding road down through the wadi of the Litani below Nabatieh and then passed through the UN lines on the other side of the river, we might be able to enter Tyre from the east. The Israelis would assume travellers from that direction were local farmers or shopkeepers whose homes were in Tyre and would not bother to block traffic. At the Qaaqaaiyet Al-Jisr bridge over the Litani, a newly installed UN unit of Finnish troops had taken control, but Major Haddad's militia had erected a checkpoint 20 yards on the northern side of the bridge. The teenage gunman looked at us suspiciously.

'Where are you going?' To the UN. 'Do you have a cigarette?' I gave him a cigar. '*Habibi*, good luck.' The Finns waved us through.

It was dusk. Our car banged into the two-foot-wide potholes on the road. We turned on the radio. The Israelis had reported heavy casualties in their headquarters. There would be a three-minute silence all over Israel in memory of the dead. Israel was in mourning. Ten miles south of the Litani, an Israeli jeep stood at a road junction. A soldier with a rifle pointed to the left-hand road. To reach Tyre on this laneway meant another 20 miles driving. Another Finnish checkpoint in the darkness. There was a UN officer standing next to a big armoured vehicle. 'The Israelis are not on this road. Keep going. I think you'll make it.'

Tyre was blacked out. Israeli troops stood in the darkened doorways as we crept slowly through the city, keeping the light on inside the car so that the soldiers would see we were civilians. Above the houses, we could see a white glow from the direction of the headquarters.

We drove right up to the rubble. The horror that had overwhelmed the Israelis had made them lose all sense of security. The moment we climbed from the car, we were cloaked in a thin white dust. The floodlit rubble of the pancaked eight-storey building lay in sharp relief like a stage set, and the Israelis stood beside it in shock and amazement. They had pulled 75 of their men from the ruins, all dead, many of them Shin Bet agents. From the tons of concrete, they also pulled the corpses of 15 Lebanese and Palestinian prisoners.

Many of the Israelis stared in silence at the huge cakes of cement and concrete that had killed their friends and colleagues. They said nothing. I thought we would be arrested. No one spoke to us. 'We haven't seen enough,' Joelsson said. I followed her to the other side of the road, past a tent strewn with maps where two officers with general's insignia were talking. Behind them was a large metal warehouse with a light shining from beneath the door.

We pushed the door gently open. The dead Israelis lay on the floor, wrapped in long, glossy white bags. Under the arc-lights inside the building, they seemed somehow unreal – as if death was absent – until a rabbi in a dark jacket walked into the building and began repeating prayers over the corpses. Row after row of them lay on the floor, in lines, regimented in death. I found it hard to believe. The Israelis had appeared so invulnerable, so omnipotent. They had seemed immune. Now the soldiers who entered the warehouse to collect the bodies seemed touched by the same astonishment. Three of them stared across the building without speaking, as if waiting for the dead themselves to provide an explanation. The dust moved slowly past the arc-lights.

We watched them struggling to lift one of the white bags and lay it on a stretcher, the body cumbersome and unwieldy, unwilling to accept death. There was an Israeli lieutenant outside with a face lined by fatigue and sweat, leaning against a jeep. 'You see that cement over there?' he asked, pointing to a stump of concrete three feet high from which wires protruded at crazy angles. 'That was the central foundation of the whole building. They had no chance.'

Such events always heighten emotion, but there was one particularly dreadful argument going on beside the warehouse which served as a temporary mortuary. Outside the doors, there stood an ambulance in which two Palestinians lay on stretchers, their faces contorted with pain. They had been found in the rubble and taken to a hospital in Tyre, but now the International Red Cross wanted to transport them to Israel for treatment. The Israelis were prepared to look after them but insisted that the helicopter be used for taking bodies home. There was no room on board for the wounded Palestinians.

I asked one of the two Palestinians his name but he could only move his lips a fraction of an inch. Many of his bones had been broken and he was bleeding slightly from his mouth. The Red Cross said that three of the Palestinian dead had been found with their hands bound in iron shackles.

A Swiss Red Cross official was pleading with a young Israeli officer beside the ambulance. 'I know your feelings,' he said. 'I know these are your dead and you want to take them home. But the bodies are, forgive me, dead. And these two people are wounded and we cannot take paraplegics by road to Israel. Please let us have your helicopter.' But the Israeli was firm in his denial. 'I agree with you one hundred per cent,' he replied. 'But my people have made up their minds. We are taking the bodies on the helicopter. I am very sorry.'

A few minutes later, the rabbi and the three soldiers carried the first of the bodies to the helicopter and the ambulance bounced off unsteadily over the track outside the warehouse, the Palestinians inside strapped to their stretchers for safety. The Red Cross official shrugged his shoulders. 'The Israelis took the other Palestinian wounded in their hospitals and accepted all my recommendations,' he said. 'There was nothing else I could do.'

Out by the main road, the two generals had been joined by junior officers and the maps had been hung on a wall. A temporary headquarters was taking shape amid the dust. But what caused this carnage? The Israeli government had announced that it might have been a gas leak, although there were no mains in Lebanon, only bottled gas. The soldiers seemed sceptical of this. An automobile engine and fragments of clothing had just been flown to Israel for forensic examination. If the building had been destroyed with explosives, then the bomber had died too. A *suicide* bomber? The idea seemed inconceivable.

On the main road, beside a radio truck, there stood a tall, bespectacled Israeli soldier, a thoughtful man with a gentle face who seemed almost too tired to speak. Did he think Israel's enemies had attacked his friends? Was Tyre still safe for the Israelis? He looked north where the main road disappeared into the darkness. 'There may be Palestinians out there,' he said. 'I don't know how many terrorists are still there. I guess nobody really does.' The old self-confidence with which the Israelis used to greet strangers here seemed to have gone.

There was no traffic on the dark road north between the orange groves; not one human being was to be seen until we reached the Litani River bridge. On the other bank, a convoy of Israeli army lorries was lined up on the highway. We drove past them slowly with headlights on low beam, but we could clearly see the soldiers standing beside them, eyes narrowed, rifles at the ready, deep in the wilderness of occupation.

In Beirut, the carnage to the south was seen as another reason why the MNF should not expand its area of operations. The Marines had been asked by Washington to reconnoitre Sidon so that MNF troops could move south when an Israeli withdrawal appeared imminent. Colonel Mead drove to the city with Lebanese army officers, took one look at the chaos and damage, at the wreckage of Ein Helweh and the frightened Israeli foot patrols on the streets, and returned to Beirut with his mind made up. Under no circumstances, he told Washington, should the MNF be sent south. The Marines were safe in the capital and that is where they would stay.

There had been only one incident to suggest that the Americans had enemies in Beirut. On 11 November, the same day that the Israeli headquarters had been blown apart in Tyre, a Marine was wounded in the hand when a car bomb blew up near his position on the western side of the airport. The explosives, hidden under the back seat of a gold-coloured Volkswagen saloon, had been triggered by a wristwatch and sent heavy pieces of shrapnel past the heads of the Marines. The first reaction of the Americans was to take cover and load their rifles. For US troops in Lebanon were under instructions not to carry live rounds in their weapons, an intriguing military order that did not, of course, go unnoticed in west Beirut. In its search for culprits, the Lebanese press contrived to mention almost every army in Lebanon. The only certain fact was that the multinational force now appeared to have enemies.*

And the dream continued. The French cleared mines, grenades and unexploded shells from miles of laneways and overgrown boulevards between east and west Beirut, bulldozing aside thousands of tons of earth and concrete. Beirut's teeth were being drawn. For the first time

---

* The US contingent had suffered its first casualty on 30 September when a Marine on mine-clearing duty set off an unexploded Israeli cluster bomb near the airport. The Americans did not announce publicly that it was Israeli ordnance but they showed us the triangular metal pouch with a hole in the side that killed the Marine and said that the bomb had originally been dropped from the air. Only the Israelis bombed from the air around Beirut.

since I visited Lebanon as a tourist back in 1972, I could drive from the museum to Galerie Semaan on the direct route, a dustbowl boulevard that now ran through a ghost town of ruined homes, offices, factories, gas stations and shops. No one had lived or worked here for seven years. In one shattered office block, I found a telephone on a desk, the receiver hanging loose on a rusting wire, just as the subscriber must have dropped it when he or she fled in panic in 1975. Like visitors to the wreck of the *Titanic*, we looked into the past with a mixture of fascination and reverence. These were the first ruins of Lebanon's war. Little did we realise, even then, how essential they were to Beirut's own identity. At the museum, Amin Gemayel inspected units from the three MNF contingents, declaring that east and west Beirut no longer existed. There was, he said, only one Beirut.

It was untrue. Gemayel wanted to be seen in front of the banners of the international army; the stars and stripes and the tricolours of France and Italy were dipped in salute before him. A Lebanese army band played a rendering – faithful to the melody if not the rhythm – of the three national anthems. But just down the road, the Phalangists maintained their usual checkpoint. The Israelis had left Gemayel with a capital in which the balance of military power had fallen so overwhelmingly on the side of the Christian Maronites that the only militia still able to roam the streets, at least in east Beirut, were the Phalangists. The president could scarcely castrate the force to which he himself still belonged. The triangular cedar tree symbol of the Phalange still hung over the streets of Christian Beirut, which was why a journey from west to east Beirut meant crossing from one city to another.

The Lebanese army had collected weapons from the homes of almost every Muslim family in west Beirut. In east Beirut, not one Phalangist gun had been confiscated. If west Beirut had been disarmed, east Beirut remained an armed camp. We had realised as early as September that this imbalance of power could prove to be a catastrophe. When Israel withdrew from east Beirut – leaving the Phalangists still in control – the status of the international army was immediately thrown into doubt. US Marines were under orders to support the Lebanese army in arresting armed men in west Beirut. But in east Beirut, the American and French troops drove through armed Phalangist checkpoints without making the slightest attempt to seize the militia's weapons.

It was difficult, I wrote in a dispatch to *The Times* that September, to escape the suspicion that Israel had deliberately sucked the MNF into this situation. Israel, one theory went, had fallen so far in international esteem that it had lured the international army into a trap, so that Western powers would share Israel's discredit.

In west Beirut, the search for arms continued for weeks. When I drove through the Fakhani district, where Arafat's headquarters had been located, I would find the streets lined with mobile anti-aircraft guns, the pavements piled with rocket-launchers and artillery shells. The most spectacular discovery came *beneath* the Palestinian camps. The Lebanese army, together with French and Italian troops, found a catacomb of concrete-lined tunnels stretching for at least four miles under the camps, some of them filled with rockets, mortars and small-arms ammunition. One tunnel through which I walked with Italian soldiers ran almost the entire length of the Chatila camp. Eight feet high and six feet wide, it included a series of concrete chambers in which were stored crates of Grad two-stage missiles. Most of the ammunition bore Russian, Czech or Polish markings together with hundreds of military manuals in English and Russian. Several tunnels opened into large rooms filled with guerrilla camouflage uniforms, belts, berets, *kuffiah* scarves and books.

The tunnels proved conclusively that the Palestine Liberation Organisation was capable of safely storing huge quantities of ammunition despite the heaviest air strikes that the Israelis staged against the camps. They also suggested that the PLO had far more ammunition at its disposal in the last days of the siege of Beirut than anyone imagined at the time. One tunnel, lined with boxes of grenades and mortars, went on for 300 yards, and Italian bomb disposal officers eventually turned back because the tunnel was so long that it was passing beneath territory held by the French MNF contingent. The French dutifully descended to explore their own section of underground passageways. During their occupation of west Beirut, the Israelis had failed to discover even one of the tunnels.

Israel's Phalangist allies were the only Lebanese to profit from the government's renewed control over west Beirut. And their leader remained the murdered Bashir Gemayel. He was dead but he was also alive. In east Beirut, Maronites would say that after Bashir was found amid the rubble of his Phalangist party office on 14 September, he walked alive into an ambulance. The story was nonsense. Gemayel was pulverised by the bomb that exploded next to him and his body so mutilated that his wife Solange was only able to identify him by his wedding ring. But the story lived on. Not only did Bashir walk from the smashed building; he climbed unaided into an ambulance bearing the figures '90' on its door. The Beirut city authorities did not possess an ambulance number 90 but the legend grew: Bashir did not die on 14 September; he left only temporarily, to return like King Arthur in Lebanon's hour of need and free the nation from her oppressors. Among the less realistic of Bashir's followers, the idea became a fixation and the Phalangist leadership was quick to take up the theme.

On the fortieth day after his death, the Phalangists held a memorial service to honour Bashir, an uneasy ceremony of regret and reincarnation.

Fadi Frem, the colourless new militia leader, did not address the mourners. In a eulogy that was as eerie as it was disquieting, he looked up towards the Valhalla in which the murdered man now resided, and spoke directly to Bashir:

Nobody can believe that your absence implies your death or that your death is final. We await your return each morning and evening. Before every decision ... we turn our gaze to your office, half hoping to see the light burning. But seeing the room dark, we say: 'The Leader has not yet returned.'

The eulogies were not confined to militiamen. Father Boulos Namaan, the leader of the Maronite Order of Monks, saw Bashir's death as martyrdom on a divine scale. 'Like Christ and with complete understanding of his Christian mission, Bashir sacrificed everything ... for all Lebanese,' he announced. The living God. Fifteen minutes after the start of the requiem mass, two Israeli Kfir fighter-bombers swept over east Beirut and the Phalangists looked up. 'The Israelis want to remind us that they made Sheikh Bashir king,' one of the militiamen said to us. The jets came back twice more, just as they had flown in tribute over Gemayel's funeral cortège in the mountains 40 days earlier.

But who killed Gemayel? The Phalange considered the possible culprits and even arrested a sad-faced youth whom its news agency accused of assassinating Bashir on Syria's orders. But after the Israelis blamed the Phalangists for the massacre at Sabra and Chatila, the Phalange artfully suggested that the Israelis might have assassinated their leader because he would not bow to their demands for a peace treaty. The Phalangists did not shoot the man they accused of killing their leader. How can a man be executed for murdering a man who is not dead? For Bashir played a parallel role to that of the hidden Twelfth Imam of the Shiite faith. Like Lebanon's own missing Imam, Mousa Sadr, Bashir was going to return.

It was a strange winter in Beirut, insulated from the suffering and chaos of the rest of Lebanon. The Lebanese government insisted that it was only a matter of time before Lebanon's sovereign territory − all 10,452 square kilometres of it, as Bashir Gemayel was in the habit of pointing out − was again under Lebanon's control. T-shirts with the magic figure of 10,452 appeared in the boutiques of Hamra Street. On the sidewalks, we could buy both the *Jerusalem Post* and the Syrian party daily *Al Baath*. Outside my apartment, truckloads of US Marines flying the Stars and Stripes would grind up from the port with supplies as the US Sixth Fleet littered the Mediterranean horizon. The American presence was bringing back investors. Money was again pouring into Beirut. The Lebanese pound, which had touched six to the dollar, was now back at three to the dollar. Expatriates reinvested in their pulverised businesses. In rue Allenby, a German water-colour painter was captur-

ing the beauty of the ruins before they were torn down to make way for
the new Beirut.

Even in what we then called the 'bad days', I used to go out at night.
Now it was a relief to drive to the *Grenier* restaurant – a hostelry of
high wooden ceilings, ancient lanterns, low seats and massive Arabic
mezze dinners – without having to talk my way past three militias on the
way. But now so many people were venturing out at night that the
Grenier was full. It was necessary to book tables two days in advance;
this being Lebanon, no dispensation was made for customers who
faithfully turned up in the 'bad days'. The telecommunications ministry
promised new phone lines. A German company began to lay new water
pipes through west Beirut.

Along the seafront Corniche, new palm trees were planted. Roads
were re-surfaced. Rafiq Hariri, a Lebanese-born Saudi philanthropist,
donated millions of dollars to clear the streets of his native capital, using
40 trucks, 100 bulldozers and 1,300 workmen. From the ruins of the
city, they created an evil-smelling mountain of rubble beside the port
that spread into the water and gave the sea a unique crust of cheese-
coloured filth. The new, internationalised Beirut received foreign ministers, diplomatic missions and business delegations. In the wreckage of
Bourj al-Barajneh, on the edge of the Palestinian camp, Princess Anne
visited a medical clinic maintained by the Save the Children Fund,
shaking hands with Shia schoolgirls beneath pictures of Imam Mousa
Sadr. She spoke, too, with Palestinian children, although this caused a
convulsion in the British Embassy in Beirut who were fearful of offending
Amin Gemayel's regime. David Roberts, the ambassador, arrived in the
Commodore Hotel on the night of the royal visit, exploding with wrath
that journalists should have even suggested the princess might have met
Palestinians. For the Palestinians, of course, were no longer supposed to
be the issue in Lebanon.

Imperceptibly, the massacre which had brought the multinational
force back to Beirut was being forgotten. The protection of the Palestinians
was now giving way to a political, strategic goal: the withdrawal of all
foreign armies, the restoration of Lebanese government sovereignty, the
internationalisation, the *Westernisation* of Lebanon. The results of the
Israeli invasion were still evident, for anyone who cared to look, and it
was still possible, amid the new economic growth and noisy optimism of
Beirut, to come face to face with something infinitely terrible.

When I took a foreign visitor to the Chatila camp in late November,
black-ribboned wreaths shook in the rain squalls over the sunken mass
grave. We had walked down the mud of a laneway towards what had
been an execution wall – the wall in front of which Jenkins and Tveit
and I had found a pile of bodies in September – when a young girl,
dressed in black but with a face of smiles, ran up to us. 'Take my

picture? Take my picture?' she asked, and beckoned us to follow her. She had been wounded in the summer air raids and she limped down the lane like a hobgoblin, shrieking, in her delight at seeing visitors, that yes, she had lost all her brothers, her sister, her uncle and one of her parents in the massacre.

Then when we reached the wall against which those young men had been shot down – its surface still pocked with bullet holes – she stood on the quicklime dust, turned to us in the rain and posed like a creature in a freak show. We took her picture in disbelief.

It snowed. All down the mountain chain from the cedars of Bsharre to the lower Chouf, the snow swept fiercely across Lebanon. Even around Hazmiyeh and in the suburbs of Beirut it snowed, for the first time in more than 20 years. The heights of Sannine glistened, blinding and jewelled above the city. In a blizzard of snow and ice, Foley and I drove past the Israeli–Syrian front line below Sofar. On the mountain sides, US Marine helicopters brought food for hundreds of motorists trapped in their cars. They were greeted by Syrian troops. Were not the Marines on a humanitarian mission? More than 50 people died in the blizzard. Israeli line troops, in their furs and frost masks, claimed that 300 Syrian soldiers had been frozen to death. But this was untrue. What was being frozen that winter was less tangible than the men on the ridge-line above Beirut.

When Foley and I drove out of the fog and clouds on the Damascus highway, down that wide boulevard from which we had watched the Israeli air raids in June, we could see only too clearly what was happening to Beirut. The Mediterranean bay had become a basin for the American fleet. The frigates and cruisers cresting through the surf represented more than the multinational force which they were intended to support. Lebanon was no longer the object of a humanitarian mission. It was acquiring a military importance of its own. The country was becoming a strategic asset. Beirut bay, with its American, French and Italian warships, was turning into a NATO base.

Day after day, we were helicoptered out to the fleet. I requested to visit every warship that arrived off Beirut. 'Your chopper – go!' the Marine at the heli-base beside the airport would shout, and I would go running over the apron, strap myself into the Chinook and go off above the MEA Boeings, the coast road and the Ouzai surf to sleek grey warships heaving on the Mediterranean swell. How quickly we accustomed ourselves to this reporting. After struggling for years with the transliteration of Arabic names into English, we were suddenly recording the movements of the USS *Iwo Jima*, the USS *Harlan County*, the *El Paso*, the *Austin*, the *Portland* and the *Eisenhower*.

Instead of giving up our Beirut assignment and moving back to the West, the West had come to us. When we climbed off the helicopters on to these ships, or clung to the wire that dropped us on their decks, we were greeted by US naval officers in immaculate uniforms, their faces bright with self-confidence, flourishing photographs of their captains and vessels, handing out folders extolling the virtues of their unique sea-borne firepower. A big blue folder enclosed the history of the USS *Independence*, the uncomfortable old aircraft carrier which provided air cover for the multinational force in Beirut. The documents referred to the carrier as the 'Guardian of Freedom' and proclaimed that we were now 'aboard the Navy's finest carrier'. The ship was there 'to maintain freedom of the seas'. The language was patriotic, hygienic, automated. The squadron of A-6E Intruders on the flight deck, we were told, were prepared for 'all-weather ordnance delivery missions'. There were EA-6B Prowlers for electronic warfare, A-7E Corsairs for the 'precision delivery of weapons', SH-3H anti-submarine warfare helicopters for 'plane guard missions', F-14A Tomcats for 'fleet air defence and weapons delivery'. The squadrons, we were told, were 'a winning team'.

This was even more surreal than Beirut. Foley and I had a pretty good idea what 'ordnance delivery missions' were like and we knew just how precise 'precision delivery' was. These clean young men on the carrier had little notion. Their lectures and briefings were a strange amalgam of political naivety, pseudo-scientific jargon and Christ-like goodwill. To report their words was to travel far further than the few miles that separated the warships from Beirut. It was always the same. We were introduced to the officers – American wire agencies reported their home towns and medals as a statutory duty, especially if they had served in Vietnam – who would then announce their mission in the language of the examination room. Vice-Admiral Edward H. Martin, the Sixth Fleet Commander (home town: Savannah, Georgia; holder of the Silver Star, the Defence Superior Service Medal, two Legions of Merit, the Distinguished Flying Cross, two Bronze Stars, two Navy Commendation medals and a Purple Heart), announced that he was in the Mediterranean 'to introduce US forces as part of a multinational force presence in the Beirut area and to establish an environment which will permit the Lebanese armed forces [LAF] to carry out their responsibilities in the Beirut area ...'

Martin's 'Task Force 60' was being monitored by both the Israelis and the Soviets, the latter represented by a chunky little intelligence gathering vessel called the *Vertikal*. Israeli missile boats sailed at night between the US ships, filming them with infra-red cameras. The *Vertikal*, with its forest of receivers and scanners, listened to both the Americans and the Israelis. They had never anticipated this serious a commitment from the United States.

The Soviets had now invested almost as much political and military prestige in a newly rearmed Syria as the Americans had in Gemayel's government in Beirut. Moscow had re-equipped Assad's air force and provided him with new SAM-5 missiles. Three batteries of long-range SAM-5s had been installed, two of them close to Damascus and the third near Deraa. They were crewed by Soviet military personnel.* Assad had been assured during a visit to Moscow that while the Soviets would not interfere if Syrian forces were in combat again in Lebanon, there would be an immediate airlift of Soviet troops into Syria if the Israelis attacked Syrian territory. The American military presence in Beirut had allowed Moscow to increase its own military presence in Syria. The balance of power in the Middle East had now been dramatically altered and its future depended upon the ability of Gemayel's Phalangist government to persuade the proxy armies of the two superpowers — the Israelis and the Syrians — to leave his country.

But Gemayel was now complaining that both adversaries were prevaricating over a mutual withdrawal. The Israelis would not move if the Syrians did not leave. Assad, however, believed that if the Syrians withdrew, this would amount to a tactical victory for the Israelis; and Assad did not intend to allow the Israelis to gain anything from their invasion of Lebanon. Besides, the Syrians had been 'invited' to enter Lebanon in 1976 by the Lebanese president. The Israelis had invaded. How could the two armies be compared? Assad's premise was simple: the Syrian presence in Lebanon was legitimate; the Israeli presence was not.

But Syria could hardly claim that all her allies in Lebanon possessed an equally valid right to be in the country. Nor had the Americans any excuse to continue under the illusion that they had no enemies in Lebanon. In Baalbek in the Bekaa Valley, several hundred Iranian revolutionary guards, in uniform and carrying their own rifles, had installed themselves not far from the Roman temples. They had set up a military headquarters in a deserted modern hospital complex and begun proselytising among the city's largely Shia Muslim population on behalf of their Islamic revolution. Three hundred yards from the market in Baalbek, the guards opened a two-storey propaganda office. When Scheherezade Faramarzi of the Associated Press and I visited this building, we found a notice on the front door, describing the occupants as 'lovers of martyrdom'. Iranians were giving lessons in the Koran to children in the district. Baalbek was strewn with placards and banners denouncing Israeli and American 'imperialism' and exhorting the Lebanese to find salvation through martyrdom.

---

* The SAM-5s, with a range of over 160 miles, were in their turn protected by five batteries of SAM-3s, six batteries of SAM-6s and belts of SAM-2s. The sites were locked into a system of 30 early warning stations that spread more than halfway across Syria towards Iraq. They represented the most complex and modern air defence system brought into the Middle East by the Soviet Union. It was a missile trap for the Israelis.

I had travelled often to Iran and these slogans were familiar. So were the revolutionary guards. I had been under fire with them in the Gulf War. Their reputation for fearlessness was well deserved. Theirs was a belief in God that rarely faltered under bombardment. Their naïvety curiously paralleled that of the Americans, but for quite different reasons. They believed that the power of God could overcome all enemies. The Americans put an equal faith in their technology. Faced with an opponent, the Americans could rely upon the hardware aboard the USS *Independence*. The Iranians could call upon the Shia cult of martyrdom. If these two forces ever came into conflict in Lebanon, who would win: the F-14 or the suicide bomber?

The revolutionary guards in Baalbek were no different from their colleagues in Iran but there was something unnerving about their presence. It was not so much the fact they were there; foreign armies were spread all over Lebanon. But if the theological certainties of the Iranians could be grafted upon the Muslims of Lebanon who had suffered so cruelly, if they recognised the same enemies, then the Iranians in Baalbek represented an immensely powerful influence in the country. Iran was undergoing a religious renaissance. Lebanon was broken, its institutions long ago corrupted. It was like pouring boiling water into a fragile glass.

If the citizenry of Baalbek initially showed themselves largely unresponsive to the heroic sentiments of the Iranians, they nonetheless felt the presence of the reticent and bearded young men who closed off the streets of the city for the *Ashoura* ceremonies commemorating the death of Hussein, grandson of the Prophet. Many Lebanese girls in Baalbek had been compelled to wear the chador and revolutionary guards walked the streets with rifles in their hands. Machine-gun posts, reinforced with sandbags and earth, protected their offices, while in one street a 35-foot mural of Iranian women shrouded in black robes urged Lebanese women to remember their modesty.

None of the Iranians appeared to have fought against Israeli troops, although they claimed another contingent of Iranian forces — camped at one point on a hillside near Dar al-Baidar — might have been in action along the Israeli lines. Gleaning information about their activities was not easy. The revolutionary guards were suspicious of strangers and they explained their presence in Lebanon in the elliptical style of Ayatollah Khomeini's own teachings. When we asked to speak to the guards' leader in Baalbek, a young, unsmiling man in a pale green uniform, wearing a black shawl around his neck and sporting a green badge depicting a miniature Koran, unlocked an iron gate and led us into a wasteland of dirt and garbage behind the propaganda office. What did we wish to know? Why were we in Baalbek? We told him we wanted to know why *he* was in Lebanon, and there ensued a brief, extraordinary conversation that at times fell somewhere between incomprehension and farce.

The young man stared at the ground when he replied, for fear of looking at Faramarzi. His modesty was profound. He spoke in a monotone, as if reading a set of responses. 'We want to guide and inform [sic] the people of Lebanon,' he said in Persian. 'Our only goal is to Islamicise the place and, as the Imam Khomeini says, we have to export the Islamic revolution to the world. So like any other Muslims, we have come here with the aim of saving the deprived Palestinians and the deprived Lebanese.'

But did the Palestinians need his assistance? Most of them were Sunni Muslims. Why did the Iranians come to Lebanon? Another young and bearded man appeared, more thoughtful than his colleague, even less prone to humour. 'I will answer your questions if you will put our propaganda in your newspaper,' the newcomer announced. 'Why don't you print *The Times* in the Persian language?'

But there were moments of clarity in all this. The second man had fought against the Iraqis at the battle of Khorramshahr and he sensed that something had gone wrong with Iran's response to the Israeli invasion of Lebanon. 'The *fatwa* [teachings] of Imam Khomeini have made it clear that the Israeli war against Lebanon was a conspiracy aimed at getting Iran to send its troops to Lebanon and to forget the war with Iraq,' he said. 'As the Imam has announced, we can only reach Jerusalem through Iraq. Therefore most of the Iranian troops who came here have returned. The reason we came? — maybe it was a mistake.'

But there were clues as to why the Iranians might have arrived in Baalbek. Up at the hospital complex — originally built with Iranian money — revolutionary guards drove in and out of the gates in brand-new trucks, all but one of which carried Syrian registration plates. The Syrian army was supposed to control Baalbek but the Syrians may not have felt able to keep watch on the Shia population now that hostilities were in progress less than 40 miles away. There would be no better way of keeping an eye on them than by encouraging the Iranians to move into Baalbek. If the Iranians chose to see their mission as part of their Islamic revolution, why should the Syrians worry? The Iranians, after all, were not in Syria.

We all had vague presentiments of catastrophe about this time, although there was little evidence to support them. In the AP office in west Beirut, Terry Anderson was now deputy bureau chief to Tatro. He spent dozens of muddy, cold nights with the Marines around the airport, huddled and wet in their foxholes and dugouts, returning at dawn, exhausted but astonished at the ignorance of the Americans.

Anderson, his wife and daughter moved into a seafront flat in the same block as myself, bringing with them a massive South African ridgeback dog and two diminutive, gentle cats. Anderson was among the toughest journalists I knew, able to go for days with little sleep, able to drink a bottle of wine, go out to a long dinner and then edit a final lead for the New York wire. Physically, he resembled his dog — big, bullish, outwardly aggressive and outrageously energetic. His experience in South Africa had taught him to despise racial prejudice. He once stormed out of a dinner with a British army officer in Beirut when the latter referred to Lebanese militiamen as 'niggers'. Anderson stood up, pointed to the officer and asked: 'What exactly do you mean by that expression?' The officer replied: 'I call a nigger a nigger — a nigger is someone who's black and has curly hair.' Anderson could barely restrain himself from hitting the British soldier. 'In my country, Sir, we don't use that kind of language about human beings,' he said, turned his back on the officer, and walked out.

In other ways, Anderson did not resemble his dog. When shells fell around our house, the animal would hide in the bath. Anderson would go onto the streets, just as he did under Israeli fire during the siege of Beirut. He was idolised by his seven-year-old daughter Gabrielle. She would sit on the windy balcony of their home above the sea in the evenings and watch her father and me opening champagne, shrieking with delight when we tried to fire the cork in such a way that it lodged in the fronds of a palm tree below Anderson's flat. His small, mischievous, piggy eyes would flash from behind his thick-lensed glasses as the dog careered through the house at the sound of the popping bottle.

We were happy, I think. But both Anderson and I knew that it could not last. We felt the Lebanese mood change alarmingly. Gemayel was refusing to make concessions that would give Muslims a larger role in the government. The Phalange, still supported by the Israelis, saw no reason to relinquish their hold on the administration. The Shia and the Druze were prepared to allow the Maronites to retain the presidency but they wanted this to be a nominal post with real power vested in a Muslim prime minister. The ambassadors of the nations contributing to the MNF urged concessions upon Gemayel. At first, he said his government was too weak to make concessions. Once his army had been retrained by the Americans, he believed he was strong enough to rule without concessions. Thus the international army became the sustaining instrument of Christian Maronite Phalangist power.

Each day, a bus would pass our homes carrying American special forces officers up to the Lebanese army barracks near the airport where they were training a new Lebanese commando force. Gemayel's government was purchasing millions of dollars' worth of American and French guns and tanks. There were constant patrols of French and US troops. A tiny contingent of British soldiers arrived to support the MNF. Reagan had wanted a battalion of the Black Watch regiment. Mrs

Thatcher contributed 100 men of the Queen's Dragoon Guards 'to assist in the restoration of the Lebanese government sovereignty and authority over the Beirut area ...' They patrolled from an abandoned Syrian army billet beside a tobacco factory at Hadeth, just inside Israeli-occupied territory, their uniforms laundered by an old Maronite who had performed precisely the same task for the British forces which invaded Lebanon in 1941.

The fighting between Christians and Druze in the Chouf intensified. Living in Beirut was now like perching on top of a giant pack of cards in a stiff breeze. Without structural alterations, the framework would inevitably collapse. But instead, even while gale-force winds were tearing at the edifice, more cards were being added to the top of the pile. The evidence of disaster was now clear. Our daily narrative became a series of vignettes, both ludicrous and horrific.

On the roof of the British 1st Queen's Dragoon Guards headquarters at Hadeth. The commander of British Forces Lebanon – 'BRITFORLEB' – is Lieutenant-Colonel John Cochrane. It is dusk and the Druze have started shooting again at the Phalange in the hills to the south. The young officers of 'C' squadron are standing on the low roof parapet, sipping glasses of rum punch and enjoying the evening show. 'Having quite a go at each other tonight, aren't they, Sir?' says a major. 'Oh boy, look at that.' From the tip of a mountain, still just visible against the pale evening sky, a bright pink line of tracer comes hosing down towards the main road at Kfarshima.

The junior officers put up a moan of despair. 'What a bloody rotten shot,' one of them shouts and there are hoots of laughter. A massive explosion shakes the building. 'Not bad, not bad. But they did better last night, didn't they, Sir?' Cochrane watches without comment. An artillery piece begins firing from behind the building. 'Too bloody slow,' comes another taunt. 'The old Phalangos will have to do better than that.'

Cochrane is watching a small cluster of trees in the darkness 300 yards from his headquarters. He knows there is an Israeli Merkava tank there. 'When the Israelis have let them have a go at each other, or if their firing gets too close to the old Sidon road, they shut them up,' he says. The shooting continues. The British have told both sides not to shoot at them. The combatants' rules are clear-cut: shoot at each other, not at the multinational force. When an artillery round hisses over the British headquarters, a sergeant whistles through his teeth. Tracer zips into the trees where the Israelis are watching. There is a tongue of yellow flame from the hidden Merkava, a clap of sound on the hill and the shooting stops. 'OK, that's it for tonight,' announces the sergeant and we finish our drinks downstairs.

In the AP bureau, we hear a thunderous explosion that brings Nassar to his feet. 'Car bomb,' he roars. 'Quickly, quickly – get Tatro, get Anderson.' We drive through panicking crowds to Kantari. Two Lebanese Squad 16 paramilitary police are running down the street, carrying Walid Jumblatt on their shoulders. The Druze leader's face and shirt are soaked with blood, his eyes seem to be popping out of his head. There are cars on fire. Jumblatt's car is wrecked. One of his bodyguards is lying beside it with a huge wound in his stomach. Pieces of his kidneys have been blown around the inside of the vehicle. Jumblatt had been returning from lunch at the Myrtom House, the Austrian restaurant on the other side of the road. Pieces of the car bomb have been pitched dozens of yards down the street.

There is a middle-aged woman in the road wearing a black skirt, shrieking and beating her face with her hands, standing beside a small car that is smothered in flames. A French Paratrooper is tearing at the door, burning his hands white in the fire. After 30 seconds of fearful pain, he reels from the vehicle and we watch helplessly as the flames consume the interior. Camera crews cluster round the car. There was a woman inside, she was driving down the street when the bomb exploded 20 yards from her. For two minutes we wait while the ignited petrol engulfs the Volkswagen, the television crews silently filming the cremation. After four minutes, the flames die and the heat slackens and a Red Cross man tears off the door. In the iron-ribbed remains of the driver's seat, there sits upright a blackened skeleton, the skull slightly turned, the last juices of mortality dripping from its bones. A Lebanese deuxième bureau man with a two-way radio climbs onto a truck and shouts to his plain-clothes men. 'Stop them. Stop filming. Go home.'

Outside the American University hospital, hundreds of Druze gather to find out if Jumblatt is alive. A young man waving a pistol threatens to shoot the staff unless he is permitted to enter the building and find out for himself if his leader is still living. The mood of the crowd prompts Jumblatt to stagger from the hospital emergency room, plaster on his face, bandages round his chest, to prove he is not dead. The Phalangists condemn the assassination attempt as an effort to fracture the unity of Lebanon. The Druze do not believe them.

Now there are demonstrations over the men who were arrested by the Lebanese army and who have disappeared. The slaughter of the summer returns to haunt Beirut. A small woman in a blue raincoat pushes her way through a crowd towards me, shoving a torn photocopy of a Palestinian identification document before my face. 'It is my son,' she says. 'He is twenty but the Lebanese army took him a month and four days ago. They gave no reason. I saw him afterwards in Badaro barracks and gave him fresh clothes but when I went back they said he had been taken to Yarze military headquarters. I have heard nothing more. I want him, I want him.'

She begins to weep as other women crowd round us, pushing forward scraps of paper and shabby photographs, believing that the mere act of recording names like Shehadi Chehab, Zohair Ahmed Adlabi, Mohamed Hassan Fakhi or Bassam Abdo Salam Bibi in a British newspaper will somehow force their captors to free them or bring them back from the dead. Many of the women lost relatives at Chatila but never found their bodies. There are still 991 men and women from Sabra and Chatila whose corpses have not been found. The exact death toll will never be known. Gemayel's government has appointed the Lebanese prosecutor general, Assad Germanos, to hold an inquiry into the massacre, parallel to the Kahan commission in Israel. But the Lebanese inquiry – unlike the one going on in Jerusalem – is held in secret. No one knows how, where or how often it sits. It eventually concludes that those who died in the massacre were 'killed by persons unknown'.

The 'persons unknown', of course, lived in east Beirut. We knew some of their names. So did Amin Gemayel. The women's demonstrations were an annoyance to the Lebanese government. They were a reminder of the past. Gemayel repeated his confidence in Lebanon's future. None of us believed it. The Syrians now said they would not leave Lebanon until 'the last Israeli soldier' was withdrawn. The Israelis wanted to leave. But first they wanted a formal agreement, an unofficial peace treaty with Lebanon that would ensure for them a military presence in the south of the country, security guarantees, *something* at least, some token or souvenir that would prove their invasion of Lebanon had not been in vain. The Americans encouraged this process, refusing to believe that the Syrians meant exactly what they said.

Assad, however, knew that the Israelis would have no stomach to stay in Lebanon under constant guerrilla attack, even if the Syrian army did remain. He also knew that their desire to leave would grow with every military casualty. President Assad acquired new confidence. He wanted not just to win a political victory in Lebanon – something he could achieve by doing precisely nothing – but to teach the Israelis a lesson. There was something of the schoolmaster about Assad. He wanted his enemies to learn from their mistakes. If the Israelis were sufficiently humiliated, they would never risk another adventure in Lebanon. If America wished to share Israel's humiliation, Assad's influence in the Arab world would be all the greater.

At first, the Americans and the Israelis could be left to humiliate each other. Claiming that they wished to pursue 'terrorists', Israeli troops along the old Sidon road made a series of incursions into the US Marine zone along the trackbed of the long-disused Beirut–Sidon railway. When an Israeli tank unit tried to advance into the Marine area in January 1983, Marine Captain Charles Johnson climbed onto the leading Merkava and brandished a pistol in the face of the Israeli commander.

Caspar Weinberger, the US defence secretary, said that Johnson should be recommended for an award. The Israelis blandly announced that Johnson – a one-beer-a-day man – might have been drunk, precisely the same allegation which they had made two years earlier against Irish UN troops in Lebanon. They then followed up this libel by putting it about that the Marines were buying hashish from the slum-dwellers of Hay al-Sellum. The Marines, an Israeli spokesman said in Tel Aviv, were unwittingly providing cover for 'terrorists.'

It was not difficult to identify the demarcation line between the American Marines and the Israeli army just west of the old Sidon road. A long line of empty oil barrels, painted white but already rusting in the rains, ran though the wasteland of grass and mud from Khalde to the edge of Hay al-Sellum, the slumland where the less Islamic of the country's Shia Muslim poor once controlled the price of Lebanon's hashish crop.

On several days in the early spring of 1983, I stood on the road to watch the Israelis' morning patrol, a mud-spattered Merkava tank, turret swivelling to the west, come slithering down the broken highway. Far over the fields to the west, it was possible to see a dozen or so American Marines deploying on their side of the rusting barrels. They would walk parallel to the tank, exchanging no words with the crew, and then withdraw.

But the Israelis were still using their indiscriminate system of re-connaissance-by-fire to scare away potential attackers, firing into the fields on both sides of the road to frighten away guerrillas. In the process, the Israelis had so far killed five innocent civilians and their bullets were regularly hitting the Marine positions as well. The Israelis said that the problem could be solved if the Marines would permit regular meetings between liaison officers of the two armies. The Americans refused: if the Marines were seen to be talking formally to the Israelis, they would appear to be allies of the Israeli occupation army in Lebanon.

I once persuaded an Israeli tank commander to let me look at his map of the district. There on the other side of the barrels was a shaded area, which included the ruined science faculty of the Lebanese university, all of which was clearly marked as the American Marine zone. In mid-March, however, the Israelis claimed they knew of no such clarification between the Marine and Israeli lines. Ricocheting Israeli bullets went on smashing into the Marine bunkers.

General Robert H. Barrow, the commander of the US Marine Corps, complained to Weinberger of 'orchestrated' harassment of US forces by the Israeli troops on the west Beirut perimeter. Then on 19 March, two jeeploads of Israeli soldiers tried to enter the Marine lines near the airport. Several Marines narrowly escaped injury from Israeli gunfire. 'It's the old Vietnam tactic of "recon-by-fire",' Colonel Mead said angrily.

'It's a very poor tactic. All it does is endanger, by ricochets, other forces or civilians. It never stopped a terrorist. It's my thought that because of the frequency of the incidents, it must be greater than happenstance. And you can quote me on that.'

But the 'recon-by-fire' continued until the Israelis got their way. The Marines were instructed by Washington to hold regular meetings with Israeli liaison officers. The confrontations immediately ceased and the Lebanese Shia Muslim militiamen of the southern suburbs of Beirut, which were patrolled by the Americans, drew the inevitable conclusion: the Marines were sharing their intelligence information with the Israelis. They were right. On 1 April, Colonel Mead said that he was now prepared to pass on intelligence information to the Israelis about possible attacks to their forces outside Beirut. 'Any time there is a possible loss of life,' he added, 'I am going to pass that information on to whomever, to whatever group.'

By now, however, the multinational force had much more serious problems on its hands. On 16 March, almost exactly six months after the MNF arrived in Beirut, three attacks were made against the international contingents in west Beirut, apparently by Shia Muslim groups. Within 48 hours, ten Italians and five Americans were wounded. French troops only escaped injury because two hand grenades thrown at one of their positions failed to explode. Two of the Italians were critically wounded and left Beirut paralysed for life. Another had a foot amputated in emergency surgery during the night. The five Marines were slightly hurt when someone threw a hand grenade at their patrol from a two-storey house in Ouzai. One of the Americans saw the grenade fall from the house but had no time to shout an alarm. There was no prior warning of the attacks.

That same afternoon, a Lebanese man called the Agence France Presse to claim the attacks on behalf of *Al Jihad Al Islami*, 'Islamic Holy War'. 'No one has ever heard of such an organisation before,' I wrote in my dispatch that night. I did not connect 'Islamic Holy War' or 'Islamic Jihad' with the serious young men I had met in Baalbek. In the AP bureau, Terry Anderson dismissed the phone call as a probable hoax. Tatro was not so sure.

That night, the Italian ambassador spoke darkly of an 'organised plot' to drive the multinational force out of Beirut. MNF soldiers were no longer permitted to dine out in the city. French troops now patrolled in flak jackets. US Marines were instructed to patrol with ammunition clips in their rifles. Only inside their headquarters compound were they forbidden to carry live ammunition in their weapons. The peace-keepers were being forced to change their colours. Lebanon was turning sour on its latest visitors.

But who were their enemies? General Ibrahim Tannous, the Lebanese army commander, warned Mead that his patrols had 'an increased probability of being hit'. After 30 Shia men were detained by Lebanese troops in Bourj al-Barajneh in March, Tannous told Mead that US troops would be attacked on the last Wednesday of the month. But nothing happened. Neither the Marines nor the French could identify their assailants. In private, we repeatedly asked their officers who was attacking them. They professed frustration and genuine ignorance.

The intelligence systems of the American and French forces were locked from the beginning into the only Lebanese intelligence apparatus available to them, the deuxième bureau, which was effectively a Phalangist organisation. Individual officers and units of the Lebanese army upon whom the MNF had to rely were sympathisers – and sometimes members – of the Phalange. Information flowed both ways. The new British contingent dined a deuxième bureau officer regularly at their Hadeth headquarters. But because the Phalange were Maronite Christians, they had scarcely any knowledge of the Shia community from which the MNF's enemies were likely to come. Therefore the Western allies did not receive accurate intelligence about the Muslim militias.

By the spring of 1983, the MNF was supporting a Phalangist administration, openly acknowledging links with Israeli forces and, through the Americans, encouraging an unofficial peace treaty between Israel and Lebanon.

On 10 April, President Reagan's Middle East peace plan – proposals that called for a freeze on Jewish settlements on the occupied West Bank and the opening of Jordanian–Palestinian talks with the Israelis for Palestinian autonomy – was formally buried by King Husain in a short, dignified statement issued at his palace in Amman. The PLO, the King said, had tried to change the draft agreement under which the King was prepared to open talks with Israel.

Yassir Arafat had reneged on his agreement with Husain after being told in Kuwait that the more radical factions within the PLO refused to be represented by Jordan in talks which could not in any case meet the PLO's publicly expressed demand for an independent Palestinian state. The Reagan plan, which had been born of the ruins of the Lebanon war and the subsequent evacuation of the PLO from Beirut, thus died not of indifference but of Arab division.

The opportunities presented by the Americans would not, however, have provided the 'solution' to the Middle East conflict as Weinberger had suggested in Beirut the previous September. At most, Palestinians would have lived in a land controlled by Jordanians rather than Israelis and there would have been no national government or national flag or national passports for the Palestinians.

I flew to Jordan in mid-April to report the end of the Reagan plan and the future of the Palestinians now that American policy in the region had partially collapsed. On the night of the 17th I had dinner with Richard Viets, the American ambassador in Amman, who was a close friend of the King. Bruce Laingen, who as chargé d'affaires at the US Embassy in Tehran found himself a hostage in the Iranian Foreign Ministry in 1979, sat opposite me and the two men talked at length of the weakness of the Reagan administration, its failure to understand events, its permanent, damaging reliance upon Israel. Only in Lebanon did the United States still shoulder its responsibilities, but both men feared this mission would end in disaster.

Next morning, 18 April, I took the MEA flight back to Beirut. I drove to the AP bureau. Earleen Tatro was there, ready to pounce. 'Well, Fisk, you've deigned to return to us now you've finished wining and dining in sunny Jordan. Now I trust you won't waste *our* time. We have work to do.' Then the AP bureau shook. It did not vibrate. It literally, physically, quivered. Farouk Nassar was shouting from the other room. 'My God! What was that?' Earleen and I raced up the stairs to the roof. To the north-west a huge mushroom cloud of brown and black smoke was funnelling into the sky with enormous force, a 200-foot-high streak of flame at its centre. America's political honeymoon in Lebanon had come to a savage and terrifying end.

The US Embassy was on the seafront only 500 yards from my apartment, only 200 yards from the Tatros' flat. But Lebanese troops blocked traffic on every road. Earleen and I ran through the streets. Outside shops and offices, hundreds of people gathered to stare upwards. The smoke was growing thicker and darker, shutting off the sun. When we reached the back of the nurses' home behind the Embassy, we found a pathway that led to a tennis court. Beyond the wire at the other end, orange flames swept upwards past the trees. Earleen clung to the wire and shook it. There was no way through. 'Goddammit, how do we get through this damned thing?' I thought she might try to climb the wire like a monkey. We'll have to use the stone steps behind your house, I said. We ran down the steps into the Ein Mreisse district. A French Paratrooper stopped us. Press, we screamed at him. '*Presse française?*' *Oui.* Behind him hung a curtain of grey smoke. '*Allez-y.*'

We ran past the soldier and then stopped. The Embassy was built in a tri-form shape, a seven-storey central administration block with two wings on either side. Globes of fire burst through the murk. 'I don't believe this,' Earleen said. She was looking in front of her as she said it. 'Fisk, I don't believe this.' A sudden, gentle breeze had moved in from the sea and drawn the curtain of smoke aside. The centre of the Embassy was missing. The bottom of the two wings of the Embassy had disappeared. One half of the building had disintegrated and the upper floors of the centre now hung down in slabs as if someone had cut through it with a knife and removed the outer portion. Behind each dangling slab of floor were trapped desks, telephones, carpets and chairs. And suspended by the feet from one of the slabs, upside-down, still in his business suit, his arms dangling cruelly round his balding head, hung a dead American diplomat.

We tripped over corpses. The roadway was slippery with water, glass and blood and other, more terrible objects which a team of Lebanese Red Cross men and women were shovelling onto stretchers. In the visa section, where dozens of Lebanese men and women had been queuing for permission to visit the United States, every living soul had been burned alive. They were brought out not as bodies but as torsos, legs, lumps of intestines piled on stretchers, individual heads heaped inside a blanket. A Red Cross girl was scooping up remains in a bucket. An American Embassy security guard, still alive but temporarily deranged by the explosion which had broken his ear-drums, began walking up and down in front of the smoking wreckage yelling 'It's gonna blow, it's gonna blow' over and over again. We could see several bodies – and parts of bodies – floating in the Mediterranean.

The bomb had been driven into the Embassy forecourt in a truck. That was all we knew in the first minutes. There had been only two flimsy barriers and no warning. If the Embassy guards opened fire on the driver, it did them no good. They died instantly. The bomb was so powerful that half the Embassy simply collapsed in dust and flames, crushing to death everyone inside. A passing Lebanese military vehicle was blasted off the Corniche into the sea while the corpses of Embassy staff were tossed 50 feet through the air onto a carpet of rubble and glass outside. The bomb had killed 63 people and wounded another hundred.

It had also blasted the self-confidence and the complacency of the multinational force and destroyed the sense of security that the American presence in Lebanon had given to tens of thousands of Lebanese. Only days after the collapse of Washington's initiative on the West Bank, and at a time when the United States was still vainly trying to secure the withdrawal of Israeli and Syrian troops from the country, the bomb struck at the very heart of President Reagan's Middle East policy.

Even as the flames still curled through the Embassy, a few survivors claimed that a suicide bomber had driven the truck. Was this possible? In a message to *The Times* later that day, I expressed 'grave doubts' about this. The Lebanese valued their own lives. I suggested that the bomb might have been hidden in a police van and detonated by remote control. Again, I had forgotten Baalbek and the martyrdom espoused by those quiet young men.

Just ten minutes after the explosion, the telephone rang again in the Beirut bureau of Agence France Presse. It was the same man who had called on 16 March. He was speaking again, he said, for 'Islamic Jihad'. He spoke in a Lebanese accent, slowly, deliberately, with great care.

'The operation is part of the Iranian revolution's campaign against the imperialist presence throughout the world,' he said. 'We will continue to strike at the imperialist presence in Lebanon, including the multinational force.' And then he hung up.

Outside the Embassy, Morris Draper, one of President Reagan's negotiators, ran from his car, shaking with emotion and in tears. 'Where is my wife? Where is my wife?' he kept pleading, until someone told him she had been taken, slightly hurt but very much alive, from the building. Ryan Crocker of the Embassy's political section stood in front of the building with blood on his face, waiting like a doomed man until he saw his wife among the crowd of survivors. Each thought the other had died. They threw themselves into each other's arms.

French and Lebanese troops were still pulling corpses from the rubble at the foot of the central section of the Embassy, some of them weeping and one of the soldiers screaming uncontrollably as the extent of the slaughter became clear. A French soldier flung his beret on the ground and clambered into the burning Embassy. We saw him later, inching along a knife-edge of broken concrete 40 feet up the ruins and scrambling into a black hole in the pancaked floors to look for survivors. Out in the Mediterranean, the helicopter carrier *Guadalcanal* steamed ponderously down to take up station parallel to the Embassy, accompanied by its destroyer escort, a symbol of power made impotent.

How quickly the Americans forgot the significance of this devastation. Perhaps it was because only 17 of the 63 dead were Americans. Perhaps the fault lay with the regional CIA, whose members could not warn the US government of the terrible importance of this event because most of them were killed by the bomb. The suicide driver had wiped out virtually all the CIA's senior operatives in the region. They had been summoned to Beirut and were meeting in the central section of the Embassy when the bomb exploded.

Perhaps Ambassador Robert Dillon, tall and white-haired, only slightly flustered after being heaved from the rubble of his office, had set the wrong tone. America had got to continue her peace efforts in Lebanon, he told us that night. 'The negotiations [for Israeli withdrawal] will go ahead,' he said. 'It's a tragedy and you can imagine how sad and angered we all are but it doesn't change anything — the US mission will continue.' It did. The Marines still kept their weapons unloaded in their base near the airport. They were peace-keepers, after all.

And the Americans still sought one outstanding achievement in Lebanon: the conclusion of a Lebanese—Israeli troop withdrawal agreement, an unofficial peace treaty which would become an integral part of the United States 'peace process' in the Middle East. If Lebanon could become a friend of Israel, if Israel's northern border with Lebanon could be secure from all attack, this would be a political victory equivalent

to the Camp David treaty which had brought peace between Israel and
Egypt. It would further isolate the Soviet Union in the Middle East. It
would create a crescent of pro-Western nations from the north of Lebanon
to the Egyptian–Libyan border.

In a series of meetings – alternately held in the Israeli settlement of
Kiryat Shmona and a hastily repaired beach hotel at Khalde – Lebanese
and Israeli delegates argued over the terms of the agreement. At one
point the Israelis were demanding traffic rights for the Israeli El Al
airline at Beirut airport. Antoine Fatal, the Lebanese representative,
tried to safeguard the appearance of Lebanese sovereignty. Lebanon was
a small and powerless country, he said, but it deserved respect for its
independence. He wanted to restrict the number of Israeli troops who
would – under one proposal – have the right to patrol southern
Lebanon.

By the end of January 1983, Fatal's delegation had suggested that the
Israelis were showing scant regard for Lebanese national rights 'on the
fiftieth anniversary of Hitler's accession to power'. David Kimche, the
Israeli representative, believed the Lebanese were being intransigent. In
a two-page statement printed on vivid pink paper, he wrote that 'if
Lebanon yields to the pressures and dictates of the Arab states, it will
slip back into a period of weakness and instability and an atmosphere of
violence and terrorism.' Since Israel had invaded seven months earlier,
the Lebanese believed that the 'pressures and dictates' had come principally from Israel, not from the Arab world.

But Kimche's real error was obvious to anyone standing outside the
Khalde hotel. As we waited for the delegates to emerge from their
meetings, we could hear the thump of shells high in the Chouf mountains.
The civil war between the Druze and the Maronites grew more ferocious
as spring approached. Lebanon *was* already slipping back into 'weakness
and instability' even as the delegates argued at Khalde, and it was doing
so *inside* an area occupied by Israeli troops. The Phalangists told us later
that Sharon threatened to pull Israeli soldiers back to Sidon without
giving any support to the Christians left in the mountains – a step
which would automatically doom the Phalange in the Chouf – if the
militia did not give its support to the withdrawal talks.

In a hopeless effort to persuade Syria to accept the Lebanese–Israeli
withdrawal agreement, George Shultz, the US secretary of state, flew to
Damascus. After a bleak four-hour conversation with a polite but evidently
hostile President Assad on 8 May, Shultz arrived in Beirut to announce
that 'it is fair to say that they [the Syrians] are hardly enthusiastic about
the agreement.' Shultz hoped that the Saudis could soften Assad's
anger. Gemayel wanted American and French MNF troops to enter the
Chouf when the Israelis left, an idea that did not commend itself to the
Americans. On the morning of Shultz's arrival in Beirut, the hillsides

above the airport had been smothered in fire and explosions as the Druze fired 120mm shells along the west Beirut perimeter into east Beirut. In the Christian sector of the capital, artillery rounds were exploding every ten seconds. Phalangist gunners could be seen firing back from a gash in the hill above Colonel Cochrane's British headquarters. Both sides obligingly suspended their hostilities just before Shultz flew into the airport. The moment he left, they resumed.

At first glance, the Lebanese—Israeli troop withdrawal agreement of 17 May provided for the independence of Lebanon, respect for its sovereignty and the abrogation of all treaties or laws hostile to either side and the end of the 'state of war' which had notionally existed since 1948. About 25,000 Israeli soldiers would leave Lebanon. But a 'security annex' forced Lebanon to accept Haddad militiamen into Lebanese army units which would patrol most of the south of the country in the company of Israeli soldiers. The Israelis would be based in two 'Security Arrangements Supervision Centres' inside southern Lebanon. And both Lebanon and Israel would 'prevent entry into, deployment in, or passage through its territory . . . by military forces . . . of any state hostile to the other party.' In other words, the Syrians had to leave Lebanon.

It was therefore little wonder that Assad claimed the agreement 'undermines Lebanon's sovereignty and independence, subjugates Lebanon to Israeli and imperialist dominance, and constitutes a grave danger to Syria's security.' To a group of West German diplomats at his palace in Damascus, the Syrian president graphically explained his fears. He ordered one of his functionaries to unfurl a giant map of Syria, Lebanon and northern Israel and then, holding a ruler, knelt on the floor and pointed out how Israel could attack Syria if the Lebanese—Israeli troop withdrawal agreement was put into practice.

He was quite specific. If Israel wanted to make trouble for Syria in the future, she would send her armies back into Lebanon. If the Lebanese objected to this through the newly envisaged Lebanese—Israeli 'joint liaison committee', the United States — under the terms of the agreement — would have the casting vote in the tripartite committee and could therefore permit Israel to attack Syria from Lebanese territory. Assad's ruler began to sweep across the map, from the Bekaa over the Syrian frontier towards Homs, from northern Lebanon up to the city of Hama. Syria, he announced, was better off with the Israelis staying in Lebanon than living under the 'threat' of the Lebanese—Israeli agreement.

For Assad, the 17 May agreement also provided Israel with a reward for its invasion of Lebanon. To destroy this prize he had only to keep his army in the country and maintain his support for those Lebanese politicians and militias who opposed the American-conceived treaty.

Syria's response was immediate. Driving across the floor of the Bekaa Valley, I found Syrian troops building massive new earth fortifications, concrete tank revetments and anti-tank ditches, installing radar stations around the village of Terbol south of Baalbek and bringing truckloads of Palestinian guerrillas into the country from Damascus. Hours after the 17 May agreement was signed — Draper's signature represented the Americans — Syria announced that Philip Habib, Reagan's senior negotiator in the Middle East, was no longer welcome in Damascus.* For more than a day, all roads through the Syrian lines in the mountains above Beirut were closed. The implications of this were obvious: if Gemayel ratified the treaty with Israel, then he would have no influence in Syrian-occupied Lebanon.

With every step the Lebanese government took to consolidate the pact, Assad increased the cost to Gemayel. When the Lebanese parliament ratified the treaty on 15 June, Syrian radio announced that the parliament members had 'sold their country to the devil'. The Druze and Shia militias were urged by Syria to 'turn their guns' not only against the Israeli army but against the Lebanese government as well. While promoting a split within the PLO, the Syrians allowed Yassir Arafat to re-enter Lebanon to meet his guerrillas in the Bekaa.

Reagan's darkest suspicions of Soviet intentions were given free rein in Washington. The association of things Western with things good, of things anti-American with things bad, had long been a theme of American policy in the Middle East; the Soviets had an almost identical policy which operated in reverse. Grafted on to the Middle East, these themes became grotesquely distorted but impossible to dismiss. So US personnel were encouraged to believe that Moscow's hand lay behind Syrian actions.

Menachem Begin, the Israeli prime minister, had fostered this idea, although George Shultz, the US secretary of state, did not share it, suspecting that Assad was a confident enough man to act on his own. But American Embassy officials in Beirut told journalists that there were 'reliable' reports of Soviet military personnel in the Bekaa Valley. We suspected these stories were deliberately fostered by the Americans in an attempt to secure domestic support for a Lebanon policy which was

---

* Habib's undoing stemmed from a ceasefire he had arranged between Israeli and Syrian forces during the Israeli invasion of Lebanon in 1982. According to the Syrians, the truce on 10 June was accepted on the understanding that there was to be a complete withdrawal of Israeli troops from Lebanon as soon as the ceasefire was implemented. Assad claimed he possessed a document to this effect drawn up by Habib. The Americans denied there was any such document and rather unconvincingly put the confusion down to a 'misunderstanding'. For Assad, Habib's later role in promoting the Lebanese–Israeli withdrawal agreement was the final double-cross.

already meeting considerable opposition in Congress. We could never substantiate the rumours.*

Yet the Soviets were certainly prepared to give intelligence assistance to the Syrians. In mid-June, the Soviet navy sent the 4,750-ton Kashin class destroyer *Szderzhanny* to within five miles of the Lebanese coast, in the company of a frigate and an intelligence-gathering vessel. The three ships cruised the coastline south of Beirut, presumably listening to Israeli military radio traffic in an attempt to find out when the Israeli army intended to pull back from the Chouf. At night, an Israeli jet fighter dropped 'chaff' to distort the Soviet communications monitoring equipment. A Soviet hospital ship put in to the Syrian port of Latakia; we suspected this was in case the Israelis bombed the new Soviet-crewed SAM-5 sites.

American nervousness was palpable. Every evening, Terry and I sat on his seafront balcony with his wife and daughter, watching the lights of the US destroyers and frigates moving in pairs up and down the coast, speeding round the tip of the Beirut peninsula and then suddenly turning to port and repeating their path southwards. They were ordered to keep on the move, always, for the US navy now feared that frogmen would attach mines to the hulls of their vessels. Crewmen armed with automatic rifles were posted day and night on the prow of each ship with orders to shoot at anyone in the water. Next to the building where Anderson and I lived, the British Embassy now served as a temporary American Embassy. A US Marine amphibious armoured vehicle was stationed below our balcony. Heavy steel anti-rocket screens were hauled to the roof of the Embassy and draped down the sides of the building. It was like living next to a bomb.

The Western powers were now trapped. Gemayel had failed to win a political consensus in his country, his regime was controlled by the Phalange, and Syria regarded his government as illegitimate. With no Syrian withdrawal, the 17 May agreement − America's only political achievement in Lebanon − was stillborn. And if the Israelis left the Chouf in its current state of anarchy, Gemayel's government army would become involved in the fighting; which meant that the Western armies in Beirut would become participants in the Lebanese civil war.

Gemayel was in Washington on 20 July when the Israelis announced that they would soon withdraw from the mountains. The Western ambassadors in Beirut were appalled. French Foreign Legionnaires had been provisionally ordered to accompany Lebanese soldiers into the Chouf while the Marines deployed down the coastal highway as far as

---

* On four separate visits to the Bekaa, the most suspicious Russian I saw was the Soviet military attaché in Damascus on his regular weekly visit to Chtaura in the Bekaa Valley to purchase cheap whisky and cigarettes. Since British diplomats in Damascus performed precisely the same ritual, this hardly counted as further superpower involvement in Lebanon.

the new Israeli front line on the Awali River. But the Druze, who dominated the highway as well as the mountains, said that the Lebanese soldiers would allow the Phalange to massacre the Druze population. What price would Reagan now have to pay for his commitment to Lebanon's sovereignty?

Syria intended to make sure it was a high one. Assad poured Katyushas into the Chouf for the Druze and encouraged Jumblatt to set up a 'national salvation front', a parallel administration to Gemayel's government. Syria was bringing more Iranian revolutionary guards into Lebanon. In Baalbek, the Lebanese flag was torn from the governor's office. In the city's streets, the only banner we saw was that of the Islamic Republic of Iran. If the Chouf burned nightly, it would illuminate a gleam of satisfaction in Damascus.

But Syria was not alone in her disgrace. Up in the Chouf, the Israelis had virtually abdicated all responsibility for the mutual slaughter of Druze and Christian. The Israelis claimed this was a 'centuries-old quarrel'. But it had been dormant from 1860 until the Israelis installed the Phalange in the Chouf in 1982. Now, for the 400,000 civilians living in the 200 square miles of mountains and valleys, life had become a nightmare. While the Phalange and the Druze shelled each other, freelance gunmen from both sides raped and murdered villagers of the opposite faith.

Near Deir al-Qamar, scarcely 600 yards from an Israeli checkpoint, Christian gunmen kidnapped Druze motorists from their cars. They selected 15 young men, separated them from their wives and children, and forced them to walk to an old bridge over a rocky gorge. There, one by one, the 15 were marched to the centre of the bridge where a man systematically plunged a two-foot butcher's knife into their hearts. Each corpse was thrown over the bridge onto the rocks. The knife just missed one man's heart and his fall from the bridge was cushioned by the corpses of his co-religionists. He thus survived to tell the tale. Perhaps as a result, bodies were later found with their tongues cut out.

The Druze dispatched Christian captives with equal savagery, sometimes after pouring boiling water over their naked bodies in an underground torture chamber at Beit Eddine. When Tatro and I tried to drive up the Damascus highway through the Christian–Druze lines, a Maronite gunman in a black shirt ran into the road and pointed a small pistol at our car. When I stopped, he ran to our vehicle, a big man with a six-inch crucifix around his neck, and pushed the muzzle of his pistol to my head. 'Fuck you, fuck you, why are you driving through here?' Behind him, from abandoned houses and alleyways emerged a gang of slovenly, bearded men, their clothes filthy, guns and knives in their hands, advancing slowly towards us.

So this was how it was done. This must be what happened to the

Druze. They stopped for one gunman and found they were trapped by others. We smiled hard. Journalists. American, British. I gabbled haplessly about how I never knew this was a dangerous area, how I had once had lunch with Bashir Gemayel. But these were not militiamen. They were freelancers and they had been killing. We were not their usual victims. We babbled on about a non-existent appointment with the local Israeli army commander. Lunch, that was it, we had a luncheon appointment. The Israelis would be very angry if we were late. The man in the black shirt thought about this, realised we were lying, stepped back, pointed his gun back down the road and said: 'Get out of here.'

Several days later, a Druze neighbour of ours, an intelligent, pretty woman who worked as a midwife for Christians and Muslims in Beirut, tried to drive up the same road. She was stopped by gunmen and gang-raped. They cut her throat and threw her body down a well. All this was happening in an area which — as the maps issued to the press by the Israeli army always stated — fell 'under Israeli control'. But the Israelis were not protecting the civilians in their area. I watched them drive past gangs of armed men without even stopping to discover their identity. The Israelis talked daily about the need to stamp out 'terrorists'. Yet the Chouf was packed with terrorists and they were doing nothing about it.

Since the beginning of the year, well over a thousand men and women had been kidnapped and murdered in the Chouf. Tatro visited the Israelis when they arranged an exchange of hostages. Two Christian militiamen were handed to the Phalange after being beaten up moments before their release. A Druze man who had come to collect a relative was told that the man was dead and handed a bag of bones.

Was it any wonder that Lebanese ministers — and several diplomats in the US Embassy's political section — were now telling us that the Israelis wanted this anarchy to continue? If the Israelis did not restore order in the Chouf, the Lebanese army could not enter the area. And if Lebanese government authority could not be imposed there, the Israelis could claim they were justified in staying in southern Lebanon.

Rockets cascaded onto east Beirut. We could only record their effects. In the streets, Christians showed me a seven-year-old girl lying dead beside her doll, an old man beheaded by a rocket fin. On 22 July, Katyushas exploded across Beirut airport, fired from a Druze area within the Israeli occupation zone on the other side of the old Sidon road. The missiles hit the runways, narrowly missing a Cyprus Airways flight about to take off for Larnaca and forcing Lebanese air force pilots to scramble their old Hawker Hunter jets as panicking passengers and airline employees drove their cars away from the terminal. One of them died as he tried to escape down the main road. A missile smashed into a tree above him, cart-wheeled onto the roof of his car and exploded inside. I found what was left of him a few minutes later: a severed hand still holding the steering wheel of a burning Peugeot. Sixteen other people were wounded by shrapnel, including two American Marines and a US naval air controller.

On the road outside the terminal, General Angioni, the Italian commander, was examining the crater made by a missile. 'You see this, Robert?' he asked, pointing to the star-shaped imprint on the tarmac made by the rocket's explosion. 'This is a present for us from the Druze. Everyone is going to send presents now. These are generous people here. They like to give things. The Americans will receive presents now.' He looked at me to see if I understood what he was trying to convey. Did he mean that the three Western armies were now involved in the war? 'We shall see,' he said. The rockets had been fired from Bchamoun, almost a mile inside Israel's occupation area. That night, nine more Christians died under the rocket bombardment in east Beirut. The Marines were impotent. They controlled the airport but they could not keep it open. All flights were suspended.

Preoccupied by the extent of the fighting around Beirut, we almost neglected the strange reappearance of David Dodge, the president of the American University who had been kidnapped during the siege of the city in 1982. He returned to his home in America after being held for several months in Iran. Neither he nor the US government would explain what had happened to him. But President Reagan publicly thanked President Assad and his brother Rifaat for helping to secure Dodge's release. The Iran connection again. Lebanese reporters said that Dodge had passed some of his captivity in the Syrian border village of Zabedani, in a house controlled by Iranian revolutionary guards.

If the Syrians were helpful on this level, however, they remained adamantly opposed to America's plans for Lebanon. When Robert McFarlane, the former Marine officer who replaced Habib as Reagan's Middle East envoy, visited Damascus in an effort to persuade the Syrians to withdraw their troops, he was received by Abdul Halim Khaddam, the Syrian foreign minister, with a brief but pointed lecture. McFarlane was welcome in Damascus, Khaddam said, so that he could 'learn more about the problems of the region and Lebanon'. There was no mention of withdrawing Syrian troops, not the slightest hint that Assad might accept Gemayel's government. McFarlane listened in silence, made a few desultory notes on a yellow writing pad and only smiled in reply.

On 10 August 1983, Gemayel ordered his government army to respond to the Druze bombardment of Beirut. Lebanese army howitzers beside the airport road began firing into the Chouf and the Druze replied with a shower of Katyushas. When I reached the American base at the airport, I found the American Marines in their foxholes. 'We're on condition red – get in there if you don't want to die,' one of their officers said and pushed me into a trench with five Marines. One of them had been hit in the neck by shrapnel and there was blood on his blouse. The earth trembled with the vibration of the outgoing artillery fire and the impact of the Druze rockets.

After an hour of this, McFarlane arrived in a US Embassy car. I climbed out of the foxhole to see McFarlane walking briskly through a haze of smoke and dust towards the Marine operations room. Like an American reporter in a 1930s movie, I found myself walking backwards in front of him at great speed, holding up my notebook and asking: 'Any comment, Mr McFarlane?' There was another explosion of rockets and McFarlane stared at me through the smoke as if I were mad. 'What is there to comment on?' he asked, and disappeared inside the operations room.

On 16 August, Moshe Arens, the new Israeli defence minister, arrived in east Beirut – without invitation from Gemayel – to deliver a warning. Israel was not going to disarm the militias in the Chouf. Negotiations would have to start with the Phalangist and Druze forces because Israel was going to withdraw from the mountains even if the two sides had not stopped fighting. 'We have no intention whatsoever of staying in Lebanon one day more than is absolutely necessary,' he said. Not a day more. It was like a liturgy. When I asked Arens on what day he thought things had started going wrong for Israel in Lebanon, he frowned and asked: 'What do you mean by "gone wrong"? What has gone wrong?' It was as if McFarlane and Arens were deaf to the drumfire of guns that echoed across Beirut.

At the Marine base, Mead, the American commander, had been replaced by Colonel Timothy Geraghty, a born-again Christian whom comic-strip writers would have called mild-mannered; a pleasant, constantly smiling officer who did not panic and hardly ever drank. He had once tramped across County Roscommon searching for his ancestors' Irish graves, but he seemed unable to disentangle the complexities of Lebanon's war. He developed the disturbing habit of asking visiting journalists what was happening in Beirut. He may have done this out of politeness but we suspected that it merely reflected the abysmal failure of his Marine intelligence officers. In the days immediately following the 17 May agreement, Geraghty reported a number of small but disturbing incidents. During their patrols of Bourj al-Barajneh and Hay al-Sellum – the slums nearest the airport which the Americans dubbed 'Hooterville' – young men had begun to shout obscenities and throw stones at the Marines.* The Americans refused to be provoked. But

---

* Some of the finest accounts of America's disastrous involvement in Lebanon were written by Thomas Friedman, the *New York Times* correspondent in Beirut. See 'America's Failure in Lebanon', in the *New York Times* magazine, 8 April 1984.

they did not understand why this was happening. Had they not come to Lebanon to protect the Lebanese?

At the end of August, Gemayel's opponents made their first attempt at a coup d'état. In a sustained and concerted effort to take over west Beirut from the Lebanese army, the Muslim militias re-emerged from the slums of Bourj al-Barajneh and Basta and Chiyah, assaulting army positions near the airport, on the seafront and deep inside the southern suburbs. At the same time, artillery batteries in the Metn hills, to the north of the Chouf − in an area occupied by Syrian troops − fired shells into the east of the city. As Gemayel's Cabinet sat in conclave throughout the day, the artillery rounds smashing the windows of the palace, McFarlane returned to Lebanon in a mood of deep despair.

Heedless of the cost in civilian lives, Gemayel's troops fought their way out of the port area to which many of them had been driven and used tank fire to clear their way through the streets towards Hamra. The soldiers faced some of their fiercest opposition in the narrow streets of Wadi Abu Jamil, the old Jewish area where Shia gunmen − from Amal, but also from a new pro-Iranian organisation about whose provenance we were still uncertain − fired at them from the rooftops. The gunmen I saw were teenagers and many had only pistols. Their rifles had been taken away during the Lebanese army searches the previous winter. But some of them, I noticed, had small goatee beards, trimmed to a point, and bandannas upon which was written the one word *Allah*.

From the safety of Damascus, Jumblatt issued a series of histrionic statements against Gemayel, describing him as a 'butcher' and the Lebanese army's counter-attack into west Beirut as 'a new carnage similar to the Sabra and Chatila massacre'. The army's tanks fired down Hamra Street. In the AP bureau, the staff retreated to the rear of the office, emerging into the exposed telex room for brief periods to punch wire tape and send messages to New York. By late afternoon on 31 August, shells were bursting outside the office. The rooms stank of cordite. On a foray to the telex room to file to *The Times*, one shell exploded so close to the building that I saw the yellow and white flash of the detonation before hundreds of tons of sheet glass cascaded into the roadway outside.

The Lebanese army was now fully engaged. Its overwhelming superiority in firepower pushed the militias back towards the slums, but Christian radios immediately broadcast reports of a massacre of Christian families in the Metn hills. Twenty-four people, most of them women and children, they said, had been knifed to death by Druze at Bmariam in revenge for the Lebanese army's assault on west Beirut. In Bourj al-Barajneh, gunmen wearing hoods emerged onto the streets with a new array of weapons, including machine-guns and rocket-propelled grenades. At this very moment, the Israelis decided to leave the Chouf.

They gave the Lebanese army less than 24 hours' notice of their intention to depart. In the Commodore Hotel, its windows blown out by the shellfire of the previous days' fighting, there was a dark mood among the television crews and correspondents. The scale and ferocity of the fighting frightened all of us. On the night of 3 September, several of us expressed the fear that there would be casualties among journalists if we went on reporting the battles at first hand. None of us doubted that there would be massacres when the Israelis left. We knew the Israeli army had already arranged to fire flares when their last armoured vehicles left each town in the mountains, a signal to the militias there that they could now destroy each other if they wished. Several correspondents had already moved into the Chouf to await events. Most had gone to Druze villages because they believed the Druze would defeat the Phalange. Clark Todd of Canadian television, for example, had taken an ABC crew to the old village of Kfar Matta which overlooked the Mediterranean high above the coastal road. Faramarzi of AP and I decided to cover the Israeli retreat from the Christian area above Kahhale on the Damascus highway.

We arrived at two in the morning. Maronite families were standing on their balconies, waiting anxiously for the dawn, their eyes focused on the darkened ridge-lines above them. The Israeli flares glowed in a sickly way over the hills. Fired high above the mountains, they crept down, yellow and phosphorescent through the cloud cover, turning the darkness into a mustard-coloured half-light. Through this fog came dozens of Israeli tanks and trucks, half-tracks and armoured personnel carriers. And as they passed us, we saw that many of the Israeli soldiers aboard were asleep, wedged fatigued between their colleagues as they left the mountains they had entered so blithely 15 months before.

There were no smiles or waves for the army which had claimed so many months ago that it wanted to bring peace and sovereignty back to Lebanon. Only the regular booming of the Syrian guns across the Metn and the heart-stopping crash of the incoming shells a few hundred yards up the road told of their passing. A teenage Israeli leaned down towards us from a half-track in the semi-darkness. 'Hear that?' he asked. 'The Syrians know we are leaving — so they are sending us some flowers.'

They were a resigned group of men on the vehicle, some of them drowsing on the back, but they woke up when they heard people speaking in English. They had all left their positions in Bhamdoun a few minutes before and they knew where they were going. 'Home,' they chorused in the opaque light. A soldier called Moti began to sing. Did he want to leave? 'What do you think? We can do nothing here. The Christians and the Druze — they are crazy.' The Syrian shells were landing closer now and there were sharp pink and crimson flashes on the mountainside above the road.

There were at least 100 tanks and trucks jammed all the way down the mountain highway towards Beirut, crawling at 5 mph, their spotlights flicking and scurrying across the vegetation and bullet-scarred walls on each side of the road. We drove with them, past the darkened Lebanese army barracks at Yarze where not a Lebanese soldier stirred from his tent. There was one lone Lebanese sentry who approached us on a side road two miles further on and asked us what was happening. We told him the Israelis were leaving. 'So that is what all the noise is about,' he said, as if Lebanon was not his country nor the Chouf his to reclaim.

By dawn we were passing Baabda, where 15 months ago the first Israeli tank led the encirclement of west Beirut and where a young Israeli medical officer who found himself among the first ten Israelis there had tried to explain to a group of sceptical journalists that his army had come to Lebanon to restore order and put a stop to all the killings in the country. We could just see the Chouf now, its mountain tops carpeted with thick black smoke as the militias began fighting each other for control.

The Israelis looked up from their half-tracks at the hillside above them as they moved towards Khalde and the sea. Explosions rippled along the valleys, bright orange bursts that sent a long low rumble of sound towards the coast and which could be heard above the roar of the convoys. At Khalde, the Israelis had woken up. In a mist of dust and exhaust smoke, they drove past us, waving and making victory signs at the two television crews who stood beside the highway south. Two tanks flew green balloons from their radio aerials; the crew of a half-track had painted a yellow dragon on the front of their vehicle. Two soldiers in a jeep braked for a moment, turned in their seats and jerked their middle fingers derisively towards the Chouf.

A pair of Israeli jets soared overhead as the last trucks moved out. They were observed at Khalde by a small group of Israeli officers who took each other's photographs as they stood, backs to Beirut, still explaining patiently to us that the violence in the Chouf was not their affair. The Lebanese had failed to settle their differences. It was, they said, a Lebanese responsibility.

But it was also an American responsibility. Only 500 yards from where we were standing, the US Marine line troops were sitting in their bunkers, watching the last Israeli tanks leave Beirut. It was Israel's invasion that had drawn the Americans into the city. It was Israel's political ambitions for Lebanon − ambitions which the Americans had indulged and helped − that were now being abandoned by Israel. It was Israel which had installed a Phalangist presidency in Beirut. Now it had lost interest in Gemayel. It was left to the Americans to support his crumbling power in a civil war that now threatened to engulf the city. In retrospect, the Americans would say that it was Israel's retreat from the

Chouf that doomed the Marines. When the last Israeli tank drove south from Beirut, it was a fateful moment.

One forgets, perhaps, that when an army withdraws there always has to be a last tank. But there it was, thrashing past Khalde, its turret reversed, its gun barrel moving from side to side, the very rearguard of the army that had blasted the Palestinian guerrillas out of Beirut but failed to secure peace in Lebanon. Its Israeli crew tossed blue, red and yellow smoke grenades onto the side of the road so that we lost sight of it, not in dust but in a blaze of psychedelic colour. In the near silence that followed, the only thing we could hear was the sound of its receding tracks and the growing clamour of gunfire from the Chouf.

14 Beirut Addio

We are not going to let a bunch of insidious terrorist
cowards shake the foreign policy of the United States.
Foreign policy is not going to be dictated or changed by
terror.

US Vice-President George Bush, on visiting the site of the
bombed American Marine headquarters, Beirut,
26 October 1983

I personally consider this deed is a good deed which God
loves and which his Prophet − may God praise his name −
loves. I bow before the souls of the martyrs who carried
out this operation.

Hussein Moussavi, leader of 'Islamic Amal',
on the bombing of the US Marines, Baalbek, Lebanon,
27 October 1983

The two Phalangists were frightened. They sprang into the road and
pointed their rifles at Terry Anderson and myself. 'Get out, get out of
here,' one of them shouted. CLACK-CLICK. Terry Anderson was half
out of the car. Terry, get back in. Anderson stared at the man. 'Take it
easy,' he began, 'we just want to know if it's safe to carry on up the
road.' CLACK-CLICK. The other, younger gunman now. 'Fuck off,
get out. We order you out.' He saw my camera. 'No photo. Fuck you.
No photo.'

The mountainside above the highway − the very air − roared and
echoed with gunfire, and from the hills in the south there rose a thick
curtain of blue smoke where the fires had taken hold in the forests. The
younger Phalangist watched Anderson climb back into the car. He was
still shouting, as if our presence was more dangerous than the shells that
hissed overhead. 'No photo. I order you out.' Anderson and I knew that
line well, and we understood what it meant. When armies told us not to
take pictures, it meant they were losing.

We were frightened. Even in the AP bureau, we feared the next trip,
the next assignment. The shells came down in blizzards. The power was
off, François' generator was running. We dripped sweat onto the wire
machine. 'FYI situation as follows,' I messaged *The Times*:

All repeat all Israeli troops pulled out of Chouf this morning ... Result
is exactly what we expected. Militias took over all Israeli positions and
fierce fighting is now going on all over the Chouf between Druze and

Christians. The Druze gunmen have even taken over control of the main Beirut–Sidon road just opposite American Marines on the southern outskirts of the city. Shellfire is spreading into east Beirut at the moment ... Latest reports are that Syrian tanks supporting Druze militiamen trying to attack Christians in vacated town of Bhamdoun ...

Anderson hovered over my shoulder. 'Fisky, we need the wire, get your message out quick. We need the wire. The Marines are being shelled. Farouk has an "urgent". You go on so damned long, I don't know why you don't tell *The Times* to print your service messages. Then you wouldn't have to write reports ...' Anderson was nervous, perhaps because he was now the AP bureau chief. The Tatros had transferred to the Tel Aviv office. But he was also fearful. We went out again, this time towards the southern suburbs of Beirut, driving fast, looking all the time eastwards, towards those fires in the hills.

The mountains that form a semicircle around Beirut were once part of its adornment, a cloak of beauty above the brash, modern city. Now they constituted part of its torment, a gun platform for the enemies of President Amin Gemayel. On the coast road, we slowed at a Lebanese army checkpoint. The soldier was crouching behind sandbags. 'Don't stop,' he shouted at us. 'They are shelling. Keep driving.' When we drove fast, the car engine made so much noise that we couldn't hear shells unless they landed close to us. This was why we travelled with all the windows open. We learned to watch for the tell-tale signs. Pedestrians who started running. Motorists who suddenly flashed their lights.

'Fisky, stop the car.' Why? 'Stop the damned car, you don't know what you're driving into.' I pulled onto a dirt lot beside some apartments. Six mortar rounds hit the road we had just travelled. Two bracketing on each side, two on the centre of the highway, exploding with dirty brown puffs. We ran into one of the buildings. It was being repaired after the previous year's bombardment by the Israelis. The concierge was a small plump man with a moustache and a young and very pretty wife who watched us indifferently from the doorway.

'Come to the roof,' the man said. 'You're as safe there as anywhere else.' This was untrue but Anderson agreed to go. 'If you haven't any idea what's going on, you're going to get killed anyway, Fisky.' Anderson was panting with fatigue. He was still overweight but claimed he had lost ten pounds in just 24 hours. I believed him. We stood on the half-completed balcony at the back of the house, watching the battle for Khalde down the coast where the Lebanese army were trying to hold their ground under intense rocket fire. The hills to the east were streaming smoke, within which it was possible to make out small, tell-tale bubbles of flame as Phalangist and Lebanese army shells exploded around the Druze villages. Off the coast, the US Sixth Fleet glided along the horizon, a destroyer and a missile cruiser closer to the shore, their guns pointed reproachfully towards the mountains.

'We've got to get to the Marines.' No, Terry, it's too dangerous. 'What the hell are we here for if we don't find out what's going on? Come on, we can make it. The only real danger is your driving.' I drew courage from Anderson, from the knowledge that he had been in Vietnam. Later he told me Lebanon was more dangerous than Vietnam. I took a side road towards the airport. Shells were bursting in the sky and now we could hear the crack of their detonation above the protesting engine of our car. The airport seemed to have become a front line. The terminal was half obscured with smoke that drifted along the deserted road towards the Marine headquarters.

I pulled up beneath the trees. A Marine ran towards us. 'You gotta get outta here. We're on "condition one". Get your car away from this entry.' He pointed his rifle towards us. Anderson was crouching beneath the trees, looking at me with an unpleasant smile. 'Well, Fisky, do like the man says — go park your car on the other side of the road.' Shrapnel was raining down onto the tarmac. I put my foot on the gas too fast, careered over the intersection, skidded onto a pile of garbage, opened the door and ran back to Anderson. My ears hurt in the noise.

Another Marine officer appeared. 'Get out, get out, this is condition one. We're under fire. You'll be killed.' There was a tremendous explosion from a small hill inside the Marine compound and a plume of earth and dust shot 40 feet into the air. Anderson stood upright. 'Look, Sir, I'm an American, you must let us in. We can take protection with you. We want to come in.' The officer raised his rifle. 'No, you can't and get out, get out.' Anderson looked hard at me. 'Fisky, these gentlemen are obviously not going to cooperate. We might as well go home.' He looked across at our car. Pieces of metal were still clicking onto the roadway. 'No point in us *both* getting killed, uh?' He gave me a big grin. 'Why don't you go get the car?'

Farouk Nassar met us at the door of the AP bureau. 'What is this about the television man from Canada?' he asked us. 'Someone said he has been wounded.' Clark Todd of Canadian television had gone to Kfar Matta, the Druze village above the Mediterranean, with an ABC crew. I ran down to the Commodore to find the ABC field producer. Nassar was right. 'Clark got hit in the chest by shrapnel,' the producer said. 'The crew left him in a barn. The Druze are looking after him. One of the crew was hit in the foot but he made it all the way to Green Beach where the Marines looked after him. We're trying to get to Clark.'

But no one could reach Kfar Matta. The village was under heavy shellfire. An American correspondent asked the US navy if it could fly a helicopter to rescue Todd. One of the air crews on a US helicopter-carrier off the coast volunteered to fly to the village if a local ceasefire could be arranged. But the whole of the Chouf was now engulfed in civil war. If help did not reach Todd soon, he would die. He had been so badly hurt that he himself did not believe he would survive. That is why he had ordered his colleagues to run for their lives and had given his cameraman his passport, his wedding ring and a ring that had belonged to his father-in-law. Just before they left, he had asked his colleagues to tell his English wife and three children that he loved them.

Kfar Matta was one of the very few villages to be captured by the Phalangists. A week later, the Red Cross found Todd's body. We reported that he had died of his wounds. Five months later, a French television crew entered Kfar Matta. It was in ruins but they found a pillow case upon which Todd had tried to send a message to his wife. He had written out her address in Biro and added his last words to her: 'Clark Todd, Canad TV. 10 Fore Street, Old Hatfield, Herts, England. Please tell my family I love them.' Ten months after Todd's death, his widow received a letter from a local Druze, Adnan Deeb, telling her that the Phalangists had captured Kfar Matta, that they had found Todd still alive but had shot him because he was in a Druze village. 'He was a good man who knew right from wrong and that's why he died,' Deeb concluded.

Kfar Matta, autumn 1984

There were bright pink flowers in the laneways of Kfar Matta but the village was still shattered, emotionally as well as physically. Every time I asked about the events of September 1983, the men and women would begin to cry. When the Phalangists stormed Kfar Matta, they shot 110 of the villagers, 65 of them from one family, the Gharribs. All the survivors remembered Todd. Milhem Gharrib was one of them, a 58-year-old unshaven man who in better days had operated the baggage carousels at Beirut airport.

He took me to a small intersection of three roads where there was a large shell-hole. 'This was the bomb that wounded Todd,' he said. 'We took him down there.' Gharrib pointed to an old stable of cut yellow stone. He told his story slowly and deliberately:

He was very cheerful. He kept making jokes. We liked him. He was a kind man. He told us not to worry, that he was with us and that if the *Kata'ib* [Phalange] came, he would tell them not to harm us. After his friends left, he lay on the sofa in the stable. There was a nurse there, a woman from the village. In the night he felt bad and wanted to write to his wife. We had no paper so I found an old pillow case and gave him my pen to write with. Then the *Kata'ib* came into Kfar Matta. There were thirty of them. They put some of our young men in the room next to Todd's and they shot them all. They left me because I was old. But they heard Todd in the next room. They heard him moan with pain. They asked 'Who's in there?' I said he was just an American journalist, that he was hurt and they should leave him alone. One of the men went into the room and shouted: 'You son-of-a-bitch. Are you still alive?' I heard shots. Then the *Kata'ib* told us to leave.

Gharrib took me to the door of the stable where Todd had lain. On one side of the room was an old blood-stained sofa with bullet holes through the fabric. 'We are so sorry about what happened to the *sahafa* [press-man],' Gharrib said. 'Please tell his wife this. If she wants to come to Kfar Matta, she is always welcome in our homes. She can come and stay with us.'

Did Todd die like this on that terrible morning, murdered by the Phalange as he lay wounded on the sofa? The Druze lost few opportunities to blacken the name of the Phalange. The only other witness I could find was a boy of ten. Anne Todd later received a death certificate from Israel, where her husband's body had been taken. Dated 14 September 1983, it was signed by a Haifa doctor named Lichtig and gave as the cause of death: 'Penetrating chest injury. Internal bleeding.' I asked Christopher Walker, the Jerusalem correspondent of *The Times*, to ask Dr Lichtig how Todd died. Lichtig replied that 'the body was already decayed. There was no internal examination and it was impossible to say whether shrapnel or bullets killed the man . . .'

Anne Todd later erected a memorial to her husband in the family's parish church across the road from their home in Hatfield. It commemorated Todd's death and the deaths 'of all victims of terrorism'.

Beirut, 6 September 1983

We could not even reach the Marines. The shells were falling in parallel series across west Beirut, setting up columns of smoke through the fir trees near Chatila camp. Anderson and I got as far as the Italian military base and tried to find General Angioni but the air was thick with tiny fragments of steel that pattered on the roofs and roadway. When we returned to the AP office Anderson saw that Farouk Nassar had already filed a first lead on the deaths of two Marines in the shelling. The International Red Cross was seeking an immediate ceasefire to evacuate tens of thousands of refugees.

The AP wire listed a succession of catastrophes. French officer killed in shelling. France threatens naval bombardment. Bhamdoun falls. The Phalangist 'Voice of Lebanon' radio announced that the Druze were about to capture Bhamdoun, that its Phalangist defenders were being 'martyred'. Our forays out into the city merely confirmed the evidence of disaster. At the Lebanese Ministry of Defence, we found the windows blown out, trucks overturned and burning, soldiers hiding in the basements.

How long could it be before the Western armies shot back at the

Druze and their Muslim allies? On the ridge-line at Souq al-Gharb above Beirut, Lebanese soldiers of General Michel Aoun's 84th Mechanised Infantry Battalion – one of the units newly constructed and trained by the US army – found themselves under attack from Palestinian guerrillas, plain-clothes Syrian gunmen and Shia militiamen as well as Druze forces. Gemayel's government denounced the assault as an act of war, their enemies as barbarians. In one night-time attack, it claimed, a 90-man unit of the Lebanese army's 8th Brigade was overwhelmed. Its commander was killed with a hatchet and dismembered. Fourteen of his men died with him, 20 were wounded and 24 others reported missing.

Gerry Labelle had returned to Beirut from vacation to become Anderson's deputy in the AP bureau. He took a call from the Lebanese defence ministry. 'We have some bodies to show you,' the voice on the telephone said. 'Want to go look at some bodies, Bob?' Labelle asked. He was tired and chain-smoking, smiling painfully at the ironies of the drama. H. L. Mencken had nothing on this. At Baabda, the Lebanese had dumped three bodies in a back yard. One had been beheaded by a shell, another had part of his lower left leg missing. Their identity cards proved that two of them were Syrian *mukhabarrat* agents. The third was a member of the pro-Syrian *Assifa* Palestinian unit. Shells fell around the buildings, shaking the ground beneath us. Labelle was fumbling for cigarettes, his hands shaking each time he lit a match. He was wearing a cruel smile and nudged my arm. 'Are you taking me to lunch today?'

Yet the identity of these bodies was critically important, for the degree of Palestinian or Syrian involvement in the fighting would decide how far the MNF could go on defending Gemayel's government. Already, the Lebanese army and the Phalange were fighting together against their Muslim enemies. And the MNF was in Lebanon to support the Lebanese army and Gemayel's government.

Only at Bhamdoun, we suspected, would we be able to discover the depth of Syrian involvement in the war. The town lay next to the Syrian lines and the Druze had announced its capture. Lebanese radios reported that Bhamdoun was burning. It was Anderson's idea to go but there was only one way to reach the town without being killed in the fighting, a detour of more than 200 miles. We drove north, high into the snow-line above Tripoli, past the ancient cedars, over the spine of Mount Lebanon and into the Bekaa west of Baalbek. There were gunmen on the narrow roads, young men in black, wearing black scarves with *Allah* written on bands around their heads, dressed just as I had seen them in Beirut during the militia battle the previous week.

'Who *are* all these people?' Anderson asked. There were green banners on the village houses and Iranian flags hanging from mosques. The gunmen here did not smile at us. There were no friendly requests for cigarettes or newspapers, no innocent enquiries about the progress of the fighting. These people were committed to something more important than a militia war. At several checkpoints there were flags identifying the gunmen as 'Islamic Amal'. Not Amal, the Shia militia in Beirut, but *Islamic* Amal.

On the road to Zahle, we turned a corner and were stopped by gunmen wearing hoods. Syrian troops drove the roads without paying any heed to these men, just as the Israelis had left the murderers of the Chouf unmolested. Anderson drew in his breath. Nothing is so concentrating to the mind as the sight of a man in a hood. Executioners wear hoods. One of them came to the car window. His hood was made from a large glossy red bag with an open zip where his mouth was and two crude slits for his eyes. British journalist, I said. He wanted to know the politics of *The Times*. In good English, he started a discussion right there on the road, in his hood with his gun in his hand, on the ethics of press freedom, and when I told him that, yes, I really did believe the pen was mightier than the sword, he smiled. I knew he was smiling because through the slits in his hood, I could see his eyes narrow slightly.

At Sofar, just up the road from Bhamdoun, the Phalangist shells were crashing into the hillsides. The Druze, many of them with long beards and baggy trousers, knew they had won. The Druze gunman who stopped us was standing beside the Bhamdoun highway, using the sleeve of his camouflage jacket to wipe the remains of his breakfast *homus* from his unkempt black beard. Behind him a Syrian army lorry creaked into the driveway of a church whose roof had been torn off in the counter-bombardment that began the assault on Bhamdoun. The truck was heavy with 122mm ammunition and crates of two-way radios. The gunman was relaxed, confident, a man whose gratitude stretched generously in two directions.

He jerked his finger towards the truck and its large-calibre cargo. 'For this, thank you, Syria,' he said. Then he nodded in the direction of Bhamdoun and the newly captured Christian towns which had just been evacuated by the Israeli army. 'For this,' he said, 'thank you, Israel. Thank you, Syria and Israel.'

Anderson and I drove into Bhamdoun, Much of it was in ruins and at least six fires were burning out of control. It was filled with gaunt young men, Palestinian guerrillas from a PLO faction opposing Arafat, Shia militiamen with green headbands, Lebanese Communist Party gunmen. They were dirty, exultant, high on danger, laughing when artillery rounds crashed into the roofs of houses. With militia banners above them, the gunmen had set up checkpoints on the broken streets. They lounged on the smashed pavements, many of them smoking large Cuban cigars. 'This was a great victory,' one of them said, leaping to his feet and pointing excitedly through the heat haze to the distant outline of Beirut below us. 'We shall be in Beirut in two days.'

From back alleys and ridges around Bhamdoun, Druze artillerymen sent salvo after salvo of shells across the mountains towards Beirut and Aoun's army at Souq al-Gharb. The guns boomed and crashed through Bhamdoun. It lay under a cloud of dust and black smoke, almost every building blasted by shellfire and looted, even the great Lamartine Hotel on the Damascus road. A trail of tailor's dummies led from a shop to the former railway station. We picked our way over uprooted trees, along streets carpeted with spent ammunition and two-foot shell fragments.

'From where you come?'

The gunman was Palestinian, unshaven, red-eyed and suspicious. He was trying to speak in English. Press. 'Why are you here?' Anderson produced his Lebanese press card. Journalists. American and British journalists. 'America kills Palestinians.' No, no. We are journalists, press, *sahafa*, reporters. There were more gunmen round us now, holding automatic weapons, draped with ammunition belts, none of them smiling. A man in black looked at Anderson. 'America kills Muslims.' This was getting worse. 'Why you want to kill Muslims?'

This was no place to explain the search for truth. The gunmen were nervous. 'Are you a spy?' I had been afraid of that. We protested. We had a duty to be there. We wanted their help. We wanted to talk to them. We worked for newspapers that were independent of governments. We did not agree with the Americans. Anderson held out his press card again.

Something had gone wrong. For years, gunmen like these — hostile, undisciplined though they might be — had respected our jobs, respected the word *sahafa*, press, on the windscreens of our cars. They had understood what we were doing. Suddenly the connection had dried up. We were no longer journalists to these people. Our jobs meant nothing to them. We were *foreigners*.

'Who are these people?' An older man had arrived, a Palestinian I guessed. '*Ajnabi*, foreigners.' Not press, they had replied. Foreigners. 'Who are the *ajnabi*?' The man was looking at Anderson but he asked the question politely. Then he turned to his colleagues. 'These are pressmen here to see our victory. You must help them. You have a duty to protect them. Help the *ajnabi*.' He smiled. 'You are OK, you can look around but ...' he paused. 'Do not stay here too long.' The other gunmen did not smile. When we walked away, they stared at us distrustfully.

Perhaps they had not recovered from the physical shock of capturing Bhamdoun. The Israeli soldiers had withdrawn at such speed that they left their positions, their earth revetments, sandbags, barbed wire — even their checkpoint parasols and Hebrew road-signs — intact. Israel's

Phalangist allies here had been left to their fate. The Christian inhabitants had been driven out or murdered. It was not surprising that in east Beirut, Menachem Begin's promises to the Christians of Lebanon were being recalled with ever-increasing bitterness.

It was only two years and five months since the Israeli prime minister had spoken with such passion about the suffering of Christians under siege by the Syrian army at Zahle. 'All Israel wants is to stop the blood-letting,' he had said then. 'Israel will continue to assist the Christian minority just as it would any other endangered minority. As Jews, we cannot stand by quietly in the face of murderous deeds in a neighbouring country, as do many European nations.'

But now the Israelis were standing quietly by as the Phalangists publicised ever more credible reports of the massacre of Christian civilians in the Chouf.* When the Phalangist defenders of Bhamdoun were killed, Israel did nothing. It was the four nations of the multinational force — three of them European — who were now trying to arrange a ceasefire to bring the slaughter to an end.

Anderson and I drove home through the Metn hills, past the Syrian gun-line in the forests above Beirut. In the clearings between the fir trees, Syrian 155s were banging shells out of the mountains, the rounds whispering off towards Beirut. We crossed the dormant line between Syrian and Lebanese troops at Dour Choueir but the road home through Broumanna was under fire. A petrol tanker had crashed into some trees and gasoline had washed down the highway, turning the surface into a skating rink. We travelled at 5 mph, trying to keep a grip on the road by driving with our right set of wheels on the grass verge.

Every time a shell exploded, I would instinctively touch the gas and the car would move sideways into the centre of the road. Anderson was breathing heavily. 'Take it easy, Fisky. Just keep the speed down.' A set of mortars firing outgoing rounds made me literally jump in my seat. We slithered into the road again and the steering wheel spun in my hand like a roulette wheel. 'Fisky, take your foot off the gas.' When the road was dry, I gunned the car towards Beirut. There were times, I told Anderson, when I really thought I had had enough of this sort of thing. Anderson was silent for a while, holding to the seat of the car as we took the mountain bends at speed. He seemed preoccupied, trapped in some private, deep concern of his own. 'Fisky,' he said at last. 'Have I ever told you you're the worst driver in the whole fucking world?'

---

* After the capture of al-Bireh, six miles south of Bhamdoun, for example, the Christian villagers were herded into the church by Druze, Syrian and Palestinian militiamen. According to survivors, the gunmen permitted more than 40 people to return to their homes for personal belongings — but then shot all 40 as they returned to the church. Inexplicably, the other villagers were then set free.

In Beirut, the four MNF ambassadors were seeking talks with Jumblatt as well as Gemayel. It was hopeless. Shia gunmen now attacked the Marines. From Hay al-Sellum — 'Hooterville' — and from the slums of Bourj al-Barajneh, militiamen now swept the Marine positions with rifle fire and rocket-propelled grenades. After two hours, the Marines were given permission to shoot back, but only at identified targets. The Americans could not see their assailants in the warren of streets.

Ceasefires were declared, truces observed for hours or only minutes. Truce terms were all-embracing, imaginary, visionary, absolute: a total ceasefire throughout Lebanon, the return of all Christian and Muslim refugees who had been forced to flee their homes in the past eight years — *eight years*; aid for all victims of the war, UN or MNF ceasefire observers in the Chouf, Lebanese police to take over Lebanese army positions in the mountains, a 'reconciliation conference' involving both Gemayel and Jumblatt's 'national salvation front' with Syria and Saudi Arabia represented at the talks. The formulas were worked out with the same attention to detail as the artillery trajectories that were destroying Beirut.

The Italians would express their hopes for a truce. When the gunfire eased, Colonel Timothy Geraghty would helicopter his wounded Marines out to the Sixth Fleet ships for surgery, speculating that the war had ended. Gemayel announced peace terms. Jumblatt argued about the location of the 'reconciliation' conference. It would be held at Beirut airport. It would be held aboard a French aircraft carrier. It would be held in Switzerland's finest hotel. Amid the gunsmoke, everyone seemed to be signing ceasefires with everyone else.

A new US naval task force arrived off Beirut with 2,000 more Marines on board. Gemayel felt stronger. A few hundred yards from the Ministry of Defence, Lebanese army batteries were now firing alongside Phalangist guns. In the AP office, Labelle took another call from the ministry. All foreign journalists should go to Baabda at once for new press credentials. I set off with Scheherezade Faramarzi. Things must be quiet up at the ministry today.

We got no further than the sandbagged guardhouse by the main gate. When I stopped the car, we heard the shells moaning through the summer sky above us. We ran for the guardhouse. There were 30 soldiers inside and an officer who formally introduced himself with a salute. 'Lieutenant-Colonel Tarek Nujaim. Good morning. Why are you here?' To collect our new press cards. There was a stunned silence, broken by a rumble of gunfire. We were told to come, Faramarzi said. For the new press credentials. The soldiers stared at us. Was this how journalists spent their time in Beirut?

Nujaim waved our mission aside. We should be writing now about the coming victory, he said. The government would win. He was perfectly confident about that. 'We don't want a ceasefire,' he shouted toward the

soldiers crouched around us. 'We want to move forward every day.'
There was only a wall of sandbags to protect us, and the colonel did not
seem to realise that this sort of talk might tempt fate. Even when a
tannoy began cursing at us — 'Get into the bunkers, get into the
bunkers' — he seemed at ease. We were too far from the bunkers and
had to take our chances where we were. Faramarzi and I sat down on
the cement floor beside a lieutenant. Colonel Nujaim stood up, a well-
built though slightly portly man whose soldiers obviously looked to him
for confidence. 'The Lebanese people are with us,' he shouted again.
The men around us laughed and that was the moment the first shell
came in.

There was a sound of tearing, as if someone were ripping up a giant
curtain over our heads, and then an explosion that knocked the breath
out of us and made our ears sing. It was so loud that for several seconds
the world about us — the clouds of brown cordite smoke, the wicked
little pieces of shrapnel that came swishing down over the flimsy sandbags, the pieces of glass — moved in silence, perhaps in slow motion.
Then, just eight feet from us, a young soldier rose to his feet, saying
nothing, just standing up amid the mass of crouched, green-uniformed
figures, a welter of blood streaming from the top of his head and
dribbling off his chin onto his battledress blouse. He swayed slightly
until a sergeant caught him under the right arm and forced him to sit on
a camp bed.

Right next to me on the floor, the lieutenant coughed and put his
hand to his chest just above his heart, pulling open his tunic very gently
to reveal a tiny track of blood running down towards his stomach. He
frowned and pulled from his pocket a piece of tissue paper, not taking
his eyes off his wounded colleague. Colonel Nujaim was on his feet
shouting: 'Keep calm, keep calm.' Then he turned to us. 'Don't worry,'
he said. 'Shells never strike twice in the same place.' He was wrong.

The badly wounded soldier was being held up by two of his colleagues,
his head flopping from side to side in near delirium, as another soldier
pulled out swathes of bandages and dressings and pressed them to the
top of his head to stanch the blood. The lieutenant picked away nervously
at the spot of blood on his chest. There was a high rushing sound of jet
aircraft as Lebanese Hawker Hunters began a strafing run on the hills
above us. Incredibly, Gemayel was sending his vintage air force of six
Hawker Hunters into action against the Druze. The colonel was on his
feet again. 'We are not afraid,' he announced. 'Get more sandbags.'

Then we heard the screaming sound again and were on our knees
before the detonation blasted over us. Tiny pieces of metal — some no
more than an eighth of an inch — rained down on our hair and backs;
and then there was a loud, clear shout. 'Soldier wounded. Soldier
wounded.' The shell had burst on the other side of the sandbags but had

splintered its way into a small concrete guard post 20 feet further away where four soldiers had been huddled for safety.

The troops around us did not want to show their fear, although Colonel Nujaim had physically to push one of them out of the sandbagged enclosure to fetch a car for the wounded men. 'It's the Syrians and Palestinians who are doing this,' another of the soldiers shouted. They were all convinced that the shells were being fired at them by Palestinians or Syrians, not by the Druze, not by their own Lebanese people. For if they believed that, then they were participating in a civil war.

We were all frightened. Every time the shells came in, we would huddle tightly on the ground and afterwards a tremendous tiredness would overtake us. Three soldiers stretched out half asleep. 'You have been in Lebanon seven years?' the colonel asked me. 'Why, you should have a Lebanese passport.' A roar of laughter from the soldiers, another shell, more smoke.

'Truly,' he said later, 'we have for the first time got a government that gives us orders. That is why we don't want a ceasefire. That is why we will win.' It did not feel as if anyone was winning. And in the moment they told us to leave the emplacement and run the 150 yards to the bunkers in the ministry, it did not seem to matter. Pounding across the grass and shell splinters and concrete of the parade ground, running as fast as ever I could remember, suddenly there was warmth and trees and light; and when we reached the other side, exhilaration.

Two basements down, we found Colonel Tom Fintel, the senior US army training officer in Lebanon, his hooded eyes reflecting a total confidence in all things Lebanese. So how were things going today? It was like checking on the cricket scores or the state of play at Wimbledon. 'Not too bad. The Lebanese are taking a lot of fire at Souq al-Gharb but they're OK.' Really? Was Fintel quite certain of that? 'Sure. Aoun's got an armoured brigade up there. No one can get through that.'

But Fintel was apparently wrong. On the night of 18 September, the Lebanese army reported that the Druze had captured most of Souq al-Gharb and Aoun's new American tanks were firing at their enemies over open sights. The Americans would later claim that the Lebanese army had been lying, deliberately exaggerating their predicament in order to involve the US navy in Gemayel's war. But at the time it seemed only hours before the Druze and their allies would break through. The Lebanese army were building a new defence line beside the defence ministry. If that collapsed, the militias would be in central Beirut. Gemayel's government would fall and the MNF would be disgraced. Had not the multinational force come to Lebanon to support Gemayel and his army?

Robert McFarlane, Reagan's senior negotiator, saw only one solution.

The US navy would have to lend gunfire support to the Lebanese army. American warships would have to shell the Druze lines at Souq al-Gharb. Under fire in his Marine base, Colonel Geraghty argued vainly against the proposal. The Americans had repeatedly stated that they would only take military action against a direct threat to their own forces in Lebanon. Just once before, on 8 September, the frigate *Bowen* had fired shells at a Druze gun battery that was shooting into the American compound beside the airport.

But the moment the Sixth Fleet opened fire to help *Gemayel*'s forces, the Marines in Beirut would become participants in the civil war. The very second that the first US navy shell landed among the Druze at Souq al-Gharb, the Americans would have aligned themselves with the Phalange in open war against the Muslims of Lebanon. Every self-imposed rule of the 'peace-keeping' force would have been broken.

I was having breakfast with my landlord on the morning of 19 September. We sat in his garden, among yellow and red flowers, his song-birds in a string of cages along the walls. It was hot. Butterflies settled on the flowers. My landlord was a Druze. He thought the Druze would win the battle at Souq al-Gharb. We were drinking our third or fourth hot sticky Arabic coffee when we saw the American destroyer *John Rodgers* making smoke as she moved north along the seafront. She passed close to us. We could even see the naval crew on the upper deck and the Stars and Stripes drifting in the warm breeze.

The vessel turned sharp to port, her wash tossing a few small fishing boats that were riding the swell off the Corniche. Then, when the *John Rodgers* was almost parallel with the tip of the peninsula, there came from her a hollow, popping sound. It was a very dull series of reports, as if someone was playing tennis underneath the sea. There was nothing warlike about it. Curious at the noise, a few strollers on the Corniche paused to watch the destroyer. My landlord fetched his binoculars and I focused on the warship. There was the American flag floating at her stern, two seamen leaning over a rail near the bridge.

The glasses caught a puff of smoke, nothing more than a smudge near the for'ard 5-inch gun. I kept the glasses trained on the gun. A few seconds later, there was another pop and then I saw a shell case — a brass shell case glinting gold in the sun — bounce onto the deck and spin right off the ship into the sea. Pop-pop. Another bright gold casing splashed into the water. Thus did the Americans go to war in Lebanon.

'The Sixth Fleet is shelling Souq al-Gharb.' I know, Terry. I've just been watching them. Anderson was holding out an AP 'bulletin', a single paragraph datelined Washington. US warships, it announced, were firing into the mountains above Beirut. Druze shellfire was threatening the Marines and the US ambassador's residence. The US navy was therefore firing in support of American forces in Lebanon. So that was going to be the excuse. Perhaps the world would believe this but the Lebanese would not. They realised that Washington was trying to save Gemayel. And their perspective, in the end, was the one that mattered.

By mid-afternoon, the *John Rodgers* had been joined by the missile cruiser *Virginia*, both laying a carpet of shells through Souq al-Gharb, killing government forces as well as militiamen in their fire. Within the city, the naval guns sounded more menacing, blasting hundreds of rounds up into the Chouf ridge-line. On the seafront, the destroyer and cruiser now moved at speed, attended by two French warships and the US amphibious assault ship *Tarawa* carrying 1,200 Marines. There were more warships in the bay. And more clarifications from the Americans.

From within the American ambassador's office in the British Embassy, there came one of those craftily constructed statements that admit one truth in order to conceal another. 'The naval gunfire support,' the Embassy now said, 'was conducted on military targets threatening Lebanese armed forces defending Souq al-Gharb. Successful Lebanese armed forces' defence of the area is vital to the safety of US personnel, including the US multinational forces, other US military and the US diplomatic corps personnel. The naval gunfire support missions are defensive actions.' This was a new and exclusive version of America's one–two–three school of Middle East politics. Labelle was that day in one of his Mencken moods. 'US policy in Lebanon,' he said, 'can now be summed up in one word: Bang.'

American statements did not convey – indeed never mentioned – the fact that these 'military targets' were Druze, that the Americans were shooting at Lebanese in order to defend Lebanese. That would have been to admit that US forces had taken sides in the civil war. Gemayel's government played along with this. Lebanese state radio now transmitted martial music, ending its midday broadcast with Elgar's *Pomp and Circumstance*. The battles were portrayed as a patriotic, nationalist war against foreigners. To this end, the government invited journalists to the Lebanese military hospital at Badaro.

Inside an old French medical ward on the fifth floor lay the wretched figure of a wounded Palestinian guerrilla, his face contorted with pain and a Syrian army jacket round his shoulders. As the dying man groaned in agony – he had a massive wound in his back – two Lebanese women reporters shrieked questions at him, eliciting only that his name was Fadi Abdul-Mowla, that he lived in the Syrian town of Deraa and belonged to the pro-Syrian Palestine Liberation Front's 'fourth battalion'. Asked who was supporting him, he replied with unconscious irony: 'Artillery.' He died three hours later.

Each day brought deeper US military involvement in the war and more devastating evidence of Lebanon's disintegration. On a visit to Souq al-Gharb on 20 September, Anderson spotted seven senior US

Marine officers under shellfire, running from a Lebanese armoured personnel carrier. Anderson concluded they were acting as forward artillery observers for the US navy and discovered that they had been in Souq al-Gharb on the day the *John Rodgers* opened fire. If only in token strength, the Marines had now entered the Chouf. Asked to comment, the American Embassy said that it was 'seeking guidance' from the State Department.

The Lebanese air force – all six planes of it – was meanwhile growing smaller. The Druze shot down a Bulldog reconnaissance aircraft over the Chouf; they left the body of the pilot to rot in a ditch for more than a week. One of Gemayel's Hawker Hunters was hit by ground fire and crashed in the Mediterranean; its pilot was rescued by the US navy. Another Hunter was damaged over the Chouf and flew to an RAF base in Cyprus for repairs. The Lebanese air force was therefore reduced to just three Hunters which used the four-lane motorway north of Jounieh as an emergency landing strip. The US navy now continued its bombardments into the night.

The absurdity of all this was evident to everyone but the Americans. Back in Washington, it presumably made sense. The United States was fighting for Gemayel's embattled democracy against the forces of Soviet-backed Syria. In Lebanon, the perspective was different. The Americans were fighting for the Phalange against the Muslims. The tragic contradictions of Lebanon played no part in White House planning. Exhumed by an American administration so enamoured of the big screen, the resurrection of the 40-year-old 45,000-ton battleship *New Jersey* for duty off Lebanon was surely the most preposterous symbol of America's folly.

This massive warship had been re-equipped with sea-to-air missiles and sent off to support the Marines in Beirut, its 16-inch guns, the largest in the US navy, capable of firing 20 miles into Lebanon, far over the Chouf and into the Bekaa Valley. It had been built – and used in the Pacific war – to destroy beachheads before invasions. The one-ton shells of this behemoth, the navy told us, were as big as Volkswagens, their impact so enormous that they spread devastation across the area of a football field. The shells had been made at the time of the Korean war. The *New Jersey* was thus a true representative of US policy in Lebanon: unthinking, unwieldy, hopelessly out of date. So old were the ship's computers, that they still contained moving parts.

If we wished to understand the treacherous dichotomy between Beirut and Washington, we had only to take one of those helicopter rides out to the Sixth Fleet. We applied to go aboard the *Virginia* which had been shelling the Chouf with such gusto. Sure enough, there were the immaculate young officers with radiant faces ready to welcome us aboard. They talked about the 'quality' of their work as if they were selling fine art, they talked about 'excellence' as if they were in business school.

Even the for'ard gun crew of the *Virginia* – the men who had been firing at Souq al-Gharb – performed with 'excellence'. It actually said so on the port side of their 5-inch gun, the first letter 'E' underlined three times to demonstrate their competence on three successive occasions on practice ranges in the Caribbean. Everyone on the *Virginia* was confident the gun crew had performed just as well these past three days, although no one seemed to know exactly what the ship had been firing at. Two hundred and thirty-eight shells the *Virginia* had sent off towards the mountains east of Beirut, and not a soul aboard could say where they went.

Even the hostile nature of the *Virginia*'s business was firmly rejected by Lieutenant-Commander Al Diamond from the commander's flagship *Iwo Jima*. 'The term "fired in anger" is not appropriate,' he announced to us in the wardroom. 'That's a very old cliché which really is not appropriate for use here. You can say that we have fired "on other than a training mission".' Down in the armaments room, a gunner's mate called Kelly Hardin was more forthcoming. 'We don't know what we're firing at,' he said. 'They just tell us to shoot the gun.' He tapped a console behind him. 'One man on this panel runs the whole show.'

The 'show' was a rather antiseptic affair on the *Virginia*. Her targets were assigned by Commander Morgan France of the *Iwo Jima*. No disconcerting names like Aley or Bhamdoun or Souq al-Gharb, but a set of clean map coordinates, just a series of figures that were fed into the computer in the glow-worm darkness of the *Virginia*'s 'combat information centre'. The computer then checked – or was supposed to check – that the latest projectile in support of President Gemayel's government really did land where it was meant to land.

Lieutenant Jack Stumborg, the *Virginia*'s ordnance officer, attempted to explain this mystical process. 'After we've done firing on a target,' he said, 'we have a means of calling up the target's grids on the computer in relation to the ship's grids and we can back-plot and kind of see where our last fall of shot went to ... up to this point, we feel we've been shooting where we thought we were shooting.' The ship's commander, Captain Joseph King, believed that his ships hit within 'fifty yards' of their targets. What these were he would not say, although the commanders of the frigates and cruisers in the Sixth Fleet gunline had been told they were shooting at tanks and missile-launchers.

Did these men understand that they were contributing to America's most serious military involvement since Vietnam? The significance of events seemed to escape them all. A young engineer told me he watched the Chouf battles at night. 'You can see the mountains getting lit up,' he said. 'I don't know why these people do these things to each other. I feel sorry for them. But I wonder how long it will be before the people we are shooting at start shooting back.' Only privately did some of the crew mention that when the *Bowen* opened fire, a mortar round was seen to land in the sea a mile away.

One of Captain King's officers did recall reading Joseph Conrad's description of a nineteenth-century warship firing symbolically into the impenetrable jungle of the African coast yet somehow, amid the iced teas and coffees of the ward-room, the red-jacketed waiters and the hiss of the ship's air-conditioning, it was difficult to remember its relevance. Even the explosions in the mountains three and a half miles away reached us only as distant thumps, a far away drum-beat.

Up on the sunlit decks, the sailors were staring eastwards where a panorama of black and brown smoke was funnelling up from 12 fires spread along the hill ridges, a dark stain that spread a mile high then moved across the Mediterranean. Through field-glasses, we could see the individual shell-bursts in the Chouf. And there on deck, we shared with the crew warm rolls and hot sausages with onions, pickles and lashings of mustard. Hot dogs while Lebanon burns.

It burned well. In west Beirut, we could smell the wood-smoke from the forest pyres of the Chouf, set alight by days of shelling. The entire Italian army ammunition dump blew up. A shell touched off the depot in east Beirut sending a 300-foot-wide bulb of flame exploding into the sky. It burned for more than a day, its black smoke moving like a canopy over the mountains, to Tripoli, across the Bekaa, even spreading its darkness over the Syrian frontier. American jets flew at rooftop height over Beirut. French Super-Etendards streaked up the wadis above the east of the city. The British sent a flight of Buccaneer fighter-bombers across the Lebanese capital.

It was intended as a warning to the MNF's enemies. Look at our weapons, it was meant to say. Think what will happen if you go too far. Be careful. We do not want to use our awesome power. But the Lebanese saw a different message. They knew all about armies and invaders. These planes meant that the MNF would attack. The planes were going to bomb. They were preparing for war. This was a challenge.

The French contingent was attacked again with rocket-propelled grenades on the Fouad Chehab ring-road near the city centre. It was close to another Shia area which, like Bourj al-Barajneh, was slipping out of the Lebanese government's control. When the French MNF headquarters were shelled, President Mitterrand personally sanctioned a Super-Etendard air strike against gun batteries in the Metn hills. For the French, that single raid was to be as critical a political event as the American decision to shell Souq al-Gharb. But the US naval bombardments were now routine. They no longer merited 'urgent' bells on the AP wire. The bells would be reserved now only for a *New Jersey* broadside. The Lebanese Cabinet resigned, allegedly to make way for a government of national unity. There were rumours that Gemayel was going to renege on the Lebanese–Israeli withdrawal agreement. Almost 30 NATO warships were riding the seas off Beirut.

Anderson's AP staff were under as much pressure as they ever were during the Israeli invasion. Foley had transferred to *Time* magazine after winning a Pulitzer prize for his pictures of Chatila. But the Beirut bureau had been augmented by a young photographer, Don Mell or, to be more precise, 'Donald C. Mell the 3rd'. He was only 21, with doe eyes and a pencil-thin moustache that made him look like early photographs of Marcel Proust. His lunatic courage under fire helped to compensate for his habit of repeating himself, over and over again, when he chose to explain the political future of Lebanon. It was Anderson's belief that reporters should do the thinking and that 'snappers' should confine themselves to what the AP called 'art work'. It was several weeks before we realised that Mell's monologues on the problems of Lebanon were not as foolish as they at first sounded.

Taking photographs of Lebanese army soldiers, he began to hear whispers of disaffection. Muslim troops in the 6th Brigade, he discovered, felt abused by their Christian officers. Mell spent a lot of time with the Marines and sensed their fear that something terrible might overwhelm them. They believed they might have to move into the mountains under fire and that this would involve heavy casualties. Day after day, Mell would sit with the Marines in their dugouts as bullets spattered into the sandbags. 'The whole thing's a bag of shit,' he proclaimed one afternoon. 'Those guys hate it there. They can't advance. They don't hold the high ground. And some of them have begun to tell me not to take pictures.' No photos. The familiar smell of a dispirited army.

Mell and I spent several afternoons on the roof of the battalion landing team headquarters – the BLT – the gaunt, cavernous, four-storey building in which most of the Marines slept next to one of the airport car parks. It had been held by Shia militiamen during the Israeli siege, so the Marines' enemies were familiar with the structure. It included a mess, chapel, a radio centre for the US navy, sleeping quarters for hundreds of men and a small lorry-park underneath the building. On the roof, the Marines maintained two permanent observers' posts.

From here, they looked out across the empty airport to the smouldering foothills of the Chouf or into the slums of Hay al-Sellum. Mell and I would watch the shells crashing onto the deserted runways, the Marines logging each explosion. They were thorough men who welcomed our presence. We shared their rations and wore their flak jackets during the bombardments. The ships of the Sixth Fleet moved steadily across the horizon. Less than three months earlier, the fleet had boated us out to the carriers for Independence Day celebrations. I still had my invitation. 'Dress is casual – picnic attire. Boats will run all afternoon from Green

Beach to bring you out to join us ... 1 PM: Lebanon's folkloric touristic group onboard USS Iwo Jima ... 5 PM cake cutting/reception for honored guests, hanger deck ... 6 PM Final Farewells.'

In the afternoon heat, the bitumen roof of the BLT would melt onto the soles of our shoes. We would be given coffee and then, when Mell had finished his 'art work', we would run to our cars and drive home. Somehow, we felt less secure when we were leaving. On the roof of the BLT, despite the falling shells, we felt safer. The Marines there did not panic. They were almost academic about the war; and if they could regard it with such apparent nonchalance, so could we. On the roof, we felt protected.

Another ceasefire was called when Gemayel agreed to a 'national reconciliation' conference. But in mid-October, Shia gunmen in Bourj al-Barajneh attacked the Marines again. A Marine was shot in the chest and killed while driving a jeep along the airport perimeter road. Bullets had been passing through the trees and long grass around the American positions for ten minutes from Hay al-Sellum — from 'Hooterville' — before the Marines obtained permission to fire back. They were still supposed to be on a peace-keeping mission. Another badly wounded Marine died as he was being taken by jeep to the contingent's medical centre.

A Lebanese ceasefire committee was operating the new truce, a member of each militia represented under the chairmanship of a Lebanese army officer. On 14 October, the Shia members of the committee withdrew. They complained that punishments had been meted out to Muslim soldiers of the Lebanese army who had refused to fire on militiamen of the Shia faith during the recent fighting. More shots were fired at the Marines. Like the naval bombardments, Marine shooting incidents no longer merited 'urgent' bells on the AP wire.

Beirut, 23 October 1983

The first distant, soft tremor wakes me up. It is a bright morning and the sea outside my balcony is splashing in a friendly way against the promenade. Bomb explosions, shell-bursts, are heartbeats in Beirut now. I decide to sleep in. It is Sunday morning. A few seconds later, another gentle quake, a very slight, intimate change in the air pressure in the house. A second bomb. I lie in bed for another four minutes. The phone rings. It is my landlord who lives on the ground floor. His voice is breaking with urgency. *'MR ROBERT, MR ROBERT, IT IS ME, GET UP, GET UP. THEY HAVE BOMBED THE MARINES. MR TERRY AND FOLEY ARE LEAVING.'*

They cannot have bombed the Marines. Where? In the street, Anderson is running for his car, Foley beside him, cameras dangling from his shoulder. Terry, wait for me. Anderson would have gone without me. He drives fast, viciously, down the Corniche. Foley's face is fixed on the road and he talks without looking at me. 'They got the Marines and they got the French. Car bombs. That's all the radios are saying.' How? Foley is angry. 'How the hell do I know? It may be a load of crap but I heard the explosions.'

The French battalion headquarters is in a nine-storey building called the 'Drakkar', beyond Raouche, before the airport. When Anderson turns off the road, Foley says 'Holy fuck' and we are out of the car amid hundreds of French Paratroopers and Lebanese soldiers. There has been an earthquake. The entire headquarters of the French 1st *Chasseurs-Parachutistes* regiment, all nine floors of it, has disappeared. I run up to a smoking crater, 20 feet deep and 40 wide. Piled beside it, like an obscene sandwich, are the nine floors of the building. There are legs and arms lying in the muck, a French officer's chest, medals still pinned to the battledress, but no head. A man pulled from the concrete with his intestines spilling out, his guts dragging along the muck beneath him. 'How many do you think can survive that?' a soldier asks us. 'How many? How many?' He puts out a hand in a sad, kindly way, wanting to show a sort of respect for something that lay on the ground between us. 'Please be careful where you walk.'

Lieutenant-Colonel Philippe de Longeaux gazes fearfully into the burning crater, staring at the catastrophe that has struck his men. He talks slowly in a dreamy kind of way, in shock:

'We have found three people who are alive. There are about a hundred soldiers still under there. The bomb lifted up the building. Right up, do you understand? And put it down again over there.'

He points vaguely to the wreckage. *The bomb lifted the nine-storey building into the air and moved it 20 feet. The whole building became airborne. The crater is where the building was.* How could this be done? 'It was a car bomb,' he says. 'A suicide driver, just like the American Embassy.'

Behind the officer, a teenage Paratrooper is being dragged from the masonry. He stands up, covered in blood, and lashes out at the doctors who surround him. When his officer approaches, he draws a commando knife and tries to kill him. He has gone mad. Another soldier just beside me, a teenager, takes off his beret and holds it in his hand and screws it up very tightly. Then he sits down in the dirt and wails like a child.

From a jagged cavern in the crunched cement, a hand emerges, a small chain bracelet round its wrist. A French soldier crawls to the hole and holds the hand in his own. The hand clasps him, grips him, seizes his arm and clings to him until its owner dies.

'Fisk, we're going.' Anderson is dragging my arm. 'I got to get to the

Marines.' The airport road is deserted but there is a cloud of white smoke steaming upwards from the far end where the Marines are based. 'We'll find Bob Jordan. You try to find him in the press room, I'll look for him in the BLT.' Jordan is the Marine press officer. But when Anderson stops the car, he is frowning. Marines are shouting and screaming from behind their barbed wire fencing and there are heavy explosions but it is not this which is troubling Anderson. 'Where's the BLT?' At the other end of the fence, Terry. 'It's gone.' It's behind the smoke. 'It isn't. It's fucking disappeared.'

Anderson throws himself at the fencing. 'AP, AP, I gotta come in. You've *got* to let me in.' There is a young Marine guard there, perhaps only 18, and he pulls the wire aside for Anderson and myself. We run forward across rubble and tree branches and through smoke and there in front of us are heaps of bodies, some in Marine uniform, others naked, broken-backed, bone-crushed, arms and legs twisted into impossible positions. 'Who did this?' Anderson shouts at the young Marines. There are three of them now. They look stupidly at Anderson. Only the youngest talks. 'Guy with a bomb. He came in a truck. He went up with the bomb.'

Behind a wrecked jeep, I come across the bodies of ten more Marines, lined up on the ground as if on parade, their faces covered by tarpaulin, their bare feet, black with dust, poking incongruously from the bottom. One of the sheets has fallen away and the body beneath is quite naked but still covered in thick dust. His mouth is open and I wonder if he is alive and trying to talk. But the top of his head is missing.

From the curtains of brown and white smoke that rise funereally behind them come the regular, gloomy vibrations of underground explosions as the heavy ammunition dump beneath the ruins of the American Marine headquarters begins to explode. A tunnel of fire 20 feet high spurts out of the rubble. When a shell detonates itself across part of the airport, the three Marines throw themselves to the ground. 'Get yourselves down.' Only when the youngest Marine has taken cover with me behind an ambulance do I notice that he is weeping, holding his rifle in his left hand and wiping the tears from his eyes with his right.

Thomas Friedman, the *New York Times* correspondent, runs through the fence to us. He looks into the fires and smoke and shakes his head. 'Fisky, this is incredible. It is the most brilliant act of terrorism.' I stand thinking about this expression, the cruel, accurate use of the word 'brilliant' and the implication of its truth: that this was the most professional massacre ever perpetrated in Lebanon.

Down a narrow path to our left, Major Robert Jordan appears. Never a humorous man, he looks stunned. There is blood smeared down his arms, on his uniform, on his face. 'I've been pulling guys out,' he says. There are more explosions from the heaps of masonry in front of us. A young Marine is being led away from it, a black soldier whose head lolls from side to side like a doll and whose legs give way just as his colleagues catch him under the arms.

Jordan has no explanation for what has happened, no careful military excuses. 'Someone drove a truck with explosives into the compound. He crashed through the south gate and into the lobby of the building. He detonated the explosives inside, collapsing all the walls down on themselves.' There are more explosions, a softer but deeper rumble this time, and two more Marines are brought out of the ruins, both on stretchers, one with his arm dangling carelessly over the edge, his hand trailing savagely through the rubble and broken glass.

Anderson and I walk to the Marine operations room. Colonel Timothy Geraghty has returned from inspecting his battalion headquarters. Only he doesn't have a battalion headquarters any more. He is grey-faced, his jaw bunched up, his cheeks pinched, his eyes empty. Behind him, the Americans are dragging tubes and oxygen bottles onto the smoking debris of the BLT, pushing the pipes into the heated interior of the hundreds of tons of collapsed concrete and iron. The BLT has been utterly destroyed, blasted open from beneath like a volcano, atomised by 4,000 pounds of explosives. A Marine says there are 60 dead so far. He must know there are *hundreds* dead. All around the crumpled grey and steaming rubble, uninjured Marines are sitting in their armoured vehicles, dutifully guarding the headquarters that is no longer there to be guarded.

The twisted iron gate through which the suicide bomber has driven lies in pieces to the south of the ruins. The explosion has torn at the trees around the perimeter fence, carpeting the rubble and concrete in a premature autumn of dark green leaves. There are papers too, the bureaucracy of military administration and personal life, scattered in their thousands across a square mile. Anderson and I pick up a pile. Classified documents on sniper locations, instructions on how to board helicopters, Marine unit newspapers, letters from home. A blue-shaded envelope from South Carolina still waiting to be opened by a relative who is probably already dead. Page 22 of a classified Marine file lies beside the ruins, a cheerful memorandum telling the Pentagon of the friendly relations between the Marines and the Lebanese. 'You only have to see how the Marines get on with the Lebanese to know this is the finest advertisement the Marine Corps could have,' it says.

By the roots of a tree, I find a copy of the 24th Marine Amphibious Unit magazine, *Root Scoop*. It is dated 15 September 1983, just five weeks ago. On page 2, 1st Lieutenant Miles Burdine has written an article entitled 'People depend on Marines'. He complains that the mosquitoes are driving him insane, that he is exhausted from standing on duty, drenched in sweat and wanting to talk to a girl. But:

to see people who merit pity, go into 'Hooterville' and look at what the people live on, the food they eat and the clothes they wear. Look at the faces of the children and realize the death, destruction and poverty many have experienced ... we will depart this country in a short time for the benefits of home ... But the Lebanese people are home right now. They are depending on us to help restore peace, so they can rebuild their economy, their city, their homes and their lives. As a result of our efforts, Beirut someday will possibly be a comfortable home for its people just as America is now.

The papers blow across the ruins. A Marine aboard an amphibious vehicle by the trees has given up any pretence at soldiering. He sits behind his machine-gun, shoulders heaving, his head in his hands. One of his officers puts an arm around him. Then he turns to Anderson and myself and the camera crews who have come trailing into the Marine base. 'You can film,' he says, 'but please don't take pictures of bodies. Remember, there are guys right now who'd like to shoot you. There's a lot of grief down there.' Out through the hot sea mist, we can see a giant shape gliding along the horizon. It is the *New Jersey*, creeping up the Mediterranean, having lost the battle before it ever fired its guns.

The two suicide bombers killed 241 American servicemen, most of them Marines, and 58 French Paratroopers. They were France's first combat casualties since the Algerian war. Not even in Vietnam did the Americans lose this many men in a single day. An old Lebanese who ran a snack bar in the BLT died in the bombing. So did the wife and children of the Lebanese concierge at the French headquarters. When President Mitterrand arrived to view the devastation, he found the concierge – who had briefly left the building to buy cigarettes when the bomber arrived – sitting silently alongside his mother-in-law beside the crater, waiting for a miracle. Mitterrand gently embraced the weeping woman and shook hands with the man. The youngest of his three children, the concierge told Mitterrand, was only three months old. He waited beside the pit for five more days before the French dug the decomposing remains of his wife and children out of the earth.

The Americans promised retaliation. This was a 'terrorist' attack. The AP had hitherto assiduously avoided the word when referring to attacks on the Israelis. Now that the Americans had been bombed, 'terrorism' became a vogue word. The AP reports out of Washington called it 'international terrorism'. In Beirut, Geraghty and the other Marine commanders had little doubt that Iran or Syria – or both – had a hand in the bombings. No freelance group of Shia gunmen could plan and execute a military assault on this scale.

The first bomb exploded at the Marine headquarters at 6.20 am. The second suicide driver immolated himself beneath the French headquarters exactly 20 seconds later. A French survivor recalled that he had been shaving when he heard the first explosion and walked to the balcony of his room because he thought the Marines might have been attacked. Then the second bomb detonated at the basement of his building. Twenty seconds. This was scientific, precision timing. It was the product of systematic preparation and design that must have taken weeks. Whoever arranged these attacks had to have planned for alternative targets, dummy runs to obtain accurate timing, back-up resources in case equipment failed.

The two MNF contingents attacked were those who had involved themselves in the war – the Americans with their naval bombardments, the French with their air strike. Seconds after the two bombs destroyed the two military headquarters, General Angioni placed hundreds of his Italian soldiers around their base at the northern end of the Beirut airport road, lying in their revetments, automatic weapons trained on every truck that approached them.

'We waited for our turn,' Angioni told me later. 'We waited and waited. You cannot imagine what those seconds were like. You think we were spared because we had not fought the militias? I am not so sure of that. We waited for the bomber who had been sent to destroy us. If he was not there in reality, he was there in our minds. I do not remember how long we waited. Then we realised he was not going to come. Maybe he couldn't start his truck. Maybe his lorry broke down at the last moment.'

American intelligence officers had received one warning of the attack: a CIA report of an overheard conversation in a Paris café that a 'complex' would be attacked in Beirut. It had been ignored. French MNF officers, who now called on the resources of French deuxième bureau officers in Damascus, were told that a group of Iranian revolutionary guards led by two mullahs had passed through Syria a month before the bombings and had been taken by the Syrians to a small Iranian camp south of Baalbek from where they were smuggled across the mountains to Beirut.

American diplomats in Lebanon put it about that the bombers were Iranian, that they had been blessed before their mission by Sheikh Mohamed Hussein Fadlallah, a fundamentalist Shia cleric in the Bir Abed district of west Beirut. With other reporters, I questioned Fadlallah about this. He denied the report. I spoke with dozens of Shia militiamen. They too denied the story. Why would the suicide bombers need to be blessed by Fadlallah? they asked me. If they believed they were performing God's work, they did not need Fadlallah to assure them of this. They already knew that paradise lay beneath the shadow of the sword.

We read carefully through every statement about the bombings made by America's enemies in the Middle East. Jumblatt condemned the massacres as 'tragic attacks'. The Libyans praised the bombings as 'courageous actions undertaken by nationalistic forces in Lebanon'. The Iranians denied any involvement. The Syrians said nothing. On 22 October, however, a day before the bombings, Syria had warned that it was prepared to use missiles against American vessels of the Sixth Fleet if President Reagan tried to 'terrorise' Syria. US Marine officers now offered the 'confidential' information that only the Syrian intelligence service was skilful enough to arrange a bombing attack of such sophistication and scale.

From Washington came graver suspicions. Soviet or east European agents may have been involved. Western embassies in Beirut dutifully relayed this information. Since the Soviets were allied to Syria, since the East Germans had helped train the Syrian *mukhabarrat*, it was only natural to include them among the possible culprits. It seemed only a matter of time before Lebanon crystallised into an object of superpower rivalry, at least in President Reagan's imagination.

If Lebanon was to be gifted with such a status, it would place a final, devastating commitment upon the international army in west Beirut. After returning to Lebanon to protect the Muslims of the capital, after aligning themselves with Gemayel's government and involving themselves on the Phalangist side in the new civil war, the MNF would then become a Cold War bulwark of the West against Soviet subversion. On the day after the bombing of the US Marine base, President Reagan discovered that this was indeed the very reason why the MNF were in Beirut. Lebanon, he announced:

> is central to our credibility on a global scale. We cannot pick and choose where we will support freedom, we can only determine how ... If Lebanon ends up under the tyranny of forces hostile to the West, not only will our strategic position in the eastern Mediterranean be threatened, but also the stability of the entire Middle East, including the vast resource areas of the Arabian peninsula.

It was a brutal irony that in Lebanon this fantasy was shared only by those against whom Reagan now promised retaliation. The young Iranians in Baalbek, the Lebanese Shia groups which identified Israel and America as a common enemy, the growing number of Muslim militiamen who drew their inspiration from Iran's titanic conflict with Iraq – they also believed that they were threatening the United States. They were indeed 'hostile to the West'. They were happy to be reassured that they were helping to destabilise the West's interests in the Middle East. To these young men – to the suicide bombers themselves – the conflict was on a global, epic scale. Were they not struggling to drive Satanic America out of the Islamic world?

But the forces which America was supporting or opposing around Beirut bore no relation to this exotic scenario. The Palestinian gunmen of Bhamdoun, the Druze militiamen in the hills above the airport, the

Syrian troops in the Bekaa would have been amazed to discover that they were playing a historic role in destroying the Western world's strategic position in the eastern Mediterranean, let alone threatening anything so grand as the 'vast resource areas' of the Arabian peninsula. They would come to believe it, however, if the Americans withdrew, a retreat that was made inevitable the moment Reagan discovered vital strategic interests in Lebanon. Thus did the film actor contrive to reassure his enemies of the reality of their mission.

While Reagan was defining the MNF's elaborate new role in Lebanon – and invading the small Caribbean island of Grenada, where some more American vital interests had been unearthed – we were still trying to answer two questions: who bombed the Marines, and how? The second question was easier to answer. Anderson and Labelle interviewed every surviving member of the 24th Marine Amphibious Unit prepared to talk to them. All agreed that the truck driver had been seen before the bombing. All who saw the truck said that it had turned left off the airport road into a car park used by airport employees and had circled the lot twice before smashing through the flimsy iron gate to the Marine compound.

Why had he made the double circle? Possibly because a car blocked his way before his initial attempt to ram the gate. Possibly because he was timing his attack to the second; the two bombers were obviously supposed to detonate their charges at the very same moment. Twenty seconds was their margin of error. Labelle immediately saw the significance of a large notice outside the American military compound, an instruction to the Marines which could be read by anyone passing the entrance to the US headquarters. 'Caution,' it said. 'Unload weapons before entering compound.' The Marines had been ordered to take their ammunition magazines out of their rifles when they went into their base.

Hour after hour, I sat in the Beirut offices of the American television networks, watching their video rushes of interviews with the Marines in case we had missed some clue. In the NBC bureau, I found tape of Lance Corporal Calhoun, a 27-year-old Marine who appeared on the screen with ear-plugs. His ears had been damaged by the explosion. He told the story of a colleague who was guarding 'Marine post 7' outside the BLT. The truck, he said, broke through the gate and, as it went by, his Marine comrade:

> tried to pull out a magazine – because we're not allowed to have one in our weapons. He tried to pull the bolt home. And by the time he got everything loaded, the bomb had exploded. He said all he could remember was that the man was smiling as he drove past.

Because we're not allowed to have one in our weapons. That was it. The Marines were ready for an attack outside their compound. But the Americans guarding their headquarters had no bullets in their rifles.

The Marines who had to protect the very heart and nerve-centre of their battalion – the most powerful unit within the multinational force – were effectively unarmed. Because the Marines were peace-keepers. Because they were only in Beirut to help the Lebanese, to support the Lebanese government. They had committed the cardinal error of so many foreign armies in Lebanon: they wanted to be liked by everyone and therefore persuaded themselves – against all the evidence to the contrary – that they *were* liked. The suicide bomber was smiling. Of course he was smiling. He was going to paradise.

Off-duty Marines in the American base had never been permitted to carry ammunition clips in their rifles but the rule had apparently been extended to the Marines on guard duty who were not actually at the compound perimeter. This meant that the bomber was almost invulnerable once he breached the compound fence. One Marine – a sergeant who was in the parking lobby of the BLT itself – did appear to have had just enough time to load his rifle and fire five rounds on automatic as the truck hurtled towards him and crashed through his sandbagged emplacement. He was killed, either by the lorry or the subsequent blast of 4,000 pounds of explosives which vaporised the suicide bomber and disintegrated even the truck's engine block of solid iron.

The Americans had received a more than adequate warning of what might happen to them: the destruction of the Marine base was an almost exact replica of the truck bombing of the American Embassy in April of the same year, an attack which was followed by an 'Islamic Jihad' promise to make further attacks on 'the imperialist presence in Lebanon, including the multinational force'. The Reagan administration's advisers – Geoffrey Kemp of the National Security Council, for example – did not hesitate to blame the disaster on 'military incompetence'. But the Marines died, too, through political incompetence. The visitors who came to Lebanon could not distinguish between the dream and the reality until it was too late.

Two days after the bombings, the stench of human decomposition was so dreadful that the Marines were issued with face masks. The Americans lined their perimeter fence and threatened to shoot anyone who approached their main gate. Outside my own home, I saw plain-clothes US security guards run from the joint British–American Embassy carrying shotguns. 'Get out of the way, they're coming here – there's a truck bomb on the way,' one of them shouted. All day, the Marines reported huge and mysterious lorries driving at speed along the airport road, weighed down at the axles, manned by smiling drivers. Beside the BLT ruins, a noticeboard had been erected with a pencilled message: 'Keep out – crime scene.'

US Vice-President George Bush arrived to view the desolation. The Marines were under rocket-propelled grenade attack so Bush put on a flak jacket and helmet to walk through the powdered cement of the BLT. 'We are not going to let a bunch of insidious terrorist cowards shake the foreign policy of the United States,' he declared. 'Foreign policy is not going to be dictated or changed by terror.' But it was. For America's enemies in Lebanon were not hit-and-run drivers. However insidious they were, cowardice was not their weakness. They were, to use a favourite American phrase, 'highly motivated'; more than that, they were absolutist. And secretive.

For despite the CIA investigations, the official inquiry into the bombing, the inspired leaks in Washington and Reagan's own abiding belief in 'international terrorism', the Amerians still have – to this day – no idea of the identity of the two young men who destroyed themselves when they drove their trucks into the US and French bases on 23 October 1983.

Our own inquiries gathered just a few details from Shia friends, including militiamen who were related by family to members of the pro-Iranian Hezbollah. These people insisted that the bombers were Lebanese, not Iranian, that they were Muslims – they would not make the distinction between Shia and Sunni – and that they were later honoured as martyrs. Their photographs, we were told, were pasted up on the walls of west Beirut with all the other militia martyrs. But on the posters, the circumstances of their death were obscured. The captions announced that the men had been 'martyred' in a Shia area of the city while fighting 'the enemies of Islam'.

The only other clue to their identity came in the inevitable telephone call to the Agence France Presse news agency. It was 'Islamic Jihad' again, the same man as before, speaking in Arabic. 'We have carried out this operation against the fortresses of reactionary imperialism to prove to the world that their naval and artillery firepower does not frighten us. We are the soldiers of God and we are fond of death. We are neither Iranians nor Syrians nor Palestinians. We are Lebanese Muslims who follow the principles of the Koran.'

In their search for culprits – any culprits – the American Embassy suggested that the Amal leader, Nabih Berri, might have been behind the bombings. The claim was vigorously denied by Berri, who said he had offered his condolences over the 'massacre' to an unnamed American diplomat. But he was unable to speak for Hussein Moussavi, the former vice-president of Amal who had been expelled from Berri's movement a year earlier in a dispute over the political direction of the militia and who now led a rival 'Islamic Amal' in Baalbek. 'I don't have to defend Hussein Moussavi,' Berri said. '. . . I'm not here to defend the others [sic].'

*   *   *

Baalbek, 27 October 1983

Anderson and I arrive outside Moussavi's house to find it guarded by several dozen armed and bearded young men, some of them in US Marine and Ranger uniforms. They offer no explanation for this. They speak of their movement not only as 'Islamic Amal' but as *Hezbil Allah*, the 'party of God'. Moussavi's office is behind the ruined Baalbek *serail*, a hundred-year-old villa with brightly painted shutters and a flowerpot outside the front door containing a dying plant. The hallway is clustered with posters of Ayatollah Khomeini and Imam Mousa Sadr. There are black flags around the building and cloth banners advocating 'Death to America'. The word 'martyr' appears on almost every one.

Moussavi is a former schoolmaster, a slim, effete man with a pointed, greying beard and aquiline features. His eyes are very dark. He shakes hands with us gravely, asking us our nationalities, who we work for. We ask him the old crank-handle question for difficult interviews. How do you see the situation, Mr Moussavi? He looks at us carefully, inspecting us, knowing full well that we have not come to Baalbek to seek his thoughts on national reconciliation. He talks for ten minutes about the aggression of foreigners. Anderson comes to the point. The American government says it suspects Moussavi's organisation staged the Marine bombings. Is this true?

Moussavi answers at once. 'As to this question – which is why you have come to Baalbek – I will tell you. I personally consider this deed is a good deed which God loves and which his Prophet – may God praise his name – loves. I bow before the souls of the martyrs who carried out this operation.' Moussavi sits back in his chair and glares at us with his dark eyes. They are not cruel eyes, nor are they suspicious. They are *watchful*, the eyes of a schoolmaster inspecting potentially unruly children.

I raise the question of martyrdom. Would Mr Moussavi like to explain this to us? He has still not answered Anderson's question. 'It is the duty of each Muslim whom Israel, America, France and all those other evil forces have oppressed or killed or helped to kill, or destroyed his home or occupied his land – it is the duty of every Muslim to counter evil with evil.' A black-turbaned mullah enters Moussavi's office and mutters in his left ear. Moussavi picks up where he was interrupted.

'God is capable of giving Muslims victory, whether the aggression comes from France or America or Italy or any other force. The Imam Ali says that we may throw the stone back from where it has been thrown and that evil cannot be repelled except by evil. Our Prophet Mohamed – praised be his name – has invoked us to carry the sword to defend our honour.'

But Moussavi has some decidedly political views with which he tries to justify his belief in violence. The Americans, he says, have come to Lebanon 'to achieve the results that America wants'. The MNF is a NATO force and America is dealing with 'some traditional leaders' in Lebanon while ignoring what Moussavi calls 'popular Islamic elements'. Then he answers Anderson's question. 'I insist that we have no relation whatsoever to last Sunday's incident on the Americans and the French. If all peace-loving peoples want peace with the Muslims, their only choice is to pressure their governments to withdraw their forces. Definitely there will be new operations against them ... I hope to participate in future operations.'

When Anderson and I are leaving the gaily painted, neat little house, one of the men in a US Ranger uniform demands Anderson's passport. Not mine. He only wants American passports. Anderson and I sit on the porch of the house and the man returns bearing a tin of Danish pastries. We each take a biscuit, thank him and wait. A few minutes later, another bearded gunman appears and gives Anderson his passport. He has made a photocopy of the passport; he is holding it in his hand, with Anderson's photograph clearly visible alongside his age and place of birth. We dismiss the incident as a symptom of their xenophobia. What on earth is the point of making a copy of Anderson's passport when we are *leaving*?

The bombings left Beirut in a state of siege — mental as well as physical — that often bordered on paranoia. It was obvious to everyone except the MNF that the Americans were going to leave. Thousands of Lebanese queued outside the American and French embassies for visas. Two of Anderson's Lebanese staff asked for his promise to evacuate them before the Marines left. Anderson called me down to his flat one afternoon to watch a battery of Hawk anti-aircraft missiles being installed on the roof of the neighbouring apartment, where many of the US Embassy security staff were housed. The Americans told us they had been warned by Washington that they should expect 'Shia suicide pilots'.

The Lebanese deuxième bureau — the very organisation that had failed to anticipate the suicide bombings — now warned the Americans that Soviet troops had been seen in the Bekaa, that a Soviet colonel had taken up residence in the village of Dour Choueir to command Syrian anti-aircraft batteries and forward artillery positions. The deuxième bureau, we suspected, had acquired this information from the Phalange, who were in turn still liaising with the Shin Bet security agency in Israel.

The reports were very specific. Russians had been seen in Chtaura. Not Soviet diplomats from Damascus, not even plain-clothes military personnel, but real live Soviet troops in grey uniforms with fur hats and a red star on the front, the whole shebang. I set off from Beirut one morning, travelling through checkpoints of the MNF, the Lebanese army and the Syrian army, and tramped around Chtaura, asking the bemused shopkeepers of that bucolic town if they had seen any Soviet troops driving past their stores. Of course, no one had.

I drove to Dour Choueir. The Soviet colonel and his staff officers, we had been told in Beirut, were living on the second floor of a building in the grounds of the Syrian brigade commander's requisitioned villa. The house in which the Russians allegedly lived was large, and it had a red roof. When I turned up at the villa I was taken to the Syrian deputy commander, who with much merriment escorted me to the house with the red roof. On the second floor, I found living not a Soviet colonel but the Lebanese man who maintained the garden in front of the brigade headquarters.

However firmly their correspondents in Beirut tried to 'kill' these specious reports, US television networks would give them currency, quoting 'reliable' Pentagon or State Department sources for their information. The wire agencies repeated these stories out of New York. Charles Douglas-Home called from London one afternoon. 'Bob, are you absolutely, really certain these reports are untrue? The Americans seem very sure about their facts.' But there *were* no facts.*

For every chimera we were able to destroy, the Americans produced another even more fanciful. Iranian suicide pilots were installed in Baalbek, we were informed. They were planning to attack the Sixth Fleet in gliders which had already arrived in Baalbek from Syria and were now stored in large metal containers in the surrounding countryside. The gliders had been manufactured in the Soviet Union. And they were made of wood.

It was a sign of our infinite weariness that Labelle and I actually set off for Baalbek one morning to interview these ghostly aviators beside their wooden flying machines. The only containers we found lay rusting in some fields south of the city, inhabited by destitute Kurds, their washing flapping from the branches of a tree.

It was fantastic, ludicrous. We were driving around Lebanon looking for the substance of dreams and nightmares. The Western powers were daily feeding their imagination with the danger of evil conspiracies against them. The Plot. In this sense, the success of the suicide bombers continued long after the fork-lift truck at Beirut airport had slotted the last of their victims in metal caskets aboard the Hercules that was to take them home. The West was on the run.

---

* McFarlane is reported to have believed that the Soviets were behind the chaos in Beirut. It was Reagan himself who had started the rumours on 8 October when he asked, apropos of Lebanon: 'Can the United States or the free world stand by and see the Middle East incorporated into the Soviet bloc?'

Gemayel and the *zuama* of Lebanon eventually held their 'reconciliation' conference in Geneva. I flew there from Beirut to watch the rituals. Suleiman Franjieh publicly embraced Gemayel, thus apparently ending the blood feud between the two families. Chamoun spoke to Franjieh for the first time in five years. Jumblatt took a camera to the conference chamber to take pictures of the old men, 'these antiques' as he called them. They agreed on Lebanon's 'Arab identity', a definition which cracked the formula that Lebanon belonged neither to East nor West. Gemayel agreed with Jumblatt, Franjieh and Berri that he would not ratify the 17 May withdrawal agreement with Israel but would search instead for a replacement treaty to guarantee the departure of Israeli troops.

America's torture was exquisite. Desperate to prevent a further round of fighting in Beirut, US diplomats urged Gemayel to compromise with his pro-Syrian opponents. But to do this, Gemayel had to abandon the 17 May treaty. The Americans were thus forced to assist in the burial of their only political achievement in Lebanon. Even as they did so, the suicide bombers attacked again, this time against the new Israeli military headquarters in Tyre, killing 60 Israelis and Shin Bet prisoners.

When I returned to Beirut, I found that nothing had changed. The Marines were sniped at by Shia militiamen in Hay al-Sellum. Anderson, Mell and Faramarzi spent a hair-raising afternoon with the Shia gunmen, running from wall to wall as the Marines fired 'flechettes' — rockets that turned a human body into purée — onto the roofs of the civilian houses. Some of the gunmen were Hezbollah, but Anderson risked his life with them. 'The Marines have gone mad,' he said on his return. 'Have they any idea what they're doing?'

Anderson and I attended a Marine press briefing by three US officers responsible for media relations. Theirs was a weekly meeting which we attended even though our fear outweighed our spirit of journalistic inquiry. The airport road was under mortar fire, the USS *Biddel* was firing into the Chouf and the Marines' howitzers were shooting in the same direction. After a few minutes, incoming shells exploded around the Marine base and we were ordered into the bunkers.

And there, deep beneath the ramparts of earth, the three young American officers dedicated to the preservation of truth and good press relations read off a list of recent incidents together with the latest statement from the White House on America's participation in the multinational force. 'The point you guys have to remember,' one of them shouted above the din of gunfire, 'is that we are still here on a peace mission.'

On 17 November, the French attacked the Iranian revolutionary guards and militiamen of Hussein Moussavi's 'Islamic Amal' at Baalbek. The two groups had recently expropriated the local Lebanese army barracks above Baalbek and this was the target which the French tried to destroy. For an hour and a half, 14 Super-Etendard fighter-bombers — taking off at dusk from the French carrier *Clemenceau* off Beirut — raided the hilltop of Ras al-Ain, a classical necropolis high above the Roman temples at Baalbek.

The French government boasted that their air force had scored 'direct hits' on the barracks and on the Khawam Hotel which served as a headquarters for 'Islamic Amal'. In Baalbek, I found that the French planes had missed. The Iranians took me into their 'Imam Ali barracks' where a few rockets had exploded, but most of the bombs had detonated on a series of small hills half a mile away, destroying no more than some olive trees. The Khawam Hotel was undamaged. Not a single pane of glass in its windows had been broken. The only damage inflicted on Baalbek as the planes came in over the Temple of Bacchus was a small hole in the roof of the famous old Palmyra Hotel, where a piece of shrapnel entered the bedroom of the local Swiss International Red Cross delegate.

The Americans and French built massive defensive walls around their compounds in Beirut, reinforcing 20-foot earth revetments with concrete and iron grids. Around the four-mile circumference of the airport, the Marines — who were, according to one of their own commanders, living in a 'threat-a-day environment'* — built an underground warren of cellars, tunnels and ventilation shafts, deeper, more elaborate than any defences previously erected in Beirut. They filled a million and a half sandbags to line their subterranean world. Politically unable to withdraw to their ships, militarily incapable of controlling the city, they now retreated downwards, into the earth. Not since the Crusades had so many soldiers built so complex a defensive system in Lebanon. Their enemies would have no chance of striking again.

But they would. Even as the Marines at Beirut airport were using lumber to shore up their underground bunkers beside the Mediterranean, the American and French embassies were being devastated by massive explosions — in Kuwait. The Kuwaitis arrested 17 men, several of them Lebanese, all of them members of 'Islamic Jihad'. The Americans had claimed that there was an international conspiracy against them, but they had not believed their own propaganda.

Certainly, the Americans now made no attempt to disguise their growing military alliance with Israel. In November 1983, Lawrence Eagleburger, the US under secretary of state, offered to 'reinvigorate the strategic dialogue' with Israel, which had been suspended after the Israeli raid on the Iraqi nuclear reactor and then again after the invasion

---

* Still deluged with useless intelligence information from the Lebanese deuxième bureau, Brigadier-General James R. Joy remarked at a Marine news conference on 21 November 1983 that 'we could probably paper the bulkhead with threats — and we take every one of them very seriously.'

of Lebanon. Moshe Arens, the new Israeli defence minister, even hinted that Israel might coordinate military action with the US in Lebanon.

Yet the Americans were still trapped in Beirut, still supporting Gemayel's government. And so were the French, even if their commitment to restore Lebanon's sovereignty had undergone a subtle shift of emphasis. This was captured in a phrase used by Claude Cheysson, the French foreign minister, on 2 December 1983, when he said that the French would not 'abandon the Lebanese'. He hoped that Gemayel's government would 'represent Lebanon in its entirety so that the process of national reconciliation can continue and lead to a truly representative force.'

In Cheysson's view, it would be 'irresponsible' of the MNF to leave Lebanon at such a critical time. This became a new refrain, increasingly adopted by the Americans: that the MNF was in Lebanon to give the Lebanese more time to work out their differences. The battles between MNF troops and the militias, the naval bombardments, the sacrifice of so many lives in Beirut, all were apparently now part of the MNF's duty to buy time for Lebanese politicians. The MNF was to be a timekeeper, a referee ready to judge the degree of reconciliation before calling an end to the match. Yet France's determination not to 'abandon the Lebanese' paid little heed to the fact that a very large number of Lebanese now wanted to be abandoned by the MNF.

Under Shia and Druze mortar fire in December, the Marines called for naval fire support and two warships took up station in Jounieh bay to shell the Metn. There seemed no end to the lengths the United States would go in this meaningless war. The naval bombardments did not prevent the shelling of the Marines. Would they now use their enormous maritime air power?

We knew the US naval air squadron wanted to involve themselves in the battle. Their pilots had told us this themselves when we visited the carrier *Eisenhower* off Beirut that autumn. They had painted a new insignia on their F-14s. On each tail fin stood a skeleton cowled in a black shroud and holding a crooked sword. From the end of the sword dripped blood. They called themselves the 'Ghost Squadron'. They could not wait to visit Lebanon.

When they did, it was a débâcle. On 4 December, the Americans staged an air raid against Syrian batteries in the Bekaa. One of their aircraft was shot down by a missile and its pilot killed. His co-pilot was captured by the Syrians and only released in January 1984 through the intervention of Jesse Jackson, the black American Democrat who was an opponent of Reagan.

There was only one weapon still to be used, and we all knew what that was. On 14 December, Farouk Nassar and I were discussing the violent mutiny within Yassir Arafat's PLO when a concussion wave smashed against the walls of the AP office. It was not a car bomb. The noise was too all embracing, too deep, too powerful even for Lebanon's suicide bombers. The whole city rang with the sound. We climbed to the roof. There was another great explosion, exactly as before. The blast wave passed right over us. Then another. It was Nassar who noticed that 30 seconds after each blast, we could hear a small, muffled explosion, far way in the mountains to the east. Then we understood. I drove Nassar down to Raouche, to the windy clifftop above the Pigeon Rocks, and there, two miles offshore, steaming northwards amid an escort of missile cruisers and destroyers, was the great leviathan, the final instrument of American policy in Lebanon. The old monster was being used at last.

It was like a spell, an inverted magic that held you in its awe for half a minute. The barrels would bloom fire, a big tulip of golden flame as long as the battleship, a gaseous sunlit balloon that would evaporate in the evening sky. In silence. The sound took 30 seconds. Then the concussion wave would swamp us as the wind might slam a dungeon door in a great castle. Nassar was transfixed. '*Habibi*, this is in-cre-di-ble.' The flame again, an onion-burst of light reaching out greedily from the for'ard guns, sweeping up the sky above west Beirut. And then the little, tell-tale, harmless reverberation far across the mountains. 'For the violence done to Lebanon ...'

Tibiyat, central Lebanon, 13 February 1984

Wadad Swaid is lying in her hospital bed, bending her head away from us so that we should not see the full extent of the burns and cuts that have slashed across her face. There is a dark blue weal across her forehead and a series of vivid crimson marks that run down her cheeks. Her white scarf falls from her hair as she describes the night on which the *New Jersey* — retaliating for attacks on the Christian sector of Beirut, according to President Reagan — fired onto her village. Less than a week ago the Americans agreed to leave Lebanon, but the war has not ended. Mell and Faramarzi of AP are with me, leaning close to the woman's bed to hear her words.

Wadad Swaid is 51, the mother of nine children and one of 250 people who live in Tibiyat, a Druze village that rests in a narrow valley of vines and pine trees east of Beirut, just inside the area occupied by the Syrians. Her brother-in-law has been killed in the *New Jersey's* bombardment and she talks about God when she describes her loss. She speaks softly, anxious not to lose control of her emotions:

We were hiding in the basement of the house. We had turned two rooms into a shelter in the basement. There were twenty-five of us, including children. We were sitting on the floor and lined up next to one another.

At first we heard a huge explosion, then the wall fell on our heads. I could not breathe. The wall next to me came on top of me. I looked for my husband and saw concrete on his head. All of us started screaming.

Fifteen of Wadad Swaid's neighbours inside the house have been wounded. The villagers tell us that two of them were children so mentally disturbed by the experience that they were taken screaming in an ambulance to Damascus with six wounded men. The Druze militiamen in Tibiyat say that 24 civilians were killed and 115 wounded in the 30 miles of Metn and Chouf foothills by the American naval bombardment and, given the state of some of the wounded women in the Al Jebel hospital, the figure is plausible. Many have bright pink, purple faces and burnt arms. They are suffering from flash burns.

We walk through the cold forest outside Tibiyat. The craters are fringed with snow but they are not hard to find. The *New Jersey*'s shells have smashed five feet deep into the forest floor west of Hammana, opening wounds in the earth 15 feet in width and blasting the pine trees for a quarter of a mile in every direction. Mell climbs into a crater and pulls hard on a piece of steel. It has already acquired a thin veneer of rust from the night rains. I help him pull it from the earth, a foot long, three inches thick, so heavy we have to carry it together back to our car. There are 18-inch shards with razor-sharp edges that have snapped off the branches of tall trees like matchwood and punched holes in the wall of a house beside the mud track.

In Tibiyat, a huge crater lies beside the broken basement where Wadad Swaid and her family took shelter. Inside the crushed and snow-covered building, we find the beds and mattresses, some of them blood-stained, on which the families were trying to hide from the shellfire.

But there are unanswered questions in the Metn hills upon which the *New Jersey* has vented its anger. A young girl who follows our car in the village of Tibiyat is prevented from talking to us by a Druze militiaman. In the hospital, another Druze gunman takes three doctors aside before we are allowed to ask questions of medical staff. There are rumours in the area that Syrian officers were killed in the bombardment. A Druze militiaman becomes nervous when we ask about Syrian casualties. 'Do you speak Russian?' he suddenly asks. Were there, perhaps, Russians in Hammana, just as there had been American Marines secretly staking out the hill ridges around Beit Meri? Who were the six wounded men taken to hospital in Damascus with the two deranged children? Or are we now suffering from the same delusions as the diplomats in Beirut?

Or did Lebanon induce this neurosis in all who lived there, Lebanese and foreigners alike, an inappropriateness of response that left the adversaries endlessly repeating themselves? Amid another burst of militia fighting in west Beirut, a proposal for another 'reconciliation' conference, a set of constitutional reforms that would deprive Gemayel of real political power and turn him into a figurehead, transferring the Lebanese army from Christian to Muslim control. All this amid the shellfire. Lebanon turned Clausewitz on his head. It made politics the logical extension of war.

We lost count of the ceasefires that winter. Marines under fire. US navy bombards Druze. Israel attacks targets in Bekaa. The sub-headings on the AP wire induced nervousness rather than boredom. We would check the computer date at the bottom of the page. Was this today's copy or last week's, or last month's? Had history doomed everyone in Lebanon to a series of repeat performances? In December of 1983, MNF warships assisted in the evacuation of Yassir Arafat and his PLO from Lebanon. Had we not reported this in 1982?

With more passion perhaps. Arafat's last stand in Lebanon was a miserable affair. His guerrilla organisation had broken apart after the evacuation from Beirut, just as we suspected it would. In adversity, the PLO discovered its own corruption and sought to cleanse its movement by indulging in that most contemptible of disputes, a murderous, fratricidal war. Those who wished to purge Arafat's ranks of the PLO men who had made money from the Lebanon war, of those who had run away from southern Lebanon at the start of the Israeli invasion, of those who dared to talk of recognising Israel, found an ally in Damascus.

With more determination to destroy the PLO politically than Israel ever demonstrated militarily, Assad's government indulged and funded a mutiny. A rival PLO office opened its doors in Damascus wherein sat Mahmoud Labadi, Arafat's factotum of just 18 months before. Through coercion and weakness, the Palestinian guerrillas in the Bekaa were suborned. Of the 10,000 who remained behind after 1982, only 4,000 stayed loyal to Arafat, and they were driven north across the mountains of the cedars to Tripoli.

In that northern city, Arafat then endured his last trial in Lebanon, a struggle not against the 'Zionist aggressors' but against Palestinians who only a year and a half before had defended west Beirut under Arafat's command. The two Palestinian camps of Badawi and Nahr al-Bared were besieged by the mutineers, assisted by Lebanese Baathists and Syrian artillery batteries which shelled not only Arafat's men but the civilian population of Tripoli. Arafat's ally was a fundamentalist Sunni militia that wished to turn all Lebanon into an Islamic republic.

The siege of Tripoli – which painfully, if on an infinitesimally smaller scale, re-enacted the siege of Beirut – was one of the most shameful episodes in the PLO's history. Anderson and I would drive through the shattered city, run through the shellfire to the 'Islamic hospital' and ask for the number of victims. Outside the building there stood a refrigerated meat lorry packed with civilian bodies, each wrapped carefully in a plastic sack. 'Is this yours?' I heard the driver call to a family one afternoon as he pulled a young girl from her sheath. Her long, golden hair tumbled across his arms, her head fell, turning as if in life to look at us.

Arafat was at his most tenacious, irritating, resourceful and ruthless. He bargained for ceasefires just as he had in Beirut. He sat one day bareheaded, quite bald, in his little office, pleading with me not to ask about the friends who had betrayed him. 'Please do not ask me this, you must not ...' He had put his head in his hands. He blamed Syria, he blamed traitors, he blamed Israel and America. He blamed The Plot. On 20 December, he announced that the Palestinian cause remained sacred, that the blood of his martyrs would assure his people ultimate political and military success. Then he set off on a fleet of Greek cruise boats with his 4,000 guerrillas, bound for Tunis on another seaborne evacuation, escorted by five French warships and an aircraft carrier. When we arrived on the 1983 Tripoli quayside, we watched 1982 Beirut all over again.

There were the same victory signs, the same bursts of gunfire, in many cases the same faces. We had seen them all before and here they were again in another expensive production of the same old epic. After humiliating defeat, Yassir Arafat turns disgrace into mythical victory, persuading his 4,000 men that they are on their way to Palestine and sailing off into the sunset on a dreamboat appropriately named *Odysseus*. They left behind them, as usual, another Lebanese city they had helped to destroy.

They took everything with them, their Mercedes limousines, their broken lorries, torn blankets, used tyres and garbage cans, like children unwilling to part with old toys lest they leave anything for the Syrians and the Palestinians who had betrayed them. It was pathetic and demeaning, an image of a homeless people in retreat and a leader with nowhere to lead them. The Lebanese policeman on the quayside put it succinctly. 'Finito,' he said.

The ritual of defeat had become almost as familiar as the story of Palestine, which always seemed to involve people arriving from exile or going into exile on boats. One noticed how old they had become, Arafat's loyal 4,000, how some of them walked the dockside with the aid of sticks, not because they had been wounded but because they had been fighting far too long; and how quickly some of the younger men forgot the damning reasons for their jubilation.

There was a youth on the quayside who raised his left hand in the victory salute, balanced an anti-tank rocket-launcher on his shoulder, opened his mouth to protect his ears from the air pressure and loosed off a missile across the heads of the thousands around him. Only when we smelled his breath did we realise he had been drinking. Three Israeli jets flew overhead, but Arafat's warriors threw hand grenades into the harbour for amusement, the underwater explosions banging like a hammer against the hulls of the ships that were to rescue them. A local Sunni militiaman, unshaven, newly acquired PLO gun in his hands, lounged opposite the ships and sneered at the evacuees. 'They were worthless and now we are free to do what we want.'

There were other images. There were young men tired from combat, embracing wives but still unable to stop looking backwards to the mountains above Badawi where they lost their last battle. There was a girl, a very pretty young woman with dark hair, who stood at one end of the quay dressed in a black suit and scarf, watching silently, without moving, for an hour.

And there at the finale, as always, was Arafat, travelling to the *Odysseus* in a Range Rover so thick with bodyguards that you could not see him through the glass. Just once on the stern we glimpsed him, kissing a young man on both cheeks, grinning and giving a double-handed victory salute before his bodyguards ordered him from the sight of potential assassins.

In Beirut, the end came equally dramatically but with less rhetoric. In January, Malcolm Kerr, the president of the American University who had fought so hard for US funds for his Lebanese students, was murdered on his campus by 'Islamic Jihad', shot in the head with a silenced pistol. The Druze and the Shia fired at the Marines again. A pervasive anti-Western mood took hold in the streets. Posters of burning American flags appeared on the walls. In Hamra, an American woman was stopped on the pavement by a bearded young man who pointed at her head with his finger and said, very quietly and slowly, 'Bang-bang.' Then he walked away without smiling.

In February, Shia militiamen in Bourj al-Barajneh attacked the Lebanese army across eight square miles of slums. Anderson drove to Galerie Semaan with Mell and me. The sunlit ruins echoed with tank and sniper fire. Mell took one look at the Lebanese soldiers and their Phalangist allies – the two forces were now fighting together, in some cases joining each other's units in opposition to the Muslims – and curled his upper lip. 'They are losing,' he said. He had told Faramarzi that the previous day. How did he know?

'Listen to them, Robert. Listen to the way they are speaking.' The Phalangists and soldiers talked to us about national unity. A militiaman called Walid showed us a shell crater. 'The shell came from the Druze in the mountains. They killed five soldiers here.' He was raising his voice. 'One had his arm cut off. One had his legs cut off.' Walid pointed to a wall and walked up to it and knelt on one knee against some dried blood at the bottom of it. He was shouting now. 'I found one like this, on one knee, and I wondered what was wrong but his head had come

off. The Druze did it.' The bombardment was growing noisier and a
steady crashing sound was drowning his words as shoals of bullets raced
between the apartment blocks to the west. The ground trembled every
few seconds but Walid was still shouting. 'The Druze. The Druze.'

He walked back to a little office in a basement. He kept touching a
hand grenade at his belt, then he unhooked the grenade and began
playing with the pin. 'This is normal for me,' he said. 'Killing doesn't
matter to me. When I saw my friend's head blown off, my mind was so
hard. It is normal now to kill and kill everybody — everybody who
wants to partition Lebanon.' One of Walid's comrades came in, a
civilian with an automatic rifle who nodded vigorously at everything
Walid said. 'We are fighting against all the people, against all the world.
We are fighting against Khomeini, Sri Lanka, Filipinos, Iran ... We
are not impressed by America. They are strong in their bombs but they
need two million years to become like a 15-year-old boy in Lebanon. We
are used to this battle and to killing.'

Mell whispered to me: 'See what I mean?' Outside, we found an old
man standing in a cracked doorway, a woman and two children beside
him. We walked over to the man as he stood listening to the battle,
watching a Lebanese tank manoeuvre clumsily into a narrow street to
fire at the Shia militias behind the crumbled masonry of St Michel's
church, the same church where Cody and I had watched the Palestinian
boys singing their revolutionary song at the end of the first civil war
eight years before.

He was a refugee for the third time, he said. The Druze had twice
driven him out of Hammana and the Shia had thrown him out of Galerie
Semaan. Eight years ago, hooded gunmen had cut the throat of his
eldest son because they thought he was a Maronite Christian. He was a
Catholic. The old man had not shaved for many days. 'I have lost my
homes,' he said. 'I have lost everything. I have nowhere to go. All I can
do is watch this.'

On the airport road that afternoon, 5 February 1984, I saw Lebanese
soldiers abandon three tanks and walk into the southern suburbs. They
were deserting. With half his capital under shellfire, Gemayel now
accepted the resignation of his Cabinet in the hope that a national
coalition government could be formed to prevent the civil war consuming
all Beirut. Chafiq Wazzan, his prime minister, handed in his resignation
with the words: 'I hope — rather I insist — that you accept it immediately.'
In the evening, I drove the airport road again. There were bearded Shia
gunmen now. The Marines were cut off.

Next morning, the dam broke. Anderson and Faramarzi, travelling
back from the Marines, saw hooded gunmen running down Corniche
Mazraa. At Raouche, Mell caught sight of militiamen staging a company
attack on an armoured unit of Lebanese troops. He jumped into the

army post, took several photographs of the soldiers and realised that they were fighting for their lives. With grenades exploding above him, he ran away.

In Hamra Street, there were bursts of rifle fire. The Lebanese soldiers guarding the Information Ministry would not talk to me. They sat in the foyer, guns at their sides, refusing to fight. And then a mass of shouting, terrified motorists began driving crazily out of the commercial centre of west Beirut, fists bunched over their horns, sometimes colliding with each other, their vehicles leaping onto the pavements surrounded by screaming pedestrians, all fleeing Hamra. I stood in a doorway and down the road came a motorcycle, and on the cycle was a man wearing a black leather hood, holding the handlebar in his right hand while his left gripped the stock of a Kalashnikov. The gunmen were back.

Outside the Moscow Narodny bank near the prime minister's office, I came across a green-uniformed militiaman. He had a smart, thin beard and wore a camouflage jacket with a Koranic quotation on the breast pocket and beneath it the symbol of a white, curved Arabic sword. He was directing traffic, ordering some young men to guard the nearest apartment blocks from looters, all the time grinning benignly at the frightened motorists. Our new protectors had arrived.

Two days earlier, President Reagan had admitted that 'the situation in Lebanon is difficult, frustrating and dangerous. But this is no reason to turn our backs on friends and to cut and run. If we do, we'll be sending one signal to terrorists everywhere: they can gain by waging war against innocent people.' Now, this very afternoon, with the Marines cut off, with west Beirut in the hands of Muslim militias, Reagan spoke again. 'The commitment of the United States to the unity, independence and sovereignty of Lebanon remains firm and unwavering.' Truly, Washington was a universe away.

That night, the Lebanese army – or rather the Christian units still loyal to Gemayel – shelled west Beirut mercilessly with the new artillery that Gemayel had purchased from the Americans. Almost a hundred civilians were killed in the bombardment, which set houses on fire across the city. We had seen nothing like it since the Israeli siege. The Lebanese government army had broken apart into rival Christian and Muslim factions. There was no longer a Lebanese army for the multinational force to support. An American diplomat in Beirut called it 'our worst nightmare'.

A few hours later, Reagan announced that the Marines in Beirut would be 'redeployed' to their ships in the Mediterranean. Redeployed. Like Napoleon's redeployment from Moscow, as an American cartoonist suggested. Like Custer's last redeployment. Like the British redeployment from Dunkirk. It meant the collapse of America's policy in the Levant, the final denouement to Israel's bloody adventure in Lebanon.

The British contingent scuttled out of Beirut first, without telling its MNF colleagues that it was leaving, driving at speed to the port of Jounieh and departing with such haste for a British warship that it left two of its military trucks on the quayside for the Phalange. The Italians stayed longer, guarding the Palestinian civilians whom they had faithfully protected for 17 months until they were satisfied that the Amal militia would perform the same humanitarian mission. Their trust was fatally misplaced. *'Beirut Addio'* one of the Italian soldiers wrote in letters five feet high over his command post in Ouzai. Goodbye Beirut.

The Americans and British airlifted most of their citizens to warships which took them to Cyprus.* Anderson's wife and daughter Gabrielle left. Gabrielle's school had been shelled the previous night and she was frightened. Anderson had called me to his apartment and asked me whether I thought his family should leave. I asked Gabrielle if she wanted to leave Beirut. She sat there in her pigtails and big spectacles and said nothing for almost a minute. Then she nodded and looked at her mother. Anderson put them both aboard the US navy helicopter.

American and British college teachers and businessmen and their families climbed aboard the helicopters taking them out to the ships. I saw an American girl, a student from New York, arguing with the Marines who were to remain behind and guard the British–American Embassy next to my home. 'You wasted your time here,' she told four of them. 'You failed in everything you did.' A black sergeant interrupted her. 'We were fighting terrorism. We're getting you out for your own safety.' The girl was in tears. 'You're not,' she shouted. 'You came here and turned my friends into my enemies and my home into a place of fear.' The black Marine shrugged and walked away.

Four days before the last of the American MNF contingent were due to leave, Reagan acknowledged that the reason for their 'redeployment' was because 'once the terrorist attacks started, there was no way that we could really contribute to the original mission by staying there as a target ...' Indeed not. Reagan was walking away from Lebanon like a man abandoning a wrecked car.

Abu Mustapha from Baalbek inherited the American land base in Lebanon. A burly man with a massive black beard and the smile of a giant, he drove through the rusting metal barrier of the Marine head-

* So embarrassed were American diplomats by the turn of events in Beirut that they initially tried to prevent press coverage of the evacuation. When Don Mell of AP arrived on the Corniche to photograph the departure, US Marines forbade him to take pictures, even though friendly militiamen with rifles were passing through the American checkpoints. When Mell asked John Stewart, the US Embassy press officer, for an explanation, Stewart replied: 'It's not because your camera is dangerous. It's because some people consider the results, the reactions to the photographs, might be dangerous or – I don't know how to put it – damaging to the foreign policy or something like that.' (Notes of conversation in memorandum of 9 February 1984 from Eileen Powell of AP to Terry Anderson.)

quarters in a stolen Lebanese army personnel carrier with a picture of Imam Mousa Sadr plastered over the front. His Shia militiamen saluted him when he turned to look at the last US troops sailing out to sea. 'We're here to stop anyone taking over,' he shouted. 'Want to come up here on my tank? Welcome.' *Sic transit gloria.*

The first thing the militiamen found were the body bags left behind by the Americans, heavy green plastic sheets that were dutifully paraded before a beaming Abu Mustapha. The scavengers were at work across the bunkers and sandbagged emplacements even before the last Marines had left the beach. They came out of the ground, out of the man-made shell-proof holes, with old chairs and boxes of dehydrated food and mattresses and American milk, ignoring the two beautifully groomed sad dogs which lay panting in the sun by a bunker labelled 'Hotel Company', waiting for their faithless masters to return. There were old copies of *Stars and Stripes*, a million and a half sandbags, some empty beer cans and the words 'Bronx—Manhattan—New Jersey' spray-painted on a wall. The Americans' bequest to Lebanon.

Perhaps the garbage that retreating armies leave behind does not tell you much about them. The Marines had been decent young men, for the most part, desperate to be liked, hopelessly ignorant of the world to which their president had sent them. Like the Palestinians who had left Lebanon only two months before, they knew it was not a famous victory. Although Reagan, had he been standing there in the Lebanese sand, would have applauded their passing. Golden flares trickled down the pale blue spring sky, Old Glory snapped from the radio aerials of the great armoured amphibians approaching the water, and the very last line troops crouched in the dunes by the main gate like a frieze from one of those old wartime movies that Reagan enjoyed.

The Marines shrugged when we asked them what they thought had gone wrong. Some said it was the Lebanese army. They did not understand how soldiers could refuse to obey orders. 'It just didn't work out,' one said. Staff Sergeant Jerry Elokonich, the very last Marine to leave, was whimsical. 'We did our job,' he said. 'And you see that surf down there? That tells it all.'

Not quite, for there were ghosts around the Marine perimeter. Without ceremony or memorial, the Americans left a broken concrete platform beside the airport, all that remained of that dreadful day in October when Lebanon showed Americans how bloody was their travail in this land. Up on the hills behind the remnants of that army, a phosphorus shell exploded like a memento, a fluffy white cloud that drifted cynically along the mountain ridge to remind Americans of the war they failed to stop. Their militia enemies had surrounded them in their last days. Where were their enemies now?

The American navy found some an hour after the last Marines were at sea. They brought the old battleship *New Jersey* towards the shore for one long broadside, to the astonishment of the Lebanese strolling along the beach. There again was the golden fire spreading out across the sea, the cataclysmic sound. It would look good on prime time television in the States that night.

What was the ship firing at? It had no effect on the Shia Muslim militiamen who calmly drove into the last American bastion on the tideline at Green Beach and hoisted a green Islamic flag where the Stars and Stripes had been lowered a few hours before. Thus the Americans left Lebanon, their last boats trailing a wake through the polluted water to the sound of gunfire.

Six days later, the commander of the *New Jersey*, Captain R. D. Milligan, was interviewed by the Associated Press at the El Pasha nightclub in the Israeli port of Haifa. 'I think the battleship is a definite weapon of peace,' he said. 'And I hope we have made some impact on bringing peace to Lebanon.'*

---

* *Daily Star* (Beirut) 5 March 1984, quoting AP report from Haifa of 4 March.

15 The Retreat

> Airplane come down to us,
> Fly us off to Lebanon,
> We will fight for Sharon,
> And return in a coffin.
>
> Israeli soldiers' song, set to the melody of a Hebrew nursery
> rhyme, southern Lebanon *January 1983*

The pariah of Lebanon became the honoured guest of Syria in just 24 hours. When Amin Gemayel arrived at Damascus airport on 29 February 1984, President Assad accorded him a 21-gun salute. The man who had been denigrated as a lackey of America and Israel, as a Phalangist stooge who had no legal status in his country – whose Cabinet had for months been insolently described on Damascus radio as 'Gemayel's Phalangist government' – was now welcomed by Assad as 'His Excellency President Amin Gemayel of Lebanon'. Israel had lost the war.

The Israelis had known they were losing for more than a year. Between September 1982, when the Israeli army had pulled out of Beirut after the Palestinian massacres, and mid-January the following year, Lebanese and Palestinian guerrillas killed 17 Israeli soldiers and wounded more than 70 in grenade, mine and shooting attacks.[*] In November 1982, the Israeli press reported that 'a number of terrorist cells ... are being reactivated by PLO officers who are believed to have infiltrated back into southern Lebanon.'[†] Two months later, Rafael Eitan, the Israeli chief of staff during the invasion, was warning that 'the war in Lebanon is formally over – but in effect, it goes on.' Israel could expect 'another hundred years of terror'. This was not the prospect which had filled the hearts of the Israeli soldiers who fought their way up to Beirut in June 1982, and who had – by the beginning of 1983 – suffered 455 dead and 2,460 wounded.

Gemayel's visit to Damascus now consecrated Lebanon's 'Arab identity' and formed a prelude to the official abrogation of the treaty which his

---

[*] See *The Times*, 14 January 1983, 'Israel's fed-up troops look to home' by Christopher Walker.
[†] *Jerusalem Post*, 1 November 1982.

country had solemnly signed with Israel the previous May.* Four days after returning to Beirut, he announced that the Lebanese–Israeli accord would henceforth be considered 'null and void'. In the months to come, particularly at the second 'reconciliation' conference which was held in Lausanne in the spring of 1983, the Lebanese were at pains to emphasise the American pressure that had been applied to them to accept the accord. 'You cannot imagine what the Americans put us through to sign,' the Lebanese minister, Elie Salem, told me in Lausanne. 'Their pressure was immoral. "If you do not sign this, we will abandon you," they said. What could we do? We are a small country.'†

The Israelis tended to blame not American pressure – which in Israel's case only came in very small spoonfuls – but American over-confidence. David Kimche, who as director-general of the Israeli foreign ministry signed the agreement for Israel on 17 May 1983, said that he was impressed by US assurances that Assad would withdraw Syrian troops from Lebanon. 'We had a very persuasive guy breathing down our necks, Philip Habib, who was pushing us and pushing us and pushing us to get this agreement done,' Kimche said. 'If we get this done, he told us, the United States will see to it that Syria withdraws its troops as soon as we sign the agreement. This was a very important factor for us. Phil Habib was saying: "Don't worry – we'll deliver. You guys don't have to worry about this."' The agreement, Kimche said, was 'not so much a "peace treaty" but as near as we could get to a *de facto* relationship, as near to peace as we could get in the circumstances.'‡

In occupied southern Lebanon, however, Israel's own policies ensured that such a peace could never be obtained. The withdrawal agreement spoke of 'mutual respect' and non-belligerency between Israel and Lebanon, but the Israeli military authorities were already giving the overwhelmingly Shia Muslim population of the south a taste of what Israeli friendship meant. Even while west Beirut was under siege, the Israeli army was expanding its control across a thousand square miles of

---

* Gemayel's decision to fly to Damascus was taken when the Americans made it clear they were deserting him. After the last MNF Marines had left Beirut, Gemayel asked for further US naval fire support for Christian units of his army in their battle with the Druze. The Americans, who had no desire to send their Marines back to what Weinberger now called 'a particularly miserable assignment', very sensibly turned him down.

† Salem committed the familiar Lebanese mistake of drawing strength from a totally illusory idea of his country's importance in world affairs. Lecturing the foreign press in a gallery of pseudo-Impressionist art at the Sursock museum in east Beirut on 27 January 1983, he had acknowledged Israel's claim that Lebanon should 'never again be used as a base for operations against it' but refused to allow military monitoring stations on Lebanese soil 'that might compromise the security of Lebanon, the security of Syria . . .' The presence of Israeli troops in southern Lebanon, he said, was unacceptable. But his speech was marred by an emotional claim that the partition of Lebanon would bring about the end of the human race. Even Reagan had not gone quite this far.

‡ David Kimche, interview with the author, Tel Aviv, 16 April 1987.

occupied Lebanese territory by creating new private armies to augment the already existing Christian-led militias. While Major Haddad's men moved into Sidon in the company of the Phalange, Shin Bet operatives hired hundreds of local gunmen — some of them former members of Amal — to control the Shia villages, sometimes inside the United Nations operational area.

By late June 1982, the UNIFIL force in the south discovered — to quote its own report — that 'new armed groups, re-equipped and controlled by the Israeli forces, appeared in parts of the UNIFIL area. These armed persons, recruited from the local population and variously referred to by the Israeli forces as "national guard" or "civil guard", attempted to establish checkpoints and patrol the villages. In some locations, the ill-disciplined behaviour of these irregulars led to friction with other inhabitants ...'* In many cases, the 'national guard' turned out to contain local criminals or gunmen who had previously worked with the Palestinian guerrillas in the south.

While senior Israeli officers settled into the Lebanese governor's administrative headquarters in Sidon — they evicted him from his office at 24 hours' notice and deposited his files on the road outside — the Sunni inhabitants of the city and the Palestinian survivors in Ein Helweh camp came under the local military orders of Phalangists and Haddad militiamen. The bodies of Palestinians were regularly found on a small road leading to the Christian sector of Sidon.

Leaflets appeared under doors demanding the deportation of every Palestinian in Lebanon.

'To all Lebanese,' one of them began:

the sun was founded to light up our land and also to burn those who desecrate it; to cleanse it of all who have abused and who still continue to abuse its beauty and security ... Honourable sons of Sidon ... help us to expel the outsiders from the land of Lebanon; particularly from the heroic city of Sidon which has long suffered under the Palestinian oppression and destruction. Our aim is not to allow any Palestinian to remain on Lebanese soil, and we are determined to carry this out. No obstacle will stand in our way ...

This leaflet, which circulated in Sidon in early February 1983, concluded with the words 'Long Live Lebanon' and was signed 'The Cedar Revolutionaries'. No one in Sidon had heard of the 'cedar revolutionaries'. They belonged to the world of anonymous Lebanese terror which journalists gifted with the word 'shadowy'. The Palestinians, however, thought these were very dark shadows indeed. In Ein Helweh, they suspected these leaflets were the work of another Christian militia, the notorious 'Guardians of the Cedar', which had now found favour with Israel.

* UN report by Timur Göksel, 24 March 1983.

The extreme right-wing 'guardians' were rightly feared by Palestinians. In the 1975–6 fighting, they routinely mutilated their Palestinian or Muslim prisoners before putting them to death, often in dreadful circumstances. Their captives were dragged alive behind cars through the streets of east Beirut and then, their bodies torn and their bones broken, were chained to the back of taxis which trailed their corpses up the motorway to Jounieh. There, the cadavers were ceremonially thrown into a dried-up wadi. Their leader, Etienne Saqr – Abu Arz, Father of the Cedars – had an equally chilling reputation. He took as his militia's slogan 'No Palestinian will remain in Lebanon', an aphorism which he later officially amended to: 'It is the duty of each Lebanese to kill one Palestinian.'* This motto could still be seen on some walls in east Beirut. There were well-documented cases of Saqr's men cutting off the ears of Muslim prisoners and tying them to their belts. His militia symbol was a white sword in a blazing fire. Anyone who doubted Saqr's psychopathic personality had only to listen to his speeches, which were usually flavoured with his favourite proverb – 'He who cooks poison, poison shall he eat.'

Palestinian and Lebanese Muslim suspicions that Israel had sought the friendship of Saqr and his gunmen were correct. In December 1982, Saqr was officially invited to Israel to meet Menachem Begin, a visit which he used to defend the Sabra and Chatila massacres and to demand the expulsion of half a million Palestinians from Lebanon. On Israeli radio, Saqr thanked Israel for her 'humanitarianism' in Lebanon and for freeing Lebanon from the 'nightmare of Palestinian terrorism and Syrian occupation'. Only on a second visit to Israel – in which he was the guest of the new prime minister, Yitzhak Shamir – did Saqr confirm that his gunmen were operating in southern Lebanon on Israel's behalf alongside Haddad's militia 'because I think it's better for us to have one army in the south than three or four armies.'† The Israelis confidently insisted Saqr had reformed, although they provided no evidence for this. 'He is a good friend of Israel,' an Israeli official told *The Times*.

The Israelis preferred to make no official comment on the record of murder and intimidation around Sidon. It reflected little credit on the occupation authorities. Two bodies were found on 26 January 1983 – one was identified as Nabil Shaqawi, a Palestinian – and three other corpses in a state of decomposition were discovered nearby. A day later, gunmen began to evict Palestinians from the Abra suburb of Sidon. On 29 January, Ahmed Subai, a Palestinian, was murdered outside his home in Qia'a. Two days later, someone threw a bomb at his sister's

---

* Statement of 'Abu Arz, commander-in-chief', published by 'Guardians of the Cedar', 20 June 1976.
† *Jerusalem Post*, 24 January 1984.

home. On 9 February, three bodies – all mutilated – were found near Ein Helweh.

Lebanese residents of Sidon made no secret of their feelings when we visited their homes. In February of 1983, I sat with an old man and his wife in the arched hallway of their home next to Sidon's main boulevard as they complained about the Israeli-hired militias. 'We liked it when the Israelis came,' the old man said. 'They cleaned out the Palestinian scum and we thought we were going to have our Lebanon back again.' His wife poured coffee into tiny painted cups. 'That's what we thought,' he repeated. 'But look outside the house. The Israelis are still here and they are arming the local gangs. All kinds of strangers are coming into Sidon with guns and taking control and the Israelis are bringing them in. Look down the road and you'll see what I mean.'

We peered out of the front door and there, sure enough, in the centre of the road a hundred yards away, stood two gunmen. Each held an automatic rifle, one wore jeans and an Israeli army jacket, the other a cowboy hat. They were stopping cars and questioning motorists. Just behind them, two Israeli soldiers were reading newspapers on top of an armoured personnel carrier. This image, recreated hundreds of times all over southern Lebanon, created a deep impression on the Lebanese. The Israelis were establishing collaborators, just as they had in the Palestinian West Bank after their victory in 1967. They intended to stay. The Israeli-paid vigilantes appeared all across the south of Lebanon. The UN invented a new acronym for them: LAUI, which stood for 'Lebanese Armed and Uniformed by Israel'.

Muslim religious leaders had recognised at a very early stage that these groups represented a profound danger. To be occupied by a foreign invader was humiliating; to be repressed by one's own country-men in collaboration with an invader was corrupting. Even while the Israelis were still besieging west Beirut, the Higher Shia Council – representing the largest religious community in southern Lebanon – met in the encircled city to condemn 'the establishment of local adminis-trations in south Lebanon under various names and pretexts, which are ignoring and bypassing the official Lebanese authorities.' Sheikh Mohamed Mehdi Shamseddin, who was deputy head of the council – the leader being the missing Mousa Sadr – urged Lebanese 'to reject the occupation and not to cooperate in any way with the Israeli-imposed local administration.'

The Israelis ignored these signs of discontent. More leaflets were distributed in Sidon, typed and mimeographed. On a visit to Sidon, I found one of them pushed behind the windscreen-wipers of my parked car. The document told Muslims to ignore those who called upon them 'to wage war against ... Zionism' in the name of Arabism and Islam, and instead to rally behind Christians in expelling 'foreigners'. The

Palestinians were the 'foreigners'. 'Let us crush the spirit of life that has remained in the venomous snake that still works in darkness, on propaganda which is meant to destroy what we have started to build and to create conflicts between us and those who must be our partners in the fatherland,' the leaflet said. 'Remember, germs live on decay.' The Palestinians were meant to be the germs. It was signed 'The Voice of Lebanese Sidon' and may have been the work of the Phalange.* Muslims in Sidon said they thought the Israeli Shin Bet may have been behind it.

Further south, the Israelis attempted to break the opposition of the *mukhtars*, the village leaders, to the squads of newly hired gunmen who now patrolled their land. A confidential UN intelligence summary in January 1983 concluded that Israeli soldiers were now using 'pressure, detention and blackmail' in the UN area to force village leaders to comply with their wishes. In Tibnin, in the Irish UN battalion zone, for instance, Israeli troops told village leaders 'to provide ten men in each village for militia – also they would be obliged to collect tax to pay them. If they refused, militia would come from other villages.'* The Shia were going to have to pay for their own oppressors.

From Beirut, we made forays down to Sidon and the villages of the south, the first of dozens of journeys deep inside Israeli-occupied Lebanon. On each trip, the mood of occupied and occupiers would subtly change, towards us as well as towards each other. They exhibited the familiar fear of people who wanted to hide from the unknown. 'Please don't use my name' became a feature of every interview. Our reports were therefore filled with first names, as if the people to whom we spoke had lost part of their identity. I would travel south with Anderson, Faramarzi or Paola Crociani of AP. The corruption of occupation moved ever more deeply into the people. The Muslims were increasingly resentful, the Christians disdainful, aware of their power.

---

* Leaflet entitled 'Communiqué: The Palestinians in Sidon and its Vicinity', dated 23 February 1983.
* UN operational report, Naqqoura, 30 January 1983. The summary also said that the UN believed Israel would 'use and exaggerate' every incident 'capable of proving to the world that the United Nations ... are not capable of giving them a guarantee of a safe northern border.' It recorded instances of 'harassment of villages' by Israeli troops and 'impolite and undisciplined behaviour of IDF personnel towards UNIFIL personnel'. In an incident on 4 January 1983, the report described how 'a green BMW car with a German registration arrived at checkpoint 7-23D 1791–2869. The occupants were in civilian clothes and were in possession of Israel ID [identity] cards. On the back seat was one M-16 rifle. This car was followed by a white Peugeot pick-up in which there were two men dressed in IDF [Israel Defence Force] uniform and armed with M-16s. While the occupants of the first car were being checked by UNIFIL personnel, the passenger of the second car – an IDF captain – got out of his vehicle, complained of the delay and pointed his rifle at the UNIFIL soldier's head.' In one month, the Israeli authorities refused UN helicopters permission to fly out of their Naqqoura base on 25 occasions. Two of these flights had been scheduled for the UN commander, General William Callaghan, and a third for the transfer of the body of a dead Finnish UN soldier.

On a visit to Sidon with Crociani of AP on 9 February 1983, these two characteristics were both evident and frightening.

We gave a 70-year-old road-worker called Hassan a lift in my car across town and he invited us into his home for coffee. He broke down almost as soon as we were inside. 'The Israeli officer comes to see me once a week,' he said. 'He keeps telling me that if I give him information about the *moharebbin* [terrorists], he will have my son released from Ansar prison camp. But he lies. I have given him information, but he has not released my son.' He stared at the floor then looked up at us. 'If you can get my son released, I will give you information too.'

On a road running along the hillside east of Ein Helweh, the body of a Palestinian had been found lying in a ditch, the back of his head blown away. We called at the nearest house. George and Tony lived there. Tony's wife made coffee and produced some locally made chocolates in shiny golden paper. His two small boys stood at the open door and watched us, stroking the feathers of a tiny bird they had found. The two men wore the olive-green fatigues of the Phalange.

'The Israelis got rid of the Palestinian murderers,' George said, 'and now we have peace here. The Palestinians used to rape our girls and steal cars. They were filth.' What about the Palestinians' bodies that had been found only a few hundred yards away? 'We know nothing about it,' George said. 'We do everything according to the law, but Palestinians are foreigners here and have no right to property in Sidon.' George shouted rather than talked. 'Bashir Gemayel was our leader – a God to us – you cannot understand – a God – a patriot, leader.' We suddenly realised that the two small boys in the doorway were tearing the wings off the live bird.

In the old vaulted souk later, seven Israeli soldiers were walking down the road in crocodile fashion, rifles at hip level, right hands playing around the triggers. They used to like having pictures taken of them on patrol. 'No photographs,' the officer screamed at Crociani. 'We want your film.' He was wearing dark glasses and looked like Peter Fonda. The crowds stopped to watch. 'Give me that film.' But another soldier stepped from the line. 'Why no pictures?' he shouted at the officer, and he walked forward, unshaven, grinning, hand held out. 'You are my friends. You can take pictures.' We had never seen him before. The crowd still watching, silent and unsmiling. When the soldiers had gone, a shopkeeper approached us with a forced smile. 'Are you from Israel?' No, we have come from Beirut. The people in the crowd nodded their heads. It was all right, the *sahafa* had come from Beirut.

Sidon was a market centre for Lebanon's orange grove country, but I could not buy a Lebanese orange there. In the cold, windswept market beside the souk, I could not find a Lebanese lemon or a Lebanese avocado. I could not find any Lebanese fruit at all. Every box of oranges, every crate of fruit had come from Israel. It was being brought across at the Israeli border post at Rosh Hanniqra, collected at the frontier by trucks whose drivers threatened journalists who tried to take photographs. Israel's exports were helping to put Lebanese farmers out of business. If there were still no political relations between Lebanon and Israel, trade relations already existed.

Above Sidon, above Ein Helweh, lay the small Palestinian camp of Mieh Mieh. In the spring of 1983, it was muddy. It oozed fear. Rain guttered off the broken roofs and swamped the shell holes in the track that ran between the huts. Graffiti had been scrawled over a faded painting of a Palestinian flag on the wall of a lavatory. But through the glassless window frames, we could see people watching us. A boy was standing in the shelter of a piece of rusting corrugated iron, clutching a pile of schoolbooks. He looked frightened when we approached, his eyes — discoloured a deep yellow by hepatitis — moving up and down the road. Yes, he said, he would take us to some relatives, and we walked through a filthy yard to an iron door where a woman stood in a long dressing-gown. There were none of the usual generous Arab greetings. 'Who are you? Where are you from?'

In six weeks, 12 Palestinians had been murdered in Sidon and strangers were not welcome. The United States government had warned Israel there might be another massacre up on the freezing hilltop at Mieh Mieh. 'When the Israelis first came in here last June, they told us they had come to protect us,' the woman said as she turned up a sputtering oil lamp on the floor. A younger girl sat with her and an old man with a white moustache who watched the fire as we spoke. 'But the Israelis took all the men away as prisoners to the Ansar and then the Phalangists came here in the autumn and burnt some houses. Some of our women went to the *serail* in Sidon to complain to the Israelis but the intimidation didn't stop.'

There was a noise outside the house, the sound of a car moving slowly up the road; it was enough to make the family stare through the broken doorway for several seconds. 'Ever since then,' the woman went on, 'the militia of the Phalange and of Saad Haddad have been sending men into our camp. The men attack our people and then the Phalange come along and say that the men are crazy and that they are not responsible. And then two weeks ago, a bomb went off at one end of the camp. It ruined fourteen houses. Part of our own roof came down and the glass from the windows crashed onto our beds as we slept.'

The car outside was driving away but we could hear footsteps crossing the muddy back yard. 'They are trying to drive us out of our houses and we are terribly exposed up here. We live in fear. We have no protection.' A boy appeared at the doorway, out of breath. 'The Phalange have seen your car,' he said to us, and the woman rose to her feet, clenching her hands in front of her. 'Please,' she said. 'Tear up your notes. Don't show them anything, tell them we said no one was harming us. Tell them we are happy.' We left hurriedly – for their sake, not ours – and found three young, unsmiling men on the roadway watching us.

The Christian village of Mieh Mieh began just 200 yards away, on the other side of a low barbed-wire fence. Outside the village church stood two middle-aged men. There was snow on the mountains to the east and the men wore coats against the wind that whipped through the narrow street. 'Journalists?' one of them asked. He wore a round, tightly fitting hat. 'Why don't you press people forget about the Palestinians and write about us? We were terrorised here for eight years by these people.' His friend, bespectacled with long, sensitive fingers and precise but heavily accented French, joined in. 'Lebanon is for Lebanese, not for foreigners. You must print that in your newspaper, that we are patriots.' He was a university teacher, a Greek Orthodox who had been born in the village.

He took us down a lane near the church and pointed to a wall above the road. Clearly marked upon it was a series of bullet holes. 'They killed three of our people there in 1975,' the man said. 'The Palestinians suspected them of being close to the *Kata'ib* [Phalange]. It was not true but the Palestinians called them from their home and murdered them there.'

A hundred yards away lay the man's home. He insisted upon his anonymity but wanted us to sit inside his cosy but damp little house. We followed him through a garden deep in grass and wild flowers, an old vine creeping over the door lintel. Inside stood his mother, an elderly, frail lady who spoke the immaculate French that the Lebanese middle classes had cultivated during the French mandate. There were bookcases lining the walls, volumes of Arabic and English literature and – a tell-tale slim volume in the corner – an Arabic–Hebrew dictionary. The man saw us looking at it. 'The Israelis came here to save us. They saved us all. Now we no longer live in fear of the terrorists ... Lebanon and Israel will be strong together because of their joint civilisation. Do you understand me?'

He sensed we did not and almost ran to the bookcase. He pulled out an Arabic translation of one of Sir Maurice Bowra's classic works, and then a novel by Khalil Gibran. 'You see?' he shouted. 'This is your literature and our literature. The Lebanese – the Christians – we are the people of civilisation, people of the West. We are the only progressive people of the region apart from the Israelis. The Muslims are a reactionary people.' He walked to the other end of the bookcase and pointed to a French-language Bible. 'And there our histories are intertwined,' he said. 'What have the Muslims to offer us in Lebanon?' He picked up the Hebrew dictionary. 'Yes, I am trying to learn some of this, I think it will be useful for us.'

This view was not shared in the Shia hill villages further south. The only culture to which they were being introduced was the practice of paying taxes – for the militiamen chosen by the Israelis. Colonel Haim of Israeli army intelligence was a peripatetic man. There was scarcely a village in southern Lebanon to which he had not paid what he referred to as a social call. Greying, a little plump, he exuded good humour.

'Colonel Haim is not here,' Colonel Haim told us when we came across him in heated discussion with Mohamed Yussef al-Ali, the village *mukhtar*, in the main square at Haris. He had forgotten that we had met before. Around him in the square were four Israeli officers, the *mukhtar*, three gunmen from Haddad's militia and a Dutch officer from the UN force. 'How did you know we were here?' an Israeli shouted at us. Colonel Haim raised his hand, still smiling. 'Please,' he said. 'No photographs.'

But the villagers had made no secret of his presence. 'Two weeks ago,' one of them said, 'Haim came here and told our *mukhtar* to pay fifteen thousand Lebanese pounds [five thousand dollars] a month to raise a local militia. The Israelis want the United Nations out and they want to put Haddad's men in here with guns. They have ordered us to pay for them. The *mukhtar* is refusing.'

Was this true, we asked Haim? 'We have not discussed money,' he said. Another Israeli tried to reply. 'Look, you people in England pay taxes, so why shouldn't the Lebanese?' But why were the *Israelis* talking about Lebanese taxes? 'Listen, these people want help, they want protection. They have said so on many occasions. I think we should support this. There are men who can do this job.' With Israeli guns? 'They have enough guns of their own.' With Israeli uniforms? 'We will give them uniforms if they need them. If the villagers don't want to pay, they don't have to.' At which point Colonel Haim interrupted. 'Maybe we did talk about money,' he said. 'Goodbye.' The smiling colonel and his staff then climbed into a yellow Mercedes without licence plates and drove off escorted by Haddad's gunmen.

The *mukhtar* would say nothing. Another villager leant towards us. 'We have asked the UN to stay here but Haim has given us to the end of the month to pay.' There was equal anxiety in a village not far away, a filthy, poor Shia hamlet whose elderly *mukhtar* refused to give his name and begged us not to identify his village. He was sitting in a darkened room surrounded by 70 villagers – all men – who watched us with concern when we asked if the Israelis had been demanding money. 'How do I know you are not working for the Israelis?' the *mukhtar* asked, and he shuffled through our passports. He seemed satisfied. 'Yes, I will tell you, an Israeli called Haim came here this morning with some soldiers. They want four thousand Lebanese pounds a month from this village but we have no money. What can we do?'

Was the village going to pay? we asked. 'If we don't, there will be trouble for us from the Israelis and the Haddad men. Haim says he wants this money from twenty-eight villages and that he needs the money to pay people to protect us from terrorists. But we want the United Nations soldiers here. Haim was very polite, very quiet. I told him that if the other villages pay, then we will.' The old *mukhtar* took from his jacket pocket a small piece of paper. Written on it in Arabic was the message: 'This is an order from the leader of the Haddad army. You must pay four thousand pounds to pay for people to protect your village. Signed: Haddad militia, with thanks.' The note was dated 27 February.

As we left the darkened room, a woman in a headscarf standing outside beckoned to us. 'I will tell you what the *mukhtar* is too frightened to tell you,' she said. 'There are twenty men from this village who are in the Israeli prison camp at Ansar and they have told us that these men will not be released until we agree to pay the money. They are taking over our village in this way, they are taking over our land and we want to be Lebanese.'

The suspicions of the Lebanese Shias were compounded by an unprecedented and highly detailed Israeli army census of well over a quarter of a million civilians living under occupation in southern Lebanon, an exercise that would provide the Israelis with intelligence on the lives and activities of the population in almost a quarter of the country. A 27-page questionnaire asked *mukhtars* for information ranging from the names of refugees and 'foreigners' in their villages to the engine numbers of privately owned cars and the names of pregnant women.

The documents sought information about the infrastructure of every village — its electricity, water, medical, telephone and postal services, even details about 'sites of religious or archaeological interest'. If the reasons for some of these questions seemed obvious — most of the 'foreigners' were Palestinians and automobile engine numbers might help to identify the provenance of car bombs — they gave the overall impression that Israel was planning to stay in southern Lebanon for a very long time.

Guerrilla attacks on Israeli troops were still largely confined to the area north of Sidon where the Israeli 162nd Division under the command of Brigadier-General Amnon Lifkin was taking most casualties. Lifkin was a 39-year-old veteran of the 1973 Middle East war with tousled grey hair, a deeply sunburned face and a clandestine military connection to Beirut which he chose not to mention to the journalists he met in Lebanon. Ten years before, he had been commander of a squad of Israeli soldiers and Mossad agents who had landed in west Beirut and killed several Palestinian officers in the 'Black September' movement, the group which had massacred the Israeli Olympic team at Munich in

1972. The wife of one of the Palestinians was shot in the face when Israeli gunmen stormed into her husband's home. There had been Israeli casualties in the 1973 raiding party, two of them shot dead by Palestinians outside a guerrilla office.*

Now Lifkin suffered further casualties in Lebanon. Two of his troops were killed and seven wounded in at least eight ambushes in late February and March 1983. He believed that his soldiers could go on sustaining such attacks while still maintaining a measure of security. 'It's not an easy job but it's not a mission impossible,' he told us on 24 March. He was wrong. Lebanese and Palestinian guerrillas attacked his men every day; only rarely did the Israelis capture their assailants, most of whom approached their lines from the Syrian-occupied area of Lebanon.

Crossing the lines between the armies, talking to Palestinians, Israelis, Syrians and Shia villagers was like passing through a glass darkly. In the home of a Palestinian family in Mieh Mieh, the Israelis and their allies presented a threatening, forbidding presence outside the window. Sitting with Israeli soldiers, the Palestinians out in the night seemed intrinsically menacing. We always shared the fear of those to whom we were talking. For we knew that an Israeli or a Phalangist who found us in the home of a Lebanese Muslim guerrilla would regard us with precisely the same hatred as the Palestinian who saw us talking to Israelis.

In late March 1983, Tatro, Faramarzi and I travelled up to an Israeli front line company headquarters in the Chouf. It was the first evening of Passover and a thick, sticky fog lay heavily over the half-ruined villa which served as Israeli Major Hillel's base outside Aley. Everyone there expected an ambush, but at the tables inside, the young Israeli soldiers sat around us, chanting and shouting the recitation of the *Haggadah* with genuine happiness. There was sweet wine on the tables and bitter herbs and the unleavened bread that reminds all Jews of their unprepared flight from Egypt.

Rabbi Tsvi asked his soldiers the ritual question of all *seders*: 'What makes this night different from all other nights?' And it was just a few minutes later that the first loud, deep thunderous explosion shook the building. We sat together and the chorus of singing voices died away into an empty silence. Rabbi Tsvi glanced at Major Hillel at the top table. All the soldiers had talked about a Palestinian attack on the first night of Passover but no one seemed to have believed it. The Rabbi started to recite the next prayer but he was interrupted by the second explosion that rumbled on and on across the darkened countryside.

It was enough. The door of the Passover feast is left open by tradition for the Prophet Elijah but now it was thronged with running soldiers.

---

* Lifkin's 1973 activities in Beirut are recounted in *The Quest for the Red Prince* by Michael Bar-Zohar and Eitan Haber (New York, William Morrow and Co, 1983), pp. 176–7.

As Rabbi Tsvi stood in the centre of the room beneath the naked light bulbs, still reading from the *Haggadah*, the Israelis grabbed their Galil assault rifles and leapt from the tables. The reservist on my left – a civil engineer from Jerusalem – looked up from his meal. 'I think it has happened,' he said, and we ran after him out of the room. There was another louder roar and that ever-so-slight change in air pressure that had become familiar to us. A cluster of flares broke open above us in the foggy night in an umbrella of light.

Each new flare popped and hissed in the sky, turning the fog-twisted laneway into a landscape of running and shouting soldiers. There were bursts of automatic rifle fire from 200 yards away and a heavy machine-gun began firing. A radio whispered in Hebrew, then talked, then shouted. An Israeli first lieutenant walked up to us out of the murk. 'The terrorists have fired rocket-propelled grenades at one of our patrols on the road outside,' he said. 'They hit the first vehicle. I know nothing more yet.' There was more radio static and he looked up. 'I think we have lost someone.'

The emotional transition had been extraordinary, a miniature version of the shock waves which overwhelmed the Americans when they came under attack in Beirut. At the Passover table, the soldier had cajoled Rabbi Tsvi to finish his recitation so they could start their dinner. A reservist stood up and recited his own verse about Menachem Begin, expressing the hope that the Israeli prime minister would be re-elected. Earlier still, the soldiers had sat with us in the company medical centre, trying to justify their war and occupation of Lebanon, asking again and again why the international press had turned against them, why America wished to hurt Israel, why no one understood what they were doing. They still saw nothing wrong in their occupation. Had we not seen the photographs of the Lebanese welcoming their army last June?

There followed the old arguments: that if the Israelis left there would be chaos, that Galilee had been under such constant 'terrorist' attack that they had to invade. But why invade all the way to Beirut? There was much discussion about this. Two soldiers believed Ariel Sharon should have pushed right on into west Beirut in June 1982. Another thought the advance should have stopped at the Awali River north of Sidon.

There was another soldier on our right who thought about his words carefully. 'Lebanon is a land without a future,' he said. Someone talked about 'destroying' the PLO but the reticent man interrupted him. 'Pressure, not "destroy",' he replied. 'The problem is not the Palestinians or the Israelis but their leaders. There is only one way to stop the PLO doing these terror things – that is by making friends with the Palestinians.'

But then those explosions blew all moral rectitude from the room.

There were curses and shouts of anger and out of the clammy fog six hours later came the Israeli first lieutenant. 'One of our people was killed in the command vehicle,' he said. 'The other two were wounded. The terrorists got away. This is all we found.' And he held up a chequered black and white Palestinian *kuffiah*.

By mid-May, General Amnon Lifkin's optimism had evaporated. At a news conference, he claimed that the Chouf fighting had escalated as a direct result of US Secretary of State George Shultz's intervention in the Lebanese–Israeli troop withdrawal talks. Instead of promising security, he declared that his occupied area of the Chouf was 'a catastrophe'. He was subdued and defensive. The Israelis made no attempt to restate their political or military objectives in Lebanon, and Lifkin scarcely bothered to blame the Syrians for the Chouf fighting. Beside the door to the Israeli military spokesman's office where the news conference was held, the usual brochures documenting the Israeli view of the Lebanon war had disappeared. A pile of old broadsheets advertising the benefits of Israeli–Lebanese cooperation lay in a corner, tied up with string and covered with dust.

In the six months since the Israelis left west Beirut, they had suffered 118 fatalities – more than a quarter of their entire death toll since the invasion. Of the 2,489 Israeli soldiers listed as wounded, 361 received their injuries in the six months after September 1982. The 'terrorists', it seemed, had not been beaten after all. In the south, Colonel Haim and another Israeli officer – who identified himself by the name 'Abu Noor' – had persuaded several Shia villages to pay money to the gangs of militiamen which the Israelis now referred to as the 'Territorial Brigade'.

Lebanon was acquiring all the accoutrements of a client state. The Israelis apparently ignored the Old Testament warnings of the fate which awaits those who involve themselves in the violence of Lebanon. Across its new front line, from the Awali River north of Sidon, up the steep and beautiful gorge of the River Bisri to the plateau below the heights of Barouk, the Israeli army was constructing a complex system of military bases, helicopter pads, radar tracking stations, tank parks and concrete and brick barracks, as if it was planning to stay in Lebanon for years rather than a few more weeks.

In June 1983, plain-clothes Shin Bet agents protected by Israeli troops began a series of raids into the Palestinian camps around Tyre, arresting up to 60 men in one day. In the lower Bekaa, the Israelis were building a completely new highway across the centre of the valley to avoid the ambushes on the old road north. Around Lake Karaoun in the lower Bekaa, there were 35 guerrilla attacks against the Israelis in a month. A new militia force was raised under Israeli auspices in Tyre, run by a Lebanese named Hartawi, while Ibrahim Farhan, who had previously controlled the port of Tyre on behalf of the Democratic Front for the Liberation of Palestine, now ran the harbour for the Israelis.

Of all people, the Israelis needed the Shia of southern Lebanon to be their friends. When they returned to their own borders, the Shia would be their neighbours. 'Better a close neighbour than a distant brother ...' the tourist postcards printed in the Israeli town of Herzlia proclaimed around a picture of a cedar tree beside a Star of David. Yet almost every action Israel took only alienated and embittered these people. Israel encouraged more of its newly created militiamen to raise cash. Israel continued what was in effect a campaign of extortion. Haddad gunmen from Beit Lif under the command of a Lebanese Shia, Ahmed Shibli, descended on the village of Yater one morning and demanded money and men to build fortifications for the Israelis. The *mukhtar* of Yater delivered a letter to the local company headquarters of the Dutch UN battalion. It read: 'Are we living in the state of Israel, the state of Ahmed Shibli or the state of the devil?'

In the West Bank, Israeli raids, paid informers and armed local collaborators had kept the Palestinians docile. Now the same system was being applied to Lebanon. But the Lebanese were not Palestinians. Their own burgeoning Shia guerrilla movement had the weapons, battle training – and the theological conviction – which the Palestinians in the occupied territories lacked. When the Palestinians of the West Bank demonstrated against the Israelis, they threw stones. The Lebanese fired bullets. The Lebanese knew all about guerrilla warfare. The Israelis did not.

On 10 June 1983, the Israeli crews of two armoured vehicles were driving out of the Shia village of Deir Qanoun en-Nahr when they were ambushed by up to ten gunmen. The guerrillas ran at them through the orange orchards on both sides of the narrow laneway and killed three of the Israelis before a shot was fired in return. Shin Bet men swarmed into the Palestinian camps of Tyre once more, searching for young men. But the attackers were Lebanese.

Southern Lebanon was turning into a death trap for the Israelis, a place of constant ambushes and booby-traps in which the most powerful army in the Middle East seemed unable to defend itself. Still the Israelis continued to impose their militiamen on the Shia villages. The *mukhtar* of Yater had paid the first instalment of money but then refused to give any more. Yater was a tiny Shia village south of the Litani River, a peaceful hamlet lying in the folds of three hills that petered out in a stony wadi three miles from the nearest main road. Now, to punish the *mukhtar* for his intransigence, the Israelis positioned two gunmen from Haddad's militia at the end of the only road that led to Yater. Whenever a local taxi left the village, the driver was ordered to pay five Lebanese pounds, about two dollars. Drivers of tractors and lorries had to pay twice as much. An Israeli half-track stood guard over the two tax collectors.

Not far away, in the Shia village of Jibchit, the Israelis were committing errors which would have graver effects in the future. Jibchit was a pretty village that sat rather pompously across two hills 12 miles from the sea. There were straggling vines and old trees that clambered from behind cheap, green-painted breeze-block walls. The local Shia Imam, Ragheb Harb, had condemned the Israeli invasion and now he was urging his flock to refuse all cooperation with the occupation authorities. In June 1983, a convoy of Israeli army trucks drove into the village, the black-bearded young cleric was put aboard one of the lorries with his hands tied, and driven away to Tyre. A peaceful village which had hitherto been known for its ability to grow olive trees on rocky soil now bore a new and bitter fruit.

A visit to Jibchit was in itself an education in the future of Lebanon. A clutter of torn black flags cracked in the breeze over the shabby blue village mosque, the *Husseiniya*, where Harb used to preach. Around the courtyard hung cotton banners which displayed that unique ability of Shia Muslims to combine naïve political aspirations with intimations of physical self-sacrifice. 'No peace in Lebanon without peace in the South,' said one. Another – scripted in white on a black cloth – announced: 'Death for us is merely a custom: God's generosity is martyrdom.'

Inside the mosque, a group of men sat on the old carpets, day and night, to protest the unseemly departure of the Imam who did not like collaborators. In an office in the mosque – a neat little room decorated with posters of Khomeini and Mousa Sadr – sat a bearded young man who introduced himself to me as 'Jihad'. He spoke slowly and talked about the 'Great Satan America'. Only afterwards did I learn that he was a member of the Iraqi Dawa party, the secret pro-Iranian opposition group which wished to depose Saddam Hussein. Only two hours later, talking to an old friend in the village, would I be told that this earnest young man was a member of 'Islamic Jihad'.

His beard was cut short, his brows furrowed. He was polite. 'My name does not matter. You may call me Jihad. Our Imam was under Israeli surveillance for some time. For several months, an Israeli intelligence officer called Abu Noor tried to talk to him but the Imam always refused to see him. On 17 March, the Israelis came at night and arrested him at his cousin's house, tied his hands with rope and took him away.'

The Israelis had treated Jibchit as they treated other Shia villages in the south. They appointed six gunmen to watch over the village, local men who signed up for the 'National Guard'. A week after Harb's detention, these men drove to the Shin Bet headquarters in Nabatieh, handed back their guns and formally resigned from the militia. Their gesture had no influence on the Israelis.

Just as the Israelis had promoted the status of Major Haddad's half-peasant army into 'the shield of Galilee' — a phrase used by one of Israel's less articulate liaison officers — so now they threw their confidence into an even more deeply flawed militia. Senior Shin Bet agents were drafted into Lebanon to arm these men with AK-47 rifles, train them in radio communications and send them off into villages to keep the peace for Israel. The Israelis trumpeted their achievement and then, as usual, believed their own propaganda. Thus in Jouaya, for example, five bed-raggled and unshaven gunmen represented the new Israeli 'Forces of Kerbala'. South of Tyre, another militia, the 'Partisans of the Army', was organised by the Israelis to control a checkpoint where the gunmen extorted money from the drivers of lorries carrying food and supplies.*

The leader of the 'Forces of Kerbala' was Haidar Dayekh, a local petrol station proprietor with a large, unkempt beard who met me at his headquarters in Jouaya in a dark green fatigue uniform which he said once belonged to a PLO guerrilla. In the shade of a cluster of trees, Dayekh — with a pistol at his hip, wearing sun-glasses and holding a golfing cap — talked of his loyalty to Lebanon and his independence from Israeli control, a conversation that suddenly changed in emphasis when a tall stranger sat down silently beside him.

The newcomer, a slightly plump but distinguished-looking man with thick grey hair and a T-shirt with a Hebrew inscription, constantly interrupted Dayekh and suggested replies that he should give to my questions. When I recognised the man as 'Abu Noor', he snapped back: 'How did you know my name?' Dayekh was an Amal gunman before the invasion. He had been wounded by the PLO and cared for in a hospital in Haddad's town of Marjayoun. Therein lay his new-found loyalty to the Israelis. When he began to criticise the Phalange in Beirut, 'Abu Noor' muttered in his ear: 'Shut up.'

Shawki Abdullah was a more impressive man than Dayekh. As head of the 'United Southern Assembly' — another institution dreamed up by 'Abu Noor' and his friends — he held court in a little office on the Tyre seafront where he had been installed by the Israeli army. He greeted me there in a natty white safari suit, sitting in a large leather-backed chair, insisting that everyone was his friend. True, someone had thrown a bomb into his money-changer's shop the previous February — he was at a loss to know why — and when he opened a metal cupboard on the left of his desk, it was possible to glimpse three Israeli rifles nestling against a wall. Just in case.

'I'm not a complicated man,' Abdullah announced, summoning coffee

---

* A list of 'taxes' applicable for drivers from 1 August 1983 at the Ras al-Bayada checkpoint included 60 dollars for a truck carrying video recorders, tapes or radios, 110 dollars for a six-wheel truck carrying tyres, 80 dollars for a six-wheel truck carrying agricultural materials or insecticides, 72 dollars for a lorry containing sugar, rice, flour, seeds, vegetables or fruit.

from a youth in olive-green fatigues who had a pistol stuffed in his belt. 'I just want to solve the problems of my people. Sometimes Colonel Haim of the Israeli army comes here for advice and sometimes Palestinians come to see me. They ask me to free their relatives from the Ansar prison camp and sometimes I succeed.' Abdullah did indeed sometimes succeed, for he was one of those men who gain prominence in any land controlled by a foreign army, essential to the occupiers and the occupied in almost equal measure.

He was a balding man with large eyes and a small, very neat moustache. 'Listen,' he said, picking up a creased piece of paper torn from a school exercise book. 'There are forty-seven names on this list – Lebanese and Palestinians whom the Israelis have arrested. They have just imprisoned three hundred more people in Ansar. At the weekend, perhaps I can get fourteen released. I will go through the list with the Israelis and we shall discuss it. It is not many – fourteen out of three hundred – but it is better than none.'

The youth re-entered the office holding a tray of coffee and leading a middle-aged man whose hands were clasped in front of him in a pleading, supplicating manner. The Israelis had just arrested his son, he said, and he produced another piece of paper. Abdullah sympathised with him and promised to take the matter up with Colonel Haim. 'You see?' he asked. 'Do you see how the people need me?'

Abdullah did not discuss how he came to be appointed but agreed that the Israelis vetted applicants for his pseudo-democratic parliament. He handed over a list of his latest candidates. 'Colonel Haim approved these people,' he said. 'The Israelis are here in southern Lebanon. It is a fact. If they withdraw, the Palestinian army will come back and the Syrian army will come back. No one wants this to happen. Soon the Israelis will leave the mountains outside Beirut and they will need the roads here in the south to be safe. There must be no ambushes. If there are bombs here, the Israelis will close the port. People will lose money. No one wants that. So we have to talk to everyone ... When the people understand what I am doing, there will be no danger for me.'

Abdullah was a Shia. A picture of Mousa Sadr hung outside his office. 'Please,' he said to me, his voice rising in intensity. 'Tell all the world that I am a Lebanese patriot and that I work for my country. I am not an Israeli or a Syrian or a Palestinian. I am faithful to Lebanon.'

Publicly, the Israeli army still claimed that it had achieved its military objectives in Lebanon. When the army left the Chouf, Amnon Lifkin's order of the day stated that 'the terrorist organisations were defeated and their infrastructure destroyed. The Syrian enemy, where they encountered our troops, could not stand against us.' But the message contained its own contradiction, for it added: 'We are in a country that is split between armed populations, among them elements hostile to the

IDF.' Its conclusion was also of interest: 'Remember! Morality of arms is a prime value in the IDF. Use your weapons only in self-defence and avoid harming non-combatants.'* Worthy though this advice may have been, it had already been so flagrantly ignored that the Lebanese no longer believed in the Israelis' 'morality of arms'.

As they withdrew back to the Awali line north of Sidon, some Israeli intelligence officers were aware that the slipshod village militias raised by Colonel Haim and his colleagues would not be sufficient to protect the Israeli army. They learned of plans to attack their Tyre headquarters at least 11 months before the suicide bomber succeeded in blowing it apart on 4 November 1983.[†]

If the Chouf was a 'catastrophe', Israel was now moving its occupation force into the clutches of a guerrilla army which fed on the hatred that Israel was creating in the villages of southern Lebanon. More than 25,000 Israeli soldiers with 330 tanks, 450 armoured vehicles and 100 artillery pieces — all merged into five armoured brigades — settled in behind their concrete underground bunkers, from the Mediterranean, across the snows of Barouk to the Syrian frontier east of the Arkoub.

The Israeli line troops faced north, towards the land which they had left in chaos, towards the 'terrorists'. But this was Lebanon, and the Israelis were looking into a mirror that reversed reality. Most of their enemies lay in wait *behind* them, in the south.

The Lebanese Christians would have been the first to strip Israel of its illusions about the Shia Muslims of the south. If Sunni orthodoxy condemned the Shia as theological heretics, the Christians saw them — in the words of one Lebanese academic — as 'the Albigensians of the Middle East'. In Lebanese politics, heresy meant betrayal, and the poverty of the hill villages of southern Lebanon, the historical neglect under which they had suffered for so many years, had secreted layers of suspicion deep inside the framework of Lebanese Shia society. We would encounter this ourselves on visits to the south. Shia friends whom we had known for months, family members with whom we had stayed for weeks — men and women who had protected us during periods of fighting, who had repeatedly helped us compile our newspaper reports — would turn to us suddenly, without warning, at breakfast or on a car journey and ask: 'Are you a spy?'

These questions were not prompted by animosity towards the West, although this was growing. They were a symptom of a much deeper

---

* IDF Order of the Day, issued by commanding general, northern sector, Lebanon, 4 September 1983.
† The report of the Israeli military commission of inquiry into the bombing specifically stated that 'the security forces compound at Tyre ... was known as an objective which the terrorists intended to attack, since the beginning of 1983.' See the 'main findings' of the commission's reports to Lt.-Gen. Moshe Levy of 11 and 24 November 1983, p. 2.

fear, which had its roots in the isolation of Shiism in Lebanon, its traditional exclusion from real political power in the country, its inability to improve the conditions under which its people lived in the tired land of the south. The condition of impoverishment in which the Shias lived led them to assume the functions of government in their own areas of Lebanon long before the country began to disintegrate elsewhere. It was not by chance that the Imam Mousa Sadr's political organisation had been named the 'Movement of the Deprived'. Mousa Sadr had founded schools and a vocational training centre outside Tyre. He was an Iranian, a representative of the only Shia power in the Middle East. Iran was now renascent, free of its former Western oppressors, winning successive victories on the battlefields of the Gulf War. In Iran, the 'deprived' had struggled and won. In Lebanon, too, therefore, the Shia could triumph over their oppressors.

These emotions manifested themselves in an unfamiliar symbiosis of political demands and theocratic conviction. Peace and security in southern Lebanon became intimately bound up with the Shia cult of martyrdom. Hence the cotton banners that floated outside the shabby *Husseiniya* mosque in Jibchit. Under the repressive measures instituted by the Israeli army in southern Lebanon, the Shias sought comfort in the suffering of Hussein, the Third Imam, grandson of the Phophet, whose death at Kerbala had given to their faith the cult of martyrdom. The righteous Hussein rebelled against the power and wealth of the Umayyads. He was killed at Kerbala while travelling to help the people of Kufa whose hearts, according to a Shia poet, were with the pious Imam but whose swords were with his enemies. Betrayal and suspicion lay at the heart of the epic of Shiism.

Every blow struck at Shiism in southern Lebanon was therefore a re-enactment of Hussein's suffering. Harb's arrest was seen by the Israelis as part of their crusade against 'terrorism'; by the Shias, it was regarded as proof of Israeli duplicity. Naming a gang of pro-Israeli collaborators — Haidar Dayekh's 'Forces of Kerbala' — after the place of Hussein's martyrdom was blasphemous. The Israelis had long deluded themselves into thinking that they had — in the words of Uri Lubrani, the Israeli government's 'coordinator of Lebanese affairs' — an 'honest and friendly relationship' with the Shias up to 1982. But even this was untrue. Most of the Shia population of the Beirut slums were refugees from Israel's bombardment of southern villages in the 1970s. The Shias of Bourj al-Barajneh, Chiyah and Hay al-Sellum also suffered grievously during the Israeli siege of west Beirut.

Now their homeland in the south was under an increasingly repressive Israeli occupation. In early October 1983, the Israelis threatened to close the Awali River bridge, the only road upon which the Shias of the south could travel to Beirut. Mehdi Shamseddin, the deputy leader of the Shia higher council, then called upon the Shias to show 'total civil resistance against Israeli occupation in Lebanon'. It needed only one incident to start a revolt.

The incident occurred in Nabatieh, the spiritual centre of Shiism in Lebanon, where each year at *Ashoura*, the tenth day of the Muslim month of *Moharem*, the Shias commemorate the Imam Hussein's martyrdom. In the streets thousands of young Shia men dressed in symbolic white shrouds, some of them carrying swords, were flagellating themselves with razors, knives or chains. On *Ashoura*, on 16 October 1983 – a day of deep spiritual significance – an Israeli army convoy drove into the thousands of worshippers. The Israelis were stoned, their trucks overturned and burned. The soldiers, facing a frenzied crowd, some pointing knives at them, opened fire. They killed two of the worshippers and wounded another seven, then denied that anyone had been hurt and dismissed the incident as a mistake. The convoy had taken a wrong turn.

A second Israeli version of the incident claimed that the soldiers had come under 'small arms and grenade fire' and had shot back at 'terrorists', but made no mention of the religious ceremonies. The Israelis said they had checked the local hospitals and that no one was injured. Like their denial of the deaths, this Israeli statement was a lie.

When I reached Nabatieh the following day, one of the half-burned Israeli trucks still lay outside the gates of the mosque, its tyres in cinders, its axles melted onto the road. Doctors at the Hekmat hospital had records of two patients suffering from gunshot wounds, one of whom was sent to Sidon in critical condition. His name was Hussein Diaa and I found him in Sidon, lying in great pain in a third floor ward surrounded by relatives, a glucose drip running into his right arm and a tube extending from a bullet wound in his stomach.

At the Jnoub hospital opposite the Nabatieh mosque, doctors had treated three people, one a young woman suffering from gunshot wounds. At the Najdeh hospital, they sent two patients to Sidon. One of them, Hussein Makhzoum, was suffering from severe abrasions to the face. The doctors said he was beaten with rifle butts. The other was Soheil Hammoura. He was shot. He was 19 and he was buried in an overgrown Shia cemetery just down the road from his family home in the village of Meiss al-Jebel.

In the Hammoura house, I was taken to a dark, crowded room of mourning relatives where Ali Hammoura, who was a doctor in Nabatieh, recounted his brother's death with a detached, clinical precision. 'Soheil came down from Beirut at the weekend to spend Sunday with me in Nabatieh. He is not particularly religious but he wanted to see the celebration of *Ashoura*. He went down with the crowds and I was working in the hospital when he returned. He just came into the entrance of the hospital and said: "I'm wounded." Then he slumped forward on his face.'

Soheil Hammoura's father seemed resigned to his son's death. He sat in a smart white *kuffiah* in an upper room of the family home, his hands in his lap, his eyes staring at his hands. The mother wept loudly downstairs with her three daughters. Ali Hammoura shuffled through the family snapshots and handed them to me one by one: Soheil swimming, Soheil diving, Soheil at a birthday party, a thin young man with a tiny moustache. 'He was shot in the back by the Israelis,' Soheil Hammoura said. 'What can we do? I cannot talk about these things. We are under occupation forces. But our feeling is that of hatred for an occupation force.'

Within a week, the Israeli army in southern Lebanon came under sustained guerrilla attack. The Shia clergy condemned all militiamen working for the Israelis as traitors. By the new year, some of the collaborators had deserted to Amal, while others were assassinated. On 25 January 1984, Mohamed Atef Farhat, the head of the pro-Israeli militia in the village of Kfar Rumman, was shot dead near his home. Israeli troops were attacked with grenades, mines and rockets nine times in one week. Some of the mines demonstrated a new technical understanding on the part of the guerrillas, who had now worked out the melting temperature of explosives and were manufacturing bombs in wash-basins. Italian Shachi mines with three detonators were found in culverts beside the roads.

The Israelis accused Sheikh Ragheb Harb and another local preacher, Sheikh Abbas Harb from Hallousiyeh — the two men were not related — of encouraging young men to join 'terrorist organisations'. But the Israeli army's own activities ensured a steady flow of recruits to the guerrilla movement. In January 1984, Israeli troops used a bulldozer to destroy Abbas Harb's home in Hallousiyeh. They drove it from the little road near the mosque, smashing through the front room and bringing down the back roof on a pile of children's toys. When I visited Hallousiyeh, the bulldozer's tracks could still be seen running through what had been the Sheikh's drawing room. The villagers had piled some of his broken furniture and crockery in the rubble. Over the ruins, they had draped a large Islamic banner containing a message for the Israelis, a series of angry, violent quotations from the Koran.

According to the Israelis, the 27-year-old Sheikh was arrested and his house destroyed because he was 'suspected of terrorist activities'. Terrorism. Having failed to crush the PLO, the Israelis were now following their obsessions into the Shia hill villages. The Shia of southern Lebanon did not want to destroy Israel. They did not want to attack

Galilee. They wanted the Israelis to leave Lebanon. But now they, too, were 'terrorists'.

In Abbas Harb's absence, the spiritual welfare – and no doubt the political opinions – of his flock were in the hands of Sheikh Adel Mowanis. He had the obligatory ascetic expression and carefully groomed beard. 'The Israelis brought in a large force of men and took Abbas Harb away in a helicopter,' Mowanis said. 'On Sunday, they brought him back. His face did not look normal. He did not have his turban on and his hands were swollen. The Israelis were holding him by the shoulders ... they told Abbas Harb to call the names of five people to come forward so that they could arrest them. Then they took him and the five people away in helicopters.'

Rumours circulated that the Israelis intended to murder Ragheb Harb, the Jibchit Imam who had been seized by the Israelis in June 1983, and subsequently released. Ragheb Harb had visited Iran and met *Hezbollah* officials in Beirut. In late February 1984, he was murdered in Jibchit, hit by three bullets fired from behind his garden wall. His bloodstained body was carried through the streets. When Shia men attempted to parade the corpse around neighbouring villages, they were attacked by members of Israel's 'home guard' who wounded four of the men.

The ambushes on the Israelis increased. By February of 1984, there were an average of 15 a week. Prisoners in Ansar were shot by the Israelis 'while trying to escape'. The village *mukhtars* opposed the Israelis but it was the Imams, the spiritual leaders, who now led the political opposition to the occupation force. They maintained links with Iran but insisted that they received no instructions from Khomeini's regime.

In the village of Adloun, south of Sidon, the 64-year-old Sheikh, Ali Mahdi Ibrahim, knew Khomeini well; he had studied in the Iraqi city of Najaf, where Khomeini lived in exile for 15 years. 'We do not receive any teachings from anybody,' he said. 'We get our teachings from ourselves. Iran takes its lessons from us.'

The Sheikh's lessons were studied closely by an admiring group of young men. When I sat in his living room, these men hung on his every word, nodding their vigorous agreement. Some of them introduced themselves as Hezbollah members. Outside Sheikh Ibrahim's house one day, two Israeli jets streaked overhead at low altitude and one of the Hezbollah men grabbed me by the arm and pointed at the planes. 'They are not powerful,' he shouted above the noise of the jets. 'They have no power.'

Israel's declining power was daily more perceptible. In January 1984, Saad Haddad, Israel's most faithful retainer, died of cancer. The Israelis replaced him with a humourless, uninspired retired Lebanese major-general called Antoine Lahd, who was the object of repeated assassination attempts.* Dozens of his 'South Lebanon Army' militiamen of Shia faith deserted to the resistance with their weapons. Even outside the gates of the Israeli base at Kfar Falous, I came across Christian SLA men who openly called the Israelis 'pimps who make us do the chores'. As we travelled around Lebanon that spring, Israel's political and military will was draining away. The Israeli soldiers to whom we spoke were dispirited and depressed.

Eleven pm. An Israeli roadblock outside Marjayoun. It is cold, and Moshe holds a greatcoat round him, his rifle under his arm. 'I don't want to be here in this land under the stars like this. I want to be home in my country with my family. Things have not gone right. Bashir was killed. Syria has become strong. Jumblatt is in control now. Who is attacking us? I don't know. They don't seem to be organised. Some do it for money. They put their explosives beside the road and run off to the fields and detonate their explosives from there.' Another Israeli soldier walks up and squints through the window of our car. His name is Ishiah. 'It is a disaster here. Sharon, I think he is crazy.'

Israeli television cameras record Israeli troops singing a parody of a Hebrew nursery rhyme. The soldiers we meet know the words:

Airplane come down to us,
Fly us off to Lebanon,
We will fight for Sharon,
And return in a coffin.

The oranges of southern Lebanon were dying. All down the coast road south, we could tell the moment we looked at the trees, for that golden blaze of light in the orchards had faded. The fruit was grey. The Israelis had torn down the orchard walls and the winds were now cutting into the trees. The resistance had attacked the Israelis from behind the walls, so the Israelis destroyed their cover. They kept a tank on the main road south of Sidon for this very purpose, a converted Merkava with a bulldozer's shovel attached to the front. A wall-breaker.

Everywhere else, the Israelis were building walls, ditches, moats around their military bases. Revetments 30 feet high, 200 feet long, barricades of concrete eight feet thick. They travelled in buses and trucks escorted by tanks, their rifles poking from the windows. Their convoys looked like armoured porcupines. Their jets began to bomb Damour, south of Beirut, again. Raids against 'terrorist bases'. They

---

* Lahd was gravely wounded by a woman who called at his front door and shot him with a pistol in 1988. Born in the village of Kfar Katra and married with a five-year-old son, he expressed his unease with his Israeli controllers when I interviewed him at his home in Marjayoun on 19 April 1984. 'If the Israelis want security on their northern border — and if we can give it to them — then there is no excuse for them to stay,' he said. But the resistance overwhelmed entire platoons of Lahd's 'South Lebanon Army' and the Israelis were still keeping hundreds of occupation troops in the far south of Lebanon in 1990.

had done this before the invasion. Now, two years after their invasion and partial retreat, they repeated their raids. So why did they invade? The Israelis had caught the neurosis of repetition that afflicted all those who sought advantage in Lebanon.

Their enemies were perfecting a new weapon. Just after 3.30 on the afternoon of 12 April 1983, a schoolboy in his late teens called Ali Safiadin was sitting in a green Fiat car on a little bridge just west of Deir Qanoun en-Nahr. Several people saw him sitting in the car. One of them noticed that he seemed distracted and asked if he felt unwell. 'Give my family my regards,' he said. Dola Harmanani, a 15-year-old schoolgirl from the village, passed Safiadin as she walked home from the house of relatives. He seemed to be thinking. In retrospect, she thought he might have been crying.

A few seconds later, two Israeli armoured personnel carriers came up the road towards the village and Safiadin started his car. Dola Harmanani did not see what happened next but she heard the explosion. She was hurled to the road, cutting her face on the stones, as Safiadin rammed his car between the Israeli vehicles and detonated a huge bomb which he was carrying in the car. It tore him to bits − the villagers had to pick up the pieces afterwards − and turned one of the Israeli carriers into an inferno of exploding ammunition.

This was one of the first times that the identity of a suicide bomber became known. Was he, as the Israelis immediately claimed, a member of a 'fanatical terrorist gang'? For days, we inquired through the hill villages. His story was as appalling as it was instructive. Ali Safiadin's brother had been arrested by the Israelis in 1983 and imprisoned in the Israeli military interrogation headquarters just south of Tyre when another suicide bomber − whose identity was never revealed − drove a truck loaded with explosives at the building in November. The brother was one of the handcuffed prisoners killed in the explosion. *And Ali Safiadin blamed not the bomber but the Israelis for his death.* Deir Qanoun was his revenge.

My journeys to southern Lebanon became more and more difficult. The Israelis often turned back reporters from Beirut at the Awali bridge or at their checkpoints at the Bater bridge high in the mountains. Thousands of Lebanese queued here for days, pleading, crying, bribing their way through the checkpoints in both directions. The Israeli front line effectively partitioned Lebanon, and in their way these people, who insisted on travelling backwards and forwards, however many days they were forced to wait, constituted a form of resistance. They were refusing to accept the partition of their country.

Jibchit again. It had become a centre of resistance to Israeli rule. I lost count of the journeys we made there, down the laneways between the olive and tobacco plantations. Israel's SLA militia had paid a visit to

Jibchit and left their victims on the road. There were women among them, girls. It was the first time this had happened in southern Lebanon. The militia said it was meant to be a search for 'terrorists'. The villagers talked of their hatred in a cruel, unforgiving way.

They had buried Khadija Abbas Atwi in the rough grass cemetery above Jibchit not far from the crumbling road where she bled to death. Her gravestone was quite explicit about what happened to her, although, like most obituaries, it did not tell the whole story. 'This is the grave of the Holy Warrior Martyr Khadija Abbas Atwi,' it said, 'who fell in confrontation with the Zionist enemy during the invasion of the village. Died 28 March, 1984.'

On her sideboard, Khadija's mother kept a framed portrait of her 18-year-old daughter, a tall, well-built girl in a pink scarf staring uneasily into the camera. Her father was a broken man. He wept and sobbed beside me. 'How do you want me to feel when I come into the house and find three of my children shot, one of my girls dead? I have no mind left.'

There were other parents like him in Jibchit and there were villagers too, whose minds — far from being vacant — were now filled with enmity and loathing. Jibchit was becoming a Lebanese tragedy, a mirror of all that had happened there since the invasion. In the mosque, I found another preacher, Abdul Karim Óbeid,* a successor to the murdered Ragheb Harb, and another group of ascetic young men. He was talking about the UN Security Council, about the Israelis they were all supposed to hate. 'Any Muslim who leaves Islam will die.' The young men murmured their consent. In the poverty and stones of Jibchit, religion was radicalising the young because politics had failed. It was the sort of place the Israelis would have done well to keep away from.

Everyone — including the Israelis — agreed that among the first armed men to enter the village were the SLA. Hassan Fahas was the first to be hit, wounded by an SLA bullet that came through the window of his home and hit him in the arm. On a small road on the other side of the *Husseiniya* mosque, Mohamed Atwi and his two sisters Khadija and Fatma heard the shooting as dawn broke. They went into the street to throw stones at the soldiers. Mohamed Atwi said they were Israelis. 'When I came out of the house, they started shooting, all of them together. Khadija was shot in front me, I bent down to pick her up. Then I was shot. I couldn't tell where the bullet came from. Then they shot Fatma in the stomach and a bullet came out of her back.'

An Israeli military doctor tried to help Khadija. According to her

---

* Obeid was to be kidnapped from his Jibchit home by Israeli troops in July 1989, an abduction which led to the murder of American UN hostage Col. William Higgins and a death threat against a second US captive.

brother, she yelled at him: 'You shoot at us and then you want to treat us.' There was a checkpoint of SLA and Israeli troops outside the village. According to Mohamed Atwi, 'they would not let the wounded leave the village. They kept us lying on the ground four hours. Khadija bled until three in the afternoon at the checkpoint. Then she died.'

Hanna Obeid was luckier. She was 16 and lay in bed in a white gown and scarf, a small girl with delicate features that belied her words. 'When the Israelis came to the village, I went up to the mosque. I collected some stones on the way to throw at them. When I threw the first stones at the Israelis, a soldier fired between my feet. I ran down the road to the square. I stood in front of an Israeli vehicle and threw stones at the soldiers in it. Then the militiamen came. I ran away ... but while I was running with my back to the militiamen, one of them shot me in the neck.' Why did Hanna Obeid throw stones? 'Because the soldiers had come to take our men. They had come to fight Islam. We have been taught in school and in the mosque to fight the Israelis. Our school books tell us that Israel is our enemy and that it is our duty to confront it.' Hanna Obeid's mother interrupts her. She too was throwing stones. 'Our faith is our weapon,' she said. 'If my daughters have to die for Islam, so be it.'

Others died that day. Sobhieh Ali Akhtar, a mother of ten, was shot dead when she ran into the street holding her skirt full of onions – the villagers had learned that onions smeared around the eyes reduce the effects of tear gas. Sobhieh Akhtar was shot in the heart; the militiamen apparently thought she was carrying a bomb. Haj Hassan Harb, the uncle of Rhagheb Harb, was shot dead. Twelve men fled the village during the shooting. They were all members of the resistance.

At the village of Maarakeh, the Israelis arrested a hundred young men. A green banner appeared over Maarakeh's main street. 'Repression strengthens us,' it said. 'Arrests and torture only make us more persistent.' Then the Israelis released 40 prisoners from Ansar 'to mark the blessed feast of *Al Fitr*,' as the Israeli military governor of Nabatieh said. There was a perversity about this conflict; repression and moderation went hand in hand, as if the struggle were a charade.

A new and more terrifying war began. Dozens of Shin Bet agents arrived in southern Lebanon, showing Israeli security passes at UN checkpoints and then driving into villages and shooting young men, always in 'self-defence'. The Lebanese believed they were death squads. All their identity cards were signed by an Israeli officer. The commander of Shin Bet operations was based at the Israeli army's intelligence headquarters in Tyre. His operatives used four cars – often without number plates – which were familiar to many villagers in southern Lebanon.

Early on the afternoon of 14 June 1984, three carloads of Shin Bet security men in civilian clothes arrived at a UN roadblock outside

Bidias, the home village of a prominent *Amal* leader called Daoud Daoud. There were 15 men in the cars and they showed their passes to the UN, each marked 'Israel Defence Force/*Sherut Bitachon* (Shin Bet)' and each signed by an Israeli colonel. According to the villagers, the first car, a white Mercedes, pulled up outside a garage belonging to Morshed Nahas, an Amal official. A man with blue eyes and blond hair in the back of the car called out Nahas' name.

The two other vehicles circled the small square at speed, apparently to prevent villagers from approaching. Eight of the Israelis armed with M-16 rifles took up positions in doorways round the square. When Nahas' mother Sawzieh reached the square, she said she saw her son being pulled into the back of the Mercedes, his legs dangling on the road, but that she was pushed aside by one of the gunmen. A village girl, Latifa Ghamlouche, said she heard one of the men say to Nahas: 'Choose the kind of death you want.'

Then they let him climb from the car. He walked away. Members of Nahas' family were present. They said he walked some yards from the car and that four gunmen in blue and yellow T-shirts ran behind him and shot him repeatedly in the head. One of them threw something on the ground. Daoud Daoud handed it to me later. It was a hood. Nahas had been ordered to join Israel's village militias, he said. This had been a warning to others. The Israelis said Nahas was shot 'while resisting arrest'.

The Shin Bet men entered other villages and walked into the homes of known guerrilla leaders, warning them of the consequences of continued opposition. But the identity of the Israeli agents was equally well known to the Muslim villagers. The Israelis liked to use Arab code names, imitating the Lebanese resistance and the PLO before them. In Nabatieh, the Israeli in charge of Shin Bet was 'Abu Yussef'. His deputy was 'Abu George'. In Kfar Falous, the senior Israel intelligence officer was 'Major Sami'. The leader of the Shin Bet unit that killed Nahas at Bidias was 'Abu Gharze'. The guerrillas had already put 'Abu Yussef' on a death list because they believed he paid almost 3,000 dollars to have Sheikh Rhageb Harb murdered. In Beirut, the Amal militia executed one of its men because they believed he had carried out the assassination for 'Abu Yussef'.

The effects of Israel's repression in southern Lebanon vibrated through west Beirut. Posters appeared of resistance exploits, drawings by an officially appointed Amal war artist which idealised the struggle against the Israelis. Cruder pictures were printed of the Star of David encircled by a swastika, of hook-nosed Israeli soldiers kicking women, of American and Israeli troops together plundering a south Lebanese village. West Beirut remained under the control of Muslim militias and of the Lebanese army's largely Shia 6th Brigade which had now become a tool of Amal.

This new mood in west Beirut was bound to be reflected in its violence. One of the few remaining Jewish residents of west Beirut was killed that July of 1984. Raul Sobhi Mizrahi ran a small electrical tool store in the Sanaya district, a harmless man of 54, a member of one of only five Jewish families still left in west Beirut. He was dragged from his home in handcuffs by three unidentified gunmen and found later on a deserted beach near the airport. Until his wife and brother were taken to view the body, Mizrahi's remains lay unidentified in the mortuary of the Makassed hospital. The Beirut newspapers treated the corpse with equal indifference. They buried news of the murder away in their inside pages, the longest report only two paragraphs.

For the Westerners who had stayed behind in Beirut, the world was also growing darker. In January 1984, an American academic, Frank Regier, and a French construction engineer, Christian Joubert, were kidnapped. Two months later, Amal gunmen freed them from the hands of 'Islamic Jihad'. What did 'Islamic Jihad' want? The multinational force had left Beirut. The Israelis were retreating. On 7 March, Jeremy Levin, the Beirut bureau chief of the American Cable News Network, was abducted on his way to work. 'He just left home at the normal time,' his wife told us later. 'He never got to the office.' We heard nothing more. A week later, William Buckley, described as a political attaché at the US Embassy in Beirut, was kidnapped as he left home in Raouche. Later — much later — the American government confirmed that he was the CIA station chief in Beirut. By then, he was dead.

The very last US Marines left on 31 July 1984. They were the last hundred men who had stayed behind to guard the British–American Embassy complex next to our home. Once more — just once — we saw the American warships on the horizon, a helicopter carrier and a frigate, grey in the haze, waiting to evacuate the last US military personnel in west Beirut. Anderson, Faramarzi, Mell and I sat on the roof of Anderson's and my apartment block and watched the helicopters thundering across the sea towards the Corniche. Anderson and Mell were pleased to see the Americans go. We were tired of their armoured vehicles outside our door, of their military orders bellowed at all hours from windows and sandbag guard posts, of the long-tailed rats that thrived on their piles of garbage in the street.

But we were all aware of what this departure meant. It was not that we felt abandoned. We were at home in Lebanon. Our friends were Lebanese. I felt much easier without the battery of Hawk missiles on the neighbouring roof. But we knew that this tiny, almost symbolic withdrawal would leave a vacuum quite out of proportion to the American departure. The kidnappings still did not cause us deep concern. Of the four abducted Westerners, two had been released. There was no definite indication that this was a campaign against foreigners. Anderson had decided to spend at least another three years in Lebanon. But there was something uncanny about that day, as if nature tried to warn us of something.

In a month when the country never saw rain — not in living memory — it poured in torrents, lashing the first helicopters that arrived roaring off the Corniche, their rotor blades slicing into the sea spray that rose majestically around them. A bank of grey, blustery clouds moved over the sky. They were not really ominous but they communicated something unspoken. Like that moment in *The Cherry Orchard* where Madame Ranevsky and her friends are picnicking and there is a distant breaking sound as if a cable has snapped far away in a mineshaft. A portent of an upheaval yet to come.

Three minutes before the last Marine helicopter was to leave, Anderson sneaked down the wall from our landlord's apartment with a camera and walked right up to the Marines. Their lieutenant-colonel was swigging champagne on the Corniche. 'Take this picture and I'll smash your camera,' he told Anderson. The Marines left by stages, the last six from their bunkers at opposite ends of the block, walking backwards from each end towards the helicopter, rifles at hip level, ready to shoot. As the rotors cut into the air, they sprayed Anderson with gravel and he snapped the last photographs of the Marines in Beirut. When he returned to us, Anderson was pulling up his trouser leg and grinning. There was a cut on his ankle and a smear of blood. 'Look what the Marines did with their helicopter,' he said. 'I've got my first war wound.'

Our difficulties then were with the Israelis. At the Awali River bridge, an Israeli officer identified as 'Lieutenant Albert' shouted abuse at a CBS television crew and refused them permission to cross to southern Lebanon. When the crew argued, an Israeli soldier fired bullets around their car. 'Albert', according to his Israeli colleagues, was a Lebanese Jew from Sidon. Israeli officers insisted that we obtain Israeli passes to visit the south. Israeli soldiers asked to read our notebooks. We always refused. I would accept a pass for identification purposes, but not as a permit to travel. I called Charles Douglas-Home, my editor, for his thoughts.

His reply was straightforward. '*The Times*,' he said, 'does not recognise an Israeli "Raj" in southern Lebanon. There is no reason why we should not accept a pass from Israeli military authorities in the south but this must not be accepted as permission to travel. You are a British citizen and *The Times* is legally in Lebanon and covers southern Lebanon from Beirut. There is to be no accepting an Israeli refusal to let *The Times* move in southern Lebanon because it does not have a pass. You may cross the Awali anywhere you like. There must be no provocation. But your notes are under absolutely no circumstances to be given to Israeli troops ...'

I crossed and re-crossed the Awali, sometimes in private cars, once on foot through the water. The deputy editor of *The Times*, Charles Wilson, visited Lebanon at my request and I drove him around the south of the country. Labelle and Faramarzi travelled with us. He asked to speak to the Israelis outside Sidon to hear 'their point of view'. The moment we arrived, we were all arrested by an Israeli officer wearing a yarmulka with lieutenant's insignia. 'You should not be here,' he said. 'You are ordered to return to Beirut immediately. These are military orders. I am sending you back to Beirut.' When I explained to him that an executive from *The Times* was present, he shrugged his shoulders.

Then the lieutenant – I suspected he was the 'Lieutenant Albert' who abused the journalists at the Awali – turned to four gunmen from the SLA. 'Get these bastards out of here,' he said. I said goodbye to the Israeli, addressing him as Lieutenant Albert. 'I am not Lieutenant Albert,' he said, and handed our deportation papers to the SLA gunmen. When we reached the Bater bridge, one of them said to us: 'Go – and don't come back.' Then he tossed the Israeli papers into a rubbish bin from which – when he turned away – I retrieved them and pushed them into my pocket. The documents were signed in Hebrew, 'Lieutenant Albert Cohen, Israeli defence force no: 272632/K'.

When we reached Beirut, Anderson was not interested in our story. Someone had blown up the American Embassy in Beirut, the new one. A suicide bomber. 'Islamic Jihad' had claimed responsibility. 'They wounded the US ambassador and the British one too,' Anderson said. 'A British security man shot the driver before the blast. What the hell is going on?' I think then we both knew. The war against the West was still going on in Beirut. But surely against embassies, diplomats. Not journalists.

Lieutenant Albert Cohen had every reason to want us out of southern Lebanon. Discipline was collapsing within the Israeli army. Israeli troops were vandalising houses around Maarakeh – we watched them tipping olive oil over beds, mixing sand in the village rice store, smashing furniture with hammers. When the Nahal Paratroop Brigade was sent east of Tyre to reimpose order, it lost a lieutenant on the first day in a rocket ambush. At the Tibnin River bridge, an Israeli officer walked up to an Irish army lieutenant and slapped him in the face.

It was not difficult to believe the frequent allegations of looting. In west Beirut, we had seen Israeli troops stealing property from houses near the airport; video players, radios, televisions. When I accompanied a British citizen back to the home he had abandoned during fighting near Chatila, we found that the Israeli troops billeted in his house had smeared Hebrew graffiti on the walls with excrement.

Examples of Israeli indiscipline were matched by evidence of their incompetence. Twenty per cent of their casualties during the 1982 invasion, it now emerged, had been caused by 'friendly fire', by their own rifles, tanks and aircraft. US officials were quoted as describing the Israeli army as 'an inept, undisciplined horde'.* Even the Israeli air force had managed to kill 34 of its own soldiers in an air attack in the Bekaa Valley.† In Israel, the police discovered that 4,000 hand grenades, 300 Galil rifles, 200 M-16 rifles, seven bazookas, 45 light mortars and two heavy machine-guns had been filched from Israeli army stores in Lebanon and were presumed to be in private Israeli hands.‡ Israeli troops were found leaving Lebanon with hashish bought in the Bekaa. A reader told the *Jerusalem Post* that 'Begin has dragged our flag through the mud long enough. I now pray that we will leave Lebanon soon, as our soldiers are being corrupted there. The longer we stay, the more we are degrading ourselves.'§

The Lebanese and the Palestinians watched this process of humiliation. They understood it only too well. When Israel tried to discredit the Western journalists who reported the 1982 siege of west Beirut, it sounded familiar. The thousands of civilians who died did not die. And those who died, according to the Israelis, were not always killed by those who killed them. It was the Palestinians, they said, who burned children with phosphorus and then called in the gullible media to demonstrate the results of Israeli shelling. Kemal Salibi, the Lebanese historian, learned something from this Israeli distortion. 'We Arabs are always rewriting our own history,' he told me. 'When we lose a war, we say we have won it. When we do something wrong, we say that others did it. I think somehow we are beginning to understand Israel, to see her as another Middle Eastern country.'

The Israeli press, which had supported the 1982 invasion in its initial days, now flayed the Israeli government and army. The army, the *Jerusalem Post* recognised, had 'instituted a destructive policy of trying to bring the Shiites to their knees while simultaneously trying to make a giant out of the South Lebanon Army.' The Israeli defence establishment

---

* See the conservative *Washington Times*, 27 August 1984: 'Israeli "ineptitude" blamed for "friendly fire" casualties'.
† I learned this quite by accident. Studying a list of Israeli military awards for the 1982 invasion, I noticed medals for courage under air attack. Dr Moshe Daniel, an Israeli army battalion medical officer, for example, received a citation from the Israeli chief of staff for treating and evacuating wounded Israelis after an air strike south of Lake Karaoun on 10 June 1982 (Awards 'for service above and beyond the call of duty', published Israel, 30 March 1983). I knew that no Syrian aircraft had bombed the Israelis during the invasion. The Israelis subsequently admitted that 'a tragedy' had occurred in the Bekaa. General Specter, the Israeli air force officer I interviewed in Israel, said that the Israeli pilot responsible for the disaster was 'short of fuel on a support mission . . . he was not responsible enough. He was given a hell of a punishment.' He would not disclose what this punishment was.
‡ See *Jerusalem Post* 23 January 1984 and 1 October 1984.
§ *Jerusalem Post*, 24 November 1982.

was being 'taken in by myths'.* More important still, the Israeli army had lost what we used to call The Threat. This was a distant cousin of The Plot. The Threat was that the ultimate war against 'terrorism' would involve a wholesale Israeli invasion of Lebanon.

If 'terrorism' did not cease, the Israelis would visit their wrath upon Lebanon. But they had come and now they were retreating. The Plot was always present but The Threat could not be used again. The Israelis were no longer feared. They could be killed and humiliated, too. The Israeli army, a writer lamented in the Israeli magazine *Newsview*, was 'no longer mysterious and terrifying to the enemy. Barricaded behind earthworks, sending out patrols of jumpy paratroops, it hardly deters.'† By the end of 1984, two of Israel's leading military writers blamed Sharon for the misery of the invasion and summed it up thus: 'Born of the ambition of one wilful, reckless man, Israel's 1982 invasion of Lebanon was anchored in delusion, propelled by deceit, and bound to end in calamity.'‡

In Beirut that September of 1984, I found a scruffy office in the ruined Palestinian camp of Bourj al-Barajneh. Scrawled in chalk on the breeze-block wall outside, the letters uneven as a child's, were the words: 'Popular Front for the Liberation of Palestine — General Command'. Up the dirty tile staircase sat six Palestinians. One wore a camouflage uniform, an old US Marine issue that was handed out to the Lebanese army. Another carried a small black pistol in the back of his trouser belt. A third man introduced himself as 'Mahmoud'. He seemed uneasy when I entered the room, anxious to present the PFLP–GC, which is among the most extreme of the PLO groups, as a political rather than a military organisation. 'We believe that the liberation of Palestine is impossible without the gun,' he said. 'But we have no military purpose here. We have no enemies here.'

Mahmoud and his friends had opposed Arafat and they were in Beirut on Syria's behalf, to keep the survivors of the camps firmly outside Arafat's control. They were watched by the Syrians and by Amal, which did not want Palestinians to interfere in its nationalist Muslim rule of west Beirut. In Chatila, the pro-Syrian Saiqa movement had set up office in a little hut, and in Mar Elias, just outside Chatila, I came across another grubby office with 'Fatah Revolutionary Council' on a sign beside the door. This was Abu Nidal's organisation, the cruellest of

---

* *Jerusalem Post Magazine*, 8 June 1984.
† *Newsview*, 29 May 1984. 'A question of morale' by A. E. Norden. See also Benny Morris in the *Jerusalem Post*, 5 June 1984: '... perhaps the worst outcome of the war for Israel is the perception in Lebanon and Syria that Israel "shot its bolt". Before the invasion, Israeli military power was held in awe by Lebanese from the various communities, by Palestinians and, to a degree, by the Syrians. That awe no longer exists.'
‡ Schiff and Ya'ari, *Israel's Lebanon War*, p. 301.

all the Palestinian movements. Abu Nidal's men were in Beirut. The Palestinian guerrillas whom Israel swore would never return to Beirut were back.

The Litani River bridge, southern Lebanon, 16 August 1984

Danny is an Israeli reservist, blond, short hair, blue eyes, an 18-year-old drafted for nine months, born in Washington, now living in Kibbutz Ein Simourian. He wants to study political science at the Hebrew University. He voted, he says, 'to the right' of the right-wing Likud Party in the recent Israeli election. The heavy machine-gun slung across his waist only emphasises his youth and vulnerability. He is too young to have participated in the 1982 invasion.

From behind him the sea roars on the beach at Sarafand. His sweat trails down his flak jacket. It is hot on the Litani.

In the plantation to the east, a Lebanese man is working in an orchard, watering the ground beneath the banana trees. Danny's eyes flicker towards the man. 'You see that man over there? Well, he may be OK. But he sees what we do every day and then he tells a brother or a friend. And he tells someone else. They see our APCs [armoured personnel carriers] moving and our jeeps and trucks. They know where we are going. They know everything about us. My platoon was ambushed last week. We were on a patrol in a banana plantation. There was a bomb beside the road ... my men were in the field. When the bomb went off, they got shot. Two of my men were hit, one in both legs.'

Danny points his index fingers at his knees. 'I know that when we do something aggressive to these people, we are bound to get attacked the next day. We have to search people. We look for terrorists. They hate us for this. I wish I could speak in Arabic to these people. I can only say to them "Do this" and "Go there". I wish I knew how to say "Please". I wish I knew how to say "Sorry".'

Kfar Falous, southern Lebanon, 17 August 1984

The Shia Muslims are queuing in the heat – hundreds of them – for a red and green pass merely to travel out of Israeli-held territory to Beirut, to their own capital. The SLA holds the crowd at bay. They smell of sweat.

A young Israeli soldier walks through the crowd. A pretty Shia girl waves at him and he waves back, smiling and shouting 'Hi!' The girl goes on smiling but she is cursing him in Arabic. 'What, are you still alive?' she asks. 'May God curse you people.' She is beautiful. The insult is all the more wicked because the Israeli cannot understand it. He innocently goes on smiling, waving again at the girl.

In late September 1984, the SLA committed a massacre in the Shia village of Sohmor. Three Druze members of the Israeli-recruited militia had been shot in an ambush. So Druze SLA men surrounded the village where the killings occurred, lined up the menfolk in the square and opened fire on them all. They murdered 13. When the Israelis arrived, another 30 wounded were lying in the square in their own blood. Part of Lahd's militia, the 'shield of Galilee', had disintegrated into an ethnic gang.

From Beirut, from the Bekaa, Shia Muslim gunmen now flocked to the south. At first unwilling to become involved in the war against the Israelis, Amal was now anxious to establish itself as the principal nationalist movement in southern Lebanon. Iran's influence within the Hezbollah meant that a separate pan-Islamic resistance was growing within the villages east of Tyre. Further east still, in the Arkoub, Lebanese leftist groups attacked the occupation army. A few PLO men made their way south so that Arafat's army could be represented, however fraudulently, in the history of the last struggle against the occupiers. The Sunni Nasserite militia formed the nucleus of the resistance in Sidon. The guerrilla organisations cooperated, but their desire to assault the retreating Israelis was prompted as much by the need to earn political credentials and hold territory for the future as to prove their patriotism.

If Amal allowed the Hezbollah to lead the struggle in the south, then Amal would lose Tyre and the surrounding villages to their Shia rivals when the Israelis left. On the Gulf war battle fronts, Iran was threatening to break into Iraq and surround Saddam Hussein's army in Basra. If the Islamic Republic's protégés could triumph over the Israelis in Lebanon, then Khomeini could claim that his goal of exporting an Islamic revolution was coming true.

As the guerrilla war in southern Lebanon reached its climax, the casualties were as high as the stakes. In December 1984 the Israeli army were attacked a hundred times. They lost three dead and 27 wounded. In the same period, gunmen killed 17 of Lahd's militiamen and eight Israeli collaborators. Fourteen guerrillas − at least one of them a Palestinian − were killed. The PLO brought Katyusha rockets across the Israeli lines. In the first week of January 1985, lists containing the names of 60 alleged informers were plastered around the walls of Tyre. Etienne Saqr's armed bands found their cars booby-trapped. By 11 January, 15 collaborators had been 'liquidated', according to what was now called the 'Lebanese National Resistance'.

On 6 January 1985, a combined Israeli army−Shin Bet patrol was attacked with a roadside bomb west of the village of Abbasiyeh. When the soldiers left their vehicle to investigate, another culvert bomb exploded 60 yards away. The patrol fled towards Tyre under small-arms fire. On the same day, near Deir Qanoun en-Nahr, an old woman waved down the car of a collaborator, known to the locals as 'Ringo'. He stopped. Four men emerged from the bushes behind the woman and shot him dead, wounding his companions. Haidar Dayekh, the leader of the 'Forces of Kerbala' whom I had interviewed in Jouaya, resigned from the militia. He did not want to die. Too late. A few days later, outside his home, Dayekh was shot in the face. He died instantly.

In Abbasiyeh, four hooded men walked into the local coffee shop and pointed to a 37-year-old Palestinian called Yussef Abdul Ghani. 'This is a collaborator,' one of the hooded men screamed. 'We are the national resistance.' The Palestinian was bundled into the trunk of a car. Several days later, in a ditch near the village of Bourj Rahal, he was found, a towel over his head, hands tied and his back torn open by three bursts of automatic-gunfire.

The Israelis brought their Golani Brigade to the Awali, left a battalion in Tyre and installed their 7th Armoured Brigade in the mountains at Bater. These were units which journalists usually described as 'élite'. In December, the Sayeret Matkal unit, the commandos who had rescued the hostages at Entebbe, were sent to search the villages east of Tyre. They went in on foot, through the orchards, and found nothing. But every search was accompanied by fierce beatings of young men in Shin Bet operatives. New code names were being used by the Shin Bet men now; 'Abu Mousa', 'Younis' and 'Colonel Gaby'. Unable to keep the roads open, the Israelis began to fly their troops to forward positions in helicopters. The 'élite' soldiers of Israel's finest regiments could not restore order. The Israeli front line north of Sidon was no longer a line but a series of besieged fortifications. At night, their enemy swarmed around them.

Everyone in Sidon knew the Israelis were leaving. Everyone – Muslims and Christians – said they wanted the Lebanese army to take control. I stayed with a Shia family in the Sidon suburb of Qia'a, on a street adjoining the Christian district of the city. Every night, we would see the flares dripping over the Israeli positions on the Awali. Every evening, frightened young men would call at our door. What did we know? Was it true the Phalange would attack Sidon when the Israelis left? Israeli spokesmen in Tel Aviv spoke of a bloodbath when the Israelis left Sidon. It would be like the Chouf. Worse. The Israelis patrolled the streets now only with tank support.

On the night of 6 February, two young men came to our door. They were polite, formal, full of hope. There was to be a meeting of all the people of the neighbourhood, they said. At four o'clock, at Omar Hariri's house. Would we come along? We were not surprised. All over Sidon, Muslims and Christians were meeting together to reassure themselves that they would not kill each other when the Israelis left.

When we arrived at Hariri's blue-shuttered apartment, there were almost 50 people in the dining room, sitting on wooden chairs, all men, middle-aged, thoughtful, smoking heavily, dressed in their best suits. Most were Sunnis and all looked very serious. They were watching a tall, dark-haired Christian called Camille Mamari explaining why everyone should trust each other in the coming critical days.

He was a personable young man. He smiled a lot, he moved his hands when he talked and he used the word *ta'awan* many times. It meant 'cooperation' and there was good reason why it should appeal to Camille. For he was also the local Phalangist official in Qia'a, and cooperation was exactly what the Phalange were going to need from the large Sunni population if the Christians were not to be driven from their homes. 'The Lebanese army is going to come,' he told the men around him. 'If we are not united in our hearts in wanting them, we will fail ... Look what happened to the multinational force and the Americans in Beirut — they left. If we are really united, the Lebanese army could come without their guns and they would be successful.'

Camille's message was not without obvious attractions to his audience. No one had wanted the Palestinians in this area, he said, and the people had carried out their promise not to have them here. No one in the room dissented from this view. 'We have been stupid in the past,' Camille said. 'We have been the stupidest people in the world — because we have destroyed our own homes.'

Cigarettes were handed round and a water jug and plastic cups of coffee. But there were questions that disturbed a few of those present. What could be done, a man in a grey suit asked, if car bombs were left in the streets? Camille assured him that efforts would be made to prevent this. And what, an old man wanted to know, about the hooded men he had seen on the streets? No such hooded men had appeared, Camille insisted. Not so, the old man went on. 'We've seen them.' Camille replied at once. 'They did not belong to our organisation.' But there was a silence afterwards, long enough to be eloquent.

Every journey around Sidon became dangerous. A visit to the supermarket near Riad Solh Street. Next door is a coffee shop and petrol station owned by a Sunni family. From the coffee shop, I use the telephone to call Beirut. Colleagues at the AP take my copy and telex it through to *The Times* in London. Outside, two thunderously loud reports. Bombs have detonated next to an SLA militia patrol. The SLA gunmen fire bullets through the windows of the coffee shop. An Israeli tank pulls up outside. Slowly and deliberately, the tank reverses into the wall of the petrol station. The nearest structure to every bomb is always destroyed. This is an Israeli punishment. An Israeli officer goes into the gas station and vandalises the shop inside, pushing tins of paint and motor oil across the floor. He emerges smiling. One of his soldiers begins shooting in the air.

A visit to the bakery at Abra to buy *manouches*, the big hot cheese sandwiches which the Lebanese eat at breakfast. Almost at the top of the Abra hill, I catch sight of an Israeli foot patrol walking in the same direction in front of my car. The soldier at the back turns and begins waving. I think for a moment that he is greeting someone in the house across the road until suddenly he is in front of my car, rifle hunched in to his shoulder, pointing the muzzle at my face, screaming through the closed window. He thinks he is confronting a car bomber.

For just a millisecond, I find myself wondering what it is like to be shot. I think the young Israeli is contemplating what it feels like to shoot someone. He has a European face with round, frameless glasses like a student and his hair sticks out like a child's from under his green poncho hat. Then he lowers his rifle with almost as much relief as I ease the car into reverse and slide away from him.

On the road to Naqqoura, three Israeli soldiers from the Golani Brigade. Rafi is 19, anxious to talk to foreigners. 'I've been ambushed lots of times. When you get bombed the first time, it's bad. After that, all the ambushes are the same and you can take it. We got hit for the first time in Sidon. It was a bomb beside the road. It was a Palestinian who did it.' What happened to the Palestinian? 'What do you think? What do you think we do with people who set off bombs for us?' There is a long, awkward silence. Morality of arms.

An old man is walking very slowly up the road towards us, towards the barricade of stones that the Israelis have laid across the road. He wears a *kuffiah* and he stumbles because he is blind. Rafi walks into the road and moves the stones. Then he steps towards the man and takes him by the arm. With infinite care and gentleness, he leads the blind Lebanese up the lane, the man all the while thanking him, unaware that it is an Israeli who is being kind to him.

In early February, at Kfar Falous, the collaborators were summoned to see the Shin Bet officers. 'Colonel Gaby' was there. They could expect no further protection, they were told. A few were offered asylum in Israel. Others were ignored. Later, they would be dragged from their homes by gunmen. The best-known collaborator in Sidon called himself 'Abu Arida'. I saw his name on many walls. 'Death awaits Abu Arida,' it said. At first, 'Abu Arida' scorned these bulletins. He was a feared man. He was a tough man. Now the Israelis were leaving and it was Abu Arida who lived in fear. For two years, he had handed to the Israelis the names of Palestinians who he said were 'terrorists'. Some of those Palestinians were among the corpses found on the roadway east of

Sidon back in 1982. In mid-February 1985, 'Abu Arida' clambered aboard a boat in Sidon harbour with two dozen of his men and set sail into the Mediterranean.

There was terror in Sidon. On a wall near the Phalangist office, I saw the spray-painted words: 'The spy passed this way.' Another wall. 'All agents will receive their rewards.' Many of the collaborators had graduated from the Ansar prison camp. I met one, frightened and alone, in the coffee shop one afternoon. 'The Israelis said to me: "Work for us and I'll let you go." They said my wife was young and beautiful, that there were many men who wanted her, that she would sleep with them while I rotted in Ansar. I wanted my wife. I worked for the Israelis.'

Another collaborator. 'An Israeli came. He was called Michel, about thirty-five, European, handsome, wearing casual clothes. He was very polite, blond, he had a big stomach. He interrogated me in the tobacco factory at Nabatieh. He let me go, then I received word through the "national guard" that he wanted to see me again. He told me to pass by an Israeli position between Zahrani and Nabatieh. "We'll stop you and make it look natural. See you at four. The checkpoint will stop you." I didn't go. So Michel told the resistance about me, that I was a good agent. Twice they tried to kill me in Jibchit.'

At night, I heard shooting. In the morning, the Israelis announced they had caught 11 Palestinian infiltrators on the Awali. All had been shot in a fire-fight. Later, the collaborators put about a different story; all 11 had been captured, disarmed, lined up by the river and shot. Executed. A firing squad. 'What do you think we do with people who set off bombs for us?'

Mustapha Saad was head of the Nasserite militia. His presence in Sidon was considered essential if a civil war was to be prevented when the Israelis left. But a bomb exploded outside his apartment. His daughter was killed, he was gravely wounded, brain-damaged. The United Nations prepared a helicopter to take him to the American University hospital in Beirut where his life could be saved. I spoke to Timur Göksel, the UN's spokesman in Naqqoura. 'The Israelis delayed permission for our helicopter to fly for half an hour,' he said. Why? Göksel preferred not to speculate. Saad lived, almost blind, after brain surgery in the United States. But he was not in Sidon in the vital days that followed the Israeli retreat.

I went to see my friend in Mieh Mieh, the Christian university teacher who read Maurice Bowra and Khalil Gibran. When I wrote about him in The Times, I called him Louis. As I explained to readers, the names were changed – as they used to say in American police movies – to protect the innocent. In Mieh Mieh, to protect the guilty as well. For there had been a sinister change on his windy little hill above Sidon. There was a red car parked not far from the teacher's home. In the driver's seat was an Israeli soldier with the acronym 'IDF' in Hebrew on his shirt. In the back seat sat two men in black leather jackets with Uzi submachine-guns on their knees. And there was another man, a Lebanese with a goatee beard, who wanted to know what a reporter was doing in Mieh Mieh. Two more men approached, Antoine and Elias. Why did I want to talk to the teacher? Was I bringing a message?

They grudgingly let me ring his door bell. I waited for him to appear. When the door opened, I saw a wraith. He had not shaved for many days. His shirt was dirty, his eyes bloodshot. When I walked into the house, so did Antoine and Elias, uninvited. The teacher was frightened. The two men sat opposite us with dull, expressionless faces. Louis' mother emerged and smiled weakly. Something was dreadfully wrong. So we talked about Wordsworth. The teacher stood up and fetched the manuscript of a book he had just completed on nineteenth-century French poetry, filled with references to the English Romantics and to T. S. Eliot's essays. Then the telephone rang. Louis took the call, listened for a few seconds, then replaced the receiver. 'There are some men coming to meet you here,' he said, and then sat down on the other side of the stove. Who were they, I asked? 'I don't know,' Louis replied with a sorrowful, apologetic smile. We sat there in silence until there was a knock on the door.

The two new men who entered were abrupt. The same questions. Identity? Where did I live in Beirut? Did I have an Israeli pass? How had I met my schoolmaster friend? A third man arrived. He ignored Louis and his old mother. There was just a hint of dark metal showing above his belt. He had a thin suspicious face. Then, just as suddenly, he left. It was made clear that I could leave, too, if I wished. It seemed a good idea. Louis looked at me soulfully. 'In war,' he said, 'words die.'

Outside in the street, the red car slid past me, the two Israeli Shin Bet intelligence men in the back seat. An Israeli army truck and a jeep were parked down another lane. What was going on in Mieh Mieh? A Phalangist official told me later that the villagers were divided. Some wanted peace with the Palestinians down the hill in advance of the Israeli withdrawal and had made contact with them. Others, he said, were working for the Israelis and wished to provoke the Palestinians. My schoolteacher friend had decided, after much reflection, that he wanted peace – with both the Palestinians and the Muslims of Sidon. He had wanted to speak out. He said he believed in democracy. He claimed he was a Lebanese patriot. Shin Bet had come to his home and placed Phalangist gunmen outside. He would be moved from his home soon, to Beirut. There would be no more talk of peace in Mieh Mieh.

In my report to *The Times* that night, I wrote that 'it would be fascinating to discover just what Shin Bet are doing in the village. And why, one wonders, are four Israeli soldiers billeted down the hill from the village in the fourth floor of a building, firing occasionally during the day in the direction of the Palestinian camp at Ein Helweh? Whatever the answers, it seems likely that we shall hear the name of Mieh Mieh again ...'

The Lebanese 'national resistance' stuck a new flyposter on the walls of Sidon. With grim humour, it announced a change of address to accord with Israel's withdrawal. 'Closing down sale. We pay in blood, not dollars. Very definitely the last chance to hit a tank. We are moving our address further south.'

When the Israelis left Sidon, the Lebanese army moved in. The Israelis dropped leaflets from the air, promising to strike 'without mercy or second thought' against anyone who attacked their soldiers. Christians and Muslims rejoiced together, briefly. Only later were we to hear of Mieh Mieh again. And everything we heard would be bad.

No sooner had the Israelis retreated to a line along the Litani River than the guerrillas attacked again. Two Israeli officers, including Colonel Avraham Hildo, described as the principal adviser to Antoine Lahd, the SLA leader, were killed in ambushes near Nabatieh. The Israeli army closed the Litani River bridge and tried to prevent soldiers of the French UN battalion from travelling to Beirut. When an Israeli pointed his gun at a French soldier, the two armies began a fist fight on the road, which continued until the French gave the Israelis an ultimatum to clear the road or be subjected to a company attack with firearms. Seeing the French troops deploying in the fields with heavy machine-guns, the Israelis opened the road in 30 seconds.

Israel now instituted what it called its 'iron fist' policy against the guerrillas of southern Lebanon. Shia villages would be raided, often at night, usually during the day, by hundreds of Israeli troops. In the morning, three or four bodies would lie on the hillsides outside the town, guerrillas 'shot while trying to escape'. Again, the Israelis refused to allow any journalists travelling from Beirut to enter their occupation zone. Don Mell, the AP photographer, and I set off through Jezzine, high in the mountains south of the Chouf, and penetrated the Israeli lines in a snowstorm, driving our car between two withdrawing Merkava tanks and waving cheerfully at the Israeli guards on the road. It was easy to understand why the Israelis did not want us there.

In Tyre, on 23 February 1985, I wrote a long letter to Charles Douglas-Home to explain the background to the reports I was filing each day on the collapse of morale in the Israeli army. Israeli raids on villages were growing ever harsher. 'It is now quite normal for me to arrive in a village,' I wrote, 'and listen to men with bruises clearly visible on their faces who have been "questioned" by Israeli troops ... In three recent raids east of Tyre, the UN have found men afterwards, shot through the head. In the raid on Bazzouriyeh ... the Israelis say they shot two men trying to escape with weapons. Privately, the French UN contingent have told me (in the shape of one of their intelligence officers) that from the bullet wounds in their heads, the men were simply led away by the Israelis and "executed" ... In one raid just over a week ago, the French army entered a village after the departure of the Israelis to find Koranic texts torn to pieces littering the floor of the mosque. The French intelligence man says he has no doubt the Israelis did this ...'

The resistance leader for southern Lebanon was now Khalil Jerardi, who was nominally a member of Amal but in fact a supporter of the Hezbollah. He lived in Maarakeh, inside Israel's occupation zone. He was a small man of 25, dressed in a blue raincoat, with a long, pointed beard, intense, angry, firm in the belief that the most fundamentalist of the resistance fighters represented both Islam and Lebanon. In a room surrounded by portraits of Islamic leaders, including Khomeini, he told me that Israel could expect further suicide bombings.

'The brutality of the Israelis has proved to everyone in southern Lebanon that the Israelis want to humiliate them,' Jerardi said. 'So they are more determined to resist the occupation — both civil resistance and military resistance.' This was standard rhetoric. But Jerardi understood the psychology of oppression — and its usefulness to the resistance.

'The brutal practices of the occupation army are in the interests of the resistance,' he said. 'The arrests the Israelis make are of ordinary people. When this happens, the people become more united. The resistance needs this badly.' Who is the resistance? Jerardi's voice did not change. 'The resistance is national, but its ideas are those of Islam. And it is based on the principle that God opposes tyranny. This is the truth of the resistance. Some statements issued in Beirut in our name are untrue, Yassir Arafat says untrue things. The resistance is not led by commanders — by a Mr X or a Mr Y, as the media say — it is directed by the ideas of Islam.'

He spoke more literally than I realised. Only later would a village sheikh tell me the reality behind this 'direction' of the resistance. The village Imams, he said, were asked to mention certain words in their sermons. The requests came from Beirut, often from the Hezbollah; sometimes, not always, the code-words were devised by Iranians. These words — 'great books', 'olive groves', 'sweet fruits', there was no limit to the combinations — would mean nothing to the village sheikhs. Nor to most of their worshippers. But a few, perhaps only one man, in the mosque would understand their import. They would be a message. That is how the suicide bombers of Lebanon used to receive their orders.

Only hours after hundreds of Israeli troops raided Maarakeh on 3 March 1985, Jerardi and his closest colleague in the resistance, Mohamed

Sa'ad, held a press conference in the village. They had been hiding in caves beneath Maarakeh during the raid; we heard them talking over military radio sets during the Israeli searches. 'We are still here,' we heard them say. 'We can say no more.' Once the Israelis had left the village, Jerardi appeared in a narrow, crowded office above the mosque, dressed in a brown combat jacket, grinning at his supporters, claiming that he had never left the village during the Israeli raid, indeed had watched it from a neigbouring window.

'Next time our villages are attacked,' he said, 'we are going to be serious about attacking the Galilee villages in Palestine. The Israelis did not capture me or any of my fighters in the Tyre area. We shall continue to fight the Israelis to the end.' I sat watching Jerardi, sitting on a sofa in the crowded little office. The end would come almost exactly a day after the Israelis had left Maarakeh, the time it takes the hour hand of a 24-hour clock to complete one revolution.

A bomb exploded on the roof of Jerardi's office on 4 March 1985. It killed almost all the resistance leaders: Jerardi, Sa'ad and ten other guerrillas were blown apart. Almost the entire French UN battalion was drafted into Maarakeh to hold back the screaming crowds and dig through the rubble. The French found pieces of the electrical mechanism of the bomb, parts of which read 'Minnesota Mining Company'. It had been manufactured in West Germany. 'This is the work of Israel,' one of Jerardi's colleagues shouted. 'The Israeli soldiers placed this bomb when they left Maarakeh.' The French intelligence officers who moved into Maarakeh agreed. 'If you're talking about guerrilla warfare,' one of them said to me, 'this is perfect terrorism − or counter-terrorism. This is what we did in Algeria.'

The corpses were laid out on a large slab of stone in a courtyard near the mosques, heaps of human remains covered in blankets from which dribbled streams of blood. There was, of course, nothing more cruel about the killing of the guerrilla leadership in Maarakeh than there had been about the deaths of countless Israeli soldiers in southern Lebanon, nor was there anything exclusive about Maarakeh's grief. A savage and merciless guerrilla war was now going on here.

On the eve of his death Jerardi had turned to me and uttered a terrible, prophetic warning. 'I assure you,' he said, 'that Israel will not be able to crush the people of southern Lebanon. They are more powerful than the Israelis. The fingers of the people of southern Lebanon are between Israel's teeth. Both sides are biting. Who will scream first?'

There was no doubt who Jerardi believed would bite hardest. Locked into a savage conflict with thousands of civilians as well as guerrillas, the Israeli army was now experiencing the first defeat of its existence, a tactical and strategic retreat from one of the greatest military blunders in recent Middle East history. Academics, especially in Israel or the United

States, liked to attribute Shia Muslim radicalism in southern Lebanon to some form of revolutionary inspiration from Iran, as if Ayatollah Khomeini exerted a physical power over the region. They ignored the fact that this radicalism was partly created by Israel. Even more seriously, they ignored the fact that the Iranian revolution did not begin in the Iranian city of Qom or in Tehran. It began in southern Lebanon.

Mousa Sadr, whose portrait now hung over the ruins of the homes destroyed by Israeli troops, was not just a missing Imam, almost a Twelfth Imam to the Shias of southern Lebanon. He was Iranian. He was born in Qom. Even more crucial, he was the principal link between the Iranian opposition to the Shah and the Ayatollah Khomeini when the latter was enduring his bitter exile in Najaf. Mousa Sadr lived in Tyre. His sister, Rabab, married Hussein Charefiddin, from one of the most prominent Lebanese Shia families in the city. In the grey days of Iranian opposition to the Shah, almost all the figures who were, after 1979, to be the kingmakers and spiritual leaders of Iran visited Tyre.

To Mousa Sadr's Jebel Amel college outside the city came Mehdi. Bazargan, Khomeini's future prime minister. Bazargan's deputy, Sadeq Tabatabai – still one of Khomeini's closest aides – visited Tyre each year. So did Ayatollah Mohamed Beheshti, who was later to become leader of the Islamic Republican Party and Iranian minister of justice. Sadeq Qotbzadeh, who advised Khomeini in Paris and became his foreign minister, travelled to Tyre each year.

Mustapha Chamran, who was to be Khomeini's minister of defence, was one of the founders of the Jebel Amel college and taught there for several years. One of his pupils, a young electrical engineering student, was Mohamed Sa'ad who, years later, was to be Khalil Jerardi's leading explosives expert in the resistance movement. Jerardi and Sa'ad both attended prayers at the same mosque as Beheshti. So did many other Lebanese teenagers from the villages around Tyre.

Many of these villagers traced their ancestry to Iran. In Maarakeh, which had born the brunt of Israel's 'iron fist', at least five families could trace their roots to Iran over the past hundred years. Thus Jerardi and Sa'ad and their friends grew up amid the power and conspiracy – theological as well as physical – of revolution. In the years to come, Beheshti would be killed in the bombing of his party headquarters in Tehran. Chamran would die mysteriously on the Iran–Iraq war front. These were martyrs whom the southern Lebanese had known and could emulate. Qotbzadeh died an official traitor before Khomeini's firing squad. The Shias of southern Lebanon now showed an equal lack of mercy to their own collaborators.

For many people in southern Lebanon, it was Israel that finally brought two doctrinal national revolutions together when its army raided the Jebel Amel college. The Israelis beat many of the pupils there. One of the students, Hassan Qassir, enraged by what had happened, drove an explosive-laden car into an Israeli army vehicle. Iranian and Lebanese Shia Muslim cults of martyrdom were now politically joined.

And so, in the last months of its occupation around Tyre, Israel's army had become ensnared by the most powerful force it had ever confronted. All the trappings of a brutal police state now existed in the occupation area. There were midnight arrests, hooded prisoners, beatings at Shin Bet headquarters. There were killings and curfews every night and reprisal raids on civilian homes and a total Israeli military ban on independent press coverage of the war. Or almost.

Mell, Faramarzi and I stayed on in Tyre and its villages with two or three other Western reporters from Beirut, sheltered by Shia families at great risk to themselves. The Israelis arrested the man who placed our telephone calls to Beirut and London. They detained Mell at night and forced him to drive through Tyre alone during the curfew. Below the homes in which we stayed, Israeli troops picked up civilians at random, hooding them in the street, dragging them on ropes to their intelligence headquarters. Civilians were forced to lie on armoured personnel carriers so that the resistance would not attack the vehicles.

I left one family with whom I was staying after Shin Bet arrested two of their relatives. In the early hours of the morning, in a filthy Tyre hotel, an Israeli Shin Bet agent guarded by uniformed border police pounded on my door and ordered me from my room. The moment I saw him, I recognised the man who the Irish army had told me – four years earlier – might have been present at the murder of their two soldiers, Barrett and Smallhorn. 'Abu Shawki'. I was tired and I was frightened of this man. 'Were you there with Barrett and Smallhorn?' I asked him. The Shin Bet man looked up sharply. He shouted at me with venom. 'You are dirt. Get back into your room.' I had not accused him of anything. But he understood. He knew the names. *He knew*. When I reopened the door a few seconds later, he had gone.

On 9 March 1985, a massive car bomb blew up near Sheikh Mohamed Fadlallah's office in Beirut. The Americans had claimed that he blessed the car bombers who destroyed the US Marine barracks. Only later would the *Washington Post* reveal that CIA operatives planted the bomb. It killed more than 80 people, almost all of them civilians. The Hezbollah hung a banner above the ruined buildings and the human remains. 'The work of the United States,' it said. They were right.

Another suicide bomber attacked the Israelis, ramming his car into a convoy above Marjayoun, killing 12 Israeli soldiers. New rules were introduced. No one was to drive alone in southern Lebanon. The Israelis believed no one would share a car with a suicide bomber. But in revenge, the Israelis turned ferociously on the village of Zrariyeh, north of the Litani, driving their tanks over cars whose passengers had no time to escape. Gunmen, old men and women were killed without quarter.

'This is the revenge of the Israeli army,' the Israeli soldiers wrote in red paint on the village square before they left. A survivor described how a Lebanese soldier had advanced from his guard post outside the town, laid down his rifle and raised his hands in surrender. An Israeli officer walked up to the man, he said, and shot him in the temple.

In Tyre, the curfew was imposed with a new cruelty. A taxi driver, Hassan Skeiki, was shot dead in his car. He had been travelling alone. When his body was brought to the hospital, most of his face had been cut away, apparently with a knife or a hatchet. Faramarzi and I travelled to the scene the next day. On our way back, we were stopped by Israeli soldiers on a road through an orange orchard. Some held bottles of beer and wine in their hands. One of them, standing by the roadside without a helmet or beret, was holding an axe. We said we were journalists and they just watched us, saying nothing, as we drove carefully away.

I returned to Beirut on 15 March, through the wreckage of the night's guerrilla bombardment of the Israeli positions on the Litani River. Smoke curled up from burning supplies. The soldiers' faces were rimed with dirt and tiredness. Mortar explosions still vibrated through the plantations as I drove over the river. Beirut lay just two hours in front of me, comfort and safety where I could bathe and eat out and sleep in my own bed.

In the AP bureau, I filed a dispatch about southern Lebanon to *The Times*. Anderson was there, cheerful if a little nervous. I talked to him in his private office about the south, the savagery of both sides in the guerrilla war. How was Beirut? 'OK,' he said, and he paused. 'Don't tell my family, but a funny thing happened yesterday. Four guys in a Mercedes tried to head me off outside the *Bain Militaire*, when I was driving back to work from lunch at home. I turned sharp left and got away. If you tell my family, they'll only be frightened. There's no need. It was probably just a bunch of freelancers trying to frighten me, having a joke at the expense of an American.'

That night, I sat drinking with Anderson on the floor of his apartment, the doors open to the night breeze off the sea. Mell was there, and Faramarzi. We did not mention the strange incident of the four men but we talked about the kidnapping of Jonathan Wright, a Reuters correspondent who had been abducted by Palestinians in the Bekaa in September 1984 and later escaped from his captors. We talked, too, about the 24-hour captivity of four Lebanese AP staffers a month later. Anderson made some cutting jokes about an attempt which had been made to kidnap me the previous year, when four armed men had tried to stop my car and then chased me through the streets as if in a scene from *The French Connection*.

Mell was planning a tennis match against Anderson in the morning. Anderson, drinking his favourite Lebanese Musar red wine, insisted that Mell would be in no mood to get up for tennis after drinking. Mell was notorious for sleeping in.

I was tired but I went on talking about kidnapping. Anderson tried to provoke me. 'Fisky, you only drove away from those guys last year because you happen to be crazy and because you drive like a maniac anyway. I've thought a lot about this. Almost all the people who've been kidnapped have been set free after a while. It's always sorted out in the end.'

Terry, I said, I think you have to fight, I think you have to struggle, I don't think we should let ourselves be taken, whatever the cost. I remembered those words for years afterwards. Was I right or wrong?

'Fisky, you're out of your mind,' Anderson said, refilling my glass of wine, grinning at me through his pin-point eyes and thick spectacles. 'These guys have guns. You don't have a chance. You were just lucky last time. If they come, it's better to let them take you.'

They came for him next morning.

16 Wait for Me

Madeleine, my love, my heart, I saw our daughter on TV
the other night and I cried for joy. I only saw her for 2 or 3
seconds, enough to notice your black hair and beautiful
bright eyes. But I can't describe how it felt to end months
of not knowing. Our guards had seen the piece on the early
news and brought in the TV for the later cast ... I never
cease thinking about you − I talk to you (in my head)
every night and in the early mornings. Those are the
difficult times, and thinking of you helps ... I miss you
terribly. I didn't think it was possible to hurt this much.

American hostage Terry Anderson, west Beirut
8 November 1985

Wait for me, and I'll return
Only wait very hard ...
Wait. For I'll return, defying every death.
And let those who do not wait, say that I was lucky.
They never will understand that in the midst of death,
You with your waiting saved me.
Only you and I know how I survived.
It's because you waited, as no one else did.

Konstantin Simonov

'Terry Anderson has been kidnapped.' Impossible. I was in my car, just
parking outside my house. Rod Nordland, the *Newsweek* correspondent,
was there, in a taxi, shouting at me through the window. 'It's true.
They got Terry by the mosque in Ein Mreisse. He'd been playing
tennis. Mell was with him.' Impossible. 'You better watch out. They
got him just down the road − the Ein Mreisse mosque.' The mosque
with the faded, soft grey stones and the delicate minaret, maybe 900
yards away. Yes, Mell lived in a flat on the other side of the road.

In the house, Madeleine, pregnant with Terry's second child, sat on
the sofa, her head in her hands, wailing with grief. Foley was bending
over her. 'It'll be OK, it'll be OK.' When he saw me, he straightened
up, left Madeleine and came over to me. 'It's true. Mell was put against
a wall. There were three guys. Mell's OK, he's at the AP. They took
Terry into Wadi Abu Jamil.' The old Jewish quarter. Now Hezbollah
held the area.

I drove to the AP in another world. The Mediterranean breakers, the
palm trees flicking by the windscreen, the strollers already drinking

coffee on the Corniche. Terry had been kidnapped. Big, strong, un-stoppable, reliable Terry who had the habit of flicking his hand to the right side of his face to show that you should stop worrying, the man who knew how to stay alive.

Labelle was in the telex room, raising New York, telling AP they had just lost their bureau chief. He looked at me quickly. 'Fisk, it's all true. I don't have time to talk. Mell's out there.' He pointed to the newsroom balcony. Mell was standing there, staring into the street, reliving something. Don, from the beginning, what happened? Where is he? All Mell's noisiness, his repetitiveness, his instinctive wisdom, his youth, seemed to have been punched out of him.

'We went to play tennis. Terry took me back to my place afterwards to change. When we pulled up, another car came in front of us, a green Mercedes kind of pulled in with three guys inside. I'd seen the car when we were starting to play tennis and when we stopped, but I hadn't thought much about it. The men had beards. I said: "Terry, I don't like the look of this." Then they pulled open his door. One of them put me against a wall and pointed a pistol at me. He didn't say anything. No, he didn't say a thing. The other two dragged Terry away. They bear-hugged him and dragged him backwards up the road. He just looked at me, as if he was waiting for me to do something. He said something to me. I couldn't hear it.' Mell was near to tears. 'He looked at me, Fisk, just looked. His glasses dropped off on the road. They put him in the back of their car. It had a curtain in the back. I couldn't see him. The car went left, into Wadi Abu Jamil.'

Yes, the car would go left into Wadi Abu Jamil. The Amal militia used to have a checkpoint there, but not any more. The kidnappers chose a road without a checkpoint, down towards the ruins of the front line. 'I took Terry's car and drove down there but I didn't see anything. They've got him, they must have been waiting for him.' Mell glared at the street as if able to summon Anderson back with his anger. 'There were people there Fisky, people, lots of them, they saw — they must have seen what happened. They didn't do anything.' Of course not. It was just another Beirut kidnapping.

I returned to Anderson's home. Madeleine was weeping in Foley's arms. 'Robert, look, look at what Terry wrote last night, on the pad on the refrigerator door. He wrote down the groceries we needed in Arabic. It's not very good Arabic but he was learning.' Tears streamed down her face. 'For the love of God, they cannot harm him.' Madeleine fumbled for a gold chain round her neck. Attached to it was part of a Koranic inscription. 'I have half of the inscription, he has the other half. Surely when they see it, they will be kind to him, surely they will not harm him.' She started crying again, in a high-pitched, uncontrollable way.

I travelled to the mosque at Ein Mreisse. Anderson had been grabbed

on the narrow pavement opposite, below a big wall painting of Nasser.
'Light – unity,' it said beside Nasser's face. There was a sandbagged
guardpost on the road opposite but no Amal militiaman was there. There
were no American diplomats to appeal on Anderson's behalf. After all
the threats from Reagan, after all the speeches about 'international
terrorism' and walking tall and keeping the flag flying, the US diplomats
in west Beirut had 'redeployed' to east Beirut. Even there, they had
been bombed. But on the other side of the mosque lived an Irish
diplomat, Pieras Mac Einri, an old friend from Dublin. He knew Terry;
he would help.

In a gesture of great courage – which typically went unrecognised by
the Americans – Mac Einri called the US Embassy in east Beirut and
asked if he could represent the United States on Anderson's behalf in
west Beirut. Who would ever request to wear the clothes of the Great
Satan in west Beirut? Armed with his new and dangerous role as an
American representative, Mac Einri set off for the Amal offices. We
were offered tea, coffee, newspapers to read, by busy officials who had
problems of their own. The Amal 'security office' near Chatila. 'What is
your friend's name?' Terry Anderson. 'Mr Anders.' No, Anderson,
A–N–D ... The phone. 'Excuse me.' The end of the call. 'The
Israelis have struck at another of our villages in the south.' But our
friend. 'Yes, please, what is his name?'

Anderson. 'He is with the Irish Embassy?' No, no – he's a journalist,
a *sahafi*, one of the most important foreign correspondents in Beirut. Of
course he was. That is why he was kidnapped. They must have watched
him for days. The four men in the Mercedes on the previous day, the
ones Terry told me about. 'Your friend, he is Irish?' American. The
phone again. 'The Israelis are advancing near the Kharroub.' The man
leaves the room. Mac Einri and I look at each other hopelessly. The
man returns. 'I have to go now. I am sorry.' Mac Einri leans across the
desk. 'Please, this is very important. This is an American citizen who
has been kidnapped. He is our close friend. He is a good man. Please
help him.' Handshakes. So many handshakes. All day, we shook hands
with people. All day, we were promised the earth. Such goodwill. As
we left the Amal office, I noticed the man had written down next to
Anderson's name, 'Irish'. He hadn't listened.

Another Amal official, a quiet thoughtful man whom I knew personally. 'Robert, I cannot help you. You remember Frank Regier and
Christian Joubert? We rescued them. You know how I did that? I knew
one of them was sick, he was on drugs. So I sent our people to every
pharmacy in west Beirut until we found a chemist who'd supplied the
medicine. Then we got the name of the man who asked for it. That's
how we identified the kidnappers. That's how we managed to free them.
But then I was told never to do this again. People came to us. I was

threatened with death. I had to resign one of the party jobs. I cannot help you. I am sorry.'

Islamic Jihad. The two words did not sound 'shadowy' any more. They were real. In the AP, Labelle still hoped that Anderson's kidnapping was a mistake, that the gunmen had thought Anderson was a diplomat, that once their error was clear, they would release him, perhaps after a day or two, with expressions of embarrassment. Both Labelle and I knew deep down that this was not true. Anderson had been targeted. Labelle's wife, Eileen Powell, had arrived from New York six months earlier. She worked in the AP bureau with him, a tiny woman with long, brown hair who had the habit of raising administrative questions in the middle of breaking news stories. She turned out now, like her husband, to be tough and courageous.

She too went round the militia offices. She went to the Druze, to Amal again, to the remnants of the Sunni Mourabitoun militia, to the office of the Lebanese prime minister. She argued and fought for Anderson. Labelle telexed AP's stringer in Damascus to ask for Syrian help. West Beirut was under militia control but the Syrian army held most of the Bekaa. In the afternoon, Labelle called a news conference. His face was haggard. He was smoking too much. Years later, I would watch the video-tape of this news conference again and realise that Labelle had changed, matured into the senior Beirut correspondent in 24 hours. He had taken charge. 'We have no news. We are still looking for Terry. In the meantime, we're going on reporting the news in Lebanon.'

Others were not. Journalists started to leave. Eileen Powell drafted a memorandum to her husband that told the whole story: 'US embassy has taken out at least 29 people in last few days, some of whom are diplomats. Charles Wallace of *LA* [Los Angeles] *Times* ordered out of west Beirut. NBC crew, including one American, ordered out of Lebanon by their offices. Derwin Johnson of ABC, despite pleas that he was needed here, is out of west Beirut and out of country tomorrow. Reuters: Betts is taking leave earlier than he would have. Maclean is in east Beirut. Andrew Tarnowski and Jonathan Kahoot in Commodore. Cannot go out at night. Masland (*Philadelphia Inquirer*) not leaving house. Kifners (*NY Times*) are in Amman. Gerald Butt (BBC) ordered out, he said ...'

I took a call from CBS radio in New York. Was this a turkey-shoot of all the Westerners in Lebanon? a voice in Manhattan asked. I didn't know. I should have. Buckley had been kidnapped in May 1984, but he was a diplomat. Levin of CNN disappeared but he had just escaped, in February 1985. There were rumours that his company bought him out, although it always denied this. There had been other Westerners kidnapped. Peter Kilburn, the librarian at the American University, was picked up near his home in west Beirut on 3 December 1984. An American Catholic priest, Lawrence Jenco, was abducted in west Beirut on 8 January 1985.

Amid the chaos of the Israeli retreat in southern Lebanon, I had scarcely had time to understand the significance of the kidnapping of two Britons. On 14 March 1985 – just two days before the gunmen came for Anderson – Geoffrey Nash, a British metallurgist working for the Lebanese industry institute, was abducted near his home in Makhoul Street by three gunmen in a yellow car. On the following day, only 12½ hours before Anderson's kidnap, Brian Levick, the British general manager of the Coral oil company, was dragged from his Buick on rue Australie by five gunmen and driven away towards the suburb of Sakiet al-Janzir. Why? For ransom? What had Britain done to earn the hatred of Lebanese Muslims?

We knew that kidnap victims were often taken to the Bekaa Valley. Levin had been transported there – he escaped, or was set free, near Baalbek. Would Terry be taken there too? I sat down with Labelle. Gerry, we've got to think like the kidnappers. We've got to be kidnappers in our minds. What would *they* do now? Labelle was not amused. 'Robert, right now I have enough trouble trying to be a news reporter without trying to be a fucking kidnapper.' Yes, but what would *you* do if you'd just kidnapped Anderson? 'Feed him less so he'd get his weight down.' Seriously. I was taking notes on what Labelle said. 'I'd hold him somewhere and then when things had quietened down, I'd get him out of Beirut.' Where to? Labelle shrugged. 'The Bekaa?' he asked. 'Baalbek?'

The AP's driver, Muhieddin Habbal, sat with us. A Sunni Muslim from Tripoli, he had been kidnapped with three of AP's Lebanese staffers the previous October. When the gunmen said they only wanted the other three, Habbal refused to leave his friends and entered captivity with them. Anderson had been instrumental in securing their release. I asked Habbal if he thought the same as Labelle. 'Why not, *habibi*?' So would Habbal come with me the next day to Baalbek? I had an idea. If we drove the mountain road to the Bekaa – the road on which the kidnappers might take Terry – and if we stopped at every militia checkpoint on the way and handed out Terry's picture to every one and then went to Islamic Amal and the Hezbollah in Baalbek, even the Syrian security men in the Bekaa, then *maybe* they would later identify Anderson in the back of a kidnapper's car. Would Habbal come with me? 'Why not, *habibi*?'

Habbal and I set off at dawn on 17 March. Mell and Zoheir Saade, the AP's Beirut photo editor, printed 60 file pictures of Anderson together with photocopied texts describing his job and the details of his kidnapping. I drove my own car with Habbal beside me, holding the pictures. Out of the corner of my eye, I saw him looking at Terry's photograph, shaking his head, smiling in a sad, kind way. 'He is a good man, why did they ever do this?' Because he's an American, Muhieddin. '*Habibi*, there are many Americans in Beirut.'

So why did they take him? Habbal was silent for all of five minutes. We drove along the Ouzai seafront, towards Khalde, past the Shia gunmen standing atop the old US Marine bunkers. 'Because he is not just an American,' Habbal eventually replied. 'He is a *mudir*, a boss. He is a big *mudir*. Everyone knows him. He was on television here after we were kidnapped last year. People knew him. He went to Baalbek after the Marine bombings. You were with him.' Yes, of course he did. Terry went to Baalbek. He talked to Moussavi. Afterwards they gave us Danish biscuits. And then they photocopied his passport. Of course. *They photocopied his bloody passport, the page with his photograph on it, when we were leaving.*

At the broken remains of the old Marine landing stage at Green Beach, we handed Terry's picture to the Shia gunmen. They were friendly, they smiled, yes, they had heard of our friend's kidnap on the radio. At Khalde, we gave one of the pictures to the Druze gunmen of Jumblatt's 'Progressive Socialist Party'. Habbal laid one of the photographs on the dashboard of the car. Terry looked at us while we drove. The portrait was serious. Anderson, fleshy-faced, eyes looking straight into the camera, moustache neatly groomed, the sort of picture we had seen a hundred times before. Every time a Lebanese was kidnapped, relatives printed up these old pictures of their missing husbands and brothers and sons and friends. Now it was Terry. Kidnapping happened to other people, but not when the other people were your friends. Were. Habbal found that we kept referring to Anderson in the past tense. Terry was a good bureau chief. He had no enemies. *Was. Had.* As if Terry no longer existed, had somehow fallen down a black hole, was no longer of this world.

Habbal and I headed for Bhamdoun. There, in the ruined streets in which Anderson and I had been confronted by gunmen under shellfire during the Chouf war 18 months before, we handed out his picture to bearded militiamen. Terry had stood here with me, on this very road, and argued about our press credentials. *Even then, we had been* ajnabi, *foreigners, rather than journalists. The trust was fading even then.* The gunmen were now unfailingly sympathetic, polite, 'Don't worry,' one of them shouted at me as I let out the clutch. 'We will find your friend.'

In Baalbek, Colonel Mohamed Asmi of the Syrian *mukhabarrat* confirmed that he had already been ordered by his government in Damascus to look for Anderson. Did we have photographs? He took ten of them. He gave us the names of Syrian army officers through the Bekaa. Asmi showed me a telexed military instruction from Damascus, in Arabic, ordering a search for Anderson in Baalbek. So the Syrians thought he might be there, too. 'Give each one of them a photograph,' he said. 'Good luck.' The Iranians were in Baalbek. We gave them pictures, too. They thanked us, unsmiling. Moussavi was not in. We gave his gunmen pictures. Please help us, we said. Help, help. Like those women who came up to us in Beirut with their pathetic photographs, their tired, rehearsed descriptions of unwitnessed kidnappings.

On the way to Zahle, Habbal talked to a Syrian paratroop officer. We gave him a picture. He invited us to talk to his men. I made an impromptu speech before 50 Syrian soldiers, about how I wanted them to help my friend. At the end, they grinned and their officer clapped. It was pathetic. For me, they represented hope for Terry. For them, I was an amusing break in a long, boring afternoon.

All the way back to Beirut, we watched the cars in the other direction, in case we saw Terry. 'If we see them, *habibi*, stop slowly and I will talk with them.' Habbal wanted to talk to them. Of course we would talk to them, chat to these professional kidnappers. Hi Terry! Listen you guys, you've got the wrong man. Terry Anderson is a reporter. He risked his life to report what the Marines were doing to the Shia civilians of Bourj al-Barajneh in 1983. He risked his life in 1982 to cover the killing of civilians by Israeli shellfire. We're not your enemies. Terry is a good guy. Won't you let us have him back? Sure they would. Of course they'd give us time for this painful, long-winded explanation. They'd sit there in their cars, windows open, Terry sitting in the back, listening to us. Habbal and I both knew the truth. If we found Terry, we would be killed. Habbal and I were frightened, terrified. If Anderson had been kidnapped by Hezbollah, how long would it be before the Muslim gunmen in Baalbek to whom we had handed Terry's picture chased after *us* and abducted us too? Still we stopped at checkpoints in Sofar, in Aley. Habbal would not let his friend down. Terry Anderson mattered to him.

We still hoped the kidnappers might be freelancers. 'Please God, not Islamic Jihad,' Eileen Powell had said. That night, the final illusion was blown away. Reuters news agency in west Beirut received a call. The man spoke Arabic. 'The Islamic Jihad organisation, in the name of God the most merciful,' he began:

> Punishment is the curse of God, the angels and all people. The detention of Terry Anderson, Brian Levick and Jerry [*sic*] Nash comes within the framework of our continuing operations against America and its agents. We are definite that Islamic Beirut is full of agents from all sides and accordingly we are working day and night to purge our region of any subversive element of the Mossad, CIA or allied intelligence agencies. We address a final warning to foreign nationals residing in our Islamic regions to respect our hospitality and not to exploit their presence among us to undertake subversive activities against us. Assuming the profession

of a journalist, merchant, industrialist, scientist and religious man will from now on be of no avail to spies staying among us. They have been exposed and their punishment is well known . . . we have delayed releasing this statement until the three were taken outside Beirut.

This was terrible. Terry Anderson was not a spy. We were not agents. The lie in this statement could be used to kill him. Surely a message of such theocratic content, surely men who could talk of God's mercy and the angels, would understand mercy? That night, at Anderson's home, I broke the news to Madeleine that Islamic Jihad had claimed Terry's kidnap. I had typed up the message and she took it into the kitchen to read on her own. When she returned, tears were running down her cheeks. 'What do you think, Fisky?' I told her I thought Anderson was still in Beirut, that if he had been taken out of the city, the kidnappers would have no reason to say so. I said I thought this could take longer than other abductions to clear up. I said it could be a few months. 'Yes, I think so too,' she said.

Eileen Powell went on struggling for Anderson. She went back to Amal twice a day. Habbal drove Farouk Nassar to Sheikh Fadlallah's house. Anderson had interviewed Fadlallah, one of Hezbollah's spiritual guides, the day before his kidnap. The Shia gunmen of Beirut certainly knew who Anderson was. Fadlallah promised to do all he could for Anderson. 'He was in my home and therefore he is under my protection,' he said. 'I regard him as my friend.'

Eileen thought Gerry Labelle was now at great risk. He stayed in the office, slept at night across the road in the Commodore Hotel. I offered to take him to lunch in my car, fast, to the *Rigoletto*. I careered through the streets. It was becoming familiar to me. In the coming months, the coming years, I would drive through Beirut like this. How do you feel Gerry? I asked him as we swept down the road from Raouche to the *Bain Militaire*. 'If you want to know, Fisky, fucking frightened.' Of being kidnapped? 'That and your driving.' The restaurant was only 200 yards from the spot where Anderson had been kidnapped. What would happen? 'What will happen to any of us now?' he asked. 'Maybe we'll see Terry tomorrow. Maybe next week.' He looked at me very coldly. 'Maybe we'll never see Terry again.' It was unthinkable. He could not be dead.

He was not. We did not know it then. We would not know it for many months. But at that moment, Terry Anderson was less than half a mile from us, in the dank basement of a ruined hotel on the Beirut front line, in complete darkness, chained to a wall like an animal, weeping in despair, waiting every moment for his execution.

I drove Labelle back to the office. Was he going to leave? 'Not till we've found Terry.' How long? 'I don't know.' Did Labelle realise he might be next? 'I think about it. So should you.'

I did. The previous November, a carload of gunmen had tried to stop me, after dark, as I drove through rue Madame Curie. I had spent that morning in November 1984 listening to a Christian telling me about his experiences as a kidnap victim. All day, I had dwelt on his description of being released, of being taken into the sunlight in a blindfold and finding the heat so strong he thought he was about to be tortured. I was still thinking of him that night when the car behind me put its lights on high beam and the driver pressed the horn. He kept on pressing it as he drove past, the passenger door swinging open to reveal a gunman waving an AK-47 rifle, pointing to me and gesturing to the roadside.

The car was full of men and all I could think of was that they all seemed to have wild, flying hair. The mind works strangely on such occasions. I thought 'This is it.' *This is it*. I said it out loud. 'This is it.' 'It's happening.' I was trying to shake myself out of my ordinary, happy life and into the darkness. The gunman at the door of the car was screaming at me now, ordering me to stop.

I realised then that there was still a gap to the left of his car, a small one but wide enough for my vehicle. I slowed as if to stop, obeying the orders of the gunman, then swerved wildly to the left and put my foot on the accelerator. I was shaking so much I could hardly turn the wheel. It was fear, not courage, that made me do it. My headlights swished across the back of the gunmen's car. It was a battered green American saloon and there seemed to be four men in the back seat. Their driver turned sharp left across the road to cut me off, my rear mudguard caught his front mudguard with a crack, then he was behind.

In films, it looks easy, but it is not. I put two cars between us. He overtook one; I could see the gunman hanging out the door, waving his rifle, outlined by the street lamps. The car's headlights, still on high beam, juddered back and forth as it tried to overtake other motorists to catch up. I headed for the Commodore. My left hand was on the horn now, my right hand grasping the wheel. I crashed into a parked vehicle, then another. Every time I thought I had lost the gunmen, their car reappeared. I put four cars between us, then six, forcing drivers to the side of the road in my panic.

Liquid began to splash onto my hands, onto the steering wheel, onto my trousers. I couldn't have been wounded, not blood. It must be raining. But my window was shut. The rain must be coming through the roof. Only when I reached the Commodore and the gunmen had disappeared did I realise that it was my own sweat splashing down my face onto my shirt. A CBS producer handed me a rum and Pepsi but the stuff spilled all over the floor because I couldn't hold it. Afterwards, I called Terry Anderson and we returned to rue Madame Curie. There was the gunmen's front mudguard lying in the street, just where I had torn it off. 'Are you sure this wasn't your fault?' Anderson had asked me then. 'Are you sure you didn't just cut in on some gunmen with your crazy driving and get them mad?' I didn't think so.

In the AP bureau, Terry's photograph was now pinned to the notice-board. He stared down on us all day with displeasure and impatience. Were we doing enough? Labelle and Powell spoke to the militias every day, to Amin Gemayel's broken-backed administration, to officers of the Lebanese army's 6th Brigade. Anderson's room was left untouched, his desk still piled with papers, ready for his return. AP's Damascus stringer told Labelle that the Syrians thought they had seen Anderson in a house near Baalbek. They recognised Anderson, he said, from a photograph handed out by a foreign reporter. A moment of triumph. It lasted three seconds. The Syrians said they had been unable to rescue Anderson because he was moved to another location.

Sometimes it seemed as though the fact of Anderson's kidnapping had not penetrated to the outside world. Other journalists had been kid-napped and re-emerged. So would Terry. We thought so too. The American ambassador had moved to east Beirut and on the day of Anderson's kidnap, the best the Embassy could do was to place a phone call to Nabih Berri, the head of Amal. If anyone could find Anderson it was the Syrians, and AP's Middle East business manager was sent to Damascus to ask for Syrian government help. But why did the president of AP, Louis Boccardi, not fly straight to Damascus to see President Assad? Assad was unlikely to act unless he was personally visited by an important American. If he was not approached in this way, the Syrians would not understand the importance of Anderson's kidnapping. That is the way things work in the Middle East. In New York, AP seemed not to understand this.

Unwilling to put more Americans into Beirut, AP now flew one of its Rome staff into Lebanon, a Bolivian named Juan Carlos Gumucio. He had been to Beirut before and knew Anderson. Gumucio — or J-C as he preferred to be called — had dark skin and narrow eyes like a Red Indian. He was, as we used to say of Arabs when they were suspected of committing crimes in Europe, 'of Middle East appearance'. He had a beard. He looked like a Hezbollah, which was good protection, and he possessed something of that militia's ruthlessness. He was a big man with the energy of a hyperactive puppy dog and a deceptively mild, bland humour that concealed a dark understanding of his colleagues' weaknesses and a generally subversive view of human nature.

In a movie, J-C would have filled the role of a rich Latin American landowner, playing with his children on the veranda of a vast hacienda, a man of *machismo* who put family before political power. In real life, J-C's ambitions were confined to journalism, a profession that was almost a religion for him. He understood the Lebanese in a way that we did not. He felt their fear before we did and he appreciated the reasons for it. He also despised the clumsy, over-confident role that the Americans had ordained for themselves in the Middle East, behaviour which he identified – no doubt from a Latin American perspective – as arrogance. He saw it as a form of irresponsibility. There was something vain in J-C, in his contempt for weakness. But he was the most resilient man I was ever to meet in Lebanon.

And in the spring of 1985, we all had reason to feel weak, vulnerable, fearful. In southern Lebanon, a civil war broke out. For no reason which they were able to explain, the Phalange militia, led now by Samir Geagea, opened fire on the Palestinian camp of Ein Helweh and on the centre of Sidon. The Phalangists set up their artillery in Mieh Mieh, that tiny Christian village on the heights east of Sidon where my university teacher friend lived. The Israeli Shin Bet were still behind the Phalangist lines. Geagea poured shells across Sidon and departed. Within 24 hours. He started a war and then left the Christian minority to await the onslaught of the Muslims. The good will for which those Muslims and Christians had searched during that nervous meeting at Hariri's house in Sidon a few weeks earlier had been incinerated. The Christians of Mieh Mieh and the villages to the east fled in terror.

When I reached Sidon the next day, the Muslim militias and the Palestinians of Ein Helweh had already overrun Mieh Mieh village. My teacher friend, who had wanted peace with his Palestinian and Muslim neighbours, had disappeared. His house was on fire, his books strewn across his garden. The Christians' houses were looted and torn down. A Palestinian family had taken up residence in one ruin. I found them sitting on the floor outside as blue smoke drifted through the village, the woman making coffee on a cooking stove, her elderly husband looking through a photograph album.

They had found it in the house. Colour snapshots of a family. A little girl at her first communion. The same little girl on the beach just north of Sidon. The little girl crying in the arms of a well-dressed father. The father and mother, their arms round each other, standing at the Spanish Steps in Rome, family parties, the men drinking arak round a table, grinning inanely at the camera, a whole life bound inside a cheap album, thumbed through by the aliens who had until this moment lived half a mile away. The Muslim looked at the Christian family, pored over the pictures, showed a photograph of the little girl to his wife. Yes, they agreed, she was a very pretty little girl. Then they went on to discuss how good it was going to be to have a pleasant home, to live in the house which they had taken from the little girl's family.

Christian refugees flocked south, towards Israel. It had happened again. Israel was once more leaving blood and fire in its wake. Just like the Chouf. Why did the Phalange open fire on Sidon, provoking this destruction upon the Christian minority? Why did the Israelis let them do it? Why had the Shin Bet men taken over Mieh Mieh in the last days before the Israeli withdrawal? And why was my teacher friend put under house arrest? In principle, Israel needed a strong, united Lebanon. But it did not want a strong, united *anti-Israeli* Lebanon. Muslims and Christians now fought each other again, just as the Israelis had said they would.

Every assignment would now be attended by an added fear. When we were not trying to avoid incoming shellfire, we were watching for mysterious cars, for Mercedes limousines with curtains over the back windows, for bearded drivers, Hezbollah signs, Iranian flags. Each time we returned to the AP bureau, we would ask about Terry Anderson. 'Any news of Terry?' As if Anderson had disappeared during an earthquake or a snowstorm, victim of a natural disaster who might still be found by rescue workers.

The kidnappers of Islamic Jihad allowed Benjamin Weir, the Presbyterian minister, to write a letter to Church officials in New York containing the terms of his release. They were demanding freedom for the 17 men – some of them Lebanese – imprisoned in Kuwait for bombing the French and American embassies there in 1983. This would also be the condition for Terry's release. Weir's letter said the captors would kill their hostages if anyone – including Syria – tried to rescue them.

The kidnappers followed a classic Lebanese tradition, of deluding strangers into a path of false hope and then of commensurately greater fear. Weir was released, to take a message to Washington. He had been with Terry. He had talked to him. Terry had sent his love to his friends. The early days of his captivity had been the worst, lying alone in darkness for weeks, chained to a wall. Perhaps his torment would soon end, like Weir's. Nash and Levick, the British hostages, were released. Both had been mistaken for American diplomats. Islamic Jihad did not want British hostages. Not yet. But they wanted Frenchmen. On 22 March, they took two French diplomats in west Beirut, Marcel Fontaine and Marcel Carton.

Then on 25 March, a British writer was kidnapped. Alec Collett was 64, a freelance working with the United Nations, writing about Palestinian refugees. He had been driving to Beirut from Sidon and was captured by gunmen a hundred yards from the Amal checkpoint at Khalde. When I drove to Khalde, the Amal men were all ignorance. But I found out what had happened. Collett possessed two passports, one for Lebanon, another marked with an entry stamp to Israel. He had been writing about the occupied Gaza Strip and had been to Israel. At the Amal checkpoint, he had shown the gunmen the wrong passport.

His kidnapping was claimed by the 'Revolutionary Organisation of

Socialist Muslims', which we thought was part of Abu Nidal's Palestinian organisation. He was not released. The Beirut kidnappings were a contagion. More journalists left. The gunmen were driving us out. The hostages' names and biographical details were typed up on lists and posted in the AP newsroom. If one was released, we crossed his name off the list. If another Westerner was seized, we typed his name onto the end of the list. Americans came at the top. Terry's name came first because it began with 'A'. A scorecard. AP's list began to stretch down the wall — it would eventually be four feet in length — and was headed 'Kidnaps-at-a-Glance'.

At first, it was only a few inches long, consigned to a wall behind the new computer screens which Anderson had introduced into the AP bureau shortly before his abduction. That was all it was then worth. For journalists were being killed as well as kidnapped. On 22 March, the Israelis began firing shells across 16 miles of Shia villages south-east of Sidon. They wanted to stop 'terrorists' attacking them before they withdrew from Tyre. J-C, Mell and I drove south together with Foley, through Aanqoum and Kfar Melki. The villagers were leaving in panic, piling bedding onto their family cars as shells smashed into the fields, the roadway, the roofs of houses. Keith Graves of BBC television was there with an NBC crew. CBS had sent two local Lebanese crew members, Tewfiq Ghazawi and Bahij Metni, to film the bombardment and they went to Kfar Melki. The Israelis were using Merkava tanks parked on a plateau of land at Hounin, well aware that the surrounding villages were occupied by civilians, shelling them indiscriminately all the same.

Gunmen were everywhere, not Amal men but those youths with pointed beards and ribbons round their heads with '*Allah*' written on them, Hezbollah men who were not afraid to die. J-C and I met some of them beside a ruined church above Kfar Melki. They walked up to our car with brand-new rocket-propelled grenades in their hands, the projectiles still in grease-proof paper with Russian writing on the outside. 'Do you want to come with us and fight the Israelis?' one of them asked. J-C beamed back. 'Not today. We can't.' He looked at his watch. 'We are reporters, we have to work.' The gunman smiled in a beneficent way, like a preacher at a laying-on of hands. 'Come with us,' he said. 'We will meet later in Paradise.'

We drove away. J-C turned to me. 'You want to go to Paradise?' No. 'You can always change your mind and we can turn back.' No. 'Are you sure?' Yes. 'Fisky, you think we should try to get to Hounin?' No. With time, I would be asking for J-C's advice. He drove down towards Hounin with Foley. I was a coward. I stayed in the village of Aanqoum. It was a mistake. While J-C sat in a field watching the tanks fire, I cowered in Aanqoum as their shells crashed through the village. One round landed so close that its percussion physically blew me through a doorway into a house. I was so frightened, I ran away from the village, down the road west, away from the shellfire, until J-C and Foley came speeding along in the car. Graves was behind them, grinning evilly at me. 'You bloody coward, Fisk.'

By the time we reached Sidon, there was nothing to laugh at. Ghazawi and Metni had been brought to the hospital there in pieces, blown apart by a single Merkava round. Impossible. I had seen them set off from the CBS office that morning, from the same building in which AP had its bureau. We had nodded to each other, no more. We all knew what Israeli bombardments were like. Outside the Sidon hospital, another Lebanese camera crew arrived, from one of the Western television agencies. They demanded permission to film what was left of the corpses. Mell was there, aghast. 'Those bastards are filming their friends in bits. Their own fucking colleagues get blown away and they want to film that obscenity?' Mell was again close to tears.

In AP, the wire machine was running a dispatch from Tel Aviv. An Israeli military 'source' was announcing the death of 'twenty-one terrorists' in Israeli tank fire in southern Lebanon. Terrorists, terrorists, terrorists. Mell looked blankly at the machine. 'These people are sick,' he said. In the CBS bureau, Walid Harati ran through the video-tape that Ghazawi and Metni were making when they died.

They had got close to the tanks. The film flicked between two Merkavas in a poppy field, their barrels jerking, the soundtrack picking up the shells as they hissed across the fields. One of these two tanks was about to kill the camera crew. The camera moved along behind a ditch. On the track, I could hear one of the two Lebanese — possibly Metni — praying in Arabic for God's protection. The film showed a village, some old men, a shell-smashed car. Then the tape stopped. Ghazawi was changing the tape in the roadway when the shell landed between his feet. The villagers were scraping parts of their bodies off the walls for the next two days.

What followed was humiliating, shameful. CBS in New York accused the Israelis of murder. The Israelis claimed that the crew had been 'advancing with terrorists'. They had not. They could not even be seen in the village. A few hours later, the Israelis said that their tank gunner might have mistaken the CBS camera for a rocket-launcher. He had not. He had not seen the crew. The shell just landed on them — as an identical round had landed near me in the next village — because the Israelis were spraying the area with indiscriminate artillery fire. They killed gunmen, a camera crew, some men and women in Kfar Melki. Then they called them all 'terrorists'.

CBS sent a senior executive to Israel from New York. He was permitted to interview the commander — but not the gunner — of the tank that fired the fatal round at the Lebanese crew. Then CBS announced that the Israelis had apologised, that the Israelis had not *meant* to kill the CBS crew. It was incredible. The Israelis had not known – or cared – who they were killing at the time. They were shooting in a wide trajectory across the country, a tank version of 'recon-by-fire'. They just did not happen to know CBS was there. But CBS accepted this. To the Western journalists still in Beirut, this was like forgiving an arsonist who burned your mother to death in a crowded hotel – on the grounds that he had not known your mother was in the building when he set fire to it. If the Israelis could get away with this, what were our lives worth? Mell sat in the AP bureau in despair. 'What's the point of going on?' he asked.

On 22 May, Michel Seurat, a French researcher, and Jean-Paul Kauffman, a journalist with the Paris weekly *L'Evénement du Jeudi*, were abducted on the airport road, a favourite kidnap ground that ran next to the southern suburbs. It was Shia territory. And it was the only road between the airport and the city. Six days later, Islamic Jihad took another American, David Jacobsen, the director of the American University hospital.

AP ordered Mell out, for his own safety. Foley was to leave in the early summer. Labelle and Powell visited New York on holiday and were told not to return to Lebanon. Madeleine stayed in west Beirut amid Terry's books, clothes and furniture until she left to have her baby in New York. J-C moved into an apartment in my block. In the evenings, we sat on the balcony over the sea and talked about the future. J-C was more optimistic than I was. 'Lebanon is a great human tragedy. We've got a duty to go on reporting it. We *can* do it. We've just got to be fucking careful. And *you've* got to be especially careful.' He was right, of course. On 27 May, gunmen approached a British teacher at the American University in Beirut. He apparently struggled with them. So they shot him in the head.

The AP office was host to other newsmen, from London, from Greece. But no more Americans. I carried on with my assignments, to southern Lebanon, to the northern city of Tripoli which was now under the total control of Sunni Muslim fundamentalists, to Cairo, to Amman, to the Gulf. The airport road was an agony of suspense. I drove fast, sometimes at more than 100 mph. I flew out of Beirut with a glass of champagne in my hand, celebrating my safety, and I flew back in with acid burning through the inside of my stomach. I kept my name off the passenger manifest. At the arrivals barrier, Muhieddin Habbal or his AP driver colleague Hussein Kurdi would be waiting for me with a mixture of concern and friendship on their faces. '*Habibi*, things are not so good.' We would drive the airport road fast, slinking through sidestreets behind Corniche Mazraa.

In my own car, I drove around Beirut like a lunatic Nikki Lauda, foot touching the gas pedal at traffic lights in case gunmen approached. At a junction on Corniche Mazraa, I saw a man in the mirror. He was walking to my car door and I crashed the traffic lane, swerving round trucks, a policeman screaming at me. Only when the mirror's panorama increased did I see that the man was a street tout trying to sell me a ticket to the national lottery.

When the Israelis finally left Tyre, the Shia militiamen renamed the Litani crossing the 'Khalil Jerardi bridge'. In Maarakeh, a dozen black-scarved gunmen stopped my car. They took me to the village's new resistance leader. Another young man called Jihad. The guerrillas, he said, would fight 'until all southern Lebanon is free'. For the Israelis had created another line, along the ridges which Major Haddad and they had controlled before the 1982 invasion. Behind that line, Israeli troops remained. So did village militias. The families of Shia men who would not join Israel's latest proxies were deported from their homes and sent north. The United Nations troops watched impotently.

There was an early heat-wave in 1985. Never was a spring more forbidding. The earth of Lebanon gave forth its secrets again. In sand dunes north of the power station at Jiyeh, a grisly charnel house was vouchsafed to the press. Would the *sahafa* like to see an example of Christian Phalangist brutality? Jiye lay on a strip of coastline which had been held by the Phalange until the end of April 1985, when it was captured by the Druze. Just by the Maronite church, we found the evidence: an ancient well choked with corpses and a vault containing the body of a murdered policeman. A group of Muslim gunmen all claimed it was the work of Christians.

Some of the dead had been burned on the sand — there was part of a backbone on the stones and a lock of long, dark, woman's hair. The policeman's body lay on its back, arms spread, still in its uniform, the head missing, bones protruding from the trousers. Down the well were a mass of bones and a dead man, tipped upside-down into the pit, his legs upwards against the wall. According to an Amal gunman — for Amal had assisted in the Druze victory at Jiye because they wanted some of the territory — a bird-hunter had smelled the corpses while walking along the beach and noticed that the lid of the well had not been closed.

In the previous two years, both Christian Phalangists and Druze militiamen in the hills above Jiye had engaged in kidnappings. Mass graves were rarely found, although outside Kfar Matta, where Clark Todd was killed, the Druze found the skeletons of villagers which had lain so long unburied in the fields that bushes and young trees had begun to grow through their bones. A skeleton dressed in the tattered rags of a woman's clothes was found holding a tiny skeleton in its arms. Here in Jiye, the Druze could provide clues to the murderers. The remains of the policeman were identified as those of Tewfiq Dakdouki, a Sunni Muslim who worked in the gendarmerie at Jiye but whose home was in the Muslim village of Barja above the coast. Dakdouki had been kidnapped by Christians in the local power station in 1983.

The Amal officer, who identified himself as 'Abu Ali', said the man who had been tipped upside-down into the well was almost certainly the husband of a Shia woman who lived near the church. 'The Phalange stopped him in his car three weeks ago,' the militiaman said. 'He was never seen again. But when Jiye was captured last week, the man's identification and car papers were found in the pocket of a dead Phalangist militiaman.'

There were no Christians left now in Jiyeh, only their church with its huge bullet-spattered altar mural depicting St George killing the dragon. The church had been desecrated. 'The Christians did this to their own church,' a Druze gunman said as I wandered through the building. I did not believe him. A week after our visit, just to make sure the Christians did not covet their old village, the Druze placed explosives along the walls of the church and blew it up. Then Shia Muslim refugees moved into the wrecked Christian houses. The Druze did not want the Shias so close to the Chouf. So they evicted the refugees and levelled the shells of the houses in which they had been living.

J-C and I were repeatedly invited to visit such places. In Sidon, Sunni militiamen from the Nasserite movement and Palestinian gunmen found a mass grave. 'The Israelis did this – they murdered their Palestinian prisoners here,' Beirut radio announced. J-C pondered our role in the new Lebanon. 'Are we news writers, are we analysts?' he asked me on the way south. 'I think I'm going to become a mass graves correspondent.'

There were bones everywhere, on the grass, in the caves beneath the little hill within which the remains had been found. Some of the bones had been cut through with a sharp instrument. At least 50 – maybe 100 – men, women and children had been buried here. A Palestinian gunman walked up to us. 'The Israelis – they shoot them,' he said in English. True, there used to be an Israeli position on top of the hill. But J-C and I were puzzled. The skeletons wore no watches. Perhaps the watches had been looted. But there were no belt buckles, no pieces of nylon shirt or rubber-soled shoes. I walked into a cave, holding a sputtering match in front of me. The place was deep in fragments of carbonised wood. J-C picked up a brown bone, a femur, and pressed it against his leg. 'These were very small people,' he said. The mass graves correspondent already realised something was wrong.

There was a flurry of activity on the grass outside. Some of the most important policemen in all Sidon had arrived, accompanied by the city coroner, a fussy, bespectacled man with a briefcase and slightly inaccurate French. He examined some of the bones, took samples of the wood fragments and walked back to his car. I bounded down behind him. Excuse me, Sir, when were these people killed? He gave me a withering look. 'About two thousand years ago,' he said. An Israelite massacre of Philistines – or the other way round. No wonder the dead possessed no watches. That night, Beirut radio announced another Israeli 'atrocity' in the south – the discovery of hundreds of murdered Palestinians outside Sidon.

Each return to the AP office provided another shock. Elie Hobeika, the Phalangist who had led the murderers of Sabra and Chatila, was appointed to the leadership of the Christian militia – to replace the disgraced Geagea and to appease Syria. *To appease Syria.* The Israeli commission of inquiry into that massacre recalled how Hobeika was asked by a Phalangist colleague over the radio what should be done with 50 Palestinian women and children prisoners. He had replied: 'This is the last time you are going to ask me a question like that. You know exactly what to do.'

But now Hobeika had uttered the magic words 'Arab identity'. Lebanon had an Arab identity. Syria, he announced, 'has a major role [in Lebanon] in view of geographical, historical and fateful [*sic*] links.' Massaged with this confirmation that the Phalange had at last accepted Syria's protective role, Damascus smiled upon Hobeika. A Beirut newspaper referred to him as a 'discreet' man; the paper itself was discreet – it failed to mention his role in the 1982 massacre. Later, when Geagea staged a counter-coup, Hobeika fled to Damascus and the Syrians set him up with a rival Christian militia in Zahle. Arafat and the PLO said nothing.

J-C and I watched these events with new eyes. I had been in Lebanon now for nine years, J-C only two months, but we both understood that the images we witnessed were changing too quickly, that the glass was fracturing in front of our faces, that we could not account for the events we saw. I began to forget friends who had died. Mounir, the engineer who serviced my car, had started a new job in the visa section of the American Embassy in 1983 on the day the suicide bomber arrived. He was killed with the other 46 Lebanese. Then there was Fuad Es-Said, the Sunni student who set up the radio transmission system for Tatro and myself during the Israeli siege of 1982. As he was driving his father Rafiq home from Sunday lunch in early 1985, a group of Kurds began shooting at each other in a neighbouring street. A stray round pierced Fuad's head. He died in a coma.

Sometimes, it was the conversation that was so shocking. A Druze friend, chatting to me near the fish restaurants in Raouche, pleased with himself: 'I saw two Phalangists over there. I knew who they were. They had a bomb in their car. I called the PSP [Progressive Socialist Party] and they took them off for questioning.' What happened to them? 'Well, they knew what would happen to them, they knew there was no hope. They were questioned here for a couple of days and then they were taken up to Beit Eddin.'

What happened there? 'There's a centre. They don't survive. There are people there who just press them until they talk. They put things into a man's anus until he screams. Boiling eggs, that sort of thing. They kill them in the end. It's only a few days and it's all over. I don't really like that sort of thing. I really don't. But what can I do?'

The casualness of it. 'You want to see the bodies of the Israeli informers?' The medical staff at the Sidon hospital were busy but the girl led me across a flower-edged courtyard filled with sunlight, through a hallway and into a dingy alley. A man pulled open a rusting iron door. The three bodies lay in a heap in the corner, covered in flies, dumped like sacks with neither care nor respect. Their families had not chosen to claim them so they were given a common, unmarked grave, like dogs.

Shia gunmen from Amal hijacked a Jordanian Alia airliner to Beirut and burned the aircraft on the runway after releasing the crew. An Amal official led us onto the tarmac to watch it burn, gloating because he thought that the Jordanian security police on board had been left to die in the flames. A Lebanese then hijacked a Lebanese MEA Boeing the same day to protest at the hijacking of the Jordanian plane. One of the American passengers on the Alia flight had been transferred to the MEA jet, hijacked twice in a day by two different people.

There was no accounting for this. A Lebanese airport security guard hijacked an MEA flight to Larnaca to protest at his low pay. The plane was forced to take off with its doors open, its escape chutes hanging from the fuselage. A passenger was sucked out of the Boeing and hurled onto the runway by the backthrust of the jets which killed him instantly. An old Lebanese man on a Larnaca–Beirut flight hijacked the plane by waving a Pepsi-Cola bottle which he said was filled with gasoline. He ordered the pilot to fly to Beirut – the plane's destination – and then summoned Shia militiamen to the airport. I sat in the terminal, ordered to stay there by armed airport cooks, watching every kind of gunman and mullah arrive to talk to this latest hero of the Islamic revolution; until they discovered that he was deranged. The Pepsi bottle had been filled with nothing more lethal than the hijacker's urine. The mullahs drifted home from the airport. The old man was allowed to walk away across the airport runways to the southern suburbs.

How could we go on reporting this with any sense of priority? When we wrote about such incidents with humour, we made a mockery of the country and of the tragedy we were witnessing in Lebanon. When we reported them at face value, we fuelled the belief that there was something unsound about the people there, that there was a contagion, a plague let loose. 'Why do you people always assume that the Lebanese have to behave like Europeans?' J-C asked me one night. Yet the Lebanese possessed the same values as ourselves. Most of them condemned hijackings and murders. I thought that these people had been invisibly mutilated by events. And many of the terrible things which had so damaged their soul had been brought about by outsiders, by foreigners. Because Lebanon was savagely attractive to foreigners, to foreign armies, to regional superpowers, to businessmen, spies, soldiers, militias, journalists, to us.

Spies. *Jsous.* 'Are you a spy?' a close Lebanese friend asked me in the *Chez Temporel* restaurant one night. No, I replied, as one might deny an interest in French opera or Romantic poetry. A Lebanese family who invited me to dinner at their home avoided the subject of kidnappings until the wife asked, very pleasantly but without apology, if it was true 'that all foreigners are spies.' The Plot. What, she asked, about George Blake? Well, I explained, Blake was a Russian spy and he had been to Lebanon. But I volunteered the suggestion that the family may also have been thinking of Philby. 'That's right, Philby, he was a spy. He was a journalist and he was a spy.' But he was working for the Russians, and besides no one could seriously think all foreigners were intelligence agents. Could they?

In the AP bureau, Farouk Nassar is staring at a blurred photograph. Anderson. Islamic Jihad have delivered a photograph. It is Terry's face all right, with a strange moustache, drooping like a Druze moustache, a suspicious look in his eyes. He does not have glasses. Madeleine is on the phone. 'Fisky, he cannot see without his glasses. He is blind without his glasses.' What is Terry thinking in this picture? That he must cooperate with his jailers in order to survive? That only by looking into this camera will Madeleine see him?

We began to understand the helplessness of the hostages and their relatives. In December, I had interviewed the friends of a young Lebanese woman, Nayifa Najjar Hamade. A middle-class woman of 37, whose picture showed her to be a chic, pretty woman. She worked as a secretary at the *An Nahar* newspaper. Her 13-year-old son Ali had been kidnapped in March 1984 and disappeared. She wrote a series of letters to her parents and friends, even to Ali. 'What am I going to say to those people who want to wish me a Happy New Year in the next few days?' she asked in one of her handwritten messages. Then she took a bottle of insecticide and swallowed the contents.

On 9 June 1985, another American was abducted. Another name on 'kidnaps-at-a-glance'. 'Thomas Sutherland, aged 54, Scottish-born acting dean of agriculture at AUB, on leave from Colorado State University . . . Islamic Jihad has claimed his abduction.' One afternoon, I found J-C staring at Terry's photograph on the wall, comparing the AP file picture with the ghoulish face which Islamic Jihad had sent us. 'We're all becoming Lebanese,' J-C said. How so? 'We're being treated just like them now.' Yes, we were being kidnapped too. The glass bowl in which we had been protected had been smashed forever. The foreigners were no more immune than the Lebanese; they were in even greater danger. Lebanon was reaching through the splinters at the *ajnabi*.

Suspicion of foreigners could perhaps blunt sensitivity to the disgrace of Beirut's militias. In the late spring of 1985, Nabih Berri tried to consolidate his power in west Beirut by sending his Amal militiamen against Arafat's guerrillas who had re-emerged in the camps. Shia militiamen assisted by the Lebanese army's 6th Brigade then began a systematic assault on Sabra, Chatila and Bourj al-Barajneh. Berri was protected by the Syrians who – having no desire to send their own army back to west Beirut – were content to allow the Shia to crush the Arafat loyalists. Assad still wanted the PLO to be a creature of Damascus. The Palestinian camps, smashed by bombs, devastated by shellfire and bull-dozed into the ground, were now to be turned to grey dust. The survivors lived underground.

For Berri, however, the reason for Amal's attack on the Palestinians was more important than a mere favour to Damascus. The geographical location of the camps had virtually cut the southern suburbs off from the centre of Beirut; and it was in the suburbs that Iran's influence was strongest. Across the Shia Lebanese side of the Bourj al-Barajneh camp flew Iranian and Hezbollah flags. The Iranians opened a medical centre in the slums and donated money to the Shia poor. Pan-Islamic revolution and Lebanese Shia nationalism confronted each other across the waste-land of the Palestinian camps; this was a prelude to a war between Amal and Hezbollah. The PLO in the camps provided a barrier between Berri's political ambition and Iran's involvement in Lebanon.

We had watched the metamorphosis of Nabih Berri over the years. Only one photograph of the Amal leader used to appear on the streets of Beirut, a grainy, seven-year-old monochrome of the young Lebanese lawyer shaking hands with Imam Mousa Sadr. But now we could buy Berri lapel badges, Berri posters, we could paint Berri – were we so minded – with specially manufactured stencils, even wear a Nabih Berri T-shirt, the sleek, slightly ageing features captured on a black background.

Over the previous two years, the head of the 'Movement for the Deprived' had become the country's most powerful militia leader, min-ister of justice in the Lebanese government, minister of southern Lebanon, self-styled minister of the Lebanese 'national resistance', ally of Syria, uncrowned king of west Beirut. After he ordered his gunmen to liquidate the Sunni Mourabitoun militia in April 1985, Berri actually referred to Beirut as his crown, a clear sign to those who watched his political progress that power, even if not necessarily corrupting, could certainly destroy humility. Yet his achievement was considerable. He was one of those rare Lebanese who was given a seat among the *zoama* without the status of family ancestry. He believed, he said, in social consensus. Not in family consensus. He was an upstart.*

Theologically too, Berri was a parvenu. His was a political rather than a religious movement. Hence those early photographs with Mousa Sadr. They linked the political and the divine. His Shia opponents would have no truck with Lebanon. The Hezbollah was founded on faith, not patriotism. The living image of that faith was Khomeini. Thus we could identify the differing persuasions in the Shia streets of Beirut. Posters of Berri and Khomeini would rarely be seen together. Berri represented Lebanon, Khomeini represented the party of God. The Hezbollah. At some point, the two would collide. When they did for the first time, the world's press returned to west Beirut — and failed to comprehend the meaning of the conflict.

In June of 1985, Hezbollah members hijacked a TWA airliner on an Athens–Rome flight and ordered it to fly to Beirut. Sometimes we wondered if hijackers really wanted to fly to Beirut, or whether perhaps the word 'hijack' had acquired so close a linguistic association with the word 'Beirut' that gunmen were no longer capable of demanding any other destination. This at least would account for the number of armed men who ordered MEA pilots to fly there when Beirut was already the planes' scheduled destination. But the TWA gunmen knew exactly what they were doing.

They ordered that the plane be flown to Beirut where women and children among the passengers were released, then to Algiers where the aircraft was refuelled. It was flown back to Beirut, where the hijackers shot Robert Stetham, a US navy diver who was travelling on the plane. The gunmen were from Islamic Jihad, the hijack was planned by a Hezbollah member called Imad Mougnieh and they wanted the release of the 17 Islamic Jihad prisoners in Kuwait. Mougnieh's brother-in-law was one of the 17. The hijackers also demanded the release of 753 Lebanese Shia prisoners who had been imprisoned by the Israelis after

---

* Berri's roots and upbringing were an education in Lebanese mores. Like many south Lebanese Shia Muslims, his businessman father made his money in Africa. Berri was born in Sierra Leone, but liked to believe that he belonged to his family's home village of Tibnin. He trained as a lawyer, acquired a French education at the *Faculté de Droit* in Paris, but his shrewd, often over-legalistic mind found its fulfilment in Mousa Sadr's 'Movement of the Deprived'. Yet if he represented the Shia of Lebanon, he was also a sophisticated Westerner, a man who liked snappy suits, French cigarettes and what might be called the American way of life. He held a residence permit for the United States and his first wife still lived in America with two of Berri's children. He regarded Washington in much the same way as some of Ayatollah Khomeini's Western-educated associates in the early days of the Iranian revolution; fascinated by its power, appalled by the way that power was used.

their 'iron fist' raids against the south Lebanese villages. These prisoners had been transferred— against international law — to jails in Israel.

Thus began a drama which revealed a great deal about the cultural gap between East and West, the mutually incomprehensible rhetoric of America and Islam and the theatrical role of television. The United States, Israel, Syria and the Shia militias of Lebanon instantly became involved in the fate of the American tourists on board TWA flight 847. President Reagan promised that Washington would never give way to the forces of 'international terrorism'. Israel said that it would never capitulate to 'terrorists'. Syria said that the Lebanese Muslim prisoners should be released. So did the Shia Muslims of southern Lebanon who felt that at last the world would understand their agony. Berri saw advantage in all of this.

Shortly after the Hezbollah gunmen had killed Robert Stetham, Amal gunmen boarded the plane and succeeded in hustling all but nine of the passengers onto trucks and taking them to Bourj al-Barajneh. Almost all were American citizens and it was Berri's intention — as he made clear in a series of press conferences — to safeguard their lives in return for the release of the Shia prisoners by Israel. Berri hoped that he would thus achieve America's goodwill by saving the lives of its citizens, the support of the Shias of southern Lebanon by freeing their relatives from Israeli detention, the humiliation of Israel by forcing it to free its prisoners, and the favour of Syria by sending the freed hostages off to Damascus.

But events conspired to ruin this ingenious plan. When the TWA jet was hijacked, there were scarcely ten foreign correspondents left in Beirut. When J-C, Faramarzi and I arrived at Beirut airport on the morning of the plane's first arrival, we were the only foreigners there. Once the hostages were taken from the plane, however, news crews poured back into west Beirut from around the world. This was a story worth any risk, for a few days at least. And American television reporters decided that since Berri was now holding the captives, he was a 'terrorist'. If he was not, why did he not free the American citizens whom he admitted he was holding? Berri wanted the world to know that he had rescued the Americans from the Hezbollah. But he could not explain this — since Hezbollah had held on to nine men from the plane, either because they were US military personnel or because their captors believed they were Jews. Furthermore, Syria did not want Berri to damage its relations with Iran which was, as Berri well knew, supporting the Hezbollah.

Berri produced an American hostage, a self-proclaimed spokesman for the passengers, a man who had 'discovered' Islam and who now parroted Amal's demands for the release of the prisoners in Israel. Berri quietly dropped Hezbollah's original condition: the freeing of the 17 'Islamic

Jihad' men in Kuwait. This went unnoticed. Day after day, young American reporters — many of them from small television stations in the American heartland, abroad on their first big story — would stand outside Berri's office in Corniche Mazraa, blue-suited, serious, all apparently identical, talking to camera about Lebanese 'terrorism', Berri's 'terrorism', the 'terrorists' whose release Berri was demanding, the likely fate of the 'terrorists' — and of the hostages.

In reality, the hostages' lives were out of danger the moment they fell into Amal's hands. But this was not the message that went out to the world. Amal's attempts to set the record straight predictably foundered at a press conference in Beirut airport at which gunmen beat up reporters who tried to talk to hostages. For the American press, this was a test of Reagan's rhetoric: would his action measure up to his words? Beirut seemed to be a curse on the Reagan administration.

The deaf then spoke to the deaf, in the same language if not with the same fluency. Reagan said he was 'considering' the closure of Beirut airport. Asked to comment, Berri condemned Reagan's 'bullying' of the Lebanese people. Each statement was flashed from Beirut to Washington and back again by the television networks and both sides felt constrained to reply to each other. Attempting to support Reagan's tough words, the Pentagon let it be known that the Sixth Fleet was lurking just over the horizon off Lebanon. There was, of course, little the Sixth Fleet could do to help the hostages, who had been split up, held in different houses and moved around the Beirut slums by heavily armed men. But the American networks showed tape of the US battle fleet steaming purposefully up and down the Mediterranean.

So what did Mr Berri think? He was, he announced, demanding the withdrawal of the Sixth Fleet as a condition of the hostages' release. It was a fact that Berri could scarcely prevent a fishing boat sailing down the Lebanese coast, let alone a warship. But within minutes, American television and radio stations were interrupting their programmes to report Berri's dramatic new condition. Those identical young men in their blue suits now speculated to camera about the shifting alliances within Amal which might have brought about this apparent stiffening of Berri's resolve.

Those of us who had sat through Berri's interminable press conferences over the previous years realised that he ordered the withdrawal of the Sixth Fleet because it was the first thing that entered his head. It was a recurring problem of all militia leaders in Lebanon. The moment they were confronted by a dozen television cameras or a telephone line from an American anchorman in New York, they felt the overriding necessity to say something — anything — to avoid the impression of weakness or dumb silence. Like the *New Jersey*, Berri had to go on firing even when there was nothing to shoot at.

The whole sordid business came to an end when the hostages, including the missing nine, were released to the care of Syrian army officers in Bourj al-Barajneh and freighted off to Damascus to be welcomed by the Syrian government. Assad subsequently accused the Americans of reneging on a promise to persuade Israel to release its prisoners. In fact, Israel's Shia hostages — for that is what they were — were freed over the next two months, dressed in tracksuits, handed to the International Red Cross just north of the Lebanese border and then interrogated by Amal to discover if any of them were informers. I saw Amal gunmen seizing several alleged collaborators from Swiss Red Cross cars. At least two were later publicly executed by firing squad in Tyre. Still in their tracksuits.

The TWA hijack ultimately involved three victims. The first was Robert Stetham. He was viciously clubbed over the face and body before he was shot in the head and thrown from the plane by Mougnieh's friends. I saw his body in the mortuary of the American University hospital, grey-faced, hair tousled, lying next to a fat Palestinian woman who had been just been shot in a gun battle between Shia militiamen and the PLO. A fly moved between the two corpses, settling on the woman for a moment, on Stetham, on the hands of the mortuary attendant who gently laid the covers back over Stetham's face.

The second victim was Alfred Yaghobzadeh, an Iranian Christian photographer covering the TWA hijack for the French SIPA Photo agency, who was kidnapped outside his hotel in west Beirut by Hezbollah gunmen. SIPA officials immediately made contact with the Iranian Foreign Ministry, with President Assad, with Fadlallah, with leading Sheikhs in the Hezbollah movement. It took 60 days of negotiations before Yaghobzadeh was freed, on the orders of the Iranian Embassy in west Beirut. I saw him minutes after his release. 'They treated me OK,' he said, 'I was underground. They had other prisoners there. One of the jailers said to me that the prisoners were informers or captured SLA men. Sometimes they were sent to Baalbek. That meant they were going to be liquidated. Other times, I heard them being dragged to a small room and I'd hear one of the jailers shout "Bring the *karaba*."' *Karaba* means electricity. 'I would hear screaming and then nothing, absolute silence.' He had not seen Terry Anderson, the third victim of the TWA hijack.

We had been told we would see him. AP reporters chased after the bus carrying the freed TWA passengers to Damascus, expecting to see Anderson with them. The State Department had hinted that Anderson and the other Americans would be released.

Later, years later, J-C and I would watch a re-run of the events on my video set, a feature film based on the TWA hijack called *Delta Force*. Made in Israel by Israelis, it provided the outcome Americans wanted to remember. In the movie, Israel supports an American commando team which storms into west Beirut, kills hundreds of Amal militiamen and rescues the American passengers, flying them out under fire on the hijacked airliner. Every Arab in the film — save for a Christian priest whose parish was supposed to be in the Shia slums — was cowardly and sadistic. America won. Israel won. The Lebanese Muslims lost. The only lie left untold was the rescue of Terry Anderson. He was never mentioned.

Nor were the Palestinians. Throughout the hijack, Berri's militiamen continued their battle against the PLO, tracking their shell trajectories across the rubble of Sabra and Chatila. By the time a ceasefire was declared — on Syria's orders, because Berri's men were failing to crush the PLO — 600 people had been killed. When J-C and I entered Bourj al-Barajneh, we found hundreds of houses lying pancaked on top of each other in a grey sea of ruins, the walls still standing scorched by fire and broken open by shells. A few skeletal, leafless trees stood amid the trash of acres and acres of Palestinian homes in which just occasionally some washing flapped. People still lived there. High Wood on the Somme could not have looked much worse.

The Palestinian dead had been buried beneath the floors of houses, basements and subterranean garages. Underground cemeteries where the gravestones were in darkness. The mass grave of the 1982 Sabra and Chatila victims was a dustbowl of splintered trees and concrete. Many of the survivors of that massacre had fled Chatila before the Amal offensive opened on 19 May 1985, and had squatted in shelters at Mseitbeh or in the ruins of the American Embassy on the Corniche. Refugees from the refugee camps.

Just after Amal began shelling the Palestinians, the Iranians offered me a visa to visit Tehran. Calling at the Iranian Embassy in Beirut was an eerie experience. These were the people, I felt sure, who controlled Terry's destiny, yet there I was, obediently turning up to collect a visa, as if the Iranian Embassy near Fakhani were any other diplomatic compound. The guards outside were bearded members of Hezbollah. I was given tea and some books to read on martyrdom, big glossy magazines that had lain on the coffee table, containing hundreds of colour photographs of dead Iranian soldiers from the Gulf war, their faces smashed, their limbs torn off. Then the consul had handed me my visa and said: 'Have a nice day.'

'Good trip to the Iranian Embassy, Fisker?' J-C asked when I returned to the AP bureau. 'I guess they let you read their literature.' He looked at me, one eyebrow arched. When I returned from Tehran less than two weeks later, he had slipped a note into my office pigeonhole. 'It's not a massacre like the last one,' he said, 'but you better read this.' Attached was a typed sheet of paper, containing J-C's observations on a visit to the area of the Palestinian camps at the height of the Amal-PLO fighting:

> The first indications of mass killings I had were statements by a man and a woman who said they had fled Sabra but didn't say how many, or when. They said there were a lot of dead people in the streets. That was all. Then a friend of mine, a Lebanese, said he saw 45 corpses piled up at the AUH [American University Hospital] morgue and that not all of them were fighters ... Other indication was the Acca hospital. One doctor there told me they were not taking any wounded because they were afraid Amal men would come and kill them or take reprisals against the hospital for helping Palestinians ... I was also highly suspicious because Amal ringed the camps and had strict instructions not to allow ... any reporter into the area. I had shots fired over my head twice in warning. I was stopped by angry men several times.

Another note, dated 10 June 1985, was from Richard Dowden, a *Times* correspondent who had covered Beirut for me while I was in Iran. He said he had spoken to an engineer at the Sabra hospital who 'said that Palestinians had brought one of their wounded fighters to the hospital on May 21 and left him there. Amal collected him, tied his hands and shot him in the back of the head. He also said they took away 20 Palestinian hospital workers.' Dowden added a few observations of his own:

> The destruction of Sabra is so great that few not living below ground can have survived. The way in which Amal and the Palestinians fought in the corridors of the hospital for the old in Sabra while the patients were still there indicates that neither side cares too much for civilians caught in crossfire. The way in which the Palestinians build their houses over the bunkers must make civilian casualties inevitable. But they want it both ways. If you ask how many fighters they have they say all Palestinians are fighters, men, women and children. But then they yell if a woman or child gets killed ...

On 6 June, Madeleine gave birth to Terry Anderson's baby in New York. A daughter, Sulome.

While the Palestinians died in their slums, the Lebanese now staged a new assault on the PLO's Israeli enemies. It was as if there was a sudden new propensity for suicide. To kill oneself out of grief – like Nayifa Hamade, who swallowed insecticide because she had lost her 13-year-old son – might be understandable. But to seek *happiness* through self-immolation was a new experience for the Lebanese. The Lebanese loved life, but now they began to excel themselves in seeking death, deliberately, with great purpose, with martyrdom aforethought. Ibtissam Harb and Khaled Azrak killed themselves on 9 July, driving separate cars into SLA checkpoints in southern Lebanon.

Harb was an attractive dark-haired young woman. One of the pro-Israeli militiamen saw her coming in her white Peugeot 504, her face 'twisted into a grimace'. He opened fire and Harb's car turned into a rolling ball of fire that moved through the checkpoint. Her companion Azrak performed the same feat in eastern Lebanon, near the town of Hasbaya, killing 15 people, at least two of them SLA men, the remainder civilians.

Harb belonged to the Syrian Social Nationalist party. She was cremating herself for political, not religious reasons. And there she was on television four hours after her death, the video delivered just in time for the news show, Ibtissam Harb's public farewell. She sat in a cocky red beret and a combat jacket, her dark hair pushed back, her face made up with just a hint of lipstick and eye shadow, for all the world like an actress preparing to play a resistance heroine in a World War Two movie. Her words, however, were less attractive. A disembodied, Mephistophelean voice asked why she was prepared to kill herself. 'I hope to kill as many Jews and their agents as possible,' she calmly replied to the camera. 'I hope my mission will be successful . . . so this will be a lesson to every enemy and traitor.' She wounded two SLA men.

J-C and I found ourselves travelling to SLA checkpoints in the far south to view the scene of the atomisation of young men and women, driving back to west Beirut just in time to see their video performance on television. Suicide bombers at-a-glance. Another list on the wall of the AP bureau: 'July 15, '85, Hisham Abbass, 20, blew himself and nine others up (2 SLA and 7 civilians) when he rammed his car into an SLA checkpoint near the village of Kfar Tibnit . . . July 31, '85, Ali Ghaleb Taleb, 22, rammed his car into an Israeli army patrol policing the south Lebanon town of Arnoun . . . Aug 6, '85 Jamal Sati, 23, riding a donkey laden with 400 kilos of TNT, blew himself up and his mount near the headquarters of Israel's military governor in the town of Hasbaya . . .'

The AP suicide list stretched two feet down the wall. In three months, there were nine suicide attacks, one of them by a woman of only 18. Several of the dead had lost relatives in guerrilla actions against the Israelis earlier in the year. But for a Westerner, it was difficult to comprehend how their minds worked. J-C produced a book on Japanese kamikaze pilots of World War Two. 'Read this, Fisker, and you'll find some parallels.' The book was filled with descriptions of funeral rites and ceremonies of martyrdom for pilots before their final take-off. They too wore cloths round their foreheads, bands of martyrdom. Their greatest pain was suffered when their missions were cancelled. Were we losing touch with the Lebanese among whom we had been living for so many years? And what chance did Terry Anderson have in the new Lebanese society that was taking shape around us?

For Anderson's birthday, Madeleine and his sister, Peggy Say, made a short video film of his family, including pictures of his tiny daughter, and successfully persuaded the Lebanese state television authorities to transmit the tape in the hope that he might be permitted to watch the broadcast. In November 1985, Anderson was allowed to write a private letter to his family. It was an expression of agony and pain, written to Madeleine, to his sister, to his father and brothers:

Madeleine, my love, my heart, I saw our daughter on TV the other night and I cried for joy. I only saw her for 2 or 3 seconds, enough to notice your black hair and beautiful bright eyes. But I can't describe how it felt to end months of not knowing. Our guards had seen the piece on the early news and brought in the TV for the later cast – all in Arabic, but at least I saw my family and the picture ... I never cease thinking about you – I talk to you (in my head) every night and in the early mornings. Those are the difficult times, and thinking of you helps. God has been good to us and I'm sure this is only an interruption of our lives together, one that if He wills, won't last much longer ...

We tried to imagine Terry's mind. That so broad an outlook, so formidable a personality, should be so 'cabin'd, cribb'd, confined', must have thrown him back on an inner courage that he had never before tested. Evidently, he had found comfort in religion. Madeleine realised this at once, gently revealing a Terry whom I had never known. 'He was thinking a lot about God before he was kidnapped,' she said. 'I remember when we went to church one Sunday near my sister's home in the north of England, he began crying during the service.'

In captivity, Terry said in his letter, he held religious services with Jenco and Weir, each taking it in turns to read from the Bible. He referred with great warmth to 'Pastor Ben' Weir, who had been released by Islamic Jihad earlier in the year. 'I hope you get a chance to talk to Pastor Ben,' Terry wrote.

... he's a gentle and kind man whose faith never wavered – much like Father Jenco, who is one of the three men confined with me. They and the Bible I was given after the first few weeks have kept me sane. We have services twice a day, and choose readings in turn ... Keeping occupied is our main problem. It's the only way to keep away the depression. I miss you terribly. I didn't think it was possible to hurt this much.

As J-C and I read this letter, we kept drawing in our breath. We were peering into a dark, terrifying world, one in which Terry's soul was searching outwards, redefining the life he had led before he was taken away.

I have been seeing bits and pieces of news about Peg (his sister) & Judy (another sister) & Dad and their efforts to get someone to do something – it's about the only encouragement we get. I love you all for it – how much I will only be able to tell you all when I'm home again. I realize now how much I have cut myself off from you over the years, and how much I've lost by doing so. I want to see all of you again so badly, and I pray for each of you every night ... I dream every day of the place at

Batavia (New York State), & of building a small cottage by the stream & working to clear the pond in the summers. I hope David (Peggy's husband) has been able to re-open the well – if it's not dead winter when I get out, I'd like to stay there awhile. I hope the AP will give me a few months off so we can enjoy the family. In nearly a decade overseas, I haven't spent much time with them ...

Photographs. We were surrounded by snapshots. Pictures of Lebanese Muslims missing in Beirut, a snapshot of William Buckley, the CIA station chief, taken just before he died after torture. Terry, we learned, had to carry Buckley's corpse out of his basement prison. Pictures in Kuwait. In the back copies department of the newspaper *Assayad*, a row of photographs. The Kuwait 17, the men whom Terry's captors want freed. Some are smiling. Elias Fuad Saab, alleged to have prepared booby-trapped cars for the 1983 US and French Embassy bombings, has a neat moustache and a big, generous face, the kind of man I might meet at a checkpoint and talk to, wishing him safety as I drive away. Others of the 17 glower at the camera. One looks like Hussein Moussavi of Baalbek.

On 1 October 1985, it was the Russians' turn. Three diplomats kidnapped, one of them – Arkady Katkov – shot and dumped on waste ground in west Beirut. This time, it seems to have been Sunni fundamentalists, trying to persuade the Soviet Union to halt Syrian military action against the *Tawheed* militia in the northern Lebanese city of Tripoli. Katkov's body was identified by his closest friend, Konstantin Kapitanov, a Soviet journalist from *Literaturnaya Gazeta*, based in Beirut.

I knew Kapitanov well. We played tennis together. I thought he was a KGB agent. He always sneered at my suspicions. Now he was sitting in the Soviet Embassy compound, tears in his eyes, swigging beer. 'Bob, he was my friend, my good friend. I valued this man. I would have risked my life for him. I could not believe he was dead, even when I saw his dead face in the morgue.' Kapitanov crying. I could scarcely believe it. 'We shall find the people who did this,' he said.

They did. The Soviets sought help from the Druze. A brother of one of the supposed kidnappers was abducted. Later, so we heard, his family received one of his fingers in an envelope. Then another. The two surviving Soviet hostages were freed unharmed. Kapitanov always denied the story. The Soviet Union had 'friends', he said, who saved the other two men.

Terry's glasses. I kept thinking about his spectacles. A Lebanese acquaintance, a Shia, offered to try to make contact with Islamic Jihad. Would I like to send Terry's glasses to him? Maybe some photographs of his daughters? J-C and I debated the wisdom of this. I found a picture of his elder daughter Gabrielle and asked Madeleine for a snapshot of Sulome. I wrote 'Fisky' on the back of each, because that is what Terry called me. I took his glasses — the ones that had fallen on the road when he was kidnapped — to a west Beirut optician for a copy.

The acquaintance arrived to collect the pictures and the glasses. He had been asked for my address. I wrote it down and attached a letter. 'My dear Terry. This is to send you my very best wishes and prayers for your safety and early release ... I think of you all the time. I pray that your captors will be kind enough to allow me to see you ... As ever, Fisky.' My acquaintance handed over the glasses, the pictures and the letter. He said later that he watched the photographs being examined, the lamination being peeled back from the print. I heard no more.

Terry Waite arrived in Beirut. The Archbishop of Canterbury's envoy had been invited by Islamic Jihad. He was massively built with a confidence to match. He stayed in Terry's flat, two floors below me. J-C and I talked with him, long into the night, about Anderson. Waite received a telephone call, from a man called Ali. He was to meet Ali at a gas station in the suburbs. But Waite did not know if 'Ali' was real. We watched the realities of Beirut worm their way into Waite's self-confidence. His greatest concern, in those early days, was that a Lebanese group hostile to Islamic Jihad might try to kidnap him. We debated how 'Ali' could be tested. Ask him where Terry Anderson spent Christmas 1984. No good. Too many people knew that Anderson had spent Christmas morning snowballing his AP friends in the mountains. Ask for details of Anderson's previous posting. But that was in South Africa; the kidnappers might misunderstand and believe that Terry approved of the regime.

It took us an hour to think of a question. 'Ali' called back. 'Please ask Terry Anderson for the name of Fisky's Finnish friend.' Surely Islamic Jihad would never know who Christina Joelsson was. I watched Waite talking into the phone. 'Yes, that's right, "Fisky's Finnish friend". Finnish as in Finland with two "ns".' A few hours later, the phone rang again. 'Ali' said 'Christina' and Waite left for his first meeting with the men who had bombed three American embassies, one French embassy, the American and French military headquarters in Beirut and an Israeli headquarters in Tyre.

Just before midnight Waite returned, fatigued, depressed, frightened. The kidnappers had blindfolded him and sat him in a chair to talk to him. He fought for the lives of the American hostages. Islamic Jihad gave him a message to take to Washington. Waite left Beirut. He met Vice-President Bush and — as we later learned from the Tower Commission report — he talked to Oliver North, one of President Reagan's staff. He returned twice more to Beirut. Waite thought he had a deal, a promise from the Kuwaitis that they would not execute three of the 17 prisoners who had been sentenced to hang, permission to visit the prisoners in Kuwait; at the very least, a promise that all 17 could write to their families.

Waite was told by Islamic Jihad that he could deliver letters from the family and friends of the Western hostages in Beirut. J-C and I sent Terry a Christmas card, telling him in a single sentence of our prayers for his early release. We signed it. He would know we were still in Beirut.

Just before Christmas, the Kuwaitis said Waite could not visit the Islamic Jihad prisoners in their country. The Americans had failed to put pressure on the Kuwaitis. There were no letters. Waite asked Islamic Jihad's permission to see the prisoners' relatives in Lebanon. He was told to leave within two days. 'The message came on the phone,' Waite told us. 'He said: "We are very unhappy at what you have done, Mr Waite. Your mission is over. You have forty-eight hours to leave Lebanon."' Waite left, immediately. During his visits, gunmen had sat outside our apartment block, watching Waite, watching the house. Young, bearded men had followed me – at a distance – as I went to buy groceries. But when Waite left, they left too.

'I don't think we'll ever see Terry alive again,' J-C said. I sat in his apartment. What had gone wrong? What could the kidnappers really want? Waite had travelled to Washington. Anderson was not released. '. . . if it's not dead winter when I get out,' he had written in his letter to Madeleine. Christmas passed with no word from him.

More kidnapping. A four-man French television crew from Antenne 2, their abduction in the southern suburbs claimed by the 'Revolutionary Justice Organisation'. We assumed, correctly, that this was Hezbollah. One of the Frenchmen was to admit later that he tried several times to kill himself in his basement cell. Michel Seurat, the abducted French researcher, died of cancer in Islamic Jihad's captivity; his kidnappers released a photograph of his dead face, in a coffin, claiming they had 'executed him'.

Our journeys in and out of Beirut were now made in great fear. The airport road haunted me. Only four Western journalists were left in west Beirut: J-C, Agneta Ramberg of Swedish radio, Julie Flint of ABC radio, and myself. We were now outnumbered almost two-to-one by the journalists held hostage in Beirut.

Kidnapping again. Two British teachers, Leigh Douglas and Philip Padfield, were abducted by armed men outside a nightclub in Makhoul Street on 28 March 1986. Two weeks later, President Reagan ordered the bombing of Libya. Washington was on the warpath against 'international terrorism' again, having accused Libya of participation in a discothèque bombing in West Berlin in which an American had been killed. The West Berlin bombing later turned out to be the work of

Syrians. But Reagan decided to avenge himself against the 'Mad Dog of the Middle East'.

Ghaddafi, a facile, ruthless dictator with an economy that was collapsing under the fall in oil prices, was singled out for America's retribution. He was sentenced to death by the Americans, every bit as crudely as the Ayatollah Khomeini was later to sentence the British writer Salman Rushdie to death for 'blasphemy'. The Americans denied they were trying to kill Ghaddafi. But someone in the Pentagon worked out the bombing coordinates for Ghaddafi's home. The Americans attacked his house, missed him, wounded his family, killed an adopted daughter, destroyed three military establishments in Tripoli and Benghazi and dropped a stick of bombs on a row of civilian houses.

J-C and I watched the bombing from our bedroom balconies in the Kbir hotel above Tripoli harbour. We attended the mass funerals afterwards. One of the bodies was that of a Lebanese–Palestinian girl who was on holiday from her school in London. Mass graves correspondents. That night, word came from Beirut that Douglas and Padfield had been found shot dead in the foothills of the Chouf. So had Peter Kilburn, the American librarian. He had been held in isolation 17 months, only to be murdered at the end of his imprisonment. His family had been trying to buy his freedom. Libyan agents in Beirut had raised more money. They bought Kilburn, just as they bought the two British teachers from freelance kidnappers. The Libyan agents tried to buy the other American hostages. They tried to buy Anderson.

Collett's death was announced next. A video film was released to Reuters in Beirut showing a corpse twisting on a gallows. It was dressed in Alec Collett's clothes – the trousers and shirt he was wearing in a video-taped message to his family at Christmas. A British television reporter, John McCarthy of Worldwide Television, was still in Beirut when the Americans bombed Libya. He fled for the airport. Again, too late. Gunmen caught him not far from the airport road. In our Tripoli hotel, J-C walked up to me in a state of great emotion. 'AP have told us we cannot go back to Beirut,' he said. 'Even though I'm Bolivian, they won't change their minds.'

We decided that somehow we would go on reporting from Lebanon. It *could* be done. The hostages were there – that in itself was one of the world's most important news stories – but so were the Israeli and Syrian armies. So were the Iranians. The Hezbollah were now mounting mass attacks against the Israelis' militia allies in southern Lebanon.

In the elevator of the Kbir Hotel one morning, J-C said: 'Are we going to go back to west Beirut?' Yes. He held out his hand. J-C immediately took leave of absence from the AP and travelled back to Lebanon.

Friends came from unexpected directions. Konstantin Kapitanov, the Soviet journalist with whom I played tennis, arrived in Tripoli. Ghaddafi, he and his colleagues agreed, was a small-town dictator only exalted to fame by American obsessions. 'Robert, you will return to Beirut?' Yes. 'If you need my help, call me. I can come to the airport to pick you up. Nobody is going to kidnap Soviet citizens in Lebanon.'

The next months were appalling. J-C and I lived in constant fear of the carloads of bearded men who cruised the streets of west Beirut. I still worked from the AP bureau. Farouk Nassar was there with a band of Lebanese women reporters, Hala Jaber, Rima Salameh, Rudeina Kenaan. '*Habibi*, take the greatest care, the very greatest care,' Nassar would say as I set off for southern Lebanon. Hussein Kurdi, the AP driver, would take me to the airport, sandwiched between his wife and baby, Nassar's young son and Salameh. They would loyally come to pick me up when I returned from Cairo or the Gulf. Who would dare touch so many women to kidnap a Westerner, even if they caught sight of the lonely Briton amid the women? Or so our fatuous argument ran.

J-C spent days in the south of Lebanon. In Deir Qanoun en-Nahr, he was introduced to an old woman who had discovered why the Israeli military headquarters in Tyre had blown up in November 1983 – the explosion which the Israelis said was caused by a gas leak. The woman's son had gone missing that day in the family car, and she had never seen him again. In her home, the family kept tape cassettes of Koranic readings and one day in 1986 – three years after her son disappeared with the car – she played a cassette of the first *surah* of the Koran. After a few minutes, however, her son's voice broke in on the tape. He was saying goodbye to her, telling her he kissed her and his father goodbye, that he was leaving them to martyr himself. The scores of Israeli dead I had seen that night in November 1983, laid out in lines across the floor of the floodlit warehouse, had been killed by a suicide bomber after all.

In early June 1986, I lunched with a Shia official in west Beirut. Every time I met members of Shia movements, I pleaded for Terry Anderson's release. 'Things are going to be OK,' he said. 'The Americans are in Tehran now.' He could not – or would not – explain what this meant. I did not understand. That US government representatives should visit Tehran was unthinkable.

The Palestinian camps war erupted with ferocity again. The Shia and Druze militias fought for control of west Beirut. There were promises of government reform but the militias had to be involved in every shift of power; and the militias brought with them all their contradictions. More kidnaps. Frank Reed of the International School, 9 September 1986; Joseph Cicippio, American University financial controller, 12 September 1986. 'Kidnaps-at-a-glance' was now five feet long. Edward Tracy,

American resident, 21 October 1986. Their friends and relatives pleaded for them in public demonstrations in Beirut. Lebanese students bravely paraded in the streets to appeal for their release.

Father Jenco was freed in 1986 with messages from the kidnappers to the Pope and President Reagan. He met Peggy Say, Anderson's sister, in Damascus. Terry still did not know his father and brother were dead. He had received photographs of his daughters with 'Fisky' written on the back. He had been given the Christmas card J-C and I sent with Waite. But no spectacles and no letter from me.

When David Jacobsen was released that autumn, there was a message for me. I was covering a series of riots by Muslim students at Egyptian universities. From Cairo, I called Jacobsen at his California home. He sounded tired, wearied. 'Terry is very worried for you,' Jacobsen growled down the line. 'He said: "Tell Fisky to get out of Lebanon. Tell him to go find another war, to go to Nicaragua or Guatemala." ' Jacobsen was very specific. 'They are after you,' he said. 'They are obsessed with Terry's flat, with the people who live in the same block. I was there when they were asking about you. They wanted your address. They wanted to know all about you.'

I called *The Times*. Douglas-Home had died of cancer in October 1985. Charles Wilson, who had visited me in Lebanon in 1984 and had met Terry, was now the editor. He had already received a phone call from the British Foreign Office telling him I should not return to Lebanon. 'I don't care about those fuckers at the Foreign Office,' he said to me. 'I want to know what *you* think.' I said I should return to Beirut at once to find out if this threat really existed. If it did, I would have to leave. 'OK matey. Good luck.'

I called Kapitanov, my Russian friend. 'Don't worry, Bob, I'll meet you at the airport.' Please, Konstantin, I have to rely on you totally. 'Trust me,' he said. The flight to Beirut was bad. The wind knocked the old Boeing around the sky as it approached Lebanon. At the airport, gunmen were lounging in the arrivals terminal. I couldn't see Kapitanov. 'Why you here?' someone asked. A bearded man in a long brown coat. I ignored him. I searched desperately for Kapitanov. This was before *glasnost*, before Gorbachev. The Soviets had no reason to help me. Outside the terminal, every man at the arrivals barrier seemed to have a beard.

But there he was. 'Robert, *tovarich*, welcome home.' He had brought the Soviet Embassy press attaché, Alexandrov, and the Beirut correspondent of *Tass*. They had two-way radios. Halfway down the airport road, there was a Hezbollah checkpoint. Alexandrov wound down the window. *'Safara Sovietiya.'* Soviet Embassy. The gunman waved us through. Alexandrov turned to me with a growing smile of superiority. 'Saved by the KGB, eh Robert? Where shall we take you? Home? Or to a restaurant?' I got the point. We lunched at the Spaghetteria, on *The Times*. Bottles of French champagne. Kapitanov watched me carefully. 'You think I am still in the KGB?' Yes, probably. 'No. I am a journalist. I have done this because you are a friend. I will always help you.' Nothing was ever asked in return. Kapitanov had kept his word.

So had the man who passed on the photographs of Terry's daughters. He insisted that I was not threatened. Then why, I asked him, were people frightened for my safety? Why did his people want to kidnap me? He did not understand. He would make inquiries. Three anxious days later, he explained. 'You have sent two sets of pictures. Each time, you were asked to give your address when you sent the pictures. New people took the pictures on the second occasion. They wanted to know that you were genuine, that your address was what you said it was. They were checking you were honest.'

When the Iran—Contra scandal broke, J-C and I cursed our lack of initiative. I had been told the Americans were in Tehran the previous May. I had not understood the significance of this. I had clung on in Beirut because I believed it to be the best Arab capital for a Middle East correspondent; but when I was given accurate information about the hostages, I had chosen to ignore it on the grounds that it was not credible. Neither J-C nor I had believed in Reagan's moral fervour. We had laughed at his crusade against 'terrorist blackmail'. But when he gave in to just such blackmail, we were amazed. Guns for hostages, missiles for prisoners. But we understood the significance of the revelations. Terry Anderson's predicament, like that of the other American hostages, was now far worse.

Islamic Jihad sent more photographs of him to the news agencies in west Beirut. In one he was bearded, in another clean-shaven. In a videotape, he wore glasses, probably spectacles that had belonged to the long-dead William Buckley. Madeleine placed copies of each photograph around Sulome's bedroom. As the little girl grew, she knew what her father looked like. She had soft, fragile hair and huge blue eyes. Madeleine wept often but was possessed of great courage. She waited when she was falsely told of Anderson's imminent release. She waited when all hope seemed lost. Always, she waited.

When the hijacked TWA jet was on the ground in Beirut, journalists who had returned for the story chatted about Anderson around the bar. Correspondents who had known him well speculated about his fate in much the same way as they ruminated about the future of Lebanon. 'D'you think he's still alive, Bob?' one of them asked me one night. He raised his glass. 'Well, here's to Terry.'

Still Madeleine waited. 'Will he still love me in the same way when he comes out?' she asked me once. I was sure he would. Terry's home was filled with books. I wondered whether he had read Simonov's poem, the one known by every Soviet soldier separated from his family during the Second World War.

Wait for me, and I'll return
Only wait very hard
Wait when you are filled with sorrow ...
Wait in the sweltering heat
Wait when others have stopped waiting,
Forgetting their yesterdays.
Wait even when from afar no letters come to you
Wait even when others are tired of waiting ...
And when friends sit around the fire,
Drinking to my memory,
Wait, and do not hurry to drink to my memory too.
Wait. For I'll return, defying every death.
And let those who do not wait say that I was lucky.
They never will understand that in the midst of death,
You with your waiting saved me.
Only you and I know how I survived.
It's because you waited, as no one else did.*

It seemed that Lebanon had become an epic of lost souls, of missing men and women, people who had disappeared, had been arrested and not returned, kidnapped, tortured, dead. In southern Lebanon, I travelled from village to village, talking to Shia Muslim men who had been imprisoned at Khiam, in an SLA jail in Israel's remaining occupation zone. They described being hooded and tortured, screaming as electric wires were attached to their fingers and penises. In Tyre, J-C discovered a man with a back of rotting flesh, a hunchback of 25 who had spent six months in a basement dungeon at Khiam, in darkness and filth. Israel refused the International Red Cross permission to visit this place of horror. It was, the Israelis said, under General Antoine Lahd's control. It had nothing to do with them.

In the AP bureau in west Beirut, my files overflowed with reports of hostages – Lebanese, American, British, Palestinian, even Iranian. In 1982, at the height of the Israeli siege of west Beirut, three Iranians – an Embassy official, a revolutionary guard commander and a journalist – had been kidnapped by Phalangists at a checkpoint north of Byblos. They had disappeared like all the other hostages. Only we had not reported this. When the Iranian Embassy first told me of this, I hunted back through my reports of the time, through my memoranda to *The Times*, my handwritten notes. Not once had I bothered to record their fate. They were foreigners. But they were Iranian.

The economic efficiency of hostage-taking seemed to fascinate the

---

* Konstantin Simonov, 'Wait for me'. This translation is taken from the episode *Red Star* (scripted by Neal Ascherson) in the British Thames television series *The World At War*.

Lebanese. By taking one man, you held his whole family, all his friends, as hostages. For the price of one, you cut into the hearts of a hundred others. Why not, when the Lebanese economy was now being torn apart? The dollar, which was worth three Lebanese pounds in 1976, now bought 1,000 Lebanese pounds. At my bank, I needed supermarket bags to collect my Lebanese currency.

By Christmas of 1986, I did not think I could stay much longer in Lebanon. Shark-like cars cruised the Corniche, their bearded occupants staring at me as they passed the house. I avoided the balconies. If I dined out with friends, I stayed at their homes overnight. One morning, my landlord rang the doorbell. 'Please, Mr Robert. The Hezbollah are having marches in the streets today, against foreigners. Please stay at home.' I sat reading, near the balcony, near enough to look across the Mediterranean, far enough away not to be seen from the road. I felt as though I was climbing down a long tunnel whose diameter was constantly shrinking until its walls pressed against my shoulders. The more I pushed my way down the tunnel, the tighter I became wedged between the walls.

Still we tried to do our job. Maarakeh, southern Lebanon. French UN troops shot three Shia gunmen at a checkpoint. Amal and Hezbollah attacked the French. J-C and I managed to drive the coastal highway all the way to Tyre, then inland, right into Maarakeh itself. We were sheltered in a Shia home, the French army's bullets skittering up the walls outside, gunmen firing clip after clip of automatic fire into the UN positions. We interviewed the Amal commander, drove at speed from the village and headed for Beirut. This was reporting Lebanon in the old way, it was work we understood. On the journey back to Beirut, we heard a BBC correspondent explaining to us what we had just witnessed. He had heard a Lebanese radio report and was recycling the story from Cyprus.

An Israeli air raid in Ein Helweh in 1987. 'Terrorist targets' hit again. Hala Jaber of AP and I travel south. In the Hammoud hospital in Sidon, a nine-year-old Palestinian girl lies on a bed, her face working with pain. Her name is Jihan Abu Greif. 'The planes came, the pillar of our home gave way and came down on my foot.' She begins to cry. 'Please don't take a picture of my left leg.' I cannot. She has no left leg. 'We took it off this morning,' the doctor says. 'Can you imagine what this means? She is a girl, she will want to marry, and she has only one leg.' Outside the hospital, a gunman approaches Hala Jaber. 'Who is your friend? He is a foreigner? Is he a spy?'

30 December 1986. J-C is to meet me at the airport with two Shia friends. He is on his own. 'It all fell through.' Why? 'How the fuck do I know? They didn't meet me.' J-C works for CBS now, he is the Beirut bureau chief. He has brought his cameraman, Bashir. On the airport

road, J-C turns to me. 'Fisker, things are very bad. Take your glasses off.' My glasses. Why? 'In case someone in the airport has seen you and is sending a message that you're going to be on the airport road.'

I sit in the back of the car, staring sightlessly out of the window. J-C turns to me again with a leering smile. 'Did you bring my Christmas present?' Yes. 'What is it?' A book. 'Give it to me.' I fumble through my bag. I have bought J-C a book about the Great Plague. 'Thank you,' he says, tucking the volume into his jacket pocket. 'That's just in case you get kidnapped before I get you home. I wanted my present.' He is grinning. We both know how bad things are. Bashir cuts through some Shia slums. A carload of gunmen pulls up in front. J-C watches them. But they stop only to talk to some friends. 'I thought we might be losing you there, Fisker.'

New Year's Eve, 1986. The camps war repeats itself. Amal and PLO gunmen continue to slaughter each other. Ali Hamdan of the Ministry of Information and Amal — the two institutions are now inseparable in west Beirut — says no problem. 'Of course you can visit our people there.' I find a driver I know and Hamdan provides a ministry escort. 'You've got to go, Fisker,' J-C says. 'If you pull out of this, it shows you don't trust Hamdan.' The driver and I set off for the southern suburbs. On the way, we pick up three Amal gunmen carrying Kalashnikov rifles.

'From England you come?' Here we go, just as I feared. Yes. 'England is good?' Yes. 'Lebanon is good?' Yes. There is a Hezbollah roadblock ahead of us. Right there, three guys in bandannas with yellow Hezbollah badges. The Amal men are uncomfortable now. They are supposed to control this area. But they obviously don't. They all begin to push their guns to the floor, beneath my feet. 'Why you come to Lebanon?' I'm a reporter, a *sahafi*. We are in a queue, awaiting our turn for inspection by the Hezbollah. 'Mister, I have a question.' Yes?

Our car is next in line. The Hezbollah gunman is looking at my driver. 'I have a question!' one of the Amal men in the car with me says. Yes, yes. The Hezbollah looks through the driver's window. 'Why you have a queen in your country?' asks the Amal man. What? 'You have a queen?'

Her Britannic Majesty, Queen Elizabeth the Second. Indeed, we do. And we have little blue passports and written on them it says 'Her Britannic Majesty's Principal Secretary of State for Foreign and Commonwealth Affairs Requests and requires in the Name of Her Majesty all those whom it may concern to allow the bearer to pass freely without let or hindrance . . .' I do not think the Hezbollah man cares much about the 'let or hindrance' bit.

He looks at me. His little yellow plastic Hezbollah badge reflects the sun. He waves us through. I become obsessed with the idea that I shall never return from this story. We have not even reached the southern suburbs. We drop the gunmen off on the airport road. Then turn east at the mosque with its black flags, deep into the narrow streets of Bourj al-Barajneh where Iranian banners flow from the roofs.

There are bearded gunmen on all the streets, portraits — 20 feet high — of Khomeini and martyrs Beheshti and Chamran. Ayatollah Montazeri looks scornfully at me from a hoarding, Hussein himself from another, the Twelfth Imam, his horses oozing blood on the fields of Kerbala. I am in Iran. And close to Terry. Perhaps he is in this building with the green shutters, up this narrow street with the silent young men in pointed beards looking over the balcony. Is this where he has his dungeon home and reads the Bible and thinks of building a small cottage by the stream in Batavia and clearing the pond?

Gunfire flits around our car. We are passing a mound of earth beside the Palestinian camp. For two seconds, as we clear a hump in the dirt track, I look across the Palestinian battleground, an ocean of powdered houses, and then we pull up beside a bullet-scarred building, its unpainted cement walls streaked with grime and damp. Inside, there is a picture of Khomeini. There is an Amal flag on the roof, but inside the men have Hezbollah badges. The gunmen here are metamorphosing from Amal into Hezbollah, changing chrysalis-like from Berri to Khomeini as the camps battle wears them down. At what point in this ideological-theocratic transformation have I arrived?

There is a young man at a desk. Berri's picture is on his desk, a comforting sign. He calls for tea. 'We are fighting God's war.' Silence. 'We are fighting a dirty war.' This is better. 'Abu Ammar [Arafat] has been preparing this war for years, especially against Amal.' I take this down in my notebook. How old is this man? He grins at me. 'I am young, otherwise I could not do this job. I am a football coach. I played for Lebanon.' Like Pierre Gemayel.

I am ready to leave. We all shake hands. 'Take care.' You too. My car is pulling away when a gunman knocks on the window. 'My officer wants to speak with you again.' Why? 'Come.' I re-enter the building, noting some dark, foul-smelling steps into a basement. The young man is writing on a piece of paper. 'I have a further statement for the *sahafi*.' He gives me the piece of paper. 'The Palestinians are our brothers,' it says. 'But not the men who follow Arafat.' When I saw the mosque with its black flags, I was happy. A T-54 tank, a Syrian gift to Berri, was parked beside the airport road, its crew drinking tea on the turret. I had never been so pleased to see the Beirut airport road. When I left the city several days later, Hussein Kurdi made me wear a Druze cap and take off my glasses. In disguise to the airport.

Then the Syrians came back. Another Lebanese replay in February 1987. President Assad had re-formed the Syrian 85th Brigade — the unit which had been ejected from Beirut with such humiliation in 1982 — and sent it back into west Beirut to save Berri's militia, which was in danger of being crushed by the Druze. I felt safer again. We were back under the *pax Syriana*. But for what purpose?

Terry Waite had returned to Beirut the previous month, uninvited by Islamic Jihad, and disappeared. He wanted to prove his good name, to demonstrate that he had been uncontaminated by the arms-for-hostages scandal. He asked to meet the Islamic Jihad kidnappers again. But he was swallowed up like the hostages he had come to help. After Amal and Hezbollah went to war in 1988, the Syrians — who may have provoked Amal into the conflict — moved their troops into the southern suburbs. In we walked with them, through the streets in which we believed Terry Anderson might be held. There was no sign of the hostages, although we recognised some of the Hezbollah leaders whom we knew to be in Islamic Jihad. The Iranians offered to help find Waite — if the Archbishop of Canterbury could find the three Iranians kidnapped by the Phalange in 1982, the hostages we had never bothered to write about. But they were dead.

In March 1989, Anderson marked his fourth year in captivity. The last word we had of him was from a released French hostage who talked about Terry's courage, his belief in God, his frustration. One day, he said, Terry had reached such a stage of depression that he banged his head against the wall of his basement cell until the blood ran down his face. Not long before he was kidnapped, he and Madeleine had been in London and went to see *The Killing Fields*, which told the story of how the *New York Times* correspondent in Cambodia stayed on after the Americans left and had watched his local Cambodian stringer walking off into captivity.

Terry had come away from this film deeply moved. 'Every reporter should see that film,' he said. 'It tells you why you should stay with the story after the big guys have gone home, and why you shouldn't think that the Americans are the only story. And it shows you how you should always think about your local staff.' Terry Anderson had cared very much about his Lebanese staff.

But Lebanon, as J-C and I realised, provided no happy endings. It was a place where courage had no reward. It had a near-fatal attraction to the brave, the foolhardy and to those who thrived in the half-world of civil war, who had self-consciously rejected or simply abandoned the standards by which other people lived, on the grounds that they had their own rules and codes of their own. Terry fell into the first category and possibly the second. His abductors — who regarded the tactical value of his American citizenship more highly than his integrity as a journalist — belonged to the third.

These anarchic conditions led us to misinterpret what we witnessed.

An abduction or a car bombing was like a natural, uncontrollable disaster. Getting kidnapped was bad luck, which is what Anderson thought right up to that moment on 16 March 1985 when he left the bright, cosmopolitan world of Beirut in which his other friends lived and enjoyed themselves, and moved, in the space of just a few minutes, into utter darkness. We made jokes to mitigate the terror of this black hole. If we drove through Beirut wearing hoods, surely no one would harm us – they would assume we had already been abducted. Or if we pointed a gun at a friend's head as we travelled across town, no one would stop our car – only once in Lebanon had a kidnapper ever been kidnapped. Terry Anderson never made these jokes; because he was the man who made them necessary.

When the kidnappers of Islamic Jihad eventually prevailed upon Anderson to make a video film, he must have felt truly abandoned. He seemed to slur his words and on the screen I could not see his lower teeth. Had he been beaten up? If he meant what he said on the video, then he was genuinely outraged when President Reagan negotiated the release from prison in Moscow of Nicholas Daniloff, a *US News and World Report* correspondent, by freeing an accused Soviet spy in return. Why would Reagan submit to one blackmail and not to another, Anderson asked, apparently unaware that Reagan had been trading guns for hostages from January of 1986. Reagan's argument was simple: the United States had diplomatic relations with the Soviet Union while Terry Anderson's captors were 'faceless terrorists'. But they were not. His principal captor was so well known that American agents tried to arrest him near Paris when he was on holiday in France. The French, mindful of their own hostages, forced the Americans to leave him alone. The French were obeying Lebanese rules.

We all went along with these unwritten laws. In a land where there was no active police force, no law, no right of appeal, no claim to friendship or journalistic integrity that was sufficient to free our friend, what else could we do? Terry Anderson was the man who proved this, who paid the price for staying on the story.

My files in Beirut grew ever larger. Amnesty International reports were filed by city or by torture. '"Disappearances" and Extrajudicial Executions by Syrian troops and Syrian-backed forces in Tripoli', dated 29 February 1987; 'Human Rights Violations by Amal', dated 18 March 1985. 'Amnesty International urges investigation of reports of torture in Israeli-occupied territory', dated 16 September 1986. Each page contains a reason why Lebanon will remain a tragedy. 'Over 200 people, including teenagers, women and old men, are believed to be held at Khiam. They are denied any judicial process and the right to see lawyers ...'

A middle-aged man approaches me in my travel agent's office as I buy a ticket to the Gulf. 'Mr Robert. Can you help? Please, my father disappeared at Mishrif, near Damour, in 1983. His name was Yussef Gharrib. He was sixty. We are Druze. He was taken by the Phalange from the village of Kfar Matta. He was imprisoned with women and children in a container. It was summer. They sealed the door. They all died, of thirst. All of them, you see.' How can I help? 'Please, Mr Robert. His body. I want his body. In the name of God, I only want to bury my father.'

My photographs of Terry Anderson fill an album. Terry throwing snowballs at Madeleine and myself on Mount Sannine, Terry sitting on my apartment balcony, drinking champagne beside Labelle, Terry looking thoughtfully at a pregnant Madeleine. Before he died of cancer, Terry's father made a last appeal for his son's release. In 1986, Terry's brother Glenn was to die too with an identical last request to Islamic Jihad. It was pathetic and demeaning and brave. I had his number: United States area code 716—343—3131. Ask for room 409, I was told.

'Hallo Robert, Terry told me all about you.' Glenn's voice is fractured, weak, dying down the phone line to west Beirut. 'I'm hanging on. I've been diagnosed to have cancer the same as my father and my father made a vow he would hang on and not die until he saw Terry. And I've made a vow, that I will not die until I see Terry. Unfortunately, it got my father faster than I thought it would. But I *must* see Terry before I go. I want him home and I'm asking the people holding him to send him home to me before I die. I don't want Terry to come home and find both his father and his brother dead. I need to see him just one more time before I go.'

Too late again. Glenn Anderson died two days after he spoke to me. Islamic Jihad never told Terry that his father *and* his brother had died. Three years after his father was in his grave, there was Terry on another video, still confidently asking his father to kiss his daughter Sulome for him.

In the long evenings in west Beirut, there was time enough to consider where the core of the tragedy lay. In the age of the Assyrians, the Empire of Rome, in the 1860s perhaps? In the French mandate? In Auschwitz? In Palestine? In those rusting front-door keys now buried deep in the rubble of Chatila? In the 1978 Israeli invasion? The 1982 invasion? Was there a point where one could have said: Stop, beyond this point there is no future? Did *I* witness the point of no return in 1976? That 12-year-old on the broken office chair in the ruins of the Beirut front line. Now he was in his mid-twenties – if he was still alive – a gunboy no more. A gunman, no doubt, a Muslim gunman, perhaps a kidnapper of Terry Anderson.

Each Christmas, *The Times* would ask me to write a seasonal report from west Beirut. I gave up this regular feature in 1987. How could I go on writing about joy and renewal in a place without hope? Or was this not the point? Was Lebanon merely a place of illusions, like the mirror of Beirut into which we smiled and then recoiled when at last it no longer smiled back?

One warm evening in 1986, sitting three feet from the door to my balcony, I conceived of a way in which I could enjoy the view of the sea and the Corniche outside my home without being seen by the bearded men in their cars that cruised the coast road. I fetched a large mirror from the bathroom and propped it on a chair beside the balcony. Thus I could sit in safety, unseen, hidden, watching the life of Beirut pass below me. The Mediterranean lay glistening off the rocks, the evening strollers leant over the seafront rails. I could see the coffee-sellers and the swinging oil lamps on their trolleys.

But in the mirror the cars drove in the opposite direction, the trees were on the wrong side of the road that I had watched over the years. The sea lay to the east. Lebanon was in the west. The tide swept in from the Orient, not from Europe. The sun set heavily, boiling down into the sea in the east, darkening the apartment blocks and the trees, casting shadows across the mirror. I took the mirror to the back window and the miracle repeated itself. Mount Sannine to the west, its foothills shouldering their way westwards away from the sea, its snow-line a leprous white fading into the darkness. Hold up a mirror and there were two realities, two countries, two governments, each complementing the other, fragmenting and fracturing along the fault line of the Beirut ruins under our alien gaze. Thus did Lebanon represent itself.

It was midnight, and we could see the crescent moon rising from behind Mt. Sunnin, and it looked, in the midst of the stars, like the face of a corpse, in a coffin surrounded by the dim lights of candles. And Lebanon looked like an old man whose back was bent with age and whose eyes were a haven for insomnia, watching the dark and waiting for dawn, like a king sitting on the ashes of his throne in the debris of his palace.*

* *The Broken Wings*, in *The Treasured Writings of Kahlil Gibran* (New York, Castle Books, 1980), pp. 395–6.

Epilogue

In the aftermath of the First World War, Winston Churchill recorded how the 'dreary steeples' of Fermanagh and Tyrone emerged above the receding waters of the great flood, the integrity of the Irish quarrel untouched by the cataclysm and revolution which had shaken the globe.

In just such a way, after the great revolutions of Eastern Europe in 1989, did Lebanon's quarrel remain unmoved by the new world of freedom which was created between Moscow and the West. While Europe anticipated a new unity, Lebanon had acquired two rival governments, one led by a Christian general, the other by a Sunni Muslim prime minister. Two Lebanons thus surfaced, a Christian rump state controlled by half the country's army and a powerless Muslim nation dependent upon Syria.

As the Berlin Wall was torn down, Lebanon's front lines grew in number. South of Sidon, below the Jezzine Mountains, Shia Muslims fought each other for control of four broken villages, martyring each other in the very terrain they had liberated from the Israelis. Then in east Beirut, in early 1990, the Christians of Lebanon crucified themselves. Between east Beirut and Batroun to the north, a distance of only thirty miles, four new front lines crossed the map, each defended by Christian Maronites shooting at Christian Maronites. Their mirror also fragmented.

Nowhere across the Arab world did the spirit of détente bless the land. Israel's humiliation in Lebanon was replayed in the Occupied West Bank and Gaza Strip, where the Palestinians at last began to fight back against their occupiers – albeit with stones rather than guns – with the same tenacity the people of southern Lebanon had shown half a decade earlier.

Israel's own government broke apart as its political leadership moved further to the right. Freed from the burden of his titanic and self-imposed war with Iran, Saddam Hussein of Iraq took upon himself the leadership of the Arab world – inspiring fear among most of his Arab neighbors and contempt in Syria.

The revolution started by Mikhail Gorbachev in the Soviet Union initiated another of those historical repetitions to which the Middle East seems to be doomed. Just as the Holocaust had helped to create the state of Israel, so Gorbachev's *perestroika* provided the possibility of a new, greater Israel. Instead of arriving on tramp steamers from the camps of Europe, Israel's new Jewish immigrants poured into Tel Aviv airport from the Soviet Union in the tens of thousands. Yitzhak Shamir, old Szymon Datner's pupil from the Hebrew gymnasium at Bialystok, saw their coming as a form of salvation. He spoke openly of 'A Greater Israel,' while the Palestinians and the Arab nations that had for so long claimed to be their protectors feared that a new, radically anti-Arab Israeli government would drive the entire Arab population from what was left of 'Palestine.' And if the Israelis were to do this – if they were to 'transfer' the Arabs out of the West Bank, as the most right-wing Israeli political party demanded – into which country would they be herded? Was Jordan to be the new 'Palestine'? Or would King Hussein close his borders and force the new Palestinian refugees into Lebanon?

In Iran, Ayatollah Khomeini died. But the Islamic fundamentalism which he represented did not perish with him as the United States and other Western nations – and, in truth, the Arab leaders – had hoped. Fundamentalism, or 'resurgence,' as the Arabs more accurately called it, was Islam's response to decades of political and economic humiliation. Its adherents fueled the Palestinian struggle against Israel on the west, encouraged violent opposition to the Egyptian government, struck at the power of King Hussein of Jordan and clung tenaciously to their political gains in Lebanon. In Southwest Asia, the same spirit of rebellion or renewal – the definitions depended upon whether you spoke to rulers or to their opponents – closed in on Afghanistan and Pakistan. In the southern, Muslim republics of the Soviet Union, Islam came into conflict first with the Armenians and then with the Soviet army.

As Central Europe changed and the Soviet empire disintegrated, so our map of the Middle East expanded. It appeared now to extend as far north as Baku, as far east as Islamabad. The minorities of the Arab nations, almost all of whom were Christians, responded to this with fear and anger.

Lebanon could not escape the new seismic tremors of the Middle East. In 1988, the old structure of the National Covenant at last began to fall apart. Yet again, foreign interference helped to bring about catastrophe. Having regarded Syria as the source of all regional evil during the Reagan era, the Americans under President George Bush now saw Damascus as the key to peace in Lebanon. Both they and the Syrians tried to ensure the election of a pliant pro-Syrian Christian candidate who could be relied upon to rule his country in the interests of its Arab neighbor. Regarding this as a final betrayal, most of Lebanon's Christian community opposed the plan.

On 22 September 1988, in his last hours as president, Amin Gemayel took the fatal step of asking his army chief of staff, General Michel

Aoun – the same Aoun who had defended Soukh al-Gharb against the Syrians – to lead a caretaker government until new elections could be held. Aoun was a Christian Maronite, but the Syrians saw him as a threat to all they represented in Lebanon. Aoun was a soldier with a loyal following among at least forty percent of the Lebanese National Army. His military units possessed the army's heavy artillery and almost all its tanks, purchased from France and America during the West's 1982 presence in Beirut. And since Aoun maintained an effective military alliance with the Phalange, the Israelis would give him their support. So too, President Assad feared, would Syria's Iraqi enemies. The Gulf War over, Saddam Hussein was now in an expansionist mood.

Militarily powerless but with Syrian political support, Gemayel's former prime minister, Selim al-Hoss, now claimed that he was the true leader of a caretaker government. Lebanon reflected itself across the Beirut front line. In the east, Aoun formed a military cabinet. In the west, Hoss formed a civilian cabinet. The two 'governments' forced each ministry to duplicate itself. There were two ministries of health, two ministries of defence, two ministries of the interior, each mimicking the other. Two offices issued identical passports. But Lebanese arriving at Beirut airport in the Muslim sector with passports issued in east Beirut were often turned away. Citizens of Lebanon with passports issued in west Beirut were sometimes refused permission to land by sea at the Christian-controlled harbor.

General Aoun, trained as an artillery officer at Fort Sill in the United States and a graduate of French Military College, was as ambitious in east Beirut as his rival Dr Hoss was humble in the west. If Pierre Gemayel had once taken his Christian inspiration from the discipline of Nazi Germany, now Aoun sought even more extraordinary inspiration from the Second World War. Hoss was a 'Petainist' and his 'cabinet' in west Beirut were in 'collaboration' with the occupying Syrian army, Aoun announced. He admired Napoleon and sought strength in his own exclusive assessment of General de Gaulle, forgetting that it was de Gaulle who said that soldiers make poor politicians.

In the spring of 1989, after ordering illegal Christian and Muslim militia ports to close down so that his 'government' could re-impose customs duties, Aoun's Lebanese army artillery batteries opened a bombardment against Syrian army positions in the densely populated areas of west Beirut. Aoun called it a 'war of liberation,' a theme enthusiastically taken up by the Christian Maronites and the bulk of the French press. Like American correspondents reporting from Israel, French journalists often lost their critical faculties when writing about Lebanon's Christians. French emissaries arrived to confer with Aoun. So did right-wing members of the French Assembly.

The Syrians fired back, as Aoun knew they would, devastatingly and with overwhelming firepower. The civilians of Beirut died by the hundreds throughout the summer of 1989, torn apart in the west of the city by the shells of Aoun's army and in the east by the shells of President Assad's army. For days, Beirut lay under clouds of smoke, its people gradually evacuating the capital until only a tenth of the civilian population – about 100,000 souls – remained. The surviv-ability of the city exercised a cruel fascination over those of us who stayed. For how long could Beirut be shelled before its people aban-doned it entirely, as surely as the world had now abandoned Lebanon?

I had now left *The Times*, whose increasingly right-wing opinions under Rupert Murdoch's ownership no longer reflected the impartial newspaper I had joined almost twenty years earlier. It is impossible for a reporter to risk his life under fire for a newspaper in which he no longer believes. I now worked for the new British daily *The Independent*, but my work was in many ways the same as it had always been. I was the paper's Middle East correspondent, based in Beirut. And Beirut, as usual, was at war with itself. For how many years had I driven under shellfire through the streets of west Beirut to seek shelter in the Associated Press office? It was still there, still run by Farouk Nassar and his team of women reporters, still watched over by those sorrow-ful photographs of Terry Anderson. Somewhere out in the southern suburbs under Aoun's artillery fire, in basements still guarded by his pro-Iranian captors, Terry was now enduring his fifth year of captivity.

I slept several nights on a mattress on the floor of Terry's office, waking suddenly after explosions to find the face of the friend I had not seen for four and a half years looking at me. Each picture was thumbtacked onto a large rectangular bulletin board next to Terry's desk. On the left was the Terry I remembered, bright, grinning, his spectacles making his eyes seem unnaturally small, the file picture from 1984. To the right was the other Terry, the one I did not know, staring at his kidnappers' cameras and video recorders. Terry fright-ened, his eyes wide with anxiety; Terry angry, talking to the camera, asking why President Reagan could not negotiate his release; Terry tired, weak, an overgrown moustache weighing down his cheeks. Did I know him now? He could not have been far away. Maybe he could hear the same shells that were shaking the AP bureau.

Beirut airport had been closed for months. To leave Lebanon, even for the briefest holiday, was a nightmare – an alternative between driving across the Bekaa Valley to Damascus under artillery fire from Aoun's guns for more than an hour and sneaking by night out of Aoun's port of Jounieh on a darkened ferry to Cyprus as the Syrian

Grad missiles exploded in the sea around it. The mountainsides above Jounieh glowed with fire.

I had met Aoun during his 1983 battles with the Syrians at Soukh al-Gharb. But when I saw him again in 1989, he seemed much smaller. His shellproof bunker used to be part of the presidential palace's underground car park. Outside the makeshift office was a pile of shell fragments that had been collected from his palace courtyard, the results of Syrian shelling. Then, a short man in American combat fatigues moved towards me, right hand outstretched in an artificial, slightly embarrassed way. He would have preferred to salute. His smile was drawn, tired. There were dark bags under his eyes. He had been directing his artillery all night. His face was white and unhealthy – he had already been living in his bunker for six weeks – and he had the appearance of a mole emerging from a long sleep, his eyes bloodshot and blinking. There were loyal 'apparatchiks' everywhere, in blue suits and ties, murmuring 'Monsieur le President' in Aoun's ear to catch his attention. His young daughter Mireille sat beside his desk, a look of adoration on her face as she fumbled with a tape recorder. The Napoleon of Lebanon was about to speak from his underground garage.

It was part monologue, part history lesson. Aoun wanted a Westernized Lebanon, 'like France, like America.' He could not see why this might not suit the Muslims, whom he also claimed to represent. When I suggested that his 'war of liberation' against Syria would turn into a disaster, he lectured me on how not one 'war of liberation' had ever been lost. 'History shows this,' he said with a gleam of satisfaction. 'Look at the French Maquis in the Second World War, look at the Algerian resistance to the French, look at the Vietcong.' So what were his plans, I asked? 'Plans? What plans?' Well, plans for the war, for the future of Lebanon. Aoun was frowning now. 'I am a soldier. I want the liberation of my country.' But your plans, General Aoun. 'Plans,' he said again, as if the word were in a language he did not understand. And he was silent.

The general's acolytes were fidgeting. One looked at his watch. Mireille still smiled, madonnalike, at her father. So that was Aoun's policy. He would get up in the morning and decide what to do for the day. An artillery barrage, a press conference, a live phone-in to AP radio in Washington, a meeting with the papal nuncio. Vatican scarlet always seemed to be fluttering around the bunker doors.

Yet under Syrian shellfire in east Beirut, it was easy to find something reassuring about Aoun. He and his colleagues would warn visitors not to travel to west Beirut where the Syrians – so they would have their guests believe – ruled like Nazis, where any Westerner would be kidnapped. Aoun laughed a lot, a homely chuckle. This made visitors confident.

Travel through the looking glass, across the front line to west Beirut, however, and the image became distorted. The Syrians were disciplined if ruthless. Now it was Aoun's shells that exploded around my own home in west Beirut. When I turned on my television, there was Aoun on the newscast, lecturing more journalists. Yet his laughter was now frightening, the gleam in his eyes messianic.

No one could have said that of Selim al-Hoss. Like Aoun, he had a pile of scrap metal outside his office, the results of shelling by the general's Lebanese army. It was as if the two men had cloned their contempt for each other's weaponry. There was a notice on the door, politely requesting visitors to leave their guns outside. Hoss arrived on his own, apologizing for being ten minutes late. He was a tall, professorial man, a former economist at the American University of Beirut. He was not self-righteous, but there was something overzealous about his sincerity. Walid Jumblatt once described Hoss to me as 'a Protestant preacher,' which caught something of the Sunni Muslim leader's careful goodness. Like Aoun, he sat next to a Lebanese flag. Hoss's daughter Widad, however, was present only in photographic form, framed on a table to the right of her father.

Unlike Aoun, Hoss did not talk about wars of liberation. He spoke of plans, immensely detailed, constitutional. 'What we need is a meeting of Parliament that will create a new president and put Aoun and myself out of existence. We must have a meeting of Parliament to elect a president and, at the very same sitting, there will be a debate for a speaker and a debate on political issues. This is what lies at the heart of our problem.'

But what about the Syrian army that Aoun had sworn to evict from Lebanon? 'Why talk about this now?' Hoss asked. 'We need political reform. After this we can talk about sovereignty.' Another mirror. Aoun said he wanted the Syrians out before political concessions were made. But the Muslims feared that if the Syrians left, the Maronites would give them nothing. So Hoss wanted political concessions before a Syrian withdrawal. These were the same, tired arguments upon which the Lebanese had been focusing for more than a decade. In 1983 the Western ambassadors vainly sought reform from Amin Gemayal. Just as the Americans promised a Syrian withdrawal.

Not only the ghosts of the dead haunted Lebanon. There were other phantoms, of political demands, of political refusal, of occupation and re-occupation. My own life seemed crushed by these repetitions. What more could I write about Lebanon? In the spring of 1989, another Briton was taken hostage: Jackie Mann, an elderly, retired airline pilot whose wife was left to live on, alone and in poverty, in their dingy apartment in west Beirut.

The Syrians positioned a gun battery down the road from my home. When it fired, which it did for hours every night, the walls and doors shook and the windows fractured. When Aoun's shells came back, whiffling in the darkness over the roof of my home, the floors moved with the vibration. All water supplies ended. Then the power station was hit, and electricity stopped. In the fall of 1989, my friend and colleague J-C left to join his wife and infant daughter in Madrid. He would continue to make visits to Beirut.

Only two Western journalists were now left, myself and Lara Marlowe of the *Financial Times*. We moved into J-C's old apartment overlooking the sea. No need to fear the sharklike cars and their bearded drivers on the Corniche now. The seafront was a military zone. No one dared travel there. Shells smashed into the street in front of our home. One night, Aoun and the Phalangists together shelled the Corniche, set fire to eight Syrian ammunition trucks and turned the boulevard into an inferno. A teenage Syrian soldier sat wounded in the lobby of our apartment building, clutching a bandage to his chest. For nights, we could not sleep through the shellfire but sat instead in a windowless corridor near the door, frightened, miserable and dirty. Thirteen years of reporting Lebanon had come to this.

Still the AP office functioned. On very bad nights, we hid there, drinking Farouk's fifteen-year-old Scotch. The bureau stood opposite the shell of the old Commodore Hotel, that temple of truth to the generation of correspondents who had long since decamped to Cyprus, India, Israel, or to become editorial executives in New York and London. The Syrian army now occupied the Commodore's ruins, the soldiers eating their hummus and beans in the basement. The hotel's windows were smashed, its furniture stolen by its new guests. Occasionally, in bars and restaurants still open around west Beirut, I would recognize familiar chairs, tablecloths, napkins from the Commodore. Like an old liner, the great hulk was slowly being broken up. The red-vinyl-upholstered bar around which so many of us had debated the Israeli invasion of 1982, the arrival and departure of the multinational force, the kidnapping of Terry Anderson and a score of others was still there. But it was caked with dust and grease. There remained just one reminder of the wreck's history: a brass plaque in the lobby recording the gratitude of Cairo-based journalists to the hotel's staff for staying open under Israeli bombardment. Now it stayed closed under General Aoun's bombardment, its only occupants the soldiers from Latakia, Aleppo and Homs. It was somehow fitting that they should have followed the journalists into the Commodore: reality replacing fantasy.

★   ★   ★

On beautiful mornings, after the night's bombardments were over and before the day's bombardments began, we could still walk across the green line from west to east Beirut, or east to west under that high, bright blue sky that only Lebanon produces. The bougainvillea and jacaranda trees in the ruins were in bloom. Grass grew out of the roads and sidewalks. There was rubble on the street. The lampposts were corroded, pincushioned with bullet holes. The wildflowers blossomed out of mountains of sand and from shell holes. Fourteen years of shell holes. The trees were still burned from the fighting of the Israeli invasion in 1982, grey stumps emerging from the undergrowth.

Some days, dozens of people crossed the line here, in both directions. These were the Lebanese who kept their city in existence, living on one side of the line, working on the other. Most mornings at the same time, the armies stopped firing at each other, allowing this little routine to continue. All walked quickly. It took maybe ten minutes to cross. I walked quickly, too. A single shell would set us running for our lives. By walking slowly, we would have tempted fate. By running, we would have invited disaster. So everyone walked quickly. In complete silence.

Reporting Aoun's war took on a familiar, wearying pattern. Hours of cowering in corridors, sweating in the heat, fearful of the shells, alternated with visits to Beirut's hospitals, journeys almost identical in geography and result to those we had made under Israeli gunfire in 1982. There was Dr Amal Shamaa in the wreckage of the Barbir hospital in west Beirut. In 1982, Israeli shells had torn the hospital apart. Now Aoun's shells performed the same task. No one knew why the hospital was targeted again. They even scored direct hits on the operating theatres.

The Arab League tried to secure a truce. As always, the Lebanese wished to believe in cease-fires. So did the Sfeir family from Ghadir, up in the foothills below the Maronite patriarchate at Bkerke. Fouad and Nadia Sfeir heard news of the truce in their underground shelter one evening in early May. So they headed up the road with their children and other family members to make dinner. The meal was already in the oven when they turned on the television and heard Lakhdar Ibrahimi, the Arab League's assistant secretary general, announcing that there was 'no more reason for anyone to fire another shell in Lebanon.' Seconds later, a Grad missile, fired by the Syrians in west Beirut, came directly through the window, decapitated Nadia and blasted her family around the room. When Nadia Sfeir died, her fifteen-month-old son Chadi was in her arms.

In the Pasteur hospital in the Christian port of Jounieh, I found Chadi squealing with pain, shrieking and crying and whimpering in turns, his half-severed fingers still bleeding into bandages. Nadia's brother-in-law Joseph was there too, a series of large black scabs over his face and chest. 'If Aoun wins, this will have been worth it,' he said to me. I could not believe this. It was a lie. It would not have been worth it. The Syrians were not going to leave Lebanon, and Aoun was not going to gain a square foot of territory outside his Christian enclave.

I drove up to the Sfeirs' home on the hillside afterwards. The house had been demolished by the missile. There were the remains of a child's piano, of a school report, of an identification card belonging to Nadia's gravely wounded husband. Their neighbors produced a book of snapshots which they had salvaged from the rubble. Nadia at Chadi's christening, a beautiful woman with a gentle smile. Chadi's older brother Charbel holding the baby on his lap. The family had been torn apart by the missile. And here we were, looking at photographs again.

It was as if there was a clue in these images of wounded families, dead men and women, hostages and suicide bombers and massacre victims, which would suddenly reveal the truth of history. Szymon Datner's wife Sosannah, murdered so long ago in the Bialystok ghetto, did not look very different from Nadia Sfeir. In the photographs, they were happy, both mothers, both victims-to-be. Reporting Lebanon, trying to discover why I witnessed the slaughter of so many people there, I came to view the sepia photographs, snapshots and videotapes as footprints of history, sometimes clear, sometimes so faint I could scarcely decipher them. Was there some order in which these pictures should be arranged, some secret in their constant reappearance, a significance which we missed?

I would sometimes escape during the 1989 war to southern Lebanon, the dangerous Nirvana which the United Nations army still patrolled, eleven years after it had arrived with its hopeless mandate and its illusions. I stayed with the Finnish battalion, whose area of operations was itself divided between land which the Shia militias claimed to have 'liberated' from the Israelis and land which Israel's Christian militia allies – the 'South Lebanon Army' – claimed to have kept 'free' of the Shia gunmen.

Sitting on the Finns' armored vehicles as we moved up the *wadis*, I could smell the flowers and the long grass. A buzzard circled above us for fifteen minutes as we crossed the line between 'liberated Lebanon' and 'free Lebanon.' Inside the area occupied by the Israelis and their allies, we stopped at a small house where a Lebanese Shia family described, in detail but without emotion, how one of their sons was blackmailed into joining Israel's proxy militia. If he refused, the Israelis would deport the whole family from their home, they said.

Now that the boy had joined the militia, however, the entire family were under threat of assassination by the Hezbollah.

On the way back to Beirut in a UN helicopter, I saw the Lebanese coast lying in the heat haze to the east, the Mediterranean wrinkling away, empty, to the west. But the sea was not really empty at all. For perhaps twenty miles from the coastline, it was thick with untreated sewage and garbage. In Cyprus, Syria, Israel, even Turkey, they were complaining about the filth of Lebanon washing up on their shores. When I looked down from the helicopter – so far from the coast that I could no longer see Lebanon – the country's detritus lay thick across the water. Boxes, papers, metal canisters, wood and brown slime, mile after mile of it spreading ever further out to sea, staining the waves.

Aoun's war went on through the humid summer. Desperately tired, one night I found I could no longer sit on the floor of the hot corridor as the shells came in. I went instead to sit on my balcony over the black Mediterranean. There I could see Aoun's artillery rounds soaring in through the darkness with small pink lights on them like tracers. All over the bay, lights were crisscrossing the water. I watched them with the fascination of exhaustion. After a while, they began to look like the cursors on a computer screen, racing back and forth across the page, orange, even green, their trajectories a thing of beauty rather than of horror. And there were moments between the bombardments when I could look up from my balcony and see a pageant of stars in the night sky.

Iraq's new power inevitably extended to support the man who challenged the Syrians in Lebanon, just as President Assad had guessed it would. France and Iraq now gave, respectively, political and military support to Aoun. Iraqi rocket-launchers were brought ashore from ships in Jounieh. The Syrians feared that Iraq had given Aoun Scud missiles with which he could hit Damascus. It was untrue, although Aoun did his best to fuel Syria's suspicions. After Ibrahimi and the Arab League brought about a cease-fire, the general – now under pressure to accept a truce since his war was obviously hopeless – announced that he would 'Give peace a chance.'

So it seemed, for a few weeks. The country's elderly members of Parliament were summoned to a conference in the Saudi Arabian resort of Taif, there to cobble up another settlement to the Lebanese crisis. The old men of Lebanon should have discarded the covenant and the system of powersharing which the French had introduced four-and-a-half decades earlier. Instead, they tinkered with the principles of the system, increasing the power of the Muslim prime minister, decreasing the power of the Maronite president but leaving confessionalism intact. The Maronites would continue to hold the top jobs. The Shia Muslims would continue to be underrepresented in government. No Muslim could be a president. No Christian could be a prime minister. Instead of carrying out major surgery to save the life of their dying nation, the Lebanese Parliament prescribed a few pills and sought promises of good behavior.

Aoun refused to attend the Taif meeting and subsequently denounced as traitors those Christian members of Parliament who voted in favor of limited reforms. Their homes in east Beirut were burned or bombed. The general's supporters swarmed to the palace of the elderly Nasrallah Sfeir, the Maronite patriarch who had supported Taif, and tried to force the old man to kiss Aoun's portrait – which was then pasted over a photograph of the pope. Hours before the Lebanese Parliament was to vote for a president, Aoun issued a decree 'dissolving' the assembly and promising new legislative elections.

Something unprecedented was happening in east Beirut. Aoun's men were creating a small military dictatorship. Army officers who doubted the wisdom of the general's policies were imprisoned or put under house arrest. Several fled to west Beirut. Instead of advertising their patriotism to their nation, Christian soldiers now displayed portraits of General Aoun on their tanks and trucks. They were fighting for Aoun's concept of the future Lebanon, a 'Westernized' nation run by Maronite Christians who believed they possessed a 'civilizing' mission. The forces under Aoun were becoming a colonial army, an army with a mission, just as the French had been at the time of the mandate. And the Muslims of Lebanon, who had at first admired Aoun's courage and patriotism, discovered that they did not like this new army. It was, after all, the same army which had entered west Beirut in 1982 and arrested hundreds of young Muslim men, many of whom were never seen again. When the Israelis invaded that same year, Aoun's army chose not to fight them. So why, suddenly, did it wish to fight the Syrians?

Ibrahimi and his colleagues in the Arab League persuaded the Lebanese MPs to gather again. Hussein Husseini, the Shia Muslim speaker of the Parliament, flew to Paris to plead with the Christian MPs who had fled there to return to Lebanon and elect a president. They did. And there was something honorable about the way the frightened old men came back to their country, albeit to a remote and disused military airfield at Qleiaat, out of the range of Aoun's guns, so far to the north of Lebanon that it was almost in Syria.

There they elected René Moawad as president of Lebanon. Moawad was a Maronite lawyer who accepted the nature – and presence – of Syrian power but who genuinely believed in the principle of Muslim-

Christian coexistence, so much so that he gave his only son a Muslim name. He was to survive just seventeen days.

Unable to occupy the presidential palace at Baabda – in which Aoun was still ensconced – Moawad took up residence in west Beirut, a president 'in transit' since it was presumed to be only a matter of days before Aoun capitulated. Moawad appointed Hoss as his prime minister and on Lebanese Independence Day, 22 November, he received foreign ambassadors at Hoss's office in west Beirut. Across the city, Aoun's military 'cabinet' was holding an Independence Day review of Lebanese troops. But the general was curiously absent. He remained in his bunker.

Not long after midday, Moawad left to return to his home on the seafront in a convoy of limousines, protected by Syrian troops and intelligence operatives. They had traveled scarcely seven hundred yards when an enormous bomb tore Moawad's armored Mercedes apart, tossing the rear section of the vehicle over the roof of the local prison, the front half two hundred yards into a parking lot. Moawad's body and those of his protectors were partly vaporized. When they buried him in his home town of Zghorta three days later, no one knew whether the president's coffin contained his remains or those of one of his bodyguards.

Who killed President Moawad? The list of those who might have found advantage in his death included almost every group in Lebanon and their supporters in other nations. General Aoun ostensibly had most to gain and least to lose from Moawad's murder. The Lebanese deuxième bureau, supported by the Phalange – or perhaps by explosives experts hired by Aoun's ally, Iraq – could have been responsible. Thus Iraq would have struck at Syria's supposed 'puppet' in Lebanon. Aoun denied any involvement, implausibly demanding a United Nations inquiry into the assassination.

But then there were rumors that Moawad had fallen out with the Syrians, that he had refused permission for Syrian firepower to be used to dislodge Aoun. If the Syrians meant to wipe out Moawad, they would find no shortage of assassins to do their bidding in west Beirut. But Syria's fury in the aftermath of Moawad's death seemed genuine.

There were other possibilities. Moawad's election had been a victory for Taif, a peace agreement engineered by the Saudis to favor their Sunni Muslim co-religionists in Lebanon, and few hated the Saudi regime as intensely as the Iranians. Not only had the Saudis helped to fund President Saddam Hussein's eight-year war against the Islamic republic, but in September 1989, the Saudi oligarchy ordered the beheading of 16 pro-Iranian Shia Muslims who had attempted to seize Mecca from the 'corrupt' Saudi regime. The Hezbollah vowed revenge. Could Iran have been behind the murder? Iran too would have had little trouble in finding assassins to do its work in Lebanon. Iranian leaders were widely believed to have ordered the blowing up of a Pan Am jet over Scotland in December 1988 in revenge for the destruction of an Iranian civil airliner by the USS *Vincennes* in the Gulf the previous year. Ahmed Jibril's Popular Front for the Liberation of Palestine – General Command was accused in the West of planting the bomb on Iran's behalf. Iran denied any responsibility. So did Jibril. But Jibril's men had bases at Damour, twelve miles south of Beirut.

The assassination of Moawad was not just professional. It was a perfect murder. The bomb contained 250 kilograms of explosives and it was placed inside a disused candy store. It would have taken a week for that quantity of explosives to be hidden in the old stone building – the shop itself became a bomb. People must have been seen carrying explosives in sacks or suitcases into the shop. The bomb was detonated at the very second Moawad's car passed the building – so the assassin watched the motorcade and set off the charge by remote control. He must have used a radio – since wires might have been discovered. He had to have been in a high-rise building. For protection, he would have placed sandbags around the room from which he could watch the road, and he would have opened the windows to prevent the glass shattering into his face.

All that was left of the shop was a twelve-foot crater in the ground. When I stood on the edge of the pit in the aftermath of the bombing, it was clear that only two high-rise buildings could have been used by the bomber to trigger the explosion. But no one reported any stranger in either building. No one would, for this was Lebanon – and to identify an assassin in Beirut is to die. In any other country, there would have been a government inquiry into the assassination and a murder hunt by the police and army. Yet within hours of the bombing, I watched bulldozers ploughing over the rubble, carefully and deliberately destroying any clues to the murder. A Lebanese army intelligence officer whom I knew was also there. When I asked him who killed Moawad, he raised his right hand and then turned a finger 360 degrees in the air. Everyone was a culprit. Who killed the president? Lebanon killed him.

René Moawad's coffin was borne from the crypt of his ancestral church at Zghorta on a gun carriage. There were wreaths from President Assad and his generals. The widows of Moawad's bodyguards were carried screaming into the church, one of them wearing her murdered husband's military beret in a last attempt to seek physical contact with the dead man she loved. In Lebanon, the men die and the women do the mourning. But respect then gave way to silence.

For the Lebanese government had no desire to find out the identity of the murderer. The answer might prove to be too terrible to contemplate. The act of discovery might, by chance, unlock other secrets of Lebanon and suggest the answers to other questions. Everyone knew what these questions were: Who killed Bashir Gemayel? Or who killed Rashid Karami? Or Kamal Jumblatt?

Even before Moawad – or what was left of him – was in his grave, the Lebanese Parliament elected another president, Elias Hrawi, a Christian Maronite landowner with neither the intellect nor the class of Moawad. A small, gruff man, he appointed a new army commander and ordered Aoun out of the presidential palace at Baabda. The general would not oblige him, and in early December 1989, the Syrian army moved hundreds of tanks and artillery pieces up into the mountains above Beirut.

I followed them up the Damascus highway, from Chtaura into the snow line, long convoys of trucks and 122-mm guns and T-62 tanks that moved slowly and deliberately up the mountain road through the clouds and ice. Had I not followed this very same army, perhaps these very same gun limbers, up this same road in 1976, when Syria was going to save the Christians from the Palestinians? Now they were going to attack Christian Maronite forces and capture Baabda for a Christian Maronite president. As I drove past the tank transporters and became locked into the military traffic above Chtaura, I passed the exact corner in the road where Ed Cody and I had first seen the advancing Syrian army more than thirteen years before.

The Syrians did not go to Baabda. They did not shell Aoun's army. There was talk of another 'red line,' perhaps drawn by the Americans who now supported Syrian policy in Lebanon, perhaps by the French who repeatedly dispatched warships towards the Christian Lebanese coast only to withdraw them before they appeared on the horizon.

Instead, Aoun decided to liquidate all political opposition within his Christian enclave and turned upon his Phalangist allies – the same militia which had massacred the Palestinians of Sabra and Chatila in 1982 – in a war even more savage than the one he had fought against the Syrians in 1989. Between the end of January and the end of May 1990, well over a thousand people died in Beirut, most of them civilians and almost all of them Christians. While President Hrawi and his cabinet ruled from a hotel in west Beirut, they could watch the fires burning day and night in the east of the city as the Christians destroyed themselves.

One day when I crossed to east Beirut, I found the Christian manager of a Lebanese bank, a middle-aged, well-dressed man, rotting in the sun beside the white Mercedes which he had just bought. He was curled up, as if he had fallen out of the open driver's door in a swoon. Behind him stood the abandoned Ministry of Justice. Snipers had shot the man three days earlier but no one dared approach his corpse for fear that they too would be killed. Some bodies lay in the streets for two weeks, many of them decomposing in the seats of the cars they had been driving when they died.

During the Crusades, the Christian knights fought just such a fratricidal conflict within the city of Tyre while the Muslim armies waited patiently at the gates of the ancient metropolis. Why should the Syrians intervene now, when the Maronites of Lebanon were slaughtering each other? By Easter Sunday, the Christians were fleeing Aoun's enclave, many of them still supporting Aoun but most of them seeking refuge in the Muslim, western sector of the city. Men and women who had not dared to visit west Beirut in fifteen years of war suddenly found themselves among Muslims who turned out to be friends rather than enemies. Some had forgotten their own capital and did not know their way to the shopping streets of Hamra. Six hundred Christian Maronite students returned to the campus of the American University in west Beirut. The ferocity of Aoun's latest war produced the first unity Lebanon had witnessed in a decade and a half.

Yet by midsummer, Aoun was still in Baabda while Geagea – the same Geagea who had so pointlessly shelled Sidon in the spring of 1985 – appeared in a Phalangist television advertisement dressed in a brown shirt, holding aloft a brazier of fire to the music of Wagner, his militiamen rewarding him with a Nazi salute. Aoun and Geagea each presided over half of the Christian enclave.

The two Shia militias – Amal and Hezbollah – continued their war in the streets of west Beirut and in the hills south of Sidon. Embittered by Israel's preparedness to settle its new Jewish immigrants in the West Bank and the Gaza Strip, the thousands of armed Palestinian guerrillas in Sidon began to turn once again to the 'armed struggle,' the very policy which had brought such ferocious Israeli retaliation upon the Lebanese over the past fifteen years.

Two American hostages, Robert Polhill and Frank Reed, were freed in 1990. But Terry Anderson remained a prisoner in a country ever more divided among its people. The last photograph we had of him came from his kidnappers in October of 1989. It showed Terry standing over a birthday cake, smiling mournfully at the camera. But when we studied the picture, it was obvious it had been taken a year earlier, in 1988.

There were rumors that the Western hostages were sick, that at least one was mentally ill. What could be the effect of five years of seclusion on a human being? Did the fissures in the mind of the captives reflect – through an indistinct lens – the hostage nation in which they were trapped? For from its southernmost border with Israel to its northern frontier with Syria, sixteen front lines now cut through Lebanon. Divided into fragments, each fragment deeming itself a nation.

Bibliography

Ajami, Fouad, *The Vanished Imam: Musa al Sadr and the Shia of Lebanon* (New York, Cornell University Press, 1986)

Amnesty International, *Report from Amnesty International to the Government of the Syrian Arab Republic* (London, 1983)

An Nahar Arab Report Books 4: Guerrillas for Palestine, ed. Riad N. El-Rayyes and Dunia Nahas (Beirut, 1974)

Ang, Swee Chai, *From Beirut to Jerusalem: A Woman Surgeon with the Palestinians* (London, Grafton Books, 1989)

Antonius, George, *The Arab Awakening: The Story of the Arab National Movement* (New York, Capricorn Books, 1965)

Baedeker, Karl, *Palestine et Syrie: Routes Principales à travers la Mésopotamie et la Babylone, l'Ile de Chypre* (Leipzig/Paris, 1912)

Bulloch, John, *Death of a Country: the Civil War in Lebanon* (London, Weidenfeld and Nicolson, 1977); *Final Conflict: The War in the Lebanon* (London, Century Publishing, 1983)

Chafets, Ze'ev, *Double Vision: How America's Press Distorts Our View of the Middle East* (New York, William Morrow, 1984)

Chomsky, Noam, *The Fateful Triangle: The United States, Israel and the Palestinians* (London, Pluto Press, 1983)

Churchill, Colonel Charles, *The Druzes and the Maronites under the Turkish Rule from 1840 to 1860* (London, Bernard Quaritch, 1862)

Dawisha, A., *Syria and the Lebanese Crisis* (London, Macmillan, 1980)

Deeb, Marius, *The Lebanese Civil War* (New York, Praeger, 1980)

Gibran, Khalil, *The Garden of the Prophet* (London, Heinemann, 1934); *The Broken Wings* (London, Heinemann, 1976)

Gilmour, David, *Dispossessed: The Ordeal of the Palestinians 1917–1980* (London, Sidgwick and Jackson, 1980); *Lebanon: the Fractured Country* (London, Sphere, 1987)

Gordon, David C., *Lebanon: The Fragmented Nation* (London, Croom Helm, 1980)

Hachette, *World Guides: Lebanon* (Paris, 1965)

Hammel, Eric, *The Root: The Marines in Beirut August 1982–February 1984* (New York, Harcourt Brace Jovanovich, 1985)

Hardie, Frank, and Herrman, Irwin, *Britain and Zion: The Fateful Entangle-

ment (Belfast, Blackstaff Press, 1981)

Hirst, David, *The Gun and the Olive Branch: The Roots of Violence in the Middle East* (London, Faber and Faber, 1984)

Jansen, Michael, *The Battle of Beirut: Why Israel Invaded Lebanon* (London, Zed Press, 1982)

Jidejian, Nina, *Beirut through the Ages* (Beirut, Dar el-Mashreq, 1986)

Kahan, Yitzhak, *The Commission of Inquiry into the Events at the Refugee Camps in Beirut*, final report by Yitzhak Kahan, Aharon Barak and Yona Efrat (Jerusalem, 1983)

Khalidi, Walid, *Conflict and Violence in Lebanon* (Cambridge, Mass., Harvard Center for International Affairs, 1979)

Lamb, Franklin P. (ed.), *Reason Not the Need: Eyewitness Chronicles of Israel's War in Lebanon* with a foreword by Sean MacBride (London, Spokesman Books for the Bertrand Russell Peace Foundation, 1984)

Lewis, Bernard, *The Arabs in History* (London, Hutchinson, 1970)

Mikdadi, Lina, *Surviving the Siege of Beirut* (London, Onyx Press, 1983)

Murray, John, *A Handbook for Travellers in Syria and Palestine including a short account of the Geography, History and Religious and Political Divisions of these Countries, together with detailed descriptions of Jerusalem, Damascus, Palmyra, Baalbek, and the interesting ruined cities of Moab, Gilead, and Boshan* (London, John Murray, 1892)

Nazzal, Nafiz, *The Palestinian Exodus from Galilee 1948* (Beirut, The Institute for Palestine Studies, 1978)

O'Brien, Conor Cruise, *The Siege: The Saga of Israel and Zionism* (London, Weidenfeld and Nicolson, 1986)

Owen, Roger (ed.), *Essays on the Crisis in Lebanon* (London, Ithaca Press, 1976)

Petit, Michael, *Peacekeepers at War: A Marine's Account of the Beirut Catastrophe* (London, Faber and Faber, 1986)

Randal, Jonathan, *The Tragedy of Lebanon: Christian Warlords, Israeli Adventurers, and American Bunglers* (London, Chatto and Windus, 1984)

Ruthven, Malise, *Islam in the World* (London, Penguin, 1984)

Said, Edward, *The Question of Palestine* (New York, Times Books, 1979); *Covering Islam: How the Media and the Experts Determine How We See the Rest of the World* (New York, Pantheon, 1981)

Salibi, Kemal, *Crossroads to Civil War: Lebanon 1958–1976* (New York, Caravan, 1976); *The Modern History of Lebanon* (New York, Caravan, 1977); *A House of Many Mansions: the History of Lebanon Reconsidered* (London, I.B.Tauris, 1988)

Schiff, Ze'ev, and Ya'ari, Ehud, *Israel's Lebanon War* (London, George Allen and Unwin, 1985)

Seale, Patrick, *The Struggle for Syria* (Oxford, OUP, 1965); *Asad: The Struggle for the Middle East* (London, I.B. Tauris, 1988)

Sim, Katherine, *David Roberts R. A. 1796–1864: A Biography* (London, Quartet Books, 1984)

Timmermann, Jacobo, *The Longest War* (London, Chatto and Windus, 1982)

Van Dam, Nikolaos, *The Struggle for Power in Syria* (London, Croom Helm, 1981)

Walker, Christopher J., *Armenia: The Survival of a Nation* (New York, St Martin's Press, 1980)

Warner, Geoffrey, *Iraq and Syria 1941* (London, Davis-Poynter, 1974)
Woodward, Bob, *Veil: The Secret Wars of the CIA 1981–1987* (New York, Simon and Schuster, 1987)
Yermiya, Dov, *My War Diary: Israel in Lebanon* (London, Pluto Press, 1983)

The above is a guide for readers rather than an exhaustive bibliography. The Minority Rights Group's 24-page report by David McDowall, *Lebanon: A Conflict of Minorities* (London, 1986), provides a quick but valuable guide to political traditions and loyalties in Lebanon. Readers who wish to inquire further into the events described in this book should also refer to the three Beirut daily newspapers *An Nahar*, *As Safir* and *L'Orient le Jour* and to *Middle East Reporter*, Ihsan Hijazi's monumental digest of events in Lebanon which is published daily in Beirut. The weekly English-language magazine *Monday Morning* published a useful bound volume of its editions covering the Lebanon invasion under the title *Lebanon: The Four Deadly Months* (issues from 14–21 June to 25–31 October 1982).

The only Syrian publication on the 1982 Israeli invasion is *L'Invasion Israélienne du Liban, par un groupe de chercheurs syriens sous l'autorité du général Mustapha Tlass* (Paris, J.A. Conseil, 1986), which contains a preface by the Syrian Minister of Defence, suggests that tactical retreat can be regarded as victory but provides details of the Syrian order of battle during the later stages of the conflict and some excellent combat maps.

There is a substantial body of Arabic-language literature on the Lebanon war, the anti-Israeli resistance movement and the political crisis in Lebanon. Karim Pakradouni's *Al Salam al Mafqud* (The Missing Peace, Beirut, 1982) provides a Lebanese Christian perspective on the tragedy; the more extreme Shia philosophy in Lebanon can be found in Mohamed Hussein Fadlallah's *Al Islam wa Mantaq al Quwa* (Islam and the Logic of Force, Beirut, 1985). The Lebanese government published a long and detailed volume on southern Lebanon in 1986 entitled *South Lebanon 1948–1986: Facts and Figures* (Ministry of Information Department of Lebanese Studies and Publications, Beirut), which provides an interesting analysis of Lebanese guerrilla operations against the Israeli army. The experience of the Multinational Force in Beirut in 1982–4 was the subject of a 1985 seminar in Oslo, attended by several former MNF military commanders and held under the auspices of the Norwegian Institute of International Affairs which later published the lectures of American, French, Italian, British and Lebanese participants.

By far the most harrowing personal account of captivity by any Beirut hostage is that of the French journalist Jean-Paul Kauffman, who wrote at length of his three-year ordeal in Islamic Jihad's prisons in the French magazine *L'Evénement du Jeudi* (issue of 12–18 May 1988).

Index

For names beginning with al- *see under* second element of name; journals and places remain under Al.

Robert Fisk is one of the most experienced reporters in the Middle East and holds more major British journalism awards than any other foreign correspondent for his coverage of wars in Lebanon, Iran, and Ireland. He has been an eyewitness to many of the dramatic events in Lebanon over the past fourteen years, living in west Beirut during the Israeli seige, entering the Sabra and Chatila Palestinian camps in 1982 on the day the massacre ended, and observing the destruction of the U.S. Marine headquarters in 1983.

He was one of only four Western reporters to stay on in Lebanon after Westerners became the target for assassination as well as kidnapping in 1986. Aged forty-four and the author of two earlier books, both on the Irish conflict, Fisk was Irish correspondent for *The Times* from 1972 to 1975 and Middle East correspondent until 1987. He is now Middle East correspondent for *The Independent*—still based in Lebanon.